Nuffield Co-ordinated Sciences

TEACHERS' GUIDE

**Published for the Nuffield–Chelsea Curriculum Trust
by Longman Group UK Limited**

Longman Group UK Limited,
Longman House, Burnt Mill, Harlow, Essex CM20 2JE, England and
Associated Companies throughout the World.

First published 1988
Revised edition 1992
Copyright © The Nuffield–Chelsea Curriculum Trust 1988, 1992

Cover illustration by Plus 2 Design

Filmset in Times Roman
Printed in Great Britain
by Butler & Tanner Ltd, Frome and London
ISBN 0 582 09393

The Publishers' policy is to use paper manufactured from sustainable forests.

Contents

CONTENTS

CONTENTS

Foreword

The publication of Nuffield Co-ordinated Sciences in 1988 marked an important step in the work of the Nuffield–Chelsea Curriculum Trust. Since that first edition significant changes have taken place in science education in schools.

First, the Schools Examinations Council introduced National Criteria for GCSE syllabuses in balanced science, for 20 per cent of curriculum time. The criteria gave explicit expression to the growing wish among scientists and science educators that pupils of all ages should be taught (and, ultimately, examined) about the processes and skills of science as well as about the knowledge content. They also gave official endorsement to the need to teach pupils that the work of science is done in the context of our society: of technology, of industry and of our environment. That policy commanded broad support – most importantly from the Association for Science Education and the Royal Society – and the Trust collaborated with the Midlands Examining Group in the preparation of a "Sciences: Double Award" syllabus for this course.

Secondly – and with far-reaching implications – the government introduced a National Curriculum for Science in 1989, which was comprehensively revised in 1991. When the first GCSE examination of pupils studying this revised National Curriculum takes place in 1994, Nuffield Co-ordinated Sciences will again be matched by a tailor-made syllabus specifying the work to be assessed for both double science and single science qualifications.

Thirdly, the government decided that National Curriculum GCSE assessment in each of the three sciences separately should continue. National Curriculum examinations in Biology, Chemistry and Physics will be set from 1995; and we have helped the Midland Examining Group to prepare Nuffield Co-ordinated Sciences syllabuses for these also.

The Trust has welcomed all these developments, in the belief that many of the underlying aims correspond with the aims consistently pursued in Nuffield science materials over twenty years: to teach young people the reality of science through enquiry, experimentation and investigation as much as by the transmission and testing of unchallengeable facts or formulae.

The responses to what society and examiners now require have been various. In this course the Trust is offering a way forward for the large number of science teachers who would like to carry the best elements of the three separate sciences over into a course which closely links the ideas of all three, which can provide for the whole range of pupils' and which can satisfy the GCSE criteria for double science, single science and separate sciences.

The present revision and slight expansion of the course, and this entirely new *Teachers' guide*, will serve to keep these aims alive. The Trust's purpose now is to help teachers and pupils fulfil the requirements of the National Curriculum, while continuing to teach and learn in the well-tried Nuffield spirit of enquiry and investigation.

The Trust is conscious of its debt to many groups and individuals for their advice, support and devoted work. First, to the General Editor of this revision, Mark Ellse, and to his immediate assistants Roger Norris, Alastair Sandiforth and Neill Travers; and to the General Editors of the original project, Geoffrey Dorling, Andrew Hunt and Grace Monger, who wove a multitude of strands into intellectual cohesion, and themselves wrote the final drafts of most of the pupils' material. Then to those whose thought and guidance helped to create the project: the Consultative Committee, with its energetic and enthusiastic Chairman, Professor Malcolm Frazer, and its expert members embracing the Inspectorate, the Secondary Examinations Council, the Secondary Science Curriculum Review, educators and scientists from the Universities, science advisers and, most important, science teachers; the many teachers whose response to a questionnaire helped determine the direction and content of the course; and to Professor Paul Black, the Trust's academic adviser.

FOREWORD

I am happy to record our thanks, also, to the many teachers and educators who wrote draft material for the original course, for the new material of this revision and for this *Teachers' guide*. Among them I record a special debt to Tim Turvey, who did much additional work on some of the worksheets, to Justin Dillon for his careful thought about scientific investigations and to David Barrett, Neil Ingram, Charles Lawrence and Rob Shuttleworth, for invaluable work in preparing our draft GCSE examination syllabus submissions.

None of these teachers could have made their vital contribution without the generosity of their head teachers. I must record a special debt of gratitude to Mr Rupert Lane, Headmaster of Monmouth School, Mr Ronald Wolsey, lately Principal of Wymondham College, Mr David Hitchin, Head of Stanborough School and Mr M. Brett, Head of Ashington High School.

New though this course and its revised edition are, they have nevertheless drawn on many of the pioneering ideas of Nuffield precursors, and I am happy to record our debt to all those who created our earlier courses.

Finally, and with great pleasure, I must thank all those in the Trust's office who have worked to let the materials see the light of day in worthy form – Dieter Pevsner and his predecessor as Publications Manager, William Anderson, with Simon Bell, Catherine Blackie, Sarah Codrington, Sheila Corr, Philip Ellaway, Frank Kitson, Carl Newell, Laurice Suess, Deborah Williams, David Wright and Mary de Zouche – and, finally, Andrew Ransom, Hilary Davies, Penny Kenwright and their colleagues at Longman, who continue to sustain the project with a warmth of commitment and support far beyond the norm.

K.W. Keohane
Chairman, The Nuffield–Chelsea Curriculum Trust

General introduction

Chapter 1 **About Nuffield Co-ordinated Sciences**

Nuffield Co-ordinated Sciences provides a course and an assessment scheme for Key stage 4 of the National Curriculum. It covers Years 10 and 11, the last two years of compulsory education, for pupils mostly between the ages of 14 and 16. The course comprises a broad and balanced science education while preserving the separate identities of physics, chemistry and biology. Earth-science components are integrated within the three separate sciences (see page 520).

Closely integrated assessment schemes are available, continuing the principle that what is taught and learnt should be what is assessed. The Double Award assessment scheme (examined by the Midland Examining Group – MEG) continues. From 1994, when it changes with the new National Curriculum, it will be joined by a Single Award assessment scheme. From 1995, a Triple Award suite, examining the subjects Biology, Chemistry and Physics separately, will be available.

Nuffield Co-ordinated Sciences is self contained and may be used after any course at Key stage 3, although it has similarities in style and presentation to Nuffield Science Years 7 to 9 and provides a logical continuation of that course.

The course publications

All existing components of the course have been revised for the second (1992) edition and have been joined by a new pupils' book *Earth and Space*, making a total of four pupils' books, three packs of worksheets and one teachers' guide. Schools using the first (1988) edition of the course may upgrade to the second edition by adding *Earth and Space*, the *Worksheet upgrade pack* and this *Teachers' guide* (see the table below). Differences between the first and second edition pupils' books are sufficiently small for both editions to be used side by side: page numbers and question numbers remain the same. The *Worksheet upgrade pack* will convert a set of three first edition worksheet packs to the same as a second edition set.

Either the second edition publications (1992) may be used ...	... or additions may be made to the first edition publications (1988)
Pupils' books Biology (1992) Chemistry (1992) Physics (1992) Earth and Space (1992)	**Pupils' books** Biology (1988) Chemistry (1988) Physics (1988) Earth and Space (1992)
Worksheets Biology worksheets (1992) Chemistry worksheets (1992) Physics worksheets (1992)	**Worksheets** Biology worksheets (1988) Chemistry worksheets (1988) Physics worksheets (1988) Worksheet upgrade pack (1992)
Teachers' guide (1992)	**Teachers' guide** (1992)

Differentiation

A science course that can be interpreted appropriately with the whole GCSE ability range includes more material in the texts and in the worksheets than any one girl or boy can be expected to undertake; parts of the texts are too advanced for some while other parts are too simple for others. In the same way, an assessment scheme needs to be tailored to suit the pupils. The MEG syllabus document specifies three "tiers" of entry for the examinations, called Basic, Central and Further, and targeted at final attainment levels 4 to 6, 7 to 8, and 9 to 10 respectively. Further information on this differentiation is given in the MEG syllabus document.

In the Routes and times sections of this *Guide*, we have provided Basic, Central and Further tiers of suggested routes through the course. These tiers correspond loosely with the three tiers of entry for the written examination, but the correspondence between the routes and the targeted levels is not rigid. There are many occasions where the routes for tiers B and C take pupils through material which will only be assessed at attainment levels 9 and 10; this occurs when such material is part of the Programme of study for Key stage 4 and when exposure to such material is an important part of a general scientific education. Our routes are not prescriptive – there are many alternatives. Teachers should select and modify the course to suit the needs of their own pupils.

The route for Chapter **B**1 "What's what?" is shown below as an example. Down the centre of the diagram is the Central route, to levels 7 and 8. Modifications to the route are given on the left (for the Basic route, to level 6) and right (for the Further route, to level 10), with approximate timings when these differ from those for the Central route. When there are distinct pieces of work for the Basic or Further routes, these are placed in boxes to the left or right of the Central route (as, for example, in the route for Chapter **B**12 on page 127). The routes assume that pupils will do all the questions unless otherwise stated.

Additional or alternative suggestions for Sc1 investigations are mentioned in the routes. Time allocated to these may be used for alternative investigations and is allowed for in the overall lengths of the routes. When material is identified as being optional, teachers should note that no time for it has been allowed in the routes, and it is suggested that such material is included only when there is plenty of time.

The route for Chapter **B**1 demonstrates the different timings for the different tiers. This chapter is short for tier F, but long for tier B. This leaves time later for the material that is covered by tier F and not by tier B (see, for example, the routes for Chapters **B**22 and **B**23).

Basic	Central	Further
	B1.1 Sorting things out (pages 8 and 9) **Worksheet B1A Observing different organisms** Omit Q4 and 7. *1¼ hours*	Read for homework.
	B1.2 Countless different types **Worksheet B1B How many different organisms?** Part **a** is optional; set part **b** for homework. *¼ hour*	Read for homework.
Spend more time on this activity. *¾ hour*	**B1.3 The art of survival** (class + homework) Omit Q5, 7, 8 and 11. *½ hour*	All questions are suitable.
Spend more time on using keys. *1½ hours*	**B1.4 Finding out who's who** **Worksheet B1C An identification key to some British birds** *1 hour*	Read for homework.
Omit Worksheet **B**1D	**B1.5 What's in a name?** **Worksheet B1D Using the names of living organisms** (class + homework) Omit Q1, 3 and 4. *¼ hour*	Read for homework.
Total: 4 hours	*Total: 3¼ hours*	*Total: ½ hour*

Routes for the Single Award scheme

The syllabus extracts at the beginnings of the chapters in this *Guide* show in **bold** those syllabus statements that make up the Single Award scheme of assessment. In a similar way, the bold boxes in the routes show those parts that should be covered by those preparing for the Single Award scheme.

Timing

There are many different patterns for school timetables. So we have decided to give our timings in hours, assuming that there are five hours for double-subject science in a 25-hour week in Years 10 and 11; this represents 20 per cent of curriculum time.

We have tried to ensure that the course can be taught in about 55 weeks, that is 270 hours, over two years. This allows for field trips, school exams and other events which disrupt the normal timetable. So our timings are based on about 3×90 hours for covering the basic course in the three sciences. In addition, time will be needed for such things as end of topic tests, and revision. The detailed teaching routes for each chapter give a sense of the relative emphasis to be given to each part of the course.

Science departments will have to translate the timings into a form appropriate to the school timetable. They will also have to find a way of dividing the available time between the three subjects. We imagine that in many schools the course will be taught by three teachers, but this is not the only possible plan. It could be taught by two science teachers, or even by one.

The development of Nuffield Co-ordinated Sciences

Nuffield Co-ordinated Sciences was developed and written in response to a number of new challenges to science teachers in secondary schools, embodied in the DES publication *Science 5–16: a statement of policy*. The statement suggested that pupils should spend one-fifth of their time in school studying science and that they should receive, in that time, a scientific education that is both broad and balanced.

The old forms of separate-science teaching were not ideally suited to this new aim, since one-fifth of curriculum time allows children to learn only two of the three sciences, and this can hardly be said to pass the "broad and balanced" test.

One solution was the integrated science approach – as in the Nuffield Science 13 to 16 modular scheme in use in many schools.

Nuffield Co-ordinated Sciences offered a new and different solution for the many teachers who believe that there is great merit in preserving the separate identities of biology, chemistry and physics. The knowledge content of each subject was limited so that the topics would fit into the available time. In addition, the three strands – of biology, chemistry and physics – were linked and inter-related throughout the publications.

The authors of the course have a double debt to earlier Nuffield courses. They drew on them for teaching ideas. They also relied heavily on the experience of teachers who taught the courses to evaluate the draft materials and to judge their appropriateness as part of a scheme of science for all.

Nuffield Co-ordinated Sciences was designed as a distinct alternative to Nuffield Science 13 to 16 to give schools a choice. The successor to Nuffield Science 13 to 16, Nuffield Modular Science, preserves that choice.

Significance

The "significance test", first used in Nuffield Secondary Science, was used to select topics for study in this course. The criteria used are that the science studied should:

- have immediate significance for the pupils in terms of its intrinsic interest
- be concerned with the real adult world.

This second aspect of significance can carry science beyond its usual boundaries. In the real world science does not exist in isolation from society, and social and moral problems can arise in the course of any scientific study.

Significance is also stressed by giving emphasis to the pupils' own experimental work, the spirit being one of investigating problems which are seen as real by them.

Teaching science in terms of significance means that we must be continually aware of the everyday lives of our pupils and the activities they are involved in, whether they be sport, shopping, running the home, repairing cars, watching television, or whatever happens to be the latest fashion. We must continually relate what is happening in the laboratory to real-life situations.

We have also tried to emphasize the relevance of the topics included in the course by giving attention to the applications and issues involved in the interaction of science and technology with society. We have been influenced by the Science and Technology in Society (SATIS) project of the Association for Science Education and have incorporated a number of SATIS units into the scheme.

Contexts

The syllabus for Nuffield Co-ordinated Sciences emphasizes the importance we attach to making the course seem significant to the pupils. Each topic is placed in context. Some of the contexts relate to the individual person; others are social, historical, environmental or industrial. One of the advantages of a co-ordinated sciences course is that the contexts can be chosen to suit the subject, so long as a balance is maintained over the course as a whole.

The work of famous scientists

We have tried to encourage pupils to reflect on the nature of science and the status of scientific ideas. We believe that pupils should meet the idea that scientific theories are not immutable but subject to change. In Chapter **P**10, for example, pupils are asked to evaluate two alternative theories.

We have tried to cater for pupils who in the past may have dropped science subjects at the earliest opportunity but who will now find themselves taking a core science course. We hope that by putting some of the science in its historical context we will help pupils to see that science has human and cultural aspects which they can relate to their other interests. The work of men and women scientists and technologists is described in each of the three main pupils' books.

Science and industry

We have tried to respond to the demand that schools should put across more positive images of industry and commerce. Traditional descriptions of industrial processes in textbooks have generally been impersonal and lacking in intellectual challenge. They make it seem as if all the problems involved in carrying out a process have been solved by working out the scientific principles involved.

A number of industrial processes feature in the Chemistry part of the course. As far as possible these accounts illustrate the types of jobs which people do, their responsibilities and the problems they have to tackle. They also illustrate the need for team work and the way in which people of different disciplines work together to solve technical problems. We received much help from a number of companies in preparing up-to-date accounts of these topics.

Environmental science

The diagram on page 12 shows that there is a strong theme of environmental science running through the course. Environmental topics provide opportunities for pupils to discuss problems for which there is no definite right answer. We have been concerned that such debates should be based on scientific knowledge and understanding of the issues.

Earth science does not feature as a separate subject in Nuffield Co-ordinated Sciences but we have incorporated important earth-science themes into the three separate sciences (see page 520).

Strategies

The diagram on page 8 shows the main topics in each of the three main pupils' books. In Biology and Chemistry the topics and chapters are published in an order which might be adopted as a teaching sequence. In Physics the content is arranged in such a way that each topic is revisited a number of times during the course.

We believe that learning from the written word should be an important feature of a science course. We have been influenced by the Schools Council Publication *Reading for learning in the sciences* by Florence Davies and Terry Greene (Oliver and Boyd, 1984). This book explains that in science books there are various types of text which pupils have to learn to deal with. Pupils need support and direction from teachers so that they can become effective readers. Active reading can be a group exercise which helps pupils to increase their success in learning from science texts.

"Commentary text" is included to make pupils aware of the links between the sciences: it gives hints about the ways in which the various sections of the books should be tackled, and it gives some indication of the levels of differentiation. We hope that it will help pupils to understand the purpose of what they are being expected to do.

In an attempt to develop the range of skills and processes which help to make up science, the pupils are often asked, in the pupils' books, to undertake a variety of tasks. There is clearly not time for a pupil to practise the full range of skills in any one topic. The choice of skill or process developed in a particular context has been based on the experience of the teachers who advised the editors during the writing of the material.

The pupils' books include two types of questions. One type is designed to set up a dialogue between the authors and the pupils. These questions have to be thought about while reading the text. The other type of question is intended as an accompaniment to the text. Questions of the second kind do not have to be looked at during a first reading.

Instructions for practical activities are not given in the main text. We hope that this makes it easier to adapt the course to the needs and interests of the pupils.

Interdisciplinary inquiries

We hope that teachers will want to include interdisciplinary activities as a feature of the Nuffield Co-ordinated Sciences programme. These may be of two kinds:

- case studies, which give pupils an awareness of the importance of interdisciplinary approaches to tackling technological problems;
- practical investigations, which require pupils to draw on their knowledge and skills to tackle a problem which cuts across the boundaries of the separate sciences.

Case studies

The SATIS publications include units which illustrate an interdisciplinary approach to technological problems. Pupils working on these units will have to draw on their knowledge of more than one science. Examples include: 110 "Hilltop – an agricultural problem", 204 "Using radioactivity", 304 and 305 "A medicine to control bilharzia – parts 1 and 2", 404 "How would you survive?", 506 "Materials for life – new parts for old", 508 "Risks", 802 "Hypothermia", 805 "The search for the magic bullet", 906 "IT in greenhouses" and 1004 "Lavender".

Interdisciplinary investigations

The course provides opportunities for pupils to plan and carry out their own investigations. The publications include suggestions, but these are not mandatory, so we hope that in time teachers will find examples of problems to investigate which help to illustrate the fact that many real problems are interdisciplinary.

Chapter 2 **Co-ordination issues**

Introduction

Co-ordination of the content and development of the separate sciences is the feature that distinguishes this course from independent, self-supporting courses in Biology, Chemistry and Physics on the one hand and Integrated Science courses on the other.

There are two aspects to co-ordination. First it is a process that has taken place in devising and writing the course. Secondly it is an essential process that takes place within a science department teaching this course.

Co-ordination within the course

Co-ordination in the planning and writing of the course has taken place in three ways. First there is co-ordination of content – what is developed in one science is taken up in another. Secondly, there is a co-ordination of ideas. Ideas that are common to two or more sciences are developed according to a common policy. An obvious example of a concept common to all the sciences is that of energy; the way that this has been treated is detailed on page 9. Lastly, there is a co-ordination of strategy. All three sciences are presented to the pupil in a similar way.

Co-ordination of content

The chart overleaf shows suggested pathways through the work of all three sciences, laid out side by side. The spacings of the topics are proportional to the suggested time allowances. In this way it can be seen how the content of one science is related in time to the content of another. There are two aspects to this.

First, it shows up some helpful concurrent links that can be made between the sciences. It can be seen, for example, that work on chemicals from plants, in Chemistry, starts just after corresponding work on photosynthesis in Biology. Just before work in Physics is concerned with the flow of electric currents, work in Chemistry has been concerned with more general properties of metals. Human influence on the environment is explored in Biology at about the same time as radioactivity (with its obvious social implications) is being studied in Physics.

Secondly it shows the extent to which each of the sciences can be relied upon to provide background to any particular topic. Examples of the way in which any one science takes up ideas already developed in another are given on page 13. Other examples that can be picked out are the work on cells and batteries in Chapter **C**14 of the Chemistry book, which assumes an acquaintance with energy and electricity covered in Chapter **P**17 of the Physics book. In a similar way, the work on temperature control in an organism, which is a part of Chapter **B**12 of the Biology book, relies on some previous understanding of the relationship between evaporation and energy transfer, which is developed in Chapter **P**2 of the Physics book. The study of digestion in Chapter **B**5 makes more sense in the light of work on carbohydrate molecules in Chapter **C**3; while the investigation of fertilizers in Chapter **C**16 assumes that the nitrogen cycle has been introduced in Chapter **B**15.

When devising alternative pathways through the material, schools will need to bear in mind the way the development of some major ideas has been co-ordinated across the sciences. This means that in some instances it is essential to ensure certain priorities – as, for example, in ensuring that introductory work on energy in Physics precedes the development of ideas about energy in Biology and Chemistry. These important priorities are made clear in the charts on pages 10–12, which show the development of ideas about energy, particles and the environment in all three sciences. It is also possible to construct alternative pathways so that the work taught by any one teacher includes material from more than one pupils' book. For example, some schools may prefer to teach work found in the Physics Chapter **P**3 "Radioactivity" alongside material from the Chemistry book. In this way, particular teacher-expertise can be used to best advantage.

Sequence of topics

Biology	Chemistry	Physics
B1 What's what?	**C2** Petrochemicals	Introduction
B2 Many forms of life		**P1** Building bridges successfully
B3 Light means life	**C3** Chemicals from plants	**P2** Cooking food quickly
	E2 Geology	**E1** Weather
	C4 Chemicals and rocks	**P4** Motion
B4 How do animals feed?		**P5** Controlling motion
B5 The gut as a food processor	**C5** Materials and structures	**P8** Machines and engines
B6 Diet and good health		**P9** Keeping yourself warm
B7 The breath of life		
B8 Transport round the organism	**C6** Glasses and ceramics	**P10** Ideas in physics
B9 Keeping going	**C7** Metals and alloys	
B10 Skeletons and muscles		**P16** Using electricity
B11 Detecting changes	**C8** Polymers	
B12 Keeping things under control		**P17** Energy and electricity
B13 Making sense of an environment	**C9** Foams, emulsions, sols and gels	**P13** Fibre optics and noise
	C10 Keeping clean	**P14** Making waves
B14 The webs of life		
B15 Salts and cycles	**C11** Dyes and dyeing	**P15** Making use of waves
		P6 Crashes and bangs
B16 Staying alive	**C12** Chemicals in the medicine cupboard	
B17 Farms, factories and the environment	**C13** Fuels and fires	**P7** Rising and falling
		E3 Space
B18 To destroy or to conserve?		**P18** Making use of electricity
B19 Living things multiply	**C14** Batteries	**P3** Radioactivity
B20 People are different	**C15** Soil	
		P11 Energy where it is needed
B21 Growing up	**C16** Fertilizers	**P12** Waste not, want not?
		P19 Making pictures with electricity
B22 Handing on to the next generation	**C17** The Periodic Table	**P20** Control
B23 Changing with time	**C18** Atoms and bonding	**P21** Communication

There is a third way in which the contents of the three sciences are linked to each other and to other areas of study. These are links of cross-reference and application. Examples from a range of sciences can often be used to illustrate particular scientific ideas (see page 13). It is not essential in such cases that the cross-reference is already familiar to pupils when first introduced. For example, the work on chemicals from plants in Chapter **C**2 of the Chemistry book looks forward to the use that will be made of it in future work in Biology, such as in the study of digestion. Work on optical fibres in Physics (Chapter **P**13) reminds pupils of earlier work on glass in Chemistry (Chapter **C**6) but does not explicitly use ideas from that chapter.

Cross-references of this sort are numerous and have been treated specially in the pupils' books by the use of "commentary text". This text is set apart from the normal text of the book and provides, for the pupil, a parallel commentary on the work. Amongst other things, this commentary text tells pupils where, in their other science books, they may find related material.

Finally, co-ordination of content can take place in carrying out interdisciplinary problems and investigations. It is hoped that all pupils will have an opportunity to do some of these. There are at least two ways in which the present material can be used to encourage interdisciplinary studies. In the first place, closely linked topics such as Chapter **P**12 "Waste not, want not?" and Chapter **C**13 "Fuels and fires" can be taught as an integrated unit of work. Secondly, several of the worksheets will be seen to involve ideas from more than one science, for example Worksheet **P**3B "Using radioactivity" and Worksheet **B**9A "Investigating respiration".

Earth and Space
The National Curriculum contains material on Earth sciences and astronomy. These subjects provide valuable applications of, and extensions to, work in all three sciences. In this second edition of the course, Earth and Space are integrated principally into the Chemistry and Physics components of the course and provided with additional material by their own pupils' book. Page 520 of this *Guide* gives further information about the content and the links with Chemistry and Physics.

Co-ordination of concepts and ideas

A common policy has been adopted in the development of any idea that occurs in more than one science. In this section, there follows an account of the policies adopted towards the most important of these common ideas. These are the concept of energy, the meaning of the word "particle", and the impact of science on the environment.

Energy
The approach adopted to energy is consistent with the terminology of the National Curriculum and has been influenced by a number of recent publications. The following points, made by many of the authors of these publications, have been taken up in Nuffield Co-ordinated Sciences:

There is often a confusion in pupils' minds over the scientists' "book-keeping" view of the conservation of energy and the everyday idea that energy is somehow being used up.

Accepting that processes of change usually involve the transfer of energy, the idea of an "energy cost" involved in bringing about a desired change is introduced prior to any consideration of energy conservation.

Eventually, energy cost and energy conservation are reconciled by recognizing that the dispersal of energy in the surroundings results in it being impossible to utilize this energy fully again. This is compared with the "loss" of material resources by their wide dispersal.

The idea that energy is transformed when it is transferred leads pupils to think that the energy associated with different things (chemicals, electricity, motion, hotness) is essentially different. This tends to make energy seem a material substance, rather than a quality of a system ("having energy") which, like temperature for example, can change according to the circumstances.

Consequently, the idea of energy transformation and reference to "forms of energy" has, as far as possible, been excluded from Nuffield Co-ordinated Sciences. Two special names have been retained, however; these are kinetic energy and internal energy. The first is too well embedded in the language of science for it to be easy to exclude it; the second is given limited use when it is necessary to refer to energy stored internally in a body (as the kinetic and potential energy of its atoms and molecules).

There is confusion in the use of the word "heat" both to refer to a particular manifestation of energy in relation to the temperature of a body, and as a mode of energy transfer when two bodies of unequal temperature are in thermal contact.

We have therefore decided not to use the word "heat" as a description of a "form of energy". Instead, the word "heat" is only used to describe a process by which energy is transferred from a hot body to a cold one. This means that the word "heat" is only used in the verbal sense of "to heat" and "heating". Consequently, the energy transfer required to raise the temperature of one kilogram of a substance by 1°C is described as the "specific heating capacity" of the substance.

The approach to energy adopted by Nuffield Co-ordinated Sciences can be summarized as follows:

• When things happen, energy is usually transferred.
• If energy is involved in a change, it will be transferred and re-arranged, but the total amount will stay the same.
• We become aware of energy only when it is transferred, and there are two important processes of energy transfer: work and heat.
Heat is the name of a process whereby internal energy is transferred from a hotter to a cooler body.
Work is the name of a process whereby energy is transferred when a force moves its point of application.
• Many changes involve energy being transferred to the surroundings. But the temperature rise which results is often so small that the energy appears to have vanished.

The chart below shows the way ideas about energy are inter-related in the three sciences.

Energy: co-ordination

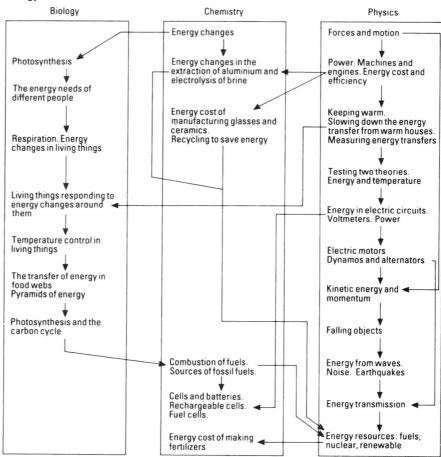

Particles

It is common to use the word "particle" in Physics as a general term for an atom, molecule or ion since in many cases, such as when developing ideas of the kinetic theory, it is inconvenient and unnecessary to draw any distinction between these different entities. In Chemistry, on the other hand, it is essential to distinguish between atoms, molecules and ions. The distinction is an important one, as for example when comparing the strong forces within molecules with the much weaker forces between molecules.

The word "particles" is also used in all three sciences to mean "small specks of matter". It is used in this way when talking of colloidal particles, dust or smoke particles.

There seemed no way of avoiding the use of the term in any of the ways listed above. In the Physics book, however, some trouble has been taken to point out to pupils that the word "particle", used in conjunction with the theory of the structure of matter, means the same thing as "atom" or "molecule" or "ion" and that it is used when distinction between these things is not important. This is reinforced from time to time by using the correct particulate term, either in brackets or on its own, particularly when a specific substance is referred to.

Elsewhere, the use of the term "particle" is generally substantiated by a reference to its precise meaning in the context in which it is being used.

The chart below shows the way the ideas about particles are taken up in all three sciences. Not surprisingly, the concept is central to work in Chemistry.

Particles: co-ordination

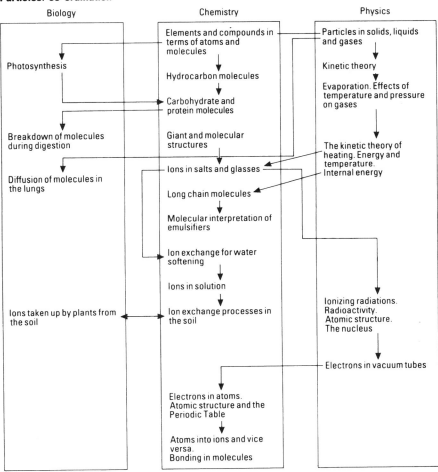

Environment

All three sciences show a common concern for the impact of the applications of science on the environment and for the impact of the environment on other things. Physics and Chemistry include topics from the Earth sciences. They also consider the impact of the environment on materials, in corrosion, and the possible pollution of the environment when considering, for example, fertilizers.

Biology includes work on the environmental factors which affect living organisms and concerns itself with matters of conservation. In Physics, the impact of things as different as noise, earthquakes and the possible effects of nuclear power are all considered at some point in the course.

The chart below shows the way we have incorporated environmental considerations into the course.

Environment: co-ordination

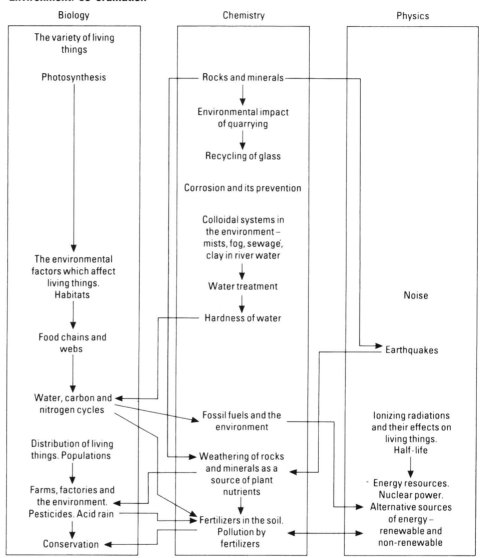

Units and conventions

We have adopted a common policy in the use of units and other conventional notation. In general, this has meant following the policy laid down by the ASE in their booklet *SI units, signs, symbols and abbreviations* (1981).

However, there are one or two points of policy adopted by the course which would not clearly follow from a reference to the ASE's publication.

Units for volume

We have adopted the litre (symbol, L) and the millilitre (symbol, ml) as the units for volume measure where no obvious shape is indicated. This decision has been taken because the litre is a familiar everyday unit of volume. Medicines are dispensed in 5-ml spoons while paints are sold in litres. For solids and one or two other cases where the use of the litre would be anomalous, the unit adopted is the cm^3 or the m^3 as appropriate. This again is in line with everyday practice (wood, for example, is measured in m^3).

As a consequence of the decision to use the litre as the basic unit for volume, the symbol L is not used for anything else.

Negative indices

Negative indices are not used in any of the books. In the case of units, the solidus (/) is used instead. In order to avoid using the solidus twice for acceleration, the convention has been adopted of giving units as, for instance, metres/second every second.

Safety symbols

The conventional safety symbols used in Chemistry have been adopted.

Chemical names

The ASE book *Chemical nomenclature, symbols and terminology* (1985) emphasizes that the names recommended are appropriate for students taking the more advanced chemistry courses. The authors of that book stress that the names used should be appropriate to the level of understanding of the student and they invite teachers to adjust the complexity of systematic names to the maturity and knowledge of the student.

We have studied these recommendations and decided not to require a knowledge of chemical nomenclature in Nuffield Co-ordinated Sciences. We have used both trivial and systematic names, but this information is not required for examination purposes.

We have tried to avoid creating barriers which will prevent pupils from seeing the connections between school science and their everyday experience. However, this does not lead to consistency when farmers still talk about "muriate of potash" while some supermarkets list a hexacyanoferrate(III) salt among the ingredients of table salt.

As a rule, systematic names have been used for the simpler inorganic and organic chemicals. Everyday names have been used for polymers and biological molecules.

Co-ordination within the science department

It is necessary when teaching this course to be aware of both the content and order of presentation of the work in all three sciences. In writing the course, duplication of work has, as far as possible, been avoided. So preliminary work essential to the development of an idea in one science may well have taken place in another. An example of this is the work on energy in Chapter **B**14 of the Biology book and Chapter **C**13 of the Chemistry book. Both of these pieces of work assume that the pupils are already familiar with earlier work on energy covered by Chapters **P**8 to **P**10 in the Physics book.

Similarly, Chapter **C**18 of the Chemistry book, which deals with atoms and bonding, assumes that pupils have already met ideas about atomic structure and electrons, covered in Chapters **P**3 and **P**19 of the Physics book.

The sample pathway through the contents of the three main books, given in the chart on page 8, takes note of this need for co-ordination in the teaching order. Other pathways are possible, but all involved will have to be aware of the extent to which ideas developed in one science depend on ideas developed in another.

Awareness of the content of all the sciences allows co-ordination to take place in another way. Examples from all the sciences can be used to illustrate the development of ideas in any one particular science. Instances of this will be found in the pupils' books. The use of catalysts and their importance in industry is discussed in Chemistry. This can be related to the study of enzymes in Biology. In Chapter **B**3 the factors which affect photosynthesis are discussed, and this experience can be used as an introduction to the study of reaction rates in Chapter **C**15 of the Chemistry course. The processes of breaking down and building up molecules are vital in digestion and growth. These biological examples help to illustrate the chemistry of polymers and the smaller molecules from which they are made. Finally, an example from Physics: in Chapter **P**1, increasing materials' stiffness by making them into tubes is discussed. This is related, amongst other things, to the structure of plant stems. Teachers will be able to think of many more examples, all of which will help pupils to establish essential links between the sciences.

Cross-links of this sort are not confined to the three sciences. Many examples will be found where links are established between the immediate scientific ideas being studied and work in geography, design and technology, and so on. There are many links with home economics: the properties of fibres (Chapter **C8**), foams and emulsions (Chapter **C9**), dry cleaning and washing (Chapter **C10**), dyes (Chapter **C11**) and fire hazards and flameproofing (Chapter **C13**) are all part of the Chemistry course. In Biology, work on food, diet and health have similar links with home economics. Physics looks at pressure cookers and microwave ovens. Work in Biology also links with physical education through topics such as oxygen uptake and muscle contraction, and with geography in the study of the impact of human activity on land use and the environment. Physics makes a number of links with technology in areas such as engines and electronics.

Chapter 3 **Skills and processes**

An education in science

Nuffield Co-ordinated Sciences gives as much emphasis to the development of scientific skills and the understanding of processes as it does to knowledge and understanding of ideas. Having said that, it is important not to underestimate the latter. Processes and skills cannot be exercised without knowledge and ideas upon which to exercise them. But it does not follow that the knowledge and ideas have to be learned and remembered.

- Some ideas are so important that they should be learned and remembered. Often these ideas are developed as part of a practical investigation. An example of this is the way forces act on an electric current in a magnetic field (Worksheet **P**18B), which is needed to understand how electric motors work.
- At other times, pupils are given an investigation to do whose outcome (as a piece of "knowledge and understanding") is not important to the course as a whole. Here they can exercise skills in science without any feeling that there is an essential "right answer". The suggested investigations into wrapping films, methods of corrosion protection, descalers and flameproofing agents provide opportunities to plan and carry out investigations in contexts where pupils can use science skills without having to master difficult concepts at the same time.
- Sometimes, the development of an important skill or process is aided by a more extended piece of science, where short-term understanding of an idea is required. But here again, the pupil is not expected to retain long-term knowledge. An example is the study of the alum industry in Chapter **C**4 of the Chemistry course. Here is an interesting story about how alum used to be made from rock, seaweed and urine. Pupils plan and carry out an experiment to see if they can make some alum from shale by a more modern process. At the same time they use ideas about elements and compounds to explain the changes they observe. So there are planning and manipulative skills as well as opportunities to apply theory. In the end they are not expected to recall the chemical, historical and industrial details for examination purposes.

The role of practical work in this course

Many of the experiments in this course have been chosen to illustrate scientific concepts and because pupils can practise skills which are useful in their studies of science. Other activities serve different purposes. Some activities are not searches for the "right answer": they are opportunities to discover that different solutions to problems can be equally valid or that there are many criteria by which solutions can be judged. Judging the approach to the problem and having a variety of strategies has often proved to be useful.

Doing a particular experiment does not automatically lead to better understanding or more knowledge for all pupils. Sometimes experiments can cloud the issue, distract or provide opportunities for new alternative conceptions to arise. Sometimes a teacher exposition or demonstration is more effective than a rushed practical with broken apparatus, carried out in an unscientific manner. Pupils should be as aware of the limitations of their experiments as they are of their results. Pupils should be encouraged to demand to be convinced "beyond reasonable doubt". Otherwise they will revert to their "common sense" explanations, which work in their "real worlds".

Research into what children can and cannot do shows that pupils have a mass of co-existing theories about the world based on their interpretations of their experiences. As teachers, what we do with this knowledge is open to us. Some strategies will work with some pupils some of the time. We cannot expect simply to substitute our ideas for the innate understanding that children already possess. It is possible that a realization that a pupil's existing theories are inadequate may make it more likely that he or she will be willing to learn more. On the other hand, it is possible that pupils will refuse to accept that their existing theories are inadequate – something that most of us have carried into our adult lives!

Skills and processes in scientific investigation

In Nuffield Co-ordinated Sciences, we have highlighted broad categories of skills and processes, as shown in the chart below. This chart also shows the symbols that are used to bring these skills to the pupils' attention in the pupils' books. These enable pupils not only to use these skills but also to **know** that they have used them. This also helps pupils to realize when the same skills appear in the different sciences. It is important that they appreciate that the skills and processes they use are not related to particular experiments or ideas, but apply generally to all science.

	1. Planning and carrying out investigations	• relate to their everyday experience and to new contexts, involving increasingly abstract concepts and the application and extension of scientific knowledge, understanding and skills, where pupils need to make decisions about the degree of precision and safe working required; • promote invention and creativity; • encourage detailed planning and evaluation in the light of findings; • are increasingly complex because they involve interacting variables; • require key variables to be controlled or taken into account, and pupils to recognize that need; • require them to generate theoretical models and to test them; • may take place over a period of time and require sampling techniques.
	2. Use of apparatus and measuring instruments	• require accurate measurement, with identification and qualification of, and accounting for, experimental error and anomalous results; • give opportunities to use information technology to gather and display data from experiments, to access and organize data relevant to their study of science, and to use programmable systems to control external electronic, electrical or mechanical devices.
	3. Observation	• require them to observe variables accurately and systematically.
	4. Interpretation and application	• encourage the use of secondary sources; • encourage the systematic recording and presentation of data using, as appropriate, a full range of forms, including graphs and mathematical relationships; • encourage pattern searching in complex data and predictions requiring abstract reasoning; • involve the critical evaluation of data; • explore the nature of scientific evidence and proof but in addition they should also: – distinguish between claims and arguments based on scientific considerations and those which are not; – distinguish between generalizations and predictive theories; – study examples of scientific controversies and the ways in which scientific ideas change. • encourage them to appraise critically their investigations including consideration of errors and suggest related improvements to their methods.

Towards better investigations

In this section some suggestions are made, in the light of research carried out by the Assessment of Performance Unit, which may enable teachers to develop strategies to make their teaching more effective.

Planning and carrying out investigations

If at all possible, planning and carrying out investigations should go hand in hand. There is evidence that when pupils are asked only to plan an investigation they do less well than when they plan the investigation and then carry it out (*Assessment matters no. 6*, page 41). This is partly because we may tend to put more effort into planning when we know we are going to have to work with the plan and also partly because there is no sharp boundary between planning and doing an investigation. Often pupils become aware of possible improvements that they could make to their plans when they see or handle the apparatus or begin to take measurements.

Variables

In an investigation, we can change the values of some (or all) of the variables. We can decide to control one variable (the **independent** variable) which affects the value of another variable (the **dependent** variable) in order to look at the relationship between the two variables. For example, in looking at the relationship between the number of 10-g masses applied to a spring and the subsequent extension, we may change the number of masses (the **independent** variable) and measure the extension (the **dependent** variable). In this example, the independent variable is described as **discrete**, that is we could increase the number of masses in discrete steps (one, two, three, four etc.). Some variables are **continuous**, that is they have more than integral values. In some experiments, the variables are said to be **categoric**, for example, which food (a categoric variable) tastes the sweetest. Not only does the **number** of variables in an investigation affect its difficulty, the **type** of variables has an effect as well.

Measurement

The use of measurement in the context of an investigation involves an interaction between children's skills of using measuring instruments, and their conceptual understanding of the importance of measurement in scientific activity and their conceptual understanding of the variables under investigation.

Assessment matters no. 2: Measurement in school science, page 7.

It is not unusual to hear science teachers bemoaning pupils' abilities to measure: "They can't even use a ruler properly." It is possibly just as likely that pupils do not see the need to, or that they do not want to, use a ruler "properly". When and when not to measure accurately can be confusing to pupils, especially when working with a variety of apparatus, some of which is clearly incapable of measuring as accurately as other apparatus in the same experiment. It is not just how and what to measure that is important, it is when. Pupils should be taught to:

- distinguish when it is and when it is not necessary to measure;
- decide how accurate to be when they measure (this will vary from one situation to another);
- decide what variables to measure;
- decide how to measure the variables identified.

The **how**, **what** and **when** of measuring should be emphasized in different contexts as and when necessary. Pupils may not see the importance of accuracy in measurement – indeed, they may not bother to record what or how they measure in written accounts of their work. In making oral and written reports of investigations, pupils should be encouraged to report on the measurement techniques that they used. They can also be encouraged to discuss with the teacher, or with each other, their reasons for choosing one measuring instrument instead of another and to report on the possible errors involved in their measurements.

Throughout their science education, pupils should be developing their measuring skills. They should become more able to use measurement to test their hypotheses and to justify their conclusions. They should become increasingly able to detect and select which features of an object or which variables in a situation need measuring and/or controlling. Pupils should encounter measurement in different contexts as they progress, so that the quantitative approach is seen to complement and, often, to illuminate a qualitative appreciation.

Teachers should also take account of APU data which suggests that pupils may use measurement less to justify similarities than differences and that, as they get older, pupils appear to rely less on measurement to justify their experimental conclusions.

Observation

Scientists' observations of phenomena depend on their training, the tools available and their prior knowledge. Observation is a "before, during and after" cognitive activity which involves the interaction of knowledge and understanding as the process of selection of what, how and when to observe, the observation itself and the interpretation of the observation, again in the light of previous experience.

Pupils should be encouraged to regard observation as involving elements of measurement, interpretation and control of phenomena. In order to observe a phenomenon, pupils may need to impose some degree of control – of one or more variables, for example – in an experiment. They should be aware that observation may be quantitative or qualitative and that they must exercise judgement when selecting their observation strategies.

Observation, like the other science process skills, involves progression. Care should be taken to match the demands of any task to both the learner and the complexity of the concept involved in a particular situation. The teacher's job will also involve focusing the pupil on the relevant features of a phenomenon or object without foreclosing the pupil's interest.

Drawing and interpreting graphs

APU research indicates that there are strategies that teachers should consider using when pupils are involved in drawing and interpreting graphs:

* Providing a space for a "variable name" and its "units" increases the likelihood that pupils will correctly label the areas and indicate the units.
* Pupils may benefit more from deciding their own scales than from using scales provided by the teacher (unless they are very straightforward).
* The most difficult aspect of constructing graphs which is frequently encountered is plotting a line of "best fit". Teachers should encourage pupils to see the graphs as representing a continuous event, not a series of separate events.
* Pupils should be encouraged to translate graphs into words, and vice versa, in order to develop their understanding of the use of graphical representations.

Further reading

Qualter, A., Strang, J., Swatton P. and Taylor, R. *Exploration: a way of learning science* Basil Blackwell, 1990.

Assessment of Performance Unit, Assessment matters series, School Examinations and Assessment Council 1990 and 1991:
　　No. 2 "Measurement in school science"
　　No. 5 "Profiles and progression in science exploration"
　　No. 6 "Planning and carrying out investigations"
　　No. 7 "Patterns and relationships in school science"
　　No. 8 "Observation in school science"
(These contain guidance on incorporating investigations into science lessons, including suggested assessment strategies.)

School Examinations and Assessment Council, *Key stage 3 School assessment folder (science part 3): (Materials to support the assessment of Sc1,* 1992.

National Curriculum Council *Strands in Attainment Targets*, NCC, York, 1991.

Chapter 4 Nuffield Co-ordinated Sciences and the National Curriculum

The order laid before Parliament in December 1991 contained provisions relating to the Attainment targets and Programmes of study in science under Section 4 of the Education Reform Act 1988. This curriculum for science comes into force for Key stage 4 on 1 August 1992 for first examination in 1994. The order specifies four attainment targets for science:

Sc1 "Scientific investigation",
Sc2 "Life and living processes",
Sc3 "Materials and their properties", and
Sc4 "Physical processes".

This chapter shows how the 1992 edition of Nuffield Co-ordinated Sciences matches that National Curriculum.

Attainment target 1: Scientific investigation

The Programme of study and Statements of attainment for Sc1 define the scientific processes covered and assessed in the National Curriculum (see pages 22–25). The Programme of study states that:

Pupils should develop the intellectual and practical skills which will allow them to explore and investigate the world of science and develop a fuller understanding of scientific phenomena, the nature of the theories explaining these, and the procedures of scientific investigation. This should take place through activities that require a progressively more systematic and quantified approach which develops and draws upon an increasing knowledge and understanding of science. The activities should encourage the ability to plan and carry out investigations in which pupils:

(i)   ask questions, predict and hypothesize;
(ii) observe, measure and manipulate variables;
(iii) interpret their results and evaluate scientific evidence.

The National Curriculum Council identifies the three strands (i) to (iii) to clarify ideas of progression in Sc1 and to enable a clear framework for assessment to be developed. They should not undermine the integrated nature of scientific investigations, nor reduce science lessons to simply an exercise in skills training.

Investigations
Investigations require pupils to:

* formulate questions or statements, based on existing knowledge and understanding, which they can test;
* put together a sequence of investigative skills (such as identification of key variables, observing and measuring) into an overall method to solve a problem;
* evaluate their findings in the light of the original problem;
* refine and develop the way they tackle problems, and what they know and understand.

They include planning, predicting, hypothesizing, designing, carrying out, interpreting results, evaluating evidence, drawing inferences and communicating plans, tasks, procedures and results, and should give the pupils the opportunity to use and build on their existing ideas, knowledge and skills. Investigations which are too demanding in terms of the concepts necessary and the skills required may hinder rather than help learning and will affect pupils' confidence in themselves.

Though pupils may benefit from relating their work to their everyday experience, there is a danger that this will distract them from the investigation in hand. Everyday life provides a stimulus to activity but it can also bring with it a vocabulary and "non-scientific" ideas that will hinder the development of "scientific thinking".

There is more to practical work than doing investigations, and observation exercises, illustrative experiments and the practising of individual skills all have their places in the course. Though practical work is an integral part of the course, the value of clear demonstrations and teacher exposition of concepts cannot be underestimated.

There are other activities, such as DARTs (Directed Activity Related to Text), that can lead to the development and reinforcing of scientific concepts, and there are opportunities for such activities throughout the course.

There is a wide range of opportunities to develop investigative skills throughout this course, as indicated in the table on pages 22–23 which summarizes the Programme of study for Attainment target 1 at Key stage 4 and lists some activities in which these skills may be exercised and assessed.

Monitoring progress in scientific investigation

There are two aspects to the assessment of skills in scientific investigation. The first of these relates to the continuous monitoring of the progress of pupils' skills throughout the course. The second relates to the provision of final assessments of Sc1 for GCSE. This section of this *Guide* relates to both of these, but definitive guidance on the second is available from MEG.

The assessment of Sc1 must be carried out in the context of scientific investigations. Discrete practical tasks that lead to the assessment of specific practical skills in isolation do not allow pupils to fulfil the requirements of the Attainment target. Investigations are integral parts of the course and not "bolt-on" assessment exercises. There should be an obvious point in doing an investigation: it should not be seen simply as an assessment exercise. For assessment purposes, there are no prescribed time limits for investigations, but sufficient time must be allowed for pupils to demonstrate their abilities to plan, carry out and consider their results and to communicate their findings.

The MEG syllabus document states that:

Assessments may only be based on investigations which are capable of providing evidence of performance related to **every one** of the three strands (i), (ii) and (iii).... These are referred to as **complete investigations**. Thus candidates will be required to make some input into deciding what is to be investigated and how, as well as carrying out the investigation and evaluating the outcomes. [However, if a student needs help with one strand, it may still be possible to assess the investigation for the other two.]

Complete investigations may occupy [as little as] one hour of laboratory time, although some [particularly at the higher levels] may be spread out over a longer period of time.

The levels assessed for a particular candidate may be based on one, two or three investigations [providing the best level for each strand] and all records relating to these assessed investigations must be available for moderation.

To facilitate such assessment, in this *Guide* we have provided outlines of 15 such complete investigations (five each for Biology, Chemistry and Physics), together with specific criteria by which they may be assessed. These experiments are not compulsory, nor are they intended to restrict the choice of complete investigations that teachers might devise. They are intended to provide a pattern which may be extended to the investigations that teachers decide are appropriate for their pupils. For those investigations which occur early in the course, criteria are given for assessment between levels 4 and 6. The range of levels progresses through the course so that for those that occur late, criteria are given for assessment between levels 7 and 10. Teachers may, of course, extend these ranges by matching a pupil's performance in an investigation directly to the general criteria of the National Curriculum. These investigations, and the levels they cover, are listed here. Further details on the individual investigations may be found in the teaching notes for the relevant chapters.

"Investigating photosynthesis" in Chapter **B**3, covering levels 4 to 6 of Sc1;
"Investigating the starch–amylase reaction" in Chapter **B**5, covering levels 4 to 7 of Sc1;
"Investigating respiration" in Chapter **B**9, covering levels 5 to 8 of Sc1;
"Investigating an object moving through water" in Chapter **B**10, covering levels 6 to 9 of Sc1;
"Investigating the growth of duckweed" in Chapter **B**15, covering levels 7 to 10 of Sc1;
"Investigating digestion" in Chapter **C**3, covering levels 4 to 6 of Sc1;
"Investigating rusting" in Chapter **C**7, covering levels 4 to 7 of Sc1;
"Investigating dyeing" in Chapter **C**11, covering levels 5 to 8 of Sc1;
"Investigating fuels" in Chapter **C**13, covering levels 6 to 9 of Sc1;
"Investigating reactions of marble with acids" in Chapter **C**15, covering levels 7 to 10 of Sc1;
"Investigating cantilevers" in Chapter **P**1, covering levels 4 to 6 of Sc1;
"Investigating frictional forces" in Chapter **P**5, covering levels 4 to 7 of Sc1;
"Investigating the cooling of coffee" in Chapter **P**9, covering levels 4 to 10 of Sc1;
"Investigating the efficiency of an electric motor" in Chapter **P**17, covering levels 7 to 10 of Sc1;
"Investigating the relationship between current and voltage" in Chapter **P**17, covering levels 7 to 10 of Sc1;

To show the pattern for Sc1 investigations, sample criteria covering the range of levels from 4 to 10 are given on pages 24–25 for one investigation – "Investigating the cooling of coffee" from Chapter P9. There are two columns for each strand: on the left are the National Curriculum Statements of attainment, and on the right are examples of pupil work which match these criteria. The examples show the progression of skills and processes through the attainment levels of the strands. But the examples are not definitive and teachers will have to use them, with their own judgement, to compare their pupils' own work with National Curriculum statements. The skeleton tables in other chapters omit the National Curriculum statements and contain merely the sample criteria for the different strands and levels. (See, for example, the skeleton table for "Investigating the cooling of coffee" on page 426.)

Prompt sheets for investigations
Photocopy masters for two prompt sheets for pupils are given on pages 26 and 27. The questions prompt pupils to consider the skills and processes they are employing.

Attainment targets 2, 3 and 4

Whereas Sc1 defines the scientific processes in the National Curriculum, the Programmes of study and Statements of attainment for Sc2, Sc3 and Sc4 define the scientific content of the National Curriculum:

- Sc2 "Life and living processes" is almost entirely covered by the Biology component of Nuffield Co-ordinated Sciences;
- Sc3 "Materials and their properties" is mostly covered by the Chemistry component, but there are significant contributions from Physics and from Earth and Space;
- Sc4 "Physical processes" is mostly covered by the Physics component, with the addition of some material from Earth and Space.

Pages 28–39 tabulate the Programme of study and Statements of attainment for each of these Attainment targets. Teachers may wish to use the Programme of study tables to find out quickly in which chapter of the course a particular part of the National Curriculum is covered. The Statement of attainment tables indicate opportunities for the internal assessment of pupils and for monitoring their progress through the levels of attainment.

Programmes of study relating to Sc1

Pupils should be encouraged to develop investigative skills and understanding of science in activities which:	Nuffield Co-ordinated Sciences
• relate to their everyday experience and to new contexts, involving increasingly abstract concepts and the application and extension of scientific knowledge, understanding and skills, where pupils need to make decisions about the degree of precision and safe working required	This is the context in which **all** investigations should be carried out.
• promote invention and creativity	**C**15D, **P**1A, **P**4A, **P**18C, **P**21B
• encourage detailed planning and evaluation in the light of findings	See the list of experiments on pages 20–21
• encourage the use of secondary sources	**B**1C, **B**1D, **B**13B, **C**1, **P**13B, **P**13C
• are increasingly complex because they involve derived and/or interacting variables	See the list of experiments on pages 20–21
• require key variables to be controlled or taken into account, and pupils to recognize that need	**B**2D, **B**3B, **B**5.2, **B**7F, **B**7H, **B**8A, **B**9C, **B**12.2, **B**13C, **B**13D, **B**16.2, **B**16A, **B**16C, **B**17B, **C**3.2, **C**7.4, **C**10.4, **C**13.5, **C**15A, **C**15B, **C**15C, **C**16A, **P**1A, **P**1B, **P**4E, **P**5A-E, **P**6C, **P**8B, **P**9A, **P**9C, **P**17E-G
• require them to generate theoretical models and to test them	See the list of experiments on pages 20–21
• may take place over a period of time and require sampling techniques	**B**4D, **B**11A, **B**13A, **B**13D, **C**7.4, **C**11C, **P**13C
• require accurate measurement, with identification and quantification of, and accounting for, experimental error and anomalous results	This is a standard procedure for **all** experiments.
• encourage the systematic recording and presentation of data using, as appropriate, a full range of forms, including graphs and mathematical relationships	**B**3H, **B**5C, **B**6B, **B**7E, **B**8B, **B**9A, **B**12B, **B**15A, **B**15B, **B**16D, **B**19D, **B**20A, **B**20B, **B**21.2, **B**21.4, **B**22B, **C**15A-C, **P**3.6, **P**4C, **P**7A, **P**8.5, **P**9, **P**17
• encourage pattern searching in complex data and predictions requiring abstract reasoning	**B**4A, **B**4B, **B**4D, **B**4E, **B**6A, **B**6B, **B**14.1, **B**14A, **B**20C, **P**3.6
• involve the critical evaluation of data	**B**1B, **B**10A, **B**11A, **B**11.3, **B**12.2, **B**12B, **B**12C, **B**12D, **B**16A-D, **B**22A-E, **B**23A-D, **C**13E, **C**17.2
• give opportunities to use information technology to gather and display data from experiments, to access and organize data relevant to their study of science, and to use programmable systems to control external electronic, electrical or mechanical devices	**B**12E, **C**15A-D, **P**4A-E, **P**5A-E, **P**6A-E, **P**13C, **P**20A-D, **P**21A-C
• explore the nature of scientific evidence and proof	**E**2.2, **E**2.5, **E**2.6, **E**3.5, **E**3.6, **E**3.7
• distinguish between claims and arguments based on scientific considerations and those which are not	**P**7C, **P**7H, **E**3.7
• distinguish between generalizations and predictive theories	The results of many experiments are generalizations. Pupils working towards higher levels will progress to producing predictive theories where appropriate.
• study examples of scientific controversies and the ways in which scientific ideas change	**B**23, **C**4A5, **C**18, **P**5, **P**10, **E**2.2
• encourage them to appraise their investigations critically, including consideration of errors, and to suggest related improvements to their methods	This should be done in **all** investigations.

The Statements of attainment relating to Sc1 follow on page 24.

Statements of attainment relating to Sc 1

As well as listing the National Curriculum Statements of attainment, this table also gives examples of criteria for assessment over levels 4 to 10 for the investigation "Investigating the cooling of coffee" from Chapter P9

Level	Strand (i) Ask questions, predict and hypothesize		Strand (ii) Observe, measure and manipulate variables	
	Statements of attainment	Examples	Statements of attainment	Examples
4	a) Ask questions, suggest ideas and make predictions, based on some relevant prior knowledge, in a form which can be investigated	*Suggest that volume matters and suggest how the rate might depend on the volume*	b) Carry out a fair test in which they select and use appropriate instruments to measure quantities such as volume and temperature	*Control initial temperature and time how long it takes two different volumes of coffee to cool to the same final temperature*
5	a) Formulate hypotheses where the causal link is based on scientific knowledge, understanding or theory	*Suggest that a large cup of coffee cools more slowly than a small cup of coffee because there is more coffee there*	b) Choose the range of each of the variables involved to produce meaningful results	*Time how long it takes two different volumes of coffee to cool over a meaningful range of temperature*
6	a) Use scientific knowledge, understanding or theory to predict relationships between continuous variables	*Suggest that the larger the volume, the slower the cooling because there is more coffee there*	b) Consider the range of factors involved, identify the key variables and those to be controlled and/or taken account of, and make qualitative or quantitative observations involving fine discrimination	*Time how long it takes a range of different volumes of coffee to cool over a meaningful range of temperature*
7	a) Use scientific knowledge, understanding or theory to predict the relative effect of a number of variables	*Suggest, with reasons, that size of container, volume of liquid and initial temperature all affect the rate of cooling, and that the most important of these is volume*	b) Manipulate or take account of the relative effect of two or more independent variables	*Time how long it takes different volumes of coffee to cool, starting from a range of initial temperatures*
8	a) Use scientific knowledge, understanding or theory to generate quantitative predictions and a strategy for the investigation	*Suggest, with reasons, that the time to cool between the same two temperatures is doubled if the volume of coffee is doubled and suggest a relevant investigation; also suggest repeating the experiment*	b) Select and use measuring instruments which provide the degree of accuracy commensurate with the outcome they have predicted	*As above, measuring temperatures to 0.5 °C and volumes to 0.5 ml*
9	a) Use a scientific theory to make quantitative predictions and organize the collection of valid and reliable data.	*Suggest that the time to cool between the same two temperatures is doubled if the volume of coffee is doubled and suggest a relevant investigation; also suggest repeating the experiment*	b) Systematically use a range of investigatory techniques to judge the relative effect of the factors involved	*Carry out the above procedure systematically*
10	a) Use scientific knowledge and an understanding of laws, theories and models to develop hypotheses which seek to explain the behaviour of objects and events they have studied	*Suggest that the time to cool between the same two temperatures depends on the ratio of surface area to volume*	b) Collect data which is sufficiently valid and reliable to enable them to make a critical evaluation of the law, theory or model	*As above, and calculate surface area; check thermometer*

Strand (iii) Interpret their results and evaluate scientific evidence

Level	Statements of attainment	Examples
4	c) Draw conclusions which link patterns in observations or results to the original question, prediction or idea	*Conclude that a big cup of coffee cools more slowly than a small cup of coffee*
5	c) Evaluate the validity of their conclusions by considering different interpretations of their experimental evidence	*Conclude that a big cup of coffee cools more slowly than a small cup of coffee, but qualifying the conclusion*
6	c) Use their results to draw conclusions, explain the relationship between variables and refer to a model to explain the results	*Conclude that increasing the volume reduces the rate of cooling because the larger volume has more energy*
7	c) Use observations or results to draw conclusions which state the relative effects of the independent variables and explain the limitations of the evidence obtained	*Conclude that the volume of coffee has a bigger effect on the rate of cooling than the initial temperature over a range of volumes and temperatures between 60 °C and 80 °C*
8	c) Justify each aspect of the investigation in terms of the contribution to the overall conclusion	*Explain why the volume was kept constant for a range of temperatures and why the temperature interval was kept constant for a range of volumes*
9	c) Analyse and interpret the data obtained, in terms of complex functions where appropriate, in a way which demonstrates an appreciation of the uncertainty of evidence and the tentative nature of conclusions	*Use the data from repeated experiments to draw graphs of results and to show that the rate of cooling decreases with volume; comment on the accuracy of the experiment*
10	c) Use and analyse the data obtained to evaluate the law, theory or model in terms of the extent to which it can explain the observed behaviour	*Use the data from repeated experiments to draw graphs of results and to show that the rate of cooling depends on the ratio of surface area to volume; comment on the accuracy of the experiment*

Prompt sheet for investigations (levels 4 to 6)

The planning stage	The reporting stage
Some points to consider	**Some points to consider**
1 Why are you doing this investigation?	12 What did you do?
2 What do you think is going to happen?	13 What were your observations and measurements?
3 Explain your answer to question **2**.	14 What errors are there in your observations and measurements?
4 How are you going to make sure that the investigation is a fair test?	15 What explanations can you give for your results?
5 Which apparatus have you selected to aid your observations and to take measurements?	16 What are your conclusions?
6 Why have you selected that apparatus?	17 Do your conclusions answer your original question?
More difficult questions	**More difficult questions**
7 What are the key variables?	18 What is the relationship between the variables?
8 Which variables are you going to control or take account of?	19 How can you explain your results using scientific ideas?
9 What ranges have you chosen for your variables?	
10 Why have you chosen those ranges?	
11 What relationships do you predict between the continuous variables?	

This sheet may be photocopied for distribution to pupils within the institution purchasing this book.

Prompt sheet for investigations (levels 6 to 10)

The planning stage	The reporting stage
Some points to consider	**Some points to consider**
1 Why are you doing this investigation?	9 What is the relationship between the variables?
2 Explain carefully what you think is going to happen.	10 Explain your results using scientific ideas.
3 What are the key variables?	11 What were the relative effects of the variables?
4 Which variables are you going to control or take account of?	12 Explain why you did each part of the investigation.
5 What relationships do you predict between the continuous variables?	13 How could your results have been affected by errors?
More difficult questions	**More difficult questions**
6 What strategy have you chosen for the investigation?	14 How sure are you of your conclusions? Explain your answer carefully.
7 Which variables do you think will have the most effect on your investigation?	15 In the light of your results, how useful is the original law on which you based your conclusions?
8 Try to predict the amount of changes of the variables.	

Programme of study relating to Sc2

Strand 2(i)	Life processes and the organization of living things	NCS chapter
2(i)I	Pupils should extend their study of the major organs and organ systems and life processes	B3, B4, B5, B6, B7, B8, B9, B10, B11, B12, B19, B20, B21
2(i)2	They should explore and investigate sensitivity, co-ordination and response, and should relate behaviour to survival and reproduction in plants and animals	B1, B2, B10, B11, B12, B19, B20
2(i)3	They should investigate limiting factors in photosynthesis, and the use of photosynthetic products in plants	B3
2(i)4	They should explore how the internal environments of plants and animals are maintained, including water relations, temperature control, defence mechanisms, solute balance, for example, *sugars, carbon dioxide, urea, and the human embryonic environment*	B7, B8, B9, B12, B20
2(i)5	In the context of their study of the major human organs they should consider the factors associated with a healthy life-style and examples of technologies used to promote, improve and sustain the quality of life	B4, B6, B8, B9, B10, B11, B12, B20, B21
2(i)6	They should consider how hormones can be used to control and promote fertility, growth and development in plants and animals, and be aware of the implications of their use	B20, B21, B22
2(i)7	Pupils should have opportunities to consider the effects of solvents, alcohol, tobacco and other drugs on the way the human body functions	B7, B8, B11, B21
Strand 2(ii)	**Variation and the mechanisms of inheritance and evolution**	**NCS chapter**
2(ii)1	Pupils should use keys to assign organisms to their major groups and have opportunities to measure the differences between individuals	B1, B2
2(ii)2	They should consider the interaction of genetic and environmental factors (including radiation) in variation	B22
2(ii)3	They should be introduced to the gene as a section of a DNA molecule and study how DNA is able to replicate itself and control protein synthesis by means of a base code	B22
2(ii)4	Using the concept of the gene, they should explore the basic principles of inheritance in plants and animals and their application in the understanding of how sex is determined in human beings and how some diseases can be inherited	B22
2(ii)5	Using sources which give a range of perspectives, they should have the opportunity to consider the basic principle of genetic engineering, for example, *in relation to drug and hormone production,* as well as being aware of any ethical considerations that such production involves	B12
2(ii)6	They should consider the evidence for evolution and explore the ideas of variability and selection leading to evolution and selective breeding	B22, B23
2(ii)7	They should consider the social, economic and ethical aspects of cloning and selective breeding	B22

Strand 2(iii)	Populations and human influences within ecosystems	NCS chapter
2(iii)1	Pupils should make a more detailed and quantitative study of a habitat, including the investigation of the abundance and distribution of common species, and ways in which they are adapted to their environment	B10, B11, B13, B14, B16
2(iii)2	They should explore factors affecting population size, including human populations	B13, B16
2(iii)3	They should have opportunities, through fieldwork and other investigations, to consider current concerns about human activity leading to pollution and effects on the environment, including the use of fertilizers in agriculture, the exploitation of resources, and the disposal of waste products on the Earth, in its oceans and in the atmosphere	B17, B18
2(iii)4	They should relate the environmental impact of human activity to the size of population, economic factors and industrial requirements	B17, B18
2(iii)5	The work should encourage pupils to use their scientific knowledge, weigh evidence and form balanced judgements about some of the major environmental issues facing society	C4, C13, P12
Strand 2(iv)	Energy flows and cycles of matter within ecosystems	NCS chapter
2(iv)1	Pupils should consider energy transfer through an ecosystem and how photosynthesis initiates this process	B14, B15
2(iv)2	They should consider how food production involves the management of ecosystems to improve the efficiency of energy transfer and how such management imposes a duty of care	B15, B17
2(iv)3	They should explore cycling of the elements and biological materials in specific ecosystems, for example, *seas, farms and market gardens*, including the role of microbes and other living organisms in the cycling of carbon and nitrogen	B15
2(iv)4	They should relate their scientific knowledge to the impact of human activity on these cycles and ecosystems and to the disposal of waste materials	B15, B17

Statements of attainment relating to Sc2

Pupils should:

Level 4		NCS chapter
2.4(a)	be able to name and locate the major organs of the human body and of the flowering plant	B3, B4, B5, B7, B8, B10, B11, B12, B19, B20
2.4(b)	be able to assign plants and animals to their major groups using keys and observable features	B1, B2
2.4(c)	understand that the survival of plants and animals in an environment depends on successful competition for scarce resources	B13
2.4(d)	understand food chains as a way of representing feeding relationships in an ecosystem	B14
Level 5		**NCS chapter**
2.5(a)	be able to name and outline the functions of the major organs and organ systems in mammals and in flowering plants	B3, B4, B5, B7, B8, B10, B11, B12, B19, B20
2.5(b)	know that information in the form of genes is passed on from one generation to the next	B22
2.5(c)	know how pollution can affect the survival of organisms	B17, B18
2.5(d)	know about the key factors in the process of decay	B15
Level 6		**NCS chapter**
2.6(a)	be able to relate structure to function in plant and animal cells	B3, B7, B8, B10, B11, B19
2.6(b)	know the ways in which living organisms are adapted to survive in their natural environment	B1, B2, B10, B11, B12, B13, B14, B16, B19
2.6(c)	know that variation in living organisms has both genetic and environmental causes	B22
2.6(d)	understand population changes in predator–prey relationships	B13, B16
2.6(e)	know that the balance of materials in a biological community can be maintained by the cycling of these materials	B15
Level 7		**NCS chapter**
2.7(a)	understand the life processes of movement, respiration, growth, reproduction, excretion, nutrition and sensitivity in animals	B4, B5, B6, B7, B8, B9, B10, B11, B21
2.7(b)	understand the life processes of photosynthesis, respiration and reproduction in green plants	B3, B9, B19
2.7(c)	understand how selective breeding can produce economic benefits and contribute to improved yields	B22
2.7(d)	know how population growth and decline is related to environmental resources	B16
2.7(e)	understand pyramids of numbers and biomass	B14

Level 8		NCS chapter
2.8(a)	be able to describe how the internal environment in plants, animals and the human embryo is maintained	B7, B8, B9, B12, B20
2.8(b)	know how genetic information is passed from cell to cell and from generation to generation by cell division	B22
2.8(c)	understand the principles of a monohybrid cross involving dominant and recessive alleles	B22
2.8(d)	understand that the impact of human activity on the Earth is related to the size of the population, economic factors and industrial requirements	B17, B18
2.8(e)	understand the role of microbes and other living organisms in the process of decay and in the cycling of nutrients	B15
Level 9		NCS chapter
2.9(a)	be able to explain the co-ordination in mammals of the body's activities through nervous and hormonal control	B12, B20, B21
2.9(b)	understand the different sources of genetic variation	B22
2.9(c)	understand the relationships between variation, natural selection and reproductive success in organisms and the significance of these relationships for evolution	B16, B23
2.9(d)	understand the basic scientific principles associated with a major change in the biosphere	B17
2.9(e)	understand how materials for growth and energy are transferred through an ecosystem	B14, B15
Level 10		NCS chapter
2.10(a)	understand how homeostatic and metabolic processes contribute to maintaining the internal environment of organisms	B12
2.10(b)	understand how DNA replicates and controls protein synthesis by means of a base code	B22
2.10(c)	understand the basic principles of genetic engineering, selective breeding and cloning, and how these give rise to social and ethical issues	B20, B22
2.10(d)	understand how food production involves the management of ecosystems to improve the efficiency of energy transfer, and that such management imposes a duty of care	B15, B17

Programme of study relating to Sc3

Strand 3(i)	The properties, classification and structure of materials	NCS chapter
3(i)1	Pupils should carry out a more detailed study of selected elements and their compounds, covering metals and non-metals, in order to understand the limitations and different ways in which elements can be classified and ordered in the Periodic Table	C1, C5, C13, C17
3(i)2	They should recognize patterns in the properties of elements in groups and periods and relate these to the electronic structures	C1, C5, C17, C18
3(i)3	Pupils should be able to make predictions from the reactivity series of metals	C4, C7, C14
3(i)4	They should investigate the process of neutralization	C10, C11, C12
3(i)5	Pupils should study the properties, structure and uses of materials, including metals, ceramics, glass, plastic and fibres	C2, C5, C6, C7, C8, C13
3(i)6	Pupils should have the opportunity to separate and purify the components of mixtures and to make different types of mixtures which have important everyday applications, such as emulsions, foams, gels and solutions	C2, C3, C4, C7, C9, C10, C11
3(i)7	They should be introduced to the idea of composite materials, illustrated by some common examples including reinforced concrete, glass-reinforced plastic, bone and synthetic fibres	C8, P1
Strand 3(ii)	**Explanations of the properties of materials**	**NCS chapter**
3(ii)1	Pupils should investigate the quantitative relationships between the volume, temperature and pressure of a gas, and use the kinetic theory to explain changes of state and other phenomena	C5, C9, C18, P2
3(ii)2	They should develop models to explain the difference between elements and compounds in terms of atoms, molecules, ions and ionic and covalent bonds	C1, C3, C5, C11, C13, C16, C18, P1, P2
3(ii)3	They should use their knowledge of the structure of the atom to explain the existence of isotopes and radioactivity	P3
3(ii)4	Through demonstration experiments pupils should become aware of the characteristics of radioactive emissions and determine the half-life of a nuclide	P3, E2
3(ii)5	Pupils should study the different methods of detecting ionizing radiation and its effects on matter and living organisms, developing an understanding of the beneficial and harmful effects	P3
Strand 3(iii)	**Chemical changes**	**NCS chapter**
3(iii)1	Pupils should investigate a range of types of reaction, including thermal and electrolytic decomposition, ionic reactions in solution, salt formation, oxidation and reduction, fermentation and polymerization and, where possible, relate these to models and to everyday processes such as corrosion and the manufacture of new materials	C2, C3, C4, C6, C7, C8, C10, C11, C12, C13, C14, C15, C16, C18
3(iii)2	They should investigate the different factors affecting the rate of chemical reactions and relate these to the practical problems associated with the manufacture of new materials and to everyday biochemical change	C16
3(iii)3	Chemical and electrolytic reactions should be represented first in word and later in symbolic equations and these should be used as a way of describing and understanding reactions	C1, C2, C4, C12, C16
3(iii)4	Pupils should begin to explore through experiment and the use of data the quantitative aspects of chemical equations, including masses of solids and volumes of gases	C5, C10, C12, C15

3(iii)5	The work should involve determination of formulae and, subsequently, quantitative electrolysis	C12, C15, C18
3(iii)6	Pupils should study chemical reactions in which there is energy transfer to and from the surroundings	C2, C13, C14
3(iii)7	At a later stage they should become aware that the energy transfer is associated with the making and reforming of chemical bonds and can be determined quantitatively by experiment and the use of data	C13, C14
3(iii)8	Pupils should study the energy requirements and the social, economic, environmental and health and safety factors associated with the manufacture of materials	C2, C4, C6, C10, C13, C16
3(iii)9	This should involve studying the processes involved in metal extraction, cracking oil, the chlor–alkali industry and the production of plastics and fertilizers	C2, C4, C8, C13, C16
3(iii)10	Pupils should relate this research to experimental methods used in the laboratory	C8, C11
3(iii)11	During the work they should be made aware that some reactions are significantly reversible and may reach an equilibrium, and that this may be a major consideration in some manufacturing processes	C16
Strand 3(iv)	**The Earth and its atmosphere**	**NCS chapter**
3(iv)1	Pupils should study, through measurement and by other means, the principles which govern the behaviour of gases in the atmosphere, and the nature of the energy transfers which drive their motion	C10, E1
3(iv)2	They should study atmospheric circulation, including the qualitative relationship between pressure, winds and weather patterns	C10, E1
3(iv)3	They should study the origins of the atmosphere and the oceans, and be aware of the chemical and biological factors which maintain atmospheric composition	E1, E3
3(iv)4	Pupils should study, through laboratory and fieldwork, the evidence which reveals the mode of formation and later deformation of rocks, and the sources of energy that drive such processes	C4, E2
3(iv)5	Pupils should study the scientific processes involved in the weathering of rocks, transport of sediments and soil formation	C4, C15, E2
3(iv)6	Pupils should understand how geological timescales are measured	C4, E2
3(iv)7	They should examine data which suggest that the Earth has a layered structure, including contrasting densities between surface rocks and the whole Earth, transmission of earthquake waves and magnetic evidence	P15, E2
3(iv)8	They should investigate the evidence that favours the theory of plate tectonics including the nature of the rock record	E2
3(iv)9	They should consider how plate movements are involved in the recycling of rocks and the global distribution of the Earth's physical resources	E2
3(iv)10	They should consider theories from earlier times concerning movements of the Earth's crust, and how these were changed through advances in several fields of science and technology	E2

Statements of attainment relating to Sc3

Pupils should:

Level 4		NCS chapter
3.4(a)	be able to classify materials as solids, liquids and gases on the basis of simple properties which relate to their everyday uses	C5, P1
3.4(b)	know that materials from a variety of sources can be converted into new and useful products by chemical reactions	C3, C6, C7, C8, C11, C14, C16
3.4(c)	know that the combustion of fuel releases energy and produces waste gases	C2, C13
3.4(d)	know how measurements of temperature, rainfall, wind speed and direction describe the weather	E1
3.4(e)	know that weathering, erosion and transport lead to the formation of sediments and different types of soil	C4, C15, E2
Level 5		NCS chapter
3.5(a)	know how to separate and purify the components of mixtures using physical processes	C2, C4, C7, C9
3.5(b)	be able to classify aqueous solutions as acidic, alkaline or neutral, using indicators	C12
3.5(c)	understand that rusting and burning involve a reaction with oxygen	C7
3.5(d)	understand the water cycle in terms of the physical processes involved	C10, E1
Level 6		NCS chapter
3.6(a)	be able to distinguish between metallic and non-metallic elements, mixtures and compounds using simple chemical and physical properties	C1, C17
3.6(b)	understand the physical differences between solids, liquids and gases in simple particle terms	C5, P2
3.6(c)	understand oxidation processes, including combustion, as reactions with oxygen to form oxides	C4, C7, C13, C16
3.6(d)	be able to recognize variations in the properties of metals and make predictions based on the reactivity series	C4, C7, C14
3.6(e)	know that some chemical reactions are exothermic, while others are endothermic	C2, C13
3.6(f)	know about the readily observable effects of electrolysis	C4
3.6(g)	understand how different airstreams give different weather related to their recent path over land and sea	E1
3.6(h)	understand the scientific processes involved in the formation of igneous, sedimentary and metamorphic rocks including the timescales over which these processes operate	C4, E2
Level 7		NCS chapter
3.7(a)	be able to relate the properties of a variety of classes of materials to their everyday uses	C5, C7, C8, C10, C11
3.7(b)	know that the Periodic Table groups contain families of elements with similar properties, which depend on their electronic structure	C1, C17
3.7(c)	understand changes of state, including the associated energy changes, mixing and diffusion in terms of the proximity and motion of particles	C9, C18
3.7(d)	understand the relationships between the volume, pressure and temperature of a gas	P2

3.7(e)	understand the difference between elements, compounds and mixtures in terms of atoms, ions and molecules	C1, C5, C10, C11, C16, C18
3.7(f)	understand the factors which influence the rate of a chemical reaction	C15, C16
3.7(g)	be able to relate knowledge and understanding of chemical principles to manufacturing processes and everyday effects	C4, C10, C11, C13, C14, C16
3.7(h)	understand how some weather phenomena are driven by energy transfer processes	E1
Level 8		**NCS chapter**
3.8(a)	know the major characteristics of metals and non-metals as reflected in the properties of a range of their compounds	C1, C17
3.8(b)	understand the structure of the atom in terms of protons, neutrons and electrons and how this can explain the existence of isotopes	C18, P3
3.8(c)	understand radioactivity and nuclear fission and the harmful and beneficial effects of ionizing radiations	P3
3.8(d)	be able to relate the properties of molecular and giant structures to the arrangement of atoms and ions	C3, C5, C6, C7, C8
3.8(e)	be able to explain the physical and chemical processes by which different chemicals are made from oil	C2, C8, C13
3.8(f)	be able to use symbolic equations to describe and explain a range of reactions including ionic interactions and those occurring in electrolytic cells	C1, C2, C4, C10, C12, C16
3.8(g)	understand how the atmosphere has evolved and how its composition remains broadly constant	B3, E3
3.8(h)	be able to interpret evidence of modes of formation and deformation of rocks	E2
Level 9		**NCS chapter**
3.9(a)	understand how the properties of elements depend on their electronic structure and their position in the Periodic Table	C5, C17, C18
3.9(b)	understand the nature of radioactive decay, relating half-life to the use of radioactive materials	P3, E2
3.9(c)	be able to interpret chemical equations quantitatively	C5, C10, C12, C15
3.9(d)	be able to use scientific information from a range of sources to evaluate the social, economic, health and safety and environmental factors associated with a major manufacturing process	C4, C11, C16
3.9(e)	be able to use appropriate scientific ideas to explain changes in the atmosphere that cause various weather phenomena	E1
3.9(f)	be able to describe and explain the supporting evidence, in simple terms, for the layered structure of the inner Earth	E2
Level 10		**NCS chapter**
3.10(a)	be able to use data on the properties of different materials in order to make evaluative judgements about their uses	C6, C7, C8, C14, P1
3.10(b)	understand chemical reactions in terms of the energy transfers associated with making and breaking chemical bonds	C13
3.10(c)	be able to relate the bulk properties of metals, ceramics, glass, plastics and fibres to simple models of their structure	C6, C7, C8, C11
3.10(d)	be able to interpret electrolytic processes quantitatively	C18
3.10(e)	understand the theory of plate tectonics and the contribution this process makes to the recycling of rocks	E2

Programme of study relating to Sc4

Strand 4(i)	Electricity and magnetism	NCS chapter
4(i)1	Pupils should study the use of electricity for the transfer of energy, the measurement of energy transferred, and its relation to the costs of using common domestic devices	P11
4(i)2	Such work should also develop an understanding of the dangers of electricity and the standard features and procedures which protect users of electrical equipment	P16
4(i)3	They should develop an understanding of unbalanced charges involving the movement of electrons to interpret common electrostatic phenomena and should consider the dangers and use of electrostatic charge generated in everyday situations	P19
4(i)4	Pupils should study electromagnetic effects in common devices	P11, P18
4(i)5	Pupils should investigate principles of electromagnetic induction as applied to the generation and transmission of electricity and devices such as *dynamos and transformers*	P11, P17, P18
4(i)6	Pupils should be given opportunities to extend their quantitative study of electrical circuits	P11, P17
4(i)7	They should use measurements of voltage and current to derive measurements of electrical resistance, charge, energy transferred and electrical power	P11, P16, P17
4(i)8	Pupils should continue to investigate the properties of components in controlling simple circuits using switches and relays, variable resistors, capacitors, diodes, transistors and logic gates	P16, P17, P20
4(i)9	They should investigate the behaviour of bistable circuits made from two logic gates	P20
4(i)10	They should consider the role of bistables in simple memory circuits to perform useful tasks	P20
4(i)11	They should investigate the effects of feedback in a control system and consider the implications of information and control technology for everyday life	P20
4(i)12	They should use knowledge of electronic systems, both analogue and digital, to solve problems	P20, P21
4(i)13	Pupils should develop an understanding of common electrical phenomena in conductors in terms of charge flow, including electrons and ions, and extend this to the study of thermionic emission and the production of X-rays	P19
Strand 4(ii)	**Energy resources and energy transfer**	**NCS chapter**
4(ii)1	Pupils should investigate the ways in which energy is transferred in a variety of personal and practical situations, including combustion of fuels	P8,.P9, P10, P11, P12
4(ii)2	These investigations should include transfer by conduction, convection and radiation, particularly in domestic contexts, including the effects of insulation	P9, P10, P11
4(ii)3	They should further develop ideas of energy conservation and efficiency of energy transfer	P6, P8, P9, P10, P11, P12
4(ii)4	They should investigate the relationship between potential and kinetic energy and link these to the concept of work	P6, P7
4(ii)5	They should be introduced to the idea of power as rate of energy transfer or doing work	P8
4(ii)6	The study should include the idea that although energy is always conserved, it may be dissipated and so it becomes harder to arrange for useful transfers of energy	P8, P9, P10
4(ii)7	They should be introduced to the ways electricity is generated in power stations from a range of resources, both renewable and non-renewable	P12
4(ii)8	By analysis of data, pupils should understand that some energy resources are limited and consider the longer term implications of the worldwide patterns of distribution and use of energy resources, including the "greenhouse effect"	P11, P12
4(ii)9	They should be given opportunities to discuss how society makes decisions about energy resources	P11, P12

Strand 4(iii)	Forces and their effects	NCS chapter
4(iii)1	Pupils should investigate the effects of forces on movement and the relationships between force, mass and acceleration	P1, P4, P5, P8
4(iii)2	They should explore examples of motion including free-fall, circular motion and the movement of projectiles and be aware of the effect of friction	P4, P5, P7
4(iii)3	They should consider the use of ideas of momentum and energy in relation to motion in systems, for example, *in collisions, rockets and jet propulsion*	P6
4(iii)4	They should investigate pressure and everyday applications of hydraulics	P8
4(iii)5	Pupils should investigate the relationship between forces and their effects in relation to the properties of common materials and how these determine the design, testing and strength of relevant artefacts and structures	P1
4(iii)6	They should apply their knowledge of the turning effect of forces and develop their understanding of centre of mass	P5, P8
Strand 4(iv)	**Light and sound**	**NCS chapter**
4(iv)1	Pupils should explore the fundamental characteristics of sound, including loudness, amplitude, pitch and frequency	P14, P15
4(iv)2	They should have opportunities to improve their understanding of the properties and behaviour of sound by developing a wave model, for example through observations of waves *in ropes, in springs and on water*	P14
4(iv)3	This should be related to pupils' experience of sounds and musical instruments, acoustics, electronic instruments and recording	P15
4(iv)4	They should be given the opportunity to investigate devices, for example microphones and loudspeakers, which act as transducers	P21
4(iv)5	They should understand the importance of noise control in the environment	P13
4(iv)6	Pupils should investigate the characteristics and effects of vibration, including resonance, in a range of mechanical systems	P15
4(iv)7	They should extend this study to include some uses of electronic sound technology in, for example, *industry (cleaning and quality control), medicine (pre-natal scanning) and social contexts (musical instruments)*	P15
4(iv)8	Pupils should investigate the fundamental characteristics of light, such as reflection, refraction, diffraction, interference and polarization	P13, P14, P15
4(iv)9	They should relate these characteristics to the wave model	P13, P15
4(iv)10	They should investigate the types of electromagnetic radiation, their uses and their potential dangers in domestic situations (microwaves, infra-red, ultra-violet), communication (radio, microwaves, light), and medicine (X-rays, gamma rays)	P15, P21
4(iv)11	They should study the process of transmission of waves through different media, including the relationship between speed, frequency and wavelength	P14
4(iv)12	They should understand the working of a range of optical devices	P13, P15
Strand 4(v)	**The Earth's place in the Universe**	**NCS chapter**
4(v)1	Pupils should have opportunities to use the idea of gravitational force to explain the movement and positions of the Earth, Moon, Sun, planets and other bodies in the Universe	E3
4(v)2	The idea of gravitational force should also be applied to tides, comets and satellites	P7, E3
4(v)3	Pupils should consider the possibilities and limitations of space travel and the use of the data gained	E3
4(v)4	Pupils should know that other planets are geologically active and that their present composition is related to their distance from the Sun	E3
4(v)5	Pupils should understand that the Sun is powered by nuclear fusion processes	E3
4(v)6	Pupils should examine ideas that have been used in the past, and more recently, to explain the character and origin of the Earth, other planets, stars and the Universe	E3
4(v)7	They should study the "life cycle" of stars	E3

Statements of attainment relating to Sc4

Pupils should:

Level 4		NCS chapter
4.4(a)	be able to construct circuits containing a number of components in which switches are used to control electrical effects	P16
4.4(b)	understand that an energy transfer is needed to make things work	P8, P11, P12
4.4(c)	know that more than one force can act on an object and that forces can act in different directions	P5
4.4(d)	know that light travels faster than sound	P15
4.4(e)	be able to explain day and night, day length and year length in terms of the movements of the Earth around the Sun	E3
Level 5		**NCS chapter**
4.5(a)	know how switches, relays, variable resistors, sensors and logic gates can be used to solve simple problems	P16, P20, P21
4.5(b)	understand that energy is transferred in any process and recognize transfers in a range of devices	P6, P8, P9, P10, P11, P14
4.5(c)	understand the difference between renewable and non-renewable energy resources and the need for fuel economy	P12
4.5(d)	know that the size and direction of the resultant force on an object affects its movement	P1, P5
4.5(e)	understand how the reflection of light enables objects to be seen	P13
4.5(f)	know that sound is produced by a vibrating object and travels as a wave	P14
4.5(g)	be able to describe the motion of planets in the Solar System	E3
Level 6		**NCS chapter**
4.6(a)	understand the qualitative relationships between current, voltage and resistance	P11, P17
4.6(b)	understand that energy is conserved	P8
4.6(c)	understand that the Sun is ultimately the major energy source for the Earth	P12
4.6(d)	understand the relationship between an applied force, the area over which it acts and the resulting pressure	P2, P8
4.6(e)	understand the relationship between speed, distance and time	P4
4.6(f)	be able to relate loudness and amplitude, pitch and frequency, of a sound wave	P13, P14, P15
4.6(g)	know that the Solar System forms part of a galaxy which is part of a larger system called the Universe	E3
Level 7		**NCS chapter**
4.7(a)	understand the magnetic effect of an electric current and its application in a range of common devices	P11, P18, P21
4.7(b)	understand how energy is transferred through conduction, convection and radiation	P9, P10, P11
4.7(c)	be able to evaluate methods of reducing wasteful transfers of energy by using a definition of energy efficiency	P8, P9, P10, P11

4.7(d)	understand the quantitative relationships between force, distance, work, power and time	P8
4.7(e)	understand the law of moments	P2, P8
4.7(f)	be able to use the wave model of light to explain refraction at a plane surface	P13, P14
4.7(g)	know that gravity acts between all masses and the magnitude of the force diminishes with distance	E3
Level 8		**NCS chapter**
4.8(a)	be able to explain charge flow and energy transfer in a circuit	P11, P17
4.8(b)	be able to use the quantitative relationship between change in internal energy and temperature change	P9, P10
4.8(c)	understand the quantitative relationship between force, mass and acceleration	P5
4.8(d)	understand the quantitative relationship between speed, frequency and wavelength	P14
4.8(e)	be able to explain resonance in oscillating systems and how this can be advantageous and disadvantageous	P15
4.8(f)	be able to use data on the Solar System or other stellar systems to speculate about the conditions elsewhere in the Universe	E3
Level 9		**NCS chapter**
4.9(a)	be able to use the quantitative relationships between charge, current, potential difference, resistance and electrical power	P16, P17
4.9(b)	be able to evaluate the economic, environmental and social benefits of different energy sources, using quantitative secondary sources of information	P11, P12
4.9(c)	be able to use the quantitative relationships between mass, weight, potential energy, kinetic energy and work	P6, P7
4.9(d)	be able to relate the physical properties of the main areas of the electromagnetic spectrum to their uses and effects	P15
4.9(e)	be able to relate the theory of gravitational force to the motion of satellites	P7, E3
Level 10		**NCS chapter**
4.10(a)	understand the principles of electromagnetic induction	P11, P18
4.10(b)	understand that in many processes energy is spread out into the surroundings and shared amongst many particles, so reducing the possibility of further useful energy transfers	P8, P9, P10
4.10(c)	understand the concept of momentum and its conservation	P6
4.10(d)	be able to relate an understanding of the nature of electromagnetic radiation to its behaviour in the processes of interference, diffraction and polarization	P13, P15
4.10(e)	be able to relate current theories about the origin and future of the Universe to the astronomical evidence	E3

Chapter 5 **Safety**

As part of the reviewing process these publications have been checked for safety. In particular we have attempted to ensure that:

- all recognized hazards have been identified (and especially those covered by the COSHH regulations),
- suitable precautions are suggested,
- where possible the proposed procedures are in accordance with commonly adopted general risk assessments,
- where general risk assessments are not available, procedures are judged to be satisfactory and of an equivalent standard.

However, teachers should be aware that mistakes can be made, and in any case different employers adopt different standards. Therefore, before carrying out any practical activity, teachers should always check that what they are proposing to do is compatible with their employer's risk assessments, and does not need modification for their particular circumstances. Any local rules issued by the employer must always be followed, whatever is recommended here.

General risk assessments have been taken from, or are compatible with:

Hazcards (CLEAPSS, 1989)
Topics in safety (ASE, second edition, 1988)
Microbiology: an HMI guide for schools and FE (HMSO, 1990)
Safeguards in the school laboratory (ASE, ninth edition, 1988)
Hazardous chemicals: a manual for schools and colleges (SSSERC/Oliver and Boyd, 1979)

It is assumed that:

- pupils are taught safe techniques for such activities as heating chemicals, smelling them, pouring from bottles, or handling flammable chemicals or micro-organisms,
- good laboratory practice is observed when chemicals and living organisms are handled,
- eye protection is worn whenever there is any recognized risk to the eyes (including activities involving heating substances, those involving toxic, corrosive or flammable chemicals, or those where high temperatures may result from a chemical reaction),
- care is taken with normal laboratory operations, such as heating substances and handling heavy objects,
- rules for student behaviour are strictly enforced,
- fieldwork takes account of any guidelines issued by the employer,
- practical work is conducted in a properly equipped and maintained laboratory,
- mains-operated equipment is properly maintained,
- dissection instruments are sharp, as much more harm is done with blunt ones,
- any fume cupboard used operates at least to the standard of *Design note 29*.

Teachers can find more information and detail about the operation of COSHH in schools in invaluable articles by Dr Peter Borrows in the January 1990 and June 1992 issues of *Education in Science* (Association for Science Education), and in two articles in the March 1992 issue of *The school science review*: one by Peter Borrows and Ray Vincent about safety policy and the other by Paul Taylor about risk assessment.

Hazard symbols on the worksheets alert pupils to particular dangers. A careful safety check and review by the pupils is an essential part of designing and carrying out their own investigations, but teachers will still need to monitor their plans carefully before they start practical work.

BIOLOGY

Introduction to Biology

The Biology course introduces the biological principles which will help pupils to explain many of the phenomena they will observe in the natural world. It also will help them towards a greater understanding of the functioning of their own bodies and their behaviour and should encourage a responsible attitude towards all organisms and the environment in which they live.

The course content is divided into four themes:

The variety of organisms
The processes of life
Living organisms and their environment
The continuity of life

The topics are presented in this order to allow time for some ideas to be introduced in Chemistry or Physics. It is also necessary, in some cases, for purposes of co-ordination. For example, it is helpful if pupils have gained some knowledge of the molecular structure of carbohydrates from Chapter **C3** "Chemicals from plants" before they study photosynthesis in Chapter **B3**.

The more difficult ideas encountered in genetics and evolution are at the end of the course where a greater maturity will be of benefit.

There has to be some flexibility, as another factor which always has to be taken into account in biology courses is the seasonal nature of some topics. This is particularly true of ecological work, which needs to be carried out at a time of year when the weather conditions are likely to be favourable.

For each theme there is a suggested sequence but there are alternatives, both in the order in which the chapters can be used and in the order within chapters.

Differentiation

In Nuffield Co-ordinated Sciences the biological topics are introduced with a familiar phenomenon or with a practical activity as a starting point. This is designed as a worthwhile exercise for all pupils.

Most of the material in the chapters of the pupils' book is suitable for all pupils but there are some concepts which only those aiming for the higher attainment levels need to understand. For example, all pupils should know that sex hormones are produced by the ovaries and testes but only those aiming for higher grades need to know of the co-ordinating role of the hypothalamus and pituitary gland. All pupils should be able to recognize the different trophic levels in a food web but it is only necessary for some to understand that the flow of energy through an ecosystem limits the number of trophic levels. Differentiation has also been introduced into the questions asked in the pupils' book and teachers will want to choose questions at an appropriate level to suit the individual needs of their pupils.

Differentiation has been allowed for in the worksheets. All of the worksheets are suitable for most pupils to use. It is the level of analysis and interpretation of results which allows for differentiated treatments. Teachers may need to give guidance but pupils will often make their own decisions about the depth of interpretation of results.

Worksheets

In the Biology part of the course many of the worksheets are not concerned with work of a strictly experimental nature. This applies to the worksheets associated with the first two chapters. Here observation is the skill which is important. Identifying organisms is a necessary part of a biologist's training and the use of a key to identify a selection of common birds is a useful practical exercise although it is not experimental in nature. It also gives useful practice in making decisions and following instructions.

Other examples are the worksheets which give guidance for investigating the structure of a joint (Worksheet **B**10B) and those dealing with the structure of other organs such as the heart (Worksheet **B**8D) and lungs (Worksheet **B**7D).

As well as worksheets which give instructions and guidance on carrying out practical work, there are those which give descriptions of experiments performed by other people and provide data collected by others. These save time and give pupils access to data which it would be difficult for them to collect for themselves. The emphasis is usually on the interpretation and analysis of the data provided.

The worksheets concerned with giving instructions for carrying out practical work will undoubtedly be modified as a result of their use with classes. This should be seen as a normal and essential part of their function.

Topic B1

The variety of organisms

Chapter B1   What's what?

The syllabus section

Context

Opportunity should be given to observe a variety of animals and plants, giving emphasis to common or familiar ones. All organisms within a group show certain common characteristics that have been used to place them in that group. Organisms have a large number of different characteristics, many of which enable them to survive in the ecosystem in which they live. The principles of biological classification (including the definition of species, rules for naming and the hierarchical structure of the classification system) can be presented using a wide range of organisms as examples.

Knowledge and understanding

Syllabus statements	PoS	SoA
Appreciate the diversity of different species of plants and animals.	—	—
Be able to use keys and observable diagnostic features to identify organisms and assign them to their major group.	2(ii)1	2.4(b)
Know the features of plants and animals (e.g. size, shape, colour, behaviour and life cycle) which enable them to survive in their natural environment.	2(i)2	2.6(b)

Tier: B C F

Opportunities for co-ordination

Classification of chemicals and the Periodic Table in **C**1, **C**8 and **C**12; of soils in **C**15.

Routes and times

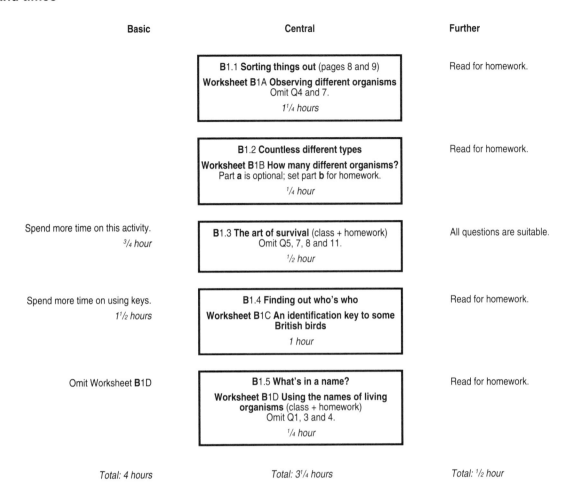

	Basic	Central	Further
		B1.1 Sorting things out (pages 8 and 9) **Worksheet B1A Observing different organisms** Omit Q4 and 7. *1¼ hours*	Read for homework.
		B1.2 Countless different types **Worksheet B1B How many different organisms?** Part **a** is optional; set part **b** for homework. *¼ hour*	Read for homework.
	Spend more time on this activity. *¾ hour*	**B1.3 The art of survival** (class + homework) Omit Q5, 7, 8 and 11. *½ hour*	All questions are suitable.
	Spend more time on using keys. *1½ hours*	**B1.4 Finding out who's who** **Worksheet B1C An identification key to some British birds** *1 hour*	Read for homework.
	Omit Worksheet **B**1D	**B1.5 What's in a name?** **Worksheet B1D Using the names of living organisms** (class + homework) Omit Q1, 3 and 4. *¼ hour*	Read for homework.
	Total: 4 hours	*Total: 3¼ hours*	*Total: ½ hour*

The pupils' book

B1.1 Sorting things out

It is an interesting feature of human behaviour that people are good at sorting different objects into groups on the basis of their similarities and differences. This section introduces the idea that characteristics which show variation can be used to classify a number of objects into different groups. From the outset, the criterion of a successful classification is one that is useful to the classifier.

Worksheet **B**1A contains two simple observation exercises, but it is not necessary to complete both parts unless there is plenty of time. The first part of this worksheet requires pupils to sort woodlice into various groups. It is relatively easy to distinguish the different types of woodlice, but much more difficult to describe exactly why the organisms have been so arranged. It is important that the pupils be encouraged to describe the similarities and differences between the groups in a table or a short written account; they need not be put off by the fact that they do not know what the different parts of the anatomy of the woodlice are called, or the correct names of the different types of woodlouse themselves. Indeed, pupils might even be encouraged to make up their own names for the parts of the anatomy and the species.

Part 2 of Worksheet **B**1A involves the comparison of a number of photosynthetic protists from a pond, and provides an opportunity to make accurate observations and draw simple diagrams.

The section ends by describing a species in terms of discrete breeding groups, which may or may not show structural or behavioural differences. This should be covered by all groups.

B1.2 Countless different types

Worksheet **B**1B involves interpreting a pie-chart for the total number of species of animals in the world. (The estimates provided are conservative ones.) Pupils like record-breakers, and the organisms featured at the end of the worksheet are considered to be some of the oldest of their type in the world. It is worth pointing out that, just as very few humans live to 120 years of age, so very few of these organisms actually survive to the ages stated.

B1.3 The art of survival

It is interesting to note that some plants are able to survive for very much longer than animals. In the absence of competition, and because of its indeterminate growth, the creosote bush (so called because it gives off a smell reminiscent of wood creosote) has been growing in the Mojave desert for at least 10 000 years.

This section is designed to show that the creosote bush is able to extract moisture from its inhospitable habitat, and will carry on growing indefinitely in the absence of competing species. This can form a prelude to work in the chapters on ecology (especially Chapter **B**13). Details of useful video material are given in this chapter under Further information.

Organisms survive because they have special features. Different species show different features. Without these, the organisms would not be able to survive inhospitable conditions.

Answers to selected questions

3 This plant germinated at a time when the last glaciers were disappearing from Britain, and when Neolithic culture was beginning to become established in the Middle East. This single plant is as old as our civilization.

5 The plant must have a minimum water loss, extract sufficient water from the soil, capture any moisture condensing from mists and avoid excessive grazing by desert herbivores.

6 Few plants will be able to compete with it for moisture or light, and relatively few herbivores will be able to tolerate such extreme conditions.

7 The creosote bush consists of a large number of creeping stems which gradually spread outwards in a ring across the desert. As it does this, the older stems tend to die away, leaving a circle of ground in the centre of the plant. In the absence of competition, the circle grows larger and larger – the oldest is 25 m across. Although the individual stems in the rings are not, themselves, very old, the single organism has managed to survive for many thousands of years.

8 Growth in animals is determinate, stopping when a maximum size is reached.

9 Ephemeral plants germinate, grow, flower, set seed and die within a few days. Their seeds are very resistant to high temperatures, and can survive for many years in dry, hot sand. It is a feature of such plants that they produce copious numbers of seeds.

10 Shortage of food and moisture, temperature regulation and predation.

B1.4 Finding out who's who

The use of keys to identify organisms is an important skill, and one which pupils should acquire in these lessons. One aim of this section is to familiarize pupils with common garden birds that can be seen almost everywhere. If teachers can show pupils how to use keys whilst generating some interest in local birds, then the aims of this section will certainly have been met.

The key, presented in Worksheet **B**1C, should be used in two ways. It is essential that pupils be given the chance to use the key to identify the photographs of the birds in the pupils' book. Identification keys that are robust enough to identify birds in the field are difficult to produce, and are not easy to use. By concentrating initially on the photographs, pupils should become familiar with the mechanics of the key, as well as with the shapes and colours of the birds themselves. (Details of useful video material are given under Further information.)

Pupils should now be encouraged to try to identify some of the birds in the locality. It will rapidly become clear that the species included in this key are only a few of those that can be seen. Any pupils who become interested in this activity will need more comprehensive field guides to help them; many of these are available quite cheaply.

Answer to selected questions
The birds in figure 1.11 are:

a	missel thrush	**b**	magpie
c	wood pigeon	**d**	swift
e	starling	**f**	jackdaw
g	blue tit	**h**	female chaffinch
i	male chaffinch	**j**	collared dove
k	crow	**l**	song thrush
m	coal tit	**n**	tree sparrow
o	male blackbird	**p**	house martin
q	robin	**r**	female blackbird
s	redwing	**t**	great tit
u	male house sparrow	**v**	jay
w	stock dove	**x**	female house sparrow.

12 The birds in the key that have different male and female forms are the blackbird, chaffinch and house sparrow.

B1.5 What's in a name?

All scientists recognize the need for a standard system of naming organisms. The system adopted is the one proposed by Linnaeus. Worksheet **B**1D provides an opportunity to establish the rules for naming organisms.

Activities

Worksheet B1A Observing different organisms

REQUIREMENTS

Each group of pupils will need:
Containers suitable for the organisms, such as beakers
Coverslips
Forceps
Light microscope with low and high power objective lenses
Microscope slides
Cavity slides
Paintbrush, small thin
Pencils, sharp
Rulers
Tray, large plastic, covered with white paper

Access to:
Photosynthetic protists, several different species (for example, *Spirogyra, Cladophora, Euglena, Chlamydomonas*)
Woodlice, a collection, preferably containing several different species

The procedure is detailed on the worksheet. Pupils are asked to try to use their own descriptions of the similarities and differences between the specimens.

Worksheet B1B How many different organisms?

REQUIREMENTS

Each group of pupils will need:
Photographs in figure 1.7 of the pupils' book

The procedure is detailed on the worksheet.

Answer to selected worksheet question
The ages quoted in *The Guinness book of records*, 1992 (see under Further information) are:

Human	120	years
Tortoise	152	years
Lobster	50	years
Ocean quahog (mollusc)	220	years
Buprestid beetle	47	years
Andean condor	72	years
Boa constrictor	40	years
Tarantula	28	years
Sturgeon	82	years
Salamander	55	years

Worksheet B1C An identification key to some British birds

REQUIREMENTS

Each group of pupils will need:
Photographs in figure 1.11 of the pupils' book
A videotape of British garden birds may be of value (see under Further information for details)

The procedure is detailed on the worksheet. Pupils should identify the birds in the photographs and a (carefully chosen) selection from the videotape, if used. They can then be encouraged to observe birds in their own locality.

Worksheet B1D Using the names of living organisms

REQUIREMENTS

Each group of pupils will need:
Normal writing materials

The procedure is detailed on the worksheet.

Further information

Further information about garden birds can be obtained from the Royal Society for the Protection of Birds, based at The Lodge, Sandy, Bedfordshire, SGI9 2DL. The society provides free information packs for teachers, and organizes a Young Ornithologists Club.

The Guinness book of records 1992 Guinness Publishing Ltd, 1992.

Videos
Section **B**1.3 "The art of survival" can be graphically illustrated by a sequence in programme 6 of "The Living Planet" by David Attenborough. The entire series of programmes is available on four tapes, with teachers' notes, from BBC Education Information (see Appendix).

The BBC has produced a video called "The BBC Videobook of British Garden Birds", which features many garden birds (including all of those in the identification key in Worksheet **B**1C). It is obtainable from BBC Education Information (see Appendix).

Chapter B2 Many forms of life

The syllabus section

Context

Opportunity should be given to observe a variety of animals and plants, giving emphasis to common or familiar ones. All organisms within a group show certain common characteristics that have been used to place them in that group. Organisms have a large number of different characteristics, many of which enable them to survive in the ecosystem in which they live. The principles of biological classification (including the definition of species, rules for naming and the hierarchical structure of the classification system) can be presented using a wide range of organisms as examples.

Knowledge and understanding

Syllabus statements	PoS	SoA
Appreciate the diversity of different species of plants and animals.	—	—
Be able to use keys and observable diagnostic features to identify organisms and assign them to their major group.	2(ii)1	2.4(b)
Know the features of plants and animals (e.g. size, shape, colour, behaviour and life cycle) which enable them to survive in their natural environment.	2(i)2	2.6(b)

Opportunities for co-ordination

Classification of chemicals and the Periodic Table in **C**1, **C**8 and **C**12; of soils in **C**15.

Routes and times

Basic	Central	Further
	B2.1 The kingdoms of the Earth Worksheet B2B **The kingdoms of the world** *½ hour*	Read for homework.
Spend more time on observing diagnostic features of different organisms. *2 hours*	**B2.2 Inside the animal kingdom** (class + homework) Omit Q2, 3, and 13. **Worksheet B2C Seafood platter** Omit Q1, 3–6, 11, 14 and 15. *1½ hours*	All questions in section **B2.2** and Worksheet **B2C** are suitable. *1 hour*
Omit Worksheet **B2D** and all questions in section **B2.4**. *½ hour*	**B2.3 The silent producers** Worksheet B2D **The silent producers** Side 3 is optional; select material to suit the class; do Q1, 6 and 9 only. **B2.4 The other three kingdoms** (homework) *1½ hours*	Read for homework.
Total: 3 hours	*Total: 3½ hours*	*Total: 1 hour*

The pupils' book

B2.1 The kingdoms of the Earth

In this book a five kingdom classification has been adopted, although the controversial nature of this system could be emphasized to more able groups. (It is hoped that teachers who prefer other models will accept that the most important aim of this section is briefly to give the pupils a "feel" for each of the major groups. The simplest way to do this is to give all the groups "kingdom status".)

The classification recognizes five kingdoms: animals, Monera (including bacteria), protists (including heterotrophic and autotrophic unicells and their immediate multicellular descendants, algae), plants and fungi. The classification is, in essence, that outlined by R.S.K. Barnes, 1984 (see under Further information). Worksheet **B2B** makes the point that some people do not think viruses are living organisms, and that those who do feel that viruses ought to be in a separate kingdom of their own (making six kingdoms).

Using photographs in the pupils' book and the descriptions in Worksheet **B2B**, pupils are asked to which kingdom various organisms belong. Two photographs (figures 2.1d and 2.1h) are viruses. It would be possible to use these photographs as a summary, and to present other living or preserved material in the classroom. These organisms need to be chosen carefully, as some material will be needed for the next section.

Answer to selected question
The photographs of the organisms featured in the pupils' book are:
a Carp, *Carassius*, animal
b Field mushroom, *Agaricus campestris*, fungus
c *Peranema*, protist
d Influenza virus
e *Mucor hiemalis*, fungus
f *Amoeba*, protist
g *Cephalanthera*, plant
h *Herpes*, virus

i *Actinia equina*, animal
j *Treponema* bacterium, Monera
k Coconut palm, plant
l *Streptococcus* bacterium, Monera.

B2.2 Inside the animal kingdom

The aim of the next two sections is to allow the pupil to develop an awareness of the diversity of animals and plants. A detailed understanding of the differences between the groups is not required; the emphasis should be on providing an enjoyable glimpse of the living world, rather than a surfeit of taxonomic detail. Section **B**2.2 leads into Worksheet **B**2C – a study of the animals that we eat as , "seafood".

Answers to selected questions
4 Centipedes (on the right) have one pair of legs on each body segment, whilst millipedes have two pairs.

10a The method of reproduction and the shelled egg are reptilian characteristics.
b and **c** Homoiothermy is associated with birds and mammals. This animal's temperature is around 30°C (lower than other mammals), although it is subject to wide fluctuations.
b Webbed feet and a bill are characteristic of birds.
c Fur, an external ear and milk production are uniquely mammalian characteristics. The mother platypus lacks nipples, and milk is produced from enlarged sweat glands and oozes over the fur of the abdomen. That this animal is a primitive mammal is beyond dispute.

11 Whilst the embryos are developing inside the uterus, no additional eggs can ripen in the ovaries. Once the young embryos are inside the pouch, the normal reproductive cycle can recommence. Marsupial animals can thus increase the number of young raised in any season.

13 As ungulates are often hunted by swiftly moving carnivores, their likelihood of survival is increased if the offspring can run as soon as they are born.

B2.3 The silent producers

This section considers plants, but it is important to remember that autotrophic protists are also producers, and form the basis of the food chains that will be encountered in Chapter **B**14. The brief treatment in the pupils' book is augmented by the examination of photosynthetic protists in Worksheet **B**2D. Parts of this worksheet are quite difficult, and could be omitted if time or circumstances so demand. There is a potential overlap between the specimens used in Part 2 of Worksheet **B**1A and those used in Worksheet **B**2D. Material should be chosen with care, so that pupils are not forced to examine the same examples twice. They can, of course, be asked to recall what they viewed earlier.

Worksheet **B**2D also contains an experimental design exercise (in the section on conifers). Pupils will need to obtain several cones of similar size, and place them in damp and dry atmospheres. They will also need to devise some method of measuring how "open" the cones are (for instance, by measuring any change in width).

B2.4 The other three kingdoms

This brief section develops ideas about bacteria, fungi and protists. It is suitable for use as a homework exercise.

Answers to selected questions
15 The role of fungi as agents of decomposition needs to be mentioned here. Cycles of matter are covered in Chapter **B**15.

16 Bread, alcohol and soy sauce need fungi.

17 The protists, such as *Euglena*. (Viruses too if they are considered to be organisms.)

Activities

Worksheet B2A Names and addresses

REQUIREMENTS

Each group of pupils will need:
Writing materials

The procedure is detailed on the worksheet.

Worksheet B2B The kingdoms of the world

REQUIREMENTS

Each group of pupils will need:
Photographs in figure 2.1 of the pupils' book

The procedure is detailed on the worksheet.

Worksheet B2C Seafood platter

REQUIREMENTS

Each group of pupils will need:
Specimens of crab, lobster, prawns,
   shrimps, cockles, whelks and mussels
or
Photographs in figures 1.7b, 2.2, 2.12
   and 2.13 of the pupils' book
Sea water, if living specimens are collected

Access to:
Hot and cold water
Soap
Towel

Dishes
Forceps
Hand lens

Safety note:
Remind pupils to wash their hands at the end of the activity.

The procedure is detailed on the worksheet.

Worksheet B2D The silent producers

REQUIREMENTS

Each group of pupils will need:
Ferns (*e.g. Dryopteris*)
Mosses or liverworts, showing sporangia (*e.g. Mnium, Funaria, Marchantia*)
Photosynthetic protists, unicellular **and** multicellular (*e.g. Euglena, Chlamydomonas,
   Spirogyra, Cladophora, Fucus, Laminaria*)
Maize, barley (both monocotyledons), broad bean and pea seeds (dicotyledons), washed in
   1% sodium hypochlorite solution and soaked overnight in distilled water
Maize, barley, broad bean and pea seedlings grown in Knop's solution (see *Note*)
Cones, male **and** female, of different ages, from a conifer (*e.g. Scots pine*)

Polystyrene cement or clear nail varnish
Drawing paper
Microscope slides
Cavity slides
Coverslips
Microscope with high and low power objective lenses
Paper, white
Pencils
Forceps
Mounted needles

Note:
Culture the seedlings in gas jars lined with blotting-paper. The specimens used should be large enough to see expanded leaves and roots.

The procedure is detailed on the worksheet.

Answers to selected worksheet questions
2 Osmosis and the permeable nature of the cell wall are covered in Chapter **B**10, and need not be discussed in any detail here, where it is sufficient to observe that water and minerals will have to enter the organism across the cell wall. The question is useful because it introduces the idea of transfer of materials between an organism and its environment.

7 This is a difficult question. The many small leaves of the moss give it a greater ratio of surface area to volume than the liverwort.

13 There are two sorts of cones. The male cones produce a large amount of pollen that is carried by the wind to the female cones. The female cones contain the ovules and eggs. If an egg is fertilized, its ovule develops into a seed, and the female cone will eventually contain ripe seeds.

Further information

Barnes, R.S.K. *A synoptic classification of living organisms* Blackwell Scientific Publications, 1984.

Videos
BBC videotape material, "Life on Earth" and "Trials of life" in particular, can be used to illustrate many of the organisms considered here. Interested teachers should contact BBC Education Information (see Appendix).

Topic B2   The processes of life

Chapter B3   Light means life

The syllabus section

Context

This section examines the physiology of photosynthesis, and how it relates to agriculture and food production. The value of photosynthesis as an oxygen-producing process is examined and related to the maintenance of the atmosphere.

Knowledge and understanding

	Tier		Syllabus statements	PoS	SoA
B	C	F			
			Be able to relate the structure of a leaf to the processes of photosynthesis.	2(i)1	2.4(a) 2.5(a) 2.6(a)
			Know how to test for the presence of starch in leaves.	2(i)1	—
			Understand the significance of chlorophyll as a light-absorbing molecule.	2(i)1	2.7(b)
			Understand the requirements for photosynthesis, the nature and use of the products formed, and the effects of altering the conditions on the rate of photosynthesis.	2(i)1	2.7(b)
			Know the factors that limit the rate of photosynthesis.	2(i)3	2.7(b)

Opportunities for co-ordination

C3 deals with carbohydrates and **C15** with soil. Energy is also the subject of **P8** (energy cost and efficiency), **P11** (energy transfer), **P12** (fossil fuels) and **P15** (the electromagnetic spectrum). **P3** deals with radioactivity. **E3** links photosynthesis to the maintenance of the atmosphere.

Routes and times

Basic	Central	Further
Replace the colours of the spectrum and chlorophyll in section **B**3.1 with Worksheet **B**2D side 3 (parts **k–o**). Omit Worksheet **B**3A, the section "What do plants need in order to make glucose (or starch)?" and Q8. *1¹/₄ hours*	**B3.1 A leafy world** **Worksheet B3A Using simple chromatography to investigate plant pigments** (optional) **B3.2 Why is photosynthesis important?** Omit Q7. *³/₄ hour*	Omit Worksheet **B**3A.
Do Worksheet **B**3B (up to part **j**). *1¹/₂ hours*	EITHER **Worksheet B3B What happens when light is kept from a part of a variegated leaf?** (up to part **j**) OR **Worksheet B3C Leaves and light** *1¹/₄ hours*	Do Worksheet **B**3C for homework after brief discussion. *¹/₄ hour*
Omit Worksheet **B**3D.	**Worksheet B3D What happens if there is no carbon dioxide in the surroundings of plants?** (demonstration) *¹/₂ hour*	
		Worksheet B7A Do plants and animals alter the environment around them? *Optional*
Omit Q3, 4 and 6 from Worksheet **B**3E. *1 hour*	**B3.3 Leaves and gases** **Worksheet B3E Looking at the surfaces of leaves** (parts 1 and 4 only) *³/₄ hour*	
Omit Q3–7 from Worksheet **B**3F. *1¹/₄ hours*	**Worksheet B3F Looking at the internal structure of leaves** Omit Q5–7. **B3.4 Made for the job** **Worksheet B3G What is a leaf like?** (optional/homework) *1 hour*	
Omit Worksheet **B**3H and section **B**3.6.	**Worksheet B3H Which factors affect the rate of photosynthesis?** Omit Q3, 5 and 6 and last paragraph. **B3.6 What are the best conditions for photosynthesis?** (class + homework) *1¹/₂ hours*	All of Worksheet **B**3H is suitable.
Total: 5 hours	*Total: 5³/₄ hours*	*Total: 4³/₄ hours*

Monitoring the progress of Sc1

Investigating photosynthesis

Students should investigate what affects the amount of starch present in leaves. This investigation may be carried out instead of or after worksheet **B**3B "What happens when light is kept from a part of a variegated leaf?".

Sample criteria are given below for an assessment between levels 4 and 6.

Strand (i) Ask questions, predict and hypothesize, e.g.	Strand (ii) Observe, measure and manipulate variables, e.g.	Strand (iii) Interpret their results and evaluate scientific evidence, e.g.
4(a) Suggest that light may be a factor	**4(b)** Control type of leaf and compare masked and unmasked parts of leaves after 48 hours	**4(c)** Conclude that leaves of a plant grown in the dark contain less starch than leaves grown in the light
5(a) Suggest that a leaf grown in the dark will contain less starch than a leaf grown in the light because light is needed to produce starch	**5(b)** As above, but examining leaves after 24 and 48 hours	**5(c)** Conclude that the longer a plant leaf grows in the dark, the less starch will be found in the leaf, but qualifying the result
6(a) Suggest that the longer the leaf is kept in the dark, the less starch will be present because light is needed to produce starch	**6(b)** As above, but trying experiment with green leaves, variegated leaves and green leaves grown in air which contains no carbon dioxide	**6(c)** Suggest that it is the amount of light that is a major factor and that the light source provides energy

The pupils' book

B3.1 A leafy world

The aims of this section are to explain why leaves look green, and to introduce chlorophyll as a remarkable molecule which "harvests" light energy. It would be possible to set up a demonstration of the light-absorbing properties of a solution of chlorophyll, using a design developed by the pupils as a result of discussion of question 5. Worksheet **B**3A separates the coloured pigments in leaves, using paper chromatography.

Answers to selected questions

2 Some colours (red, blue, indigo, violet) disappear almost entirely whilst others (orange, yellow, green) are practically unaltered.

3 The pupils might well suggest that the missing colours have been absorbed by the chlorophyll solution.

4 Some pupils may need a little help to reason that if chlorophyll absorbs the red and blue light, then most of the light that passes through the leaf (*i.e.* is transmitted) is green light, so the leaves look green when looked at from underneath.

5 An arrangement such as the one shown opposite should be suggested.

B3.2 Why is photosynthesis important?

This section provides an important opportunity for pupils to design controlled experiments to investigate the factors that control the rate of photosynthesis. Worksheet **B**3B introduces the basic experimental techniques that can be adapted to test a variety of hypotheses, while Worksheet **B**3C provides experimental data for analysis by those who are not able to design and perform their own experiments. It is important, however, that **all** pupils are familiar with the technique of testing leaves for starch (see Worksheet **B**3B), and can

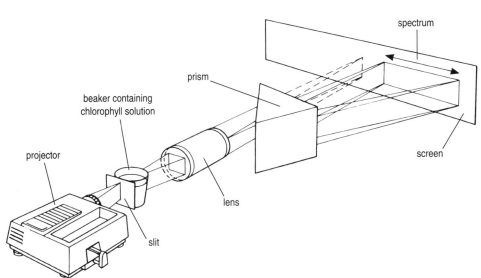

Possible apparatus to determine the effects of passing light through chlorophyll.

perform it safely and as a matter of routine. This section stresses the significance of photosynthesis as the source of energy both for plants and for the animals that depend upon plants for food; the basis for all food production is the process of photosynthesis.

Answers to selected questions

7 Sugar cane is the obvious example of a plant that makes only sugar, and wheat is likely to be suggested as a plant which makes starch as well.

8 The need to use identical containers and materials for the plants should be stressed. Sodium hydroxide pellets absorb carbon dioxide gas. Black paper or aluminium foil can create dark conditions for the plants. (Note that both illuminated and dark plants should be kept at the same distance from a light source, so as to maintain approximately equal temperatures.)

B3.3 Leaves and gases

Photosynthesis plays a crucial role in maintaining the delicate balance of carbon dioxide and oxygen in the atmosphere. The numbers used in this section are designed to let pupils appreciate the importance of photosynthesis. They are **not** meant to be memorized!

Worksheet **B**3D investigates the importance of carbon dioxide in the surroundings of plants.

B3.4 Made for the job

Leaves can be visualized as "factories" for photosynthesis. The structure of a leaf is of major significance in allowing this process to occur efficiently. This section, combined with Worksheets **B**3E, **B**3F or **B**3G, should reveal how the structure of a leaf is closely related to its function. At the end of the section, pupils should appreciate which structures in a leaf enable photosynthesis to occur effectively. These include:

1 A large ratio of surface area to volume, which ensures the absorption of as much light as possible and a large surface across which gases can be absorbed.
2 Transparent cells on the outer surfaces of the leaf, through which light can be transmitted.
3 Holes (stomata) in the surface of the leaf, which allow carbon dioxide and oxygen to diffuse in and out. In most plants stomata open in the daytime and close at night, and a mechanism by which the size of the pore is regulated must exist.
4 The presence of most chlorophyll in the upper surface of a leaf, where the light will be most intense.
5 Spaces between the cells in the leaf, which allow movement of gases between the leaf cells and the air.

6 A well developed water supply in the veins which carry water to the leaf cells from the roots, and a transport system which removes the food products away from the leaf. Other general points which could be mentioned are:

7 Ideally, a leaf has a very thin structure, with the result that no cell is too far from the surface.

8 The leaves grow, bend and turn to form a leaf mosaic, which means they do not overshadow each other.

B3.5 More about photosynthesis

This section is a difficult one, in which pupils should relate the consumption of carbon dioxide to glucose production. It should also become clear that the oxygen given out by a plant during photosynthesis comes from water (which is split into hydrogen and oxygen), and not from carbon dioxide. It is the hydrogen released from the water molecule that reduces the carbon dioxide to glucose. It is intended that the pupils should become familiar with the idea of chemical reactions occurring in and around the chloroplast, rather than have a detailed understanding of the different stages of the photosynthetic reactions.

Answer to selected question

9 It will help pupils to refer to figure 3.6 when answering this question. The molecule of carbon dioxide enters the leaf through a stoma and passes into an airspace. From here, it diffuses through the cell wall and cell membrane of a mesophyll cell and into a chloroplast, where it is reduced to glucose.

B3.6 What are the best conditions for photosynthesis?

By this stage, pupils should be familiar with the requirements for photosynthesis. It is reasonable to ask whether the rate of photosynthesis can be increased indefinitely by increasing the concentrations of the various "raw materials". This leads to a consideration of the idea of limiting factors in the process of photosynthesis (and also their relevance to agriculture and horticulture). The relationship between the rate of photosynthesis and such factors as light intensity, wavelength and carbon dioxide concentration can be investigated using Worksheet **B**3H.

Answers to selected questions

10 Light, an appropriate concentration of carbon dioxide, temperature and the availability of water all affect photosynthesis.

11 The light intensity is highest when the lamp is nearest to the water plant; therefore the rate of photosynthesis is directly proportional to the light intensity.

12 Lamp C.

13 Much of the output of light from lamp C is at the red end of the spectrum. As red light is absorbed by green plants, the bulb could be useful. The results of Worksheet **B**3H will confirm, for instance, that the rate of photosynthesis is faster in red light than in green light of the same intensity.

14 Some factor, other than light, must be limiting the rate of photosynthesis; it is most likely to be the concentration of carbon dioxide in the atmosphere.

15 In this case a different limiting factor is operating – possibly light.

16a It is most likely to be light.

b It is not likely to be temperature or light; it is most likely to be carbon dioxide.

c In these conditions it is not likely to be temperature or carbon dioxide; light is the most likely limiting factor.

Activities

Worksheet B3A Using simple chromatography to investigate plant pigments

REQUIREMENTS

Each group of pupils will need:
Leaves, fresh green (*e.g.* busy lizzie, grass, nettle, spinach or bamboo)
Leaves, variegated or red (*e.g. Coleus*, copper beech)
Propanone (acetone) – FLAMMABLE – 40 cm^3
Beaker, 250 cm^3
Boiling-tube
Bung, split
Capillary tube, fine
Filter paper
Funnel
Glass wool
Pencils
Pestle and mortar
Scissors

Access to:
Receptacle for waste solvent

The procedure is detailed on the worksheet.

Worksheet B3B What happens when light is kept from a part of a variegated leaf?

REQUIREMENTS

Each group of pupils will need:
Leaves, a selection from the following: variegated leaves (e.g. *Pelargonium, Coleus*), green leaves
  (*e.g.* privet, young ivy, lime, busy lizzie) which have been in the light, green leaves which have
  been kept (on the plant) in the dark for 48 hours, green leaves which have been kept (on the plant)
  without carbon dioxide for 48 hours
Ethanol – FLAMMABLE
Iodine in potassium iodide solution
Boiling-tube in which to heat ethanol
Cork and pins *or* aluminium foil *or* black paper and paper clips, to cover areas of leaves
Dropping pipette
Forceps, blunt
Petri dish or white porcelain dish
Eye protection

If leaf discs are used:
Cork borer
Wooden board or white tile

Access to:
Water bath, electrically heated
Receptacle to receive used ethanol containing chlorophyll
Water

Notes:
Leaves with thick cuticles or very hairy surfaces are not suitable because the reagents do not
penetrate the leaf.
  Leaf discs may be mounted on slides for examination under a microscope. They are more
transparent if mounted in 50 per cent glycerol, thus making the distribution of starch easier to
observe.

The worksheet can be developed in a number of ways. Variegated leaves such as *Pelargonium* or *Coleus* can be used to show that the distribution of chlorophyll is linked to starch synthesis. The importance of light for photosynthesis can be investigated by testing leaves from a number of plants that have been kept in the dark for at least 48 hours before the practical, and the role of carbon dioxide can be studied by using leaves that have been kept without carbon dioxide – by enclosing them in a conical flask containing soda lime (sodium hydroxide – CORROSIVE) – for 48 hours before the experiment starts.

Worksheet B3C Leaves and light

REQUIREMENTS

Access to:
The pupils' book

This worksheet consists of descriptions of three investigations, with results for the pupils to interpret. The investigations could be set up as demonstrations in order to help pupils visualize what is happening (see under Demonstration experiments, below).

Worksheet B3D What happens if there is no carbon dioxide in the surroundings of plants?

REQUIREMENTS

Each group of pupils will need:

Well-watered potted plants (such as *Pelargonium*) which have been kept in the dark for 48 hours

Ethanol – FLAMMABLE

Iodine in potassium iodide solution

Sodium hydroxide pellets – CORROSIVE – wrapped in a muslin bag

Boiling-tube in which to heat ethanol

Bungs, split rubber

Clamps to support conical flasks

Conical flasks, boiling-tubes or plastic bags, in which to enclose selected leaves

Cottonwool

Dropping pipette

Forceps, blunt

Lamp

Petri dish or white porcelain dish

Scissors

Eye protection

Access to:
Water bath, electrically heated

This worksheet utilizes the technique developed in Worksheet **B3B**.

Worksheet B3E Looking at the surfaces of leaves

REQUIREMENTS

Each group of pupils will need:

Leaves (such as privet, ivy-leaved toadflax, lilac, busy lizzie)

Beaker in which to boil water

Bunsen burner

Coverslips

Forceps, blunt

Gauze

Microscope with high power (×40) objective lens

Microscope slides

Nail varnish, clear, or clear adhesive

Tripod stand

Eye protection

The procedure is detailed on the worksheet.

Worksheet B3F Looking at the internal structure of leaves

REQUIREMENTS

Each group of pupils will need:
Prepared slides of leaf sections
Microscope with low and high power objective lenses

The procedure is detailed on the worksheet.

Worksheet B3G What is a leaf like?

REQUIREMENTS

Access to:
The pupils' book

The procedure is detailed on the worksheet.

Worksheet B3H Which factors affect the rate of photosynthesis?

REQUIREMENTS

Each group of pupils will need:
Elodea, free of dirt and filamentous algae
Sodium hydrogencarbonate
Beaker or flask to hold water for filling syringe
Bench lamp fitted with 60 W bulb
Capillary tubing, narrow bore, 30 cm length
Clamp
Graph paper
Means of shielding apparatus from other light sources
Retort stand
Rubber tubing, short length
Rulers
Scissors or razor blade
Stopclock
Syringe, plastic, 20 cm^3
Eye protection

If wavelength is investigated:
Other light sources and filters

Safety note:
The use of razor blades demands special vigilance by the teacher. One-sided razor blades, which shatter easily, should not be used.

This worksheet can be developed in a variety of ways to suit the ingenuity and ability of the pupils concerned. It would be possible to set each group a different problem to solve, asking them to report back at the end of the practical session.

Demonstration experiments

The investigations described in Worksheet **B**3C can be performed as demonstrations, before the pupils analyse the data provided in the worksheet. The additional apparatus required is listed below.

Investigation 2

REQUIREMENTS

Leaves, freshly picked, such as privet or
    busy Lizzie

Hydrogencarbonate indicator solution,
    previously equilibrated with atmospheric air

Water, distilled

Aluminium foil *or* black polythene

Aquarium tank, transparent plastic

Forceps, blunt

Light source (must be powerful)

Rubber bands

Stopclock

Syringe, $2\,cm^3$

Test-tubes with rubber bungs, 3

Metal test-tube rack

Thermometer

Investigation 3

REQUIREMENTS

Elodea, free of dirt and filamentous algae

Potassium hydroxide solution,
    concentrated – CORROSIVE

Potassium pyrogallate solution– CORROSIVE

Beaker, large tall, $500\,cm^3$ minimum

Capillary analysis tube, J-shaped, with greased
    adjustment screw held firm by rubber tubing

Funnel, glass, with short stem

Light source, strong

Paper towels

Plasticine

Rulers

Test-tube

Trough, bowl *or* sink of water at room
    temperature

Further information

Science and Technology in Society
SATIS unit 201 "Energy from biomass", which develops the ecological aspects of photosynthesis, could bridge this chapter and Chapter **B**14, where the theme of food webs is developed.

Chapter B4 How do animals feed?

The syllabus section

Context

This section examines how the structure of the teeth reflects the diet of the organism. Human dentition is examined, and the causes and prevention of dental decay are considered.

Knowledge and understanding

Syllabus statements	PoS	SoA
Be able to name and locate the major organs of digestion in the human body.	2(i)1	2.4(a)
Be able to name, locate and outline the functions of the different types of teeth in carnivores, herbivores and humans (omnivores).	2(i)1	2.4(a) 2.5(a)
Understand the role of bacteria forming acids in the mouth, leading to tooth decay, and the effect of life-style on tooth decay.	2(i)5	2.5(a)
Understand the part different types of dentition play in the life process of nutrition, and relate this to the relative amounts of food needed to keep omnivores alive.	2(i)1	2.7(a)

Opportunities for co-ordination

Links to **C**10 (fluoridation of water supplies) and **C**12 (chemicals in the medicine cupboard).

Routes and times

Basic	Central	Further
	B4.1 Lazers or grazers? **B4.2 Different ways of feeding** **Worksheet B4A How much do animals eat?** (optional/homework) *¹/₄ hour*	
Spend more time on this section. *1¹/₂ hours*	**B4.3 Different teeth for different food** **Worksheet B4B Looking at teeth** Set part **k** and questions for homework. *1 hour*	Revision only; select material as necessary. *³/₄ hour*
Spend more time on this section. *1¹/₂ hours*	**B4.4 Teeth should last a lifetime** **Worksheet B4C Cleaning your teeth** *1 hour*	Omit Worksheet **B4C**. *¹/₂ hour*
Spend some class time on this section. *¹/₂ hour*	**Worksheet B4D How healthy are your teeth?** (optional/homework) **B4.5 Prevention is better than cure** (homework)	
	Worksheet B4E Is it something in the toothpaste? (optional) **Worksheet B4F How good is the toothpaste you use?** *³/₄ hour*	Omit this section.
Do page 48 only from section **B4.6**.	**B4.6 Different guts for different diets** (class + homework) *¹/₂ hour*	Use this section as revision homework.
Total: 5 hours	*Total: 3¹/₂ hours*	*Total: 1¹/₂ hours*

The pupils' book

B4.1 Lazers or grazers?

The aim of this section is to introduce the idea that the type of food that is eaten (meat or vegetation) has consequences on the life-style of the animals concerned. This theme runs throughout this chapter and the next, since the type of food also affects the dentition and the digestive systems of the consumers.

Answers to selected questions

1 "Hunting or grazing" is an acceptable generalization.

2 The lions must get sufficient energy and nutrients from their food to enable them to feed only intermittently.

B4.2 Different ways of feeding

This section should be completed in conjunction with Worksheet **B4A**, which gives data on the amount of food eaten by tigers and elephants. It provides an interesting development of questions 1 and 2 in the previous section, and is a suitable exercise for homework. The photographs of animals feeding in figure 4.2 can be supplemented with appropriate video sequences (see under Further information).

Answer to selected question
3 Herbivores: **d** panda, **g** elephant, **e** slug.
Carnivores: **a** praying mantis, **b** ladybird, **c** owl, **f** hyena, vulture and lion.

B4.3 Different teeth for different food

This section should be completed in conjunction with Worksheet **B4B**. This allows differences between the dentition of herbivores and carnivores to be investigated, and the theme of human dentition, which will be developed in the subsequent sections of this chapter, is also introduced.

Answers to selected questions
6 Sheep lack upper incisors and canines.

7 Canines, and the upper premolars and lower molars called carnassial teeth. These teeth are for tearing and cutting flesh.

8 The cheek teeth of a plant-eater have a series of grooves and enamel ridges running across them. The ridges of the teeth in the upper jaw fit into the grooves in the teeth in the lower jaw. Similarly, the ridges in the teeth of the lower jaw fit into the grooves in the teeth of the upper jaw. When these animals eat, they move their jaws from side to side, and the teeth scrape against each other, grinding any food caught between them into small pieces.
　　The cheek teeth of a meat-eater fit tightly together when the jaw closes. Their sharp edges cut flesh and the flat surfaces crush hard materials such as bone.

9 The mammals will have similar types of teeth to ours, although there will be some variation in size, number and shape.

B4.4 Teeth should last a lifetime

The idea of dental hygiene is developed in sections **B4.4** and **B4.5**. This section develops understanding of the causes of tooth decay – and the reasons why it can be so painful! The remaining parts of Worksheet **B4B** can now be completed. The accumulation of plaque can be revealed by disclosing tablets, using the method in Worksheet **B4C**.

B4.5 Prevention is better than cure

This section concentrates on dental hygiene. It should be supplemented by Worksheet **B4D**, a survey of dental health, the results of which can be compared with national figures for the 1960s, 1970s and 1980s. Analysing the amount and type of sweets eaten by pupils in the class can lead to interesting discussions on diet and health, which can lead into Chapter **B6** "Diet and good health". The effectiveness of different toothpastes in killing bacteria can be investigated, using Worksheet **B4F**, and the effectiveness of fluoride can be considered, using Worksheet **B4E**. (Question 1 on this worksheet might make a suitable homework exercise.)

Answer to selected question
10 Regular cleaning to remove plaque, neutralization of the mouth contents after eating sweet or acidic food and reducing the amount of sugar kept in the mouth for long periods (chewing and swallowing sweets is better than sucking them).

B4.6 Different guts for different diets

This section resumes the theme of the first two sections, and serves as an introduction to the next chapter. It points out that mammalian plant-eaters and meat-eaters differ not only in their dentition, but also in their digestive systems.

Answer to selected question
11 A ruminant herbivore has an enlarged section of its digestive system, which contains the micro-organisms that break down the plant fibres. This is not the case with carnivores.

Activities

Worksheet B4A How much do animals eat?

REQUIREMENTS

Each group of pupils will need:
Pens

The procedure is detailed on the worksheet.

Worksheet B4B Looking at teeth

REQUIREMENTS

Each group of pupils will need:
Skulls of rabbit, sheep, dog, cat (at least 1 herbivore and 1 carnivore)
Dental mirror
Drawing paper

Notes:
Skulls can be bought from dealers, or with a little patience can be prepared at school. If fur, skin and flesh are removed and the skull then heated in a pressure cooker, it becomes an easy matter to scrape it perfectly clean. It should then be scrubbed with a stiff paste of calcium chloride before being bleached with hydrogen peroxide. Take care that the bones do not become brittle and that fixed joints do not separate. Teeth should be glued into their sockets.

Very interesting results will be obtained if pupils can compare the teeth of older friends and relatives with their own. Modern (usually alkaline) toothpastes and fluoridation of drinking water, together with a greater knowledge of and interest in personal hygiene, have caused pupils to have better teeth than their parents. This will be revealed most clearly if the age at which the older generation lost their teeth can be determined.

The worksheet asks pupils to work out dental formulae for a herbivore, a carnivore and an omnivore. Details of the formulae should not be memorized. Typical examples are:

		Incisor	Canine	Premolar	Molar
Human	upper:	2	1	2	3
	lower:	2	1	2	3
Rabbit	upper:	2	0	3	3
	lower:	1	0	2	3
Dog	upper:	3	1	4	2
	lower:	3	1	4	3

Note that these figures are for one half of the mouth, and need to be doubled in order to calculate the total number of teeth.

Worksheet B4C Cleaning your teeth

REQUIREMENTS

Each group of pupils will need:
Disclosing tablets, fresh (1 per pupil)
Water, drinking, in a disposable cup or beaker
Tissues or paper towels
Dental mirrors
Toothbrush (brought from home by each pupil)
Toothpaste

Access to:
Sink or bowl

This lesson can be developed in a number of ways. For example, brushes of differing hardness or different toothpastes could be used, or one different style of brushing could be employed. Similarly, an investigation could be made into the recent diet of the children, and an attempt made to relate this to the amount of plaque.

    Very careful consideration must be given when pupils are the objects of investigations: there must be no pressure on them to take part, and the educational advantage of any procedure must be judged in relation to the hazards involved.

Worksheet B4D How healthy are your teeth?

REQUIREMENTS

Each group of pupils will need:
Pencils
Writing paper

The procedure is detailed on the worksheet.

Worksheet B4E Is it something in the toothpaste?

REQUIREMENTS

Each group of pupils will need:
Pencils
Writing paper

The procedure is detailed on the worksheet.

Worksheet B4F How good is the toothpaste you use?

REQUIREMENTS

Each group of pupils will need:
Prepared plastic Petri dish with nutrient agar
  and microbes (see Procedure below)
Forceps, blunt
Rulers

Access to:
Chinagraph pencil or marker pen
Adhesive tape
Toothpaste, 4 brands
Filter paper discs, 5 mm in diameter
Hot and cold water
Soap
Towel

Safety notes:

1 Spills must be reported to, and dealt with by, the teacher or a technician. Use disposable gloves and cover the spill with a cloth soaked in an appropriate solution of a clear phenolic disinfectant (or a freshly prepared 1% chlorate(I) solution) for ten minutes. Then mop up with cloths if necessary. Put the cloths in an "autoclavable" bag, loosely seal it and autoclave. Contaminated clothing should be placed in the disinfectant solution before cleaning. You should record microbiological spillage incidents.

2 Be vigilant to ensure that pupils do not open the Petri dishes for examination.

Procedure

The culture recommended is actively growing *Micrococcus luteus* in a nutrient broth. Prepare nutrient broth by adding 13 g of powder to 1 litre of distilled water. Mix well. Dispense into McCartney bottles as required and then sterilize at 121°C and 100 kPa (15 lb/in^2) for 15 minutes. Inoculate cool nutrient broth the day before the class session and then incubate at 25–30°C.

Prepare nutrient agar by suspending 28 g of nutrient agar powder in 1 litre of distilled water. Bring to the boil to dissolve completely. Dispense into McCartney bottles as required and sterilize at 121°C and 100 kPa (15 lb/in^2) for 15 minutes.

On the day of the class session, prepare agar plates inoculated with the microbial culture, as shown in the diagrams on the next page. After pouring, rotate each dish on a flat surface to make sure that the agar is evenly distributed and allow to cool before inoculating with the culture.

Allow the pupils to add the toothpaste to filter paper discs and place them on the surface of the agar with sterile forceps. Ensure that the plates are sealed with adhesive tape, and **do not allow pupils to open them again**.

Incubate the sealed Petri dishes, upside down, for two days at 25°C and allow the pupils to see the results in a later lesson. (Growth can be slowed down by keeping the plates in a refrigerator once good results are apparent.) Pupils should wash their hands thoroughly after examining the dishes.

At the end of the investigation, put all Petri dishes in an autoclavable plastic bag, seal it and sterilize in an autoclave before disposal of the unopened bag. Wipe the benches with an antibacterial wipe.

Further information

Science and Technology in Society

Two SATIS units could provide useful background material to this chapter. They are units 606 "The Tristan da Cunha dental surveys" and 401 "Fluoridation of water supplies" (both available in revised forms in *SATIS Update 91*).

Video

Video sequences of herbivores and carnivores feeding can be found in programme 11 of the BBC series "Life on Earth"; the series "The velvet claw" deals with the natural history of carnivores. Write to BBC Educational Information (see Appendix).

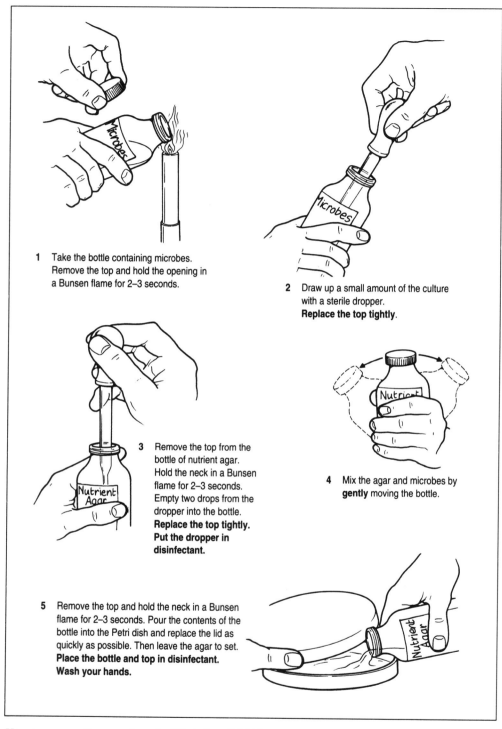

1 Take the bottle containing microbes. Remove the top and hold the opening in a Bunsen flame for 2–3 seconds.

2 Draw up a small amount of the culture with a sterile dropper. **Replace the top tightly.**

3 Remove the top from the bottle of nutrient agar. Hold the neck in a Bunsen flame for 2–3 seconds. Empty two drops from the dropper into the bottle. **Replace the top tightly. Put the dropper in disinfectant.**

4 Mix the agar and microbes by **gently** moving the bottle.

5 Remove the top and hold the neck in a Bunsen flame for 2–3 seconds. Pour the contents of the bottle into the Petri dish and replace the lid as quickly as possible. Then leave the agar to set. **Place the bottle and top in disinfectant. Wash your hands.**

How to prepare the agar plates for Worksheet **B**4F (*Society for General Microbiology*).

Chapter B5　The gut as a food processor

The syllabus section

Context

Digestion is presented as a means of transforming complex food substances into smaller soluble molecules prior to absorption into the body. The functions of the human digestive system are examined. This section also provides an opportunity to explore the role of enzymes as catalysts in this process.

Knowledge and understanding

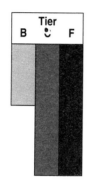

Syllabus statements	PoS	SoA
Be able to name, locate and outline the functions of the organs of the human digestive system.	2(i)1	2.4(a) 2.5(a)
Be able to relate how the structure of the human digestive system enables it to: (i)　move food by peristalsis (the role of circular and longitudinal muscles), (ii)　digest food by enzyme action (the effect of pH, temperature), (iii) absorb the soluble products of digestion through the villi.	2(i)1	2.7(a)

Opportunities for co-ordination

The use of enzymes in household and industrial situations is in **C**10, protein structure in **C**2, the chemistry of carbohydrates and proteins in **C**3, the separation of large and small molecules using membranes in **C**3, the emulsifying action of bile salts in digestion of fats in **C**9, acids and alkalis in **C**12, soil in **C**15 and emulsions in **C**9.

Routes and times

Basic	Central	Further
In section **B**5.1, start just after Q2 and omit Q2 and 6–10. Omit section **B**5.2. *¹/₂ hour*	**B5.1 Food on the move** (class + homework) Omit Q6 and 11. **B5.2 Digestion** Omit the experimental design. *³/₄ hour*	All questions are suitable.
Spend more time on this section. *1³/₄ hours*	**Worksheet B5A What happens when starch is mixed with amylase?** Omit Q2; start on experimental design. *1¹/₂ hours*	
Spend more time on this section. *1³/₄ hours*	**Worksheet B5A What happens when starch is mixed with amylase?** (continued) Carry out the investigation. *1¹/₄ hours*	
Do the second paragraph only from section **B**5.3. *¹/₄ hour*	**B5.3 The faster the better** *¹/₂ hour*	
	B5.4 A little more about enzymes **Worksheet B5B Digestion of proteins** (optional) **B5.5 A matter of digestion** *³/₄ hour*	Omit Worksheet **B**5B and the questions in section **B**5.5.
Omit Worksheet **B**5C.	**B5.6 An absorbing activity** **Worksheet B5C The value of villi** (optional/homework) **B5.7 The waste pipe** *¹/₂ hour*	
Total: 5 ¹/₂ hours	*Total: 5 ¹/₄ hours*	*Total: 5 ¹/₄ hours*

Monitoring the progress of Sc1

Investigating the starch–amylase reaction

Students should investigate the effects of amalyse on starch. This investigation may be carried out after Worksheet B5A "What happens when starch is mixed with amylase?".

Sample criteria are given below for an assessment between levels 4 and 7.

Strand (i) Ask questions, predict and hypothesize, e.g.	Strand (ii) Observe, measure and manipulate variables, e.g.	Strand (iii) Interpret their results and evaluate scientific evidence, e.g.
4(a) Suggest that temperature may be a factor, and suggest how the rate might depend on temperature	**4(b)** Control the amounts of starch and amylase solutions, and time how long it takes for starch to be broken down at different temperatures	**4(c)** Conclude that a warm solution of amylase breaks down starch faster than a cool solution
5(a) Suggest that a warm solution of amylase will have a quicker effect than a cool solution because the reaction will be faster	**5(b)** As above, but timing how long it takes starch to be broken down over a meaningful range of temperatures	**5(c)** Conclude that a warm solution of amylase breaks down starch faster than a cool solution, but qualifying the result
6(a) Suggest that the higher the temperature, the faster the rate of loss of starch because the reaction will be faster	**6(b)** Time how long it takes a range of different volumes of starch solution to be broken down over a meaningful range of temperatures	**6(c)** Conclude that raising the temperature increases the rate of reaction because the warmer solution has more energy
7(a) Suggest, with reasons, that temperature, amount of starch and presence of salt all affect the rate of breakdown, and that the most important of these is temperature	**7(b)** Time how long it takes a range of different volumes and concentrations of starch solution to be broken down over a meaningful range of temperatures	**7(c)** Conclude that the temperature of the amylase–starch solution has a bigger effect on the rate of breakdown of the starch than the initial concentration of starch over a range of concentrations and over temperatures between 15 and 35 °C

The pupils' book

B5.1 Food on the move

This section begins by getting pupils to think about what happens to food once it is in their mouths. The mechanical breakdown by teeth (and cutlery) is described briefly; pupils should appreciate that small pieces of food are easier to swallow than large ones. The cream cracker exercise in question 11 is designed to show that the food must also be moist.

After completing section **B5.3** on enzymes it would be possible to refer back to **B5.1** in order to develop the idea of smaller pieces of food offering a greater surface area for enzymes to work on. At this point, more able pupils could be asked to design an experiment to test this.

The role of muscles in squeezing food along the gut (peristalsis) can be a difficult idea to understand, but it is hoped that the variety of approaches mentioned in the text will help to overcome any difficulties. A useful model (which is easy to make and which can be passed around the class) is a length of flexible pipe with a ball-bearing inside to act as a bolus of food. A piece of Bunsen burner pipe will do – it works better if the inside has been lubricated with oil. Pupils can squeeze the ball-bearing along the tube to simulate peristalsis, in which the circular muscles contract behind the bolus and the wave of contraction spreads down the gut. This is analogous to the finger squeezing the rubber pipe and moving down the length of the pipe.

Answers to selected questions

2 Height × width × depth.

6 The gut contents are not normally opaque to X-rays.

B5.2 Digestion

This section aims to establish that digestion is essential if food molecules are to get from the gut into the bloodstream. The food molecules need to be small enough to pass through the gut membranes. A useful analogy to explain the need to produce small molecules can be made with reference to soccer supporters: if the soccer supporters (glucose molecules) hold hands (chemical bonds) to form a long chain (starch molecule), they cannot get through the turnstiles into the ground (cell membrane). However, if their hand grips were to be broken (digestion), the turnstiles would no longer be a barrier.

Worksheets **B5A** and **B5B** allow pupils to investigate digestion. Opportunities also exist to design experiments that test certain hypotheses about amylase. The experimental design exercises could be set for homework, although the pupils should be given the opportunity to carry out their own experiments in class. Re-evaluation of experimental designs in the light of experience is a valuable way of developing expertise in this area.

B5.3 The faster the better

This section aims to establish the nature of the substance found in saliva which helps with digestion. The term enzyme is used for the first time, and some of the general properties of these essential protein molecules are introduced. More able pupils will be able to link the information in this section to their findings in the investigations of the previous section.

Answers to selected questions

12 pH 7.0.

13 At high temperatures enzyme molecules are permanently altered. They are said to be denatured. At low temperatures molecules have less kinetic energy, so it is less likely for an enzyme molecule to make contact with a substrate molecule. Pupils could be asked to design an experiment to show that enzyme molecules are not denatured by low temperatures.

B5.4 A little more about enzymes

This section aims to show that enzymes are found in living organisms other than humans. It is also important to establish that enzymes can control the synthesis of large molecules from smaller ones.

B5.5 A matter of digestion

Pupils are expected to appreciate that the gut is not just a simple pipe, but has specialized regions in which particular tasks are carried out. In this section pupils are introduced to the events taking place in the stomach. Worksheet **B5B** allows them to investigate the effect of protease on egg white.

Answers to selected questions

15 Approximately pH 2.

16 It will reduce its activity because a pH of 2 is far from the optimum pH at which salivary amylase is most active.

17 It will neutralize the acid and provide the optimum pH for the pancreatic enzymes – about pH 8.

18 It will increase the surface area of the fat for the lipase enzyme to work on, thereby helping to speed up the breakdown of the fat into fatty acids and glycerol. It is important that pupils do not think that it is bile which converts fats into fatty acids and glycerol.

B5.6 An absorbing activity

This section continues the theme that the gut has specialized regions along its length. A portion of the gut devoted principally to the absorption of digested food products is one essential area. In question 19 pupils are asked to suggest the features such a portion may have. This can lead into a consideration of Worksheet **B**5C, which compares the growth of a child lacking villi with that of a comparable healthy child.

Answer to selected question
19 The region would need to be long enough to provide a large surface area (in relation to the space taken up) for absorption. Pupils will need help to appreciate that the surface area can be, and is, increased by the presence of millions of tiny projections called villi. An opportunity to see microscope slides of transverse sections through the small intestine may be of some use at this stage.

B5.7 The waste pipe

The large intestine is the final specialized part of the gut to which pupils are introduced.

Answers to selected questions
20 Water is absorbed from them.

22 X = stomach; Y = duodenum; Z = ileum.

Activities

Worksheet B5A What happens when starch is mixed with amylase?

REQUIREMENTS

Each group of pupils will need:
0.5% amylase solution
Benedict's solution
Iodine in potassium iodide solution
0.5% starch suspension (not containing reducing sugar)
Water, distilled
Bunsen burner
Dropping pipette
Eye protection
Spotting tile
Stopclock

Syringe, 20cm³
Test-tubes and rack
Tissues or paper towels

Access to:
Amylase solution through which cigarette smoke has been bubbled
Sink
Sodium chloride
Water baths at various temperatures (*e.g.* 25°C and 35°C)

Notes:
Check that the syringe plungers move freely and allow pupils to practise delivering single drops from a syringe.

The requirements for the experimental design exercise have been written in the *Access to* list. Cigarette smoke can be bubbled through an amylase solution, using a U-tube attached to a filter pump. One end of the U-tube is attached to the pump, and the other end to a cigarette. The suction from the pump is sufficient to draw the smoke through the amylase solution. This should be done as a demonstration in a fume cupboard.

The starch is largely converted into maltose; the action of amylase serves to illustrate the process of digestion.

Worksheet B5B Digestion of proteins

REQUIREMENTS

Each group of pupils will need:
Egg white suspension, 10 cm³
10% protease solution, 5 cm³
Eye protection
Stopclock
Syringes, 5 cm³, 2
Test-tubes, 2, and holder

Access to:
Dilute hydrochloric acid
Dropping pipette
Water bath at 37°C
Thermometer

Safety note:
Use of the hydrochloric acid solution must be closely supervised.

The procedure is detailed on the worksheet.

Worksheet B5C The value of villi

REQUIREMENTS

Each group of pupils will need:
Graph paper
Pencils
Rulers

The procedure is detailed on the worksheet.

Answers to selected worksheet questions

2 Between 4 and 9 years old.

3 The normal boy grew 20 cm in this 3-year period, the coeliac boy only 10 cm. Yearly rates of growth are therefore 6.67 cm and 3.33 cm respectively. Rates calculated from the graph will, of course, depend upon its accuracy.

4 The normal boy grew twice as fast.

5 Almost all the commonly observed clinical features of coeliac disease arise as a consequence of poor absorption of food. They include loss of body mass, diarrhoea, muscle weakness, skin abnormalities, anaemia and, in children, a failure to grow.

6 He must be given a gluten-free diet for the rest of his life.

It is worth noting that some baby foods are gluten free, and point this out on their labels. Pupils could be asked to look out for these and to bring the labels into school. A discussion of the various other substances besides gluten which are left out of baby food would provide a link with Chapter **B**6, which deals with diet.

Further information

The industrial applications of enzymes (for instance, in washing powders, malting, cheese making and immobilized enzymes) are covered in SATIS unit 710 "What is biotechnology?".

Further information about coeliac disease may be obtained from The Coeliac Society, PO Box 220, High Wycombe, Bucks HP11 2HY.

Chapter **B6 Diet and good health**

The syllabus section

Context

This section allows ideas of healthy eating to be discussed in terms of the biological requirements of a balanced diet. Sensible eating patterns (including the dangers of excess sugar, salt, saturated fats and additives) should be discussed. The value of high-fibre foods and vegetarianism should be considered. Strategies for successful slimming can be developed in the light of the dangers of obesity and anorexia nervosa.

Knowledge and understanding

Syllabus statements	PoS	SoA
Understand that a balanced diet contains sufficient energy to maintain life, and that the energy requirements of a person vary with age and activity.	2(i)1 2(i)5	—
Understand why fibre and vitamins are needed for health. Appreciate the unhealthy effects of eating too much fat and salt.	2(i)1 2(i)5	—
Know that the thyroid gland controls metabolic rate.	2(i)1 2(i)5	2.7(a)

Opportunities for co-ordination

Proteins link to **C**3, salt to **C**5, carbohydrates to **C**8, food additives to **C**9. Food as an energy source or fuel is also in **C**13 and **P**12.

Routes and times

Basic	Central	Further
Spend more time on this section. *1¼ hours*	**Worksheet B6A Your daily diet** Omit if time is short. **B6.2 Why do you need food – and what food do you need?** (class + homework) *¾ hour*	Omit Worksheet **B6A**. Some of section **B6.2** should be done for homework. *¼ hour*
	B6.3 Getting the energy balance right Omit Q4. **Worksheet B6B How much energy do you need?** (homework) **B6.5 Controlling your appetite** *½ hour*	All questions are suitable.
Omit section **B6.4**.	**B6.6 Everything you need to know about cholesterol** Omit Q13 and 14. **B6.7 Cutting down on salt** **B6.8 The importance of fibre in the diet** **B6.4 Too fat or too thin?** Select material from this section. *1 hour*	Q13 from section **B6.6** is also suitable. *¾ hour*
Total: 2¾ hours	*Total: 2¼ hours*	*Total: 1½ hours*

The pupils' book

B6.1 What would you like for supper tonight?

This section allows pupils to begin to think about what they eat and why. It may be developed by using Worksheet **B6A**.

B6.2 Why do you need food – and what food do you need?

Sensible patterns of eating could include meat, but need not. The emphasis in this section, and indeed in the whole chapter, is that pupils should think carefully about what they eat and develop balanced diets that suit them.

Answers to selected questions
2 Cereal grains, seeds (such as beans or pulses) and nuts are all sources of protein, as are new vegetable products such as Quorn.

3 Some vegetarian diets are probably healthier than diets rich in animal fats and low in fibre. Nonetheless, both vegetarian and meat diets need to be carefully planned.

B6.3 Getting the energy balance right

Worksheet **B6B** develops the idea that a balanced diet contains the right daily intake of energy. The number of kilojoules of energy needed each day will vary with the individual's age, health and activity.

Answer to selected question

4a Fat acts as an insulator against heat loss in cold climates.

b Protein is required for repairing damaged or worn body tissues.

c Women can lose a lot of blood during their menstrual periods: the amount varies widely between individuals. The loss of iron compounds in the blood may cause anaemia. Additional iron makes up for what is lost in this way.

d Glucose can be readily absorbed into the body, and is immediately available for respiration in muscle cells. It can be thought of as an additional source of energy.

e Pregnant women require additional food in order to nourish the developing embryo. A strict vegan diet may not provide enough food or the correct minerals, particularly calcium and iron, for the embryo, as dairy products and meat are not eaten.

B6.4 Too fat or too thin?

Pupils often worry about their physical appearance, and this section needs to be taught with sensitivity. It makes the point that deposition of fat usually results from a surplus intake of energy and too little exercise. Anorexia and bulimia are topics that needs especially gentle handling, since their origins are psychological.

Answers to selected questions

7 Fat people are more prone to heart disease, high blood pressure and diabetes than people of normal mass.

10 Strong contenders should include biscuits, pies, fish and chips, and sweets. Of more relevance is the idea that in moderation these foods are not "bad". Taken together, or eaten to excess with the exclusion of other foods, they can form an unbalanced diet.

B6.5 Controlling your appetite

Fortunately, most of us are able to eat sufficient food to avoid the dreadful consequences of protein deficiency. Two-thirds of the world's population are not so fortunate. Pupils with an inclination (or a need) to diet should be warned of the potential dangers of excess dieting. All pupils ought to become aware of the dietary problems that face far too many of the world's population.

B6.6 Everything you need to know about cholesterol

This section provides useful guidance on the dangers of excess cholesterol and fats in the diet.

Answers to selected questions

13a The risk increases by a factor of 1.29, *i.e.* by about one quarter.

b The risk increases by a factor of 2.11, *i.e.* it more than doubles.

14 Trim the fat off the lamb, use shortcrust instead of flaky pastry, eliminate (or reduce) ice cream and cream, perhaps replace the sweet course with cheese and biscuits and try reduced fat cheese (e.g. low fat cheddar).

B6.7 Cutting down on salt

This section continues the examination of diet by considering salt.

Answer to selected question

16 Certainly do not add it to the food that is on the table. Avoid excess convenience foods.

B6.8 The importance of fibre in the diet

Fibre is an important element in our diet. Fibre levels can easily be raised by eating wholemeal bread instead of white bread.

Answer to selected question
17 About 6 slices of wholemeal bread, 10 slices of wheatmeal bread and 18 slices of white bread.

B6.9 Food additives

It is important that pupils realize that not **all** substances with an "E" number are harmful. Indeed some, like ascorbic acid (vitamin C, E300) are positively beneficial. Even so, certain additives can cause reactions in some people.

Activities

Worksheet B6A Your daily diet

REQUIREMENTS

Each group of pupils will need:
Variety of food labels giving nutritional information

Access to:
Nutritional information, especially concerning size of regular portions

One approach to the analysis of diet is described on the worksheet. There are many ways in which this analysis can be developed. Pupils should be encouraged to bring in labels from tins and packets of food, which give many details of minerals, vitamins, fibre, salt, sugar, preservatives and colouring matter. Charts, tables and other forms of display could be prepared. Pupils may need help in estimating how much of each food they eat at each meal. From this they can work out their daily intake of energy and food substances into the body.

Worksheet B6B How much energy do you need?

REQUIREMENTS

Each group of pupils will need:
Graph paper
Pencils

This exercise could be used as a basis for a class discussion on the energy requirements of different people. It is also suitable for use as a homework exercise.

Further information

Science and Technology in Society
There are a number of SATIS units that could provide background information for this chapter. They include units 703 "Vegetarianism", 102 "Food from fungus", 108 "Fibre in your diet", 404 "How would you survive?" (a study of malnutrition), 104 "What's in our food? – a look at food labels" and 208 "The price of food". Of these, units 108 and 404 are updated in *SATIS Update 91*.

Chapter B7 The breath of life

The syllabus section

Context

This section provides an opportunity for investigating how pressure changes inside the thorax lead to inspiration and expiration. The exchange of gases between the alveoli and the blood capillaries is also considered. The dynamics of the breathing rate are emphasized by studying the effects of exercise on breathing.

The effects of asthma and industrial pollution on the normal functioning of the lungs are developed. The effects of cigarette smoke on health are considered. The reasons why people smoke are discussed.

Knowledge and understanding

Syllabus statements	PoS	SoA
Be able to name, locate and outline the functions of the diaphragm, pleural membranes and intercostal muscles which enable inhalation and exhalation in animals; pressure changes in the thorax and the antagonistic nature of the intercostal muscles.	2(i)1	2.4(a) 2.5(a)
Understand how the structure of alveoli and blood capillaries enable gaseous exchange to occur; the importance of diffusion in gaseous exchange across the alveoli.	2(i)1	2.4(a) 2.5(a) 2.6(a)
Know and understand the effects of tobacco on the way the human body functions.	2(i)7	—
Understand the role of goblet cells and phagocytes in keeping the lungs free from infection.	2(i)4	2.8(a)

Tier: B C F

Opportunities for co-ordination

Gas pressure links to **P2**. Gas exchange in the maintenance of the atmosphere is dealt with in **E3**.

Routes and times

Basic	Central	Further
Omit Q2 and 3 from section **B7.1** and Q5 from section **B7.2**. *³/₄ hour*	**B7.1 Holding your breath** **B7.2 Gas exchange** Omit Q4. *¹/₂ hour*	All questions are suitable.
Omit Q9 from Worksheet **B7B**. *1¹/₂ hours*	**B7.3 Breathing in and breathing out** **Worksheet B7B How you inflate your lungs** **Worksheet B7C The pleural membranes** (optional demonstration) *1 hour*	
Omit Q9–11 and 13 from section **B7.4**. *1¹/₂ hours*	**Worksheet B7D Looking at the lungs of a mammal** (demonstration) Omit parts **f** and **g** but draw attention to the pulmonary blood vessels. **B7.4 From air to blood** Omit Q11. *1 hour*	All questions from section **B7.4** are suitable.
		Worksheet B7E Size and gas exchange This may be used as extension material.
Spend more time on this section. *1¹/₂ hours*	**B7.6 Smoking and health** (class + homework) **Worksheet B7G Investigating cigarette smoke** (demonstration) **Worksheet B7H Starting, stopping and carrying on …** (optional/homework) *1 hour*	
Omit section **B7.5** and spend more time on Worksheet **B7F**.	**B7.5 The pipe cleaners** **Worksheet B7F Exercise and breathing** Especially Q3. *1 hour*	
Total: 6¹/₄ hours	*Total: 4¹/₂ hours*	*Total: 4¹/₂ hours*

The pupils' book

B7.1 Holding your breath

Most pupils will have tried to hold their breath for as long as possible at some time in their life, and no doubt they will have competed with each other to see who could last out the longest. This common experience serves as a useful introduction to breathing.

Pupils will be amazed at the breath-holding ability of Robert Foster. In fact, he did hyperventilate with oxygen for 30 minutes before his attempt. This information has been omitted from the text to avoid pupils trying to hyperventilate before they next dive into a swimming pool, unaware of the danger they are subjecting themselves to. It must be left to the discretion of the individual teacher whether to teach pupils about hyperventilation or not.

This is an important section that develops the idea that the composition of air is modified by being drawn into the lungs. The data enable simple calculations to be made.

Answers to selected questions

2 Changes in the percentage of each gas are: nitrogen $+0.49\%$
oxygen -4.56%
carbon dioxide $+4.07\%$.

Note that exhaled air also contains higher levels of water vapour.

3 Oxygen is removed from the air in the lungs and carbon dioxide is added. The **amount** of nitrogen is unchanged, but its **proportion** changes because the quantities of the other gases change.

B7.2 Gas exchange

The apparatus in figure 7.4 in the pupils' book can be easily assembled and used for a demonstration. Interpreting the exchange of gases in this situation is relatively straightforward. Although limewater is a specific test for carbon dioxide, hydrogencarbonate indicator is more sensitive to slight changes in its concentration.

Worksheet **B**7A provides an additional experiment that is more complex. The interpretation of the changes in the levels of carbon dioxide in the community can form a challenging exercise for practically minded groups. Less able groups can either attempt it when Chapter **B**9 has been completed, or be guided through it now.

B7.3 Breathing in and breathing out

The models in Worksheets **B**7B and **B**7C provide a useful way of visualizing the changes in the thorax during inhalation and exhalation. When using these models it is important to emphasize the ways in which they are like the actual thorax, and the ways in which they are unlike the thorax. The relationship between pressure and volume can be developed from Chapter **P**2 in the Physics pupils' book.

B7.4 From air to blood

It is important that pupils realize that the lung is not like a large bag filled with air, but has a more complex structure. They can examine the actual structure of the lungs, using Worksheet **B**7D. The X-ray photograph in figure 7.6 in the pupils' book begins the process of revealing the internal structure. Looking at actual X-ray photographs interests pupils, and hospitals will often respond favourably to a request for a suitable supply – particularly if you live near enough to make a personal visit.

The lung histology shown in figure 7.9 continues the examination of the internal structure. Prepared microscope slides should be used to supplement the photographs in the pupils' book.

The idea of the diffusion of gases into and out of the blood is developed from it consideration of experimental data. There are opportunities to expand on this theme, using the approach adopted in Chapter **C**18 of the Chemistry pupils' book – that of there being weak attractions between molecules in liquids and gases.

Answer to selected question
11 Collapsing the lungs decreases the mammals' volume, reducing the upward force of the water (the upthrust) on them. It also means that nitrogen is not absorbed into their blood, and hence prevents them getting "the bends".

12 This question allows pupils to observe directly the change in volume of water they displace when they breathe out, shedding light on question 11.

B7.5 The pipe cleaners

This section is important because it considers aspects of human health in relation to lung structure and function. Section **B**7.6 develops the theme further.

Answer to selected question
14 Although a **moist** surface is required for the alveolar membrane to be permeable to

gases, too much fluid will impede gas exchange. (In the extreme – as in drowning – there will be no room left in the lungs for the gases.) An accumulating volume of stagnating fluid in the alveoli will also provide ideal conditions for reproduction of bacteria and possible infections, *e.g.* pneumonia (which in turn would lead to production of more mucus, hence decreasing the efficiency of the gas exchange surface still further).

B7.6 Smoking and health

A graphic demonstration of the nature of cigarette smoke can be undertaken, using Worksheet **B**7G. The harmful effect of cigarette smoke on the health of individuals is discussed in this section. Smoking also affects athletic performance, although this is often not recognized by those athletes who are also smokers! Worksheet **B**7F develops the idea that exercise affects the breathing rate. The corollary of this is that if smoking reduces the efficiency of the lungs, then smokers must find exercise more strenuous than comparable non-smokers.

This important section is further supplemented by Worksheet **B**7H, which asks pupils to conduct a survey into why some people smoke and why some people continue to smoke.

Activities

Worksheet B7A   Do plants and animals alter the environment around them?

REQUIREMENTS

Each group of pupils will need:
Elodea, free of dirt and filamentous algae, about 5 cm long
Water animals, such as water snail or *Gammarus*
Hydrogencarbonate indicator solution, equilibrated with atmospheric carbon dioxide
Water, distilled
Box or cupboard, light-proof
Chinagraph pencil

Clingfilm as covering material for tubes
Rubber bands to fix Clingfilm, 8
or
Fitted caps, thin rubber
Light source
Silver sand, well washed
Specimen tubes, 11 flat-bottomed, 7 cm × 2.5 cm; 3 of these should have stoppers
Syringe and needle, 2 cm³ (or larger)

Notes:
Both tubes and syringes should be very carefully washed to remove all traces of contamination.

This experiment should run for 12 hours so it may be convenient to set it up beforehand. Allow the students to inject the indicator solution, observe the colour changes and discuss their meaning.

Freshly prepared indicator solution should be used. Useful comparisons can be made if three tubes are prepared beforehand to show the colour of the indicator when in equilibrium with atmospheric air (normal levels of carbon dioxide), with exhaled air (increased levels of carbon dioxide) and with air containing no carbon dioxide. This can be done as follows:
1 Stoppered specimen tube with indicator solution, to show colour in contact with normal air.
2 Stoppered specimen tube with indicator solution, which was breathed into before the stopper was inserted.
3 Specimen tube with indicator solution, above which some granules of soda lime are held in place in a piece of muslin wedged in position by the stopper. (This should be set up some hours in advance.)

The indicator solution in each of these demonstration tubes should be diluted so that the concentration corresponds to that produced when 2 cm³ of indicator solution are injected into each of the experimental tubes.

A full interpretation of the changes in the levels of carbon dioxide in the tubes will possibly elude all but the most able until Chapter **B**9 is covered, since it is necessary to establish that animals and plants respire (and thus produce carbon dioxide) all of the time, but plants also photosynthesize in the light, and take in carbon dioxide. In bright light, the rate of

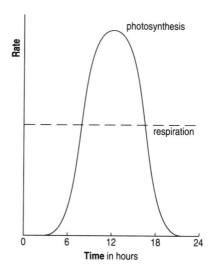

Changes in levels of photosynthesis and respiration over 24 hours.

photosynthesis of plants exceeds the rate of respiration of both plants and animals, so the levels of carbon dioxide in the tubes actually fall, as shown by the purple colour of the hydrogencarbonate indicator. The diagram on the left gives an indication of how photosynthesis and respiration vary over a 24-hour period.

Worksheet B7B How you inflate your lungs

REQUIREMENTS

Access to:
Parallelogram model of human ribcage
Syringe model of human thorax, as described for Worksheet **B7C** below

The ribcage model can be used to illustrate the movement of the intercostal muscles. Note that the two sets of muscles are antagonistic, and that contraction of one set pulls the other set back to its original length.

In the diagram below, the band between P and Q represents the external intercostal muscles, which cause the ribs to move upwards and outwards. A band stretched between R and S would represent the internal intercostal muscles, which cause the ribs to move downwards and inwards.

Parallelogram model of the ribcage.

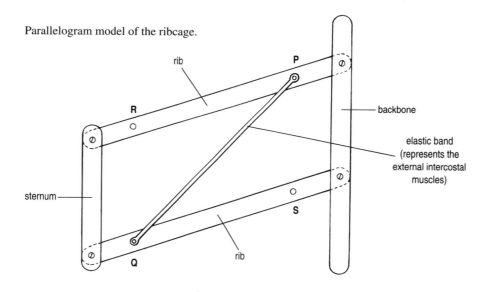

Worksheet B7C The pleural membranes

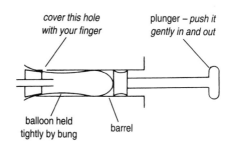

Syringe model of the thorax.

REQUIREMENTS

Each group of pupils will need:
Water
Microscope slides, 2
Pipette

Syringe model of human thorax
Wood, strips

Access to:
Glue to hold wooden strips in position

Note:

The syringe model can be assembled as shown on the left. A finger over the hole in the syringe casing will enable the pressure in the barrel of the syringe to change when the plunger is moved. The plunger simulates the human diaphragm, and the syringe barrel represents the thorax. Note that the balloon almost fills the syringe, as do the lungs in the thorax.

The procedure is detailed on the worksheet.

Worksheet B7D Looking at the lungs of a mammal

REQUIREMENTS

Each group of pupils will need:
"Pluck" of sheep or pig
Beaker of water
Forceps, blunt
Hand lens
Scalpel
Scissors

Seeker
Eye protection

Access to:
Hot and cold water
Soap
Towel

Safety notes:
The use of scalpels demands special vigilance by the teacher. Remind pupils to wash their hands after handling the "pluck". After the activity, the pluck should be disposed of quickly, either by incineration or by placing it, wrapped, in a dustbin or container for food wastes that will **not** be fed to animals.

A "pluck" consists of lungs, heart, trachea, larynx, oesophagus and parts of the diaphragm; it can normally be obtained from a local butcher, and can be kept for a day or two in a refrigerator. Make sure the butcher does not leave the liver attached, as it is not needed in this worksheet and can raise the price of the "pluck" considerably. A "pluck" always arouses a great deal of interest and can be used to train the pupils' powers of observation, as the tissues vary greatly in texture and colour. Encourage pupils to discuss their observations and record the information in as much detail as possible.

Be alert to the religious, moral and cultural sensitivities in the class concerning the handling of material from dead animals; models or videos might be offered as alternatives.

Answers to selected worksheet questions
3 Lung tissue floats if it contains air; it sinks if it has been taken from an animal that has drowned, because water has entered the tissue. It also sinks if it is from a baby born dead, because air has never entered it.

5 The atria must pump blood only as far as the ventricles. They collapse on death.

6 Arteries have thicker walls than veins, and therefore appear less red. They contract on death and appear smaller than veins.

9 The cartilage in the trachea prevents it from collapsing. Note that the rings are incomplete where the oesophagus runs alongside the trachea.

11 The glandular tissue near the larynx is the thyroid gland. Its function is to produce the hormone thyroxine, which is important in the control of growth, development and the body's metabolism.

Worksheet B7E Size and gas exchange

REQUIREMENTS

Each group of pupils will need:
Graph paper
Pencils

Access to:
Wooden blocks to simulate organisms, ideally cubes of side 1 cm

The concept of the ratio of surface area:volume is a difficult one; the use of wooden building blocks is a good way of helping the pupils to visualize it. The pupils should be allowed to build the model "animals" from the building blocks if they wish to.

Answers to selected worksheet questions

1 *Cubus major.*

2 If the linear dimensions of each "cell" are 1 cm, then the shortest distance will be 0.5 cm for *Cubus minor* and 1 cm for *Cubus major*.

3 6 cm^2 for *Cubus minor* and 24 cm^2 for *Cubus major*.

4 6 cm^2 for *Cubus minor* and 3 cm^2 for *Cubus major*.

Pupils ought to appreciate that larger animals have less surface area per cell available for gas exchange than smaller animals. An increase in available surface area is clearly of benefit to large animals – hence the discussion about size.

Worksheet B7F   Exercise and breathing

REQUIREMENTS

Each group of pupils will need:
Stopwatch

Safety notes:
This activity is probably most safely carried out in a gymnasium.

    Very careful consideration must be given when pupils are the objects of investigations: there must be no pressure on them to take part, and the educational advantage of any procedure must be judged in relation to the hazards involved. It is wise to check with the form tutor or PE department that all pupils in the class are fit for the suggested ways of exercising. Any pupil who is known to be epileptic, asthmatic or to suffer from other bronchial conditions and/or is excused from the **normal** PE activities should not take part in this investigation. (See also *Safeguards in the school laboratory*, ASE, 9th edition, 1988.)

This simple activity is best done in pairs. Pupils should sit quietly and still for about two minutes at the start of the lesson in order to establish a resting breathing rate. This is a good Friday afternoon activity!

Worksheet B7G   Investigating cigarette smoke

REQUIREMENTS

The teacher will need:
Universal Indicator solution
Chinagraph pencil
Cigarettes, 4
Clamps, 2, with stands and boss heads
Conical flasks, 2, with rubber bungs, each fitted
   with 2 bent glass tubes
Cottonwool
Dish for collecting ash from burning cigarette
Filter pump

Matches
Rubber tubing, short lengths
"T" piece, glass
Tubes, hard glass, 2, with bungs, fitted with
   tubes shaped to act as cigarette holders

Access to:
Fume cupboard
Balance

In this experiment it is worth comparing high and low tar cigarettes. The acid nature of cigarette smoke can be investigated by bubbling it through Universal Indicator solution.

Worksheet B7H   Starting, stopping and carrying on...

The procedure is detailed on the worksheet.

Demonstration experiments

The apparatus for detecting increased levels of carbon dioxide in human exhaled air, featured in section **B**7.2, would make an excellent demonstration. (This is affectionately called the "suck–blow" apparatus.)

Worksheets **B**7D and **B**7G will probably be performed as demonstrations.

Further information

Barrett, D.R.B., "Pleural membranes: a simple model", *J.Biol.Educ.*, **18** (1), 15, 1984.

Bell, G.H., Emslie-Smith, D. and Paterson, C.R. *Textbook of physiology* 10th edition, Churchill–Livingstone, 1980. (Earlier editions entitled *Textbook of physiology and biochemistry*.)

Beckett, B.S. *Biology: a modern introduction for G.C.S.E.* Oxford University Press, 1986.

The Guinness book of records 1992 Guinness Publishing Ltd, 1992.

Head, J.J. *A student's collection of electron micrographs* Edward Arnold, 1976.

Royal College of Physicians of London *Health or smoking?* Pitman, 1983. (Follow-up report to *Smoking OR health* Pitman, 1977.)

Chapter B8 Transport round the organism

The syllabus section

Context

This section allows transport systems to be examined at length. The need for transport systems in large organisms is considered, together with the ways in which the major transport systems of plants and mammals function.

This section also allows aspects of the human blood system that relate to healthy living to be considered, in particular, acclimatization to altitude, anaemia, carbon monoxide poisoning, blood groups, strokes, heart attacks and shock.

Knowledge and understanding

| | Tier | | | | |
B	C	F	Syllabus statements	PoS	SoA
			Know the location of the heart.	2(i)5	2.4(a)
			Know that dead xylem cells transport water and mineral salts through a plant, as well as providing internal support.	2(i)1	2.4(a) 2.5(a)
			Know that living phloem cells transport the products of photosynthesis away from the leaves.	2(i)1	2.4(a) 2.5(a)
			Understand that the heart acts as two muscular pumps side by side, one side receiving deoxygenated blood from the body and sending it to the lungs, the other carrying the oxygenated blood from the lungs to the body.	2(i)1	2.5(a)
			Understand the role of arteries, veins and capillaries and how their structure relates to their function.	2(i)1	2.5(a)
			Be able to relate the structure of xylem, phloem and red blood cells to the process of transport in plants and animals.	2(i)1	2.6(a)
			Be able to describe the roles of phagocytes, antibodies and platelets in defence mechanisms.	2(i)4	2.6(a)
			Understand the effect of life-style on the human blood system (e.g. effects of diet, exercise, smoking).	2(i)5, 7	—
			Be able to describe how water content is maintained in plants.	2(i)4	2.8(a)

Opportunities for co-ordination

C18 links with radioactive carbon tracing. **C9** deals with blood plasma as a colloidal system. **P15** links with blood groups.

Routes and times

Basic	Central	Further
Spend more time on this section. 1¼ hours	**B8.1 Delivering the goods** **B8.2 Transport in plants** Omit Q1, 2 and 6. ¾ hour	Brief revision only (class + homework) ¼ hour
Omit Worksheet **B8A**.	**Worksheet B8A Measuring the water taken up by a leafy shoot** Omit if time is short; omit Q4. 1¼ hours	
Spend more time on Worksheet **B8B** and on discussing the results of Worksheet **B8E**. 2 hours	**Worksheet B8B Measuring the rate of water loss from leaves** (class + homework) **Worksheet B8E Transport in plants** (optional) ¾ hour	
Omit Q13–15 from section **B8.4**. Section **B8.6** should be covered in class; omit Q21. 1½ hours	**B8.3 Transport in animals** **B8.4 Looking at blood** Omit Q13. **B8.5 More about red blood cells** ("Carbon monoxide poisoning" only) **B8.6 Liquid protection** (homework) 1 hour	Worksheet **B8C** "Looking at diffusion and mass flow", could be done after section **B8.4** (optional). All of section **B8.5** is suitable.
Omit section **B8.10**. 1 hour	**B8.9 The blood vessels** **B8.10 Severe bleeding** (optional/homework) ¾ hour	
	Worksheet B8D Looking at a heart Include parts **f** and **g** and Q4–8 from Worksheet **B7D**. **B8.8 The perpetual pump** Q31 is suitable for homework. 1½ hours	Spend less time on this section. 1 hour
	This is an alternative position for Worksheet **B**12E "Changes in pulse rate" (optional).	
Total: 7¼ hours	*Total: 6 hours*	*Total: 5 hours*

The pupils' book

B8.1 Delivering the goods

This section aims to introduce the idea that a transport system is essential in large organisms in order to service all the cells adequately. Some of the consequences of a "faulty transport system" are considered later in the chapter.

B8.2 Transport in plants

This section introduces the idea that an effective transport system is also essential to land plants. The use of radioactive tracers to investigate the distribution of photosynthetic products around the plant can be introduced, developing ideas from Chapter **B**3. Alternatively, the role of aphids as "phloem-sap extractors" can be discussed. Both are techniques that have been exploited to show that the products of photosynthesis (primarily carbohydrates, but also indirect products such as amino acids) travel through the living cells of the phloem.

Worksheet **B**8E enables pupils to investigate the movement of dye in a plant with a translucent stem (such as *Impatiens* or celery). More able candidates could be asked how they could use the technique to investigate the rate of water movement in the xylem. Alternatively, the investigation could be performed as a demonstration, or pupils could be asked to interpret figure 8.6 in the pupils' book.

The bubble potometer is a useful piece of apparatus for measuring the uptake of water into a plant stem. This is the same as the amount of water lost through transpiration, provided that the plant cells are turgid during the experiment. Although the apparatus is useful, it is also temperamental, and teachers might like to provide some of their pupils with working sets of apparatus if they are unable to assemble it for themselves. Worksheet **B**8A allows either option to be followed. For those teachers preferring to do this exercise as a demonstration, Worksheet **B**8B provides experimental data for analysis by the pupils.

Answer to selected question

3 In addition to sugars, the liquid in the phloem also contains low concentrations of amino acids, which are required by the aphids. In order to get adequate amounts of amino acids, the aphids have to ingest large volumes of sap. As a result, they produce vast quantities of sugary exudate, called honey-dew, which can make the leaves of a tree feel quite sticky, particularly at the height of summer. Ants are attracted to the honey-dew. (In some parts of the world, honey-dew is used to make cakes.)

B8.3 Transport in animals

Worksheet **B**7E developed the idea that large organisms have ratios of surface area:volume that are too small to enable them to obtain sufficient oxygen by diffusion across the surface of their bodies. An internal transport system is a logical consequence of having a specialized region of gaseous exchange that is remote from most of the cells. It is interesting to note that whilst movement into and out of the capillaries is by diffusion, the transport around the body is by mass flow. Diffusion will be discussed further in Chapter **C**18 "Atoms and bonding", whilst Worksheet **B**8C allows pupils to compare the rates of diffusion and mass flow experimentally.

B8.4 Looking at blood

The red blood cell has a biconcave shape, which increases its surface area by comparison with a sphere of the same volume. Simple models can illustrate this concept. The remainder of the section aims to develop an awareness of the huge numbers of red blood cells in the body. More able pupils could compare the oxygen-carrying capacity of equal volumes of water and blood.

Answers to selected questions

13 $(5\,000\,000) \times (5 \times 1\,000\,000) = 2.5 \times 10^{13}$ red blood cells.

14 Blood is 63 times better.

B8.5 More about red blood cells

This section discusses anaemia, the effect of high altitude, "doping" and carbon monoxide poisoning, all of which can be understood through a knowledge of the role of red blood cells in the body.

Answers to selected questions

16 The first part of this question was tackled in question 4c in section **B6.3**. Infants are prone to anaemia if iron levels in breast milk are low.

18 The response ensures that the cells of the body receive sufficient oxygen.

19 The team should arrive with enough time to spare for the increase in the number of red blood cells in the body to take place before the main tournament.

B8.6 Liquid protection

This section develops the theme of the body's defence against injury and cuts. The ideas are complex, but important. They need to be explained carefully.

B8.7 Blood transfusions

This section introduces an important topic with which all pupils need to be familiar, although a detailed analysis of blood groups in terms of surface antigens and antibodies is probably beyond the scope of all but the most able. The section will need to be taught carefully.

B8.8 The perpetual pump

The heart should be considered simply as a twin pump that allows blood to circulate between the lungs and the body. Worksheet **B8D** allows the internal structure of the heart to be investigated.

Britain has an appalling record for problems associated with heart disease. For this reason the text includes some information to help to educate pupils in this important area. This could be linked with the work on diet in Chapter **B6**. It could also provide an opportunity to discuss ethical problems. For example, with limited funds available to the National Health Service it is very difficult for decisions to be made about where the money should be allocated – to heart surgery and transplants, or to other essential operations.

The section ends with an exercise in measuring the pulse rate. Most people know that it can be used to measure the heart rate; the exact relationship between the contraction of the heart and the pulse rate need not be evaluated. Data concerning the pulse rate before and after exercise can be collected and analysed graphically. The **increase** in heart rate can be calculated for each pupil and related to fitness. The time taken to return to the normal pulse rate is also related to fitness.

The topic of fitness and, in particular, the identification of those pupils who are not fit can be an emotive issue, and needs to be handled sensitively. There should be no compulsion on students to carry out the activity, nor should it become competitive.

B8.9 The blood vessels

It is hoped that pupils will be able to link the description of the blood vessels in the text to the transverse sections in figure 8.19. The terms artery, vein and capillary will need to be explained carefully in terms of whether they carry blood to or from the heart. The use of microscope or photographic slides could help to make pupils more aware of the differences between these blood vessels.

B8.10 Severe bleeding

It is important that pupils are aware of what happens when people bleed profusely. This section provides valuable information on how to deal with such a situation.

Activities

Worksheet B8A Measuring the water taken up by a leafy shoot

REQUIREMENTS

Each group of pupils will need:

Leafy shoot, with stem just wide enough to fit
   PVC tubing
Absorbent paper
Beaker, 250 cm^3
Bung with hole wide enough to take shoot
Capillary tubing, about 15 cm long, with a
   90° bend
Flask, 250 cm^3, with side arm
PVC tubing, short length
Retort stands with bosses and clamps, 2
Scale, such as Scalafix or a piece of graph paper,
   attached to one length of capillary tubing

Scalpel
Stopclock
Syringe, 10 cm^3, and needle
Eye protection

Access to:

Sink or large bowl of water in which
   shoot can be inserted into PVC
Bench lamps
Electric fan
Polythene hoods

Notes:

The choice of shoot is very important if this investigation is to succeed. A young woody shoot that is not easily crushed is ideal.

   The success of this investigation also depends on air not collecting below the cut end of the shoot; the end of the shoot should be placed in water immediately after it has been cut or, better, be cut under water. Care should be taken when setting up any equipment under water – a good fit is required and it is helpful to trim the end of the shoot with an oblique cut.

   This is a very adaptable piece of apparatus. Once it has been set up, results are obtained with ease and the apparatus can be transported to different conditions. Readings can be obtained for long periods and it is light, cheap and easy to use. It is a great improvement on conventional potometers.

Safety note:

The use of scalpels demands special vigilance by the teacher.

Worksheet B8B Measuring the rate of water loss from leaves

REQUIREMENTS

Each group of pupils will need:
Graph paper
Pencils

Pupils are required to interpret data obtained from investigations with potometers.
A complete interpretation would include a consideration of the diffusion of water vapour molecules from open stomata, and the effect of the atmosphere around the stomata.

Worksheet B8C Looking at diffusion and mass flow

Part 1: Method A

REQUIREMENTS

Each group of pupils will need:
Agar jelly, cubes with sides 2 cm long, 2 (allow
  pupils to cut their own cubes – see *Notes*)
Potassium manganate(VII) solution, 150 cm³
Beakers, 2
Filter paper or blotting-paper
Rulers
Eye protection
Scalpel
White tile

Access to:
Water for washing cubes

Part 1: Method B

REQUIREMENTS

Each group of pupils will need:
Cubes of agar jelly in which eosin has been
  incorporated, with sides 2 cm long, 2 (allow
  pupils to cut their own cubes – see *Notes*)
Hydrochloric acid, dilute
Filter paper or blotting-paper
Eye protection
Rulers
Scalpel
Test-tubes, 3
Test-tube rack
White tile

Safety note:
Warn pupils to use the hydrochloric acid with care, and supervise its use. The use of scalpels also
demands special vigilance.

Notes:
Agar is most easily prepared by purchasing tablets, adding water as directed and heating in a pressure
cooker. The liquid is then poured into a Petri dish and allowed to set. Larger blocks can be prepared
by pouring the liquid to greater depths in other dishes or beakers. Eosin can be added before the agar
and water are heated in the pressure cooker.

   The agar for both methods should be prepared to a depth of 2 cm, so that pupils can cut their own
cubes.

Part 2

REQUIREMENTS

Each group of pupils will need:
Bungs, 4
Chinagraph pencil
Clamps, stands and boss heads, 2
Cottonwool
Dropping pipettes, 2
Forceps
Glass rod, at least 20 cm long
Glass tubes, 20 mm diameter and 30 cm long, 2
Eye protection
Litmus paper, red
Rulers
Scissors
Stopclock

Access to:
Ammonia solution, 2M
Ammonia solution, 9M – IRRITANT
Water
Fume cupboard

Part 3

REQUIREMENTS

Each group of pupils will need:
Chinagraph pencil
Cottonwool
Dropping pipettes, 2
Forceps
Glass rod
Glass tube, 20 mm diameter and 30 cm long
Eye protection
Litmus paper, red
Retort clamp, stand and boss head
Rulers
Scissors
Stopclock

Access to:
Ammonia solution, 2M
Ammonia solution, 9M – IRRITANT
Water
Fume cupboard

Safety note:

Warn pupils to use strong ammonia solution with care, and supervise its use; ventilate the room well or, better, use a fume cupboard.

Notes:

These notes apply to Parts 2 and 3 of this worksheet.

Prepare 9M ammonia solution by diluting 0.880 ammonia solution – CORROSIVE – with an equal volume of water. 2M ammonia solution can be prepared by diluting 11 cm^3 of 0.880 ammonia solution with 89 cm^3 water. Each group of pupils requires about 4 cm^3 of each solution.

It is useful to prepare a blue colour standard with which the litmus paper can be compared before the timed change has been judged to have taken place.

Worksheet B8D Looking at a heart

REQUIREMENTS

Each group of pupils will need:
Heart
Beaker large enough to contain heart
Dish or tray
Forceps, blunt
Means of taking measurements
Scalpel
Scissors
Seeker
Eye protection

Access to:
Bag for waste material
Top-pan balance
Hot and cold water
Soap
Towel

Safety notes:

Warn pupils not to look over other dissections while pupils are working with sharp scalpels. Dispose of the heart quickly, either by incineration or by placing it, wrapped, in a dustbin or container for food wastes which will not be fed to animals.

Notes:

Frozen hearts can be used, but such material bought from the butcher often lacks the main blood vessels and even part of the aorta. It is worth explaining requirements well in advance to butchers, as they are often willing to provide complete hearts if given time to collect them.

Be alert to the religious, moral and cultural sensitivities in the class regarding the handling of material from dead animals; models or videos might be offered as alternatives.

Worksheet B8E Transport in plants

REQUIREMENTS

Each group of pupils will need:
Leafy shoots, transparent, 2 (*e.g.* groundsel, celery, flowering spinach), which have been in a weak dye solution for about 2 hours before the lesson
Water
Coverslip
Hand lens

Light microscope
Light source
Microscope slide
Razor blade
Rulers
Scalpel, blunt
Eye protection

Safety note:

The use of scalpels and razor blades demands special vigilance by the teacher.

The procedure is detailed on the worksheet.

Demonstration experiments

Worksheets **B**8A, **B**8C and **B**8E could be performed as demonstrations.

Further information

Bell, G.H., Emslie-Smith, D. and Paterson, C.R. *Textbook of Physiology* 10th edition, Churchill-Livingstone, 1980. (Earlier editions entitled *Textbook of physiology and biochemistry*.)

Heart Research Series. 16 booklets published by the British Heart Foundation, 102 Gloucester Place, London, WIH 4DH. Available from health clinics at no charge.

Bulletins of the Institute of Medical Ethics – published monthly, by I.M.E. Publications, 151 Great Portland Street, London, WIN 5PB.

Revised Nuffield Biology *Teachers' guide 2* and *Text 2 Living things in action* Longman, 1975.

Richardson, M., Studies in Biology No.10 *Translocation in Plants* 2nd edition, Edward Arnold, 1975.

Selkurt, E.E. *Physiology* 5th edition, Little, Brown & Company, Boston, 1984.

Simpkins, J. and Williams, J.I. *Advanced Biology* Bell & Hyman, 1984.

Science and Technology in Society
SATIS unit 603 "The heart pacemaker" (updated in *SATIS Update 91*) could be of interest.

Chapter **B9** **Keeping going**

The syllabus section

Context

This section introduces respiration as a process of transferring energy from food (*i.e.* glucose) to the cells of an organism. Some of this energy is, however, transferred to the environment as heat. Oxygen is normally required for respiration, and carbon dioxide is produced as a waste product.

The applications of an understanding of anaerobic and aerobic respiration to athletic training and performance are discussed, and fermentation is considered as an example of anaerobic respiration.

Knowledge and understanding

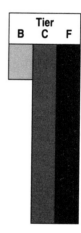

	Tier		
B	C	F	

Syllabus statements	PoS	SoA
Appreciate the effect of exercise and training on respiration.	2(i)5	—
Know that anaerobic respiration can occur in human muscles. Lactic acid accumulation will cause this process to stop.	2(i)1	2.7(a)
Know that aerobic respiration involves transferring energy from glucose to a cell; oxygen is needed, carbon dioxide is produced. Some energy may be transferred to the environment as heat.	2(i)1	2.7(a), (b)
Understand the role of respiration in maintaining solute balance in plants.	2(i)4	2.8(a)

Opportunities for co-ordination

The human body as an engine is in **P8** and **P12**. **C13** deals with fuels. **E3** discusses the role of respiration in maintaining the atmosphere.

Routes and times

Basic	Central	Further
Omit Worksheet B9A.	**B9.1 The living engine** B9.2 **Fuel for the living engine** **Worksheet B9A Investigating respiration** (class + homework) *1 hour*	Section **B9.3** "The power stations of the cell" is also suitable.
Omit Part 2 Worksheet B9C.	**Worksheet B9C Some investigations using yeast** B9.5 **Respiring without oxygen** (up to and including "Fermentation") *1½ hours*	
Omit this section.	**B9.4 Hard work** Supplement with relevant information from Worksheet B9B "Active transport" for role of respiration in maintaining solute balance. *½ hour*	
Omit section **B9.5**. Concentrate on section **B9.6** but omit Q12 and 13.	**B9.5 Respiring without oxygen** (from "Anaerobic respiration in animals") **B9.6 Speed *versus* stamina** *½ hour*	Section **B9.7** "Chemical reactions in cells" is also suitable. *Optional*
Total: 3 hours	*Total: 3½ hours*	*Total: 3½ hours*

Monitoring the progress of Sc1

Investigating respiration

Students should investigate the effect of temperature on the production of carbon dioxide by yeast. This investigation may be carried out instead of Worksheet **B**9C "Some investigations using yeast".

Sample criteria are given below for an assessment between levels 5 and 8.

Strand (i) Ask questions, predict and hypothesize, e.g.	Strand (ii) Observe, measure and manipulate variables, e.g.	Strand (iii) Interpret their results and evaluate scientific evidence, e.g.
5(a) Suggest that warm yeast solution produces carbon dioxide more quickly than cool yeast solution because the reactions happen faster at higher temperatures	**5(b)** Control the amounts of yeast and sugar, and measure the rate of production of carbon dioxide at two different temperatures	**5(c)** Conclude that warm yeast solution produces carbon dioxide more quickly than cool yeast solution, but qualifying the result
6(a) Suggest that the warmer the yeast solution, the faster the production of carbon dioxide because the reactions happen faster at higher temperatures	**6(b)** As above, but measuring the rate of production of carbon dioxide over a meaningful range of temperatures	**6(c)** Conclude that raising the temperature increases the rate of production of carbon dioxide because the warmer solution has more energy
7(a) Suggest, with reasons, that temperature, volume of solution and concentration of yeast solution all affect the rate of respiration, and that the most important of these is temperature	**7(b)** Measure the rate of production of carbon dioxide over a range of temperatures, using different volumes of solutions	**7(c)** Conclude that the temperature of the yeast solution has a bigger effect than the volumes of the solutions over a range of volumes and over temperatures between 5 and 35 °C.
8(a) Suggest, with reasons that the rate of production of carbon dioxide is doubled if the temperature is doubled; suggest a relevant investigation	**8(b)** Measure the rate of production of carbon dioxide over a range of temperatures using different volumes of solutions, measuring temperatures to 0.5 °C and volumes to 0.1 ml	**8(c)** As above, but explaining why the volume was kept constant for a range of temperatures and why the temperature difference was kept constant for a range of volumes

The pupils' book

B9.1 The living engine

This section compares the human body with a mechanical engine. The analogy is a useful one and can be developed further. Both need a source of energy, require oxygen and produce waste gases. In both cases the energy transferred from the "fuel" can be harnessed to do "useful" work. But the analogy cannot be pushed too far, as the next section shows.

B9.2 Fuel for the living engine

This section aims to show how the transfer of energy inside cells differs from simple combustion. The term "respiration" is introduced, and the ideas are developed in Worksheet **B**9A. The experiments outlined in this worksheet can be demonstrated before the pupils complete the worksheet.

B9.3 The power stations of the cell

This section illustrates the importance of enzymes in controlling the transfer of energy from food molecules. The electronmicrographs should lead pupils to realize that mitochondria are the important organelles where respiration occurs. The presence of larger numbers of mitochondria in a cell which requires a lot of energy by comparison with one which requires less could provide the necessary link.

B9.4 Hard work

This section develops the idea that organisms transfer energy from food for useful purposes. Worksheet **B9B** asks pupils to interpret data on the uptake of ions into plant roots.

B9.5 Respiring without oxygen

It is important that pupils realize that respiration can occur in the absence of oxygen. Commercially, this forms the basis of the brewing and baking industries. The importance of anaerobic respiration in yeast can be studied experimentally, using Worksheet **B9C**.

The data in figure 9.5 in the pupils' book provide an opportunity for pupils to practise their graph-plotting skills, in question 6.

Pupils can try to make their own ginger beer; some, of course, may already be well versed in the art of brewing beer at home. If there is an experienced brewer or winemaker in the class, he or she might be happy to describe the process in front of friends. Opportunities to develop a child's self-confidence when speaking to large groups ought not to be missed.

The section ends with a demonstration of anaerobic respiration in the muscles of the pupils' arms, which can be used to introduce the next section.

Answer to selected question

7 The shape of the graph is reminiscent of the typical shape obtained for the rate of enzyme controlled processes at different temperatures. This indicates that anaerobic respiration also uses enzymes to help to make energy available.

B9.6 Speed *versus* stamina

This section makes the comparison between aerobic and anaerobic respiration, using examples that pupils may find intriguing.

The cheetah is superb at running fast. The flexible spine enables the animal to achieve an enormous stride, and the small leg muscles are light and can contract quickly. However, the supply of energy to the muscles has to be so great during the fast chase that aerobic respiration is inadequate and anaerobic respiration is inevitably called upon to supply energy. It does not take long for the level of lactic acid to reach its peak; when this happens the cheetah has to drop out of the race.

The data in figure 9.11 indicate that for human athletes the proportion of energy being supplied by anaerobic respiration falls as the race gets longer. The questions which follow serve to emphasize that it is not the distance of the race which is important but the speed at which it is run. In a good long distance athlete the level of lactic acid rises slowly and, ideally, will not reach a peak until the moment he or she crosses the finishing line.

Answer to selected question

12 Because the first half of the race has been run too fast, too much energy has had to be obtained from anaerobic respiration. The rate of lactic acid build-up which results is sufficient to impair the functioning of the athlete's muscles and forces retirement from the race.

B9.7 Chemical reactions in cells

Metabolism is not an easy concept for pupils to grasp. This section aims to indicate what the word means and to illustrate the process by introducing it in terms of the chemical reactions occurring in respiration.

Answers to selected questions

19 From the list of statements it is hoped that pupils will be able to suggest that the factors which influence metabolism are body mass (see parts **a** and **e**), activity (**b**, **d**) and environment (**c**, **d**).

20 This question provides an opportunity for pupils to design an experiment to investigate the oxygen consumption in a named living organism. A suitable apparatus is shown below.

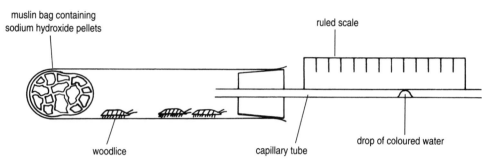

Suitable apparatus to investigate the rate of oxygen consumption in woodlice. The control should consist of the same apparatus without the woodlice. (Sodium hydroxide pellets are corrosive and must be handled with care.)

A successful experimental design should include:

1 Setting up the experiment and the control at the same air temperature.

2 Taking accurate measurements of the time taken for the water to move a known distance.

3 Subtracting any distance travelled by the water in the control tube from the readings taken for the water in the experimental tube, in order to obtain an accurate value for oxygen consumption.

4 Expressing the oxygen consumption in sensible units such as mm/minute. If the diameter of the bore of the tube is known the results could be expressed in mm^3/minute. Some pupils may even suggest that mm^3/minute/g would be sensible units to use.

It would be possible to extend this procedure to enable pupils to investigate the factors that affect the **rate** of oxygen consumption (*i.e.* size, activity or environment). This would link quite well with the statements in question 19.

Activities

Worksheet B9A Investigating respiration

REQUIREMENTS

Each group of pupils will need:
Writing materials

The procedure is detailed on the worksheet.

Answers to selected worksheet questions

2 Put seedlings into an incubator set at 95 °C for 24 hours, then find their mass. Repeat this process until a constant reading for mass is obtained.

3 The dry mass would have increased with time because the seedlings would have been able to photosynthesize.

7 A small count is produced by background radiation and naturally-occuring carbon-14 in the air.

8 The carbon atoms in the glucose eaten by the rats become the carbon atoms in the carbon dioxide they exhale. For this to happen the glucose molecule must have been changed inside the rat.

9 First, to provide a constant temperature near the optimum for the enzymes in the cells of the organism, and secondly, to ensure that the readings are taken at the same temperature and thus avoid any fluctuations in the gas volumes collected.

Worksheet B9B Active transport

REQUIREMENTS

Each group of pupils will need:
Graph paper
Pencils

The procedure is detailed on the worksheet. There is some differentiation of questions on this worksheet; teachers may find that some pupils need assistance when attempting the more demanding problems. The rate of uptake of sulphate ions is faster in aerobic conditions, which suggests that the presence of oxygen improves the ability of the seedlings to take up sulphate ions. As oxygen is used in respiration, the process by which energy is made available, it is reasonable to suggest that the data support the hypothesis that mineral uptake by plants is an active process. However, the data for anaerobic conditions suggest that in this experiment diffusion can account for the uptake of some of the sulphate ions.

Worksheet B9C Some investigations using yeast

REQUIREMENTS

Each group of pupils will need:

10% glucose solution, previously boiled to remove oxygen, corked, cooled and with fresh yeast suspension added, 10 cm³ (see *Notes*)

As above but with **unboiled** glucose solution, which will contain oxygen (for control)

10% glucose solution, previously boiled to remove oxygen, no yeast added (for control)

0.03 % diazine green (Janus Green B) solution, 4 drops

Hydrogencarbonate indicator solution, previously aspirated with atmospheric air
Paraffin, liquid, 5 cm³
Bungs to fit test-tubes, fitted with delivery tubing, 2
Specimen tubes, 2
Test-tubes, 10 cm³, 2
Test-tube rack
Thermometer
Water bath

Notes:

The mixture of glucose and yeast needs to be prepared before the lesson. The 10 % glucose solution should be boiled to remove oxygen from the water and then corked and cooled before adding the yeast suspension. Fresh yeast is preferable to dried yeast.

The experiment requires about 10 cm³ of the yeast and glucose mixture, which can be prepared by adding 12 g of fresh yeast to 150 cm³ of 10 % glucose solution. Stir the mixture thoroughly to obtain a uniformly cloudy suspension of cells. If dried yeast is used, add 6 g per 150 cm³ of 10 % glucose solution and stir the suspension very thoroughly for several minutes to make sure the cells are fully hydrated. Dried yeast takes time to become active, and the mixture should be prepared at least an hour before the lesson starts. Fresh yeast normally gives results within 30 minutes of being set up.

Some pupils can set up a control with glucose solution and no yeast, others a control with the unboiled glucose solution.

Part 2 of the experiment needs to run for at least two hours, with the temperature being recorded every 20–30 minutes.

The pupils can then design investigations to test certain hypotheses about respiration in yeast. The two hypotheses mentioned in the worksheet are not the only ones that could be tested. Pupils could be encouraged to formulate their own hypotheses, and then design experiments to test them.

Demonstration experiments

The experiments outlined in Worksheets **B9A** and **B9B** could be performed as demonstration experiments.

Further information

There are several useful references that provide background material for this chapter. These are:

Brock Fenton, M. *Just bats* University of Toronto Press, 1983.

Hawkey, R. *Sport science* Hodder & Stoughton, 1981.

Newsholme, E.A. and Leech, T. *The runner: energy and endurance* Fitness Books, 1983.

Revised Nuffield Biology *Teachers' guide 2* and *Text 2 Living things in action* Longman, 1975.

Simpkins, J. and Williams, J.I. *Advanced biology* Bell & Hyman, 1984.

Watson, A.W. *Physical fitness and athletic performance: a guide for students and coaches* Longman, 1983.

Whitfield, P. *The hunters* Simon & Schuster, 1978.

Science and Technology in Society
SATIS unit 603 "The heart pacemaker" (updated in *SATIS Update 91*) could be of interest.

Chapter B10   Skeletons and muscles

The syllabus section

Context

This section develops ideas about how organisms support themselves. Plant stems are strong and flexible, and the importance of lignin and turgidity in supporting cells is considered.

   The functions of skeletons and muscles in animal movement are developed. The sizes of legs of animals are largely dependent on the sizes of their bodies. An understanding of joints and muscles is used to discuss sports injuries, athletic training and osteoarthritis.

Knowledge and understanding

Syllabus statements	PoS	SoA
Be able to name, locate and outline the elements of support systems in plants and animals, including plant stems and bones, joints and muscles.	2(i)1	2.4(a) 2.5(a)
Be able to relate the structure of cells to the processes by which plants support themselves.	2(i)1	2.6(a)
Understand the importance of lignin in supporting woody plants, and turgid cells in supporting non-woody plants. Plant stems are strong but flexible.	2(i)1	2.6(a)
Know that a joint occurs where two bones meet. A synovial joint allows the movement of two bones. Cartilage and synovial fluid reduce friction between the bones.	2(i)1	2.6(a) 2.7(a)
Understand the importance of size and shape in aquatic and terrestrial organisms.	2(iii)1	2.6(b)
Know the functions of the skeleton and muscles in animal movement.	2(i)1	2.7(a)
Understand that muscles enable bones to move. Muscles can only contract, and are stretched back to their original length by the action of antagonistic muscles.	2(i)1, 2	2.7(a)
Appreciate how an understanding of joints and muscles can be used to discuss sports injuries, athletic training and osteoarthritis.	2(i)5	2.7(a)

Tier: B C F

Opportunities for co-ordination

P1 links with elasticity of muscles, **P**5 deals with joints, **P**7 with drag and streamlining.

Routes and times

| Basic | Central | Further |

Basic | **Central** | **Further**

Omit Q5 and 7 from section **B**10.1. Omit side 3 and Q1–3, 5–8 and 11–16 from Worksheet **B**10A.

> **B**10.1 **Propping things up**
>
> **Worksheet B**10A **Osmosis and turgor**
> Omit side 2 and Q6–8, 11, 15 and 16; side 3 is optional.
>
> *1 ³/₄ hours*

All parts of Worksheet **B**10A are suitable.

1¹/₂ hours

Spend more time on this section.

1 hour

> **B**10.2 **Limbs as props**
> Omit Q10–14.
>
> **B**10.3 **Joints and skeletons** (class + homework)
>
> *³/₄ hour*

Replace sections **B**10.4 and **B**10.5 by Worksheet **B**10B "Looking at a pig's trotter".

³/₄ hour

> **B**10.4 **Muscles and movement**
>
> **B**10.5 **Damage may occur** (homework)
>
> *1 hour*

Spend more time on this section.

1¹/₂ hours

> **Worksheet B**10C **Moving through water**
> Omit Q2.
>
> **B**10.6 **Moving through water**
>
> *1¹/₄ hours*

Total: 5 hours | *Total: 4³/₄ hours* | *Total: 4¹/₂ hours*

Monitoring the progress of Sc1

Investigating an object moving through water

Students should investigate the effect that shape has on the speed at which an object falls through water. This investigation may be carried instead of Worksheet **B**10C "Moving through water".

Sample criteria are given below for an assessment between levels 6 and 9.

Strand (i) Ask questions, predict and hypothesize, e.g.	Strand (ii) Observe, measure and manipulate variables, e.g.	Strand (iii) Interpret their results and evaluate scientific evidence, e.g.
6(a) Suggest that a narrow cone shape will move faster than a broader one because the forces on it are smaller	**6(b)** Time how long it takes cones of a range of diameters to fall over a meaningful distance	**6(c)** Conclude that reducing the diameter of an object may streamline it and reduce the drag/resistance
7(a) Suggest, with reasons, that both shape and mass affect the speed and that shape is the more important	**7(b)** As above, but also varying the mass	**7(c)** Conclude that both shape and mass affect the speed, and explain some of the limitations of the conclusion
8(a) Suggest, with reasons, that a cone twice as broad as another will fall half as quickly; suggest a relevant investigation	**8(b)** As above, measuring times to 0.5 s and distances to 1 mm	**8(c)** Conclude that both shape and mass affect the speed over a range of diameters from 3 to 15 mm and masses from 10 to 50 g
9(a) As above, and suggest a relevant investigation which involves repeating the experiment	**9(b)** Carry out the above procedure systematically	**9(c)** Use the data from repeated experiments to draw graphs of surface area against time and to show that shape affects speed; comment on the accuracy of the experiment

The pupils' book

B10.1 Propping things up

This section examines the variety of methods used by plants for support, in particular the roles of water and wood in terrestrial plants and of water in aquatic plants. Osmosis is introduced in order to show the significance of turgid cells in supporting plant structures. Worksheet **B**10A consists of simple investigations into the significance of osmosis in relation to plant turgor.

Answers to selected questions

2 Lignin is found in the xylem. The columns of xylem cells are gathered into (vascular) bundles, which are **usually** arranged around the edge of the stem.

7 Water moves into the cells by osmosis. Eventually the cells become turgid and press against each other; this internal pressure provides the support for the plant stem.

B10.2 Limbs as props

There are many examples in biology of a particular structure being linked to a particular function. This section begins by getting pupils to think about the structure and function of a variety of limbs.

The main emphasis here is to establish that as animals get bigger they have legs which are much shorter and much thicker than would be expected if proportions were being maintained.

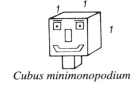

Cubus minimonopodium

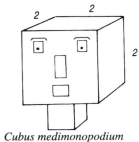

Cubus medimonopodium

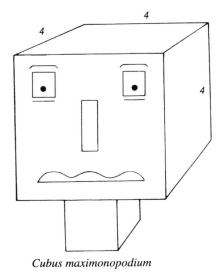

Cubus maximonopodium

Answers to selected questions

8 There are several possible suggestions that pupils could make. Increased contact between the body and the ground will increase friction and will thus make movement a more energy-demanding activity. In addition, it may be more difficult to see prey if you are the predator, or to see predators if you are the prey.

10 The plotted line is not straight and suggests that bigger animals have shorter legs than might be expected.

For more able pupils, a quantitative approach could be adopted to show that bigger animals have thicker legs than might be expected. This approach uses cubes as model "animals". Data and questions follow.

In this series of models each animal has only been given one leg – hence the "pretend" names of *Cubus minimonopodium*, *Cubus medimonopodium* and *Cubus maximonopodium*. To simplify matters, each leg is also square-shaped.

C. medimonopodium is bigger than *C. minimonopodium*, each of the sides of its body being twice as long. In addition, the width of each of the sides of the leg of *C. medimonopodium* is twice the width of the leg of *C. minimonopodium*. Similarly, the linear dimensions of *C. maximonopodium* are twice those of *C. medimonopodium*.

Each cube represents the body of the "animal" which has to be supported by single leg. The mass of the body is in proportion to its volume. The volume of cube is calculated as the (length of one side)^3.

It is the cross-sectional area of the leg – rather than the length – which is important in supporting the animal; this is equal to the (width of one side)^2.

In order to make things easy, we can say that the mass of *C. minimonopodium* equals 1 mass unit, and the cross-sectional area of its leg equals 1 area unit.

The pupils should attempt the following problems:

A Use the information in the preceding paragraphs to complete this table.

Name of model "animal"	Length of body	Mass of body	Cross-sectional area of leg
C. minimonopodium	1	1	1
C. medimonopodium	2		
C. maximonopodium	4		

Imagine that *C. minimonopodum* is a stable animal that does not fall down. This means that its body is adequately supported by its leg. We can calculate the pressure that is acting on the leg as the mass of the body divided by the area of the leg that is in contact with the body. For *C. minimonopodium* the pressure is equal to 1 unit. This represents the maximum pressure that the leg can withstand.

B Calculate the pressure acting on the leg of *C. medimonopodum* and *C. maximonopodium*. Explain why each of these animals will not be stable on its leg.

If these two animals are to become stable, the pressure acting on the single leg must not exceed 1 pressure unit.

C What must the cross-sectional area of the legs of *C. medimonopodium* and *C. maximonopodium* be if these "animals" are to be stable?

D Use these data to explain why large animals have proportionately thicker legs than small animals.

Answers to selected questions on the model "animals"

A The body masses and cross-sectional areas are calculated as the cube and square, respectively, of each of the figures in the "Length of body" column.

B The pressure acting on the leg of *C. medimonopodium* equals 2 units, whilst the pressure on the leg of *C. maximonopodium* is 4 units. In both cases the pressure exceeds the maximum of 1 unit.

C In order to achieve stability, the cross-sectional area of the leg of *C. medimonopodium* must increase by a factor of two, from 4 area units to 8 area units. Similarly, the cross-sectional area of the leg of *C. maximonopodium* must increase by a factor of four, from 16 area units to 64 area units. The larger the body of the "animal", the thicker the leg must become.

B10.3 Joints and skeletons

This section is mainly concerned with joints. It would be helpful if a skeleton (or suitable joints – obtained from a butcher) were available to be looked at. See Worksheet **B**10B.

The synovial joint is dealt with in greatest detail, but pupils may know something about the other types mentioned if they are familiar with the "soft spot" in the skull of newborn babies or have heard about "slipped" (strictly, "burst") discs.

Answer to selected question

15 The synovial fluid and cartilage reduce friction, the ligaments hold the bones together, the capsule holds the synovial fluid in place and the cartilage acts as a shock absorber and spreads the load evenly over the joint.

B10.4 Muscles and movement

This section aims to explain the relationship between muscles and skeletons that enables movement to occur. Two types of skeleton are discussed – endoskeletons and exoskeletons. Worksheet **B**10B deals with the examination of a pig's trotter; it can be used here (as recommended in the pupils' book) or in conjunction with the previous section.

Pupils can use themselves as examples of animals with an endoskeleton. It would be helpful if they could have access to living specimens of animals which have exoskeletons or hydrostatic skeletons.

Answer to selected question

24 It is an advantage for humans (and for tree-dwelling primates) to have long arms, but the extra operating distance is gained at the expense of operating force.

B10.5 Damage may occur

Pupils who are interested in sport are often aware of the injuries that can occur to their muscles, joints and bones. An appreciation of the vulnerability of joints and muscles is very necessary in this age of increased interest in sport and leisure. Pupils may have heard about repetitive strain injury (RSI) resulting from many types of repeated movement, *e.g.* in sports, musical-instrument playing and typing.

Answer to selected question

27 There are many answers to this question. They include:

Age – this affects the strength and resilience of the tissues. Muscle strength starts to decline at 30 to 40 years of age, elasticity in tendons and ligaments from the age of 30, and the strength of bone starts to decrease after the age of 50. Inactivity accelerates these natural degenerative changes, whilst exercise tends to delay them.

Personality – temperament and maturity may make an athlete more or less likely to take risks.

Experience – more inexperienced athletes suffer more injuries.

Level of training – too much or too little will increase the likelihood of injury.

Insufficient warm-up period – this makes muscle and tendon injuries more likely.

Poor technique – when jogging on hard surfaces, for example, this may injure knee joints.

Poor general health and diet, or lack of rest and steep.

The wrong equipment, particularly shoes and protective clothing. Joggers, for example, need shoes which give adequate support and which have a sole thick enough to provide shock absorption on hard surfaces.

B10.6 Moving through water

Animals have all sorts of special features which help them to move in their particular environment. This section aims to show the value of a streamlined shape for moving through water. This shape is not confined to aquatic animals; one has only to look at the shape of birds and some fast-running mammals such as the cheetah to appreciate this. The advantage of looking at aquatic animals is that it is easy for pupils to carry out an investigation in the laboratory which will test their ideas about the best body shape for moving through a particular medium. This is the purpose of Worksheet **B**10C, a practical exercise which is suitable for the assessment of several practical skills.

The theme could be developed by considering the idea that it is no use having a suitable shape for moving through water unless the shape is propelled through the water. The QE2 would not move if the propeller failed to turn. This begs the question, "What propels a fish?". The answer, of course, lies in the arrangement of the muscles of the tail; if a dead specimen is available, pupils could examine this arrangement. Like all muscles involved with movement, these are found in antagonistic pairs. Pupils may also be able to appreciate just how much of the total mass of a fish is devoted to muscle – essential for making progress through the comparatively viscous medium of water.

Some pupils may wonder why fish have fins. They appear to be a nuisance for moving forwards at speed because they provide a greater surface area in contact with the water, and so produce greater drag. Observation of living specimens will help pupils to appreciate the importance of fins.

Activities

Worksheet B10A Osmosis and turgor

Part 1

REQUIREMENTS

Each group of pupils will need:
Potato, raw
Sucrose solution, 2.0 mol/dm³, 10 cm³
Water, distilled, 10 cm³
Balance for measuring mass (accurate)
Chinagraph pencil or marker pen
Cork borer or scalpel
Filter paper
Rulers
Test-tube rack
Test-tubes with rubber bungs, 3
Tile, for cutting potato on
Eye protection

Part 2

REQUIREMENTS

Each group of pupils will need:
Potato, raw
Sucrose solution, 2.0 mol/dm³, 35 cm³
Water, distilled, 35 cm³
Balance
Chinagraph pencil or marker pen
Cork borer or scalpel
Filter paper
Pipette, graduated, 10 cm³, or syringe
Rulers
Test-tube rack
Test-tubes with rubber bungs, 6
Tile
Eye protection

Part 4

REQUIREMENTS

Each group of pupils will need:
Dandelion, inflorescence stalk
Sodium chloride 10% solution, 10 cm³
Water, distilled, 10 cm³
Chinagraph pencil
Forceps, blunt
Scalpel
Tile
Watch-glasses, 2
Eye protection

Part 5

REQUIREMENTS

Each group of pupils will need:
Onion, raw, that has not been kept in the
   refrigerator
Sucrose solution, 2.0 mol/dm³ 20 cm³
Water, distilled, 20 cm³
Bulb pipette
Chinagraph pencil or marker pen
Filter paper, 3 strips, about 2 cm × 5 cm
Forceps, blunt
Microscope
Microscope slides, 3, with coverslips
Paint brush, small, or glass rod
Pipette, graduated, 10 cm³, or syringe
Scalpel
Scissors
Test-tube rack
Test-tubes, 3
Tile
Eye protection

Safety note:
The use of cork borers and scalpels demands special vigilance by the teacher.

Teachers might like to arrange these practicals in a "circus", and to allow pupils to report their findings to the rest of the group. Alternatively, one or two experiments could be completed. Parts 1 and 5, for example, are easy to perform and informative; they can even be performed concurrently. If time is a problem, then the apparatus could be set up beforehand, but this is, for several reasons, a less satisfactory way of completing the worksheet.

   If time is available, Part 2 is certainly worth attempting as it gives valuable experience in making a series of dilutions and gives accurate results. Remember, however, that the potato tissue should stand in the sugar solution for one hour (45 minutes would be an acceptable minimum). Results are not satisfactory if the material is left overnight, although they may be acceptable if the test-tubes are kept in the refrigerator.

Worksheet B10B Looking at a pig's trotter

REQUIREMENTS

Each group of pupils will need:
Pig's trotter
Dissecting dish
Forceps
Scalpel
Scissors

Eye protection
Plastic gloves

Access to:
Hot and cold water
Soap
Towel

Safety notes:
These cuts require some force, and pupils should be advised to take care. Remind them to wash their hands at the end of the activity. The dissection may be done as a demonstration by the teacher.

   Dispose of the trotters quickly, either by incineration or by placing them, wrapped in a dustbin or container for food wastes which will not be fed to animals.

Pig's trotters are easily obtained from a butcher. They can be stored frozen, but allow plenty of time for them to thaw out before attempting the dissection.

Be alert to the religious, moral and cultural sensitivities in the class regarding the handling of material from dead animals; models or videos might be offered as alternatives.

Worksheet B10C Moving through water

REQUIREMENTS

Each group of pupils will need:

Balance	Tube, glass or clear plastic, at least 1 m long,
Bowl for tube to stand in	2 cm diameter, fitted with a rubber bung at the
Chinagraph pencil	lower end
Lead shot	*or*
Plasticine	Measuring cylinder, very large
Retort stand and clamp, with extra load on base	Wallpaper paste, about a 3 % solution
Stopclock	

This experiment provides a good opportunity to discuss the processing and presentation of results. The pupils will find that the fish shape drops more quickly than a cube or sphere, and should conclude that the streamlined shape decreases drag.

Pupils should be reminded that fungicidal wallpaper pastes may be toxic.

Demonstration experiments

The dissection in Worksheet **B**10B and certain experiments in Worksheet **B**10A could be performed as demonstrations.

Further information

Barrett, D.R.B., "Body size and temperature: an extended approach", J. *Biol. Educ.*, 17 (1), 7–8, 1983.

Bell, G.H., Emslie-Smith, D. and Paterson, C.R. *Textbook of physiology* 10th edition, Churchill Livingstone, 1980. (Earlier editions entitled *Textbook of physiology and biochemistry.*)

Hardy, R.N., Studies in Biology No. 35 *Temperature and animal life* 2nd edition, Edward Arnold, 1979,

Revised Nuffield Biology *Teachers' guide 2* and *Text 2 Living things in action* Longman, 1975.

Selkurt, E.E. *Physiology* 5th edition, Little, Brown & Company, Boston, 1984.

Soper, R. and Tyrell Smith, S., *Modern biology for first examinations* Macmillan Education, 1979.

Science and Technology in Society
Also relevant are SATIS units 707 "Artificial limbs", 503 "Paying for National Health" (contains information on hip replacement operations) and 509 "Homoeopathy – an alternative kind of medicine".

Chapter B11 Detecting changes

The syllabus section

Context

All organisms respond to changes in their environments, and this section explores some of the ways in which they do this. The growth of emerging shoots towards the light is explored experimentally, and a variety of human senses are discussed in terms of sensory receptors sending nervous impulses to the brain. The effects of drugs and alcohol on the human body are considered as causes of physical and emotional dependence. There are recommendations for drinking sensibly.

Knowledge and understanding

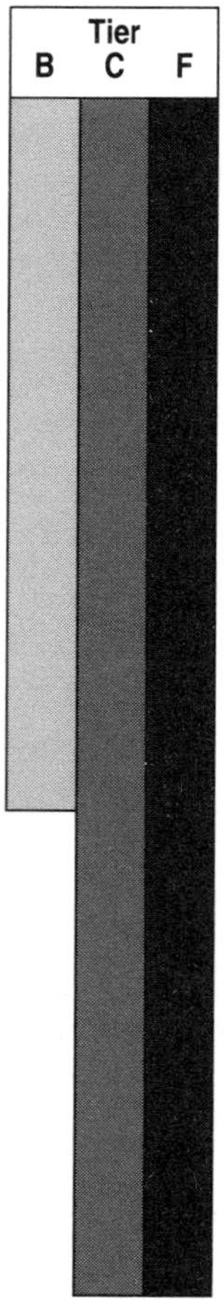

Syllabus statements	PoS	SoA
Be able to name, locate and outline the functions of the principal receptors in animals.	2(i)1	2.4(a) 2.5(a)
Be able to relate the structure of a neuron to its function.	2(i)1	2.6(a)
Be able to explain reflex actions as a way in which body activity of a mammal is co-ordinated through nervous control.	2(i)2	2.5(a) 2.6(a)
Know behavioural features of plants and animals which enable survival and reproduction.	2(i)2 2(iii)1	2.6(b)
Understand the effects of solvents, alcohol, tobacco and other drugs on the way the human body functions.	2(i)7	—
Understand the life process of sensitivity in plants and animals: (i) appreciate that external stimuli can be detected by organisms, and may result in responses, (ii) appreciate that the responses of organisms to stimuli may increase their chances of survival, (iii) appreciate that the receptor converts the stimulus into a form that can initiate a response by the effector. (These principles should be developed with reference to the growth responses of plants to light and gravity and the response of humans to visual stimuli.)	2(i)1,2	2.7(a)
Appreciate how technology can be used to improve sight in humans.	2(i)5	2.7(a)

Opportunities for co-ordination

Light and sound are dealt with in **P**13, colour and wavelength in **P**15, the behaviour of sound in **P**15, sensors as transducers in **P**15, problems of drug abuse in **C**12, communications in **P**21 and kinetic energy and momentum in **P**6.

Routes and times

Basic	Central	Further
	B11.1 Well-behaved plants Omit Q4. **B11.3 Animal responses** **B11.4 Light for sight** (homework) *1 hour*	All questions are suitable.
Concentrate on the range and function of sense receptors.	**B11.6 Other senses** (class + homework) EITHER **Worksheet B11C How good is your sense of touch?** OR **Worksheet B11D The skin as a sense organ** *1¼ hours*	Briefly discuss section **B**11.6 (class + homework). Omit Worksheets **B**11C and **B**11D. *½ hour*
	B11.7 The faster the better **B11.8 Nerves and nerve cells** *¾ hour*	Section **B**11.9 "The brain" may be used as extension work.
Omit all this section.	**B11.2 Light matters** **Worksheet B11A How plants respond** *1 hour*	
Concentrate on the basic structure of the eye. *1 hour*	**Worksheet B11B Looking at the eye of a mammal** **B11.5 How the eye works** (class + homework) The use of technology to improve sight might be included here (see teachers' notes for Worksheet **B**12D1 "Keeping life going"). *1½ hours*	
	B11.10 Altering things **Worksheet B11E Poisonous substances** Select material from either of these (class + homework). *1 hour*	
Total: 5 hours	*Total: 6½ hours*	*Total: 5¾ hours*

The pupils' book

B11.1 Well-behaved plants

This section introduces pupils to the idea that the growth response of plants towards light is an example of behaviour (defined in the pupils' book as the responses that organisms make to stimuli) and that it has survival value. The section presents the important concept of:

STIMULUS → RECEPTOR → (MESSAGE) → EFFECTOR → RESPONSE

This is the main theme running through all of the examples in this chapter.

Answer to selected question
4 The hairs are the receptors and the hinge mechanism is the effector.

B11.2 Light matters

Having established that plants respond to light in a way which favours their survival, we still need to know how the response is achieved. Following the principles underlying this chapter, we need to discover how the receptor cells in the plant convert the stimulus into a form that can initiate the growth response by the effector. This section examines the idea by referring to simple experiments; it can be supplemented by Worksheet **B**11A.

B11.3 Animal responses

The data in figure 11.5 in the pupils' book were obtained by 14-year-old pupils, using pitfall traps. Explaining data such as these presents a challenge to the pupils, because a number of variables may be involved in addition to light. Animals at night may be less visible to predators and less prone to dehydration and they may find their prey more abundant at night. Pupils should be encouraged to develop hypotheses to explain the responses of invertebrates to light in terms of the principles of this chapter. If time permits, they could also plan and carry out investigations to test their hypotheses.

B11.4 Light for sight

This brief section introduces one of the most important receptor organs we possess – the eye. The structure and functioning of the eye are examined in later sections; the importance of having two eyes is investigated here.

Pupils enjoy working out their sight capacity. If class data are collected, the results could provide an opportunity to show the variation that is found whenever a characteristic is measured in a sample of humans. From the range of values obtained, an average can be calculated. This can be taken as the representative value.

B11.5 How the eye works

This section relates the structure of the eye to its function, and should be completed with Worksheet **B**11B. The emphasis should be to show how the eye converts electromagnetic radiation into nerve impulses that can cause the central nervous system to initiate a response. Sufficient factual detail should be included to allow these principles to be developed, but care should be taken to avoid overloading pupils with too much incidental detail.

B11.6 Other senses

This section includes material on the ear, the skin and the tongue. The aim is to develop the principles outlined at the start of this chapter. Teachers should select certain parts of this section, depending on which examples they have chosen. Worksheets **B**11C and **B**11D could be used at this point.

B11.7 The faster the better

This section deals very simply with reflexes, stressing their survival value to the organism. A distinction between reflexes and spinal reflexes is not made in the text, but it could be mentioned that the reflex pathways which do pass through the brain do not pass through those higher centres of the brain that are involved in the making of conscious decisions.

B11.8 Nerves and nerve cells

This section develops the previous one with a consideration of the structure of nerves. These should be considered as a means of transporting the "message" to and from the co-ordinating centre of the body.

To get some idea of just how many nerve cells there are in the human body, pupils could be asked to work out how long it would take them to finish counting 28 billion cells if it took one second to count each one – taking into account rounding-up of numbers, the answer is about 900 000 years!

Answer to selected question

27 The fatty material acts as an insulator around the nerve, preventing the impulse from "leaking away" from it.

B11.9 The brain

A brief consideration of the brain completes the material on the ways in which humans detect and respond to changes in their environment. The emphasis is on aspects that are directly relevant to the pupils. A detailed consideration of the role of each part of the brain is beyond the scope of this course.

Answers to selected questions

31 To allow the skull to be reduced in cross section to pass through the vagina at birth.

32 Meningitis is a serious disease because the inflamed meninges membranes can affect the functioning of the brain. The symptoms include fever, severe headache, photophobia, vomiting and stiffness in the back and neck. Later symptoms include drowsiness and convulsions. The bacterial form of the disease needs to be treated immediately with antibiotics if permanent damage to the brain is to be avoided. The viral form is not susceptible to antibiotics and is much less easy to treat. The Hib vaccine, introduced in the UK in 1992, offers protection against the most common bacterial form.

33 A loss of consciousness or confusion leading to a loss of memory for events before and after the injury. Recovery is often accompanied by nausea or vomiting.

34 Blood can build up inside the cranium and compress the brain. The symptoms of this are muscular twitches, convulsions or epileptic-type fits. Breathing is noisy, the pulse is slow and the pupils of the eyes may dilate (this occurs to different extents in different people). The body temperature may rise. Later symptoms are a reduction in the level of alertness and passing into a coma.

B11.10 Altering things

The significance of this section will depend upon the health education programme of the school. The importance of the idea that **all** of the drugs mentioned in figure 11.22 of the pupils' book are dangerous cannot be overstressed. None of these substances is safe, since they can all lead to dependence of one type or another.

It is worth pointing out that a carefully controlled prescription of barbiturates and benzodiazepines (*e.g.* Valium) can prove to be beneficial to some people for a short time. Long-term use is harmful since it leads to dependence. These drugs do not solve people's problems; they may, at best, increase their ability to withstand pressure and solve their problems for themselves.

The dangers of alcohol are becoming increasingly apparent, as are moves towards making it less socially acceptable to drink too much.

Answers to selected questions

38 Pleasure, curiosity, social anxiety, rebelliousness – it's a good way of being anti-authority – relief from worry or depression, fear of missing out or losing face, boredom, attention seeking and search for self-knowledge. (The last is not usually a reason within this age group, though it might be a motive for the few older teenagers who experiment with hallucinogenic drugs.)

39 Drugs which have been found to be addictive are used as little as possible. Amphetamines used to be quite widely used, for example as appetite suppressants, but now they are hardly ever prescribed. When drugs such as tranquillizers or sleeping pills are really necessary, they should be prescribed only for as short a time as possible – just to help the person over a bad patch.

Obviously there are cases when a drug's medical value outweighs the disadvantages of addiction – patients suffering from a painful terminal illness, for example, will be given morphine (heroin).

41 A larger person has a greater volume of body fluids than a smaller person. Therefore, if they both drink the same amount, the alcohol will be less concentrated in the blood of the larger person and will have less effect. Women, as a general rule, are smaller than men and have smaller volumes of body fluids. They are therefore more easily affected by alcohol.

Activities

Worksheet B11A How plants respond

REQUIREMENTS

Each group of pupils will need:
Pea seeds, germinated, 42
Compost, seed
Box, black on the inside, light-proof, with a hole
  at one end
Pots, 7.0 cm, 7

Access to:
Light source
Water

Peas give excellent results; they germinate readily and in many ways are easier to use than the traditional oats. The seeds should be soaked in water for at least 24 hours before setting up the experiment. Ten days should be allowed (at 20 °C) for results to appear.

Because the plants are hardy, a number of experiments can be set up. This worksheet gives a few ideas and then invites students to devise their own series of experiments.

Worksheet B11B Looking at the eye of a mammal

REQUIREMENTS

Each group of pupils will need:
Eye of sheep or ox, fresh
Dish
Forceps
Hand lens
Scalpel, sharp
Scissors, dissecting
Eye protection

Tile
Tissue paper, thin, 2 cm²

Access to:
Hot and cold water
Soap
Towel

Safety notes:
Remind pupils to use scalpels with care, and to wash their hands at the end of the activity.

Dispose of the eyes quickly, either by incineration or by placing them, wrapped, in a dustbin or container for food wastes which will not be fed to animals.

A great deal can be learned by studying the external features of the eye; frequently pupils fail to do this in detail because they rush to make the internal examination. Pupils who feel unable (or unwilling) to perform this dissection should be allowed to complete suitable alternative work (such as using books or models to find out the answers to the worksheet questions).

Eyes can usually be obtained from a butcher, who will require notice in advance in order to assemble a number for class use. The lens and internal surfaces will certainly be in better condition in fresh eyes, which will need to be obtained from an abattoir. Frozen material can, however, be used; if it is frozen solid it can be sawn in various planes with a fretsaw. Eyes that have been frozen may take 12 hours to thaw out fully.

If too much pressure is used to make an initial cut the aqueous humour sometimes squirts out, to the distress of more sensitive pupils. It may help to avoid this if the teacher makes the initial incision with scissors or a sharp scalpel blade.

Pupils should be encouraged to observe carefully and to think about the structures that they see.

Increasing concern about bovine spongiform encephalopathy (BSE) is making it harder to obtain any animal nerve tissue, including eyes. Some local authorities also have their own guidelines about the use of such tissue.

Worksheet B11C How good is your sense of touch?

Part 1

REQUIREMENTS

Each group of pupils will need:
Blindfold
Maze
Stopclock

Part 2

REQUIREMENTS

Each group of pupils will need:
Blindfold
Metal sheet, thin, with raised and
    depressed patterns of dots

Part 3

REQUIREMENTS

Each group of pupils will need:
Samples of Braille and Moon alphabets

Notes:
Each maze should be at least 30 cm × 30 cm (larger if possible). A maze consists of strips of card or draught-excluder strip about 3 mm wide glued onto a thick base – either cardboard or plywood.

The metal sheets should be about 20 cm × 20 cm, and have series of metal dots punched into them with a centre punch. Each pattern should consist of six dots, but the spacing between the dots and the patterns themselves should vary both on a single sheet and between sheets. Some patterns can be made with raised dots, others can be made with depressed dots.

Braille texts may be obtained from The Royal National Institute for the Blind, 224 Great Portland Street, London W1N 6AA. Moon texts may be obtained from The Royal National Institute for the Blind, Moon Branch, Holmesdale Road, Reigate, Surrey. Drawings of the two styles of text are shown in the diagrams on the worksheet; these can be examined if it proves to be difficult to obtain actual samples of the texts.

Worksheet B11D The skin as a sense organ

REQUIREMENTS

Each group of pupils will need:
Blindfold   Hairpins, wire, 2
Cork or expanded polystyrene, small pieces   Rulers

The procedure is detailed on the worksheet. It is important that the tips remain the measured distance apart; this can be achieved by pushing them through small pieces of cork or expanded polystrene.

Worksheet B11E Poisonous substances

REQUIREMENTS

Each group of pupils will need: *Optionally, access to:*
12 white cards or slips of paper   Measuring cylinder, 100 cm³
                                              Measuring cylinder, 500 cm³
                                              Wine glass
                                              Small spirits glass (whisky "tot" or similar)
                                              Empty wine bottle, spirits bottle and beer can

This activity introduces pupils to the physiological effects of alcohol and drugs and how they modify behaviour. The group activity on the worksheet provides an opportunity for pupils to pool and check their own knowledge of the effects of alcohol, and may be repeated before the work on drugs.

It is not possible to forecast blood alcohol levels reliably on the basis of what has been drunk.

As a rough guide, for an 11-stone man drinking one pint of beer (two "units") quickly on an empty stomach, the alcohol content of his blood will rise to a peak of 30 mg/100 ml after about an hour; it will than fall at the rate of one "unit" (¹/₂ pint beer) per hour. Another pint drunk quickly after two hours will again increase the level. This is an idealized picture as rates of absorption vary so much.

The elimination rate is more predictable at one "unit" per hour, so the only sure guide to being free of alcohol is to calculate the number of hours from the time of drinking on this basis. This may take several hours: someone who has had a heavy drinking session during the late evening may still be over the limit when he goes to work at 7 a.m. the next morning.

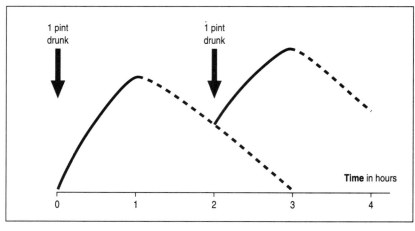

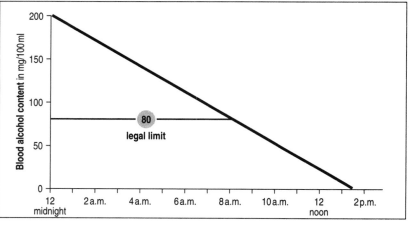

Calculation of alcohol levels.

An optional practical involves calculation of the amount of alcohol in various "glassworths" of different drinks. The glasses or bottles may be filled up with water (to represent the alcoholic drink) and the volume of water measured. Pupils may then calculate the volume of pure alcohol contained in each glass or bottle by using the approximate percentages: beer 4%, wine 10%, whisky 40%.

Apart from affecting the liver and the brain, heavy drinking affects the stomach (where it causes irritation), the heart (which can be affected by vitamin deficiencies caused by a neglected diet) and the reproductive organs. Cirrhosis of the liver is probably not caused directly by alcohol but rather by the alcohol accentuating a nutritional deficiency.

Side 2 of the worksheet may be used as a basis for the discussion of the uses and abuses of drugs and hazardous solvents. A few notes about individual drugs are given below.

- "Speed" is an amphetamine, often amphetamine sulphate.
- Cocaine (also known as "C", "coke" or "snow") may lead to damage to the nasal membranes and is of practically no use in medicine. "Crack" is a modified form of cocaine that can be smoked rather than "snorted"; it is highly addictive.
- Valium is a common tranquillizer. The barbiturates Seconal, Nembutal and Amytal are used in medicine. Barbiturates and tranquillizers can cause addiction.
- Opiates such as diamorphine (heroin) and codeine depress the thalamus, which is a critical point in the brain for the sensory impulses reaching that organ.
- Sudden death by solvent sniffing, when it occurs, may be due to the blocking of the electrical impulses which trigger the contraction of the heart muscles.
- Hallucinogens like LSD ("acid" or "sugar") may eventually cause depression and irrational behaviour. The danger with these drugs is not primarily one of addiction or of harmful effects on individual organs but of the changed behaviour of the individual. LSD is lysergic acid diethylamide.
- The effects of "Ecstasy" are similar to those of LSD; at high doses it is similar to the amphetamines. It is not physically addictive, but tolerance builds up so that ever higher doses need to be taken to get the same effect.

A further optional activity is to assemble a collection of empty containers that once held materials containing hazardous solvents, *e.g.* paint thinners, varnishes, solvent-based glues, etc. (preferably ones with hazard warning labels).

Answers to worksheet questions

1 Small amounts of alcohol slow down reaction time, and this may lead to driving or cycling accidents. Accidents in the workplace and at home may also be caused by lengthened reaction time and increased carelessness.

2 High concentrations of alcohol in the body cause, a loss of the sense of balance, blurring of vision, etc.

3 Carbon dioxide and water.

4 Some of the alcohol in the bloodstream diffuses into the lungs and is breathed out.

5 Good vision, concentration, reaction time, judgement of distance, operational control of the car (*e.g.* steering etc.) are all affected by drinking.

6 Advances in medicine have increased the search for new and more powerful drugs, and chemists have developed better methods for extracting and purifying drugs for useful purposes. On the negative side, easier travel and better communications have led to an increase in the illicit drugs trade.

7 In a search for relief from worry or depression, from curiosity or pleasure, in a search for some sort of knowledge about oneself, in order not to be "one of the crowd", etc.

8 Slurred speech, sleepiness, reduced anxiety, slower responses, etc. Many drugs also produce a "hangover".

9 The person may be tempted to increase the dose in order to get the same effect, and this may lead to ever higher doses being taken.

10 Some glues, paint thinners, some cleaning fluids, "whiteners" for blanking out writing, nail-varnish remover, solvents for inks in felt-tip pens, etc.

11 An "unreal" situation may cause a person to do something silly which he or she would not normally do, and which might lead to accidents.

Demonstration experiments

Parts of Worksheet **B**11A could be performed as demonstrations, where they could be developed to include the use of a klinostat to study gravitropisms. Demonstration material of etiolated plants could accompany section **B**11.1 or Worksheet **B**11A

Further information

Science and Technology in Society
Two SATIS units are relevant to this chapter. They are: unit 209 "Spectacles and contact lenses" (updated in *SATIS Update 91*) and unit 406 "Blindness".

Supplementary material
Braille and Moon texts can be obtained from the addresses given in the notes for Worksheet **B**11C.

Chapter B12 Keeping things under control

The syllabus section

Context

In this section, homeostasis is defined as the maintenance of constant internal conditions within organisms. The principles can be developed in a wide variety of contexts, including the maintenance of balanced water levels in the blood and fluid bathing the tissues, the regulation of body temperature in mammals, and the maintenance of glucose. The practical implications of failure of the regulating mechanisms can be considered (*e.g.* hypothermia, sugar diabetes, kidney failure), together with possible solutions.

Knowledge and understanding

Syllabus statements	PoS	SoA
Be able to name and locate the principal systems which maintain constant internal conditions in animals and humans.	2(i)1	2.4(a) 2.5(a)
Understand the significance of sweating as a method of cooling the body, and shivering as a mechanism for generating heat.	2(i)4	2.5(a)
Appreciate how mammals and lizards regulate their body temperature.	2(i)4	2.6(b)
Know and be able to explain that the kidneys remove excess water and waste products (e.g. urea) from blood plasma. Urine is produced and stored in the bladder. The composition of urine may be altered by the kidney tubules.	2(i)4	2.8(a)
Appreciate that transplants and dialysis serve as possible solutions when a kidney fails.	2(i)5	2.8(a)
Be able to explain the way in which the blood-sugar level in humans is co-ordinated through the hormonal control of insulin.	2(i)2, 4	2.9(a)
Understand the basic principles of genetic engineering in relation to insulin production.	2(ii)5	2.9(a)
Understand and be able to explain how homeostatic and metabolic processes contribute to the control of human body temperature and breathing, including the role of negative feedback.	2(i)4	2.10(a)

Opportunities for co-ordination

P20 deals with control systems, **P**2 with the kinetic theory of matter, **P**10 with energy change and temperature, **C**9 and **C**12 with dialysis.

Routes and times

Basic	Central	Further
	B12.1 Not too cold, not too hot **B12.2 Controlling the body's central heating system** **Worksheet B12A A normal temperature** *1¼ hours*	
Spend more time on this section. *1½ hours*	**Worksheet B12B Investigating heat loss from objects of different sizes** Part 2 is optional; omit Q4–6. *1¼ hours*	
		B12.3 Control of blood sugar level *¾ hour*
		Worksheet B12C Investigating the effect of different concentrations of water on blood *Optional/homework*
Omit section **B**12.4 but discuss the basic function of the kidney. Omit Worksheet **B**12D. *½ hour*	**B12.4 What goes in must come out** **Worksheet B12D Your kidneys at work** *1 hour*	
Concentrate on incubators in Worksheet **B**12D1. *½ hour*	**B12.5 What happens when a kidney fails?** **Worksheet B12D1 Keeping life going** (class + homework) *1 hour*	
		B12.6 Other adjustments **Worksheet B12F Controlling concentrations** (class + homework) *1 hour*
This is suitable for Basic level. *¾ hour*	**Worksheet B12E Changes in pulse rate** *Optional*	Omit Worksheet B12E.
Total: 4½ hours	*Total: 4½ hours*	*Total: 6¼ hours*

The pupils' book

B12.1 Not too cold, not too hot

Homeostasis is a vital process for maintaining life in organisms. This section introduces the idea by referring to various circumstances which can affect body temperature and indicating the responses needed to keep it within close limits. It can be completed alongside Worksheet **B**12A. Alternatively, the worksheet can be completed as part of the next section.

B12.2 Controlling the body's central heating system

This section aims to explain the mechanisms involved in controlling the responses needed to keep body temperature constant. In particular, the text makes a brief reference to those parts of the skin that are involved. Worksheet **B**12B may also be completed as part of this section.

The investigations using cobalt chloride paper are fun to do, and teachers might like to spend time developing these ideas. Adhesive tape can be used to stick squares of the moisture-indicating paper to the skin, but delicate areas should not be used for the investigations, as peeling off the tape could be painful! Non-allergic sticking plaster is a useful alternative.

Clearly, the investigations in the text are qualitative in nature, and so it may be necessary to establish some method of comparing degrees of moisture output. Squares of dry absorbent material can be weighed and then stuck to the skin. Reweighing after an appropriate amount of time will reveal just how much water has been released from the skin. A very sensitive balance is needed, but the results do lend themselves to further study.

The section continues with a consideration of how sweating cools the body and of the role of the hypothalamus in keeping the temperature of the body constant. Behavioural methods of regulating body temperature are also discussed.

Answer to selected question

15a By keeping its mouth open the crocodile is able to cool its body, which is being warmed by the sun. Being warm means that its muscles are able to contract quickly in order to attack prey. Presumably, if the crocodile were to spend time in the water its body would be cooler, but this would reduce its ability to move quickly; in addition, depending on how deep the water was, it might have to expend energy to keep afloat. Being warm on the river bank may also help it to speed up the digestion of food in its gut. Some pupils may suggest that having an open mouth makes it easier for birds to clean the crocodile's teeth.

b The muscles that a butterfly uses to vibrate its wings will generate heat, which will raise the body temperature until it is ideal for the flight muscles to work at peak efficiency.

c The lizards can only be active at the coolest parts of the day. In the heat of the midday sun the temperature of their bodies would soon rise to an intolerable level, and so they retreat into the shade.

B12.3 Control of blood sugar level

This section introduces the control of glucose levels as a homeostatic mechanism, and, through a brief consideration of diabetes, looks at the role of insulin within this mechanism. The section ends with a brief account of the production of insulin through modern techniques of genetic engineering.

Answers to selected questions

17 Each peak in the level of glucose in the blood occurs soon after a meal.

18 These peak levels are not permanent, and they soon fall to a constant level which is greater than zero.

19 The body controls the blood sugar level so that it is constant, despite a variable supply of glucose.

21 Diabetics feel weak because insufficient sugar is available in the blood. They may lose body mass because their fat reserves will need to be broken down to supply sugar. The lack of an immediate source of energy such as sugar will make them feel tired and weak. (The word *diabetes* means "siphon".)

22 A large volume of urine is produced because a lot of water is used to remove the excess sugar from the body. (Traces of sugar in their urine also make diabetics prone to urinary infections. The Romans tested for diabetes by putting urine out for bees.)

24 Someone who has become very heavy will need more energy just to move the increased body mass around. Such a person will therefore need more insulin too, and the pancreas may not be able to provide the extra. There is the additional factor that people get fat because they overeat – and they tend to eat large amounts of the starchy and sugary foods which produce the greatest rise in blood sugar. Again, the pancreas might have produced enough insulin to keep pace with a normal diet, but not with overeating.

B12.4 What goes in must come out

The kidney is considered in this section as a filtration unit. Details of the structure and function of the nephrons are not required. This section can be completed with Worksheet **B**12C, which emphasizes that the amount of water inside the body needs to be regulated if damage to cells is to be avoided. The kidney plays a major role in the maintenance of a constant water level in the body. Worksheet **B**12D examines the functioning of the kidneys more fully.

B12.5 What happens when a kidney fails?

This section gives a brief account of the two alternative methods of treatment – dialysis or a kidney transplant – open to someone who suffers kidney failure.

B12.6 Other adjustments

This section considers a further example of homeostasis: the effect of increased levels of carbon dioxide on the breathing rate. It can be supplemented by Worksheet **B**12E.

Activities

Worksheet B12A A normal temperature

REQUIREMENTS

Each group of pupils will need:
Graph paper
Pencils
Rulers

The procedure is detailed on the worksheet.

By comparing the average value of the small sample of boys with the national average, it is hoped that pupils will begin to appreciate the effect that sample size can have on the validity of any representative value quoted.

If pupils are to gain first-hand experience of using a clinical thermometer, the thermometers **must** be carefully disinfected before each use and the correct use demonstrated before pupils try for themselves.

Worksheet B12B Investigating heat loss from objects of different sizes

REQUIREMENTS

Each group of pupils will need:
Water, cold
Beakers, 3, of volumes $100\,cm^3$, $250\,cm^3$, $500\,cm^3$
Graph paper
Measuring cylinder
Rulers
Stands, 3
Stopclock
Thermometer (see *Note*)

Access to:
Source of very hot water (as near boiling as possible), *e.g.* electric kettle

Note:
Digital strip thermometers may be more appropriate here than spirit or mercury-in-glass ones.

It is necessary to have a source of very hot water and a safe method of transporting it around the laboratory. Care should be taken to ensure that the beakers of hot water are stable on their stands.

The calculations in the second part of this worksheet are complex and may not be appropriate for all pupils. They should illustrate the relationship between the heat loss of a body and its surface area and volume. Although the temperature falls most quickly in the smallest beaker, more energy is actually transferred per unit time from the largest beaker.

It is important that pupils appreciate the analogy that can be drawn between this example and the case of animals. Some pupils will need to be helped to understand this.

Worksheet B12C Investigating the effect of different concentrations of water on blood

This worksheet describes a simple experiment and gives results for interpretation by the pupils. The procedure for their analysis is detailed on the worksheet. Alternatively, the pupils could perform the experiment for themselves, using the requirements outlined on the worksheet.

Worksheet B12D Your kidneys at work

The procedure is detailed on the worksheet.

Worksheet B12D1 Keeping life going

This worksheet introduces pupils to a variety of technological advances in medicine which have extended or improved the quality of life. It might be supplemented by a discussion of how technology can be used to improve sight in humans and by considering kidney and heart transplants (see below).

The heart pacemaker is inserted under local anaesthetic and measures approximately $5\,cm \times 5\,cm \times 1\,cm$; its case is made of titanium coated with silicone rubber. It is usually powered by long-life lithium iodide or zinc–mercury cells although a nuclear source may also be used. The commonest type of pacemaker is the "demand" type, which works when the natural rhythm of the heart falls below its normal rate. These pacemakers are programmable and are often able to adjust the frequency of their output to correspond to the different demands placed on the heart according to the activity of the wearer. The "fixed rate" pacemaker gives impulses at a steady rate even if the heart is beating on its own.

A study of the artificial kidney machine gives an opportunity to revise dialysis. A vein in the arm is usually used to connect the patient to the machine. (The vein is usually fairly large and made surgically by connecting a normal vein to an artery.) The main parts of the artificial kidney are the dialyser, a pump, a temperature-control system, an oxygen-supply system and a means of adding an anticoagulant to stop the blood clotting on the plastic membrane. A type of cellophane (a cellulose tetranitrate) which acts as a very fine molecular sieve is used so that proteins are not removed from the blood. The differentially permeable membrane has a very large surface area to ensure adequate exchange between the blood and the dialysate, and the dialysate is continuously renewed to remove waste products. There are a number of types of kidney machine which all work on the same principle; the one shown in the diagram is the twin-coil apparatus. The dialyser in this apparatus can be easily changed and is available in sterilized packs. Kidney machines cannot remove water easily, although some machines force the blood through the machine under a slight pressure which forces some water through the membranes. Pupils should appreciate that although artificial kidneys are very effective in helping victims of kidney disease, the patients often suffer from problems such as anaemia and infections, and must spend several hours a week on the machine.

Incubators help to sustain the life of premature babies whose low weight and generally weak condition reduces their viability. The environment in the incubator can be altered to suit a range of conditions (temperature, relative humidity and oxygen concentration). A premature baby may be kept in an incubator for the first few weeks of life and all activities such as weighing, feeding and even minor operations may be performed through arm "portholes" in the incubator sides. Incubators are often fitted with a range of control devices which sound a warning or regulate the environment should the conditions in the incubator change suddenly.

Other technological applications which have helped improve the quality of life and might be mentioned here include artificial limbs, heart–lung machines and artificial heart valves.

Detached retinas are caused by localized disease or by the formation of a small hole in the retina which allows fluid from the vitreous humour to accumulate behind the retina. Fixing the retina back in position may be done by laser treatment or diathermy (electrical heat treatment). Corneal transplants may be used to restore vision in many cases where the cornea has been damaged. Modern technology has allowed corneas to be stored in "cornea banks" until required. The pupils should also consider the role of organ transplantation in enhancing and prolonging life, especially with reference to kidney transplants.

Answers to worksheet questions

1 It should be unreactive and should not dissolve.

2 So the battery can be changed easily without major surgery.

3 Because the pressure of the blood in veins is lower than in arteries. Veins are also usually wider than arteries and have thinner walls, so it is easier to insert the electrode.

4 The tip of the electrode must be in contact with the heart wall so that there is direct electrical stimulation of the heart muscle.

5 Urea.

6 Proteins.

7 Foods (*e.g.* meat) which produce a large quantity of waste products such as urea need to be avoided. Too great an intake of water may cause problems if the water-regulatory function of the kidney is not working properly, since water cannot be easily removed by the kidney machine.

8 The temperature of the blood in the kidney machine and the rate of removal of waste products.

9 Because small molecules and ions diffuse from the blood into the dialysate along with the urea. The presence of these molecules in the dialysate helps maintain the concentration of these essential substances in the blood.

10 These babies have a relatively large surface area for their size and so lose energy rapidly compared with larger children or adults.

11 To prevent dust or bacteria entering the incubator and thus maintain a clean, relatively disease-free environment.

12 To ensure that fresh air is continuously drawn into the incubator (to prevent a build-up of carbon dioxide and water vapour around the baby).

Worksheet B12E Changes in pulse rate

REQUIREMENTS

Each group of pupils will need:

Chair or stool	Pencils
Graph paper	Stopclock

Safety notes:
This activity is probably most safely carried out in a gymnasium.
Very careful consideration must be given when pupils are the objects of investigations: there must be no pressure on them to take part, and the educational advantage of any procedure must be judged in relation to the hazards involved. It is wise to check with the form tutor or PE department that all pupils in the class are fit for the suggested ways of exercising. Any pupil who is known to be epileptic, asthmatic or to suffer from other bronchial conditions and/or is excused from the **normal** PE activities should not take part in this investigation. The activity should not be allowed to become competitive.
(See also *Safeguards in the school laboratory*, ASE, 9th edition, 1988.)

The procedure is detailed on the worksheet. The results are best recorded as a graph of pulse rate against time, with the exercise period clearly marked in.

Pupils may be very interested to find out whether the physical fitness of members of the class has any relationship to the results. A "scoring method" can be devised after discussion with the class. For example, an average figure can be found for students **a** sitting, **b** standing, **c** after exercise. Each student could be given 15 points and have points deducted for figures above the mean. For example, when sitting, 1 point may be deducted for a pulse over 78 beats per minute, 2 points deducted if over 84 beats, 3 points deducted if over 96 beats (taking 78 beats per minute as the mean). However, the topic of fitness and, in particular, the identification of those pupils who are not fit can be an emotive issue, and needs to be handled sensitively.

Fitness can also be judged by allowing points for regular training, membership of teams, cycling to school, walking and so on. No doubt the pupils will be familiar with this type of assessment, as it is sometimes used in magazines and on television.

Worksheet B12F Controlling concentrations

The role of carbon dioxide in controlling the rate of breathing is discussed in the first part of this worksheet. When the carbon dioxide dissolved in the blood reaches the medulla, cells which are sensitive to changes in carbon dioxide concentration respond by increasing the rate and number of nerve impulses that control the action of the muscles involved in breathing. Both the rate and the depth of breathing are increased, and this rapidly brings the carbon dioxide concentration in the alveoli back to normal levels. The rate and depth of breathing can be controlled consciously, but this mechanism cannot continue with carbon dioxide concentrations above a certain limit. Carbon dioxide is produced by cellular respiration and the increased concentration of this gas in the bloodstream during vigorous activity results in an increased ventilation of the lungs and consequently an increased supply of oxygen to the tissues, up to a certain limit. A knowledge of this mechanism has led to advances in resuscitation techniques: carbon dioxide is sometimes added to oxygen cylinders used for resuscitation in order to stimulate the medulla.

The second part of the worksheet deals with further examples of how the kidney controls the absorption of water and sodium back into the blood, and the role of hormones in this process. As the filtrate passes down the tubules a large proportion of the molecules and ions dissolved in it are transported via the epithelial cells of the tubule back into the blood. Active transport is involved in these processes rather than diffusion, with the glucose molecules and various ions moving against a concentration gradient. As dissolved materials such as sodium ions move back into the blood, the concentration of water in the tubules increases compared with that in the blood, and a concentration gradient is set up so that water diffuses back into the blood.

The role of hormones in regulating the amount of water should be discussed at a simple level. ADH regulates the reabsorption of water by increasing the permeability to water of the cells at the far end of the tubule. The secretion of this hormone by the pituitary gland is controlled by the concentration of water in the blood. Changes in the water concentration of the blood are detected by receptors in the hypothalamus which regulate the amount of ADH the pituitary gland secretes. The hormone aldosterone acts by increasing the reabsorption of sodium ions back into the blood from the tubules and thus increases the reabsorption of water. For each sodium ion that is reabsorbed, a potassium or hydrogen ion is transported into the tubule. The pumping of hydrogen ions into the tubule helps regulate the pH of the blood, but the actual mechanism is complex. The urine can often have a pH as low as 4, even in healthy people. The role of hormones in controlling calcium levels in the blood can be discussed and provides a good but complex example of feedback mechanisms between the thyroid and parathyroid glands. At the end of the section, pupils should realize that hormones play an important part in controlling the concentrations of certain dissolved substances in the blood.

The role of respiration in maintaining the solute balance

This is an appropriate place to discuss the active transport of ions and molecules. In animal cells, an "ion pump" which depends on continued respiration drives sodium ions out of the cell and potassium ions into the cell. Active transport systems for glucose also exist. Similar transport systems exist in the membranes of plant cells, and many substances may be transported actively rather than simply diffusing through the membrane: sugars and other organic compounds (to which membranes are relatively impermeable) are rapidly absorbed when the cells are respiring. The sodium pump exists in most organisms. Active transport mechanisms involving respiration are necessary for cells in order for certain substances to be concentrated inside the cell and others to be excluded.

With some groups, teachers may consider discussing some aspects of control mechanisms of some animals and plants which live in salty surroundings. For example, bony fish which live in the sea keep their body fluids at a lower concentration than sea water by actively excreting sodium and chloride ions from their gills, and plants such as cord grass which live in salty conditions regulate their salt content by excreting sodium chloride from special glands on their leaf margins.

Answers to worksheet questions

1 0.03%.

2 Carbon dioxide: the breathing rate increased when the person breathed in air with a high carbon dioxide concentration but not when breathing a high concentration of oxygen alone.

3 To make it a fair test: different people may have slightly different breathing rates under the same conditions.

4 An increased rate of nerve impulses would increase the rate of breathing (because the impulses control the contraction of the muscles).

5 The concentration of carbon dioxide in normal air is very low. When the volunteer breathes normal air again, the carbon dioxide concentration in the lungs falls gradually.

6 The concentration of water in the tubules increases.

7 Anything causing sweating, *e.g.* vigorous activity, or reducing the amount of water taken into the body in food and drink.

8 The concentration of water in the blood increases, so the pituitary gland releases less ADH, and the cells at the far end of the tubules let less water back into the blood.

Further information

Science and Technology in Society

The following SATIS units are of relevance here: 302 "Living with kidney failure", 309 "Paying for National Health", 710 "What is biotechnology?", 1102 "Special types of hearing aid" and 1104 "Materials to repair teeth". Of these, units 302, 309 and 710 are updated in *SATIS Update 91*.

Topic B3

Living organisms and their environment

Chapter B13 Making sense of an environment

The syllabus section

Context

The ecological definition of the environment is considered, and pupils should become aware of the wide range of different factors that can compose an organism's environment. The factors that compose the human environment can be discussed. Jet lag resulting from flying, for example, is considered to be a disruption of a person's internal body clock caused by artificial changes in the rhythm of the day.

Knowledge and understanding

	Tier		Syllabus statements	PoS	SoA
B	C	F			
			Understand (by abundance and distribution investigations in a locality) that organisms may compete with each other for a resource that is in short supply.	2(iii)1	2.4(c)
			Know (through study of a locality) features of plants and animals (e.g. size, shape, colour, behaviour and life cycle) which show adaptation to an environment and enable survival.	2(iii)1	2.6(b)
			Understand that successful organisms will succeed unsuccessful ones in a habitat. Eventually a climax community might be produced.	2(iii)2	2.6(d)

Opportunities for co-ordination

P21 deals with transmission of messages of all kinds.

Routes and times

Basic	Central	Further
Spend longer on this section. *1 hour*	**B13.1 Conditions of life** *½ hour*	
Worksheet **B13A** "Looking at a community" or Worksheet **B13B** "Weather and the growth of trees" could be included here. *1½ hours*	**B13.2 Some natural communities** **B13.3 Changes – weather, season and tide** (class + homework) *1 hour*	
	Worksheet B13C A look at the way animals behave *1½ hours*	
Spend more time on this section. *1 hour*	**B13.4 Changes – competition, succession and climax communities** (class + homework) *½ hour*	
	EITHER **Worksheet B13D Sun and shade plants** OR **Worksheet B13E Weapons in the competition war** *1½ hours*	
Total: 6½ hours	*Total: 5 hours*	*Total: 5 hours*

The pupils' book

B13.1 Conditions of life

Humans are introduced first, as examples of familiar organisms, with the intention of showing that we are atypical animals because of our considerable ability to manipulate our environment, thus escaping from the environmental constraints that control or limit most other species.

The limpet is used as an example of a contrasting organism, fully constrained by its environment. Pupils are asked to decide which environmental factors determine where the limpet can live. There is every opportunity here to encourage them to use this approach for other organisms – the photographs in figure 13.4 of the pupils' book could be used as some of many examples. The pupils may need some guidance here, since it could be difficult to define the environmental influences and constraints on, for example, very mobile animals. It is relatively easy to explain why limpets must live below high tide level, but not so easy to understand why blackbirds will be found in habitats on the edges of woodland rather than in dense woodland.

Answer to selected question

4 Descriptions of the habitats of the organisms mentioned here would be more meaningful if some idea were conveyed of any major environmental influences: these might either be apparent from the photographs or be appreciated by the pupils already. Most will be familiar with the earthworm, and should appreciate the cool, damp nature of its habitat.

B13.2 Some natural communities

This section develops the important concepts of habitats, communities and ecosystems. It can be supplemented by Worksheet **B**13A.

Answer to selected question

8a and **b** The coral reef and tropical rain forest are "rich" communities because temperatures are high and there is no shortage of water. Coral reefs are at or near the water surface, so light does not become a limiting factor.

The deep ocean floor is often "poor" because of total darkness, so all food chains rely on the arrival of dead remains falling from the surface. It is also cold, and communities found in cold environments tend to have fewer species than those in warmer environments. Pupils could be encouraged to speculate about why this should be so.

The hot desert is a comparatively "poor" community because water is a limiting factor. Also, temperature variation can be extreme, both daily and seasonally, producing further potential stress for organisms.

B13.3 Changes – weather, season and tide

It is important that pupils realize that most organisms have to survive in their environment as they find it – there is usually no "escape", as there often is for humans. However, figure 13.7 in the pupils' book provides examples of behaviour patterns fitted to regularly changing environments, and some pupils may see some of these (such as migrating birds) as examples of "escape" from an organism's present environment. There is scope here for pupils to contribute their own examples.

The passage entitled "Changing the body clock" may well provide a forum for pupils to relate their own experiences of, for example, waking at the same time each day, and how the time of waking can be altered – possibly when relaxing on holiday. The hidden effects of "jet-lag" on the decisions that business travellers and politicians make after insufficient periods of adjustment could provide another area for discussion.

Pupils can also carry out practical work related to this section, using Worksheets **B**13B and **B**13C.

Answers to selected questions

9 Bird migration is more concerned with the availability of food than with the higher temperatures further south.

10 Reproducing in spring means that delicate, unprotected young are not subjected to the rigours of winter weather, and are allowed a long growing season before the first winter. Conditions for growth are probably at their best during summer, with, for example, high light intensities and high temperatures. Food may also be far more readily available.

11 Tidal currents and light intensity will vary over 24 hours. Light intensity will also vary seasonally, as will water temperature. The availability of food is more likely to change during a year than during 24 hours.

B13.4 Changes – competition, succession and climax communities

This section discusses the idea of competition, and then studies the effect that it has on the composition of species within a community. Worksheets **B**13D and **B**13E may be used with this section.

The main point to emphasize is that limited resources will cause competition between individuals, resulting in stress. The fittest individuals will be at an advantage – this has obvious links with Chapter **B**23, on evolution. The unequal competition between different species leads to succession until a climax community is established.

Activities

Worksheet B13A Looking at a community

REQUIREMENTS

Access to:
Aquarium, containing a variety of organisms
Keys or reference material for identification

One of the major problems with this exercise is providing enough aquaria for the class to study. If the laboratories have demonstration aquaria that are already established, these would be appropriate for study.

An alternative (and very effective) approach is to set up a tank of mineral nutrient solution (such as Knop's culture) in an open place, and allow organisms to colonize it. Six to eight weeks is sufficient time to establish a viable community of microscopic organisms. Pupils can take samples from the tank, using small beakers, and search for organisms, using microscopes. They will need help when trying to identify the organisms, which is probably best given in the form of keys and diagrams.

A third approach to the problem is to set up several miniature "aquaria" in beakers. In order to reduce stress, the number of fish in the beakers should be limited to one. Ideally, pond water should be used for setting up the "aquaria", although tap water can be used if it has been allowed to stand in the open air for at least one day.

Worksheet B13B Weather and the growth of trees

REQUIREMENTS

Each group of pupils will need:
Clinical, or digital strip, thermometer
Graph paper
Pencils
Rulers

Access to:
A number of reasonably long twigs (at least 10 cm in length) from chestnut tree or other tree with clear terminal bud scars
Local weather data for the last 10 years

Safety note:
Thermometers **must** be carefully disinfected before each use, for example with a freshly made solution of hypochlorite.

It will be necessary to obtain local weather data for the last ten years or so. A local weather station, a keen amateur or a local newspaper office may be able to help. It is particularly important to establish whether the springs and summers were "good", "bad" or "indifferent": rainfall, amount of sunshine and temperature are all important factors.

The material used for this worksheet should be shared and all class results collected before they are analysed.

Worksheet B13C A look at the way animals behave

REQUIREMENTS

Each group of pupils will need:
Blowfly larvae
Water, iced
Bench lamp
Dish, about 15 cm across, covered with plastic film
Graph paper
Pencils
Stopclock

Thermometer
Tubs, plastic, sealed, 2
Water bath or tin can
Teaspoons or tweezers
Hot and cold water
Soap and towel

Access to:
A blacked-out laboratory

Safety note:
Remind students to wash their hands at the end of the activity.

The procedure is detailed on the worksheet. Blowfly larvae can be kept for some days in a refrigerator.

Worksheet B13D Sun and shade plants

Part 1

REQUIREMENTS

Each group of pupils will need:
Graph paper
Quadrat, 0.25 m²
Pencils
Rulers

Access to:
Tape measure
Trees in or near school grounds (*e.g.* in a park)

Safety note:
The glass apparatus should not be used out of doors.

The procedure is detailed on the worksheet. Part 2 of the worksheet must be performed in the late spring (*i.e.* mid-April onwards), when the plant material is available.

Part 2

REQUIREMENTS

Each group of pupils will need:
Leaves of sun and shade plants, *e.g.* dandelion and dog's mercury
Hydrogencarbonate indicator, in equilibrium with air
Container, large glass, with tight sealing lid and glass well
or
Boiling-tubes with bungs, 3
Pins to fasten plants in tubes, 2

Worksheet B13E Weapons in the competition war

Part 1

REQUIREMENTS

Each group of pupils will need:
Nicotiana seeds soaked overnight (about 50)
Plant material: garlic clove, leaves of rue, rosemary, basil, potato
Petri dish, sterile, with lid, containing potato dextrose agar
Cork borer, sterile
Rulers
Scalpels or knives, 3
Tile
Eye protection

Access to:
Ethanol – FLAMMABLE – to sterilize cork borer
Incubator at 26°C
Hot and cold water
Soap
Towel

Safety notes:
Rue can cause a burn-like allergic reaction in some people; protective gloves might be considered, as well as thorough hand-washing after handling it. The use of scalpels and knives demands special vigilance by the teacher.

Part 2

REQUIREMENTS

Each group of pupils will need:
Cress or grass seeds, 100
Graph paper
Pencils
Plastic cups, 3
Rulers
Spoons, dessert, 3

Access to:
Soil from different places under a tree (the pupils should collect this themselves)
Tape measure
Water

Normal safety practice for microbiological procedures should be observed, and any pupils with open cuts on their hands should use disposable gloves when collecting soil.

The procedure is detailed on the worksheet. It might be worth trying different combinations of plants and seeds in Part 1.

The aim of Part 2 of the worksheet is to demonstrate that competition between a tree and colonizing plants can be reduced by chemicals produced by the roots of the tree. These chemicals inhibit the growth of seedlings.

Demonstration experiments

The experiment showing competition amongst mustard seedlings, featured in figure 13.10 in the pupils' book, could be demonstrated. It is very easy to perform and could be shown with many plant species. One disadvantage is the long-term nature of the experiment; fast-growing plants (such as mustard or mung beans) are therefore preferable, and the different stages of competition could be shown by staggering the time of seed-sowing. "Fast plants" have advantages in such experiments. The experiment could be developed by measuring the surface area of leaves, internode distance, numbers of flowers or seeds, and dry masses.

Further information

Further information relevant to the worksheets can be obtained from the following sources:

Worksheet B13A:
Leadley Brown, A., Nuffield Advanced Biological Science *A key to pond organisms* Longman, 1970.

Worksheet B13B:
Chandler, T.J. and Gregory, S. (eds.) *The climate of the British Isles* Longman, 1976.

McKelvie, A.D., "A school survey of the flowering time of broom in the north of Scotland", J. *Biol. Educ.*, **4** (4), 227-233, 1970.

Lowry, W.P., "The climate of cities", *Scient. Am.*, August 1967.

Worksheet B13D:
Brown, G.D. and Creedy, J. *Experimental biology manual* Heinemann Educational, 1970.

Chapter **B14 The webs of life**

The syllabus section

Context

The feeding relationships between organisms are developed as food chains, and then as food webs. Both models show the direction in which energy is transferred between organisms. Parasites feed on an organism without killing it. Opportunities exist for considering the range of parasites that can infect humans, and this can lead to a consideration of correct hygiene techniques for controlling the spread of parasites.

Knowledge and understanding

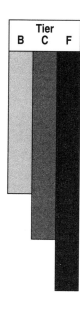

Syllabus statements	PoS	SoA
Know that food chains and food webs can be used to show feeding relationships in an ecosystem.	2(iv)1	2.4(d)
Know the role of producers and consumers in a food web; primary, secondary and tertiary trophic levels of consumers.	2(iv)1	2.4(d)
Know (through study of a locality) features of plants and animals (e.g. size, shape, colour, behaviour and life cycle) which enable survival.	2(iii)1	2.6(b)
Understand the significance of the shapes of pyramids, of biomass and numbers. Losses of energy through the ecosystem.	2(iv)1	2.7(e)
Appreciate that the flow of energy through an ecosystem limits the number of trophic levels in a food chain.	2(iv)1	2.9(e)

Opportunities for co-ordination

P10 links with transfer of energy and **C**10 with the role of water in hygiene.

Routes and times

Basic	Central	Further
Spend more time studying food chains and food webs. *1½ hours*	**B14.1 Food chains and food webs** Brief revision. **Worksheet B14A Food chains and food webs** (homework) *¾ hour*	Brief revision only. *¼ hour*
	B14.2 Parasites and food webs Especially parasite adaptation; select material to suit needs of class. *½ hour*	This should be done for homework.
Omit this section.	**Worksheet B14C How much energy is there in some foods that you eat?** Side 2 is optional. **B14.3 The flow of energy through food webs** *1¼ hours*	Both sides of Worksheet **B14C** are suitable. *1½ hours*
Omit this section	**B14.4 Pyramids in ecology** Omit Q24–26. **Reading for learning 1: Energy and beans** (homework) *¾ hour*	All questions are suitable.
Total: 2 hours	*Total: 3¼ hours*	*Total: 2½ hours*

The pupils' book

B14.1 Food chains and food webs

This section introduces food chains, taking as an example the food that humans eat. There are, of course, innumerable examples that could be given, but initially it may be preferable to use examples of food chains that include humans, so pupils can appreciate the concept in relation to their own food. It is important that they have a clear understanding of why the arrows indicating a transfer should always point from the consumed to the consumer – otherwise, they will often provide illogical arguments as to why the arrows "should" point in the reverse direction.

Worksheet **B**14A can help pupils to study feeding relationships within aquaria. While it is quite easy to set up simple food chains in such tanks, care should be exercised in the choice of organisms to be included. There should be no unnecessary suffering when secondary consumers feed, and it is inadvisable to include a higher level of consumer. (Teachers might like to use some of the ideas in section **B**14.1 of the pupils' book as background information if Worksheet **B**14A is to be used as an alternative to this section.)

Pupils are expected to work out food chains for themselves, either by observing organisms or from given data. Section **B**14.1 provides a series of guidelines applicable to any habitat for which the food web is to be worked out. It would be useful for pupils to have considered them before carrying out any field work.

Whilst it is necessary to have an approximate identification of an organism, there comes a point where it is not worthwhile trying to identify an organism any more accurately. Most vertebrates encountered and included in a food web can probably be identified according to genus or even species. In some cases dicotyledonous plants might be identified according to species, but it is almost certainly more economical of time and effort to be content with "speedwell", "dandelion", "bramble", etc. Teachers should use their own discretion here.

Invertebrates are difficult to identify because there are so many species, most of which try the skills even of professional taxonomists. Furthermore, there are often no common English names for them. This is not to say that there should be no attempt at their identification; working with a key, it should be possible to identify earthworms, slugs, snails, harvestmen, spiders, springtails, dragonflies, plant bugs and aphids, grasshoppers, earwigs, beetles, true flies, butterflies and moths, bees, wasps and ants. Many pupils, of course, will recognize some or even most of these without recourse to an identification key. Only a few will recognize all of the organisms, however, and all should be encouraged to "try their hand" at working through a key.

Answers to selected questions
5 A source book will be of obvious benefit when finding information about the ancestors of domestic pets and their original or natural diets.

If the animal concerned is herbivorous, then there may be little value in exhaustive research to discover which plant species might be expected to form the whole (or part) of the diet, and simply "plants" could be entered at the bottom of the food chain.

Cats and dogs will be the most commonly kept carnivorous pets. Dogs are thought to have originated from the wolf, an extremely successful animal that in former times ranged throughout Europe, Asia and North America. Many different animals could reasonably have been included in their diet, and therefore in the food chain, although the food favoured by wolves appears to be various species of deer.

The domestic cat is thought to have originated in the Middle East and North Africa. There are now well-established feral populations of cats, and it would perhaps be easier for pupils to consider which small animals might be available for these feral cats, around farms or on derelict urban sites.

7 Crop plants and farm livestock would be the most useful foods to establish in the Moon base. Some pupils might suggest that the best crops would be those with a high yield, fast growth rates and low susceptibility to disease. Livestock introduces an extra link in the food chain, reducing the yield available to the human population. Pupils will understand this better after section **B**14.3, but there is no harm in introducing the idea now.

Pests and carnivores would be unwelcome additions to the Moon base food web.

B14.2 Parasites and food webs

This section uses the idea that although parasites are part of a food web, they differ from predators because they (usually) do not kill their host. Worksheet **B**14B provides an opportunity to look at one such example.

The maps in figure 14.8 in the pupils' book relate the distribution of human parasitic diseases to poverty and poor nutrition. Without being categorical about cause and effect, pupils should be able to make some suggestions that link the maps, bearing in mind the proviso about parasites just mentioned. They may need guidance to show how reduced poverty and increased food intake can decrease the incidence of disease – once again there is scope for discussion.

This section and its associated worksheet (**B**14B) describe some parasitic features, which are presented as special characteristics for survival in difficult habitats. Several aspects of life cycles that illustrate this are mentioned, although no one parasite is treated exhaustively and no complete life cycles are included.

B14.3 The flow of energy through food webs

The comparison of an oak woodland with a high moorland community is included to illustrate that, ultimately, more energy is stored and is therefore available in the "rich" woodland. This is not because more energy arrives there – if both are at the same latitude, then the moorland community will actually receive more radiant energy per unit surface area, because less is lost through atmospheric absorption at higher altitudes. The difference in the quantity of stored energy in each habitat is more closely related to ease of survival – lower temperatures, severe winter weather and high evaporative water loss make the moorland generally a more difficult place to survive in.

Although pupils might not realize it, there is a temporal element in this comparison, as the stored energy needs time to accumulate – more species growing to a greater size and covering more of the surface of the ground will, over a period of time, store more energy. More habitats develop as the community develops, so that ultimately the woodland community is richer than the moorland one.

B14.4 Pyramids in ecology

This section introduces the idea of pyramids of numbers, biomass and energy. Some indication of a pyramid of numbers might be possible from a consideration of organisms in a pond or mineral nutrient tank (see Worksheet **B**14A). When the producers are small and numerous, the pyramid of numbers has a broad base. However, the example of the English oak woodland shows that the pyramids can easily be "inverted".

Pyramids of biomass are generally preferable to pyramids of numbers because the relative sizes of each organism are taken into account. However, it is less easy to collect the data. To do this properly, organisms have to be collected from a unit area or volume of the habitat and dried before weighing. Obviously, this entails killing all the organisms, and there are ethical reasons why this should not be done when teaching ecology at this level.

There are two alternative methods that could be tried by teachers who wish to explore this topic experimentally: either to use data already available, or to use fresh (live) masses of the animals and dry masses of the plants.

Teachers must use their discretion here – an area of the school grounds used for ecological study will probably not harbour rarities, so there may be no objection to collecting all the plant material from a few sample areas for drying and weighing. However, this cannot be assumed if a habitat outside the school premises is being studied. If the dry masses of producers but fresh masses of consumers are used, pupils should be aware that this will produce an overestimate of the consumer biomass. They should also appreciate that only a proportion of consumers from their sample area will have been collected. There is plenty of scope here for discussing the validity of results and for reaching conclusions from limited data.

Answers to selected questions
19 The producers in the river were photosynthetic protists.

20 If a scale of 1: 100000 is chosen, the maximum width of the diagram is 15 cm. Some pupils may note that it is not possible to draw the one tertiary consumer to scale.

Activities

Worksheet B14A Food chains and food webs

REQUIREMENTS

Each group of pupils will need:
Containers for the organisms
Sampling equipment appropriate to the habitat studied

Access to:
Appropriate keys and resources on the habitat studied

This investigation is divided into two parts. 'Teachers should select the part that is best suited to the needs of their pupils and to the time and resources available. The first part can be treated as an extension of Worksheet **B**13A or as an opportunity to explore a local habitat. The use of natural habitats for this purpose needs to be considered carefully, since it is improper for pupils to remove organisms from their natural surroundings for further study. The mineral nutrient tank discussed in the notes on Worksheet **B**13A in this *Guide* would also be highly suitable for this exercise.

The second part of the worksheet is theoretical, and involves interpreting the interrelationships between organisms in a food web. It becomes clear from this exercise that a food chain is a simplification and that a food web is more realistic.

Worksheet B14B Parasites

REQUIREMENTS

Each group of pupils will need:
Bench lamp, covered except for small aperture for light
Hand lens
Mounted needle

Access to:
Holly leaves, some of which are mined

The holly leaf miner appears to be far more common in towns than in the countryside, possibly because urban areas are warmer and have fewer frosty days. There is considerable variation between bushes in the amount of damage done by the miner, the frequency of its occurrence and the time taken for it to emerge.

Worksheet B14C How much energy is there in some foods that you eat?

REQUIREMENTS

Each group of pupils will need:

Peanuts, unroasted (see *Note*)	Measuring cylinder, 100 cm^3
Water, 100 cm^3	Mounted needle
Balance, accurate	Retort stand and clamp
Boiling-tube	Thermometer, stirring
Burner	Eye protection

Note:

It might be convenient to weigh the peanuts before the practical starts; they can then be provided in small Petri dishes with a note of the mass of each nut.

A peanut should contain around 25 kJ/g of energy. If carefully performed, this experiment is about 50 % accurate. The worksheet asks pupils to identify the major sources of error of the apparatus, to suggest improvements and to evaluate other designs of calorimeters.

One way of collecting class results is to give each pupil a sticky label on which to write results. Stick the labels onto a single sheet of paper and photocopy that sheet.

Further information

ABAL (Advanced Biology Alternative Learning Project) Unit 9 *Ecology* Cambridge University Press, 1985. (This may be useful for Worksheet **B**14B.)

Science and Technology in Society
Several SATIS units are relevant to this chapter: unit 402 "DDT and malaria" (updated in *SATIS Update 91*), units 304/5 "A medicine to control bilharzia" and unit 201 "Energy from biomass".

Chapter B15 Salts and cycles

The syllabus section

Context

The concept of cycles of mineral substances through the ecosystem is considered, and the importance of the decomposer food chains is emphasized. Practical consequences of the need for mineral recycling are stressed (*e.g.* the need for farmers to return mineral salts to the soil after they have harvested their crops, and the financial limitations on the use of chemical fertilizers).

Knowledge and understanding

Syllabus statements	PoS	SoA
Know the effect of temperature, microbes, compactness and moisture on the process of decay.	2(iv)3	2.5(d)
Know that the balance and availability to producers of materials (e.g. nitrogen, carbon and minerals) in a specific ecosystem (e.g. seas, farms, market gardens) can be maintained by the cycling of these materials.	2(iv)3, 4	2.6(e)
Appreciate the importance of decomposer (microbes and other organisms) food chains in decay and in recycling nutrients.	2(iv)3	2.8(e)
Be able to explain how organisms acquire materials for growth and energy either by consuming other organisms or by photosynthesis, and how these biological materials are cycled through ecosystems.	2(iv)1, 3	2.9(e)
Understand how food production involves the management of ecosystems to improve the efficiency of energy transfer.	2(iv)2, 3	2.10(d)

Opportunities for co-ordination

The nature of mineral ions links to Chemistry. The significance of water as a biological solvent is discussed in **C**10, soil in **C**15, the chemical aspects of the nitrogen cycle in **C**16.

Routes and times

Basic	Central	Further

Basic

Spend more time on this section.

1½ hours

Central

> **B15.1 Plant mineral requirements**
> Omit Q4, 5 and 7.
>
> **Worksheet B15A Mineral ions and the growth of duckweed**
>
> *1 hour*

Further

Omit, or demonstrate the results of, Worksheet **B**15A.

½ hour

Select material from pages 182 and 183 of section **B**15.2. Worksheets **B**15B and **B**15C are optional.

> **B15.2 Decomposition**
> EITHER
> **Worksheet B15B Decomposers (side 2)**
> OR
> **Worksheet B15C Decomposers in leaf litter**
>
> *1½ hours*

Spend more time on the carbon cycle. Omit Worksheets **B**15B and **B**15C.

¾ hour

Spend more time on this section.

1 hour

> **B15.3 Water, water everywhere**
>
> **Reading for learning 3: Case study: cholera**
> (optional/homework)
>
> *½ hour*

> **B15.4 The fixing of nitrogen**
> Select material to suit class needs.
>
> **Reading for learning 2: Sewage**
> (homework)
>
> *1 hour*

All of section **B**15.4 is suitable. Worksheet **B**15D "Nodules on legume roots" is optional.

1½ hours

This is an alternative position for Worksheet **B**17C "Our impact on the environment".

Total: 5 hours   *Total: 4 hours*   *Total: 3¼ hours*

Monitoring the progress of Sc1

Investigating the growth of duckweed

Students should investigate the effects of mineral ions on the growth of duckweed (*Lemna*). This investigation may be carried out instead of Worksheet **B**15A "Mineral ions and the growth of duckweed".

Sample criteria are given below for an assessment between levels 7 and 10.

Strand (i) Ask questions, predict and hypothesize, e.g.	Strand (ii) Observe, measure and manipulate variables, e.g.	Strand (iii) Interpret their results and evaluate scientific evidence, e.g.
7(a) Suggest, with reasons, that the presence of mineral ions and the pH will affect the growth of duckweed, and predict that magnesium is one of the most important	**7(b)** Measure the survival rates of duckweed in solutions of different mineral ions and of different pH	**7(c)** Conclude that the presence of a particular ion is more important than the pH of the solution between pH5 and pH8
8(a) Suggest, with reasons, that doubling the concentration of a mineral ion will double the number of green leaves surviving after a given time, and suggest a relevant investigation	**8(b)** As above, measuring concentrations to 0.1 mol/L and pH to 0.5 units	**8(c)** Explain why the solution composition was kept constant for various pHs and why pH was kept constant for various solution compositions
9(a) As above, and suggest repeating the experiment	**9(b)** Carry out the above procedure systematically	**9(c)** Use data from repeated experiments to draw graphs of results and to show that the presence of certain ions affects growth; comment on the accuracy of the experiment
10(a) Suggest that the growth of duckweed depends on the presence of certain mineral ions which are essential for photosynthesis	**10(b)** As above, and check purity of chemicals used	**10(c)** As above, but using knowledge of the complexing ability of various mineral ions to explain the result

The pupils' book

B15.1 Plant mineral requirements

This section outlines the mineral requirements of plants. It emphasizes the functions of ions in plants rather than the effects of ion deficiencies. Worksheet **B**15A develops this theme experimentally.

Answers to selected questions

1 Water.

3 Humus improves the soil's ability to absorb and retain moisture.

7 The high levels of salt in the water would cause the plant roots to lose water by osmosis, and the plants would wilt and eventually die.

B15.2 Decomposition

Worksheets **B**15B and **B**15C are simple investigations into decomposition. Worksheet **B**15B should be regarded as an extended study, to be carried out over several weeks. It is important that the work on decomposition is linked to the ideas of food chains and pyramids of biomass etc. developed in the previous chapter.

Answer to selected question

9 This does not contradict the conclusion that the energy source of all food chains is sunlight, since decomposer food chains start with the arrival of **dead** material into the habitat. When alive, this material formed parts of food chains which were dependent on sunlight. Without photosynthesis, there could be no food chains, and consequently no decomposer food chains.

B15.3 Water, water everywhere

The idea of the cycling of materials is an important one. This section gives an opportunity to establish the idea with an example that pupils find reasonably accessible. The more complex nitrogen cycle is covered in the next section.

Answer to selected question

13 The cycle depends upon water being either a liquid or a vapour, depending upon the circumstances. On Venus, water would be unlikely to condense to form a liquid, and on Mars it is likely to be permanently frozen

B15.4 The fixing of nitrogen

Worksheet **B**15D allows pupils to investigate root nodule formation in legumes. An appreciation of the various ways in which nitrogen can be fixed is needed only by those hoping to achieve higher grades.

In previous work on plant nutrient requirements, pupils will have been introduced to the ideas that plants need nitrate ions and that ions (including nitrates) are released back into water or the soil during decomposition. The energy released by lightning and its role in the formation of nitrates are now discussed, and figures showing the significance of this source are given. One estimate gives the frequency of thunder storms as 1800 at any one moment over the entire Earth's surface.

The treatment of nitrogen fixation is conventional, but relates it to agriculture and the cost of fertilizer.

Answers to selected questions

17 Production could fall in natural habitats for a number of reasons. Natural catastrophes such as eruptions, floods, droughts, etc. will all slow production or abruptly terminate it, but this may actually stimulate an increase in production later on. For example, abnormal flooding may drown an entire habitat, but when the flood water has subsided, the silt deposition with additional nutrients may encourage more rapid plant growth than before.

Reduced temperature always reduces production rates, as does reduced light intensity caused by dust emissions, which in turn could be caused by natural or human activities. All these examples give further opportunities for class discussion.

21 The advantages of using human waste are that it would provide a source of mineral salts, an organic component to the soil and a solution to the problem of disposal; it has a low cost, involving collection and field distribution only.

The main disadvantage is the risk of disease transmission. In some societies the risk is high, and the costs to the society caused by such diseases may balance, and will probably cancel out, the advantages of sustained food production.

In Britain, untreated sewage has long been used as a fertilizer, but recent EC legislation requires all sewage to be treated (usually by anaerobic fermentation) before use in this way.

Activities

Worksheet B15A Mineral ions and the growth of duckweed

REQUIREMENTS

Each group of pupils will need:
Duckweed (*Lemna*), 20 healthy plants similar in
size, colour and number of leaves
25 cm^3 of each of the following solutions:
complete mineral nutrient solution
complete solution lacking nitrogen
complete solution lacking magnesium
complete solution lacking iron
Containers, plastic or glass, 4 (*e.g.* crystallizing
dishes), with loose covers
Graph paper
Pencils

Access to:
Marker pen
Good light source

The procedure is detailed on the worksheet. Tablets containing balanced mineral salts can
be obtained from biological suppliers.

Worksheet B15B Decomposers

Part 1

REQUIREMENTS

Each group of pupils will need:
Graph paper
Pencils
Rulers

Access to:
A compost heap that will be undisturbed for
several months
Tullgren funnel apparatus (see diagram on
Worksheet **B15C**)
Key to identify organisms

Part 2

REQUIREMENTS

Each group of pupils will need:
Cork borer
Graph paper
Markers, 3 (to mark position of mesh bags on
soil surface)
Mesh, nylon, 3 samples (*e.g.* tights, net curtain,
plastic mesh of about 1 cm width)
Nylon string
Wooden block

Access to:
Flat leaves from one plant species (*e.g.* alder,
apple, ash, beech, oak)
Soil in which to bury mesh bags

This practical ought to be performed only by those teachers and pupils who are able to
work with sustained interest for at least a term, since the changes occur slowly.

Worksheet B15C Decomposers in leaf litter

REQUIREMENTS

Each group of pupils will need:
Leaf litter
Ethanol, 10 %
Collecting dish
Graph paper
Pencils
Trays for leaf litter and collected organisms
Tullgren funnel apparatus (see diagram on
worksheet)

Access to:
Weighing balance

The procedure is detailed on the worksheet.

Answer to selected worksheet questions
1 The animals move away from the hot, dry conditions near the light, *i.e.* downwards, and fall out when they reach the bottom.

Worksheet B15D Nodules on legume roots

REQUIREMENTS

Each group of pupils will need:
Pea or bean seeds, 4 per pot
Pots

Access to:
Running water
Various soil samples (*e.g.* vermiculite, sterile sand, sterile organic potting compost, garden soil rich in nitrates, garden soil in which beans have been growing, sterilized garden soil in which beans have been grown)

Note:
The legume seeds must be soaked in distilled water for 24 hours before germination.

The number of seeds needed depends upon the number of different soil types that are available. Vermiculite should be free from nitrates, and can act as a control; it must be watered **gently**, otherwise it tends to float. This experiment should run for several weeks in order to get good root growth before the plants are examined for nodules.

Further information

Science and Technology in Society
The importance of artificial fertilizers is considered in two SATIS units: unit 505 "Making fertilizers" and unit 207 "The story of Fritz Haber". Unit 201 "Energy from biomass" considers the conflict between adequate food production and soil fertility.

Chapter B16 Staying alive

The syllabus section

Context

This section considers the way in which a habitat can become colonized by organisms. An essential prelude to this is the successful dispersal of organisms to the habitat. Different strategies for successful dispersal to a new locality, and survival when there, are developed. The dispersal of the human species into new habitats is considered.

Knowledge and understanding

Syllabus statements	PoS	SoA
Understand the processes by which animals and plants colonize habitats.	2(iii)1	2.6(b)
Understand, through an exploration of factors affecting population size, population changes in predator–prey relationships.	2(iii)2	2.6(d)
Understand the relationship between population growth and decline and environmental resources (e.g. unusually dry, wet, hot or cold).	2(iii)2	2.7(d)
Appreciate the variety of factors limiting the growth of populations that could account for the uneven distributions of organisms in a habitat, and the significance of this for evolution.	2(iii)1, 2	2.9(c)

Opportunities for co-ordination

C18 deals with mineral ions, C16 with agrochemicals.

Routes and times

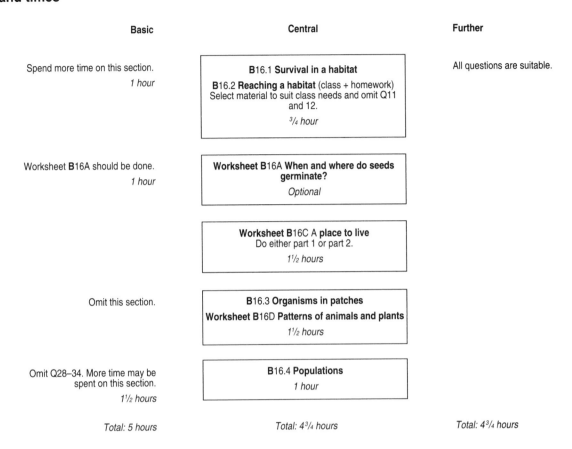

Basic	Central	Further
Spend more time on this section. *1 hour*	**B16.1 Survival in a habitat** **B16.2 Reaching a habitat** (class + homework) Select material to suit class needs and omit Q11 and 12. *³/₄ hour*	All questions are suitable.
Worksheet **B**16A should be done. *1 hour*	**Worksheet B16A When and where do seeds germinate?** *Optional*	
	Worksheet B16C A place to live Do either part 1 or part 2. *1¹/₂ hours*	
Omit this section.	**B16.3 Organisms in patches** **Worksheet B16D Patterns of animals and plants** *1¹/₂ hours*	
Omit Q28–34. More time may be spent on this section. *1¹/₂ hours*	**B16.4 Populations** *1 hour*	
Total: 5 hours	*Total: 4³/₄ hours*	*Total: 4³/₄ hours*

The pupils' book

B16.1 Survival in a habitat

In some ways the start of this chapter recalls Chapter **B**13, in that a range of environmental factors is encountered in both. Here the emphasis is on the availability of certain habitats for colonization, provided that the organisms can survive the environmental conditions.

B16.2 Reaching a habitat

This section forms the major part of this chapter, and should be developed with reference to a variety of examples. Pupils are not expected to remember the details of each example, but should appreciate how the different features and methods enable organisms to be dispersed. Worksheet **B**16A includes simple experiments on germinating seeds, and provides an opportunity for pupils to design their own experiments. Worksheets **B**16B and **B**16C are investigations into colonization and habitat preference.

The wide dispersal of the type of sea snails shown in figure 16.13 in the pupils' book is remarkable, and is related to the very long duration of their larval life. Most sea snail and other marine larvae travel much shorter distances, although with a planktonic life lasting three or four weeks considerable distances may still be covered. Unlike dispersing seeds, dispersing animals have some ability to avoid unfavourable habitats.

Answers to selected questions
11 This is a difficult exercise. Fresh sea water should be collected from an area that is some distance from the nearest barnacle colony, to ensure that it is free from barnacle secretions. The barnacle secretions could be collected by surrounding adult barnacles with

fresh sea water. This water could then be transferred to a clean tank, into which barnacle larvae are added. The larvae should be able to settle on the sides of the tank. The control experiment should consist of an identical tank, containing the same number of larvae from the same sample, surrounded by an equal volume of the sea water sample which has **not** been exposed to adult barnacles. Both tanks should be kept in identical conditions and aerated. After a time, the number of barnacles that have settled in each tank should be compared.

14 All of the organisms could be dispersed, since they all reached the islands. We cannot say anything about the relative powers of dispersal of bats and humans, since we do not know when the first bats or the first humans arrived on the islands. We do know, however, that the bats (and humans) were able to disperse themselves more effectively than most other mammals, since they were the only ones that the Maoris found.

16 Sea plantain seeds are probably dispersed by car tyres. The plant has a distinctly maritime distribution, but it extends inland along trunk roads. Its natural distribution is related to the sea salt spray that finds its way into coastal habitats. The practice of salting the roads in winter to prevent ice formation creates an additional habitat for this plant along the grass verges.

B16.3 Organisms in patches

The factors that control the distribution of certain organisms are often hard to discover. After an introduction on patterns of distribution, Worksheet **B**16D guides pupils in the study of one organism, the protist *Pleurococcus*, whose distribution is reasonably simple to evaluate. Examples are also given in the pupils' book in such a way that the pupils should be able to think about what factors might cause the uneven distribution of the organisms.

B16.4 Populations

This section takes the guppy as a model to show that population sizes are controlled. It is possible to demonstrate this practically, although it is not recommended as it is hard to avoid placing the animals under stress. Population changes in natural environments are also considered.

Answer to selected question
29 The reason for the decline in the overcrowded laboratory population is probably limited resources, particularly food and space. A large number of offspring are produced in the understocked tank, many of which survive, leading to an increase in numbers.

Activities

Worksheet B16A When and where do seeds germinate?

REQUIREMENTS

Each group of pupils will need:
Cress seeds

(The pupils should provide their own apparatus lists)

Although this exercise in experimental design works well, it can be demanding in terms of technician time, since each group of pupils requests the apparatus it requires. Obviously the pupils will need to hand in their requirements well before the lesson is due to start – the design problem needs to be set in the lesson before the practical is due to begin.

One way of limiting the pressure on the technicians is to give the pupils a list of apparatus from which they select the pieces they want. In this way, the worksheet can be tackled in a double lesson, but time will need to be allocated later to review the results of the experiment.

The exercise is useful because it teaches pupils about the need to vary just one factor at a time, keeping all the others constant. There is a number of factors that the pupils could choose to study; it is profitable for one or more groups to investigate the inhibitory effects of freshly squeezed orange or apple juice on seed germination.

Worksheet B16B Colonization – a result of dispersal

REQUIREMENTS

Access to:
Books identifying plants, lichens and protists
Tarmac or concrete paths
Walls (*e.g.* old brick, cement, shady or sunny, etc.)

The success of this practical hinges on the pupils being able to recognize the types of organism that they encounter on walls and paths. It is not necessary for them to identify the organisms accurately. It will be sufficient to recognize them as lichens, mosses, protists, flowering plants, etc. Lichens form a group that has been deliberately omitted from Chapter **B**2 of the pupils' book because they cross the boundaries of two of the groups that are defined in that chapter. Lichens are made by an association between a photosynthetic protist and a fungus.

Worksheet B16C A place to live

Part 1

REQUIREMENTS

Each group of pupils will need:
Gammarids, 5
Water weed, rotting
Dish, large
Sand or gravel
Silt or mud
Stones, large

Access to:
River or spring water
Hot and cold water
Soap
Towel

Part 2

REQUIREMENTS

Each group of pupils will need:
Woodlice, 10
Choice chamber (see *Note*)

Access to:
Drying agent (*e.g.* calcium chloride)
Water

Note:
Commercial choice chambers are obtainable from biological suppliers. Alternative models can be made following the design of figure 20, page 31, Revised Nuffield Biology *Text 3* (Longman, 1975), although teachers might prefer to use muslin or nylon mesh instead of zinc sheets.

Pupils should wash their hands thoroughly after contact with river or spring water, and any with open cuts should use disposable gloves.

Pupils should attempt only one of these investigations, unless teachers can set up both at the same time, in which case the pupils can observe both parts of the worksheet.

The first part of the worksheet provides an alternative to choice chamber work with woodlice, although it is dependent on there being an available source of fresh running water from which the organisms can be sampled.

Worksheet B16D Patterns of animals and plants

REQUIREMENTS

Each group of pupils will need:
Clipboard
Graph paper
Paper
Pencils
Quadrat, 10 cm^2 (made from transparent plastic)
String, marked at 10 cm intervals

Access to:
Trees close to the school grounds

The procedure is detailed on the worksheet. It is important that pupils are shown exactly what *Pleurococcus* looks like before they attempt to study its density on the tree trunk. Much of the success of this exercise depends upon the pupils' ability to estimate sensibly the percentage of bark covered by the protist.

Further information

Dowdeswell, W.H. *Practical animal ecology* Methuen, 1969.
This is an extremely useful source of sampling techniques (such as how to investigate the distribution of organisms in a field).

Slingsby, D. and Cook, C. *Practical ecology* Macmillan, 1986.

Bülow-Olsen, A., Penguin Nature Guide: *Plant communities* Penguin, 1978.
Many pupils find this an attractive and informative guide.

Revised Nuffield Biology *Teachers' guide 3* and *Text 3 Living things and their environment* Longman, 1975.

Chapter B17 Farms, factories and the environment

The syllabus section

Context

All organisms have the ability to change their environments. This section investigates various ways in which this can happen. Humans are extremely adept at manipulating their environments, and a number of different ways in which they do this are considered. The use of pesticides, industrial pollution (including acid rain), and the farming practice of growing monocultures are all examples of this manipulation.

Knowledge and understanding

	Tier		Syllabus statements	PoS	SoA
B	C	F			
			Appreciate current concerns about human activity leading to pollution of the environment and how the introduction of a pollutant into an environment can have complex long-term consequences for the survival of organisms in that environment.	2(iii)3	2.5(c)
			Be able to relate the environmental impact of human activity on the Earth to size of population, economic factors and industrial requirements, and understand these relationships.	2(iii)4	2.8(d)
			Understand the basic scientific principles associated with a major change in the biosphere (e.g. desertification).	2(iii)3 2(iv)4	2.9(d)
			Appreciate the need to destroy agricultural pests, the advantages and disadvantages of industrial pesticides and the principles of biological control.	2(iv)2	2.10(d)

Opportunities for co-ordination

The importance of chemical pesticides in modern agriculture is dealt with in **C**16, the environmental effects of mineral mining in **C**4, the impact of fertilisers on the environment in **C**16, the effects of waste from quarrying and industry in **C**6 and **C**4.

Routes and times

	Basic	Central	Further

Basic | Central | Further

Omit section **B**17.2.

> **B**17.1 **Necessary damage?**
> **B**17.2 **Monoculture**
> *¼ hour*

> **Worksheet B**17A **Build your own biogas generator** (optional extension work)
> **B**17.3 **Problems with pests**
> **B**17.4 **Biological control**
> *1¼ hours*

Omit section **B**17.7.

> **Worksheet B**17B **Acid rain** (sides 3 and 4 only)
> **B**17.7 **Acid rain**
> **Reading for learning 4: The story of acid rain** (homework)
> *1 hour*

Some selection of material from section **B**17.5 may be needed. Omit section **B**17.6.

> **B**17.5 **Fertilizers** (pages 213–214 only)
> **B**17.6 **Industry and estuaries** (class + homework)
> *½ hour*

All parts of section **B**17.5 are suitable.

Worksheet **B**17C is optional.

> **Worksheet B**17C **Our impact on the environment** (class + homework)
> Select material to suit the needs of the class.
> *1 hour*

Cover Worksheet **B**17C in greater depth.
2 hours

Total: 1¾ hours   *Total: 2¾ hours*   *Total: 5 hours*

The pupils' book

B17.1 Necessary damage?

The chapter begins by pointing out that it is impossible for people to exist **without** changing the environment. "Damage" is often simply a question of scale, and while undesirable effects can be minimized, it may be impossible to eliminate them entirely. The chapter addresses the problems of environmental despoliation, including both large-scale problems and more localized problems, of which pupils may well have firsthand experience. The material included is not prescriptive there are other large-scale problems which are not included. Alternatively, teachers may prefer to use examples of local damage. There is an opportunity here for pupils to investigate such problems using other published material. For example, several marine oil pollution incidents have now been documented, various initiatives concerning acid rain are under way, the Chernobyl nuclear disaster is well documented, and the ecological effects of the war in Kuwait are worth studying.

B17.2 Monoculture

Monoculture involves growing plants which are identical in as many respects as possible. Invariably they have similar flowering or ripening times and final heights; they have the same pests and need the same fertilizers. This makes cultivating and harvesting the crop easier, since it allows chemicals and machines to be used more effectively.

B17.3 Problems with pests

The increased use of monoculture means that the problem of pests is more acute. Various ways of dealing with this problem are evaluated critically in this section. The use of pesticides places severe natural selection pressures on the insect population. It is not surprising, therefore, that insect populations become resistant to the pesticides. This example of natural selection can be mentioned when evolution is considered, in Chapter **B**23.

Answer to selected question
5 To encourage survival of natural wildlife that would not be able to flourish in the artificial environment of a monoculture field.

B17.4 Biological control

Biological control is an interesting attempt to reduce the incidence of pests without using chemicals. The danger of this method is that it is easy to underestimate the complexity of the interactions within a community; there may be serious and unforeseen consequences. A general discussion may develop from question 14.

B17.5 Fertilizers

The use of fertilizers has become an essential part of modern farming practice. The consequences of surplus fertilizer for streams and ponds are considered in this section, which provides another example of the complex interactions that occur when additional factors are introduced into an ecosystem. The technique of using compost and waste materials for generating methane is now exploited in some developing countries. (Worksheet **B**17A gives some guidance for pupils to try to develop some "alternative technology" for themselves.)

The clearing of forests for agriculture is a practice that always occurs when a country is developing. The global consequences of these activities are only now being considered seriously.

B17.6 Industry and estuaries

The pressure for industry to exploit estuarine sites, with their good communications, ample water supplies and low population densities, is balanced here against the need to preserve these habitats. The tension between these two competing needs is all too real and the issues are fought out in many public inquiries. The aim of this section is to help pupils to appreciate both sides of the situation. It could provide an opportunity for a class debate or a role-playing exercise.

B17.7 Acid rain

Acid rain is, and probably will remain, a major source of pollution, destroying plants and disfiguring buildings. Worksheet **B**17B guides pupils on how to test a number of hypotheses concerning acid rain.

Activities

Worksheet B17A Build your own biogas generator

REQUIREMENTS

Each group of pupils will need:
Apparatus selected by the pupils after
  consultation with the teacher

Access to:
Water bath at 30°C
Sample of compost or manure (see *Note*)
Water
Petroleum jelly

Note:

Any manure used should be obtained by a member of staff, from a suitable source.

This is an interesting exercise that could stimulate pupils into considering the technological aspects of a topic that is becoming increasingly important. Methane gas produced in this way is being used commercially in some places to heat kilns and other industrial furnaces. In rural India, generated methane is being used to provide heating, a practice that is beginning to overcome the problem of the lack of wood for heating.

Classes undertaking this exercise must be given ample time to design and discuss their pieces of apparatus before they give their apparatus lists to the technicians. Wherever possible, pupils should be encouraged to bring suitable containers from home.

Pupils should be encouraged to make safety a major consideration when designing their apparatus, and teachers should carefully check the safety aspect of their plans before they start practical work.

The diagram below shows a possible design for a biogas generator.

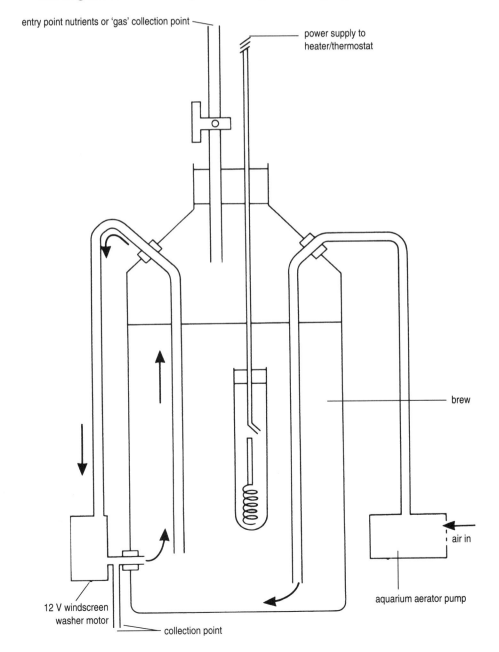

A biogas generator.

Worksheet B17B Acid rain

Part 1

REQUIREMENTS

Each group of pupils will need:
Gammarids, 10
Pond weeds
Pond water which has been adjusted to pH 4,
    pH 5 and pH 6
Beakers, 3
Jar, large, or small tank
Marker pen
Universal Indicator paper
Stones, several, small
Stopwatch

Part 2

REQUIREMENTS

Each group of pupils will need:
Damp soil samples (*e.g.* acidic, basic, neutral)
Eye protection
Container in which to collect water dripping
    through soil
Marker pen
Measuring cylinder, 250 cm³
Retort stand and clamp
Universal Indicator paper
Yogurt pots with holes in the bottom

Access to:
Ash from burnt wood
Distilled water acidified to different pH values
Rainwater
Lime

Notes:
The acidified water should be made up in advance. All pond water should be equally aerated before the first part of the practical begins.

The second part of the practical allows pupils to develop and test their own hypotheses about the effects of acid rain on soil. Different samples of soil can be made by adding peat, humus, lime or clay to a standard soil.

Worksheet B17C Our impact on the environment

REQUIREMENTS

Access to:
Reference books and other resources about the greenhouse effect, global warming and desertification

This worksheet focuses on the effects of human activity on the carbon and nitrogen cycles and on various aspects of the environment. The nitrogen cycle has largely been unaffected by the removal of atmospheric nitrogen for industrial uses but the effect of human activity on the carbon cycle is more noticeable. The levels of carbon dioxide in the atmosphere recorded in a number of places have gradually risen over a number of years. It is estimated that 23 billion tonnes of carbon dioxide will be released into the atmosphere in 1992, compared with 16 billion tonnes in 1972, and the atmospheric carbon dioxide concentration stands at 0.0356% in 1992 compared with 0.0327% in 1972. The chief sources of this increase are industrial processes such as steel production, brick and cement making and the burning of fossil fuels, rubbish and vegetation. The increase in atmospheric carbon dioxide is only a third of what would be expected from the burning of fossil fuels. Part of this shortfall may be due to increased rates of photosynthesis, but the bulk of it is due to carbon dioxide dissolving in sea water and eventually increasing deposits of calcium carbonate. The dissolved carbon dioxide may be redistributed by the ocean currents and some is liberated into the atmosphere in warmer tropical waters, but the timescale for this part of the cycle is not clear.

Carbon dioxide is transparent to visible light but absorbs infra-red radiation and cuts down the radiation of energy back into Space. Other gases, such as nitrous oxide, methane, ozone and chlorofluorocarbons (CFCs) have a similar effect. "Greenhouse effect" is the name given to the processes whereby the increased concentrations of these gases in the atmosphere reduce energy loss by radiation from the Earth and lead to global warming.

Of the seven warmest years on record, four have occurred in the 1980s. There are concerns that global warming may lead to a rise in sea level and that an increasing dryness and reduced precipitation which would accompany a rise in temperature might have serious climatological effects. There are also worries that large "sinks" such as the oceans are now unable to absorb the carbon dioxide as rapidly as it is being produced, and that the destruction of natural vegetation is causing the level of this gas in the atmosphere to increase by lowering the amount recycled through photosynthesis. One estimate suggests that the destruction of tropical rain forests alone results in about 1 billion tonnes per year of carbon dioxide being added to the atmosphere.

On the other hand, human activity also increases the reflectance of the Earth by depositing dust particles in the atmosphere which reduce the amount of energy absorbed. There is also much evidence to suggest that there have been large fluctuations in the composition of the atmosphere throughout the Earth's history. Scientists are still debating the "greenhouse effect" and many are still keeping an open mind about the long-term effects.

Deforestation also leads to problems of soil erosion and species extinction. In 1972 about 100 000 square kilometres of forest were being lost per year but by 1992 this figure is estimated to rise to 170 000 square kilometres per year. Trees absorb both thermal radiation and carbon dioxide; they moderate the effect of winds and prevent soil erosion. 40% of the land in Ethiopia was described as being "forest" one hundred years ago but by 1987 the amount of woodland had been reduced to 3%. Human activity may have been partly responsible for the desertification: collection of wood and the burning of dung for fuel may have prevented the soil from retaining its structure. The introduction of arable farming into areas which have thin soils that are more suited for grazing may also disturb the ecological balance. Cultivation also destroys the natural humus in the soil and, if nothing is done to replace the organic material, the soil is eventually eroded. Desertification may be reversed by re-establishing plant cover, reforestation, improved use of water and well-managed irrigation, and a reduction in the number of grazing animals. There are, of course, many social and economic implications of the actions required, and this makes the process of desertification difficult to prevent, especially in poorer countries.

The ozone layer is a narrow region about 25 km from the Earth's surface where ozone is present at a concentration of 0.01%. 99% of the ultra-violet rays which reach the atmosphere are absorbed by this layer. CFCs (found as propellants in some aerosols and fire extinguishers, and in blown foam packaging, foam mattresses and refrigerators) are not easily decomposed and destroy the ozone layer by free-radical reactions involving the interaction of ultra-violet radiation with CFCs. By 1975 the concentration of CFCs in the atmosphere was 1.4 parts per billion but by 1992 this value had doubled. In an area over the South Pole, the ozone concentration has fallen by 40% since 1957 and there are now worries about a "hole" in the ozone layer appearing over Europe. The results of ozone depletion, however, are complex and the theory that the increased radiation on the Earth's surface will cause a temperature rise is modified by an increase in the cooling of the stratosphere. Reduction of ozone does not occur uniformly throughout the ozone layer and the altitude at which the ozone is at maximum concentration may vary. If the average ozone altitude is lower, this will lead to a warming of the Earth's surface but if it is higher it will have a cooling effect on the Earth.

The effect of human activity on the water cycle could also be discussed. The diversion of water for agricultural uses, electrical power and paper-making may reduce the groundwater supply considerably and play a contributing part in creating poor soil conditions. The importance of trees in the water cycle could also be discussed.

Answers to worksheet questions

1 Increased burning of fossil fuels by burning ever-increasing amounts of coal, oil and gas.

2 Apart from being a product of respiration, carbon dioxide is a product of volcanic activity and forest fires.

3 Approximately 0.037% (assuming current rates of increase).

4 More carbon dioxide may dissolve in the sea, leading to increased deposits of calcium carbonate. An increased rate of photosynthesis may also help reduce the concentration of carbon dioxide.

5 Respiration, corrosion of iron etc., and combustion of fossil fuels and other materials.

6 The processes of oxygen removal from the atmosphere and from water should be shown, as well as the process of photosynthesis.

7 It is likely that the effect will be minimal because the pool of atmospheric nitrogen is very large. If the role of denitrifying bacteria is drastically reduced and the atmospheric fixation of nitrogen is increased, an effect may be noticed, but the "external" cycle will continue to function as long as the processes of decomposition etc. continue.

Further information

Science and Technology in Society
SATIS unit 301 "Air pollution – where does it come from?" includes a consideration of acid rain. Patterns of land usage, including monoculture, are covered in unit 409 "Dam problems". Units 210 "The pesticide problem" and 402 "DDT and malaria" consider pesticides, while the importance of artificial fertilizers is discussed in unit 505 "Making fertilizers". Units 1201 "Agrochemicals and the environment" and 1206 "The greenhouse effect" are also relevant. Of these, units 210, 301, 402 and 409 are updated in *SATIS Update 91*.

Chapter B18 To destroy or to conserve?

The syllabus section

Context

The conservation of natural habitats and endangered species requires an understanding of their ecology and acts of preservation. This section considers these ideas by discussing a variety of different examples, some local and others of global significance. The biological, economic and political difficulties of conservation can be developed.

Knowledge and understanding

Syllabus statements	PoS	SoA
Understand that pollution of the environment may cause extinction of a species and that it will have an effect on the remaining species in a community.	2(iii)3	2.5(c)
Know that conservation of habitats requires active management by relating this to the environmental impact of human activity on the Earth.	2(iii)4	2.8(d)
Understand the relationships between human activity on the Earth to size of population, economic factors and industrial requirements.	2(iii)4	2.8(d)

Opportunities for co-ordination

C4 deals with mines and quarries.

Routes and times

Basic	Central	Further
Do only pages 220 and 221 of section B18.1.	**B18.1 Destruction or conservation?** **B18.3 Rare species** (class + homework) *1 hour*	
	Worksheet B18A Conservation (optional) **B18.2 Conservation** Select material to suit class needs. *1 hour*	
	Worksheet B18B What to do with waste? (class + homework) *½ hour*	
Total: 2½ hours	*Total: 2½ hours*	*Total: 2½ hours*

The pupils' book

B18.1 Destruction or conservation?

This section describes a variety of ways in which humans have altered the environment. Pupils should be encouraged to predict the long-term effects of these changes on the composition of the habitat.

Answer to selected question

3 Amenities (car parks, lavatories, etc.) need to be built. Erosion of soil can occur through trampling, wild plants may be picked and shy animals may be disturbed.

B18.2 Conservation

This section develops the case study of Epping forest as an example of successful conservation. It could be related to similar examples in your area. The principal aim of this section is to show that conservation involves active management of the area. Worksheet **B**18A could be used to replace some or all of the material.

B18.3 Rare species

Pupils are often interested in rare species, and television has brought an awareness of the problems into our homes. It is easy to become angry about the destruction of habitats in developing countries without realizing the pressures that are on the leaders of those countries. Question 13 allows pupils to think about the wider implications of such development, and could be used as a basis for a debate between the "developers" and the "conservators".

Answer to selected question

16 The big difference between all other times and now is the human-caused **rate** of extinction. In the past, if one species became extinct something else may have taken its place, perhaps even leading to increasing diversity of species. The sudden loss of species over the last decades has clearly reduced the diversity of species and of genes.

Activities

Worksheet B18A Conservation

REQUIREMENTS

Access to:
Compass
Identification keys
Large-scale Ordnance Survey map of the area
Measuring tape

The amount of time that is devoted to this exercise depends upon the inclination of the pupils or the teacher. A small group of committed pupils could successfully devote as much as five lessons to this exercise and produce some worthwhile results at the end; for others, two lessons would be sufficient. It is important that the area under consideration is not too large. Assistance should be provided whenever appropriate.

Within a working group, pupils should be given various responsibilities and be encouraged to report back to the rest of the group. This could form the basis for an assessment of a number of skills.

Worksheet B18B What to do with waste?

REQUIREMENTS

Access to:
Reference books, newspaper articles and other resource materials about waste and recycling

Safety note:
When pupils are making a list of waste materials their family throws away, they should be encouraged to record the rubbish before it is thrown away and not (on health grounds) to "rummage" through dustbins.

This worksheet forms the basis for discussing the nature of waste, its disposal and the recycling of materials. It is suggested that pupils start to record the materials they throw away a week before the bulk of the activity is completed. Pupils should be encouraged to record their results in a suitable form, classifying the types of waste as necessary. It would also be useful if some indication of the quantity of each material thrown away was recorded.

In 1989 there were 1400 landfill sites in Britain, and some of these have had problems involving leakage of toxic materials and build-up of methane gas. Recent research indicates that even thick plastic or ceramic linings are not completely leakproof, whilst the problems of overflow after heavy rain have not yet been completely solved. One estimate suggests that 10% of aquifers in Britain are contaminated with chemicals leached from waste dumps.

Dumping in the sea has caused several problems, and this could be linked with a more general discussion of water pollution. In some countries, all household waste is sorted out before disposal in order to collect the recyclable materials: Switzerland and Germany, for example, have separate collection bins for glass, paper and aluminium to facilitate recycling. Excessive packaging of goods accounts for large amounts of waste plastic and paper and some countries, *e.g.* Germany, have laws which force the retailer to take back unwanted excess packaging. In Britain, 6 million glass bottles are bought every day but only one-sixth of these are recycled. Fine dust, paper, organic material, rags and plastics release energy when burnt and in some places combustion of such substances is used to heat buildings. Manchester City Council runs a scheme to make oil from organic rubbish containing up to 40% cellulose. Methane gas from several landfill sites in Britain is now piped off for use as a fuel.

Water-borne wastes such as sewage, industrial effluents and agricultural slurries may seep into rivers and sometimes cause pollution problems. Sewage sludge is the solid waste that settles out in the sedimentation tanks in a sewage treatment plant. It is usually taken to a digester tank where micro-organisms break down the sludge to methane. The treated sludge may then be used as a fertilizer or be dumped at sea.

Nuclear waste is disposed of according to the level of its radioactivity. Low-level waste is placed in containers in large concrete vaults. Intermediate-level waste is encapsulated in thick-walled drums, then packed in vaults excavated in hard rocks with suitable geological conformations well below the ground. High-level waste is concentrated and stored in stainless steel tanks enclosed in thick concrete walls; cooling coils are necessary to reduce the heating effect of the radioactivity. A new process involves putting the high-level waste into glass blocks and then placing these in stainless steel containers.

Answers to worksheet questions

1 All the unwanted substances that are thrown away by households, industry and agriculture, or discharged into the atmosphere or into rivers, lakes or seas.

2 The answers will depend on the results collected. An average British dustbin may contain 30% paper, 20% organic waste (food waste, peelings etc.) and up to 15% ash, whilst 25% may be made up of metals, glass and plastics.

3 Glass, paper and some metals like aluminium and iron can be recycled but are often thrown away.

4 Less fuel is required for recycling since less energy is required to melt or reprocess the material than to make it from its raw materials. Recycling protects the environment by reducing the amount of waste, reducing the leaching of potentially poisonous substances into the soil, water, etc., and reducing the demand for raw materials, *e.g.* trees to make paper.

6 Composting of organic materials returns minerals to the ground and provides necessary organic material for the soil.

7 Biogas might be collected by placing pipes into the rubbish tip and leading the gas off into collection chambers.

8 Resistant to water, unreactive with a wide range of chemicals, rot-proof, tough but flexible/mouldable.

9 To check that poisonous materials are not leaking into the soil and that there is no build-up of biogas.

10 For heating buildings etc.

11 Poisonous substances accumulate in larger organisms through the food chain, and the concentration of these substances may eventually build up so that even larger organisms are poisoned.

12 The gills of organisms living on the bottom of the sea may become clogged with the ash and they may die through lack of oxygen.

Supplementary material

A number of overseas aid agencies have simulation games which are helpful in understanding the delicately balanced economies of many villages in developing countries; such games have great educational value. They can be bought from the Oxfam Education Department, 274 Banbury Road, Oxford OX2 7DZ, or from TEAR Fund, 100 Church Road, Teddington, Middlesex TW11 8QE.

Further information on recycling waste is available from many local councils, Friends of the Earth, the Green Party and the Warmer Campaign (see Appendix).

The continuity of life

Chapter **B**19 Living things multiply

The syllabus section

Context

This section introduces the biological aspects of reproduction in organisms. Asexual reproduction is contrasted with sexual reproduction. The effects of grass pollen on hay-fever sufferers are considered.

Knowledge and understanding

	Tier			
Syllabus statements	B	C	F	PoS	SoA

Syllabus statements	PoS	SoA
Be able to name, locate and outline the functions of the reproductive parts of a flower.	2(i)1	2.4(a) 2.5(a)
Be able to relate the structure of gametes (sex cells) to their function.	2(i)1	2.6(a)
Appreciate the significance of the differences between internal and external fertilization in animals, and the significance of courtship.	2(i)2	2.6(b)
Know that asexual reproduction produces offspring that are identical to the parent.	2(i)2	2.6(b)
Understand the significance of "oestrus" in the reproduction of many mammals.	2(i)2	2.6(b)
Understand that sexual reproduction involves a mobile male gamete (e.g. sperm) fusing with a stationary female gamete (e.g. egg).	2(i)1	—
Understand the differences between pollination and fertilization in flowering plants, self-pollination and cross-pollination.	2(i)2	2.7(b)

Routes and times

Basic	Central	Further
Spend more time on this section. *1 hour*	**B19.1 Reproduction is a necessity of life** Brief revision. **B19.2 Different ways of reproducing** Brief revision. **B19.3 Reproduction without sex** *³/₄ hour*	
Omit the parts of section **B**19.4 which deal with self- and cross-pollination. Replace Worksheet **B**19A by Worksheet **B**19C "How pollen grows" (side 1 only). *1 hour*	**B19.4 Sexual reproduction** Omit "The mating of animals". **Worksheet B19A Differences between wind-pollinated and insect-pollinated flowers** (optional) **Worksheet B19B The pollen count** (optional/homework) *³/₄ hour*	
	B19.4 Sexual reproduction ("The mating of animals" only) *³/₄ hour*	
Section **B**19.6 is optional.	**B19.5 Sexual cycles in mammals** **B19.6 What happens as a result of fertilization?** Especially the role of the placenta. *¹/₂ hour*	
Total: 3¹/₄ hours	*Total: 2³/₄ hours*	*Total: 2³/₄ hours*

The pupils' book

B19.1 Reproduction is a necessity of life

This section introduces the idea that reproduction is a feature of all living organisms. It is a prelude to the next section.

B19.2 Different ways of reproducing

This important section presents a number of major ideas, in particular, the difference between sexual and asexual reproduction. The terms "female gametes" and "male gametes" are introduced.

Answer to selected question
1 The mature sycamore reproduces sexually (but it can also be propagated by taking cuttings). Yeast reproduces sexually and asexually. In figure 19.3 in the pupils' book *Saxifraga* has reproduced asexually, although it can reproduce sexually using flowers. *Hydra* can also reproduce sexually and asexually. Swans reproduce sexually, as do all birds and mammals.

B19.3 Reproduction without sex

This section deals with asexual reproduction, briefly in the case of animals, and at greater length in that of plants.

Answers to selected questions

2 Apples are produced by grafting stems on to superior root stocks. Budding is often used for roses.

3 Asexual reproduction enables a plant to produce a large number of (genetically) identical "offspring". This can result in the rapid colonization of an area in which the plant is established. Sexual reproduction results in (genetically) dissimilar offspring and serves to increase the ability of the plant to colonize areas with different or unstable environments.

B19.4 Sexual reproduction

This section begins by considering fertilization in flowering plants, both by self- and by cross-pollination. Pupils may investigate the differences between wind- and insect-pollinated flowers, using Worksheet **B**19A, and how a pollen tube grows, using Worksheet **B**19C. The study of the pollen count in Worksheet **B**19B can also be done at this stage.

    The section then studies sexual reproduction in animals (apart from human reproduction, which is dealt with in the next chapter). Pupils consider internal and external reproduction and what happens when an egg is fertilized.

Answers to selected questions

4 The wind-pollinated flowers are **a** (rye grass), **c** (nettle), **d** (hazel) and **f** (silver birch); the insect-pollinated flowers are **b** (apple) and **e** (crocus).

9 Not all of the eggs are fertilized, although the eggs release chemicals which attract sperms. Furthermore, the number of sea urchins that survive long enough to reproduce is limited by the resources of the environment.

15 Both reptiles and birds lay eggs with hard shells, so fertilization must occur before these are laid.

B19.5 Sexual cycles in mammals

The menstrual cycle is covered in the next chapter, but this short section prefaces it by considering the breeding season in a variety of mammals. The term "oestrus" is introduced.

Answer to selected question

17 This is less wasteful of sperm; females have enough time to wean the young born from a previous mating, before the next reproductive cycle begins.

B19.6 What happens as a result of fertilization?

The pattern of development of the human embryo is covered in detail in the chapters that follow. This short section introduces the idea that other animals may have different patterns of development. Worksheet **B**19D compares the lengths of the gestation periods of several mammals.

Activities

Worksheet B19A Differences between wind-pollinated and insect-pollinated flowers

REQUIREMENTS

Each group of pupils will need:
Hand lens
Mounted needle
Fine forceps

Specimens of insect- and wind-pollinated flowers such as those shown in figure 19.8 in the pupils' book, as available

The procedure is detailed on the worksheet.

Worksheet B19B The pollen count

Information to be studied is given in the worksheet.

Worksheet B19C How pollen grows

Part 1

REQUIREMENTS

Each group of pupils will need:
Drawing paper
Hand lens
Microscope slide
Microscope
Pencils

Access to:
Specimens of insect- and wind-pollinated
  flowers
or
Garden, school grounds or potted plants for
  collection of specimens

The procedure is detailed on the worksheet.

Part 2

REQUIREMENTS

Each group of pupils will need:
Flowers of busy lizzie or other insect-pollinated
  plants
Flowers of wind-pollinated plants
Culture solution, 2 cm^3 (15% sucrose solution,
  0.01 g boric acid, 0.01 g yeast)
Absorbent paper
Clock
Eyepiece graticule
Petri dish and lid

Worksheet B19D What happens after fertilization in mammals?

REQUIREMENTS

Each group of pupils will need:
Graph paper
Pencils
Photographs in figure 19.24 of the pupils' book

Instructions will be found on the worksheet.

Further information

Hunt, P. Francis *Discovering botany* Longman, 1979.

Chapter B20 People are different

The syllabus section

Context

This section places the facts of human reproduction in a context that is relevant to adolescent boys and girls. Opportunity is given for the social and emotional consequences of human sexuality to be discussed sensitively. For example, practical advice on hygiene during menstruation, dealing with hetero- and homosexual feelings, and the dangers of engaging in sexual intercourse at an early age can be given in ways appropriate to the pupils concerned. The dangers of smoking, drinking and taking drugs in pregnancy can also be stressed. An understanding of the effectiveness of contraceptives can be included in this section, together with a basic awareness of the major sexually transmitted diseases (including AIDS).

Knowledge and understanding

Tier B C F		

Syllabus statements	PoS	SoA
Be able to name, locate and outline the functions of the organs of reproduction in humans.	2(i)1	2.4(a) 2.5(a)
Know that the timing of puberty varies from person to person.	2(i)2	—
Know that adolescence is controlled by hormones produced by the testes or ovaries; that the male sex hormone is testosterone, while the female sex hormones are oestrogen and progesterone.	2(i)2	—
Appreciate the changes in the ovary and uterus throughout the menstrual cycle; the significance of menstruation at the end of the cycle.	2(i)2	—
Understand the biological aspects of sexual intercourse, ejaculation, fertilization and implantation.	2(i)2	—
Understand the process of birth.	2(i)2	—
Understand the effectiveness of different types of contraceptives.	2(i)2	—
Know the causes and symptoms (in simple terms) of the major sexually transmitted diseases (including AIDS).	2(i)5	—
Understand the links between human reproduction and human emotions, feelings and relationships.	2(i)5	—
Appreciate the dangers of smoking, drinking and taking drugs in pregnancy.	2(i)2	—
Understand the protection given to the embryo by the amniotic sac; the role of the placenta in transporting materials to and from the foetus.	2(i)4	2.8(a)
Appreciate the role of the hypothalamus and pituitary gland in co-ordinating the activities of the endocrine glands to produce the sex hormones.	2(i)6	2.9(a)
Appreciate how hormones can be used to control and promote fertility, growth and development in humans and be aware of the implications of their use.	2(i)6	2.10(c)

Opportunities for co-ordination

B2 introduces placental mammals. **B**11 introduces the concept of "normal" variation with regard to body temperature. **B**21 concerns the population growth of humans. Chemicals in the medicine cupboard are discussed in **C**12.

Routes and times

Basic	Central	Further
Spend more time on this section. *2 hours*	**B20.1 What is it that makes sex different for us?** **B20.2 Sexual development** Select appropriate sections for revision but omit reference to the hypothalamus and the pituitary gland. *1³/₄ hours*	Include the roles of the hypothalamus and pituitary gland. *2 hours*
Omit the role of the placenta and Worksheet **B20B1**.	**B20.3 Fertilization and development** Omit Q26. **Worksheet B20B The growth of a human embryo and foetus** (optional) **Worksheet B20B1 The foetal environment** (homework) *1 hour*	
	B20.5 Contraception Brief revision. **B20.6 Sexually transmitted diseases** *1 hour*	Spend less time on this section. *³/₄ hour*
		The use of hormones to control and promote fertility should be discussed here (see teacher's notes for Worksheet **B22B5** "Genetic issues"). *¹/₂ hour*
Total: 4 hours	*Total: 3³/₄ hours*	*Total: 4¹/₄ hours*

Note

Sex education, and AIDS education in particular, is controversial, and schools will have different opinions on how much of this material they should include in the pupils' science lessons: schools with well-developed Personal and Social Education programmes may prefer to omit much of the information in this chapter.

The school governors and head teacher are responsible for approving the programme of sex education activities and the resources used, and there may also be Local Education Authority guidelines to be followed. Teachers are advised to ensure that their approach is consistent with school policy.

The pupils' book

B20.1 What is it that makes sex different for us?

This section introduces a central idea of this chapter, that human sexuality has functions in our society other than the purely biological aim of reproduction.

B20.2 Sexual development

Since adolescents are often uncomfortably aware of the physical changes that are happening to them, this section begins by showing that there is great variation in the rate at which boys and girls mature. There is also great variation in the appearance of people's bodies. This theme is developed further in Worksheet **B20A**.

Next, the hormonal changes that accompany adolescence are discussed and the menstrual cycle is then considered in more detail. It is shown to be a hormone-controlled sequence that prepares an egg for fertilization, and then prepares the uterus to receive it if it is fertilized. Pupils learn that if fertilization does not occur the cycle ends with the period of menstruation.

The reproductive systems of the male and female are considered next.

The section now turns to the problems of coming to terms with sexual feelings. This can be a difficult area, and teachers should use the material here sensitively.

An account of sexual intercourse is included in this section.

B20.3 Fertilization and development

The section begins with the moment of fertilization. It shows how this leads to the implantation of the fertilized egg in the uterus. It then considers the development of the embryo, the function of the placenta and the growth of the foetus. It closes with an account of the birth of a baby. Spontaneous abortion is also discussed.

Worksheet **B20B** asks pupils to interpret the growth pattern of the foetus.

Answer to selected question

19 From about day 9 to day 16 of her cycle. This assumes, of course, that the woman ovulates at the mid-point of her cycle. In many women, especially younger ones, this may not be the case, and the variation in the time of ovulation can be critical. Pupils need to understand that they run a risk of pregnancy whenever they have unprotected intercourse. Obviously, this risk is greater at some times than others.

B20.4 The human population

This section contains an exercise in sampling variation. Most of us know families which consist of several boys or several girls. When averages are taken over a whole neighbourhood, however, the ratio of sexes becomes more nearly equal.

Worksheet **B20C** is relevant. This allows pupils to analyse the growth of various human populations. It echoes the issues raised in Chapter **B**18, where the economic problems of developing nations were set in an ecological context.

B20.5 Contraception

This section describes the mechanics of a variety of contraceptive devices. No attempt is made to discuss the moral or ethical aspects of contraception, and teachers may wish to decide for themselves whether to do this.

B20.6 Sexually transmitted diseases

Sexually transmitted diseases, including AIDS, are covered in this section. Teachers may like to supplement the material with pamphlets which may be obtained from the Health Education Authority.

Answer to selected question

30 Promiscuous people or even those who have the occasional casual sexual encounter are at risk from these diseases. At the time of writing, the AIDS (HIV) virus is at low levels in the heterosexual population, although it is becoming increasingly prevalent in the homosexual community and among those who share hypodermic needles. This pattern could easily change as the AIDS virus becomes established in the heterosexual population. The contraceptive sheath offers some protection against all STDS, including AIDS, but it cannot confer absolute protection. In the light of these trends, it is becoming necessary to be much more thoughtful about our sexual behaviour.

Activities

Worksheet B20A What is normal?

REQUIREMENTS

Each group of pupils will need:
Graph paper, pencils and rulers

Access to:
0.9 % saline solution
Disposable drinking cups
Scale for measuring height
Scales, bathroom, measuring in kg
Tape measure, in cm
Watch or clock

The procedure is detailed on the worksheet. It is important that pupils taste the salt solution from clean cups. As with any activity that involves tasting, this must **not** be done in the laboratory.

Very careful consideration must be given when students are the objects of investigations: there must be no pressure on them to take part, and the educational advantage must be judged in relation to the hazards involved.

Worksheet B20B The growth of a human embryo and foetus

REQUIREMENTS

Each group of pupils will need:
Graph paper, pencils and rulers

The procedure is detailed on the worksheet.

Worksheet B20B1 The foetal environment

This worksheet introduces the role of the placenta in regulating the exchange of materials between the foetus and the maternal blood system. Many substances appear to diffuse simply through the placenta and even large molecules such as some proteins may pass through this organ. Carrier molecules and enzyme systems may be responsible for the transport of larger molecules, and some molecules cross the placenta against concentration gradients. Considerable amounts of calcium may pass through the placental barrier to the foetus, and if the demands of the foetus exceed the mother's daily calcium intake, calcium is absorbed from the mother's bones and teeth. Alcohol, drugs and anaesthetics may all pass through the placenta and have harmful effects on the foetus. The amniotic fluid also provides a protective cushion for the foetus.

Answers to worksheet questions

1 Oxygen, amino acids, glucose, hormones, vitamins, minerals, water, etc.

2 To allow a greater surface area for interchange of material.

3 For the formation of bones and teeth.

4 It protects and supports the foetus.

Worksheet B20C The human population

REQUIREMENTS

Each group of pupils will need:
Graph paper, pencils and rulers

The procedure is detailed on the worksheet.

Further information

Health Education Authority *Pregnancy book* Health Education Authority, Hamilton House, Mabledon Place, London WC1H 9TX, 1984.

Supplementary material
The Health Education Authority's pamphlets on family planning and on sexually related diseases.

Chapter B21 Growing up

The syllabus section

Context

This section considers the patterns of development of a number of different organisms, including those showing complete and incomplete metamorphosis. The control of this development in terms of internal regulating chemicals is developed.

The growth and development of the human is dealt with in a series of stages. The development of linguistic and motor skills in babies is examined, together with the need for love between parents and children. The formation of the emotional bonds between parents and children can be discussed.

Maturity and old age are considered as different stages of development. The problems of old age both to the individual and to society can be discussed. The changing patterns of life expectancy and causes of death are also considered.

Uncontrolled division of cells leads to the formation of tumours. Benign and malignant tumours are compared. Treatment of cancer can be discussed.

Knowledge and understanding

Syllabus statements	PoS	SoA
Understand the methods used to measure the growth of organisms.	2(i)1	2.7(a)
Know the principal stages in the development of a human from childhood to old age.	2(i)1	2.7(a)
Know that tumours are caused by uncontrolled cell divisions; some are benign, others are malignant.	2(i)5, 7	2.7(a)
Appreciate the role of auxins in the growth of plants.	2(i)6	2.9(a)
Understand the role of thyroid hormone in controlling metamorphosis.	2(i)6	2.9(a)

Opportunities for co-ordination

C12 links with chemotherapy, P3 with radiotherapy.

Routes and times

Basic	Central	Further

Worksheet **B20A** "What is normal?" is also suitable.

1¼ hours

> **B21.1 Growth and development**
> **B21.2 Different patterns of development**
> Set Q5–8 for homework.
> *³/₄ hour*

> **B21.4 How are growth and development controlled?**
> **Worksheet B21A1 Growth hormones and cattle**
> *1 hour*

These sections are optional at Basic level.

> **B21.3 Telling the age of an organism**
> **B21.6 More about human development**
> *½ hour*

> **B21.7 Parental care**
> Select material according to the class; the questions are optional.
> **Worksheet B20C The human population**
> (optional/homework)
> *³/₄ hour*

Omit at Basic level.

> **B21.5 Uncontrolled growth**
> **Worksheet B21A People and cancer**
> (optional/homework)
> *½ hour*

Total: 2 hours   *Total: 2½ hours*   *Total: 3½ hours*

The pupils' book

B21.1 Growth and development

Growth is defined as a series of changes that can be observed and measured. Pupils are given the opportunity to try to find ways of measuring the growth of different organisms.

Answer to selected question
2 Length and mass for the animals; height and girth of stem for the sycamore tree and seedling.

B21.2 Different patterns of development

This section studies the growth of the human body from birth to adulthood and provides a good opportunity for the assessment of measuring and interpreting skills.

B21.3 Telling the age of an organism

This section concentrates on ways of telling the ages of fishes, and can be linked with the exercise on the ages of organisms in Chapter **B2**.

Answer to selected question
9 The herring was eight years old.

B21.4 How are growth and development controlled?

This section contains some important, if rather complex, ideas that may be more suited to those aiming for higher grades. Questions 10, 11 and 12 could make homework exercises.

B21.5 Uncontrolled growth

This section aims at considering the biological aspects of cancer in a helpful way – for example, by helping pupils to understand the important difference between benign and malignant tumours. Worksheet **B21A** provides additional information that may be of value.

B21.6 More about human development

Pupils are shown that the development of babies into children, and children into adults, involves acquiring a large number of skills; parents can help their children to gain these.

B21.7 Parental care

This section develops the idea of parental care raised in the previous one, by considering the roles of mother and father. It stresses that a child needs love as well as protection and suggests that men can "mother" children as well as women. The material ought to stimulate lively debate, since everyone has an opinion about parents! The section ends by considering maturity and old age.

Worksheet B21A1 Growth hormones and cattle

This worksheet introduces pupils to the ways in which hormones have been used to increase food production and discusses the drawbacks associated with the use of these chemicals, which is now banned in many countries. Cattle treated with anabolic steroids convert food to meat five times more efficiently than cattle which are untreated. The most commonly used hormones have been progesterone, testosterone and 17–ß oestradiol (naturally occurring) and trenbolone acetate and zeranol (synthetic). Natural cattle meat may contain a far higher concentration of hormones than meat from hormone-treated cattle. Although the naturally occurring sex hormones may be destroyed by digestion, some synthetic hormones may not be broken down. The banned oestrogen-based hormone DES formerly used in the USA has been shown to cause cancer, whilst the premature sexual development of a number of children in Puerto Rico in the 1980s was thought to have been caused by synthetic growth hormones used to fatten chickens. BST (bovine somatotrophin) may be obtained by genetic engineering, but this form of the hormone differs from the natural one by a few amino acids. Although BST increases milk yields and allows farmers to produce the same amount of milk with fewer cows, the over-production of meat and milk by the European Community has partly invalidated the rationale for its use in Europe. Many countries, including Britain, have now banned the use of growth hormones for increasing the yield of meat.

Hormone control and fertility
This is a convenient place to discuss the role of the hypothalamus and the pituitary gland in co-ordinating the activities of the endocrine glands to produce sex hormones and to appreciate how hormones can be used to promote fertility in humans. The hypothalamus is the region of the brain just above the pituitary gland. Clusters of nerves in the hypothalamus regulate the levels of hormones in the bloodstream by secreting a transmitter substance (releasing hormone) which travels to the anterior lobe of the pituitary gland. The pituitary gland then secretes hormones which act on other glands to stimulate specific

hormone production. LH (luteinizing hormone), manufactured by the pituitary gland, targets particular cells in the testes which are stimulated to produce testosterone, an important male sex hormone. FSH (follicle stimulating hormone) promotes the maturation of egg cells and in conjunction with LH stimulates the follicle cells to produce oestrogens, as shown below. The system is an example of negative feedback control similar to that for insulin regulation.

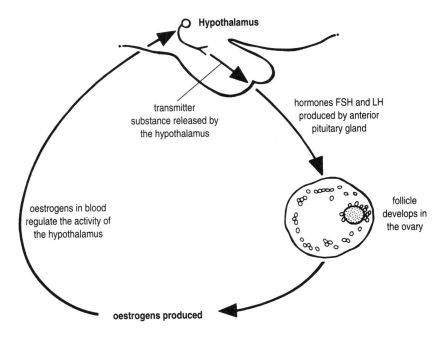

Feedback control of hormone levels via the hypothalamus.

The use of hormones to control or promote fertility should be covered either here or in conjunction with Worksheet **B22B4** "Genetic issues". Oral contraceptives contain a synthetic oestrogen and a progesterone-like compound. The increased levels of these hormones in the blood cause the hypothalamus to inhibit secretion of the transmitter substance for FSH and LH production, so that neither normal follicle development nor ovulation can occur.

Fertility in animals may be promoted by using hormones to regulate ovulation. Hormones are also used to promote fertility in humans. The LH/FSH inhibitor Buserelin is first used to reduce the natural gonadotrophic activity of the woman. Pergonal (containing a follicle stimulating hormone and a luteinizing hormone analogue) is then used to stimulate ovulation.

Answers to worksheet questions

1 Farmers can manage the supply of beef in a more flexible way because the cows grow faster and can be made "ready for market" at the appropriate time. They can also control the leanness of the meat.

2 The normal growth hormones (which are similar to the synthetic steroid hormones used) are secreted by the testes. If the testes are removed, the growth rate will be lowered because of the reduction in the natural hormone.

3 Bulls can be dangerous and difficult to control.

4 The hormones may get into people's bloodstreams after eating hormone-treated meat and cause various growth defects or lead to some kind of disease.

5 It increases the amount of food eaten.

6 Untreated cow: 0.82 kg milk per kilogram of food.
Treated cow: 0.87 kg milk per kilogram of food.

7 It would be broken down by the digestive juices.

Activities

Worksheet B21A People and cancer

REQUIREMENTS

Each group of pupils will need:
Pencils
Rulers
Graph paper

The procedure is detailed on the worksheet.

Further information

Health Education Authority *Pregnancy book* Health Education Authority, Hamilton House, Mabledon Place, London WC1H 9TX, 1984.

Chapter B22 Handing on to the next generation

The syllabus section

Context

This section develops the ideas of Mendelian genetics, through the use of "family tree" pedigree analysis, and through the results of genetic crosses. The effects of heredity and the environment on the expression of certain characteristics are considered.

The inherited nature of a number of human conditions is presented, and the value of genetic counselling can be discussed.

Technological advances in the development of cloning techniques for crop plants are considered, using the example of the oil palm.

Knowledge and understanding

Tier			Syllabus statements	PoS	SoA
B	C	F			
			Know that features can be inherited and that the information for these features is passed on from one generation to the next by genes.	2(ii)4	2.5(b)
			Know that the variation shown by living organisms is partly inherited and partly results from environmental influences.	2(ii)2	2.6(c)
			Understand, through exploration of variability and selection, how selective breeding can produce economic benefits and contribute to improved yields.	2(ii)6, 7	2.7(c)
			Know that gametes contain half the number of chromosomes of the other cells of the body. Cells do not develop normally if they contain abnormal numbers of chromosomes or if the chromosomes are damaged.	2(ii)4	2.8(b)
			Understand how the offspring of a cross can be predicted from a knowledge of the genes of the parents.	2(ii)4	2.8(c)
			Appreciate the meaning of the terms dominant allele, recessive, homozygote, heterozygote, F1 and F2 generations, phenotype and genotype.	2(ii)4	2.8(c)
			Know how sex is determined in humans.	2(ii)4	2.8(c)
			Understand how some diseases can be inherited.	2(ii)4	2.8(c)
			Understand that genetic variability is brought about in a number of ways, including reshuffling chromosomes and mutation.	2(ii)6	2.9(b)
			Know that chromosomes are found in the nucleus, and that genes are carried on chromosomes. Genes are 'coded instructions' for making proteins. DNA is the chemical which stores the coded instructions.	2(ii)3	2.10(b)
			Understand technological advances in the development of cloning techniques.	2(ii)7	2.10(c)
			Appreciate from a range of perspectives the principles of genetic engineering, in relation to drug production, selective breeding and cloning, while developing an awareness of social and ethical considerations which arise.	2(i)6 2(ii)6, 7	2.10(c)
			Appreciate the social, economic and ethical aspects of cloning techniques and selective breeding.	2(ii)7	2.10(c)

Routes and times

Basic	Central	Further
Omit Q4 and 5 and spend more time on this section. *½ hour*	**B22.1 Alike or not alike?** *¼ hour*	
Worksheet **B22A** should be done in class. *2 hours*	**Worksheet B22A Is variation inherited or due to the environment?** (optional) **B22.2 Environment or heredity?** *1 hour*	Worksheet **B22B** "Two kinds of variation" is suitable extension material.
Omit this section.	**B22.9 Are you just your genes?** **Worksheet B23C1 Artificial selection** (class + homework) *½ hour*	
Omit this section.	**B22.3 Halving and doubling** **Worksheet B22B1 How cells divide** *1 hour*	
Omit this section.	**B22.5 Boy or girl?** Refer back to section **B20.4.** *½ hour*	
Omit this section.	**B22.6 Patterns of inheritance** **Worksheet B22C Breeding with beads** (optional) *2 hours*	Spend less time on section **B22.6.** *1½ hours*
Omit this section.	**B22.7 Five toes, or maybe six?** Select material to suit class needs. **B22.8 Genetic counselling** **Worksheet B22B5 Genetic issues** (introduction only) *1¼ hours*	The mutation aspect should be stressed in section **B22.7** and more time spent on Worksheet **B22B5.** Worksheet **B22E** "Growing irradiated seeds" is optional extension work.
Omit this section.	**Worksheet B22D Patterns of inheritance** *Optional*	
		Introduction (pages 3–4) **Worksheet B22B2 DNA, genes and protein synthesis** *1 hour*
		B22.4 Cloning – science fiction or fact? **Worksheet B22B3 Making clones** (class + homework) *1 hour*
		Worksheet B22B4 Genetic engineering **Worksheet B22B5 Genetic issues** (class + homework) *1 hour*
Total: 2½ hours	*Total: 6½ hours*	*Total: 9 hours*

The pupils' book

The main object is to introduce the principles of genetics. Wherever possible, examples from human genetics are used as these usually seem most relevant. However, it is important to stress that patterns of inheritance are similar in all organisms. Otherwise, little could be learned from human genetics alone.

B22.1 Alike or not alike?

The chapter opens by picking up a theme that appeared in Chapter **B**20, that of the natural variation in characteristics found in organisms. This should encourage discussion about the causes of variation, so that from the beginning pupils realize the importance of interaction between heredity and environment.

Answers to selected questions

4 and **5** Height remains much the same; the average difference in head length is slightly greater in twins brought up together but this is probably not significant. Average differences in mass are greater and appear to be influenced by the environment. However, some recent work suggests that mass, too, may be genetically determined to a greater extent than is generally accepted. (The average differences in total height and head length are about 1% for both separated and unseparated twins. Since body mass depends on the cube of the linear dimensions, an average difference in body mass of 3% would be predicted, which is what is found in twins brought up together. The mass difference for separated twins is more than twice this, suggesting that environmental factors may be more important in determining body mass.)

B22.2 Environment or heredity?

This section introduces the idea of "nature and nurture", and can be completed alongside Worksheets **B**22A and **B**22B, in which pupils investigate variation in seeds and discontinuous and continuous variation.

The biology of the passage entitled "Why do people look like their parents?" is straightforward but it is a sensible precaution to find out in advance if there are any adopted children in the class. If so, it may be helpful to qualify the word "parent". For example, there are the "natural parents" who provide the sperm and the egg, and "real parents" who provide love, home and family; the two may not always be the same.

A thoughtful pupil might query why structures described as "long threads" actually appear in the photographs in the pupils' book as an "X" shape (the two chromatids and the centromere).

Teachers may think it appropriate to remind pupils of what they read about DNA in the Introduction to their Biology book (page 3).

Answer to selected question

7 A few of the characteristics listed are due only to heredity (*e.g.* blood groups), but most are strongly influenced by environment as well. There are links here with section **B**22.9 "Are you just your genes?". Discussion might need careful handling if there is teenage antagonism towards parents, school and the local environment.

B22.3 Halving and doubling

This section introduces the idea that all human cells have the same number of chromosomes except for the gametes, which each have half of the total.

The individual "stages" of mitosis and meiosis are not dealt with in this course, though pupils should be aware of the importance of the nucleus to the functioning of the cell.

In this chapter, the importance of a constant number of chromosomes and accurately matching pairs is mentioned. The sterility of interspecific crosses (such as the mule) can be explained simply by saying that because the two sets of chromosomes do not match up properly, the single chromosomes cannot be shared out evenly to make eggs or sperms.

B22.4 Cloning – science fiction or fact?

Since cloning produces genetically identical offspring, this section will allow pupils to contrast it with the production of variable offspring provided by the sexual method. It will also introduce them to tissue culture, an application of the principles of cloning which is becoming more and more important commercially.

It may be appropriate at this point to teach the pupils to distinguish between the terms "gene" and "allele". These terms are not defined until section **B**22.6, although the term allele is introduced here, in passing.

The difficulties of cloning animals are stressed.

Answers to selected questions

9 There are various examples: bulbs, corms, runners, layering, grafting, cuttings (sugar cane) and stem tubers (potato) are some of them. To many pupils it may be necessary to explain that a "seed potato" is not a seed at all. This question should reinforce the work on asexual reproduction in Chapter **B**19.

11 Cloning is quicker than seed production.

B22.5 Boy or girl?

This section shows how the difference in the chromosomes of the "23rd pair" determines the sex of a human being. These are the sex chromosomes. The female has XX and the male XY.

B22.6 Patterns of inheritance

All alleles are genes, but not all genes are alleles, since alleles are alternative forms of a particular gene. At GCSE level, where only monohybrid crosses are involved, the term allele can be used without any real confusion, since we only ever refer to a single **gene**. The words homozygote and heterozygote are used in the pupils' book text, but not genome. Genotype (see also Worksheet **B**22C) and phenotype are defined. Genetics is notorious for needing, even at elementary level, a whole new vocabulary in order to express ideas easily. Too many new words are daunting, but once the "language" has been learned pupils often enjoy being able to sound knowledgeable.

It is not envisaged that all teachers will use all of the material in this section with all of their classes. Enough should be done to give the pupils an understanding of how the offspring of a cross can be predicted by knowing the alleles of the parents. It may be helpful to do Worksheets **B**22C, in which pupils use coloured beads as models in breeding investigations, and **B**22D, in which they examine the pattern of inheritance in seedlings.

Teachers will probably find that the material which is most readily understood is the family tree of hair colour (figure 22.15 in the pupils' book), which is deliberately simplified to consider only red and brown hair.

Most classes will contain at least one pupil with a family tree including red hair. If the pupil is willing, this may more effectively illustrate patterns of inheritance than those in the text.

Any work on pupils' own family trees needs to be approached with caution and must always be a voluntary exercise. It is helpful to have a few family trees for the use of pupils who do not have one of their own. Pupils may not know very much about their own families, or may be unwilling to expose private family matters. Also, there may well be adoptions and illegitimacies unknown to the pupils themselves, which they might unwittingly make public. Any oddities which seem to point in this direction can usually be explained away by saying that inheritance patterns are really more complicated than those used in class. It is as well to be aware of possible pitfalls beforehand.

The sections on blood groups and red-green colour blindness (strictly, colour **deficiency**) are probably only appropriate for those who can grasp the patterns and probabilities fairly quickly. Some pupils could become confused between inheritance patterns and the antigen–antibody reactions in blood transfusions. Those who can cope will probably enjoy the challenge of working out possible combinations of the three alleles of the ABO blood groups. Alleles A and B show co-dominance, and O is recessive to both A and B.

Answers to selected questions

19 Two, one allele from each parent.

20 Each sister has one allele for brown hair, and may or may not carry a recessive allele for red hair.

21 The boy must have inherited the allele from his mother's mother (= maternal grandmother).

22 Each of the boy's parents carries a hidden recessive allele for red hair.

23 You might expect some of the father's relations to have red hair, since a number of them must carry the hidden recessive.

In this particular family, only one of the boy's great-great-uncles on his father's side is known to have had red hair. This illustrates clearly how a recessive character can remain hidden for many generations, rather than just "skip a generation" as is often the case.

24 This is the familiar "back cross to recessive parent".

Parents	Tt	×	tt
Gametes	T *or* t		t *or* t

There will be equal numbers of both tall and dwarf plants.

25 This cross is in effect the same as the original cross; the offspring are all tall. As a general point it should be stressed that it is only when there are large numbers of offspring that one can be sure that the dominant parent does not carry the hidden recessive gene. This is particularly relevant when dealing with animals that have small litters.

26 For a recessive character to show, there must be two recessive alleles present. If the alleles are similar then the organism is homozygous for that particular character.

27 Half of the F2 plants will be heterozygous.

28 Since O is recessive to both the alleles A and B, the person must carry the alleles OO.

29 One parent must belong to blood group A and one to group B. In addition, each must carry a hidden O allele: *i.e.* the parents must be AO and BO.

30 The allele for red–green colour blindness is recessive. It will show when the allele is present on both of the X chromosomes of the female. This is unlikely to happen since it would usually require a colour blind male to mate with a carrier female. Only one allele for colour blindness is needed for it to show in a mate, and it can be produced when a carrier female with normal colour vision mates with a normal male.

31 Margaret's daughters must all carry an allele for colour blindness, inherited from their father. They have normal sight as they have all inherited an allele for normal sight from their mother.

32 James inherits his normal sight from his mother. He does not inherit an X chromosome from his father.

33 Richard and Jonathan both inherit their colour blindness from their mothers.

34 Yes; whether or not she has inherited the allele for colour blindness depends on which of the two X chromosomes happened to be in the egg. She cannot know unless she has children. If she carries the recessive allele she has an even chance of producing a colour blind son.

B22.7 Five toes, or maybe six?

Most mutations do not improve the fitness of an organism. At best they may have neglible effects, but many will be harmful. Recessive genes which are harmful may be tolerated by an organism, provided that the other allele functions normally. A few mutations may, however, improve the fitness of an organism, particularly in an unstable changing environment. The theory of evolution rests upon this premise.

If irradiated barley is grown, the effects of radiation on the percentages of germination and survival past the seedling stage are very obvious. Sometimes mutations such as lack of chlorophyll can be seen. Worksheet **B22E** illustrates this point graphically. If the remaining healthy plants are grown and compared with the same number of control plants there is little difference between them, and the dry mass of the irradiated plants may even be greater than that of the control. So some plants may escape with no harmful mutations, while others might even show some improvement. Much effort has been spent in trying to use mutations to improve the yield of crop plants. There have been some successes, but they are few and far between.

Answers to selected questions

36 The parents, the grandfathers and the mother or father of the grandfathers must have carried the recessive allele.

37 The albino children will inevitably hand on the allele if they themselves produce offspring. Any of their normal brothers and sisters and aunts and uncles might pass on the allele for albinism.

B22.8 Genetic counselling

The counselling of people who are known to carry harmful alleles is becoming more and more important in Britain. It is said that most of us carry at least one harmful recessive allele. Provided we do not marry someone with the same identical allele (and, provided a husband and wife are not related genetically, the chances of this are normally low), then there will be no problems. Some harmful alleles are found more often than others in the population, however, and occasionally two normal "carriers" marry. Genetic counselling can tell these parents what chance they have of producing a child unaffected by the disease.

Cystic fibrosis is given as an example because the gene is relatively common in the population of north-west Europe, affecting about one child in 2000.

If a gene frequency of 1 in 25 is assumed, then there is a 1 in 625 chance of carriers marrying. With a 1 in 4 chance of the recessive appearing, this would mean one affected child in every 2500 members of the population as a whole. As yet, affected individuals rarely live beyond young adulthood but diagnosis and treatment improve their chances of survival. Work on the identification of carriers (at St Mary's Hospital, London) is well advanced, and can at least mean that a mother of one child already affected need not have another. Useful literature on this condition may be obtained from the Cystic Fibrosis Research Trust, 5 Blyth Road, Bromley, Kent BR1 3AS (telephone 081–464 7211).

Answers to selected questions

38 Because of the sticky mucus resulting from cystic fibrosis, the cleaning mechanism of the lung does not work properly and food in the gut cannot be digested. Enteric-coated pancreatic enzymes are taken to help digestion, especially of fats.

40 There is a 1 in 4 chance that an affected child will be born.

41 3 in 4 children will be normal.

42 2 out of every 3 normal children will be carriers.

43 There is a 1 in 4 chance that the gene will not be passed on at all.

45 1 in 2 children will have 6 fingers if the person is heterozygous.

46 No – it does not have the (dominant) allele for six fingers; if it did, it would have six fingers itself, not five.

B22.9 Are you just your genes?

It is important not to leave a study of genetics with a fatalistic attitude to life, particularly when it is realized that genes influence so many of our personal characteristics. Genes and the environment interact when producing a characteristic. You could (in theory, anyway) have a set of genes that could predispose you to become a brilliant pianist. But if you never sat at a piano you would never find this out! This is the message of this final section.

Activities

Worksheet B22A Is variation inherited or due to the environment?

REQUIREMENTS

Each group of pupils will need:
White or yellow (chlorophyll-deficient) strains of tobacco, tomato or barley seeds
Compost, damp
Petri dish with circle of moist filter paper in base, if tobacco seeds are being used
Pots, small (1 for each seed type)

The procedure is detailed on the worksheet.

Worksheet B22B Two kinds of variation

REQUIREMENTS

Each group of pupils will need:
Graph paper
Pencils
Rulers
Stopclock
Tape measure

Access to:
A variety of specimens showing measurable variation for obvious characteristics, for example:
    stick insects
    woodlice
    pods 4, of peas or beans
    branch of pine needles
    holly leaves
    bluebell flower spike
Sensitive weighing balance

The procedure is detailed on the worksheet.
    The examples given in the worksheet are only a few of those that could be selected. Teachers could choose their own examples, avoiding overlap with Worksheet B22A.

Worksheet B22B1 How cells divide

REQUIREMENTS

Each group of pupils will need:
Piece of cloth or rough surface about $^1/_2$ m $\times$ 1 m (*e.g.* dishcloth)
String
8 pieces of coloured wool, 18–20 cm in length (two pieces of each of four different colours)
Cotton thread
Scissors
Blu-Tack or Plasticine
2 small rings (to pull the threads through)
Sticky tape

Pupils are introduced to the process of mitosis by making a model. It is not intended to refer to individual "stages" in the mitotic process; the whole should be seen rather as a series of events merging into each other.

Background information
The complete replication of DNA occurs in the S (synthesis) phase, and two chromatids are formed by replication of each chromosome; the word chromatid has not been mentioned in the worksheet since it will only serve to confuse. In the next phase (the G2 phase), contractile proteins accumulate in preparation for chromosome separation, but little is known about this phase. The main stages of mitosis, in which definite microscopic changes in the cell can be observed, follow on from the S and G2 phases, and the chromosomes are gradually pulled towards the centrioles. The centrioles themselves have not been mentioned either, since we are more concerned with the replication of genetic material than with the details of the process. The division phase of the cell itself is different in animals and plants: in animals, the cytoplasm between the nuclei constricts and two cells are formed, but in plants a new cell wall and membrane are formed across the middle of the original cell where the chromosomes lined up.

The idea of genes as sections of the DNA in a chromosome which are responsible for particular characteristics can then be developed. It is sometimes the case, however, that a combination of several genes is responsible for a given characteristic. The genes along a DNA strand are not always different and sometimes multiple copies of DNA sequences occur. The base sequences not only code for particular proteins via messenger RNA, but there are many genes which code for transfer RNA.

Answers to worksheet questions
1 The chromosomes separate from their partners and move towards the poles of the cell.

2 The chromosomes have been replicated exactly, and each half of the cell contains an exact copy of each chromosome because of the way the chromosomes have separated.

Worksheet B22B2 DNA, genes and protein synthesis

REQUIREMENTS

Each group of pupils will need:
Disposable copy of side 3 of Worksheet **B**22B1
Scissors
Sticky tape

The ideas of genes as particular sequences of bases in DNA and the synthesis of proteins are introduced by a series of "cut out" models. The essence of this activity is not for the pupils to remember the details but to appreciate that:

- The genetic code represented by the sequence of bases along the DNA can be translated into a message which is read during protein synthesis, and
- Particular amino acids are coded by groups of three bases (triplets).

As an extension exercise, pupils could be asked to suggest how DNA replicates itself in terms of the nucleotide pairing.

Background information

All the stages mentioned in the worksheet are catalysed by enzymes. For example, an enzyme catalyses the unwinding of DNA, another enzyme catalyses the condensation reactions which make the mRNA, and other enzymes are responsible for binding the tRNA to the ribosomes. RNA stands for ribonucleic acid; it differs from DNA in having the base uracil in place of thymine, and having a different sugar from that in DNA. The code itself is non-overlapping; sections of the same gene are not used for more than one type of protein. The bases on the mRNA are complementary to those on the DNA. Proteins are synthesized on the ribosomes, where the mRNA and tRNA carrying the amino acids come close to each other and form specific bonds between the triplets on the mRNA and the anticodon bases on the tRNA. The codons on the mRNA are specific for particular amino acids, but many amino acids have more than one code; for example, the amino acid glycine can be coded for by GGG, GGA etc. The example on the worksheet gives GGG as the messenger code for glycine, and this corresponds to the DNA code CCC. The amino acids are attached to the tRNA earlier in the process. As the ribosomes and mRNA move over each other, the tRNAs are brought to the mRNA one by one and the protein chain is gradually built up, as shown diagrammatically below.

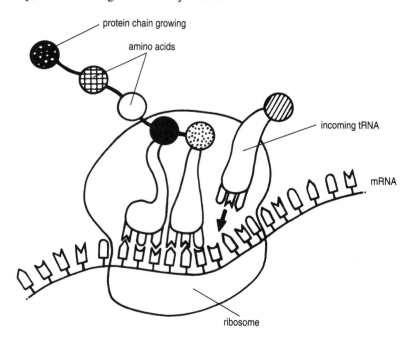

Diagrammatic representation of protein synthesis.

Answers to worksheet questions

1 A reaction in which pairs of molecules join together with the elimination of a small molecule (in this case, water).

2 The weak bonds between the bases are those which are the most likely to break.

3 Because they have a different order of bases.

Worksheet B22B3 Making clones

REQUIRMENTS

Each pupil will need:
Eye protection
Plastic gloves

Each group of pupils will need:
2 small margarine tubs
Small potato with well-developed "eyes"
Root of dandelion or dock plant
Knife

Access to:
Soil/sand mixture or potting compost
Darkened room or dark cupboard
Examples of plants showing buds developing
   into new plants, *e.g.* leeks, onions, crocus
   corms, etc.

The teacher will need:
Photographs of cloned animals (clawed toads)

Safety note:
The use of knives demands special vigilance by the teacher, and care should be taken to ensure the correct disposal of waste.

Pupils are introduced to cloning through simple observations and investigations on vegetative reproduction. Pupils should set up the activity with potatoes and dandelion roots some time in advance since the results will not be evident for two or three weeks.

Tissue cultures show that single cells of carrot phloem can grow into whole new carrot plants when kept in suitable containers and supplied with the proper nutrients and plant growth substances such as IAA. For continued cell division, cytokinins are also required. Modern culture techniques allow the continuous culturing of cells in a liquid medium in the same vessel. Unless a mutation occurs, cloned organisms have an identical genetic make-up. In the cloning of the African clawed toad, the eggs were grown to the blastocyst stage and the hollow ball of cells dissociated to form a number of genetically identical cells.

Cloning has several advantages; for example, if crops ripen uniformly, it makes harvesting easier. Cloned cells also facilitate an easier study of the actions of drugs and hormones on particular cell types. Teachers could discuss the ethical problems involved with cloning animals here or discuss it in relation to genetic engineering in Worksheet **B22B4**.

The nature of the immune system should be revised with pupils before discussing the use of monoclonal antibodies: pupils should be aware of how antibodies work in simple terms. An antigen (or imunogen) is a large molecule which is foreign to the body and which stimulates antibody formation. Small "foreign" molecules do not stimulate antibody formation unless they are attached to a larger molecule. The combining sites of antibodies are rather like the active sites of enzymes in that they are specific for particular antigens (although the specificity is not always absolute). The diverse antibody complement in the serum is the result of many different antibody-producing cells, not just one cell. Of the antibodies studied, each seems to consist of a number of long and short peptide chains, with the shorter chains having one of two possible structures. Immunoglobin G has a Y-shaped structure with a sort of hinge that enables two antigen-binding sites on the antibody to adjust their positions so that they combine with particular groups on the antigen.

Monoclonal antibodies are produced after lymphocytes have been fused with tumour cells. These "hybrid" cells are used because lymphocytes die rapidly outside the body whereas tumour cells can be readily cultured under *in vitro* conditions. The hybrid cells are then cloned under controlled conditions in order to produce quantities of one particular type of antibody. Specific drugs attached to monoclonal antibodies can be used to deliver drugs to specific proteins on the surface of a diseased cell. People suffering from leukaemia have cancerous bone marrow cells and these cells may be killed by the poison ricin. By attaching ricin to antibodies derived from cloned cells, the poison may be delivered to the cancer cells without harming the normal bone marrow cells. Monoclonal antibodies have also been used in concentrating Factor VIII for treating haemophiliacs and for purifying specific proteins from mixtures.

Answer to worksheet question

1 Bacteria which cause tuberculosis have antigens which are not the correct shape to join with the antibodies made in response to the measles virus.

Worksheet B22B4 Genetic engineering

REQUIREMENTS

Each group of pupils may need:
Wool, in two different colours; about 40 cm of each colour
Scissors
Sticky tape

The principles of genetic engineering are introduced by reference to insulin production. The process of excision and joining of sections of DNA may be modelled by making "wool genes" and cutting and inserting genes at the relevant place. Restriction endonuclease enzymes cleave the DNA, and different types of enzyme cut the DNA at specific base sequences. Plasmids are small sections of DNA which have independent existence in the cytoplasm and are not part of the ordinary DNA of the cell. They are found in many organisms and the cell can normally survive without them. To date, most genetically engineered proteins have used either plasmids or viruses to convey the "foreign" gene, not the ordinary DNA of the cell.

In the manufacture of genetically engineered insulin ("humulin"), only a small proportion of the bacterial cells are successfully "infected" with the changed DNA. A gene with antibiotic resistance is used as a "marker" to recognize the bacteria which have been successfully infected. Such bacteria containing the insulin gene may be identified by growing the bacteria on a medium containing the antibiotic: only those with antibiotic resistance will survive. Other proteins which have been genetically engineered include human growth hormone and vaccines for hepatitis B and foot and mouth disease. In 1992 genetically engineered Factor VIII was first used in the United Kingdom to treat a haemophiliac patient undergoing surgery. Such genetically engineered blood products are free from viruses such as HIV and hepatitis.

Answers to worksheet questions

1 Pupils should refer to page 149 of the Biology pupils' book.

2 The bonds between the "cut" ends of the DNA are formed using specific enzymes.

3 The genetically engineered human insulin overcomes problems of adverse reactions which might occur with the hormone extracted from natural sources.

4 The culturing of micro-organisms is easier to control and there are fewer problems with the quality of the extracted material and continued supply of material.

5 A temperature of 35–40 °C, adequate nutrients and sufficient oxygen for respiration (if the bacterium is aerobic).

6 The initial research and setting up of the industrial plant is expensive. Hygiene factors are extremely important and procedures to avoid contamination are necessary.

7 White cells are collected and the gene for interferon is isolated using "cutting" (excision) enzymes. The rest of the process follows that shown for insulin.

Worksheet B22B5 Genetic issues

Genetic engineering has many uses but some people are worried that problems may arise in the future. There are worries that slight differences which may sometimes occur between the genetically engineered and the natural product could have adverse affects on the human body. Foods which are processed using genetically engineered materials are now becoming available: several cheeses in various supermarkets contain the enzyme chymosin, which has been genetically engineered using a fungus. There are also worries that genetic engineering may lead to a new generation of "superbugs", which are resistant to antibiotics or may cause disease.

Recent advances in the diagnosis of genetic defects have opened up the possibility of eliminating hereditary diseases by genetic engineering. Genetic counselling is the general means of informing couples with a family history of genetic problems about the risk that their child will be born with, or develop, a genetic disorder. The ability of scientists to culture embryos may make it possible in the future to create organisms with certain characteristics by modifying the genetic structure of the DNA in the embryo. The "mapping" of the genes of the human chromosomes is well advanced and the genes responsible for a number of genetic diseases have been pinpointed. The possibility of correcting inherited genetic disorders poses a number of ethical and moral problems, especially regarding the status of the embryo. Although such research may in the future help to alleviate human suffering and handicap, there is a considerable body of opinion that it is morally wrong to interfere with the natural processes of the body and that the embryo should be accorded the same rights as a child or adult. The Warnock Report recommended that no human embryo should be grown for more than 14 days outside the uterus and also addressed such issues as the artificial creation of human beings with certain characteristics, *e.g.* high intelligence (researchers have suggested that by 2005 all the thousands of genes for human intelligence may have been mapped). The question of who will be the recipients of genetically engineered genes may also be a problem, because the process will be very expensive.

In vitro fertilization to produce "test-tube babies" poses several ethical problems. The "spare" embryos may be used for research into diseases and the possibility of cloning such embryos has already been hinted at. The prediction of the sex (or other characteristics) of embryos cultured *in vitro* may lead to abuse of the process, for instance parents demanding children of a particular sex or with certain characteristics. Embryo implantation has been used in livestock production. Fertility drugs may be given to pedigree cattle to stimulate the ovaries to produce a large number of eggs. The eggs are then fertilized *in vitro* by the semen from a pedigree bull and implanted in the womb of a non-pedigree cow. The calves produced will then show the characteristics of the pedigree.

The teaching notes for Worksheet **B21A1** give further information about fertility hormones.

Answers to worksheet questions

1 The virus might have harmful effects on the cells of the body.

2 The gene would have to be placed in the DNA of a fertilized egg cell. All the cells in the body are derived from this and thus contain the same genetic information.

3 Resistance to disease, increased yields due to increases in growth rates, tolerance to extremes of environment, etc.

4 Science cannot provide an answer to this question. Some people believe that the father and mother have a right to decide whether to terminate the pregnancy at an early stage because it may lead to suffering. Others believe that every foetus is a separate human being and has a right to live even though it may have a genetic disease. The possibility of genetic disease being passed on to the general population might also be considered.

5 Some of these issues are discussed in the notes above.

6 Pupils should respect the different points of view on these issues. There is a balance between the desire of the individual couples to have a child and the moral and ethical issues involved in bringing forth life by an artificial extension of natural processes. The issues relate not only to the *in vitro* fertilization but also to the use of hormones to promote fertility. Pupils should be aware that those who believe that a new life begins at conception will consider it unethical to destroy or experiment upon any "spare" embryos from *in vitro* fertilization.

7 It is possible for a woman with some kind of uterine damage to allow another volunteer woman to carry her fertilized egg for her. Surrogate motherhood not only poses ethical and moral problems but also raises the possibility of the surrogate mother bonding with the baby.

Worksheet B22C Breeding with beads

REQUIREMENTS

Each group of pupils will need:
Beads, plastic "poppet", in 2 contrasting colours; 200 of each colour
Beakers for the beads, 3
Marker pen or chalk

The procedure is detailed on the worksheet.

This simulation exercise works well, provided that the pupils fully appreciate what the beads and the beakers symbolize. It is important that the concepts of genes and alleles are explained carefully, since this is a fertile area for confusion.

Provided that the number of zygotes "made" is small compared with the number of beads in the containers it does not matter whether the beads are retained or returned after being taken out.

Worksheet B22D Patterns of inheritance

REQUIREMENTS

Each group of pupils will need:

Tomato seeds: parents and F1 generation of crosses involving variation in stem colour and leaf shape caused by single major genes	Sprayer, for watering compost
	Labels
	Seed tray
Compost, damp	Top of plastic or glass, for seed tray
Block of wood, to press compost down	Thermometer

The procedure is detailed on the worksheet.

Biological suppliers produce material that illustrates genetic variation, although it is expensive. This practical might make a suitable demonstration, particularly as the differences observed ought to be immediately obvious. If possible, parents and F1 and F2 generations should be sown. This experiment could be combined with Worksheet **B**22A.

Worksheet B22E Growing irradiated seeds

REQUIREMENTS

Each group of pupils will need:

Seeds, irradiated at several different doses	Distilled water
Compost, damp	Ruler
Filter paper for each dish	Seed tray
Petri dishes (one for each radiation dosage)	Water, distilled

The procedure is detailed on the worksheet. This practical would also be suitable as a demonstration.

Demonstration experiments   Worksheets **B22D** and **B22E** are suitable for demonstration purposes.

Further information   Cohen, N. *Discovering genetics* Longman, 1979.

Gonick, L. and Wheelis, M. *The cartoon guide to genetics* Barnes & Noble Books, 1983.

Science and Technology in Society
Unit 1202 "Mapping the human genome" is relevant to Worksheet **B22B5**.

Supplementary material
Publications of the Cystic Fibrosis Research Trust, Department PD130, Alexandra House, 5 Blyth Road, Bromley, Kent BR1 3RS (081-464 7211).

Chapter B23 Changing with time

The syllabus section

Context

The theory of evolution as proposed by Darwin and Wallace is presented historically. The operation of natural selection on gene frequencies in populations can be considered with a number of examples (*e.g.* sickle cell anaemia and antibiotic resistance). The importance of the fossil record in providing evidence for the evolution of different species is considered. The evolution of *Homo* from ape-like ancestors is examined critically.

Knowledge and understanding

Syllabus statements	PoS	SoA
Know the four observations that led to the theory of evolution.	2(ii)6	2.9(c)
Understand how natural selection can operate in populations.	2(ii)6	2.9(c)
Appreciate that the natural variation that exists between organisms has arisen through mutations.	2(ii)6	2.9(c)
Understand that environmentally-induced variation cannot be passed on to the next generation through genes.	2(ii)6	2.9(c)

Opportunities for co-ordination

C4, **C13** and **E2** link with fossils and the geological timescale.

Routes and times

Basic	Central	Further
Omit Chapter **B23** at Basic level.	Omit Chapter **B23** at Central level.	

B23.1 Unanswerable questions?
B23.2 How old is the Earth?
B23.3 What evidence is there of change?
All optional/homework

B23.4 What's Darwin got to do with it?
B23.5 The Darwin–Wallace theory of evolution
Worksheet B23A How many of each kind?
(optional)
1 hour

B23.9 The fossil record (optional)
Worksheet B23B1 Evidence for evolution
Worksheet B23C Comparing vertebrate limbs
(class + homework)
1 hour

B23.6 Are all offspring the same?
Worksheet B23C1 Artificial selection
1 hour

B23.7 How do new variations happen?
B23.8 Natural selection in action
Worksheet B23C2 Natural selection
Include factors limiting populations that account
for the uneven distribution of organisms.
1½ hours

Total: 4½ hours

The pupils' book

There are three parts to this chapter. The first deals in the main with the age of the Earth and when life began, and it develops the Darwin–Wallace theory of evolution by natural selection, using examples of the evidence on which it is based. The second part is much more relevant to everyday life in the present and shows how natural selection is happening all the time and is often influenced by humans. The last part introduces pupils to fossil evidence for evolution, emphasizing the way in which *Homo sapiens* has changed in a relatively short time.

B23.1 Unanswerable questions?

Neither scientific theories nor creation myths can ever **prove** how the universe began, nor how life developed, however much one may hope that one or other of them will. It is important to encourage pupils to look critically and objectively at scientific evidence and to keep an open mind. This is an area where strong (and often conflicting) religious beliefs may be encountered and must be respected. Science cannot hold all the answers to the questions which we may ask.

B23.2 How old is the Earth?

If pupils are to have any understanding of life history it is important to help them to understand the enormous length of geological time. As well as the clock face, a model with a scale of 1 mm for each year is quite useful. A time chart on this scale could be made as a long strip of graph paper stretching right round the laboratory, or along a school passage. Similarly, but with a change in scale to 1 mm = 1000 years, it would be possible to go right back to the creation of the Earth – this would come to 4 km, round and round the playing fields. There are opportunities for joint work with history and geography and Earth and Space Chapter **E2**, as well as the co-ordination with Chemistry Chapter **C4**.

Answers to selected questions
1, 2, 3 In the clock diagram in figure 23.2 in the pupils' book, bacteria are shown to have existed for about three-quarters of Earth history, but most other living things for only a quarter of the time (about 1200 million years).

4 The white cliffs of Dover are from the Cretaceous period. The distance involved in the journey back to this period (about 70 million years), would be 70 km.

5 The oldest rocks in Britain are about 3000 million years old and our journey would be 3000 km.

B23.3 What evidence is there of change?

Answer to selected question
6 In the past 2 million years, a number of the larger mammals found as fossil remains have become extinct.

B23.4 What's Darwin got to do with it?

Short biographies of Darwin and Wallace are included to give a historical and human background. So many accounts make the men look old and venerable, but they started off as young adventurers. Darwin's theory has had such a far-reaching effect on the way we think about evolution that it is difficult to imagine the way in which ordinary people thought in a pre-Darwinian world.

B23.5 The Darwin–Wallace theory of evolution

The evidence on which Darwin and Wallace based their theory is given here and illustrated by examples which should be relevant to pupils at all levels. The difficulties come in relating natural selection, which we can see happening today, to the evolution, not only of closely related species, but of very different forms of the same species.

The most important concept to get across to pupils is natural selection, for which there is plenty of evidence. This is summarized as four observations ("facts") upon which the theory is built. The theory is based on what has been happening in populations in recent times. It is an assumption (albeit a logical one) that these processes began a long time ago and led to the formation of the groups that we see today.

Fossil evidence shows that organisms in the past were both different from and similar to organisms which are alive today. This scientific evidence (and other evidence, based, for example, on adaptive radiation and geographical distribution) leads to theories about what may have happened in the past.

Even with the vast length of time that was available, evolution by a series of small changes alone might not have been possible. Modern theories such as that of punctuated equilibrium provide alternative explanations.

Practical work on the numbers of offspring produced by different organisms, based on Worksheet **B23A**, can be performed at this point.

Answer to selected question

7 Somewhere around a maximum of 400 eggs.

B23.6 Are all offspring the same?

Pupils should see that sexual reproduction results in organisms that show variation for characteristics. Variation is studied in populations of *Drosophila*. Ultimately (as the next section emphasizes), genetic variation arises from mutations. These occur in laboratory populations of *Drosophila*, but are less obvious in wild populations. The reasons for this are discussed.

Variation also occurs in human populations. Blood groups are an example of this. When doing work on blood groups it is important to make clear the difference between individuals and populations. With very few exceptions, a population will contain at least some individuals with each blood group.

It is important that pupils realize that only gene mutations can be inherited and that variation caused by the environment cannot be passed on to the next generation.

Answers to selected questions

8, 9 82 fruit flies have 38 bristles, which is the most common number occurring in 16% of the sample.

10 The range is from 30 to 48 bristles.

11 Any mutant form which – perhaps as a result of its wing shape – is less well able to fly will probably leave fewer descendants, since the ability to find food, find a mate and spread to new habitats will all be affected. Differences in colour and pattern might make the fly more or less visible to predators. In laboratory conditions new mutant forms will be easily recognized and can be maintained, but in the wild they may disappear.

12 The proportions of the different blood groups in gypsy populations make it seem probable that they came originally from India.

13 Blood group "O" is most common in the British Isles and is higher in Celtic groups than in the English.

B23.7 How do new variations happen?

This work is really a reinforcement of the section on mutations in Chapter **B22**. It is a useful opportunity to make sure that it has been properly understood. There are many examples of domesticated animals (such as pigeons and dogs) where mutant forms would have little chance of survival in the wild.

Because most populations remain stable the enormous potential of most organisms for reproduction is not really appreciated. Only when colonizing do organisms begin to realize this potential, and then only for a short time.

How does the environment affect organisms? This is the crucial question, for it is the environment, acting on populations which are competing for limited resources, that generates the pressure of natural selection that will lead to evolutionary change. This leads into the next section.

Answers to selected questions

16 With variegated plants, if only half the leaf area is green the plant has only half the normal amount of photosynthetic tissue and so would be at a disadvantage in competition with fully green plants in the wild. Competition for light and space is removed in cultivation. Overgrown and neglected gardens provide many examples of competition and of the survival of only the most successful individuals.

17 If all the seeds germinated at once there would be more competition and even fewer would survive. If conditions soon after the time of germination are unfavourable, all the seedlings will die. With dormancy and staggered germination, there is more chance of at least some offspring growing to maturity, however bad the conditions. In commercial packeted seed a tendency towards delayed germination is undesirable and this characteristic has largely been bred out of crop plants.

B23.8 Natural selection in action

Several examples of natural selection are given in this section; it can be completed with Worksheet **B23B** which pupils may find entertaining. Teachers should select from this section the examples that suit their needs, but should realize that their examples may be more complex than those that appear here.

Antibiotic resistance in bacteria is a timely, but rather chilling, example of natural selection that affects humans. There are now numerous examples of the development of resistant forms of bacteria. A useful point to make here is the importance of finishing the whole course of antibiotics, even if the person feels better and has apparently recovered, and never giving any doses of a medicine to someone for whom it has not been prescribed.

Answers to selected questions

22 There tend to be more yellow, banded snails in grassland habitats. Yellow snails are better camouflaged when the grass has grown in the spring. Brown and pink forms tend to predominate in woodland areas.

28 You would expect the number of S alleles in the populations where sickle cell anaemia occurs to decrease.

29 HbAA and HbSS.

30 Because only one of the alleles passes into an egg or a sperm when cells divide to form gametes, the parents could be any of the following: HbAA and HbSS; both HbAS; or one HbAA and the other HbAS; or one HbSS and the other HbAS.

31 The results in figure 23.22 of the pupils' book suggest that the presence of sickle cells prevents a person from being affected by malaria.

32a Natural selection removes the A allele because people with AA are susceptible to malaria and may die.
b Natural selection removes the S allele because people with SS have sickle cell anaemia and may die.

33 A and S are kept in the population because people who are AS are apparently immune to malaria and yet do not suffer from sickle cell anaemia.

34 The balance depends on the presence of malaria in an area, which means AS individuals tend to increase in proportion to AA or SS.

B23.9 The fossil record

Almost any fossil can provide the focus for a lesson on this topic – the object itself is much more stimulating than a photograph. For each example, it should be possible to estimate its age (give or take a few million years), the environment in which it lived and obvious similarities and differences between the fossil and its closest living relatives. Studying the past history of living things on our planet is a form of historical ecology. Pupils who have done work on ecology should have little difficulty in imagining the habitats in which the fossil animals or plants lived and how large scale environmental changes might have led to their extinction. However, it is important for them to realize that the reconstruction can only be as accurate as the information provided by the evidence, which is often scanty. Worksheet **B**23C allows pupils to think about the homology of the vertebrate limbs, which can supplement the inadequate evidence of the fossil record.

Dinosaurs never seem to lose their appeal and Carboniferous forests are probably familiar from work on fuels. Ammonite fossils are widespread and interesting because they are not like any present day molluscs. The horseshoe crab (*Limulus polyphemus*) is sometimes inaccurately referred to as a king crab, which is a different organism. Horseshoe crabs are not really crabs at all, but a form of marine arthropod with no close living relatives. The strong similarity between modern horseshoe crabs and their fossil ancestors may be due to an unusually stable environment and to the absence of competition from any organisms better able to survive.

The final passage on the evolution of humans can be completed with Worksheet **B**23D. The old misconception that "men are descended from monkeys" can be corrected here. The change in the hand, with the larger thumb set at a wider angle to the fingers, has made the precision grip possible. This would not be of much use without the ability to walk easily on two legs, which leaves the hands free, leading the way to the production of specialized tools.

The larger brain has made possible the development of those characteristics which we regard as specifically human.

Speech is possibly one of the most important human attributes, leading to the transmission of culture and tradition from one generation to the next. Humans have rites surrounding death and other events of their existence; they also have the capacity for rational thought and moral and aesthetic values.

At a more obvious and practical level the use of fire and the production of tools for future use (not just for the present moment) are specifically human characteristics.

While scientists agree that selection, natural and artificial, is taking place in species which are present in the world today there is still considerable debate about the processes by which species evolved, and whether or not a supernatural Being is the ultimate explanation. The consequences of human influence on the selection of organisms, for good or ill, is much more important than discussion about what else might or might not have happened in the past. With most groups it is probably better to spend more time on natural selection and less on evolution.

Activities

Worksheet B23A How many of each kind?

REQUIREMENTS

Each group of pupils will need:
Groundsel plant, or other example, with fruits and flowers
Mould on bread (possibly *Mucor*), in a sealed Petri dish
Hard herring roe and soft herring roe
Balance
Coverslip
Dish
Microscope
Microscope slide (with counting cell if possible)
Needle, mounted
Scissors

Notes:
The organisms suggested for practical work are easily obtainable, but many others are suitable. These include butterfly eggs on cabbages, snail eggs in ponds and many annual or biennial weeds and garden plants.

Pupils will be amazed to find the number of seeds in, for example, a tomato; they can then make an estimate of the number of fruits produced by one plant. This quantitative approach is an important aspect of biology and should be introduced whenever the opportunity arises. It is suggested that as many organisms as possible should be studied by different groups in the class.

The procedure is detailed on the worksheet. This section may be related to the work on human reproduction and contraception in Chapter **B**20.

Worksheet B23B Investigating the value of camouflage

REQUIREMENTS

Each group of pupils will need:
Clipboard, paper and pencil
Straws, 100 green and 100 red, cut to about
    10 cm lengths
Watch with seconds hand

Access to:
Patch of grass about 15 metres square
Patch of dirt or bare ground about 15 metres
    square

The procedure is detailed on the worksheet.

Worksheet B23B1 Evidence for evolution

REQUIREMENTS

Each pupil will need:
Disposable copy of side 3 of Worksheet **B**23B1
Scissors
Glue

Access to:
Plaster casts of evolutionary series of fossil sea urchins or ammonites (optional)

This worksheet should be done in tandem with Worksheet **B**23C "Comparing vertebrate limbs". Together, the worksheets consider the range of indirect evidence for evolution. The idea that mammals originated from a common ancestor which had reptilian features by a long series of small changes and the discovery of prehistoric forms of intermediate structure suggests links between the classes of vertebrates. The evidence, however, is scanty and there is little proof that any of the invertebrate phyla can be linked in this way.

Reasons for the paucity of fossil evidence could be discussed. Teachers may refer to the example of *Archaeopteryx*, which exhibits a mingling of reptilian and bird-like features (although it is closer to a reptile than to a bird). It is of evolutionary interest because it did not have pneumatic bones, as birds do, but did have feathers. The idea that flying birds were derived from such species is still the subject of much speculation. The idea that species or groups gradually evolve from each other (phyletic gradualism) was challenged by Niles Eldredge and Stephen Jay Gould in 1972. They suggested that species remain unchanged for millions of years and then go through a sudden series of abrupt changes. This theory of *punctuated equilibrium* might account for the paucity of fossil evidence for intermediate forms. The fossil record, however, does provide several examples of long-term evolutionary series showing gradual morphological change, for example fossil ammonites, sea urchins and trilobites. If casts of such series are available, teachers could use them to illustrate evolution.

Darwin's finches provide an example of the relaxation of selection pressure which may have enabled the better adapted birds to find alternative food sources. Of the thirteen species of Galapagos finch, some have stout beaks for eating seeds, others have beaks adapted for eating insects, one species has a beak resembling a woodpecker's, and another resembles a warbler. The woodpecker finch is able to drill holes in wood but has to use a cactus spine to dig out the insects because its tongue is too short. The relative isolation of the different islands in the Galapagos formed a barrier to interbreeding and allowed unique island races of finches to develop. From these emerged the different species alive today.

The geographical distribution of different groups of animals such as the lung-fish, which are found in places as widely separated as South America, West Africa and Australasia, but nowhere else, suggests that they were distributed differently in the distant geological past. It is held that migration and slow spreading of species from their area of origin, together with the movement of the continents, is evidence that certain groups of animals may be descendants of extinct species. The ancestral species had undergone evolutionary change in response to a changed environment, and isolated groups were free to evolve along different lines. Examples of parallel evolution are shown by various marsupial and placental mammals; for example, the bandicoot and marsupial mole found in Australia have parallels with the rabbit and mole found elsewhere, thus suggesting a common ancestry.

Embryological evidence for evolution rests on the perceived similarity in the developmental stages of a range of organisms. There are similarities between the larvae of annelids, molluscs and echinoderms, whilst every chordate has a similar early embryonic life in the way the cells divide and are rearranged into layers. Such evidence, however, is not always convincing. Analysis of the biochemical and genetic make-up of individual organisms provides further evidence for the relationship between species and suggests basic similarities between some groups.

Answers to worksheet questions

1 The dead remains of organisms fall to the bottom of seas and lakes, become incorporated in sediments and are preserved by mineralization.

2 The lowest layers are expected to contain the oldest fossils (assuming that no drastic Earth movements invert the layers), because the sediments are layered one on top of another in time sequence.

3 No; it is only if we can find several "intermediate" forms linking one class to another that we can be more certain that the classes originated in this way.

4 Pupils should comment on the reduction of digits 2, 4 and 5, the increases in length and thickness of specific bones in digit 3, and the formation of the hoof.

5 The foot of *Hyracotherium* was adapted to soft ground near streams by the spreading out of its digits to increase the surface area for support. *Equus* has thickened limbs for supporting its heavier body, and its broad hoof is suitable for running on firm ground.

6 They were guided from South America on the air currents coming from the south-east.

7 A rapid increase in the population of finches in the absence of predators would lead to competition for a limited amount of food.

8 Some finches developed characteristics (through natural variation or mutation) which were suited to an alternative food source, and were then no longer in competition with the "original" finch species.

Worksheet B23C Comparing vertebrate limbs

REQUIREMENTS

Each group of pupils will need:
Paper glue
Photocopy of the worksheet plan of vertebrate forelimbs, enlarged if possible (to make cutting-out easier)
Scissors
Table, arranged as in worksheet, but large enough to accommodate cut-out "bones"

The procedure is detailed on the worksheet. It is important that pupils appreciate that the original vertebrates developed by occupying a wide variety of niches. As they did so, the appearance of their limbs slowly changed as a result of natural selection over the course of many generations. Although the pattern of bones in the limbs has hardly altered, the final form of the limb has developed markedly.

Worksheet B23C1 Artificial selection

REQUIREMENTS

Each pupil will need:
Disposable copy of Worksheet **B23C1** (side 2)
Scissors
Glue or sticky tape

Pupils are introduced to the processes of artificial selection, inbreeding and outbreeding through a comparison of the characteristics of selected varieties. It is useful to start by revising natural variation in organisms. Once organisms with the desired inherited characteristics are identified, these organisms may be mated together in order to obtain not only greater numbers of offspring with the desired characteristics but also to intensify these characteristics. Selection by humans in the past may not always have been conscious: seed from crop plants may have been collected when the crop was harvested and this may have selected against late-germinating plants, for instance. The development of different breeds of cattle provides good examples of selection by humans for particular characteristics. Jersey cattle not only yield creamy milk but they mature quickly and are useful for improving native cattle in regions where heat tolerance is needed. The highland breed is very hardy, often being grazed in mountainous areas, but is slow to mature. There is some variation in Friesian (Holstein) cattle, the North American type being primarily bred for milk whereas the Dutch type is mainly used for meat. The Hereford is a hardy breed which matures early and adapts itself to a wide range of climates from near arctic conditions in Canada to the Australian outback. The Simmental is widely bred in Europe and, although used mainly for meat, it can produce high milk yields.

Continued inbreeding of animals and plants eventually reduces the diversity of the gene pool and can lead to loss of productivity and decrease resistance to disease. Outbreeding, which is especially useful for plants, involves crossing individuals from genetically distinct varieties or strains. The results from such crossings, which are called F1 hybrids, exhibit advantages such as increased fruit size and increased resistance to disease. Some commercial F1 hybrids do not exhibit a significant increase in yield but have the advantage of genetic consistency. Many commercial hybrids are single crosses but some plants, such as sweet corn hybrids, are often double crosses obtained by mating two single cross hybrids. Increased vigour results from mixing the genes so that the hybrid contains all the dominant alleles in heterozygote combinations whereas the parents may possess only some of the dominant alleles:

Parents' genotypes:	llMMnnOO × LLmmNNoo
Gametes:	lMnO × LmNo
F1 genotype (hybrid):	lLMmnNOo

Answers to worksheet questions
1 Bread wheat, because it has the characteristics required by humans, *i.e.* it has more seeds, and they are larger than those of the wild wheat.

2 Humans selected seed from the wild wheat with the best characteristics. By continued selection and breeding the modern wheat evolved.

3 The thicker stem is stronger and more resistant to the wind.

4 The Simmental has a large mass as well as being able to produce a considerable volume of milk.

5 The characteristic of hardiness, possessed by the highland cattle, may be passed on to other cattle by a suitable programme of breeding.

6 The hybrid exhibits a more vigorous shoot growth and a larger cob with more regular, closer-spaced, seeds.

Worksheet B23C2 Natural selection

The case of the peppered moth is used as an example of how the process of evolution might occur. Careful observation confirmed that predatory birds ate a higher proportion of the speckled (grey) form of the moth in industrial areas. If a mechanism similar to selective breeding is to bring about evolutionary change, the natural population must show inherited variations. These may be continuous or discontinuous, and this is an appropriate point to revise variation. Pupils should also appreciate that some variations in a species may have arisen through mutations, and that environmentally-induced variation cannot be passed on to the next generation through the genes.

The second part of the worksheet introduces the concept of species and how separate species may arise. Populations which are separated geographically for a long time may show considerable differences in their morphological or physiological characteristics, which may be related to climatic or other factors. Isolation must play some part in the formation of new species, since there must be some kind of barrier to prevent interbreeding. Geographical barriers may be provided by mountains, seas or deserts. Behavioural barriers may also reduce the possibility of interbreeding: the lesser black-backed gull and the herring gull can interbreed but they hardly ever do so because their nesting and mating habits are very different. Two populations living in the same area can also be kept isolated if they have different food sources or lay their eggs in different places. If the different groups arising from a single species are kept separate for long enough they may show variations which fit them better for the particular environment in which they find themselves and eventually develop into separate species which cannot interbreed.

Answers to worksheet questions

1 The soot emitted from the chimneys would blacken the tree trunks.

2 The left-hand diagram.

3 Dorset: speckled 12.5%, black 6.3%.
Birmingham: speckled 25%, black 53.2%.

4 The black form in Dorset, and the speckled form in Birmingham.

5 The moth is less preyed upon by birds in the area where it is better camouflaged.

6 The numbers of moths released in the two areas were not the same, so the figures are not strictly comparable.

Worksheet B23D Changes in humans

REQUIREMENTS

Each group of pupils will need:
Rulers

The procedure is detailed on the worksheet.

Further information

British Museum (Natural History) *Man's place in evolution* 1980.

British Museum (Natural History) *Origin of species* Cambridge University Press, 1981.

CHEMISTRY

Introduction to Chemistry

Topics and contexts

The Chemistry course is designed to introduce girls and boys to the everyday, industrial, and environmental importance of chemistry, while explaining sufficient theory to show them how scientific knowledge can help them to make sense of the world in which they live.

The content is presented in six topics. However, it can also be reviewed in terms of the following themes:

People and chemistry
Chemistry and the environment
Chemistry and living things
Industrial processes
Materials
Structure and bonding
Chemical change
Chemical analysis
Periodic Table.

The main interlinking ideas show how the properties of materials can be explained in terms of structure and bonding. The Chemistry course also includes material on geology (Topic **E2** in Earth and Space).

Differentiation

In most chapters of Nuffield Co-ordinated Sciences Chemistry the starting point is a practical activity. In general the suggested experiments and investigations are such that it is worthwhile for most pupils to tackle them. It is the way in which the results are analysed and interpreted which allows differentiated treatments.

Topic **C2**, for example, is devoted to the study of materials including glasses, ceramics, metals and polymers. After doing the practical work many pupils will be able to think about the relationship between the properties of these materials and the way they are used. A more theoretical treatment seeks an explanation of the properties of the materials in terms of structure and bonding.

There are several theoretical ideas which are only required of those aiming for higher GCSE levels. Most of these are boxed in the pupils' book so that the main text can be read without referring to them. Examples include the concept of amount of substance, the ionic explanation of precipitation reactions, and the descriptions of bonding in terms of electron transfer and electron sharing.

Differentiation has been allowed for in the worksheets too. For example, the worksheets for Chapter **C12** suggest a series of titration experiments to investigate antacids. Alternative methods of working out an answer from the results are given. The simpler method is based on a conversion scale. The more advanced method uses the equation for the reaction and the concept of amount of substance.

Worksheets

There are three types of Chemistry worksheets. Most of the worksheets are designed to help pupils tackle the experiments and learn practical skills.

Other worksheets are based on SATIS units (published by the Association for Science Education) intended to promote thought and discussion of issues arising from the impact of science and technology on society. We have used worksheets for some of these issues so that the topics chosen for discussion can be changed and be kept up to date and topical throughout the lifetime of the course.

The third category of worksheets has been included to help pupils to learn by studying text. These sheets are designed to promote active reading as suggested in *Reading for learning in the sciences* by Florence Davies and Terry Greene (Oliver and Boyd, 1984). This book is based on the premise that effective reading has to be an active process. It explains why pupils have difficulties with reading science textbooks, and suggests strategies for helping boys and girls to become more reflective as they read so that they will learn to study technical books.

The suggested reading activities are designed to help pupils master the various types of text found in science books. The activities are of two types. There are reconstruction activities which are essentially problem solving and have game-like characteristics. They make use of modified text. Examples of this type are Worksheets **C4D**, **C4F**, **C6C**, and **C13A**.

There are also analysis activities. These use straight text and are an introduction to study methods and note-taking. It is essential that the pupils should be able to mark a copy of the text by underlining or labelling selected words, sentences and paragraphs. Hence the need for worksheets to use alongside the main text. Examples of this type are: **C3D**, **C4B**, **C5D**, and **C17B**.

Topic C1   Raw materials

Chapter C1   The elements of chemistry

The syllabus section

Context

This section includes Chemistry topics likely to have been covered before Key stage 4.
A brief outline of the history of the discovery of the elements and a simple treatment of the
Periodic Table can be included. (See also sections **C17** and **C18**.)

Knowledge and understanding

	Tier	
B	C	F

Syllabus statements	PoS	SoA
Be able to distinguish between metallic and non-metallic elements, mixtures and compounds using simple chemical and physical properties.	3(i)1	3.6(a)
Be able to represent simple chemical reactions in terms of word equations.	3(iii)3	—
Be able to compare the physical and chemical properties of elements and know what is meant by a periodic pattern.	3(i)1 3(i)2	3.7(b)
Understand the meaning of the terms element, compound, atom and molecule, in terms of atoms, ions and molecules.	3(ii)2	3.7(e)
Be able to represent chemical reactions in terms of symbolic equations. These should be used as a way of describing and understanding a range of reactions.	3(iii)3	3.8(f)

Opportunities for co-ordination

The particulate nature of matter and kinetic theory are introduced in **P2**.

Routes and times

Basic	**Central**	**Further**
Select material suitable for revising the difference between metals and non-metals, atoms and molecules, etc. Omit word equations. *1½ hours*	**C1.1 What are raw materials made of?** Brief revision of atoms, molecules, elements, compounds, mixtures, etc. *1 hour*	Revision homework.
Omit this section.	**C1.2 When were the elements discovered?** *Optional*	Revision homework.
Omit. Revise word equations and do Worksheet **C**1A "Reacting molecules".	**C1.3 How do we write chemical equations?** Include pages 18 and 19. *1 hour*	Include further examples of equations. *³/₄ hour*
Total: 2½ hours	*Total: 2 hours*	*Total: ³/₄ hour*

The pupils' book

This chapter has been included mainly for reference and revision, so that the pupils have access to an account of the main ideas the, are meant to have gathered from their work in Key stage 3. The questions are available for use at any time for homework and revision during the two years of the course.

C1.1 What are raw materials made of?

There are no class experiments to find chemical formulae in this course. The policy is to allow pupils to have access to tables of data which give the formulae. So the Data section at the back of the Chemistry book, is used from the start. The questions in this chapter provide plenty of opportunities for the pupils to use the tables of data.

C1.2 When were the elements discovered?

We have decided that it is simpler to talk about **atomic mass** than **relative atomic mass**. Hence the decision to use atomic mass units (symbol u). This has the advantage that every physical quantity in the course is seen to have a number and a unit.

C1.3 How do we write chemical equations?

In this chapter the examples are all molecular. This complements the study of molecular compounds in Chapters **C2** and **C3**. The choice of symbols to represent giant structures in equations is not dealt with until Chapter **C5**.

This section includes one of a number of cartoons in which a girl and a boy are seen to be trying to work out the answer to a theoretical problem. This may appear artificial, but we believe that these cartoons can show pupils how they should try to work out answers to difficult questions. So the cartoons can be seen as a way of exposing the thinking needed to solve problems. We hope that teachers will work through other examples with their classes while studying later chapters in the course. Pupils may be helped by opportunities to work in groups to explore the use of symbols and equations.

Many pupils find it difficult to come to terms with symbol equations. The advantage of starting with molecular examples in Chapters **C2** and **C3** is that it allows pupils to use models to give a picture of what the equations mean.

Activity

Worksheet C1A Reacting molecules

REQUIREMENTS

Each group of pupils will need:
Copy of Worksheet **C1A**
Scissors

Access to:
Stapler

The idea of this flick book is to give pupils an animated picture of what happens during a reaction. This may help to counteract the static impression given by equations. The worksheet is also included as an example because we think that it is a useful exercise for pupils to try and make their own flick books. Pupils have to understand an idea thoroughly before they can make a flick book to illustrate it. Making flick books can be used as a homework activity. In addition to the examples suggested here, they might be asked to make flick books to show a solid melting, a liquid evaporating, or one gas diffusing into another.

Chapter **C2 Petrochemicals**

The syllabus section

Context

This section provides opportunities to explore the importance of the modern petrochemical industry and to describe some of the problems and challenges faced by people who work in the industry.

Knowledge and understanding

Syllabus statements	PoS	SoA
Know, in the context of a range of types of reaction, that the combustion of fuel releases energy and produces waste gas.	3(iii)1	3.4(c)
Know how to separate and purify the components of mixtures, using techniques such as distillation.	3(i)6	3.5(a)
Know that crude oil is a mixture of hydrocarbons.	3(i)5	—
Appreciate the ability of carbon atoms to join up in chains, branched chains and rings.	3(iii)1	—
Understand that the physical properties of a hydrocarbon depend on the size of its molecules.	3(iii)1	—
Appreciate some of the issues involved in the location of industry.	3(iii)8	—
Know that chemical changes transfer energy to and from the surroundings.	3(iii)6	3.6(e)
Understand how fractional distillation, cracking, polymerization and reforming are involved in the production of a range of useful chemicals from oil.	3(iii)9	3.8(e)
Know that materials can be converted into useful products through a range of chemical reactions, including thermal decomposition, addition and polymerization.	3(iii)1	3.8(e)
Be able to represent chemical reactions in terms of symbolic equations and to use graphical and molecular formulae.	3(iii)3	3.8(f)

The image beside the table shows the tiers **B C F**.

Opportunities for co-ordination

This section introduces the idea of thinking in terms of atoms and molecules, which links to photosynthesis in **B3**, digestion in **B5** and respiration in **B9**.

This section can touch on some of the civil engineering problems involved in the discovery and exploration of North Sea gas and so it might be useful to refer to some of the ideas about structures and forces in **P1**. Liquids and gases are also discussed in **P2**.

Routes and times

Basic	Central	Further
Omit Q6–8 and part D from Worksheet **C2A**. Omit Q7 and 8 from section **C2.2** but do Q9 using models. Omit graphical formulae. *1½ hours*	**C2.1 What are petrochemicals?** Omit Q1. **Worksheet C2A Making models of molecules: part 1** **C2.2 What are the rules for making molecules?** Omit Q9. *1¾ hours*	All questions in section **C2.2** are suitable.
Omit pages 27–32 and questions from section **C2.3**. Omit Q4–9 from Worksheet **C2B** and pages 32–35 from section **C2.4**. Replace with relevant videos. *1½ hours*	**C2.3 How can the molecules in oil be sorted out?** Omit Q10–17. **Worksheet C2B Cracking hydrocarbons** Omit Q10. **C2.4 How can molecules be broken into smaller pieces?** Omit Q18 and 19. *2 hours*	Q10–12 from section **C2.3** and Q10 from Worksheet **C2B** are suitable.
Do parts A, B and D from Worksheet **C2C** but omit Q1–5, 8 and 9. Omit section **C2.5**, apart from lower half of page 39. Replace with relevant video on polythene. *1¼ hours*	**Worksheet C2C Making models of molecules: part 2** **C2.5 How can ethene be used to build new molecules?** Omit Q25. *1½ hours*	Section **C2.6** "Why did the chickens stop laying eggs?" could be done for homework.
Total: 4¼ hours	*Total: 5¼ hours*	*Total: 5¼ hours*

The pupils' book

C2.1 What are petrochemicals?

Sections **C2.1** and **C2.3** are designed to give pupils an image of what happens in an oil refinery. Broadly the processes can be divided into three types:

- separation by fractional distillation
- conversion by cracking, reforming or polymerization
- purification by removing sulphur and arenes from fuels, and waxes from lubricants.

The focus in this chapter is on distillation, cracking and polymerization. The purification steps are dealt with in Chapter **C13**, which also includes more detail about the products of fractional distillation.

A film or video will help pupils to gain an idea of the scale of operations in the oil industry. Most of the major oil companies have produced suitable films for the purpose. Sources of films and videos are listed in the Appendix in this *Guide*.

Questions 2-6 revise the distinctions between elements, compounds and mixtures, and introduce some rather more complex molecules than those in Chapter **C1**.

C2.2 What are the rules for making molecules?

This section gives pupils an opportunity to use tables of data, and to note both that pure compounds have a particular boiling-point (under given conditions) and that there is a correlation between boiling-point and molecular size. The family name for the alkanes is introduced, but there is no need to use the term "homologous series".

Question 9 asks pupils to explore the possibility of isomerism, but a formal treatment of the concept is not required for examination purposes. This is one of many examples in the course where a topic is introduced as an opportunity for the pupils to exercise skills and processes. It should not to be taken to mean that knowledge of the idea will be assumed as an examination requirement.

This section is complemented by Worksheet **C2A**.

C2.3 How can the molecules in oil be sorted out?

Pupils are not expected to remember the details of this section. The idea is that they should have some impression of the scale of the industry and be aware of some of the problems involved.

Answers to selected questions
15a 500 tankers; **b** 1000 times a day.

16a To prevent corrosion.
b Near villages and towns for safety.
c Under roads and railways to protect the pipe.
d To make sure that it is not damaged by ploughing and other farming activities.
e To cut off part of the pipeline in case of accident.
f By checking that the flow past each point is the same.

C2.4 How can molecules be broken into smaller pieces?

This section shows that North Sea gas and oil are not just sources of fuel but are also the basis of the petrochemical industry in Britain.

This section points out the importance of people in industry. It also mentions some of the factors which determine the location of industry and the issues which have to be faced in relation to those who live nearby. These points may mean more to the pupils if they can see a film or video, about the petrochemical industry.

The problem at the end of the section (page 39) is a planning exercise. Some may come up with a workable solution with the help of table 7 in the Data section. If not they can be given Worksheet **C2B**. Attempting the planning exercise may help pupils to appreciate the design of the apparatus on the worksheet.

C2.5 How can ethene be used to build new molecules?

The terms *saturated* and *unsaturated* are introduced because they appear on household products and crop up in the debate about diet and health. (See Chapter **B6**.)

Ethene is shown to be able to add to other molecules and to itself, but the term addition reaction is **not** used. The model equations provide an opportunity for pupils to practise the use of symbols and to see why chemical equations balance.

Worksheet **C2C** complements sections **C2.4** and **C2.5**.

C2.6 Why did the chickens stop laying eggs?

A chemical plant does not run simply according to the simple chemical description of the process. This section is included to give pupils some impression of the challenging problems which can face those responsible for operating an industrial plant.

Activities

Worksheet C2A Making models of molecules: part 1

REQUIREMENTS

Each group of pupils will need:
Copy of Worksheet C2A (see note 1)
Set of ball-and-spring models (see note 2):
    4 black atoms, four hole
    4 red atoms, two hole
    10 white atoms, one hole
    4 long bonds
    10 short bonds

Access to:
Book of data or textbook giving the formulae
of alkanes

Notes:

1 The worksheet is designed for ball-and-spring/stick models and will have to be revised if alternative models are used.

2 Suitable molecular models are obtainable from Spiring Enterprises Ltd, Beke Hall, Billinghurst, W. Sussex RH14 9HF. The models are conveniently supplied in a plastic bag with a checklist on a card inside.

It is very important that pupils should have the opportunity to make their own models, here and elsewhere during the course. We think that it is well worth while buying enough models for a class of pupils working in groups.

The worksheet is largely self-explanatory, but some pupils will need help to see that double bonds are needed in oxygen, carbon dioxide and ethene molecules so that their formulae are consistent with the bonding rules. There are no detailed instructions on the worksheet to show pupils how much they are expected to write down. It is left to teachers to decide how much drawing and writing is appropriate.

Pupils who work rapidly can go on to the text and questions of section C2.2 in the Chemistry book.

Worksheet C2B Cracking hydrocarbons

REQUIREMENTS

Each group of pupils will need:
Copy of Worksheet C2B
Hard-glass test-tube
Glass rod
3 test-tubes with bungs, to collect gas
Delivery tube with bung to fit the hard-glass test-tube (see worksheet)
Bunsen valve to fit delivery tube (see note 1)
Trough, or large crystallizing dish (see note 2)
Stand, with boss and clamp
Burner and mat
Eye protection

Access to:
Mineral wool
Liquid paraffin, medicinal, in bottle with dropper; allow 5 ml per group
Broken chips of porcelain
Strips of copper gauze, 10 cm × 3 cm (optional)
Iron wool (optional)
Aqueous potassium manganate(VII) – OXYDIZING HARMFUL – 0.001 mol/L in bottle with dropper
Dilute sulphuric acid – CORROSIVE – in bottle with dropper

The teacher will need access to:
Aqueous bromine – HARMFUL – in bottle with dropper (see note 3)
Fume cupboard

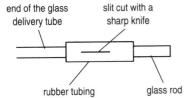

A Bunsen valve.

Notes:

1 The design of a Bunsen valve is shown on the left. It is made from glass rod and rubber tubing. Use a sharp blade to cut the slit in the rubber tube. This allows gas to escape but makes it difficult for water to suck back. Do not use old or perished rubber, as it may not be flexible enough.

2 Large plastic margarine tubs can be used as cheap troughs.

3 1,2-dibromoethane is dangerous, but very little (if any) will form if aqueous bromine is used for the test. The products should preferably be disposed of in a fume cupboard.

This practical exercise provides an opportunity for pupils to make observations and interpret them. Some skill is needed to carry out the experiment successfully. In experiments like this, the biggest problems are blocked apparatus (such as molten bungs) and suck back.

Pupils know that small molecules boil at a lower temperature than larger molecules, so the conversion of a liquid to a gas suggests that cracking has taken place. The reactions of the product with potassium manganate(VII) and aqueous bromine show that the product is more reactive than the oil which has been cracked.

Pupils who get on quickly can try the further investigations to compare alternative catalysts.

Worksheet C2C　Making models of molecules: part 2

REQUIREMENTS

Each group of pupils will need:
Copy of Worksheet **C**2C (see note 1)
Set of ball-and-spring models (see note 2):
  4 black atoms, four hole
  1 red atom, two hole
  2 green atoms, one hole
  8 white atoms, one hole
  4 long bonds
  8 short bonds

Notes:
1 The worksheet is designed for ball-and-spring/stick models and will have to be revised if alternative models are used.
2 Suitable molecular models are obtainable from Spiring Enterprises Ltd, Beke Hall, Billingshurst, W. Sussex RH14 9HF. The models are conveniently supplied in a plastic bag with a checklist on a card inside.

This follows on from Worksheet C2A. It is designed for use alongside sections C2.4 and C2.5. Pupils who work more rapidly can be asked to attempt the questions in those sections after they have finished the model-making.

Further information

Petrochemicals
The Education Service Departments of the main oil companies provide a variety of materials which can be used to complement this topic, including films/videos, worksheets, booklets and wallcharts. (See the Appendix for addresses.)

Science and Technology in Society
Unit 105 "The bigger the better" is a data analysis exercise about crackers; it covers economic aspects of the industry and illustrates the importance of ethene.

Unit 1002 "Quintonal: an industrial hazard" is a simulation exercise concerning industrial safety.

University of York Science Education Group
The unit *Transporting chemicals* in Salters' Chemistry includes a consideration of the issues involved in the location of the chemical industry. The hazard warnings used when chemicals are transported are described.

The Chemistry in Action series includes a unit called *Cracking the problem* which puts pupils in the position of a technician employed in a petrochemical plant. The problem is to discover the source of an unpleasant "gassy" smell which is annoying local residents.

Videos
"Gas separation at St Fergus" and "Teamwork on target" (both from Esso) and "Poly(ethene)" (ITV Chemistry in Action series) are useful here.

Chapter **C3 Chemicals from plants**

The syllabus section

Context

This section provides an introduction to elementary biochemistry, with particular reference to carbohydrates and proteins. It provides an opportunity to illustrate the wide variety of chemicals available from plants.

Knowledge and understanding

Syllabus statements	PoS	SoA
Know, through a range of types of chemical reactions, including fermentation and polymerization, that natural materials can be converted into new, useful products.	3(iii)1	3.4(b)
Know that sugars, starch and cellulose are carbohydrates and compounds of carbon, hydrogen and oxygen.	—	—
Know that protein molecules consist of long chains of amino acids, and that starch and cellulose are polymers of glucose.	—	—
Understand that large molecules can be separated from smaller ones by a selectively permeable membrane.	3(i)6	—
Appreciate that the bonding in carbohydrates and protein molecules is essentially the same as in simpler carbon components.	3(ii)2	3.8(d)

Opportunities for co-ordination

This section provides the chemical background needed for **B**3 to **B**6 and **B**8 to **B**10.

Routes and times

Basic	Central	Further
Slower groups should spend longer on Worksheet **C**3A and section **C**3.1. *3/4 hour*	**Worksheet C3A Plant products** **C**3.1 **What can we get from plants?** *1/2 hour*	Faster groups should spend less time on Worksheet **C**3A and section **C**3.1. *1/4 hour*
Omit Q14–17 from section **C**3.2.	**Worksheet C3B Investigating carbohydrate molecules** (side 1 only) **C**3.2 **What are carbohydrates?** (pages 48–53) Omit boxes 1 and 2. *1 hour*	Side 2 of Worksheet **C**3B is optional.
Omit Worksheet **C**3C.	**Worksheet C3C Models of carbohydrate molecules** (parts A and B) **Box 2 Experiment: Molecules big and small** *1 hour*	Part C of Worksheet **C**3C is also suitable. *1 1/4 hours*
Slower groups should spend longer on the problem in box 1. *1 1/2 hours*	**Box 1 Problem: Are all sugars equally sweet?** Sc1 assessment. *1 hour*	
Q25–27 are optional.	**C**3.3 **What are proteins?** *1/4 hour*	
Total: 4 1/2 hours	*Total: 3 3/4 hours*	*Total: 3 3/4 hours*

Monitoring the progress of Sc1

Investigating digestion

Pupils should investigate the effect of stomach acids on carbohydrates. This investigation may be carried out as part of Worksheet **C3B** "Investigating carbohydrate molecules" (side 2).

Sample criteria are given below for an assessment between levels 4 and 6.

Strand (i) Ask questions, predict and hypothesize, e.g.	Strand (ii) Observe, measure and manipulate variables, e.g.	Strand (iii) Interpret their results and evaluate scientific evidence, e.g.
4(a) Suggest that concentration matters, and suggest how rate may depend on concentration	**4(b)** Control temperature and type of carbohydrate and time how long it takes the carbohydrate to be broken down by two different concentrations	**4(c)** Conclude that a more concentrated solution of acid breaks down carbohydrate more quickly than a less concentrated solution
5(a) Suggest that a more concentrated acid will break down carbohydrate more quickly than a less concentrated acid because there is more acid present	**5(b)** Time how long it takes two different carbohydrates to be broken down over a meaningful range of concentrations	**5(c)** As above, but qualifying the result
6(a) Suggest that the higher the concentration of acid, the faster the rate of reaction because there is more acid present	**6(b)** Time how long it takes a range of different carbohydrates to be broken down over a meaningful range of temperatures and concentrations	**6(c)** Conclude that increasing the concentration of acid reduces the time for the carbohydrates to be broken down because there are more acid particles present

The pupils' book

C3.1 What can we get from plants?

This section is designed to emphasize the extent to which we depend on plants. The pictures speak for themselves. The pupils might be asked to make a collection of pictures from magazines and other sources, and to produce their own illustrated introduction to this topic in their notes.

Worksheet **C3A** is designed to be used in conjunction with this section.

C3.2 What are carbohydrates?

This can be developed in parallel with the introduction to photosynthesis in Chapter **B3**. There are only three elements in carbohydrates, but the molecules are much more complex than the hydrocarbons studied in Chapter **C2**. Pupils will need time to relate to the models and representations of molecules used in this chapter; hence the importance of Worksheet **C3C**.

The problem in box 1 "Are all sugars equally sweet?" could be used simply as a planning exercise. However, it raises problems of experimental design which will become much more apparent if the pupils are able to try out their plans. (See under Activities.)

The experiment in box 2 on page 52 is designed to show pupils that they can use their knowledge of carbohydrates to interpret results. It is worth trying this as a group activity in class. The ideas raised will be important in Biology Chapter **B5** where pupils investigate digestion. It may help to set up the experiment as a demonstration (see under Activities). For those pupils who may go on to A-level, this experiment provides a possible introduction to the concept of dynamic equilibrium. There is no need to mention the term at this stage, but discussion of the experiment can lead to the idea that the smaller molecules continue to move freely in and out of the tubing in both directions until the concentrations are the same inside and outside the tube. Thereafter the rates of movement into and out of the tube are the same and there is no apparent change.

Questions 6–9 revise photosynthesis, first introduced in Chapter **B**3.

Questions 10–15 can be answered in conjunction-with Worksheet **C**3C. The method of polymerizing glucose to make starch is different from that used to make poly(ethene). The difference is noted but the terms "condensation polymerization" and "addition polymerization" are not used here.

C3.3 What are proteins?

In Biology, the pupils need to know that proteins consist of long chains of amino acids. It also helps if they know that the five main elements in amino acids are carbon, hydrogen, and oxygen, together with nitrogen and sulphur.

The questions in this section reinforce the point that biological molecules can be understood in the same terms as simpler molecules.

C3.4 How does all this clever chemistry happen in living things?

It may seem odd to mention the process of inversion and not to use the more general and chemically useful word "hydrolysis". It is no part of this course to explain inversion in terms of the effect of sugar solutions on polarized light. Here the word is just a name for the reaction which splits sucrose into glucose and fructose.

Worksheet **C**3D is one of a number which have been designed to help pupils to study the text. This type of worksheet is discussed in the Introduction to Chemistry in this *Guide*. The worksheets can be reused if they are protected by plastic covers or envelopes. The marking of the text can then be done with washable pens and later removed. However, where possible the pupils should be allowed to keep the sheets they have worked on as models to remind them of how they studied the information.

Activities

Worksheet C3A Plant products

REQUIREMENTS

Each group of pupils will need:
Copy of Worksheet **C**3A

The teacher will need:
Set of slides (see note 1)
Slide projector

Note:

1 The idea is to have a set of slides showing local examples of plant products familiar to the pupils and in a context they recognize. The cheapest way of getting a suitable set is to ask a senior pupil, members of a photography club, or a member of staff to take them. Pupils are likely to be much more interested in examples in and around the school. They will also enjoy seeing people they know in the pictures. The captions to figures 3.1 to 3.9 in section **C**3.1 of the Chemistry book include ideas for possible pictures. (See also Worksheet **C**8C.)

Worksheet C3B Investigating carbohydrate molecules

REQUIREMENTS

Each group of pupils will need (see note 1):
Copy of Worksheet **C**3B (printed on two sides)
Copy of the planning sheet (Worksheet **C**0)
3 test-tubes in rack
Beaker, 250 ml
Tripod, gauze, burner and mat

Measuring cylinder, 10 ml
Dropping pipette
Thermometer, 0–100 °C
Stopwatch or stopclock
Eye protection

Access to:

Iodine solution (12.7 g iodine – HARMFUL – and 20 g potassium iodide in 40 ml water, diluted to 1000 ml) in a dropper bottle

Benedict's solution (see note 2) in a dropper bottle

Glucose solution (10 g in 100 ml); allow 10 ml per group

Fructose solution (10 g in 100 ml); allow 10 ml per group

Fresh sucrose solution (10 g in 100 ml); allow 20 ml per group

Starch solution (see note 3); allow 10 ml per group

Samples of glucose, fructose, sucrose and starch as solids

0.1 mol/L dilute hydrochloric acid (see note 4) labelled "stomach acid"; allow 25 ml per group

1 mol/L sodium carbonate solution (10.6 g of the anhydrous compound – IRRITANT – in 100 ml water) in dropper bottle

Indicator paper

Distilled water

Balance

Notes:

1 The pupils are asked to make their own plans for the investigation on side 2 of the worksheet, and so some modification of this list may be necessary.

2 Benedict's solution is made by dissolving 17.3 g of sodium citrate and 10 g of anhydrous sodium carbonate – IRRITANT – in 85 ml of water. Then 1.73 g $CuSO_4 \cdot 5H_2O$ is dissolved in 15 ml water and added to the citrate/carbonate solution with constant stirring.

3 The starch solution must be fresh. Make a cream of 1 g soluble starch in a little cold water. Pour this into 100 ml boiling water and continue to boil until the solution is clear.

4 The stomach acid does not have to be accurately 0.1 mol/L. Dilute 25 ml of 2 mol/L hydrochloric acid with water to make 500 ml. In order to ensure that the experiment works within a reasonabe time, however, a more concentrated solution, e.g. 1 mol/L, may be required.

For the initial tests it is convenient to supply the carbohydrates already in solution, but samples of the solids are required for the investigation on side 2 of the worksheet. This activity covers all the main carbohydrates mentioned in Chapter **C3**. Benedict's solution distinguishes glucose and fructose from sucrose and starch. There seems no advantage, at this level, in introducing the term "reducing sugar".

It will save time if each working group only tackles two of the carbohydrates for their investigation on side 2. They should then be advised to try one compound which is demonstrably affected by acid (starch or sucrose) and one which will not seem to change according to the tests used (either glucose or fructose).

The investigation on side 2 is difficult. An easier opportunity for investigation is provided in the problem in box 1 on page 49 of the pupils' book; further information on this is given below.

Worksheet C3C **Models of carbohydrate molecules**

REQUIREMENTS

Each group of pupils will need:

Copy of Worksheet **C3C** (see note 1)

Set of ball-and-spring/stick models (see note 2):

   6 black atoms, four hole

   6 red atoms, two hole

   12 white atoms, one hole

   12 short springs

   12 long springs

Notes:

1 The worksheet is designed for ball–and–spring/stick models and will have to be revised if alternative models are used.

2 Suitable molecular models are obtainable from Spiring Enterprises Ltd, Beke Hall, Billingshurst, W. Sussex RH14 9HF. The models are conveniently supplied in a plastic bag with a checklist on a card inside. There are no questions on the worksheet. Questions 10–15 and 28–32 can be answered in conjunction with these model-building activities.

Some pupils may be puzzled by the different representations of glucose molecules in figures 3.14 and 3.15. Starch is a polymer of the alpha form of glucose, while cellulose is a polymer of the beta form. With models it is easy to show the difference between these two forms and this should be enough to satisfy the curiosity of those interested. Pupils are not expected to remember the details of these differences.

Box 1 Problem: Are all sugars equally sweet?

REQUIREMENTS

The precise requirements will depend on the plans made by the pupils. For reasons of safety it will be sensible to provide:
Copy of the planning sheet
  (Worksheet **C0**)
Drinking straws
Disposable cups

Access to:
Selection of sugars (in bottles or packets which are new, or reserved for use in this investigation)
Balance
Plastic spoons (to be used as spatulas)
Measuring jugs (or some method of measuring volumes of water not using laboratory measuring cylinders)

Safety note:
This experiment should **not** be done in a chemistry laboratory.

The main purpose of this experiment is to explore the problems of designing an experiment which will give meaningful results. Different groups can try alternative approaches and then compare the results. Some of the aspects of the design of the experiment which pupils have to consider are hinted at in box 1 on page 49.

As a result of doing this investigation, the pupils will become more familiar with the nature of carbohydrates and be aware of sugars as a class of compounds.

This is one of a number of practical investigations suggested during the course. No pupil is expected to tackle all of them.

Teacher demonstration: Molecules and membranes

REQUIREMENTS

The teacher will need:
Visking tubing, 15 cm length soaked in distilled water
Strong, fine thread to tie the tubing
Boiling-tube
Test-tube rack
Plastic syringe, 25 ml
Burner and mat
Eye protection

Access to:
Glucose solution (see the notes on Worksheet **C3B**)
Starch solution (as above)
Distilled water
Iodine solution (as above)
Benedict's solution (as above)

This demonstration might be set up when the pupils are asked to think about the experiment in box 2 on page 52.

Procedure
1 Close one end of a 15-cm length of Visking tubing by tying it tightly. Wet the other end so that you can open it up.
2 Use a syringe (without a needle) to fill the tube nearly to the top with a mixture of glucose and starch solutions.
3 Tie a tight knot at the top of the tube, leaving a length of thread which you can use to hold the tubing.
4 Rinse the outside of the tubing thoroughly under the tap.
5 Put the tubing in a boiling-tube and then fill the tube with distilled water.

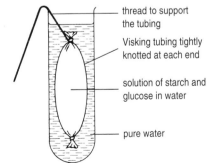

thread to support the tubing

Visking tubing tightly knotted at each end

solution of starch and glucose in water

pure water

Further information

Science and Technology in Society
Unit 1004 "Lavender" includes a demonstration of the use of steam distillation to extract a perfume.

Chapter C4 Chemicals and rocks

The syllabus section

Context

The geological timescale and the rock cycle can be used to introduce the study of rocks and minerals. The history of the manufacture of alum, the newer processes based on salt and limestone, and the extraction of aluminium can all serve to illustrate the importance of the chemical industry.

The work of Humphry Davy provides examples of the ways in which chemical discoveries are made.

Knowledge and understanding

Syllabus statements	PoS	SoA
Appreciate the economic importance of salt and limestone.	—	—
Know the scientific processes involved in weathering of rocks, transport of sediments and formation of different types of soil.	3(iv)5	3.4(e)
Know how to make different types of mixtures which have important everyday applications, and how to separate and purify the components of mixtures using techniques such as filtration, dissolving and evaporation.	**3(i)6**	**3.5(a)**
Understand the terms oxidation and reduction in terms of the addition and removal of oxygen.	3(iii)1	3.6(c)
Be able to recognize variations in the properties of metals, and sequence common metals in order of reactivity.	**3(i)3**	**3.6(d)**
Understand electrolytic decomposition and be able to describe the changes at the anode and cathode.	3(iii)1,3	3.6(f)
Be able to describe evidence which reveals the scientific processes and timescales involved in the formation of igneous, sedimentary and metamorphic rocks.	3(iv)4,6	3.6(h)
Know that materials can be converted into new, useful products through a range of types of chemical reactions, including thermal and electrolytic decomposition and salt formation.	3(iii)1	3.7(g)
Be able to represent chemical, ionic and electrolytic reactions in terms of symbolic equations.	3(iii)3	3.8(f)
Appreciate that economic, social and environmental issues may be involved when minerals are mined.	3(iii)8,9	3.9(d)

Opportunities for co-ordination

The introduction to the geological timescale is useful background for **B**23 and **E**2. The study of mineral resources and the chemical industry can be used to provide examples to illustrate **B**17.

The investigation of electrolytes as a class of electrical conductors is useful background for **P**16.

Routes and times

Basic	Central	Further
Slower groups should spend more time on Q1, 2 and 4 of section **E**2.1. Omit magnetic evidence, plate tectonics and Q3–5 from section **E**2.2.	**E2.1 Finding minerals** **E2.2 The moving Earth** **Worksheet C4A4 Drifting apart** *1¼ hours*	Omit Q1 and 2 from section **E**2.1. Replace Worksheet **C4A4** with Worksheet **C4A5** "The moving Earth".
Omit section **E**2.3. Do Worksheet **C4A2** "Making sandstone".	**E2.3 Earthquakes** Omit seismic evidence for a layered structure and Q3–6. **E2.4 Recycled rocks!** **Worksheet C4A1 Igneous rocks** *1¼ hours*	All parts of section **E**2.3 are suitable.
Omit all this section and replace with "How are rocks formed?" from section **C**4.1 (pages 57–59). *³/₄ hour*	**E2.5 How fast does it happen?** **Worksheet C4A3 Shifting sands** **E2.6 Geological time** Omit Q2 and leave explanation of radioactive dating until Chapter **P3**. *1½ hours*	Q2 and the explanation of radioactive dating are optional.
	C4.1 What is the difference between a rock and a mineral? ("What is a mineral?") Omit Q1 and 4. *¼ hour*	
Do Worksheet **C4A** rather than box 2. *1³/₄ hours*	**C4.2 How was alum made from rocks?** Omit Q5–7, 9–11, 13, 16 and 17. EITHER **Box 2 Problem: Can you make alum from shale?** OR **Worksheet C4A Making alum from shale** *1½ hours*	Do box 2 rather than Worksheet **C4A**.
	C4.3 Why is salt so important? (pages 67–69) Select material to suit class needs. **Worksheet C4D Chemicals from salt** *³/₄ hour*	
Q39 and 40 should also be omitted from section **C**4.3.	**Worksheet C4C Investigating the electrolysis of a solution of sodium chloride** **C4.3 Why is salt so important?** (pages 72–73) Omit Q27–35 and 41. *1½ hours*	Faster pupils could read about Humphry Davy (pages 70–71) and do Q25 and 26 for homework. Q41 of section **C**4.3 is also suitable.
	Worksheet C4E The Limestone Inquiry *1½ hours*	
	C4.5 Where do metals come from? Select material to suit class needs, and expand on oxidation and reduction. *1 hour*	Part of section **C**4.5 should be done for homework. *½ hour*
		Section **C**4.6 "How much?" is an optional extension exercise for faster groups.
Total: 10 hours	*Total: 10½ hours*	*Total: 10 hours*

The pupils' book

C4.1 What is the difference between a rock and a mineral?

This section provides links with work which pupils may have done previously in science or during a geography course. It provides a context for the rest of the chapter.

If possible the pupils might be shown specimens of rocks and minerals. The pupils can be asked to discuss answers to some of the questions 2-4.

Box 1 and questions 2 and 3 remind pupils of the basic rules for naming simple inorganic compounds.

C4.2 How was alum made from rocks?

The main purpose of Worksheet **C4A** is to give pupils the satisfaction of getting a good yield of an attractive product from a raw material which looks very unpromising. The emphasis is on manipulative skills. The problem: "Can you make alum from shale?" in box 2 on page 65 is included as an optional planning exercise. It is designed to help pupils to use two-dimensional line diagrams to draw apparatus.

Pupils will not be required to remember the history of the alum industry. Worksheet **C4B** is included to help pupils focus on the main points in the passage. Questions 5-17 are also designed to encourage pupils to reflect on what they are reading and relate it to other knowledge.

For example, question 5 sets political and social events alongside some of the key developments in science and technology from 1500 to 1900.

Question 13 raises some of the issues to do with the location of industry.

Question 14 includes some daunting formulae but the questions only require a recognition of symbols and are intended to illustrate the fact that chemical changes involve the rearrangement of elements.

Questions 16 and 17 are numerical problems in an unusual context.

Answers to selected questions
16 Mass of potash produced = 377 tonnes.

17a Mass of ammonia = 11 kg = 0.011 tonnes per person per year.
b Number of people required = 341.

C4.3 Why is salt so important?

Pupils are likely to have studied rock salt previously and purified it in the laboratory. The section starts with text, diagrams and questions (18-21) which revise these topics.

Electrolysis is introduced as a process which decomposes compounds and so rearranges elements. There is no need, at this stage, to attempt to explain the changes in terms of ions and electron transfer. Ions are first introduced in Chapter **C5**. Many pupils find it hard to understand the theory of electrolysis; the detailed treatment of electrode processes is delayed in the text until Chapter **C18**. By this time atomic structure will have been described in Physics.

Pupils will not be required to remember the details of the work of Humphry Davy. The account of his work is included to show that science is the result of human activity and imagination. The first, optional, demonstration repeats Davy's "capital experiment" and is worth doing if there is time. Alternatively pupils might be shown the electrolysis of lead(II) bromide – HARMFUL – as an example of the decomposition of a molten salt. This demonstration should be carried out in a fume cupboard, as the bromine vapour that is produced is corrosive. Worksheet **C4C** gives pupils some practical experience of electrolysis. They are told what to do and the emphasis is on careful investigation, accurate observations, and discussion, of the results.

Box 3 Experiment: The electrolysis of molten compounds
Box 4 Experiment: The electrolysis of compounds in solution

Two experiments are described on pages 72–3 to give pupils the opportunity to look for patterns in the results. The emphasis should be on the activity of seeking the patterns, **not** on remembering them. Discussion of questions 27–41 can follow the experiment on Worksheet **C4C**. These questions will not be suitable for all classes.

Questions 27–32 suggest this pattern:

- metals are deposited at the negative electrode;
- non-metals are released at the positive electrode.

Questions 33–41 explore what happens when water is also present. The results show that water must get involved in electrolysis.

- Metals low in the activity series are deposited at the negative electrode.
- Hydrogen is formed at the negative electrode if the metal is high in the activity series.
- Oxygen is usually formed at the positive electrode unless the salt is a chloride, bromide or iodide.
- If the salt is a chloride, bromide or iodide, then the halogen is formed at the positive electrode.

Note that there is no need to mention the complication of active electrodes which get involved in electrolysis, but this may be raised by pupils who have had experience of electroplating.

Worksheet **C4D** is included to help pupils to study and make sense of the description of the manufacture of sodium hydroxide and chlorine from salt. In this course pupils are not expected to remember details of manufacturing operations for examination purposes. They are expected to show that they have experience of using their knowledge of chemistry to make sense of accounts of related industrial processes.

C4.4 Why is limestone important?

Worksheet **C4E** is a role-play exercise about the quarrying of limestone. It highlights the importance of limestone as a raw material and raises many of the environmental and social issues involved when mineral resources are exploited on a large scale. If the pupils are unfamiliar with limestone scenery it is very desirable to show the ICI video "Limestone", which gives a picture of a large quarry at work and describes the chemistry and uses of limestone, as well as discussing the problem of what to do with a quarry when it has been worked out.

The text of section C4.4 summarizes much of the information involved in Worksheet **C4E**.

C4.5 Where do metals come from?

The extraction of aluminium is included here as another example of the importance of electrolysis. A film, video, or set of slides will help pupils to gain some impression of the scale of the process. (See under Further Information.)

Worksheet **C4F** is designed to help the pupils study this section.

Questions 47–53 cover the extraction and uses of aluminium.

Answers to selected questions

48 About 70 years.

51 The bulb will run for 150 hours.

C4.6 How much?

The question "How much?" is very important in chemistry, and so quantitative chemistry has been covered at several levels in this course. The concept "amount of substance" (measured in moles) is introduced in Chapter **C5** for the benefit of those who are likely to go on to more advanced study of the subject. In this section a simpler treatment uses atomic masses to work out the percentage of metals in metal ores.

Box 6 Problem: How can malachite be analysed?

An important planning exercise is given in box 6 on page 82. This example has been included to illustrate the importance of quantitative chemical analysis and the difficulties involved.

Pupils should be allowed to attempt any procedure which is safe even if it will not lead to a satisfactory result. In this context they will learn as much from failure as from success. The planning is best carried out in small groups in class, and questions 54–8 are included to guide the discussions-

Answer to selected question
59a 39.3 % sodium
b 70 % iron
c 77.5 % lead
d 78.8 % tin
e 34.8 % copper

Activities

Worksheets C4A1 to C4A5 relate to Topic E2 "Geology". Further information on this topic may be found on pages 524–28 of this *Guide*.

Worksheet C4A1 Igneous rocks

REQUIREMENTS

Each pair of pupils will need:
Test-tube and holder
Salol (phenyl salicylate)
9 microscope slides
Eye protection

Access to:
Oven and refrigerator
Specimens of granite, dolerite and basalt (for matching rocks to locations on the illustration)
Specimen of obsidian
Hand lens (for observing small crystals)

The procedure is given on the worksheet.

Granite forms deep below the Earth's surface, extending through large volumes. The rate of cooling is very slow and large crystals form.

Lava flows are usually of basalt which cools and solidifies quickly, forming fine-grained rocks.

"Intrusions" just below the Earth's surface of similar magma to that which forms basalt cool more slowly than lava flows. Dolerite is the name given to this rock type. However, there is every gradation of crystal size between basalt and dolerite, so that it is sometimes difficult to distinguish the two. The "Whin Sill", on which Hadrian's wall stands, is an example of a dolerite intrusion.

Obsidian is a volcanic glass, the result of extremely rapid cooling as molten magma flies through the air. It has no time to crystallize but simply freezes in a disordered structure.

Answers to worksheet question
1 Pupils should find that crystals form first in the smallest drop, which solidifies first and produces the smallest crystals. When hot microscopic slides are used, the rate of crystal growth is slower, as the cooling rate is slower. When cold slides are used, the rate is quicker.

The illustration should be labelled as follows:
Location A: quickly, fine, basalt.
Location B: less quickly, medium, dolerite.
Location C: slowly, coarse, granite.

Worksheet C4A2 Making sandstone

REQUIREMENTS

Each group of pupils will need:
Disposable syringe, about 10ml,
  with end cut off

Access to:
Petroleum jelly
Sand
Microscope
Salt solution

Sugar solution
Iron(II) sulphate solution – IRRITANT
Powdered decorating filler
Clay
Plaster of Paris
Hand lens
Samples of different sandstones
Newspaper or scrap paper to work on

This activity allows pupils to consider some of the mechanisms and requirements for the production of sedimentary rocks. The procedure is detailed on the worksheet.

Answers to worksheet questions

1 and **2** Pupils should note the irregularity of packing and the spaces between the sand grains.

3 The rock will be soft, since there is nothing to hold the grains together.

4 The cemented rocks are harder than the compacted rocks.

5 Pupils will be able to see that a good cement produces hard "rocks". They may notice that plaster of Paris is more brittle than decorator's filler and hardens more rapidly. Decorator's filler is sometimes based on plaster of Paris, with additives to reduce the speed of setting and make the final product tougher.

Worksheet C4A3 Shifting sands

REQUIREMENTS

Each pupil will need:
Disposable copies of sides 2 to 5 of Worksheet **C4A3**

In this activity pupils use maps to observe erosion and deposition on the east coast of Britain.

Answers to worksheet questions

1 On Map 1 (1820), Glebe Farm is approximately 950 m from the coast and on Map 2 (1940) it is approximately 1400m. From this observation pupils can conclude that deposition is occurring on the coast in that area.

2 Pupils might note, for instance, that Freiston Shore used to be on the shore but is not any longer.

3 Mappleton which was about 600m from the shore in 1840 (Map 3) was only 200 m from the shore in 1940 (Map 4), showing that erosion is occurring on this coastline.

4 Pupils might note the obvious danger presented to the houses in Hornsea. In addition, the presence of another village (Hornsea Beck), marked "in the sea" on Map 3, shows the effects of previous erosion.

5 A reasonable suggestion is that material eroded from the north is being deposited further south, carried along by the prevailing sea currents.

Worksheet C4A4 Drifting apart

REQUIREMENTS

Each pupil will need:
Eye protection

Each group of pupils will need:
Burner, tripod, gauze and heatproof mat
Beaker, 500ml (or 250ml if not enough large beakers)
Tweezers (to pick up crystal of potassium
    manganate(VII)
Glass tube, about 3–5 mm internal diameter, length
    about 10 cm

Access to:
Potassium manganate(VII) crystals – OXIDIZING

The teacher will need:
Eye protection
Burner, tripod and heatproof mat
Gauze (optional)
Tweezers (optional)
Safety screen
Round-bottomed flask, 500 ml or 1 litre
    (optional)
Retort stand, clamp and boss (optional)
2 pieces of plywood, approximately
    $1\,cm \times 2\,cm \times 5\,cm$
Shallow dish or tray, heat-resistant, at least
    7 cm deep, at least 15 cm diameter
2 cans of tomato soup

Safety note:
Pupils should pick up the potassium manganate(VII) with the tweezers, and must take care when heating liquids.

The aim of this activity is to introduce pupils to a possible description of how plate tectonics works. Some of the questions (3, 7, 8, 9 and 10) are only suitable for faster groups.

The potassium manganate(VII) experiment demonstrates convection in a fluid. Convection should be discussed merely in terms of circulating fluid at this stage; it is not intended to go into details about why the circulation occurs. With care, the pupils should briefly see convection cells marked out by the moving purple solution. The effect does not last long before general turbulence takes over, so it must be stressed that gentle heating and careful observation are required. The experiment may be demonstrated more effectively in a large round-buttomed flask (apparatus marked "optional" in the list above).

The tomato soup experiment shows the possible cause of the plates spreading apart as they are carried by convection cells in the mantle (however, see below). A relatively shallow tray or dish is needed. There should be enough room for the two pieces of plywood to float side by side on the soup, representing the crust on the mantle. The tray is filled with dilute tomato soup, about two parts soup to one part water, though the dilution required depends on the brand of the soup and must be determined by experiment.

Heating the soup below the join between the plywood blocks causes the blocks to separate. It is best if the heating is done without a gauze, so that heating is confined to a small area. If the soup is heated too strongly, local boiling occurs under the plywood and the steam forces the pieces apart. This is a good simulation of fissure eruptions.

Theories of the mechanism of plate tectonics have undergone revision recently. The mantle is now thought to be composed of solid mineral grains with voids, with molten material in between. The mantle behaves like a solid to passing earthquake waves but, under certain conditions, the liquid in the voids is able to migrate upwards reaching the surface through volcanoes. Hot spots occur in the mantle where there are rising convection plumes. These can cause massive volcanic activity in the crust directly above. The Hawaiian islands are a chain of volcanoes formed as the crust moves over a mantle hot spot.

Such hot spots were also thought to be solely responsible for ocean ridge volcanic activity but a different mechanism has now been suggested. Pulling apart at ocean ridges stretches the crust and the upper mantle, causing decompression and melting. This effect is something like what happens when the cap is taken off a bottle of fizzy lemonade.

Answers to worksheet questions
1 At least part of the mantle is behaving as a very viscous liquid.

2 The crust sank down slightly into the flexible mantle under the load of the ice (this is

known as isostatic depression). In post-glacial times isostatic rebound has occurred as the crust has gradually risen back to its former position. It is still rising.

3 There are fishing villages stranded several kilometres inland in Finland as the crust continues to rise and the Baltic Sea consequently recedes.

4 Because the plates under the ocean are enlarging in area.

5 The blocks are carried apart by convection currents.

6 Volcanic activity occurs along the central "rift", these are the oceanic ridges seen on bathymetric maps.

7 The magma originates from the hot liquid layer, called the asthenosphere.

8 The tomato soup is mainly liquid, and is much less viscous and circulates much faster than the real mantle. Real sea floor spreading occurs at a rate of a few centimetres a year.

9 Friction between the descending plate and the surrounding mantle causes heating of both. Magma is produced and rises because it is less dense than the surrounding material.

10 Friction also causes earthquakes in a landward descending pattern corresponding to the edges of the descending plate. Most coastal and island regions round the edge of the Pacific Ocean lie above such zones, and in a region also known for volcanoes called the Pacific "ring of fire".

Worksheet C4A5 **The moving Earth**

REQUIREMENTS

Each group of pupils will need access to:
Sealed tins containing a variety of single solid objects, for example: a marble, a cube of wood, a nut with a pair of hexagonal bolts screwed onto it.
Further complexities can be introduced by changing the interior surface of one part of the tin, for example, by packing the base with a layer of expanded polystyrene. To really puzzle the pupils, have a toy marble in one tin and in the base have some nails projecting into the tin from a piece of wood. As the marble is shaken, it will sometimes become lodged between the nails and its rolling will be inhibited until it is shaken free.

Plate tectonics represents a relatively recent scientific revolution. In describing the state of knowledge prior to the plate tectonic theory, you may be able to use evidence from the rocks in the locality of the school. In nearly every area there will be evidence of rocks being folded, horizontal strata being tilted, faults (which represent evidence of earlier earthquakes), or the existence of volcanic rocks. It should be possible, therefore, to find empirical evidence for previous Earth upheaval.

The four types of plate movements shown in figures 1 to 4 in the worksheet represent the simple elements. In actual situations, combinations can occur: along the Pacific coast of America we find lateral movement along the fault lines fairly near the surface in some places, while elsewhere the predominant feature is of plate destruction giving rise to volcanoes and deep earthquakes.

The relative neglect of Wegener's ideas before the 1960s tells us a lot about how science progresses. You might want to discuss the role of the scientific community, which decides what is acceptable science. There is little scope for an outsider to gain an audience and influence professionals, and in this context Wegener was an outsider. One advantage of talking to fellow professionals is that the discussion should be to the point, as everyone has prior knowledge of the subject, but the drawback is that everyone may share the same prejudices which blind one to new insights.

Most of our evidence about the interior of the Earth has come from the study of earthquake waves. These display reflection and refraction at the boundaries between the different layers of the Earth. In addition, transverse waves are absorbed by a liquid medium and this fact gives evidence for the rocks being molten under the surface.

The newly discovered evidence about the mid-Atlantic floor came from two techniques. One was the use of radioactive isotopes to date the rocks. Usually the potassium–argon method is used in this context (*not* carbon dating, which is used in archaeology but covers too short a time span to be useful in geology). The second line of evidence came from palaeomagnetism. As molten rocks cool, crystals of magnetic materials, for example the iron oxide magnetite, become locked into the rock in alignment with the Earth's magnetic field. At intervals the Earth's field reverses. The rocks nearest the mid-Atlantic ridge show the current orientation, then the next strip shows the reverse, and the next strip shows the current orientation, and so forth. The existence of such parallel strips can only be explained by assuming that the rocks at the ridge are very new, and as we move away from the ridge they become progressively older.

Originally the rocks in south-east England were folded up into a great arch, or anticline. The rocks forming that arch have largely eroded away, giving rise to the area known as the Weald, with the North and South Downs representing remnants of this arching rock.

Answers to worksheet questions

1 The Atlantic Ocean is widening and the Pacific Ocean is becoming smaller. The Red Sea will probably open wider.

2 to **4** The line dividing the two continents runs approximately from south-west by west to north-east by east, through the Solway Firth. As the original ocean disappeared there must have been plate destruction, as shown in figure 4. In that event we would expect to find evidence of volcanoes, and indeed they are evident in southern Scotland, Ireland and the Lake District. We would also expect to find evidence of former earthquakes, as faults in the rocks, and these too are abundant in this region.

Worksheet C4A Making alum from shale

REQUIREMENTS

Each group of pupils will need:
Copy of Worksheet **C4A** (see note 1)
Tin lid or metal sand tray
Beaker, 250 ml
Watchglass to cover the beaker
Conical flask, 250 ml
Funnel
Evaporating basin
Burner, tripod, gauze and mat
Tongs
Eye protection

Access to:
High alumina shale, 10 g per group, in
   container with spatula (see note 2)
Dilute sulphuric acid (2 mol/L) – CORROSIVE –
   20 ml per group, with measuring cylinder
Potassium hydroxide solution (2 mol/L)
   – CORROSIVE – allow 20 ml per group, with
   measuring cylinder (see note 3)
Full range, or Universal, indicator paper
Filter paper
Balance to weigh 20 g

Notes:
1 The worksheet will not be needed if the pupils have made their own plans based on the problem in box 2.
2 The high alumina shale is available from The National Stone Centre, Wirksworth, Derbyshire DE4 4FR. It should preferably be broken up into small pieces in advance.
3 Stress to pupils that alkali (potassium hydroxide) in the eye is **more** dangerous than acid of comparable strength.

The main point of this experiment is to give the pupils the satisfaction of getting a good yield of attractive alum crystals. Good results are achieved using the high alumina shale described in note 2. The shale should be broken into pieces about 0.25-0.5 cm across.

A variety of types of fired clay may be used instead of shale, and scrap unglazed pottery from the Art department can be crushed and investigated as a possible source of alum.

Trials have shown that the main part of this experiment can be completed in a double period. Filtering takes time but is quicker with fluted filter papers. The filtrate may be greenish due to impurities, but this does not affect the appearance of the crystals at the end.

During step **d** the contents of the flask should be swirled vigorously while adding the potassium hydroxide solution. This limits precipitation due to local excesses of alkali. Sometimes an orange-brown precipitate appears, so filtering may be necessary at the end of step **d** before the solution is evaporated and allowed to crystallize.

Worksheet C4C Investigating the electrolysis of a solution of sodium chloride

REQUIREMENTS

Each group of pupils will need:
Copy of Worksheet **C4C**
Electrolysis cell (see note 1)
Glass rod
2 test-tubes, to collect the gases over the electrodes
2 connecting wires, each fitted with a crocodile clip at one end and a plug at the other
d.c. supply, 6 V (see note 2)
Stand, boss and clamp
Eye protection

Access to:
Sodium chloride solution (30 g/L), allow 80–100 ml per group
Indicator paper
Splints

Notes:
1 The cell must be large enough to allow the pupils to investigate what is happening around the electrodes. A home-made cell is easily made by cutting the top off a plastic chemical bottle and fitting it with a large bung and carbon electrodes as shown in the diagram on the worksheet.
2 Make sure that the lab pack cannot give more than 20 volts.

The worksheet tells the pupils what to do: the activity is an exercise in observation and interpretation. They should be able to identify hydrogen by showing that it burns with a pop, and chlorine by its smell and bleaching action. Warn all pupils not to breathe the chlorine in deeply, and asthmatics not to breathe it in at all. The experiment illustrates the fact that the water has to be taken into account when aqueous solutions are electrolysed. This point is explored further in the Experiments described in boxes 3 and 4 on pages 72–3.

Worksheet C4E The Limestone Inquiry

REQUIREMENTS

Each student will need:
Copies of the General briefing sheets and a copy of one of the Briefing sheets (1 to 7). For a class of thirty, 30 copies of the General briefing sheets and 5 copies of each of the Briefing sheets will be needed.

Procedure

1 Preliminary
Tell the class that in the next lesson they will be taking part in a Public Inquiry about a proposed extension of a limestone quarry.

Divide them into seven groups. One group will play the role of Inspectors and organize the Inquiry. They should elect a chairperson to do the talking. Members of this group need copies of Briefing sheet 1. The Inspectors play a key role because they control the Inquiry. It is important to have pupils with appropriate personal qualities in these roles, particularly the Chairperson.

Three groups will be in favour of the quarry extension. They will represent Limeco, the quarry operators (2), the industrial users of limestone (3) and the trades unions (4).

Three groups will oppose the extension. They will represent the National Park Authority (5), local residents (6) and the local conservation group (7).

Issue each member of the class with copies of the General briefing sheets, and their

Briefing sheets (1 to 7) according to the group they are in. They should study these sheets in class or for homework (or both).

In school trials it has been found necessary to allow plenty of time for pupils to assimilate the information and discuss it together. This can be a good point to show a film/video to give pupils a picture of a quarry, and the surrounding landscape.

2 On the day of the Inquiry
Each group should spend some time together using the Briefing sheets, their notes and other sources of information to plan how they are going to present their arguments.

The Public Inquiry should as far as possible be organized by the team of Inspectors. It may be better to do this in a classroom, or laboratory where there is movable furniture, so that the Inspectors can arrange the seating suitably. The Inspectors should be encouraged to take firm control of the Inquiry to ensure that everyone gets a fair hearing.

A suggested sequence for the Inquiry is given on Briefing sheet 1.

Box 6 Problem: How can malachite be analysed?

REQUIREMENTS

These will depend on the plans made by the pupils, but each group is likely to need:
Beaker, 100 ml
Boiling-tube
Glass rod
Tongs
Burner, tripod, gauze and mat
Funnel
Eye protection

Some groups may also need some of the following:
Hard-glass test-tube with a small hole blown near the closed end
Bung and short delivery tube to fit the test-tube
Rubber tubing to connect the delivery tube to the gas supply
Low voltage, d.c. supply
2 carbon electrodes
Connecting wires with crocodile clips
Stand with clamp

Access to:
"Malachite" (i.e. powdered copper(II) carbonate – HARMFUL), allow 2-3 g per group
Dilute sulphuric acid, 2 mol/L – CORROSIVE
Zinc metal, foil or powder – FLAMMABLE
Filter paper
Balance

Safety note:
Care may need to be taken over what pupils think of doing – some procedures might be hazardous. For example, the reduction of copper(II) oxide with hydrogen (or natural gas) causes many accidents, and local Risk Assessments should be checked if this is proposed.

At the start, pupils may be shown samples of rock which contain the mineral malachite but for their own experiments they should be provided with pure "malachite" (i.e. copper(II) carbonate) on the assumption that the mineral processing stages have been completed.

The main purpose of the activity is to give pupils a chance to explore the problems involved in carrying out a quantitative analysis. Some pupils will respond to the idea that their group is competing for the contract to be awarded to an analytical firm by a mining company.

Teacher demonstration: Davy's capital experiment

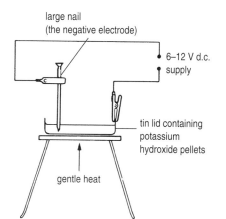

large nail
(the negative electrode)

6–12 V d.c. supply

tin lid containing potassium hydroxide pellets

gentle heat

REQUIREMENTS

The teacher will need:
d.c. supply, 6-12 V
Iron nail, 5-10 cm long
Small tin lid (about 1.5 cm deep)
Burner, tripod and mat
Stand with boss and clamp
Spatula
2 connecting wires, with crocodile clips at one end and plugs at the other

Beaker, 100 ml
Eye protection and protective gloves
Safety screens to protect teacher and pupils

Access to:
Hexane, or naphtha – FLAMMABLE
Potassium hydroxide pellets – CORROSIVE
Desiccator
Fume cupboard

The diagram shows the arrangement for this experiment; some consideration needs to be given as to how the crocodile clips and wires are to be supported away from the heat and any corrosive spray. The apparatus gives small pellets of potassium (FLAMMABLE, CORROSIVE) at the point of the nail, quite safely and reliably, provided that the conditions below are observed. The goggles and gloves are to protect against any spray from the molten alkali. The pellets may even be skimmed off, using a small spatula, and placed quickly under a hydrocarbon solvent.

Procedure

Before the lesson. Fill a small tin lid, which should be about 1–1.5 cm deep, with pellets of potassium hydroxide and warm until molten. If necessary add more pellets until a depth of at least 0.5 cm is obtained. Cool in a desiccator. It is essential that the potash should be really dry, before starting the electrolysis. Set up the rest of the apparatus but do not put the tin lid with the electrolyte in position until you are absolutely ready to begin the demonstration.

The demonstration. Adjust the nail so that its point penetrates the surface of the potash, but does not touch the base of the tin lid. Heat gently, just below the nail, and switch on the power pack at 6 V. It is only necessary to heat until electrolysis has started. After that the less heating the better. (Davy achieved fusion by using a higher voltage with slightly damp terminals.) Small silvery globules appear. Their size can be about 2 mm; optimum conditions are best found by trial and error, adjusting the voltage and rate of heating to get the desired results. Use a spatula to lift out some of the globules and put them under a hydrocarbon solvent in a small beaker. It is possible to make the potassium burn at the cathode by raising the voltage. However, this should only be attempted with a safety screen in place or in a fume cupboard, and if you are confident about doing it after preliminary practice.

The next demonstration is more familiar but is also optional. Pupils should have seen at least one example of the electrolysis of a molten compound before studying the results of the experiments in box 3 on page 72.

Teacher demonstration: The electrolysis of lead(II) bromide

REQUIREMENTS

The teacher will need:
d.c. supply, 10–12 V
Demonstration ammeter, 3A
4 connecting wires, crocodile clips and plugs
Rheostat
2 carbon electrodes
U-tube
Stand, with boss and clamp
Burner and mat
Pestle and mortar
Eye protection

Access to:
Lead(II) bromide – HARMFUL
Fume cupboard

This demonstration must be carried out in a fume cupboard because poisonous vapours are given off if the apparatus is overheated.

Note: The electolysis of lead(II) bromide is shown at the start of the video "Chemicals from salt II" (see under Further information).

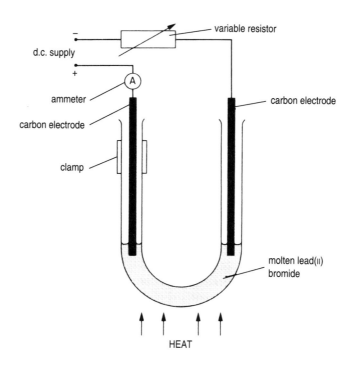

Procedure

1 Set up the apparatus above and heat the bottom of the U-tube with a small flame. You may have to add more lead(II) bromide when it starts to melt to provide an adequate depth of liquid, but this can be a tricky operation and is best avoided if possible.

2 Adjust the rheostat to give a current of about 1 A; bromine vapour (CORROSIVE) will then be seen almost at once around the positive electrode.

3 Allow electrolysis to continue for about five minutes, then pour the molten contents of the U-tube into a mortar. If you gently crush the solid lead(II) bromide you should discover a small bead of metallic lead.

Further information

Science and Technology in Society

There are three SATIS units, published by the ASE, which can be used as alternatives to the Limestone Inquiry:

Unit 307 "Chemicals from salt" places more emphasis on economic and technical problems but also includes social issues. This exercise requires the pupils to work in groups to answer a series of questions. There is no need for a debate involving the whole class.

Unit 502 "The Coal Mine Project" is more like the Limestone Inquiry, but the imaginary situation supposes that major coal deposits have been found near the school, so the pupils are thoroughly familiar with the locality which may be affected by major industrial developments.

Unit 1001 "Chocolate chip mining" is a practical, problem-solving activity linked to an analysis of data about copper mining.

University of York Science Education Group

The following units in the Salters' Chemistry course can be used as a source of alternative activities and questions: *Buildings, Minerals,* and *Making and using electricity.*

The unit *Salt solution* in the Chemistry in Action series deals with the mining of salt and the environmental aspects of potash mining.

ICI

The ICI video "Limestone" is very useful and can be purchased from the Argus Film and Video library. (See Appendix.)

ICI Mond Division have some useful resource material about limestone and salt. (See Appendix.)

National Parks

The Council for the National Parks distribute a kit that includes factsheets on many aspects of the parks including geology and mineral resources. (See Appendix.)

ITV Chemistry in Action series

The videos "Chemicals from salt I" (modern solution salt mining and the chlor–alkali industry) and "Chemicals from salt II" (the production of sodium and its uses, the alkali metals and the halogens) may prove useful in section C4.3.

The video "Aluminium" is particularly suitable for section C4.5.

Plate tectonics

The following publications provide useful information for Worksheet C4A5:

Anderson, P. and Cadbury, D. *Imagined worlds* BBC Publications, 1985.

Calder, N. *The restless Earth* Chatto and Windus, 1972.

Geological Museum *The story of the Earth* Natural History Museum, 1972 (well illustrated, and also highly recommended for pupils).

Topic C2 — Materials in use

Chapter C5 Materials and structures

The syllabus section

Context

This section is theoretical and introduces two important questions:

- How are the uses of materials related to their properties?
- How can the properties of materials be explained in terms of structure and bonding?

Knowledge and understanding

	Tier		Syllabus statements	PoS	SoA
B	C	F			
			Be able to classify materials as solids, liquids and gases on the basis of simple properties which relate to their everyday uses.	3(i)1	3.4(a)
			Understand some of the vocabulary used to describe the properties of materials, including words such as strong, weak, stiff, flexible, hard, elastic, transparent, opaque, porous, impermeable, conductor, insulator, biodegradable and rotproof.	3(i)5	3.4(a)
			Understand the physical differences between solids, liquids and gases in particle terms.	3(ii)1	3.6(b)
			Understand some of the vocabulary used to describe the properties of materials, including words such as tensile strength, compressive strength, porosity and thermal conductivity.	3(i)5	3.7(a)
			Be able to develop models in order to understand and explain the difference between elements, compounds and mixtures in terms of atoms, ions and molecules.	3(ii)2	3.7(e)
			Know that an ion is a charged particle and that the compounds of metals with non-metals are ionic.	3(ii)2	—
			Understand the distinction between a molecular structure and a giant structure with the help of a limited range of simple examples such as water, oxygen, carbon dioxide, diamond, graphite and silicon dioxide.	3(i)1,5	3.8(d)
			Appreciate that the forces holding atoms together in molecules are much stronger than the forces between molecules.	4(iii)2	—
			Understand why ionic compounds only conduct when molten or in solution.	—	3.8(d)
			Be able to recognize patterns in the properties of metals and non-metals and relate this information to their position in the Periodic Table.	3(i)2	3.9(a)
			Be able to interpret chemical equations quantitatively through experimental exploration and the use of data. The work should involve determination of formulae, and pupils should know that 'amount of substance' has a precise meaning in chemistry and is measured in moles.	3(iii)4	3.9(c)

Opportunities for co-ordination

P1 deals with the strength and stiffness of materials, **P**2 with solids, liquids and gases. Ions are mentioned in the context of plant growth in **B**15 and in the context of ionizing radiation in **P**3.

Properties of materials links with Design and Technology.

Routes and times

Basic	Central	Further
All questions in section **C**5.1 are suitable. Omit Q5 and 6 in section **C**5.2. *³/₄ hour*	**C5.1 What are materials?** Omit Q1–3. **C5.2 Why use models?** Omit Q5. *½ hour*	All questions are suitable.
Omit Q11–13 from section **C**5.3. Omit Q6 and 7 from Worksheet **C**5A.	**C5.3 Molecules or giant structures?** **Worksheet C5A Molecules or giant structures?** *2 hours*	
	Worksheet C5B Ions on the move *³/₄ hour*	
Omit Q17–19 from section **C**5.4. *1¼ hours*	**C5.4 Why is sodium chloride so different from sodium and chlorine?** (up to Q19) **Worksheet C5C Ions and electrolysis** *1 hour*	Omit Worksheet **C**5C and do section **C**5.6 for homework. *³/₄ hour*
Omit this section	**C5.4 Why is sodium chloride so different from sodium and chlorine?** (boxes 2 and 3 and questions) *1 hour*	
Section **C**5.5 should be developed into a practical activity with slower groups. *1½ hours*	**C5.5 Atoms, molecules or ions?** *½ hour*	
		C5.7 How many atoms, molecules or ions? (class + homework) Omit Q27. *1½ hours*
Total: 6¼ hours	*Total: 5³/₄ hours*	*Total: 7¼ hours*

The pupils' book

C5.1 What are materials?

This section introduces pupils to some of the vocabulary used to talk about materials. Questions 1–4 are included to reinforce the ideas in the text.

C5.2 Why use models?

The treatment of structure in this course is heavily dependent on the use of models. At some point it is likely to be appropriate to discuss the advantages and limitations of chemical models. This section can be used as a basis for the discussion.

The PEEL model of ethanol is included in figure 5.10 simply to show that there are several ways of representing the same molecule. "There is no intention that pupils should have any knowledge or understanding of the use of these models.

C5.3 Molecules or giant structures?

It may be helpful to start by exploring some of the meanings of the word ,"structure" which has different levels of meaning in science. The word is used in its engineering sense in Chapter **P**1. Microscopes reveal the microstructure of materials. X-ray diffraction reveals the crystal structure which describes how the atoms are arranged. But we are also interested in the atomic structure in terms of electrons, neutrons and protons.

The important thing is to be aware of the difficulties which pupils may have with the word "structure" and not to confuse them by going into all the meanings in detail. Here it is sufficient to discuss "engineering structures" and "crystal structures".

The suggested treatment makes a clear distinction between giant structures and molecules. The term *giant molecule* is deliberately avoided because it has two meanings. Some texts refer to diamond as a giant molecule on the grounds that the bonding in both small molecules and diamond is covalent. Other texts call polymers giant molecules.

For clarity, in an introductory course, it seems better to separate the words *giant* and *molecule*. In a giant structure there is a continuous two- or three-dimensional network of strong bonds. In a molecular structure there is strong bonding within the molecules but weak bonding between the molecules. Thus metals, diamond, silica, graphite, mica, and salts all have giant structures. Organic compounds, liquids and gases, and thermoplastic polymers are all molecular.

As a general rule the metal elements and compounds of metals with non-metals have giant structures. Non-metals and compounds consisting only of non-metals are normally molecular, but there are exceptions: principally diamond, graphite, silicon and silicon dioxide. These generalizations are illustrated by the summary at the end of the chapter in the Chemistry pupils' book; the information for completing the summary is in the Data section.

There is no substitute for making and handling models of structures. Time and cost are, unfortunately, limiting factors. Most models of the diamond structure are too small to bring out the idea of a giant structure, which is why figure 5.20 is so important. A diamond structure can also be built up using the carbon atoms from a set of ball-and-spring/stick models as used in Chapters **C**2 and **C**3 (see also under Further information).

Answer to selected question
12 Pupils may need to be guided through this question, as the Data section reveals no melting- or boiling-point for carbon dioxide, only that it sublimes. That it does this at low temperatures shows that its particles (molecules) are held together less strongly than those of silicon dioxide (giant structure).

C5.4 Why is sodium chloride so different from sodium and chlorine?

In Chapter **C4** the pupils investigate electrolysis and look for patterns in the results. At that stage there is no attempt to explain the observations. This section starts the introduction to ionic theory.

Faraday invented the idea and the name "ion" long before electrons were discovered. In the publications for this course, the idea of ions is introduced and used in Biology, Chemistry and Physics before pupils are asked to think about how it is that atoms can turn into ions.

However, some teachers may wish to explain how ions are formed here, using parts of Chapter **C18**. If so they will have to do some introductory work on atomic structure. This requires co-ordination with the treatment in Physics, but there is no fundamental problem. The approach to atomic structure in Nuffield Co-ordinated Sciences does not involve a survey of the evidence leading to the picture of a nuclear atom with electrons. We have decided to present the model and then to show that it is plausible by demonstrating the range of problems which the model helps to solve.

Worksheet **C5B** and the associated teacher demonstration give evidence that there are particles on the move during electroysis. The ionic explanation for electrolysis can then be explored with the help of Worksheet **C5C**. Worksheet **C5C** is designed to help pupils with questions 17–19,

C5.5 Atoms, molecules or ions?

This section could be developed into a laboratory activity. Pupils might be asked to use the key in figure 5.36 to work out the structures of a selection of substances, given appropriate data and apparatus for testing conductivity. Note that it may be necessary to make sure that pupils do not have access to the Data section in their Chemistry book which includes the structures of most common elements and compounds.

C5.6 How can we discover the structure of substances?

Some pupils will want to know the answer to the question in the heading to this section. The section does not answer it in detail, and pupils will only be expected to be aware of the fact that modern methods for determining structure are based on X-ray diffraction and other instrumental methods.

The importance of this section is that it shows the personal involvement of scientists in their work. It demonstrates that much scientific research is a collaborative venture which may take years to develop.

Worksheet **C5D** is designed to help pupils study this section.

C5.7 How many atoms, molecules or ions?

This section starts by extending the rules for writing equations in Chapter **C1** to cover giant structures. The data tables should help here because they show the symbols normally used in equations.

The treatment of amounts of substance, here and later in the course, is designed to emphasize the usefulness of the idea as a means of making fair comparison between equal numbers of particles. Worked examples show how measuring amounts in moles can be used to interpret equations quantitatively. The examples are highly structured. The hope is that most of those pupils who tackle this section will be able to experience some success with the questions by following the examples step by step.

Note that we have deliberately avoided the term "mole concept" which does not fit with normal usage. We do not talk about the "gram concept" or the "joule concept" either! We have also been careful to use the word "amount" in Chemistry only when referring to quantities measured in moles.

Chemical formulae are taken as given. No experiments to determine formulae are included, on the grounds that it is difficult to get good results under school conditions. Also, the interpretation of the results can make the mole seem a difficult idea from the start.

We think that it helps to work in terms of molar masses with the units g/mol. This makes it possible to include the units in every stage of calculations, leading to the correct units for the final answer as shown in box 6 on page 110. This is consistent with the use of units in Physics and Biology. It is very important that those pupils who may go on to more advanced studies in science should learn to use units in a correct and consistent way from the start.

It is better to omit the work on "amount of substance" altogether, rather than to try to find pedagogical devices to allow pupils to get the right answer without really understanding what is happening. So this topic is only required of those aiming for top grades in public examinations. We have also limited the number of types of calculations.

Questions 27 and 34 to 37 refer back to a number of important reactions introduced in earlier chapters.

Answers to selected questions
28a 1 mol
b 2 mol
c 0.01 mol
d 0.1038 mol.

29a 39 g
b 216 g
c 140 g
d 32 g
e 5.6 g.

30a 40 g
b 32 g
c 414 g
d 3 g.

31a 28 g
b 71 g
c 64 g
d 63 g.

32a 1 g
b 2 g
c 88 g
d 43 g.

33a 58.5 g
b 200 g
c 78 g
d 102 g.

34 90 g

35 11.5 g

36 1.6 g

37 560 g

Activities

Worksheet C5A Molecules or giant structures?

REQUIREMENTS

Each group of pupils will need:
Copy of Worksheet **C5A**
Tin lid
Tongs
Burner, tripod and mat
Eye protection

Access to:
Small samples of the following solids (preferably in rice-grain sized lumps rather than as powders): copper, iron, zinc, graphite, sand, sodium chloride, magnesium oxide, calcium carbonate, candle wax, glucose, polythene, ice
Fume cupboard

Restricted access to:
Polystyrene
Small lumps, or crystals, of sulphur and iodine – HARMFUL

Lumps of silicon should not be heated, as they frequently shatter explosively. Polystyrene, sulphur and iodine should only be heated in a fume-cupboard, as the sulphur dioxide formed when sulphur burns is toxic and iodine vapour can crystallize in the eye. Teachers may prefer to demonstrate what happens to sulphur and iodine. It is also important to restrict the amounts of wax and plastics which are heated.

Worksheet C5B Ions on the move

REQUIREMENTS

Each group of pupils will need:
Copy of Worksheet **C5B**
Microscope slide
2 crocodile clips with connecting wires
Power supply, 20 V d.c. (see note 1)
Pencil
Eye protection

Access to:
Filter paper and scissors
Tap water
Crystals of potassium manganate(VII)
  – OXYDIZING, HARMFUL –, with tweezers

Note:
1 Make sure that the lab pack cannot give more than 20 volts.

This is a reliable experiment and pupils should have no difficulty in observing the movement of the purple colour towards the positive electrode.

The colour of any other salts that might be used is likely to be too pale to give clear results. One possibility is to moisten the filter paper with ammonia solution and then put a crystal of copper(II) sulphate on the pencil line.

Teacher demonstration: Watching coloured ions move

REQUIREMENTS

The teacher will need:
U-tube
Stand and clamp to support U-tube
2 carbon (or preferably platinum) electrodes
2 long leads
Power supply, 20 V d.c.
Pipette, 25 ml
Beaker, 500 ml
Eye protection

Access to:
2 mol/L sulphuric acid – CORROSIVE
Concentrated solution of copper(II) chromate(VI) – IRRITANT – in 2 mol/L sulphuric acid and saturated with urea, allow 40 ml (see note 1)

Note:

1 In a fume-cupboard, dissolve solid copper(II) chromate(VI) – IRRITANT – in the minimum volume of 2 mol/L sulphuric acid – CORROSIVE – and then saturate the solution with urea to increase its density.

The arrangement for the experiment is shown below. The demonstration needs to be started early in a double period to allow time for the results to become obvious. The class can do Worksheet **C5B** while the demonstration is running and then come to the front in groups to look at the results.

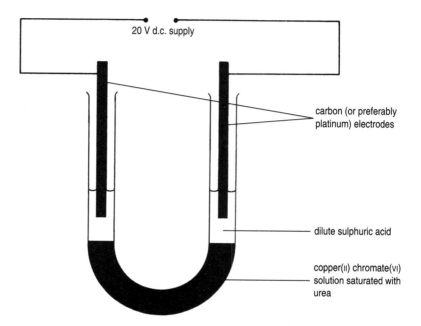

Procedure

Fill the U-tube with dilute sulphuric acid to about one-third of its depth. Run in the copper(II) chromate(VI) solution very slowly from a pipette, delivering it to the bottom of the U-tube so that it forms a separate layer and has a clear layer of sulphuric acid above it on both sides. Withdraw the pipette carefully to avoid mixing.

Insert an electrode into each arm of the U-tube to dip into the acid layer. Connect up to a source of 20 V d.c. Results should be visible after about 10 minutes and will be clear after half an hour. If the contents of the U-tube start to get hot, cool with a large beaker of cold water.

There is an interesting series of suggestions for discussing this demonstration with a class on pages 88-94 in *Visual communication in science* (Barlex and Carré, Cambridge Science Education Series, 1985).

Worksheet C5C Ions and electrolysis

REQUIREMENTS

Each group of pupils will need:
Copy of Worksheet **C5C**
Scissors
Glue, or sticky tape

Pupils can use this model in conjunction with section **C5.4** in the text. They can represent the chemical change at the electrodes by turning the ion circles over and writing the atom symbols on the back. The chlorine atoms can then be joined in pairs (with glue or sticky tape).

Unless they have already studied atomic structure in Physics, pupils cannot explain how ions lose their charges and turn back into atoms at the electrodes. This idea is developed further in Chapter C18.

Further information

Molecular models

Models of diamond, graphite, sulphur and sodium chloride are obtainable from Spiring Enterprises Ltd, Beke Hall, Billingshurst, W. Sussex RH14 9HF.

Science and Technology in Society

The following SATIS units might be used in conjunction with this chapter:

Unit 101 "Sulphurcrete"
Unit 506 "Materials for Life – new parts for old"

Chapter C6   Glasses and ceramics

The syllabus section

Context

The uses of glasses and ceramics, and the industrial methods used to fabricate articles from them, provide opportunities to investigate the advantages and disadvantages of these materials.

Knowledge and understanding

Syllabus statements	PoS	SoA
Know that common ceramic objects are made from fired clay.	3(iii)1	3.4(b)
Appreciate arguments for and against recycling materials such as glass.	3(i)5 3(iii)8	—
Understand that glass has a giant structure with a disordered arrangement of atoms.	3(i)5	3.8(d)
Be able to make evaluative judgements about the uses of ceramics and glass from their properties and structures, and by using data.	3(i)5	3.10(a)
Appreciate the bulk properties of ceramics, glass and plastic, and relate these to models of their structure.	3(i)5	3.10(c)

Opportunities for co-ordination

P1 covers the use of concrete in bridges and shows that it is weak in tension. The insulating properties of brick, concrete and glass are relevant to the investigation of strategies to prevent energy loss from houses in **P**9.

    The impact of quarrying and the problems of waste disposal are relevant to the whole question of the impact of industry on the environment, which is an important part of **B**17.

Routes and times

Basic	Central	Further
Omit pages 115–117. Include both further investigations in Worksheet C6A. *1¼ hours*	**C6.1 What are glasses?** (pages 113–117) Omit Q1–6. **Worksheet C6A Making glass** Investigation 3 is optional. *1½ hours*	All questions are suitable for homework.
	C6.2 What are ceramics? Omit questions. *¼ hour*	This should be done for homework.
Replace sections **C**6.4 and **C**6.5 with Worksheet **C**6B "Glass working".	**C6.3 How do we use glasses and ceramics at home?** **C6.4 How are glasses and ceramics used in industry?** **C6.5 How are glass and ceramic objects manufactured?** Omit Q23. *1¼ hours*	Q15–17 and 23 are suitable for homework.
Slower pupils could spend longer on section **C**6.6. *¾ hour*	**C6.6 Recycling glass** *½ hour*	
Total: 3½ hours	*Total: 3½ hours*	*Total: 3¼ hours*

The pupils' book

C6.1 What are glasses?

Some pupils will not be aware that there is a great variety of glasses. A small exhibition of objects made from different types of glass might help to put across the idea (see also the notes on section **C6.2**).

A glass may be regarded as a supercooled liquid with such a high viscosity that it is effectively a rigid solid. It does not have the regular arrangement of atoms found in crystals. One of the most obvious similarities between glasses and liquids is the fact that they are transparent, unlike polycrystalline materials in which the many internal surfaces scatter and reflect light.

Silicon dioxide glass is difficult to melt and shape, so other oxides are added to lower the viscosity and hence the working temperature. Alkali and alkaline earth metal carbonates are included in the mixture fed to the furnace. The carbonates decompose to oxides which modify the glass giant structure by reacting to break up the network of strong and directional covalent bonds, as shown below.

Doubly charged calcium ions produce stronger lattice forces than singly charged sodium ions. Calcium ions also act as a bridge between two negatively charged oxygen atoms, so they have a smaller effect on the viscosity but help to prevent a complete breakdown of the glass network.

A teacher demonstration described under Activities provides evidence for the existence of ions in glass and helps to revise some of the ideas met in Chapter **C5**.

Answer to selected question
6a Si:Ca ratio is 7:1.
b 73.8 % SiO_2 16.3 % Na_2O, 9-8 % CaO.

C6.2 What are ceramics?

An exhibition of ceramic objects might help to draw attention to this group of materials which we take very much for granted (see also the notes on section **C6.1**). This chapter concentrates on traditional ceramics based on clay. Lack of time prevents a review of the many new ceramic materials which are important for their electronic, magnetic, abrasive, refractory or piezo-electric properties.

There is some argument about the classification of ceramics and glasses. An American ceramicist, W.D. Kingery wrote as follows in his *Introduction to ceramics*:

> "We define ceramics as the art and science of making and using solid articles which have as their essential component, and are composed in large part of, **inorganic, non-metallic materials**. This definition includes not only materials such as pottery, porcelain, refractories, structural clay products, abrasives, porcelain enamels, cements and glass, but also non-metallic magnetic materials, ferroelectrics, manufactured single crystals, and a variety of other products which were not in existence a few years ago – and many of which do not exist today."

In this course we are using a more limited definition of ceramics and we distinguish ceramics from glasses. Attention is directed mainly to traditional ceramics based on clay.

Answers to selected questions

7 A kaolinite crystal about 15 mm across would actually be 0.0005 mm or 500 nm across.

8 5000 silicon atoms across the crystal.

C6.3 How do we use glasses and ceramics at home?
C6.4 How are glasses and ceramics used in industry?

There is an opportunity here for groups of pupils to make wall charts illustrating the many uses of ceramics and glasses as well as their advantages and disadvantages as materials. Leaflets, booklets, magazines and catalogues contain many pictures of materials in use.

Ceramics and glasses have giant structures and so they have high melting-points. They are made from oxides and cannot burn because they have already been oxidized. This is the basis of their refractory properties. These two aspects of their chemistry should be accessible to pupils and should be emphasized.

C6.5 How are glass and ceramic objects manufactured?

If time permits, this section might be illustrated with a film, video or a visit. If there is a pottery department in the school then a demonstration of the stages in making a glazed pot from raw clay will add interest to this section.

Worksheet **C6C** is designed to help pupils think about the Float Process. This can be a group activity in school. Clearly the pupils should not have access to their Chemistry book while doing it.

C6.6 Recycling glass

A more detailed treatment of this topic is given in Science Unit 2: *Glass*, published by the Tidy Britain Group (see Further information).

The Glass Manufacturers' Federation publishes a number of booklets, magazines and leaflets about Bottle Banks and the campaign to increase the amount of glass recycled (see Appendix).

Answers to selected questions

25 Non-return bottle – one trip 6.9 MJ
Re-usable bottle – one trip 9.7 MJ
– two trips 6.1 MJ
– five trips 3.9 MJ

26a Overall saving per tonne = 5552 MJ
b Volume of fuel oil saved   = 135 L

Activities

Worksheet C6A Making glass

REQUIREMENTS

Each group of pupils will need:
Copy of Worksheet **C6A**
Sample tube or test-tube with stopper
Crucible (see note 1, overleaf)
Tongs
Burner, tripod and mat
Pipe-clay triangle
Eye protection

Access to:
Lead(II) oxide – HARMFUL – with spatula, allow 4 g per group
Boric acid with spatula, allow 2 g per group
Zinc oxide with spatula, allow 0.5 g per group
Balance

Further investigations

The chemical resistance of glass

Each group will need:
4 test-tubes in rack
Eye protection

Access to:
Dilute nitric acid – IRRITANT
Dilute hydrochloric acid
Dilute sodium hydroxide solution – CORROSIVE
Bleach – CORROSIVE

Colouring glass (see note 2)

Each group will need access to:
Further quantities of the glass-making chemicals listed above
A few grains of selected metal oxides: iron(III) oxide, manganese(IV) oxide – HARMFUL, copper(II) oxide and cobalt(II) oxide

Notes:
1 After use the crucibles can be cleaned, once cool, in 5 mol/L nitric acid – CORROSIVE. This treatment may have to be repeated two or three times.
2 Only minute amounts of the metal oxide are needed. The teachers' notes for the Tidy Britain Group unit on Glass give more details; they suggest that simple jewellery can be made by using epoxy resin to fix coloured beads of lead borate glass to metal ring mounts. The unit also includes a worksheet showing that the colouring of glass can be investigated using borax beads. (See Further information.)

This experiment shows clearly how a mixture of powdered oxides can be converted into glass. It is also fun to do, and another example of making something useful from chemicals. The practical application of glass making can be emphasized if there is time to go on and make ornamental coloured glass beads.

Lead borate glass is not resistant to attack by aqueous reagents. The glass dissolves in dilute nitric acid overnight. Treatment with dilute hydrochloric acid results in a white, powdery surface. Dilute sulphuric acid has little affect. Bleach has no effect, but the surface of the glass is pitted after treatment with dilute sodium hydroxide.

Worksheet C6B Glass working

REQUIREMENTS

Each pupil will need:
Copy of Worksheet **C6B**
Length of glass rod, to make a stirring rod
  (see note 1)
2 lengths of glass tubing, for making a dropping
  pipette and a right-angle bend (see note 1)
One longer length of glass rod for glass blowing
Burner, tripod and mat
Tongs
Eye protection

Access to:
Glass-cutting knife or file (see note 1)
Flame spreader or batswing burner
  (one between four pupils)

Note:
1 The glass rod should be cut in advance. Cutting tubing is easier and safer than cutting glass rods, so teachers may prefer the pupils to cut their own lengths. On the other hand, cutting the tubing in advance is likely to be more economical.

This experiment will give pupils experience of the behaviour of hot glass so that they can contrast it with the melting of crystalline solids. They will also come to appreciate the skill involved in glass blowing when they find how difficult it can be to make quite simple items. In a double period the majority of the pupils will develop some ability to manipulate glass.

The worksheet has been prepared on the assumption that the teacher or technician will demonstrate the techniques first. If the technician has been trained in simple glass working, this activity is a good opportunity to remind pupils of the technical skill needed in science prep. rooms. Three of the items to be made are useful, and so the glass is not wasted. The dropping pipette is easier to make and more robust than ones made by drawing a jet.

The instructions on the worksheet suggest that the wider end of the dropping pipette is spread out by pressing it down onto a heatproof mat when hot. Better results are achieved using a moulding cone, or simply a length of graphite rod sharpened into a pencil shape as shown on the left.

The pupils are likely to be most interested in glass blowing. **It is vital that they wear eye-protection.** If they blow too hard and burst the bulb there may be fine fragments of glass in the air.

Glass blowing can be extended by asking the pupils to make a thermometer. After blowing a thick-walled bulb and letting it cool, they half-fill the tube with coloured water. Warming near the surface of the water produces steam which drives out the air. The open end is then sealed by rotating it in a flame. After cooling, the thermometer is calibrated in the usual way. This is a challenging test of manipulative skills.

The suggested tasks on the worksheet are functional and some pupils may respond to a more creative approach. It can be fun to make glass ornaments as shown below. Thin coloured rods for ornamentation can be made by drawing out coloured rod from suppliers.

Forming the end of a dropping pipette.

snail from a glass rod rolled up and shaped as shown

swan from a glass rod bent and moulded as shown

miniature scent bottle and stopper:
bottle from tube/bubble (blow a little glass bubble and flatten the end to form the base of the bottle)
stopper from rod: a glass rod is formed in a stopper shape

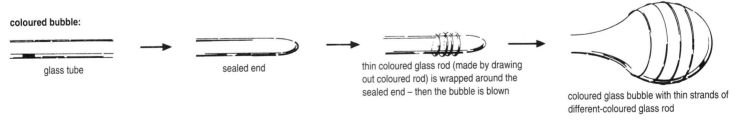

coloured bubble:

glass tube

sealed end

thin coloured glass rod (made by drawing out coloured rod) is wrapped around the sealed end – then the bubble is blown

coloured glass bubble with thin strands of different-coloured glass rod

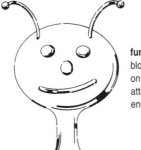

funny faces from bubble and coloured blobs and rod: make a glass bubble, stick on coloured blobs for eyes, nose, mouth, attach fine coloured rod with blobs on ends for antennae

Some simple glass ornaments which pupils can make.

Teacher demonstration: Evidence for ions in soda-lime glass

Safety note
This demonstration is potentially hazardous. Head teachers or heads of departments who permit staff to carry it out in unsafe ways could be at risk of prosecution. Appendix 5 (pages 18–19) of Chapter 3 of *Topics in safety* (ASE, 2nd edition, 1988) gives a safe procedure which involves construction of a special connector box. However, some LEAs may not permit such procedures at all and teachers must check.

Further information

The Mineral Industries Manpower and Careers Unit
Let's look at china clay is a set of curriculum materials available from the Unit (MIMCU – see Appendix). The pack includes a teachers' guide, worksheets which teachers are free to copy, a resource book for pupils and samples of rocks and minerals. A modest fee is charged. The use of this material would introduce more Earth Science into the course. Topics covered include the origins, mining, processing and uses of china clay as well as economic and environmental issues.

Tidy Britain Group
Science Unit 2: *Glass* is a kit of curriculum materials which includes teachers' notes, a set of booklets for the pupils, practical worksheets and a film strip which can be made into slides. The practical cards include experiments to investigate the toughening and colouring of glass. The text of the pupils book covers the reuse and recycling of glass in some detail and also revises some basic optics by showing how discarded and broken bottles might start fires in dry summers. (See Appendix.)

University of York Science Education Group
The unit *Buildings* in the Salters' Chemistry course includes investigations of glass and clay.

Science and Technology in Society
Unit 410 "Glass".
   This unit includes reading, questions and practical work on the manufacture, uses and recycling of glass.

Science at Work (old edition)
Section 1 of *Building science* includes experiments to investigate mortar and concrete. There is also a description of how bricks are made from clay.

Chapter C7 Metals and alloys

The syllabus section

Context

This section examines the connection between the properties of metals and alloys and their uses. A simplified model of metal giant structures is used to illustrate the way in which metallurgists seek to explain the properties of metals.

Knowledge and understanding

	Tier		Syllabus statements	PoS	SoA
B	C	F			

Syllabus statements	PoS	SoA
Know that materials can be converted into new, useful products through a range of types of chemical reactions.	3(iii)1	3.4(b)
Understand, through study of a range of reactions related to everyday processes, that rusting involves a reaction with oxygen and water.	3(iii)1	3.5(c)
Appreciate the advantages and disadvantages of alternative methods of preventing rusting.	3(iii)1	3.6(d)
Be able to explain how techniques such as chromatography can be used to separate substances.	3(i)6	3.5(a)
Be able to investigate oxidation processes, as reactions with oxygen to form oxides, in the context of a range of reactions.	3(iii)1	3.6(c)
Be able to recognize variations in the properties of metals, and sequence common metals in order of reactivity.	3(i)3	3.6(d)
Be able to relate the uses and properties, such as tensile and compressive strengths, porosity, thermal conductivity and cost, of metals to everyday use.	3(i)5	3.7(a)
Understand that metals are polycrystalline and that the atoms are arranged in close-packed layers in metal crystals.	3(i)5	3.8(d)
Appreciate that the bonding in metals must be somehow different from that in the giant structures in glasses, to account for the fact that metals can be bent and stretched.	3(i)5	3.8(d)
Appreciate that alloying can modify the properties of metals because the atoms of metals differ in size.	3(i)5	3.10(a) 3.10(c)

Opportunities for co-ordination

The properties and uses of metals link to **P1**, **P6** and **P16**: links also to Design and Technology.

Routes and times

Basic	Central	Further

C7.1 Why are metals so useful?

1/4 hour

This should be done for homework.

Omit pages 134–138 and Q5 and 6 from section **C7.2**.

3/4 hour

Worksheet C7A Properties of metals

C7.2 How can we explain the properties of metals? (pages 130–138; class + homework) Omit Q6.

1 1/4 hours

Q6 is suitable at this level.

C7.3 What are alloys, and how do they differ from pure metals?
Omit Q8 and 9 and figure 7.35.

Worksheet C7B Analysing an alloy

1 1/2 hours

All parts are suitable but faster groups spend less time on this section.

1 1/4 hours

Slower pupils may need to spend longer on the Sc1 assessment. Show the ITV video "Corrosion".

3 hours

C7.4 How can we stop corrosion?
Omit Q10.

Box 1 Problem: What is the best way to stop rusting?

Sc1 assessment on rusting.

2 1/4 hours

Total: 5 1/2 hours   *Total: 5 1/4 hours*   *Total: 4 3/4 hours*

Monitoring the progress of Sc1

Investigating rusting

Pupils should investigate the effect of salt on the rusting of iron. This investigation may be carried out instead of the problem "What is the best way to stop rusting?" in box 1.

Sample criteria are given below for an assessment between levels 4 and 7.

Strand (i) Ask questions, predict and hypothesize, e.g.	Strand (ii) Observe, measure and manipulate variables, e.g.	Strand (iii) Interpret their results and evaluate scientific evidence, e.g.
4(a) Suggest that the concentration of salt matters, and suggest how the rate of rusting may depend on the concentration of salt	**4(b)** Control volume of solution and mass of iron, and time how long it takes before mist appears in solutions of two different concentrations	**4(c)** Conclude that a more concentrated salt soltuion corrodes more quickly than a less concentrated solution
5(a) Suggest that iron will rust more quickly in a strong salt solution than in a weak salt solution because there are more salt particles in a strong solution	**5(b)** As above, but over a meaningful range of concentrations	**5(c)** As above, but qualifiying the conclusion
6(a) Suggest that the higher the concentration, the quicker the rusting because there are more salt particles in a strong solution	**6(b)** Time how long it takes a range of different amounts of iron to begin rusting over a meaningful range of concentrations	**6(c)** Conclude that increasing the concentration increases the rate of reaction because of the increased number of particles present
7(a) Suggest, with reasons, that concentration of salt, volume of liquid, amount of iron and temperature may all affect the rate of rusting, and that salt concentration is the most important	**7(b)** As above, but over a range of temperatures	**7(c)** As above, but indicating the range of concentrations and temperatures used

The pupils' book

C7.1 Why are metals so useful?

Questions 1 and 2 provide alternative ways of making pupils more aware of the importance of metals. These can be class activities or they can be set for homework. Copies of Worksheet **C7A** will be needed if pupils are asked to answer question 1.

C7.2 How can we explain the properties of metals?

If possible, pupils should be shown examples of the grain structure of metals. This can be demonstrated quickly and easily by the lead-pancake experiment (see under Activities). In schools which study a metallurgy option at A-level it may be possible to show pupils samples of polished and etched specimens of metals which have been preserved in plastic.

The lead-pancake experiment can be difficult to interpret on an atomic scale. Pupils might use a stencil to add "atoms" to a diagram such as the one to the left. They add atoms two at a time to each "grain" and see what happens when they meet.

There is no intention to distinguish the three main types of metal structure. Metallic bonding is named to distinguish it from the bonding in other giant structures such as diamond, and to point out that the forces holding metal atoms together must differ from those between non-metal atoms to account for the fact that metals can be bent and stretched without breaking. There is no attempt to explain metallic bonding.

In this diagram you can see that three crystals have started to grow. Copy the diagram using a stencil or a coin to draw the circles – they do not have to be the same size as the ones drawn here.
Now make your three crystals grow by adding more and more atoms until there is no room for any more.

Question 5 asks the pupils to reflect on their understanding of the structure of solids. Some of the suggested false deductions from the model have been shown to be common misconceptions by the Children's Learning in Science Project (see for example CLIS "Aspects of secondary students' understanding of the particulate nature of matter", January 1984).

The behaviour of layers of atoms in a metal structure can be demonstrated on an overhead projector with a bubble raft, with ball bearings in a Petri dish, or with marbles.

Figure 7.24 gives another opportunity for pupils to reflect on the difference between a giant structure and a molecular structure.

C7.3 What are alloys, and how do they differ from pure metals?

Pupils who are doing metalwork in a technology course should be able to contribute a good deal to this section of the course. Pupils are not expected to remember the details of the compositions of alloys.

The suggested practical work involves the analysis of an alloy by chromatography. A different method of analysis is given in the *Metals* unit of the Salters' Chemistry Course. Instead of analysing alloys it is possible to make and test alloys as described in the *Building materials* booklet from the old edition of Science at Work.

Answer to selected question
9 The ratio by amounts is 3 mol Fe: 0.5 mol Cr.
So the atomic ratio for Fe:Cr is 6:1.

C7.4 How can we stop corrosion?

It is assumed that the pupils have done an experiment to show that air and water are needed to make iron go rusty. In this section, the pupils should focus their attention on designing an experiment to investigate the available methods for preventing corrosion. Different groups in the class can tackle different questions. Finally, representatives of each group can be asked to give a brief report on their findings to the rest of the class.

Activities

Teacher demonstration: How do crystals form from molten lead?

REQUIREMENTS

The teacher will need:
Crucible
Pipe-clay triangle
Burner, tripod and mat
Tongs
Smooth metal plate
Beaker, 250 ml
Tongs
Spatula
Eye protection and protective gloves

Access to:
Lead metal, 30–40 g (see note 1)
Powdered charcoal
Dilute nitric acid, 2 mol/L – IRRITANT – about 50 ml
Good ventilation

Note:
1 Avoid lead shot. Lead foil can be used, but if it is thin it may oxidize rather quickly during melting. Thick lead sheet or lead piping is better.

Lead "pancake".

Procedure
1 Melt the lead in the crucible, but do not overheat. If the metal is dirty, a scum will collect on the surface. This can be removed using a spatula, preferably after adding a little powdered charcoal.
2 Pour the molten lead onto the flat surface so that it forms a pool some 30 to 50 mm in diameter. Use the spatula to hold back any remaining scum, or charcoal, as you pour.
3 Immerse the cold lead "pancake" in dilute nitric acid. Remove the specimen after 15–30 seconds when the metal crystals reflect light and sparkle. Wash with distilled water and dry. A typical etched pancake is shown on the left.

Worksheet C7B Analysing an alloy

REQUIREMENTS

Each group of pupils will need:
Gas jar and lid, or large beaker with aluminium foil cover
Chromatography paper, Whatman No. 1 (see note 1)
2 or 3 plastic paper clips
Tweezers
Eye protection

Access to:
Solvent (90 % propanone – FLAMMABLE, 5 % concentrated hydrochloric acid – CORROSIVE, 5 % water), allow 20-50 ml per group
Solutions containing the following metal ions, each at about 0.1 mol/L: Ag^+, Cu^{2+}, Fe^{3+}, and Ni^{2+}, a few drops per group
Fine glass tubes provided with each of the metal ion solutions (see note 2)
Large watchglass or dish, with 0.1 % dithio-oxamide in ethanol – FLAMMABLE –, in fume cupboard
Trough in fume cupboard with concentrated ammonia solution – CORROSIVE
String and plastic clips to act as a "washing line" for chromatograms, in the fume cupboard

The teacher will need:
Evaporating basin(s), one per sample to be investigated
Tongs
Eye protection

Access to:
Aqua regia – VERY CORROSIVE – (see note 3)
Alloy sample(s) for analysis (see note 4)
Distilled water
Measuring cylinder, 10 ml

Notes:
1 The chromatography paper should be cut to size so that it will stand inside the gas jar provided without touching the sides. Excellent results can be achieved using slotted chromatography paper; this is available from the usual suppliers. The slots prevent the spots from running into each other.
2 If there is time, the pupils may enjoy drawing their own fine glass tubes from soda-glass tubing. The technique will have to be demonstrated and pupils should be reminded of safety precautions required when glass working (see under Activities for Chapter C6).
3 Aqua regia is made by mixing three parts by volume of concentrated hydrochloric acid – CORROSIVE – with one part by volume of concentrated nitric acid – CORROSIVE – in a fume cupboard. Use the mixture immediately: do not stopper or store. It should be disposed of by pouring into a large excess of water.
4 Suitable samples include pre-decimal coins and foreign coins.

R_f values for the metal ions under these conditions are as follows: Cu^{2+}: 0.09; Ni^{2+}: 0.05; Fe^{3+}: 0.73; and Ag^+: close to zero. So copper or nickel can be separated from iron. Silver can be distinguished from copper but not very well from nickel. The spots on the developed chromatogram have different colours, and this helps to identify the ions.

The teacher must demonstrate the preparation of the solution of the unknown sample by dissolving a very small amount of the alloy in about 0.5 ml of aqua regia, which is highly corrosive. This can be done by immersing a coin in the reagent for about 30 seconds. The solution formed is diluted with about 5 ml of distilled water. The pupils can spot the diluted solution onto the paper.

This is an interesting experiment, but pupils should perhaps be told that nowadays an analyst would be unlikely to use chromatography to analyse alloys. The modern techniques include solvent extraction, spot tests, and atomic absorption spectroscopy.

Box 1 Problem: What is the best way to stop rusting?

REQUIREMENTS

Each group of pupils will need:
Copy of Worksheet C0
Petri dishes or test-tubes
Eye protection

Access to:
Warm solution of corrosion indicator (see note 1), 30–60 ml per group depending on the containers used for the samples
Metal samples (see note 2)
Cleaning agent for metal samples (see note 3)
Derusting agent for metal samples (see note 4)
Zinc foil, magnesium ribbon – FLAMMABLE – and copper foil
Various tools including snips, a file, hammer and pliers
Commercial corrosion inhibitors (see note 5)
Various types of paint, with brushes
Oil and Vaseline
Protective gloves

Notes:
1 Prepare the corrosion indicator shortly before the lesson. Make a warm solution of 5 g gelatine in 100 ml water and then dissolve 0.2 g of potassium hexacyanoferrate(III) in it. Keep the solution warm.
2 Scraps of mild steel are likely to be available from the technology department. Clout nails from a hardware store are a convenient source of galvanized steel. Tin-plated steel can be cut from tinned fruit cans (but take care with the sharp edges). Stainless steel screws or bolts can be obtained from a hardware store or from a boat chandler.

3 Dirt, grease and fingermarks will interfere with the results. A suitable cleaning agent is a solution containing 5 % sodium carbonate and 0.5 % household detergent.
4 Existing rust must be removed from samples before the experiment. Rust can be removed with dilute hydrochloric acid followed by thorough rinsing in cold water.
5 Pupils should be advised to note the safety warnings on the packs of commercial inhibitors and to handle them with care, using protective gloves if necessary.

This investigation is suggested in box 1 on page 143 of the Chemistry pupils' book. It may be helpful to demonstrate the use of the indicator with unprotected iron nails before the groups of pupils start to think about their plans.

The suggested indicator is only designed to detect iron(II) ions. With the suggested concentration of potassium hexacyanoferrate(III) it will take up to half an hour before obvious signs of corrosion appear. This allows time for the solution to gel. It also gives a clearer distinction between treated and untreated specimens. The results are more rapid if sodium chloride is added to the reagent (5 g in 100 ml).

In warm weather it may be helpful to increase the concentration of gelatine, using about 8 g in 100 ml of the solution. The standard ferroxyl indicator also includes phenolphthalein to show the regions where hydroxide ions are being formed. For most pupils it will be simpler to omit this complication, but if desired add 1 ml of phenolphthalein solution – FLAMMABLE – to 100 ml of the reagent.

In studies to see what happens when iron is linked with other metals, it is important to make sure that the second metal is tightly gripped to the iron to ensure good contact.

Further information

ITV Science and Technology series
The video "Corrosion" is useful here.

Science at Work
Section 1 of *Materials and their uses* includes a section on corrosion and its prevention by various means.

University of York Science Education Group
Chemistry in Action includes a unit called *Aluminium can...* Pupils are asked to compare the advantages and disadvantages of aluminium and steel as packaging materials for food

The unit about *Metals* in Salters' Chemistry has a section about the analysis of the alloy used to make drawing pins. Another section covers the effect of alloying on the properties of metals. Three sections deal with the causes and prevention of corrosion.

Tidy Britain Group
Science Unit 3, *Metals*, covers alloys, the shaping of metals, the conservation of metals and the effects of lead in the environment. The kit includes booklets for the pupils together with slides and practical worksheets dealing with alloys, heat treatment, corrosion, anodizing and air pollution.

Science and Technology in Society
The following SATIS units might be used in conjunction with the work in this chapter:

Unit 310 "Recycling aluminium"
Unit 103 "Controlling rust"
Unit 604 "Metals as resources".

Chapter C8 Polymers

The syllabus section

Context

This section continues to emphasize the two themes, which are the connection between the properties of materials and their uses, and the theory which explains properties in terms of structure and bonding. The theory of this section provides further examples of the important idea that the bonds within molecules are much stronger than the forces between molecules.

The everyday importance of plastics can be illustrated by looking at the variety of methods used to fabricate objects from polymeric materials.

Knowledge and understanding

Syllabus statements	PoS	SoA
Appreciate that there are both natural and synthetic polymers and know that monomers can be converted into new products by polymerization.	3(iii)1	3.4(b)
Know how thermoplastics and thermosets behave on heating and study the properties and uses of plastics and fibres.	3(i)5	3.7(a)
Know that plastics are giant molecules.	3(i)5	3.8(d)
Understand the difference between addition and condensation polymerization using simplified models.	3(iii)1	3.8(d)
Understand the processes involved in the production of plastics.	3(iii)9 3(iii)10	3.8(e)
Be able to make evaluative judgements about the uses of plastics through the study, using data, of their properties and structure.	3(i)5	3.10(a)
Understand the difference between thermoplastics and thermosets in terms of weak "between molecule" forces and cross-linking.	3(i)5	3.10(c)

Tier: B C F

Opportunities for co-ordination

The use of keys for identification is introduced in **B**1. There are links with the study of protein and carbohydrate polymers in **B**6 and **B**10.

Plastic and elastic materials are mentioned in **P**1. The strength of synthetic fibres and fabrics is referred to in connection with seat belts in **P**6. **P**9 features the use of plastics in home insulation.

There are opportunities to link work with Design and Technology.

Routes and times

Basic	Central	Further
Omit Q8 from Worksheet **C**8A. Replace section **C**8.1 with the booklet *Plastics explained* (BP Caveman series) or similar.	**Worksheet C8A Polymerization** C8.1 **What are polymers?** (pages 145–148 and 150–151) *1½ hours*	
Slower groups could spend longer on Worksheet **C**8D and identify a larger number of plastics. *2 hours*	C8.2 **How do we use polymers?** **Worksheet C8D A key to identify plastics** *1½ hours*	
Replace sections **C**8.3 and **C**8.4 with the booklet *Shaping plastics* (BP Caveman series) or similar. *½ hour*	C8.3 **What is the structure of plastics?** C8.4 **Who does what in the plastics industry?** Or a video on thermoplastics. *³⁄₄ hour*	Emphasise cross-linking and "between molecule" forces.
Omit part d and the data exercise but discuss reinforced concrete.	**Worksheet C8E Composite materials** Part d is optional. Omit Q10 and 11, and refer back to Q2 on page 88. *1½ hours*	Q9–11 should be done for homework.
Total: 5½ hours	*Total: 5¼ hours*	*Total: 5¼ hours*

The pupils' book

C8.1 What are polymers?

Teachers may like to take the opportunity to revise the work on polymerization in Chapters **C2** and **C3** with the help of molecular models. Use of models will help pupils to see the difference between addition and condensation polymerization.

Box 1 uses simple C_2 compounds to point out the advantages of the newer chemical names. However, a knowledge of formal chemical nomenclature is not an examinable part of this course. Where necessary, alternative names will be given and pupils will have access to data tables giving names and formulae.

Figure 8.12 is included to help pupils to think through the idea of condensation polymerization.

C8.2 How do we use polymers?

The modification of cellulose can be demonstrated in two ways. Part 4 of the booklet *Fibres and fabrics* from the old edition of Science at Work describes a procedure for making rayon. Details of a method for making cellulose acetate are given in the section on Activities below.

C8.3 What is the structure of plastics?

Teachers will know that the majority of pupils have difficulty in grasping the distinction between the bonding within molecules and the bonding between molecules. An appreciation of this distinction is crucial if pupils are ever to understand the contrast between molecules and giant structures. This section provides a good opportunity to develop the idea after they have used the key in Worksheet **C8D**. The first test distinguishes thermosoftening plastics which only have weak forces between the molecules and thermosetting plastics which are cross-linked. Molecular models can be used to explain the difference effectively.

Some pupils may appreciate the application of the same ideas in hair-dressing. When hair is washed in hot water, set and dried, only weak "between molecule forces" are broken and reformed. The result does not last. However a "perm" involves breaking and reforming strong bonds cross-linking the protein molecules, and the result is permanent until the hair has grown out.

In Chapter **C11** the difference in fastness between natural dyes and modern reactive dyes is also explained in terms of "within molecule" and "between molecule" forces.

More able pupils may appreciate the ICI video *Polymers* (see Appendix). The section on the mechanism of polymerization is at A-level standard; however there is an interesting sequence which illustrates the uses of a number of thermosoftening plastics and explains how their properties can be controlled. The final part shows the variety of plastics used in a modern refrigerator. The film uses systematic names.

C8.4 Who does what in the plastics industry ?

This will make more impact if the pupils can see a film or video. The ICI video "*Working with thermoplastics*" is suitable (see Appendix).

Activities

Each group of pupils will need:
2 beakers, 10 ml
Tweezers
Glass rod
Measuring cylinder, 10 ml
Protective gloves
Eye protection

Each group of pupils will need:
Disposable container (see note 2)
Glass rod
10-ml measuring cylinder
Protective gloves
Eye protection

Worksheet C8A Polymerization

Part 1

REQUIREMENTS

Access to:
Fume cupboard
Solution 1: hexanedioyl dichloride (adipoyl chloride) – CORROSIVE – in 1,1,1-trichloroethane – HARMFUL – (5 g in 100 ml solvent), 5 ml per group (see note 1), with 10-ml measuring cylinder
Solution 2: diaminohexane – IRRITANT – in water (5 g in 100 ml water), 5 ml per group

Part 2

REQUIREMENTS

Access to:
Fume cupboard
Methanal (40 % formalin – TOXIC), 10 ml per group (see note 3)
Urea, 5 g per group
Dilute sulphuric acid, 1 mol/L – IRRITANT – 5 ml per group
Balance

Note:
1 Solution 1 must be freshly made. (Cyclohexane – FLAMMABLE – may be used as the solvent, in which case the "shelf life" is at least one week.) Decanedioyl dichloride (sebacoyl chloride) – CORROSIVE – can be used as a cheaper alternative.

Notes:
2 A section cut from a plastic egg carton is suitable for this experiment.
3 Methanal vapour is poisonous and so this experiment must be done in a fume cupboard. Methanal may form a powerful carcinogen if allowed to mix with hydrochloric acid. Methanal should be stored separately from concentrated hydrochloric acid.

Close supervision of the pupils is required, and these preparations should be demonstrated if there is any doubt about their competence to handle hazardous chemicals. Do not allow the pupils to handle the nylon "rope" without protective gloves: it is, in fact, a thin tube that contains the solvent and unreacted reagent.

One possibility is for the teacher to demonstrate a larger scale version of the nylon "rope-trick" and then allow the pupils to do part 2 (working with fume cupboards).

Other polymerization reactions which can be demonstrated are given under Further information at the end of this chapter.

Worksheet C8B The label at the back: a look at clothing fibres

REQUIREMENTS

Each pupil will need:
Copy of Worksheet **C**8B.
In case some pupils are unable to carry out the survey at home it would be useful to have a range of garments available in the lesson.

This is based on the SATIS unit 405 and is in three linked parts.

Part 1 *Looking at clothing labels*
The survey of clothing labels is best done for homework, though it would be possible to bring a range of garments to the class.

Part 2 *Which are the most popular fibres?*
The class results are combined and summarized in a table.

Part 3 Questions and activities
Questions 10–14 and Factsheet 3 are intended for use only with more able students.

Worksheet C8C Polymers all about us

REQUIREMENTS

Each pupil will need:
Copy of Worksheet **C8C**

The teacher will need:
Set of slides (see note 1)
Slide projector and screen

Note:
1 The easiest and cheapest way of getting a suitable set of slides is to ask a senior pupil, members of a photography club, or a member of staff to take them. Pupils are likely to be much more interested if they are having a fresh look at familiar scenes in and around the school. They will enjoy seeing staff and pupils in the pictures. As far as possible the pictures should cover the advantages and disadvantages of plastics listed below. A range of natural and synthetic polymers should be included covering plastics, elastomers and fibres. Some possibilities are included in the table opposite.

Advantages of plastics	**Disadvantages of plastics**
<ul><li>Easily moulded</li><li>Strong in relation to their weight</li><li>Hardwearing</li><li>Waterproof</li><li>Weather resistant</li><li>Chemically resistant</li><li>Rot resistant</li><li>Fairly cheap</li><li>Clear, or translucent, but can be easily coloured</li><li>Electrical insulators</li><li>Thermal insulators</li></ul>	<ul><li>Many soften and melt at low temperatures</li><li>Flammable – and when they burn some give off poisonous fumes</li><li>May gradually change shape if heavily loaded</li><li>Some slowly break down in sunlight</li><li>Easily scratched</li><li>Not biodegradable</li></ul>

Advantages and disadvantages of plastics.

The idea here is that the pupils are shown the slides and fill in the worksheet after discussion in class.

Teacher demonstration: Making cellulose acetate

REQUIREMENTS

The teacher will need:
Beaker, 100 ml
Beaker, 250 ml
Measuring cylinder, 25 ml
Measuring cylinder, 10 ml
Watchglass
Glass rod
2 dropping pipettes
Filter funnel
Eye protection for the teacher and pupils

Access to:
Cotton wool, 0.5 g (see note 1)
Glacial acetic (ethanoic) acid – CORROSIVE – 20 ml
Acetic (ethanoic) anhydride – CORROSIVE – 5 ml
Concentrated sulphuric acid – CORROSIVE – 2
  drops
Distilled water, 150 ml
Muslin cloth
Blotting paper or paper towels
Fume cupboard

Note:
1 This experiment only works satisfactorily using pure cotton wool.

Picture/s	Useful properties of polymers shown in the picture	Limitations of polymers shown in the picture	Type of polymer (if known)
Plastic drain pipe/ Rusty iron pipe	No corrosion. Strong in relation to weight	May slowly become brittle in sunlight	Unplasticized pvc
Insulated wires in science lab	Electrical insulator Flexible. Easily coloured	Insulation melts if over – heated	Plasticized pvc
Table tennis balls – in action	Light and strong	Easily crushed. Highly flammable	Cellulose nitrate
Overloaded carrier bag with stretched handles	Cheap. Strong in relation to weight	May stretch if overloaded	Low density polythene
Melamine camping mug with enamel and ceramic mugs	Poor heat conductor. Tough. Easily coloured	Can be scratched. May stain	Melamine
Handle of iron or of a saucepan in DS room	Poor heat conductor. Thermosets do not melt	May char if overheated	Phenol-formaldehyde (Bakelite)
White electrical sockets and plugs	Electrical insulator	Brittle, may chip	Urea-formaldehyde
Stacking chairs in classroom – perhaps one damaged	Light in proportion to strength. Easily moulded	May crack or break if grossly misused	Polypropylene
Plastic litter in or near the school	Cheap and easily formed. Moisture proof. Easily coloured	Not biodegradable	Various – polythene, polypropylene
Car rear light in staff car-park	Transparent non-brittle substitute for glass. Easily coloured	Easily scratched	Acrylic
Clothing, e.g. school tie or blazer	Can be spun into fibres. Rotproof. Hardwearing	May be less absorbent than natural fibres	Polyester fibres
Resin used for fibre glass repairs or canoe building	Strong but light. Easily formed	Dangerous fumes during mixing and setting	Polyester resin
Bottle for fizzy drinks	Strong but light		Polyester film
Plastic casing of food mixer	Tough and strong. Can be formed into intricate shapes		ABS
Foam filled crash mat in gym	Light, flexible, durable, elastic	Can be a hazard in case of fire in the home. Fumes are very poisonous	Polyurethane covered with pvc
Foam plastic packaging or ceiling tiles or drinking cups	Good heat insulation. Absorbs shocks	Flammable	Expanded polystyrene
Model kit	Can be accurately moulded into intricate shapes	Dissolved by some solvents	Polystyrene
Photographic film	Transparent. Not attacked by chemicals		Cellulose acetate

Some possible slides.

Procedure

1 Working in a fume cupboard, place 20 ml of glacial acetic acid, 5 ml of acetic anhydride and 2 drops of concentrated sulphuric acid in a 100-ml beaker. Stir the reagents then add 0.5 g of cotton wool. Use a glass rod to make sure that all the cotton is immersed in the liquid mixture.

2 Cover the beaker with a watchglass and set aside in a fume cupboard for 24 hours, or until all the cotton wool has dissolved. (The viscosity of the polymer solution can be a discussion point with some pupils.)

3 Pour the mixture into a 250 ml beaker containing 150 ml of water. The cellulose acetate will now precipitate.

4 Filter the product using a cloth in a funnel. Press out as much moisture as possible and then blot dry. Complete the drying process by putting the product in an oven set at 50 °C.

Commercially this plastic is made from wood cellulose, not cotton. Fibres of cellulose acetate are produced by dry spinning using a solution of cellulose acetate in acetone (propanone).

Worksheet C8D A key to identify plastics

REQUIREMENTS

Each group of pupils will need:
Tongs
Eye protection

Access to:
Samples of plastics (see note 1) with scissors,
  or snips
Fume cupboard suitably equipped (see note 2)
Trough or large margarine tub for the float test
Washing up detergent, a few drops per group

Notes:

1 Sources of the plastic samples are suggested below. As far as possible the plastics should be free of fillers and pigments,but this is impossible for urea-formaldehye and phenol-formaldehyde plastics. The pieces provided for the heating tests must be very small. If pupils prepare their own samples, this should be carefully supervised to ensure that they do not heat and burn large quantities. Pupils should **not** heat pvc themselves, even in a fume cupboard; teachers could do this to demonstrate the technique.

2 Each fume cupboard will need: one or two medium-sized nails; tongs; burner; heatproof mat covered with large tin-lid to catch any drips; source of a small flame (such as a supply of wood splints or a candle).

Name of plastic	Sources of suitable samples
Urea-formaldehyde	light coloured domestic plugs and light fittings
Phenol-formaldehyde	dark coloured electric fittings, some screw caps for reagent bottles.
Nylon	curtain rail fittings, some plastic hinges
pvc	cling film, many transparent cooking oil or shampoo bottles
Polythene (ldpe)	sliced bread bags, bin liners, carrier bags
Polythene (hdpe)	some carrier bags and food bags (thinner, whiter and 'noisier' than ldpe)
Polypropylene	transparent film for crisps and other snack foods
Acrylic	'Perspex sheet', motor vehicle rear light covers
Polyester film	carbonated drink bottles (but not the base)
Polystyrene	disposable cups (not the expanded ones), translucent egg boxes, yoghurt pots (may be co-polymerized with butadiene)

Source of plastics for Worksheet **C**8D.

The key is only designed to work for the range of plastics listed in the table opposite. It is dangerous to allow pupils to heat any unknown plastics they may collect and bring to the laboratory.

The Tidy Britain Group worksheets include a key for identifying an even more limited range of packaging plastics. Some pupils may find this simpler to follow.

Worksheet C8D should only be used in a laboratory with fume cupboards. Otherwise it is much safer to use a key to identify fibres. Possible keys are included in the booklet *Fibres and fabrics* from the old edition of Science at Work.

Worksheet C8E Composite materials

REQUIREMENTS

Each pupil will need:
Plastic gloves
Eye protection

Each group of pupils will need:
Burner, tongs and heatproof mat
Tin-lids (for heating sulphur, sand, etc.)
2 beakers, 100ml
Dropping pipette

For part d (optional):
Selection of masses
Sticky tape
Plastic beaker, 250ml
Ruler
Other equipment as specified by the pupils

Access to:
Fume cupboard
Balance, to weigh to 0.1g
Hydrochloric acid, 2mol/L (200ml per class should be sufficient)
Samples of composite materials (all of approximately the same size if possible, e.g. $5\,cm \times 3\,cm \times 1/2\,cm$), for example: glass-reinforced plastic (polyester glass fibre); concrete; sulphur concrete (see note 1); plastic–metal laminate, e.g. aluminium-foil crisp packets; plastic–paper laminate, e.g. plastic/paper sacking; plastic–wood laminate, e.g. from kitchen worktop; bone (chicken bones or rabbit bones are a suitable size); demineralized bone (the bones are put in 2 mol/L hydrochloric acid overnight or until the minerals have been dissolved and the bones are flexible, and are then washed well in water before drying)
Samples of the following, preferably of similar dimensions to the composite materials: polyester plastic; glass fibre (in container with warning to wear gloves to avoid irritation); sulphur (roll sulphur); sand (in beaker); aluminium foil; polythene; paper (white paper bag)

Note:

1 The following recipe is suitable for making sulphur concrete. A fume cupboard must be used throughout the procedure.

Fill a metal container lined with aluminium foil (an old tobacco tin is suitable) with powdered sulphur. Place this on a gauze resting on a tripod. Heat the sulphur very gently and when it is molten, pour in sand, stirring gently until the desired consistency is reached. Then set aside to cool. The sulphur concrete cannot be stored for any length of time because it becomes powdery on its surface after a few days.

Safety note:
Burning sulphur and plastics give off toxic vapours and any experiments involving heating should be done in a fume cupboard with small amounts of material. Pupils should handle glass fibres with gloves to avoid irritation. The fibres should be such as do not produce dust that might be harmful by inhalation. Edges of all materials, especially those of wood or hard plastic, should be filed down so that there are no jagged edges.

This activity introduces pupils to the properties associated with various composite materials. The list of possible materials could be extended to include other examples, such as safety glass (which is often interleaved polyvinylbutyrate), fibre-reinforced plastics (polymethylmethacrylate) for baths, and various polyamides and polyesters used in the textile industry in conjunction with natural polymers. For example, many shirts are a mixture of cotton and polyester. The polyester is a useful addition because it is shrinkproof, creaseproof and easy to wash, whilst the cotton makes the clothes more fire resistant and warmer. Polyester–glass fibre is often worked up by hand-layering on moulds although mechanical compression is sometimes used. Extra glass fibre is often put on corners or edges as additional reinforcement. The layers are sometimes welded by using styrene monomers to form the cross-links with the unsaturated polyesters. Another method involves the direct use of the monomer with a catalyst and accelerator; the polymer then sets around the glass fibre without heating. In part d, pupils may compare the strengths of plasticized and unplasticized paper by dropping masses from different heights onto the sample stretched across a plastic beaker, or they may devise their own apparatus for testing strength.

Sulphur concrete is acid resistant and hard but is brittle compared with ordinary concrete. In practice, additives are used to prevent the plastic sulphur from reverting to S_8 sulphur molecules, but since they are not used in this work, the sulphur concrete should not be stored for long periods.

Answers to worksheet questions

1 For floors and walls in chemical factories or laboratories where spillage of acid might pose problems. (Sulphur concrete has also been used for lamp posts and kerb stones.)

2 The trade in ivory has led to the destruction of elephant herds and the use of wood must be carefully managed if particular habitats, e.g. tropical rainforests, are not to be destroyed.

3 The hardness and rigidity of the bone are due to the minerals.

4 The bones of the elderly are more brittle because they contain a higher proportion of minerals.

5 It increases the strength in both directions.

6 Polyester–glass fibre is light, stiff, fairly strong and easily moulded (although brittle in comparison with iron).

7 The polythene laminate gives additional strength and is more fire resistant in comparison with paper, in addition to being water resistant.

8 The plastic laminate is easier to clean.

9 Low density and hence ease of transport (such concrete is only used for internal blockwork).

10 The greater the density, the greater the compressive strength. (However, the data is rather limited here.)

11 Little tensile strength.

Further information

Science at Work (old edition)
Fibres and fabrics includes sections on paper, a key for the identification of fibres, as well as the nylon experiment and experiments to investigate the strength, wear resistance and the heat insulation properties of fabrics.

Building Science has a section on plastics including an investigation of stress in plastics using polarized light and some information about the moulding of plastics.

University of York Science Education Group
The unit on *Plastics* in Salters' Chemistry is particularly relevant to this chapter. The unit on *Clothing* has some helpful ideas dealing with fibres and fabrics including an investigation involving the use of a key.

Tidy Britain Group

Science Unit 4 *Plastics* could be used as an alternative but parallel approach to the one in this chapter. The unit includes booklets for the pupils, slides, worksheets and teachers' notes. A particular feature of the approach is the work on recycling plastics.

The Education Services of major oil companies

There is a wealth of material available which can be used to support or extend the work in this chapter (see Appendix), including videos such as "Working with thermoplastics" (ICI).

The Education Service of the Plastics Industry (ESPRI)

ESPRI publish a book called *A foundation course for science teachers* which covers all the ideas in this chapter and gives ideas for practical work. A variety of other resources is available from this source too (see Appendix).

Topic C3 — Chemicals in our homes

Chapter C9 Foams, emulsions, sols and gels

The syllabus section

Context

This section focuses on the wide variety of colloidal systems. The nature and properties of colloids can be explored. There are problems involved in both making and destroying colloidal systems.

Knowledge and understanding

	Tier	
B	C	F

Syllabus statements	PoS	SoA
Know that a colloid consists of one substance finely dispersed in another, and know the meaning of the words aerosol, foam, emulsion, sol and gel.	3(i)6	—
Appreciate the everyday importance of colloidal systems.	3(i)6	—
Know that dialysis is a way of separating large colloid particles from smaller particles.	3(i)6	3.5(a)
Know that colloidal systems scatter light.	3(i)6	—
Know the purpose of emulsifiers. Understand in simple terms the action of emulsifiers.	3(i)6	—
Understand the molecular explanation of Brownian motion.	3(ii)1	3.7(c)

Opportunities for co-ordination

Links with Biology include food additives in **B**6, the emulsifying action of bile salts in the digestion of fats in **B**5, blood plasma as a colloidal system in **B**8, enzyme chemistry in **B**5 and dialysis and kidney machines in **B**12.

Links with Physics include states of matter (**P**1), aerosols and Brownian motion (**P**2), and forces between electrically charged particles (**P**16).

Routes and times

Basic	Central	Further
	Central	**Further**

Omit "The effect of ions on a colloid" on side 2 of Worksheet **C9A**.

> **C9.1 What are colloids?**
> Omit Q3–5; box 1 is optional.
>
> **Worksheet C9A Investigating colloids**
>
> *2 hours*

All of section **C9.1** is suitable.

> **Worksheet C9B Surface tension**
> This is suitable for slower groups.
>
> *1/2 hour*

Omit the molecular explanation of Brownian motion.

> **C9.2 How can we recognize a colloid?**
>
> *1/2 hour*

Omit the molecular explanation of the action of emulsifiers. Omit Q9 and 14.

> **C9.3 How do we make colloids?**
> Omit Q9.
>
> **Worksheet C9C Making a cosmetic cream**
>
> *1 hour*

Omit this section.

> **C9.4 How can we destroy colloids?**
> Omit Q19–23.
>
> *1/2 hour*

Q19–23 should be done for homework.

Total: 4 hours   *Total: 4 hours*   *Total: 4 hours*

The pupils' book

C9.1 What are colloids?

The illustrations in this section are designed to emphasize the picture of a colloidal system consisting of one material finely dispersed in another. As far as possible, familiar examples are used. There is some new vocabulary; pupils will need help with it, especially where the everyday use of words differs from the technical use. Question 4 may help pupils to understand the use of the terms "continuous" and "disperse".

Colloquially the term "aerosol" is often taken to refer to a spray container and its contents rather than to the dispersion of liquid droplets in air formed when the product is in use. The difference between the everyday meaning as used in Chapter **P2** and the scientific meaning may have to be discussed with the pupils.

The use of the word "particle" may also need discussion. In this chapter it is used to mean a little bit of a solid, or a small droplet of a liquid. Elsewhere the word is sometimes used as a general term for an atom, molecule or ion. We have avoided the latter usage where possible, but in some cases it is difficult to do so without replacing it with the formally correct but difficult word "entity".

Box 1 can be used as a planning exercise. It is also an opportunity to revise work done on enzymes and proteins.

Answers to selected questions

2	**Example**	**Type of colloid**
	meringue	solid foam
	fog	aerosol
	salad cream	emulsion
	clouds	aerosol
	head on beer	foam
	jelly baby	gel
	muddy water	sol
	whipped cream	foam
	insecticide spray	aerosol
	sponge	solid foam
	crunchy bar	solid foam
	bread	solid foam
	chocolate mousse	gel/foam
	hand cream	emulsion
	lipstick	solid sol
	mascara	sol or emulsion
	rubber pillow	solid foam
	toothpaste	sol stabilized by a gel
	bubble bath	foam
	cold custard	gel
	non-drip paint	sol/gel

3 Figure 9.8:
a about 0.25 to 0.5 μm (2500 to 5000 atoms across);
b about 0.5 μm (5000 atoms across);
c of the order of 3 μm (30 000 atoms across).
Figure 9.9: about 1.4 μm (14 000 atoms across).

C9.2 How can we recognize colloids?

This section is designed to be read in the light of the experience of Worksheet **C9A**.

C9.3 How do we make colloids?

The treatment of surface tension is deliberately simplified. The main thing is to show yet another application of the idea that there are weak attractive forces between molecules.

The treatment of emulsifying agents is extended in Chapter **C**10 where the action of detergents is explained.

Answer to selected question

9a 6 cm^2

b 10^{12} cubes

c 6×10^{-8} cm^2

d 6×10^4 cm^2

C9.4 How can we destroy colloids?

Teachers may like to demonstrate the electrophoresis experiment. It is also possible to demonstrate the action of an electrostatic precipitator. These demonstrations are described under Activities. Voltage used must not exceed 40 V.

Note that the terms "lyophobic" and "lyophilic" have been avoided deliberately.

A more detailed treatment of the stabilization of colloidal systems is given in the Nuffield Advanced Chemistry Special Study *Surface chemistry*. All that is required here is summed up as follows:

- Some colloids are stabilized by the repulsive forces between the particles which all carry the same charge.
- Ions of opposite charge to the colloidal particles can bring about coagulation.
- Ions with a larger charge are more effective at coagulating colloidal particles than those with a smaller charge.

This section provides an opportunity to revise the idea that compounds of metals with non-metals are generally ionic.

Activities

Worksheet C9A Investigating colloids

The five investigations on this worksheet can be set out as a series of stations in a circus. Some of the experiments, especially "Dialysis" and "The effect of ions on a colloid", take longer than others and this will have to be allowed for when setting up the circus. Worksheet **C**9B can be used as a "buffer activity".

Light scattering

Requirements for one station:

Copy of Worksheet **C**9A (side 1)
Bright light source, or projector (see note 1)
Stoppered test-tubes in rack containing the
   following and labelled accordingly:

gelatine gel labelled "gelatine" (see note 2)
starch solution labelled "starch" (see note 3)
glucose solution labelled "glucose"
salt solution labelled "salt"

Notes:

1 This needs to be set up in a darkened area of the laboratory. One possibility is to line the inside of a cardboard box with black paper and lie it on one side. The bright light source can then be shone through a hole cut in one of the vertical sides of the box.

2 Prepare the gel by sprinkling the required amount of gelatine into hot water in a beaker. Stir well. Use at the rate of 11 g gelatine to 500 ml water.

3 Make a cream of 2 g soluble starch in cold water. Pour into 100 ml of nearly boiling water and then boil for a minute or two.

Milk under the microscope

Requirements for each station:
Copy of Worksheet **C9A** (side 1)
Several microscope slides and coverslips
Seeker
Microscope with high and medium powers
Milk (fresh or UHT)
Glass rod

Types of emulsion

Requirements for each station:
Copy of Worksheet **C9A** (side 2)
Selection of emulsions which have been lightly sprinkled with a dye mixture on labelled
  watchglasses (see notes). Do not stir after adding the dyes.

Notes:

1 Suitable emulsions include mayonnaise, salad cream, milk, cream, butter, hand cream and other
cosmetic or medical creams.
2 The dye contains equal amounts of powdered methylene blue – HARMFUL – and sudan III well
mixed. These dyes stain skin strongly and so protective gloves should be used when mixing and
using them. There is no need for the pupils to handle the dyes.

The effect of ions on a colloid

Requirements for each station:

Copy of Worksheet **C9A** (side 2)
Boiling-tube with stopper
Four test-tubes, with stoppers, in rack
Spatula
Distilled water, with 25-ml measuring cylinder
Labels
Titanium dioxide (a few grams) – see note

Sodium chloride solution, 2 g in 100 ml water,
  with 10-ml measuring cylinder
Magnesium sulphate solution, 8 g $MgSO_4 \cdot 7H_2O$
  in 100 ml water, with 10-ml measuring
  cylinder
Potassium alum solution, 15 g in 100 ml, with
  10-ml measuring cylinder
Eye protection

Note:

1 A suitable grade of titanium dioxide is supplied by Griffin & George for use with the Nuffield
Advanced Chemistry Special Study *Surface chemistry*.

Dialysis

Requirements for each station:

Copy of Worksheet **C9A** (side 2)
Dialysis apparatus which has been set up for at
  least an hour (see note 1)
Dropping pipette
Measuring cylinder, 10 ml
2 test-tubes and 2 boiling-tubes in rack
Burner and mat
Test-tube holder
Dropper bottle containing fresh or UHT milk

Benedict's solution in dropper bottle (see note 2
  for Worksheet **C4A** on page 000 of this *Guide*)
Sodium hydroxide solution, 2 mol/L
  – CORROSIVE – in dropper bottle
Copper(II) sulphate solution, 0.1 mol/L, in
  dropper bottle
Eye protection
Filter funnel
Filter papers

Note:

1 Set up the dialysis apparatus as follows: Soak a 30 cm length of Visking tubing in water until soft. Tie a
double knot at one end. With the help of a funnel pour milk into the tube until it is a little over half full. Tie
the open end with thread. Rinse the outside of the tube with distilled water and then place it in a 250-ml
beaker as shown in the diagram on Worksheet **C9A**. Add distilled water to the beaker until the liquid
levels are the same inside and outside the tube.

Worksheet C9B Surface tension

This is suggested as an optional but enjoyable extension to the circus.

Requirements for each station:
Copy of Worksheet **C9B**
Wire frames as shown on the worksheet (see note 1)
Trough
Thread
Soap solution (see note 2)

Notes:
1 The wire frames should be rigid and not too irregular.
2 Make the soap solution by dissolving 30 g sucrose in 30 ml warm water. Cool, then add 30 g propane-1,2,3-triol (glycerol) followed by 2 g of washing-up liquid. Stir well. This mixture produces very stable films.

Worksheet C9C Making a cosmetic cream

Requirements for each group:
Copy of Worksheet **C9C**
2 beakers, 100 ml or 150 ml
2 stirring thermometers, 0-100 °C
Burner, tripod, gauze and mat
Jar, or other container, for the product
Protective gloves (see note 1)
Eye protection

Access to:
Balance
Stearic acid, 15 g per group
Glycerol (propane-1,2,3-triol), 8 g per group
Distilled water, with measuring cylinder
Potassium hydroxide pellets – CORROSIVE – 0.7 g per group (see note 1)
Perfume (see note 2)
Preservative (see note 2)
Grease paint
Cotton wool

Notes:
1 It may be safer to provide preweighed samples of the potassium hydroxide to avoid any danger that the product will contain a dangerous excess of alkali. Protective gloves should be provided if the pupils are going to weigh out the potassium hydroxide themselves.
2 The perfume and preservative are optional. A suitable preservative for the emulsion is nipagin M. If no preservative is added the emulsion must be used in a short time.

There is always a risk (well-known to cosmetics manufacturers) that any cosmetic may produce an allergic reaction in some people. Teachers and pupils should be aware of this possibility, and there should be no pressure on pupils to apply the cream to their skin. It would be wise to keep containers of the chemicals for use **only** in cosmetics experiments and to ensure really clean conditions, perhaps working in the home economics room rather than the laboratory.

The emulsifier is potassium stearate which is formed when the two phases are mixed.

Pupils might be asked to cost this and other cosmetic preparations with the help of catalogues and then compare their answers with the price of commercial products.

Additional cosmetic formulations can be found in the materials listed under Further information.

Teacher demonstration: Colloidal particles and electric charges

REQUIREMENTS

The teacher will need:
U-tube
Pipette, 20 or 25 ml, with filler
Two electrodes, platinum or carbon (see note)
Connecting wires with crocodile clips
Power pack, 25 V d.c. (must **not** exceed 40 V)
Stand with boss and clamp
Gummed paper or grease pencil

Access to:

0.1 mol/L sodium chloride solution (1.5 g in 250 ml water)

1% dispersion of TiO2 in 0.1 mol/L NaCl solution containing
  3 % sucrose to increase its density, 100 ml

Note:

1 The electrodes can be held in place with extra stands and clamps. Alternatively, corks can be used if vertical grooves are cut in their sides to allow any gases formed to escape.

This experiment is described in the pupils' book (in box 2 on page 176) and teachers may well decide not to demonstrate it. The apparatus is shown in figure 9.35.

Procedure

1 Support the U-tube with the stand and clamp. Fill the bottom half of the tube with sodium chloride solution. Now fill a pipette with the TiO_2 dispersion. Carefully lower the tip of the pipette to the bottom of the U-tube and allow the dense dispersion to run in slowly. Withdraw the pipette carefully so as not to disturb the boundary between the two layers. Wait for a few minutes while the boundaries become clearer then mark their positions with gummed paper or a grease-pencil.

2 Insert the two electrodes and connect to a 25 V d.c. supply. Movement of the boundaries should become obvious in the course of a double period so it is essential to start the demonstration early in the session.

Teacher demonstration: A model electrostatic smoke precipitator

REQUIREMENTS

The teacher will need:

Van der Graaf generator (or induction coil and
  low voltage d.c. supply)

Drying tower adapted as shown

Filter pump

Connecting wires with clips

Access to:

Cigarette, or other source of smoke

This demonstration is only worth trying on days which are dry enough for the Van der Graaf generator to work. (An induction coil can be used in place of a Van der Graaf generator and may be more reliable in humid conditions.)

Safety notes:

1 Induction coils made in the last twenty years should be used as they cannot produce a current of more than 3 mA; older ones may do so and must not be used.

2 The two terminals and the related parts of the apparatus constitute a capacitor. The terminals should be shorted out across each other at the end of the experiment to remove any residual charge.

Procedure

1 The drying tower is arranged as shown. The copper foil is folded to form a collar. The inner metal rod should not touch the sides of the drying tower.

2 A filter pump is connected so that air can be drawn through the apparatus. A cigarette is inserted into some rubber tubing and connected to the lower end of the tower.

3 Once the drying tower is filled with smoke, switch on the Van der Graaf generator. The smoke is cleared rapidly and deposits of tar appear on the glass sides.

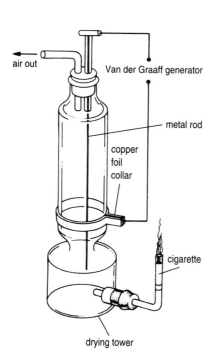

air out

Van der Graaff generator

metal rod

copper
foil
collar

cigarette

drying tower

Model electrostatic smoke precipator.

Further information

Science at work (old edition)
Cosmetics includes several sections about emulsions and cosmetics which could be used to extend the treatment in this chapter.

Photography includes a simplified account of the manufacture of a photographic emulsion.

University of York Science Education Group
In the Salters' Chemistry course the unit *Keeping clean* includes an experiment to make a cosmetic cream. The unit *Food processing* investigates the use of emulsifiers in salad dressing and mayonnaise as well as studying milk and butter.

Science Workout
The Cosmetics section contains worksheets on emulsions that are suitable (Purnell, R. *Science Workout 1* and *2*, Stanley Thorne, 1989.)

Chapter C10 Keeping clean

The syllabus section

Context

The use of detergents provides a link between this section and section **C9**, about colloids. The water cycle, water treatment and the study of hardness of water can be used to introduce theory about the chemistry of solutions.

Knowledge and understanding

Syllabus statements	PoS	SoA
Understand the processes involved in supplying pure water.	3(iv)1,2	3.5(d)
Know of some of the domestic, industrial and agricultural sources of water pollution.	3(iii)8	—
Appreciate why detergents are needed to help get things clean when washing with water.	3(iii)1	3.7(a)
Know that hardness is caused by the presence of dissolved calcium or magnesium compounds and be familiar with the behaviour of soap in hard and soft water.	3(iii)1	3.7(g)
Know that a scale of calcium carbonate may form when hard water is boiled and understand that scale removers are acids which dissolve calcium carbonate.	3(iii)1	3.7(g)
Understand how the process of ion exchange can be used to soften water.	**3(i)6**	**3.7(g)**
Know that it is hydrogen ions which make water acidic and that concentration of hydrogen ions determines pH.	**3(i)4**	**3.7(e)**
Appreciate that many precipitation reactions involve ions.	**3(i)4**	**3.7(e)**
Understand equations which describe the formation of hard water, scale formation and water softening processes.	**3(i)6**	**3.8(f)**
Understand the measurement of concentrations in mol dm^{-3}.	3(iii)4	3.9(c)

The Tier key (column at left):

Tier		
B	C	F

Opportunities for co-ordination

There are a number of links with Biology: the water cycle (**B**15), fluoridation and dental health (**B**4), enzymes (**B**5), breakdown of fats to fatty acids (**B**5) and eutrophication (**B**17).

Links to Physics include the action of fluorescors in washing powder (**P**15) and the measurement of energy transfer by immersion heaters/hot plates (**P**10).

There are also opportunities for co-ordination with Geography in the section on the water cycle/water supply and with Design and Technology in the sections about dry cleaning and washing.

Routes and times

Basic	Central	Further
Omit molecular explanation of detergents.	**C10.1 Why do we get so dirty?** Omit Q2 and 3. **C10.2 Why do we need detergents?** Omit Q9 and 10. *3/4 hour*	
Omit boxes 1–4, and Q11–14 and 27. *3/4 hour*	**C10.3 How do we get pure water?** Q15–27 are optional: omit box 4; for Single Award omit pages 190–192. *1 1/4 hours*	Box 4 is also suitable. *1 1/2 hours*
Omit section **C**10.4 and Worksheet **C**10B. Do experiments to compare hard and soft water, e.g. *Science Workout* 4.3 A–D, 4.4 A and B, 4.5 A and B.	**C10.4 Hard or soft?** Omit Q37, 39, 40 and 42, and boxes 6 and 7. **Worksheet C10B Which is the best way of softening water?** *1 1/2 hours*	
Slower pupils may need to spend more time on this section. *2 1/4 hours*	**Box 6 Problem: Which is the best descaler?** Sc1 assessment. *1 3/4 hours*	The problem in box 7 on page 197 is optional for faster groups.
Spend more time on this section. *1 hour*	**C10.5 Keeping water pollution under control** *3/4 hour*	Some of this section should be done for homework. *1/2 hour*
Total: 6 3/4 hours	*Total: 6 hours*	*Total: 6 hours*

The pupils' book

C10.1 Why do we get so dirty?

Coming before section **C10.2**, this introduction serves as a reminder of the difference between a true solution and a colloidal dispersion. Questions 2 and 3 revise the structure of ethane and ethene.

C10.2 Why do we need detergents?

This part of the chapter follows on from section **C9.3** and shows the importance of the ideas developed in the earlier chapter. The Unilever film, "Outline of detergency" gives an animated picture of the theory. (See Appendix.)

Worksheet **C10A** is related to this section.

C10.3 How do we get pure water?

Pupils are likely to be familiar with the water cycle from work in biology and geography. This section concentrates on the specifically chemical aspects of water treatment.

Several of the stages can be demonstrated. A suspension of calcium hydroxide can be shown to neutralize acids with the help of a coloured indicator such as litmus. The adsorbing properties of charcoal can be demonstrated by shaking a large spatula measure of charcoal with a dilute solution of a dye such as methyl violet (Gentian violet) and then filtering.

The ionic theory of acids, alkalis and neutralization reactions is introduced step by step in this chapter and in Chapters **C11** and **C12**. Questions 11 to 14 in box 1 on page 185 lead to the suggestion that it is hydrogen ions which make water acidic.

This section also includes the first mention of ionic precipitation reactions. Pupils are not expected to be able to write formal ionic equations which are notoriously difficult at this level. However they should be able to appreciate the meaning of diagrams such as figure 10.19. When introducing this topic teachers may wish to demonstrate a number of precipitation reactions and show that knowledge of the solubility of salts can be used to predict whether or not a precipitate will form.

The sample calculation in box 4 on page 191 shows the advantage of using units consistently. The pupils who study the working in this box will be helped if they can come to see the value of checking the consistency of units in every step.

Answers to selected questions
25b 0.64 g of sulphur dioxide

26 0.000 02 mol/L

27 1 mol/L sodium carbonate
2 mol/L potassium hydroxide
0.5 mol/L copper(II) sulphate
0.1 mol/L silver nitrate

28 188 u

29 60.6%

30 2.65 mg

31 5.3×10^{-5} mol/L.

C10.4 Hard or soft?

Pupils can deduce that calcium and magnesium ions make water hard from the evidence given in the experiment described in box 5 on page 193. The formation of an insoluble scum with soap and calcium ions is the most familiar example of precipitation for those who live in hard water areas.

Worksheet **C**10B is related to this section. The problems posed in boxes 6 and 7 on pages 196-7 can be the basis of practical investigations planned and executed by the pupils. Videos from ICI can be used to illustrate the importance of this section (see Appendix).

C10.5 Keeping water pollution under control

Study of this section should be co-ordinated with the treatment of pollution in Chapters **B**17 and **B**18. There are possibilities for practical work to illustrate this section as suggested under Further information.

Activities

Worksheet C10A Comparing detergents

REQUIREMENTS

Each group of pupils will need:
4 pieces of white fabric, 15 cm × 15 cm (see note 1)
Bowl or trough large enough for washing the fabric
  samples
Wooden stick, or other suitable agitator
Thermometer
Eye protection

Access to:
Marking pen
Measuring cylinder, 500 ml
Stains: motor oil, moist clay, powdered charcoal,
  lipstick, cooking fat, dust
Hot water, from a tap, kettle or water heater
"Lolly sticks" or spatulas to apply the stains to the
  cloth samples
Soap powder, in its packet (see note 2)
Soapless detergent powder, in its packet (see note 2)
Wall clock or wrist watch
Washing line for drying the washed samples
Balance

Notes:
1 Pupils may be able to provide their own remnant samples for washing. Each group should have four pieces of fabric made of the same material. If the different groups use a variety of natural and synthetic fabrics this will add interest to the investigation.
2 Some people are allergic to some detergents, so these should be handled with care.

Pupils will have to scale down the quantities given on the detergent packets. They will need to know the approximate capacity of a washing machine and weigh a measure full of powder so that they can work out how much powder to use in the containers provided.

Worksheet C10B Which is the best way of softening water?

REQUIREMENTS

Each group of pupils will need:
Test-tube with bung
Test-tube rack
Measuring cylinder, 10 ml
Dropping pipette
Beaker, 250 ml
Glass rod
Thermometer, 0–100 °C
Burner, tripod, gauze and mat
Eye protection

Access to:
Hard water (see note 1)
Soap solution in dropper bottle (see note 2),
  allow 25 ml per group
Calgon, allow 1 g per group
Bath salts (sodium sesquicarbonate), allow 1 g
  per group
Ion exchange column (see note 3)
Balance, to measure 0.5 g

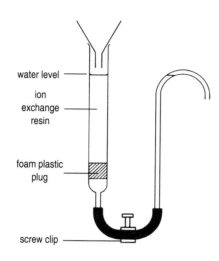

water level

ion exchange resin

foam plastic plug

screw clip

Notes:

1 If local tap water is not very hard, a sample of hard water can be made before the lesson. Bubble carbon dioxide through 100 ml limewater until the precipitate redissolves. Dilute with 900 ml tap water, then add 0.25 g of magnesium sulphate.

2 Soap solution can be made by dissolving 10 g of soap flakes (or soft soap) in 250 ml of ethanol – FLAMMABLE – and then adding 250 ml of water.

3 A suitable resin is Zeo-carb 225 (sodium form). Any cation exchange resin in its sodium form will do. A suitable mesh size is BSS 52/100.

The column shown on the left has the advantage that it cannot run dry. An old burette can be used if shortened to about 15 cm. The burette tap replaces the clip. The plastic plug can be cut from foam plastic with a cork borer several sizes greater than the column diameter.

It is **most important** that the resin should be made into a slurry with distilled water in a beaker or flask **before** being added to the column. The resin beads swell and can crack the column as they expand. The procedure would need to be repeated if the resin dried out.

Setting up the column:

Fill the empty column with distilled water. Displace any trapped air bubbles by squeezing the rubber tubing.

Saturate the foam plastic plug with water and gently push it into position with a glass rod. Do not force the plug into the tapered part of the tube.

Pour the resin slurry into the column through the burette funnel.

Adjust the glass tube so that the level of the outlet is about 5 mm above the top of the resin bed.

The column can be reused if regenerated with a concentrated solution of sodium chloride. After regeneration it should be washed through several times with distilled water.

Box 6 Problem: Which is the best descaler?

Box 7 Problem: Does descaling kettles save energy?

REQUIREMENTS

Each group of pupils will define their own requirements on the planning sheet (Worksheet **C0**).
Eye protection will be needed.

The teacher will need:

Samples of commercial descalers in their original packs (see note 1)
Kettle(s) with scale

Note:

1 Some of these commercial descalers are corrosive, and pupils should be encouraged to make safety a major consideration when planning their experiments.

2 The problems will seem more important to pupils living in hard water areas. However, hardness is widespread in Britain.

Pupils can choose to investigate one or other of the practical problems outlined in section **C10.4** of their book.

Which is the best descaler?

Manufacturers of products affected by scale have to deal with the problem whatever the nature of their own – or the school's – local water supply.

The problem of descaling might be put to the pupils some weeks before the laboratory session. This will allow time for planning and research. They can be encouraged to find out which descalers are on sale locally. They may be able to review test reports in magazines such as *Which?* in their local public library. They can find out something about the chemical properties of known descalers from textbooks.

Each group might take on one aspect of the problem so that the class as a whole can combine the findings to produce a final recommendation. The chemical principles involved include the chemistry of acids, metals and carbonates, and a knowledge of the effects of temperature and concentration on reaction rates. Pupils who have been introduced to the concept "amount of substance/mol" might calculate the amount of descaler needed in theory to remove a given quantity of scale.

In a hard water area the class could follow up its recommendations by packaging agreed quantities of the chosen descaler with appropriate labelling for use at home. The exercise can be costed to determine an appropriate pack price.

Does descaling kettles save energy?

Which? reports suggest that the effect of descaling is much more marked with kettles heated on an electric hotplate or gas ring than with electric kettles.

This problem provides some useful links with Chapter **P9**. It is only possible as a quantitative exercise using gas rings if some method of metering the gas used is available.

Further information

Videos

"Fit to drink?" (ITV Chemistry in Action series) and "What's on tap?" (BBC Global Environment series) are useful here.

Science at Work

Cosmetics (old edition) includes sections dealing with soap and hard water.

Pollution (old and new editions) has several sections dealing with water. Experimental work covers the identification of pollutants as well as biological monitoring. Water treatment is dealt with and so is the problem of oil pollution.

Dyes and dyeing (old edition) includes experiments to investigate the use of solvents to remove stains and to find out whether solvents can damage fabrics.

University of York Science Education Group

In Salters' Chemistry:

Drinks deals with water treatment, fluoridation, and sewage treatment.

Keeping clean deals with hardness of water, and detergency.

Chemistry in Action

The *Invergrog reservoir project* requires pupils to use their knowledge of chemistry to choose the site for a new reservoir which will supply a whisky distillery. The *Eboclean* unit requires pupils to take on the role of a scientist employed to analyse samples of the product which appear to be inferior and which are being marketed by a rival, unscrupulous manufacturer.

Science and Technology in Society

Unit 607 "Scale and scum" examines the claims made for a commercial water softening unit and thus covers much of the chemistry of hard water.

Unit 801 "The water pollution mystery" is a data analysis exercise about solving the problem of death of fish in a river.

Science Workout

The Cosmetics section has worksheets on hard water that are suitable for less able pupils. (Purnell, R. *Science Workout 1* and *2*, Stanley Theorne, 1989.)

Chapter C11 Dyes and dyeing

The syllabus section

Context

The use of natural and synthetic dyes linked to a study of aspects of the history of dyeing can be used both as the basis of investigational practical work and as a lead-in to aspects of chemical theory.

Knowledge and understanding

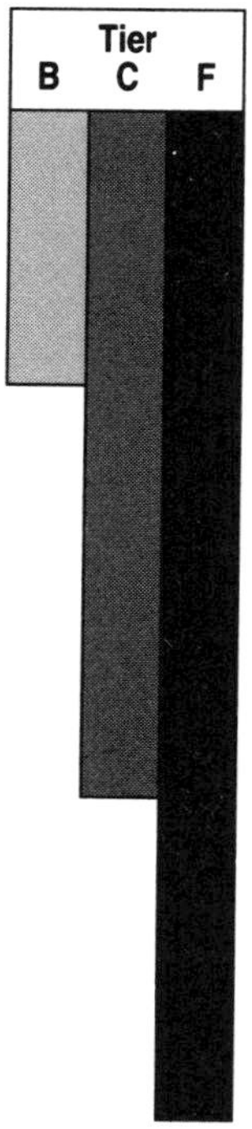

Syllabus statements	PoS	SoA
Know that materials can be converted into useful dyes through a range of chemical reactions, including ionic reactions, oxidation and reduction.	3(iii)1	3.4(b)
Appreciate the relative merits of natural and synthetic dyes.	**3(i)6**	—
Know the meaning of the terms mordant and vat dye, and understand that a good dye must be fast to washing and light.	3(iii)1	3.7(a)
Know that it is hydroxide ions which make water alkaline.	**3(i)4**	**3.7(e)**
Appreciate that the discovery of synthetic dyes made a dramatic change in the range of colours of fabrics.	3(iii)10	3.7(g)
Appreciate some of the problems involved in discovering and marketing a new chemical product.	3(iii)10	3.9(d)
Understand that dyes which react with cloth fibres are faster than dyes which are held by "between molecule" forces.	**3(ii)2**	**3.10(c)**

Opportunities for co-ordination

There are links with the work in Biology on the treatment of diseases in **B**14 and **B**20.

The topic of colour is discussed in Chapter **P**15.

There are considerable opportunities for co-ordination with Art, CDT and Home Economics. This chapter is designed to focus on the more chemical aspects of the subject. There are also opportunities for co-ordination with History, including developments in German industry up to the outbreak of World War I and changes in the range of colours available for dresses and fabrics during the nineteenth century.

Routes and times

Basic	Central	Further
Section **C**11.1 could be replaced by an appropriate video. Omit side 2 from Worksheet **C**11A. *1 hour*	**C11.1 What is a dye?** (class + homework) **Worksheet C**11A **Dyeing with indigo** For Single Award, include box 4 on page 205 here. *1¼ hours*	Section **C**11.1 should be done for homework. *1 hour*
Section **C**11.2 could be replaced by an appropriate video.	**C11.2 What is a mordant?** **Worksheet C**11B **Mordant dyeing** This could be extended as an Sc1 assessment. *1¼ hours*	Section **C**11.2 should be done for homework. *1 hour*
Omit this section.	**C11.3 How were synthetic dyes discovered?** *Homework*	
Omit section **C**11.4. *1 hour*	**C11.4 Why are modern dyes so fast?** (homework) Discuss in following lesson. **Worksheet C**11C **Dyeing with a reactive dye** This could be extended as an Sc1 assessment. *1¼ hours*	
Spend more time on this section. *2 hours*	Sc1 assessment based on the fastness of samples of dyed cloth (from Worksheets **C**11A, **C**11B and **C**11C) to washing, light and chemicals. (The practical work could be done at home after planning at school.) *1½ hours*	
Total: 5¼ hours	*Total: 5¼ hours*	*Total: 4¾ hours*

Monitoring the progress of Sc1

Investigating dyeing

Pupils could investigate the effect of the temperature of the dye bath on the final colour of the sample. This investigation may be carried out instead of or after Worksheet **C**11B "Mordant dyeing" or Worksheet **C**11C "Dyeing with a reactive dye".
Sample criteria are given below for an assessment between levels 5 and 8.

Strand (i) Ask questions, predict and hypothesize, e.g.	Strand (ii) Observe, measure and manipulate variables, e.g.	Strand (iii) Interpret their results and evaluate scientific evidence, e.g.
5(a) Suggest that a warm solution of dye will be more effective than a cool solution because the dye sticks better at higher temperatures	**5(b)** Compare the colour of two samples which have been immersed in two dye solutions at different temperatures	**5(c)** Conclude that a sample of material immersed in a dye bath of a higher temperature is more effectively dyed than one dyed at a lower temperature; qualify the result
6(a) Suggest that the warmer the dye bath, the more effective the dyeing because the dye sticks better at higher temperatures	**6(b)** As above, but with a range of samples	**6(c)** Conclude that hot dyeing is more effective than cold dyeing because bonds between dye and sample form better at higher temperatures
7(a) Suggest that the volume of the dye bath, the temperature of the solution and the time of immersion are all factors, and that the most important is the temperature of the solution	**7(b)** As above, but over a range of temperatures	**7(c)** Conclude that the temperature of the dye bath has more effect than the time of immersion, within the limit of the variables as used in the investigation
8(a) Suggest that doubling the temperature results in the same colour as increasing the time by a factor of four; suggest a relevant investigation	**8(b)** As above, measuring temperatures to 0.5°C	**8(c)** Explain why the time of immersion was kept constant for various temperatures and why the temperature was kept constant for various times of immersion

As an alternative, pupils could investigate the fastness of samples of dyed cloth to washing, light and chemicals as suggested in the Routes chart on page 000.

The pupils' book

C11.1　What is a dye?

Pupils are not expected to remember the details about the dyes. The information is included for those who may be interested.

When they tackle Worksheet **C**11A pupils should notice that the surface of the dye bath stays blue however much they stir. Those interested might be asked to suggest ways of demonstrating that it is oxygen in the air which is responsible for restoring the blue colour. This provides an opportunity to mention oxidation reactions and to review examples which they have met previously. Reduction is defined as the opposite of oxidation (see question 2).

The pupils should keep careful records of the results of all three dyeing experiments. Then they have to plan and organize tests to see if the dyes are fast to washing and light.

This can be linked to a home survey of the coloured textiles in their homes: looking for patterns in the extent to which different coloured fabrics suffer from fading in use.

C11.2 What is a mordant?

Recommended methods for mordanting cloth are based on longer treatments in hot solutions of salts. Worksheet C11B suggests the use of ammonia to precipitate metal hydroxides as a quicker way of depositing the mordant in the fabric. The text explains this in terms of ionic precipitation as a further example of these reactions which were introduced in Chapter C10. Ionic equations are used in box 1 on page 205. Pupils are not expected to be able to write their own ionic equations under examination conditions, but they should be able to show some understanding of simple examples.

C11.3 How were synthetic dyes discovered?

See Further information for details of an experiment to repeat Perkin's discovery. Pupils are not required to remember the historical details. It is more important that they should reflect on what Perkin achieved by the age of twenty, and think about the problems of exploiting scientific discoveries. A keen stamp collector may be able to produce a penny mauve stamp.

C11.4 Why are modern dyes so fast?

The superior fastness of reactive dyes over direct dyes provides an interesting demonstration of the greater strength of the bonds within molecules compared to the weak attractive forces between molecules.

The reaction between the dyes and cellulose can be explained in the same terms as one step of a condensation polymerization process. Here there is an opportunity to revise the structure of cellulose described in Chapter C3.

When pupils have completed their own series of dyeing experiments they might evaluate the dyes they have used according to the criteria in figure 11.14.

Activities

Each working group will need:
Copy of Worksheet C11A
Beaker, 400 ml
Glass rod
Tongs
Burner, tripod, gauze and mat
5 boiling-tubes in rack
Protective gloves
Eye protection

Worksheet C11A Dyeing with indigo

REQUIREMENTS

Access to:
Indigo, allow 0.4 g per group, with spatula
Sodium hydroxide – CORROSIVE – allow 1 g per group, with spatula
Sodium dithionite – HARMFUL – allow 2 g per group, with spatula
Cotton cloth for dyed samples (see note 1)
Extra cotton cloth for part 2 of the worksheet, 5 small squares per group
Balance
Absorbent paper (e.g. paper towels)
Distilled water with cylinder to measure 200 ml
Bench reagents: dilute hydrochloric acid, hydrogen peroxide (1 volume strength), and acidified potassium dichromate(VI), 0.02 mol/L, allow about 15 ml of each per group
Solution of sulphur dioxide in water – HARMFUL – about 15 ml per group

Note:
1 Rolls of plain cotton bandage are excellent because they have not been treated with surface dressings which confuse the results. It is also easy to cut suitable lengths of fabric for these experiments. **Each pupil** needs enough cotton to be able to have three samples to keep (see worksheet). Each **group** needs five further pieces for part 2.

Part 1 of this worksheet is accessible to all pupils. Part 2 introduces the idea that there are chemicals which "do the same thing as oxygen" and so can be classified as oxidants. Examples are hydrogen peroxide and acidified potassium dichromate(VI) solutions which rapidly turn the cloth blue. They must not be too concentrated or they will then bleach the indigo. There is no colour change in sulphur dioxide which is a reductant. It is impossible to exclude oxygen completely and so water is included as a control.

For the less academic, an alternative to part 2 would be to try tie-dyeing; this can work well with indigo (see Further information).

Pupils are expected to prepare one dyed sample for display under results and to keep two other samples for fastness testing.

Worksheet C11B Mordant dyeing

REQUIREMENTS

Each group of pupils will need:
Beaker, 250 ml, for the dyebath
2 beakers, 100 ml
Glass rod
Tongs
Measuring cylinder, 100 ml
Burner, tripod, gauze and mat
Cotton fabric (see note 1 under Worksheet C11A)
Protective gloves
Eye protection

Access to:
Alizarin, allow 0.2 g per group, with spatula
Alum solution (25 g potassium alum in 1 L water), allow 50 ml per group, with 50-ml measuring cylinder (see note 1)
Dilute ammonia solution (50 ml 0.88 ammonia – CORROSIVE – made up to 1 L with water), allow 50 ml per group, with 50-ml measuring cylinder
Absorbent paper (e.g. paper towels)
Balance
Fume cupboard

Note:
1 Pupils may have time to try other mordants such as iron(II) sulphate – IRRITANT, magnesium sulphate and tin(II) chloride– IRRITANT. These should be made up in similar concentrations to the alum. Tin(II) chloride and iron(II) sulphate will have to be prepared immediately before the lesson to avoid oxidation by the air.

Pupils must be reminded that they will have to keep their samples in an orderly way so that they know which is which when it comes to fastness testing (see below). They can be encouraged to make an attractive display of the dyed samples in their notes. The specimens look much better if they are cut neatly and ironed.

Worksheet C11C Dyeing with a reactive dye

REQUIREMENTS

Each working group will need:
Beaker, 250 ml
Beaker, 100 ml
Glass rod
Tongs
Burner, tripod , gauze and mat
Thermometer
Test-tube
Measuring cylinder, 10 ml
Stand, boss and clamp
Protective gloves
Eye protection

Access to:
Yellow fibre-reactive dye solution allow 5 ml per group (see note 1)
Sodium chloride, allow 2 g per group, with spatula
Sodium carbonate solution, 1 mol/L, allow 5 ml per group
Cotton cloth (see note 1 for Worksheet C11A)
Absorbent paper (e.g. paper towels)

Safety notes:
1 Fibre-reactive dyes are chemicals which can cause respiratory allergies and eye irritation in people who handle them. The powder should only be handled in an efficient fume cupboard, and dust masks might be considered advisable. Prevent the creation of dust and the breathing of dust or mist during handling. Consult a doctor if symptoms similar to hay-fever or asthma develop in any person handling the dye. Anyone who has become sensitized or has chronic chest disease should not handle this type of dye. In schools where very small amounts of the dye are involved there should be no problem if normal safety procedures for handling chemicals are followed.
2 The dye used in C11C should be supplied to the pupils in solution so that they do not have to deal with the powdered solid. In the light of this, a revised version of Worksheet C11C has been prepared and will be sent free of charge to schools who have already bought the pack of worksheets. Send a stamped addressed envelope to the Publications Manager, NCCT, King's College London, 552 King's Road, London SW10 0UA.

Note:
1 Suitable dyes are Procion Yellow MX–3R and MX–8G – both IRRITANT – obtainable from Kemtex Services Ltd, Victoria Works, Wilton Street, Denton, Manchester M34 3ND. Prepare a stock solution by dissolving 1.5 g of dye in 100 ml water (see Safety notes).
The Procion H–E range of dyes – IRRITANT – can also be used for the experiment; these are less toxic but have to be used in a dyebath at 80°C. Some hazard will therefore result from having to stir the cloth in the hot dyebath, but schools might consider this preferable to the risk of respiratory sensitization.

Pupils must be reminded to keep samples of cotton dyed with both dyes, both for their results and for fastness testing.

For some pupils this will simply be an opportunity to use a modern dye and to compare it with natural dyes for depth of colour, brightness, and fastness. With more academic pupils it provides an opportunity explain observations in terms of structure and bonding.

Further investigations: Fastness testing

This investigation lends itself to being done as a home experiment. For light fastness the pupils only need opaque paper or card, scissors, staples or sticky tape and access to a window. For washing fastness they need a basin, a source of hot water and some soap or detergent.

Some pupils can be given minimal instructions and asked to plan, execute and report on their investigations largely unaided.

Others will need more help and they can do the planning in school. If there is time the experiment can be done in school too.

Light fastness is conveniently tested by attaching the pieces of dyed cotton to thin card and then covering them with a second piece of card with windows cut in it. The samples can then be exposed to sunlight in a (south-facing) window. Significant results will be seen after three or four weeks with some dyes (depending on the weather and the time of year). The exposed parts of some pieces of cotton will be noticeably paler than the parts hidden under card.

Washing fastness can be tested following the instructions on the packet of powder for coloured cotton. (Pupils should perhaps be warned not to put the samples in with the family wash!) Wash fastness is sometimes tested by stitching the sample to a piece of undyed cotton to see if any colour transfers to it from the dyed specimen.

Pupils might be asked to set up a five-point rating scale for fastness testing ranging from 5 (no change) to 1 (very great loss of colour).

Further information

Videos
"Dyes" (ITV Science and Technology series) and "At the end of the rainbow – the link between dyes and drugs" (BBC Great Experiments series) are useful here.

Science at Work (old edition)
Dyes and dyeing includes practical work dealing with natural dyes, mordant dyeing, and fastness testing as well as tie-dyeing and Batik. There is also an experiment to make two brown dyes which involves the use of ammonia to precipitate iron(II) and chromium(III) hydroxides in the fibres of cotton. Chlorine is then used to oxidize the iron(II) to iron(III). If there is time this experiment could provide further experience of precipitation and oxidation reactions.

Science and Technology in Society
Unit 510 "Perkin's Mauve" includes details of an experiment to make a sample of mauveine.

Chapter C12 Chemicals in the medicine cupboard

The syllabus section

Context

This section concentrates on the mild painkillers and antacids likely to be found in a medicine cupboard. The history of the discovery of aspirin can be used to show how chemists modify natural substances to improve their pharmaceutical properties. The work of famous scientists can be used to introduce the idea of chemotherapy.

Knowledge and understanding

Syllabus statements	PoS	SoA
Know that salts are formed when acids are neutralized by alkalis.	3(i)4	3.5(b)
Be able to classify aqueous solutions as acidic, alkaline or neutral using Universal indicator.	3(i)4	3.5(b)
Know the meaning of the terms drug, analgesic and antacid.	3(iii)1	3.5(b)
Understand that during neutralization reactions, hydrogen ions combine with hydroxide ions to form water molecules.	3(iii)3	3.8(f)
Be able to interpret chemical equations quantitatively, through exploration of antacids or analgesics. The work should involve determination of formulae.	3(iii)4,5	3.9(c)

Tier: B C F

Opportunities for co-ordination

This section can be linked to **B6** and **B14** which deal with hygiene. The problem of drug abuse is not raised in this section but is covered in **B11**. Gastric acid is discussed in **B5**. The work on acids, alkalis and neutralization should be related to the study of pH, and acids in the mouth and stomach, which are covered in **B4** and **B5**.

Routes and times

Basic	Central	Further

Omit graphical formulae and Q2 and 3 from section **C**12.3.

C12.1 **What is the difference between a drug and a medicine?**

C12.2 **What is an analgesic?**

C12.3 **How was aspirin discovered?**
(reading homework)

Omit box 1.

$^1/_2$ hour

Omit box 2 and Q9.

C12.4 **What is an antacid?**
Omit Q5–8 and 10, and box 3. For Single Award, select material as appropriate or replace by Nuffield Science Year 9 Activity **D**25 "Making a salt".

$^3/_4$ hour

Worksheet C12A **How much gastric juice does "bicarb" neutralize?**

Optional

Do alternative 1 on side 2 of Worksheet **C**12B. Worksheet **C**12A "How much gastric juice does 'bicarb' neutralize?" is suitable.

$2^3/_4$ hours

Worksheet C12B **Analysis of a magnesia tablet**
Some time is needed to introduce the use of burettes.

$1^3/_4$ hours

Omit alternative 1 on side 2 of Worksheet **C**12B and replace with box 3 "How much gastric juice can an antacid tablet neutralize?" from section **C**12.4. Do Q10.

$2^1/_4$ hours

C12.5 **What is chemotherapy?**

$^1/_4$ hour

This should be done for homework.

Total: $4^1/_4$ hours

Total: $3^1/_4$ hours

Total: $3^1/_2$ hours

The pupils' book

C12.1 What is the difference between a drug and a medicine?

The extraction of caffeine from tea might be demonstrated here.

C12.2 What is an analgesic?

The concept of an analgesic is introduced, along with a number of related medical terms that may be unfamiliar to pupils.

C12.3 How was aspirin discovered?

The story of aspirin illustrates the importance of plants as sources of drugs. Sometimes it is possible to make the drug synthetically, sometimes not. Once the chemical structure is known it is possible to make modifications to the drug in the hope of improving its properties.

The conversion of salicylic acid to aspirin is easily demonstrated. (See under Activities.)

Our dependence on plants for new drugs is one of the arguments in favour of retaining the genetic diversity of wild species of plants and for protecting the tropical rain forests.

Some pupils will want to discuss the ethical problems raised by the testing of new drugs on animals. Animal tests include measuring the pharmacological activities of the drug while a watch is kept for side-effects. The toxicity of the drug is determined. The short-term toxicity is normally given by the LD 50 (lethal dose 50) test which determines the dose which causes immediate death in 50 % of the group of animals to which it is administered. Long term toxicity is investigated by administering smaller doses to a group of animals for about two years. At the end of this time the animals are killed and their organs examined for evidence of damage.

Animal species vary considerably in their tolerance to drugs. It is therefore considered essential that these animal studies be carried out on a representative range of different mammals before treatment of human patients is considered.

Once a drug has been passed for general use, animal testing continues as part of quality control. It is estimated that between 1955 and 1976 some 1.5 million monkeys were killed worldwide during the production and testing of polio vaccine. An alternative based on cultured human cells has since been developed.

Scientists are now responding to public pressure to reduce the scale of animal testing. Cell cultures are being used to replace tests on whole organisms. Alternatives for the assay of the potency of drug products are also being developed.

It may take from three to twenty years to discover a new drug. A further two to three years is needed to carry out and evaluate animal tests. Clinical trials of the efficacy and safety of the drug with human patients may require three to five more years before the drug can be marketed.

All this contrasts markedly with Felix Hofmann treating his father with acetylsalicylic acid.

The text shows that the traditional English and German names for salicylic acid and its derivatives are different. This provides an opportunity to point out to those who may go on with their study of chemistry that newer IUPAC names are becoming standardized internationally.

C12.4 What is an antacid?

The term *indigestion* often appears in inverted commas in medical reference books. Dyspepsia is merely an old-fashioned term for indigestion. Heartburn is a burning sensation below the breastbone which arises when some of the acid contents of the stomach are regurgitated in the oesophagus.

There is a clearly a big market for products which treat the symptoms of "indigestion".

Most of the products are formulated with hydroxides or carbonates. Apart from neutralizing hydrochloric acid, the compounds used may have other side-effects.

Sodium hydrogencarbonate (bicarbonate) works fastest but is absorbed into the bloodstream and in large quantities can upset the chemical balance of the body. It must be avoided by those on a low sodium diet.

Calcium and aluminium compounds tend to constipate. Magnesium compounds are mildly laxative. Thus many branded products are mixtures designed to avoid upsetting bowel habits.

Answer to selected question
10a 100 ml
b 15 ml
c 7.5 ml
d 122.5 ml

C12.5 What is chemotherapy?

There is an account of the work of Paul Ehrlich in SATIS unit 805 "The search for the magic bullet". This can be related to the subsequent development of sulphonamide drugs, antibiotics, monoclonal antibodies and cancer treatments.

Activities

Volumetric analysis

REQUIREMENTS

Each group of pupils will need:
Burette and stand
Burette funnel
Beaker, 100 ml
Bottle of distilled water
Graduated pipette, 25 ml, with safety filler
  (see note 1)

Access to:
Balance

Note:
1 Pupils will only need to learn how to use a pipette if they are going to tackle Worksheet C12C.

This is an introductory exercise to train pupils in the correct use of volumetric glassware. They can practise delivering volumes of water into a weighed beaker and then reweighing to find the mass (and hence volume) of water measured out. In this way they can check the consistency and accuracy with which they use a burette. Those who will do the aspirin analysis can also practise the use of a graduated pipette.

Worksheet C12A How much gastric juice does "bicarb" neutralize?

REQUIREMENTS

Each group of pupils will need:
Flask, 100 ml
Burette and stand
Burette funnel
Beaker, 100 ml
White tile, or piece of white paper
Eye protection

Access to:
Balance, to weigh to 0.01 g
Sodium hydrogencarbonate with spatula
"Gastric juice" (0.1 mol/L hydrochloric acid),
  allow 75 ml per group
Screened methyl orange indicator – FLAMMABLE –
  in dropper bottle
Distilled water with 25-ml measuring cylinder

This experiment provides an opportunity for pupils to do a quantitative experiment without having to do any calculations.

The worksheet shows the "bicarb" being weighed in the titration flask; this is simple, but not the best practice. Some teachers may prefer to use weighing bottles.

Worksheet C12B Analysis of a magnesia tablet

REQUIREMENTS

Each group of pupils will need:
Conical flask, 100 ml
Burette and stand
Burette funnel
Glass rod with flattened end
Distilled water wash-bottle
White tile, or piece of white paper
Eye protection
Balance

Access to:
Milk of magnesia tablets, 2 per group
Dilute hydrochloric acid, 75 ml per group
  (see note 1)
Screened methyl orange indicator – FLAMMABLE –
  in a dropper bottle (see note 1)

Notes:

1 If the concentration of the hydrochloric acid is 0.517 mol/L, then 1 ml of the acid neutralizes 15 mg of magnesium hydroxide. The acid concentration must be known accurately.

The easiest way of preparing for the experiment is to make an approximately 0.5 mol/L solution by diluting 100 ml concentrated hydrochloric acid to 2 L. This can be standardized by titration against a milk of magnesia tablet as described on the worksheet.

Suppose the average titre is x ml. The tablets contain 300 mg of magnesium hydroxide. Calculation (alternative one):

1 ml of the acid reacts with $\dfrac{300}{x}$ mg magnesium hydroxide

Calculation (alternative two):

The concentration of the acid $= \dfrac{10.34}{x}$ mol/L

2 Bromothymol blue is an alternative indicator with a colour change from blue to yellow, which some pupils may find easier to see.

The tablet does not dissolve completely because of the inert material used to bind the magnesium hydroxide together. This means that the solution is cloudy during the titration. The magnesium hydroxide gradually dissolves as the titration proceeds. The contents of the flask must be mixed well during the titration. In the later stages of the titration, adding a drop of liquid from the burette may temporarily turn the indicator to its acid colour, because the reaction is relatively slow. The titration should continue until the indicator shows its acid colour for some time even after thorough mixing.

An alternative procedure for doing the experiment is described in SATIS unit 709 (see under Further information).

Magnesium hydroxide tablets have been chosen because they contain only one chemical. Other antacid tablets with mixtures of chemicals may have a marked buffering action which leads to confusing titration results. Some antacid ingredients react very slowly with hydrochloric acid, and the apparent end-point continues to change for a long time.

The worksheet is designed so that there are two ways of working out the results of the analysis. Alternative one is relatively simple. Alternative two involves a calculation based on the equation for the reaction.

Worksheet C12C Analysis of aspirin tablets

REQUIREMENTS

Each group of pupils will need:
2 beakers, 100 ml
Graduated flask, 250 ml
Funnel and glass rod
Graduated pipette with safety filler, 25 ml
Conical flask, 250 ml
Burette, 25 or 50 ml
White tile, or piece of white paper
Distilled water wash-bottle
Burner, tripod, mat and gauze
Eye protection

Access to:
Commercial aspirin tablets, 5 per group
1.00 mol/L sodium hydroxide – IRRITANT – allow
   30 ml per group (see note 1)
One or more communal burettes to dispense the
   sodium hydroxide
Screened methyl orange indicator – FLAMMABLE –
   in dropper bottle
0.100 mol/L hydrochloric acid, allow 60 ml per
   group (see note 1)
Balance

Note:

1 The solutions must be accurate and are conveniently prepared from volumetric concentrates. This is only justified if pupils adopt correct titration procedures and read the burettes to at least the nearest 0.1 ml.

This is a demanding practical exercise which is likely to be suited to only a minority of pupils.

Teacher demonstration: Making aspirin from salicylic acid

REQUIREMENTS

The teacher will need:
Beaker, 100 ml
Beaker, 250 ml
Glass rod
Measuring cylinder, 25 ml
Measuring cylinder, 100 ml
Buchner funnel and flask
Water pump
Filter paper to fit funnel
Protective gloves
Eye protection for the teacher and the pupils

Access to:
Salicylic acid – HARMFUL – 5 g
Concentrated sulphuric acid – CORROSIVE – in
   dropper bottle
Ethanoic (acetic) anhydride – CORROSIVE – 10 ml
Balance
Fume cupboard

Procedure

1 Weigh out 5 g salicylic acid in a 100-ml beaker.
2 In a fume cupboard, add 10 ml ethanoic anhydride.
3 Stir with a glass rod until the solid has dissolved, then add 12 drops of concentrated sulphuric acid, while continuing to stir (still the fume cupboard).
4 Cool the mixture to room temperature (this will be quicker if an ice-bath is used) and then pour it into a beaker containing 150 ml distilled water. The aspirin is insoluble in the mixed solvent of water and ethanoic acid so it precipitates as a fine white powder.
5 Separate the solid using a Buchner filtration apparatus. Wash the solid well with about 50 ml distilled water. Suck dry.

Further information

Science and Technology in Society
The following units are related to this chapter:
Units 304 and 305 "A medicine to control bilharzia" – parts 1 and 2
Unit 609 "Hitting the target – with monoclonal antibodies"
Unit 709 "Which anti-acid?"
Unit 710 "What is biotechnology?"
Unit 805 "The search for the magic bullet".

Topic C4 Energy changes in chemistry

Chapter C13 Fuels and fires

The syllabus section

Context

This section describes the importance of fossil fuels, makes a comparison of fuels and discusses the impact of fuels on the environment. The dangers of fire and methods of fire-fighting are included.

Knowledge and understanding

Syllabus statements	PoS	SoA
Know that limewater (calcium hydroxide solution) and hydrogen carbonate indicator can be used to test for carbon dioxide and that oxygen relights a glowing spill.	3(i)1	—
Understand what is meant by the term fossil fuel.	3(i)5	—
Know, in the context of a range of types of reaction, that the combustion of fuel releases energy and produces waste gas.	3(iii)1	3.4(c)
Understand burning in terms of the fire triangle and know that carbon dioxide and water are among the products of burning hydrocarbon fuels.	3(iii)1	3.6(c)
Be able to study chemical changes in which there is energy transfer to and from the surroundings, describing the accompanying temperature changes and using these to compare the energy changes.	3(iii)6	3.6(e)
Understand the meaning of the terms endothermic and exothermic.	3(iii)6	3.6(e)
Appreciate the environmental issues which arise from the use of fossil fuels.	3(iii)8	3.7(g)
Appreciate the need for the separation, conversion and purification stages in an oil refinery.	3(iii)9	3.8(e)
Understand that energy needs to be supplied to break bonds and that energy is released when bonds are made.	3(ii)2	3.10(b)

(Left of table: Tier B C F)

Opportunities for co-ordination

Photosynthesis and respiration link to **B**3 and **B**9, food and fuels to **B**9, the carbon cycle to **B**15 and energy transfers in food webs to **B**14.

Energy transfers by heating and by working link to Physics: the concept of specific heating capacity to measure energy transfers in the home to **P**9, machines and engines, including internal combustion engines, to **P**6 and **P**8.

Questions of energy cost appear in **P**8, **C**4, **C**6 and **C**17.

There is a link also to **P**12 which reviews the various energy sources and the problem of "energy conservation".

Routes and times

Basic	Central	Further
Omit Q1 and Q6–10.	**C13.1 What is burning?** Omit Q8–10. $\frac{1}{2}$ hour	
Worksheet **C**13A "Fuels" is also suitable. Answers can be checked using section **C**13.2.	**Worksheet C13B What makes a good fuel?** **C**13.2 **What is a good fuel?** (pages 226–227 only) **Worksheet C13C Choosing a good fuel** $1\frac{1}{2}$ hours	
Do page 229 only from section **C**13.2.	**Worksheet C13D Measuring the energy released by burning fuels** **C**13.2 **What is a good fuel?** (pages 228–229 only) $1\frac{1}{2}$ hours	
		Worksheet C13D1 Burning fuels: making and breaking bonds 1 hour
	This is an alternative position for Worksheet **C**14A1 "Exothermic or endothermic?" (Omit Q5; Q4 is optional.)	
Omit pages 234–236.	**C13.3 What are fossil fuels?** Select material according to class needs. $\frac{1}{2}$ hour	
Spend more time on this section. $1\frac{1}{2}$ hours	**C**13.4 **Fossil fuels and the environment** Select material according to class needs. 1 hour	Some of section **C**13.4 should be done for homework. $\frac{1}{2}$ hour
	Worksheet C13E Air pollution – where does it come from? (class + homework) $\frac{1}{2}$ hour	
Replace section **C**13.5 with an appropriate video.	**C**13.5 **How can fires be fought?** Omit Q42. **Box 3: How effective are flame-proofing agents?** Possible Sc1 assessment. $1\frac{1}{2}$ hours	
		Section **C**13.6 "Fire on the farm" is suitable for an extension homework.
Total: 7 hours	*Total: 6$\frac{1}{2}$ hours*	*Total: 7$\frac{1}{2}$ hour*

Monitoring the progress of Sc1

Investigating fuels

Pupils should investigate how the energy transferred to the surroundings depends on the fuel burned. This investigation may be carried out instead of Worksheet **C**13D "Measuring the energy released by burning fuels".

Sample criteria are given below for an assessment between levels 6 and 9.

Strand (i) Ask questions, predict and hypothesize, e.g.	Strand (ii) Observe, measure and manipulate variables, e.g.	Strand (iii) Interpret their results and evaluate scientific evidence, e.g.
6(a) Suggest that the larger the amount of a fuel burned, the greater the amount of energy transferred to the surroundings because more energy is released	6(b) Measure the energy transferred by burning a meaningful range of masses of a fuel	6(c) Conclude that increasing the mass of fuel burned increases the energy transferred because more particles are involved
7(a) Suggest, with reasons, that type of fuel, mass of fuel and temperature of surroundings may all affect energy transfer, and that one of the most important of these is mass of fuel	7(b) As above, but with a range of fuels	7(c) As above, but indicating the range of mass and fuels used
8(a) Suggest, with reasons, that doubling the mass of fuel burned doubles the amount of energy transferred; suggest a relevant investigation	8(b) As above, measuring temperatures to 0.5°C and masses to 0.1 g	8(c) Explain why type of fuel was kept constant for a range of mass and why mass was kept constant for a range of fuels
9(a) As above, and suggest repeating the experiment	9(b) Carry out the above procedure systematically	9(c) Use the data from repeated experiments to draw graphs of mass against energy transferred; comment on the accuracy of the experiment

The pupils' book

C13.1 What is burning?

Air and burning are investigated in most introductory science courses, but for many pupils it will be necessary to revise the chemistry involved. It may help to demonstrate the experiment in box 1 on page 225. Pupils can then attempt questions 1–10 (see under Activities).

The fire triangle can be a focus for much of the work in this chapter. Note that in this course we have avoided using the word "heat" as a noun, for the reasons explained in Chapter 2 of the General introduction.

C13.2 What is a good fuel?

Worksheet **C**13A is designed to help pupils study this section. This can be a group activity: the pupils can work out the meaning of the passage among themselves, and discuss the possible words which might fill the blanks. They should not have access to the text while using the worksheet.

Worksheets **C**13B and **C**13C are also designed to be used alongside this section. Brainstorms and rounds are ways of encouraging all members of a class to contribute ideas.

During a brainstorm, no idea should be rejected however odd it may seem at first sight.

This encourages the less confident pupils to join in. All ideas should be recorded. They can be displayed on the blackboard, on a large chart, or with the help of an overhead projector.

Following a brainstorm, a round gives everyone a chance to say what they think of the ideas which have been suggested, but no-one should be forced to do so. Each time someone refers to a particular idea during the round, make a mark against that statement in the summary list from the brainstorm.

Tests of a good fuel might cover its burning characteristics (how easy it is to light, how much smoke it produces, how much ash it leaves); its convenience (how safe and easy it is to transport, store and use); and economic aspects (how cheap or expensive it is in relation to the amount of energy released on burning, and whether it is renewable). A suitable checklist is needed as a result of discussions such as those suggested on Worksheet **C**13B, so that pupils can goon to Worksheet **C**13C.

The experiment described in box 2 on page 228 is probably better considered after the pupils have done the experiments described on Worksheet **C**13D. It is included to give pupils more practice with the methods of calculation and interpretation which are introduced in Chapters **P**8, **P**16 and **P**17 and used in connection with the worksheet.

Answer to selected question

18a Energy transferred $= 25$ J/s $\times 600$ s
$$= 15\ 000 \text{ J}$$

b 15 000 J

c Energy released $= 15\ 000$ J/0.5 g
$$= 30\ 000 \text{ J/g}$$
$$= 30 \text{ kJ/g}$$

C13.3 What are fossil fuels?

There are several films available free from the libraries of major companies which can be used to illustrate this section (see Appendix). This should be co-ordinated with the work to be done in Chapter **P**12 on energy resources.

C13.4 Fossil fuels and the environment

Worksheet **C**13E "Air pollution – where does it come from?" might be set for homework and followed by reading and discussion of this section in class. Some pupils may have difficulty with the graph on the worksheet; they can be helped by being given a copy of the graph sheet with the axes already marked on it. Others may manage without this assistance.

The main pollutants discussed are carbon dioxide (greenhouse effect), carbon monoxide, sulphur dioxide and nitrogen dioxide. It should. be appreciated that there is usually a trade-off between reducing pollution and extra expense, and that many aspects of pollution are complex and incompletely understood (such as the acid rain problem and global warming).

These issues should be discussed in co-ordination with Chapter **B**17. The SATIS unit 502 "The coal mine project" might also be used to involve pupils in more of the issues raised.

The problems mentioned in this section are likely to remain topical and controversial for many years. It is important to show that it can take a long time to reach definite answers when investigating the effects of chemicals on the environment. Newspaper articles and cuttings from magazines can be used to supplement the information in the pupils' book.

C13.5 How can fires be fought?

The local fire brigade may be able to help with this section, either by allowing a visit or by sending a speaker to talk to the class and answer questions.

No time has been allowed in the "Routes and times" charts for the problem in box 3 on page 245. However, this investigation might be carried out in place of one suggested in another chapter. Pupils can make their own plans and state their requirements on Worksheet **C**0. Possible procedures for experiments are given in several of the publications listed under Further information.

C13.6 Fire on the farm

Questions 47 to 52 are based on a serious refinery fire in Europe which resulted in the death of fourteen fire fighters when a burning tank of oil "boiled over." After the accident, the investigators decided that water sprayed onto the tank had sunk below the oil. The oil at the surface became increasingly dense as the lighter fractions burned away until the hot oil sank and came in contact with the water underneath. The water rapidly turned to steam so that the tank seemed to "boil over". One possible modification is to fit pipework and valves so that liquids can be drained from the bottom of the tank in an emergency.

Activities

Teacher demonstration: What are the products of burning fuels?

REQUIREMENTS

The teacher will need:

2 test-tubes with side-arms and bungs

Beaker, 400 ml

Filter pump

Glass tubing including thistle funnel (see figure 13.2 in the Chemistry pupils' book)

Thermometer

Anhydrous copper(II) sulphate – HARMFUL – or cobalt(II) chloride paper

Limewater

Ethanol – FLAMMABLE – in a dropper bottle

Crucible

Mineral wool

Heatproof mat

Eye protection for teacher and pupils

It will only take approximately 10 seconds to see evidence of water and carbon dioxide. The water collected can be boiled, but it takes 20 minutes or so to collect enough to boil. Anhydrous copper(II) sulphate or blue cobalt(II) chloride paper can also be used as tests for the presence of water. Carbon will be seen round the thistle funnel – evidence of incomplete combustion. Thoughtful pupils might point out that the limewater would eventually go cloudy anyway because of carbon dioxide from the air. They may be able to suggest a modification to the apparatus.

The questions in the box in section **C**13.1 can be used as a basis for pupil activity during the demonstration.

Worksheet C13C Choosing a good fuel

REQUIREMENTS

Each group of pupils will need:

Copy of Worksheet **C**13C

Tin lid

Tongs

Burner, tripod and mat

Eye protection

Access to:

Variety of solids in very small pieces: wood, coke, coal, wax, paper, straw

Variety of liquids in **small** reagent bottles with droppers: methylated spirits, paraffin, unleaded petrol – all FLAMMABLE

Mineral wool

Wood splints

Waste container for hot residues

Spatula or knife to scrape the tin lid clean

This worksheet is designed for use after the pupils have drawn up a list of criteria for judging a good fuel. One approach to this is suggested by Worksheet C13B.

Safety

It is very important to control the issue of materials to be burned – especially the liquids. Some pupils will be tempted to burn far too much. It will generally be safer if the teacher dispenses the liquid fuels.

Testing liquid fuels needs to be organized particularly carefully. The liquid must be dispensed well away from flames. The liquid must not be put onto hot mineral wool or a hot tin lid. The tin lid must be cool enough to pick up with fingers before a liquid fuel is added to the mineral wool.

Be warned that several pupils have been badly burned (needing skin grafts) in recent years in incidents involving methylated spirits; teachers may prefer to use this fuel for demonstration only.

Worksheet C13D Measuring the energy released by burning fuels

REQUIREMENTS

Each group of pupils will need:
Crucible
Tin lid
Metal can (see note 1)
Measuring cylinder, 100 ml
Thermometer, 0-100 °C
Stand with boss and clamp
Heatproof mat
Eye protection

Access to:
Ethanol – FLAMMABLE – in a dropper bottle or, safer, a burner with wick (see safety notes on Worksheet C13C above and note 2)
Meta fuel – FLAMMABLE
Gas fuel burner – FLAMMABLE – (e.g. cigarette lighter - supervision by teacher is necessary if this is used)
Balance weighing to 0.01 g

Notes:
1 An empty ring pull can with a domed bottom makes a cheap, disposable calorimeter.
2 Having the ethanol in a burner with a wick, which can be weighed before and after heating, removes the need to refill the burner during the lesson.

If time is short, each group can do the experiment with one fuel and then compare results with other groups.

The calculation can be simplified if 100 ml of water are used. Then the pupils can be told that a rise in temperature of one degree corresponds to a transfer of 420 J of energy to the water.

Worksheet C13D1 Burning fuels: making and breaking bonds

REQUIREMENTS

Each group of pupils will need:
Set of ball-and-spring models:
  1 black atom, 4 holes
  4 red atoms, 2 holes
  4 white atoms, 1 hole
  4 long bonds
  4 short bonds

By using models, pupils are led to a consideration of how bond energies are used to calculate the energy change when fuels are burned. The idea is confined to covalent bonding and it should be made clear that the bonds are not small protrusions coming from the atoms. Pupils should also realise that the O=O and C=O bond energies refer to the energies of both double-bond bonds added together.

The process of bond breaking and bond forming which is introduced is only a convenient book-keeping exercise and teachers should be at pains to explain that this is not what actually occurs in chemical reactions. In reality, only certain bonds are broken in specific sequences. Energy is given out because the energy released in forming new bonds is greater than the energy required to break the old bonds. The calculation shows that 730 kJ/mol is released when methane is burned. Pupils may be curious as to why the C–H bond energy values used for methane are different from those given in question 9. The bond energies depend on the exact environment of the bond, i.e. the type of atoms to which any given atom is attached, and average bond energies for a variety of compounds have been used. Strictly speaking, the bond energy refers to specific bonds in the compound in its **gaseous** form being atomized to form **gaseous** atoms.

Answers to worksheet questions

1 1740 kJ

2 996 kJ

3 2736 kJ

4 The carbon–oxygen and the hydrogen–oxygen bonds.

5 1610 kJ

6 1856 kJ

7 3466 kJ

8 2736 kJ, 3466 kJ, 730 kJ.

9 (i) 486 kJ/mol released; (ii) 1524 kJ/mol released; (iii) 1318 kJ/mol released.

Further information

Booklet
The BP booklet *How is oil refined?*, which is part of their "Caveman" series, is ueful here.

Science at Work (old edition)
Section 1 of *Energy* includes experiments and information about fuels. (Note that section 2 is written in terms which we have deliberately excluded from Nuffield Co-ordinated Sciences.)

Science and the motor car includes experiments and information about crude oil, oil refining and lubricants.

Section 8 of *Pollution* (section 4 in the new edition) investigates the effects of sulphur dioxide on plants and includes information about air pollution.

Fibres and fabrics describes an experiment to study the effectiveness of flame-proofing fabrics.

Science and Technology in Society
The following units can be used in conjunction with this chapter:

Unit 205 "Looking at motor oil"
Unit 403 "Britain's energy sources"
Unit 502 "The coal mine project"
Unit 702 "The gas supply problem"
Unit 902 "Acid rain"
Unit 1003 "A big bang".

Science Workout

The worksheet on finding out about solid fuels, and the crossword on fire, are both suitable for less able pupils. (Purnell, R. *Science Workout 1* and *2*, Stanley Thorne, 1989.)

University of York Science Education Group

The unit *Warmth* in Salters' Chemistry includes sections about the choice of fuels and the effects of air pollution. The unit called *Burning and bonding* studies fires and fire prevention and includes a quantitative comparison of fuels.

Videos

"The greenhouse effect" and "A breath of fresh air" (both BBC Global Environment series), "The black desert" (BBC Short Circuit series), "Oil refining in the 90s" (Esso) and "Fire and flame" (ITV Scientific Eye) are all useful here. The last of these is particularly suitable for less able pupils.

Chapter **C**14 **Batteries**

The syllabus section

Context

This section is based on a study of simple and rechargeable cells as well as fuel cells. The sodium–sulphur cell can be introduced in preparation for the account of the theory of cells in **C**18.

Knowledge and understanding

	Tier		Syllabus statements	PoS	SoA
B	C	F			
			Know that a cell consists of two different electrodes dipping into an electrolyte solution.	3(iii)1	3.4(b)
			Know that changing the electrodes changes cell voltage.	3(iii)1	3.4(b)
			Appreciate that the voltage of a cell with two metal electrodes can be related to the positions of the metals in the activity series.	3(i)3	3.6(d)
			Understand, in principle, the differences between simple cells, rechargeable cells and fuel cells.	3(iii)1	3.7(g)
			Be able to make evaluative judgements about the use of various types of cell.	3(iii)1	3.10(a)

Opportunities for co-ordination

Cells link to **P**17 and **P**18. The work of Volta is also mentioned in **P**18.

Routes and times

Basic	Central	Further
	Basic	**Central**	**Further**

Omit Q3–5.

Worksheet C14A1 Exothermic or endothermic?
Omit Q5; Q4 is optional.
1 hour

All questions are suitable.

C14.1 How were batteries invented?
Worksheet C14A Investigating cells ("Volta and the activity series")
1¼ hours

C14.2 What types of cell do we use today?
(class + homework)
½ hour

Worksheet C14A Investigating cells
("A rechargeable cell")
Q6 could be developed
into an Sc1 assessment if time is available.
1 hour

Omit section **C14.4**.

C14.3 How can cells be used to store energy?
Omit Q9.
C14.4 What is a fuel cell?
³/₄ hour

Q9 is suitable for homework.

Total: 4½ hours   *Total: 4½ hours*   *Total: 4½ hours*

The pupils' book

C14.1 How were batteries invented?

There are various versions of the story of the discovery made by Luigi and Lucia Galvani which give differing degrees of credit to husband and wife depending on the sympathies of the author.

In this chapter it is necessary to distinguish clearly between cells and batteries, but elsewhere in the course we have generally used the word "battery" in its everyday sense.

C14.2 What types of cell do we use today?

Pupils are not expected to remember the technical details of the cells described. The SATIS unit 706 "Dry cells" includes a practical investigation of a dry cell but it depends on a chemical test which the pupils will not have met before. It is very important to warn pupils of the dangers of opening cells other than dry cells; even dry cells can be quite corrosive.

C14.3 How can cells be used to store energy?

The sodium–sulphur cell is described here partly because it is new, and partly because it is relatively easy to describe the chemistry of the cell as an example to illustrate the ideas in Chapter C18. Another new type of cell which is becoming available commercially is the aluminium–oxygen cell.

A battery of sodium–sulphur cells is surrounded by a double-walled container filled with glass fibre so that it stays at its operating temperature. If the cell is discharged and recharged by 80% of its capacity every 24 hours, it stays at its working temperature because the energy lost to the surroundings is replaced by the heating effect of the current in the cell.

C14.4 What is a fuel cell?

A fuel cell can be demonstrated as suggested under Activities. Fuel cells are still "exotic" but research continues in the quest for a reliable and safe cell for commercial use. Reports appear in newspapers and magazines from time to time about the progress of this development work.

Activities

Worksheet C14A1 Exothermic or endothermic?

REQUIREMENTS

Each pupil will need:
Eye protection

Each group of pupils will need:
2 plastic drinking cups with one lid (the expanded polystyrene type is best)
Spatula
Thermometer, -5 to 110 °C
Weighing boat or small pieces of paper for weighing
2 measuring cylinders, 100 ml
2 beakers, 100 ml (for acid and alkali)

Access to:
0.2 mol/L copper (II) sulphate solution, allow 60 ml per group
Zinc powder (fine grains are best but *not* zinc dust)
2 mol/L hydrochloric acid, allow 120 ml per group
2 mol/L sodium hydroxide solution – CORROSIVE – allow 240 ml per group
2 mol/L nitric acid – IRRITANT – allow 120 ml per group
1 mol/L citric acid solution, allow 60 ml per group
Sodium hydrogen carbonate (solid)
2 mol/L potassium hydroxide solution – CORROSIVE – allow 60 ml per group
1 mol/L sulphuric acid – IRRITANT – allow 60 ml per group
Balance, to weigh to 1 g

Safety note:

Pupils should be reminded that acids may be corrosive or irritant and that alkalis are corrosive. Copper(II) sulphate solution is toxic and powdered zinc may be an irritant. Zinc dust should not be used because it is highly flammable and ignites spontaneously when moist. Zinc powder which is obviously "gritty" must be used instead.

This activity forms a preliminary exercise to the work on electrochemical cells and may be linked to that section in several ways. In relation to the reaction of copper(II) sulphate and zinc and part d, teachers should refer back to the chemical activity series: cells giving the greatest potential difference are made from systems which show the greatest difference in reactivity. Pupils will note that some chemical reactions release energy but that this energy cannot be harnessed in a useful way if it is just used to raise the temperature of the surroundings. Electrochemical cells are systems in which the chemical reaction takes place in a controlled manner and the energy may be used to do a "useful job", e.g. the electric current could light a lamp.

Pupils should ensure that their measuring cylinders and plastic cups are well washed-out and dried between experiments, and thermometers should also be washed. At the end of the activity, pupils should realize that some reactions are exothermic and some are endothermic and that this depends on the bond making and bond breaking in the reactions. Pupils may need some help with the idea of energy being absorbed from the surroundings. Do not be tempted, however, to go as far as talking about the bonds of the specific compounds involved in these activities: the reasons behind the energy changes observed in these reactions are complex and involve hydration energies of the ions, etc. With faster groups, teachers may consider drawing an energy diagram, such as the one shown here, for bond making and bond breaking.

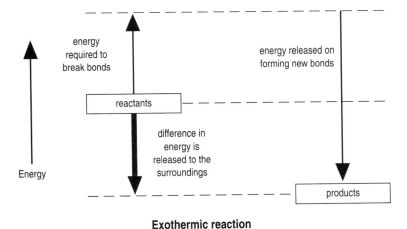

Exothermic reaction

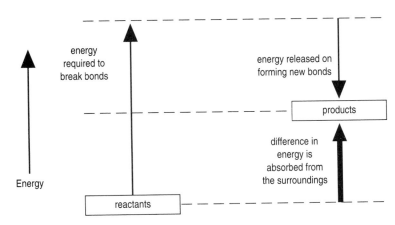

Energy diagrams for exothermic and endothermic reactions.

Endothermic reaction

Answers to worksheet questions

1 Plastic is a good insulator and prevents energy loss to the air.

2 Energy is released.

3 $Zn(s) + CuSO_4(aq) \rightarrow ZnSO_4(aq) + Cu(s)$

4 Yes; the concentrations of hydrogen ions and hydroxide ions are the same in each case. (The simplified neutralization reaction is the same in each case: $H^+ + OH^- \rightarrow H_2O$.)

5 In an endothermic reaction, more energy is required to break existing bonds than is released on forming new bonds.

Worksheet C14A Investigating cells

REQUIREMENTS

Each group of pupils will need:
2 beakers, 100 ml
White tile
2 connecting wires with crocodile clips
Voltmeter, 0-5 V (see note 1)
2 lead electrodes, 3 cm × 5 cm
Power supply, 2–6 V d.c.
Bulb in holder, 1.25 V/0.25 A
Eye protection

Access to:
Metal electrodes: copper, iron, magnesium
  – FLAMMABLE – , nickel, zinc, and others if
  available
0.1 mol/L solutions of metal salts: copper(II)
  sulphate, iron(II) ammonium sulphate, magnesium
  nitrate, zinc sulphate, 50 ml per group (see note 2)
Potassium nitrate solution, 0.5 mol/L, about
  50 ml per group
Dilute sulphuric acid, 1 mol/L – IRRITANT – ,
  50 ml per group
Filter paper
Scissors
Snips

Notes:
1 For good results a high impedance voltmeter should be used. These are likely to be in short supply. If a limited number of meters is placed at convenient access points, groups can make their cells on a mat or tray, then take them to a meter to measure the voltage.
2 The solutions might be labelled: copper salt solution, iron(II) salt solution, etc.

The pupils should have read section **C**14.1 before starting on this worksheet. They are not expected to cover all the suggested investigations. The various groups might tackle different parts and then report their findings to the class.

Teacher demonstration: A fuel cell

REQUIREMENTS

The teacher will need:
Beaker, 400 ml
2 hydrogen electrodes, platinized
Connecting wires
High resistance voltmeter
Hydrogen – FLAMMABLE – cylinder

Oxygen – OXIDIZING – cylinder
Connecting tubing
Sodium hydroxide solution, 2 mol/L
  – CORROSIVE –, 200 ml
Eye protection for the teacher and pupils

The apparatus is illustrated opposite. The voltage rises and steadies at a value just under 1 volt. Teachers need to be satisfied that they know how to use gas cylinders safely.

The advantage of this apparatus is that it is clear that the cell is continuously supplied with the fuel and the oxidant which is the essential feature of a fuel cell. A much simpler apparatus

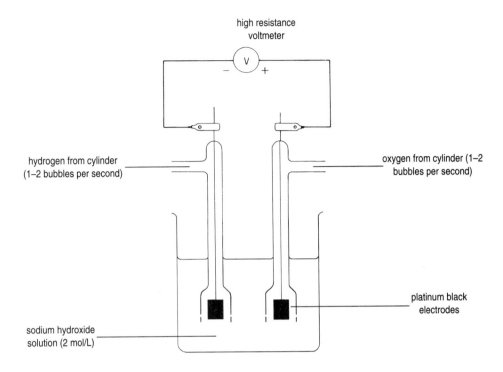

high resistance
voltmeter

hydrogen from cylinder
(1–2 bubbles per second)

oxygen from cylinder (1–2
bubbles per second)

platinum black
electrodes

sodium hydroxide
solution (2 mol/L)

was described in section A23.5 of Revised Nuffield Chemistry *Teachers' guide II*, but it suffers from the disadvantage that pupils might believe that the process of using electrolysis to generate the oxygen and hydrogen might be akin to charging up a lead-acid cell.

The disadvantage of the suggested apparatus is that it is only schools running A-level courses which are likely to have hydrogen electrodes. So this should be regarded as an optional demonstration.

Further information

Science at Work (old edition)
The booklet called *Science and the motor car* includes a section about car batteries including an experiment, pictures and information.

Science and Technology in Society
Unit 706 "Dry cells" might be used in conjunction with this chapter.

University of York Science Education Group
In Salters' Chemistry there is a topic called *Making and using electricity* which includes a series of sections relevant to this chapter.

Topic C5 Soil and agriculture

Chapter C15 Soil

The syllabus section

Context

This section looks at soil as one of the Earth's life-support systems and shows how natural processes lead to the formation of fertile soil. Factors affecting the rate of reaction can be investigated in this context.

Knowledge and understanding

Syllabus statements	PoS	SoA
Know that weathering of rocks is the result of both physical and chemical changes.	3(iv)5	3.4(e)
Know that weathering of rocks releases into the soil salts which plants need for growth.	3(iii)1	—
Understand the factors (temperature, concentration, particle size and catalysts) which influence the rate of a chemical reaction.	3(iii)1	3.7(f)
Be able to interpret chemical equations quantitatively, including masses of solids and volumes of gases. The work could involve determination of formulae or balanced equations.	3(iii)4,5	3.9(c)

Opportunities for co-ordination

Some of the living organisms found in the soil are described in **B**2 and **B**15. In **B**15 there is also an account of the mineral salts which plants need for growth. **B**15 also shows that the variety of plants in a particular district is related to the composition and pH of the soil. **E**2 deals with the formation of soils. Rates of chemical (and biochemical) reactions are discussed in **B**3 and **B**5.

Pupils use graphs in **P**4 to describe moving objects.

Routes and times

Basic	Central	Further
	C15.1 Why study soil? Omit Q1–3. **Worksheet C15A1 Breaking down the rocks** **C15.2 How is soil formed?** Omit the problem in box 1 and Q4. *1 hour*	Faster groups should also read section **C**15.3 "What is in soil?" for homework.
	Worksheet C15A Particle size and the rate of reaction of a rock with an acid *1 hour*	Omit Worksheet **C**15a.
Sc1 investigation based on Worksheet **C**15B "Concentration and the rate of reaction of a rock with an acid" and/or Worksheet **C**15C "Temperature and the rate of reaction of a rock with an acid". *2¼ hours*	**Box 1 Problem: Investigating the rate of reaction of an acid with a rock** Sc1 assessment: omit the effect of particle size. *2¾ hours*	Sc1 assessment based on all of the problem in box 1. *3 hours*
	C15.4 Why does soil pH matter? Omit the problem in box 2. *½ hour*	
The problem in box 2 should be developed into an Sc1 investigation for slower groups. *1½ hours*	**Box 2 Practical problem:** **Measuring the pH of soil** *1¼ hours*	Omit if time is short.
	C15.5 How can the pH of soil be controlled? Omit box 3 and Q21–23. *¼ hour*	Box 3 and Q21–23 are suitable.
Total: 6½ hours	*Total: 6¾ hours*	*Total: 6 hours*

Monitoring the progress of Sc1

Investigating reactions of marble with acids

Pupils should investigate the effect of particle size on the rate of the reaction between marble and acid. This investigation may be carried out instead of Worksheet C15A "Particle size and the rate of reaction of a rock with an acid".

Sample criteria are given below for an assessment between levels 7 and 10.

Strand (i) Ask questions, predict and hypothesize, e.g.	Strand (ii) Observe, measure and manipulate variables, e.g.	Strand (iii) Interpret their results and evaluate scientific evidence, e.g.
7(a) Suggest, with reasons, that concentration of acid, mass of marble, temperature and particle size all affect the rate of reaction, and that particle size is a major factor	**7(b)** Time how long it takes different sizes of particle to react at different temperatures	**7(c)** Conclude that the particle size has a bigger effect on the rate of reaction than the temperature, and quote the range of particle sizes used
8(a) Suggest that the rate of reaction will double if the mean diameter of the particles halves; suggest a relevant investigation	**8(b)** As above, measuring time to 1 second and length to 0.1 mm	**8(c)** Explain why temperature was kept constant for a range of particle sizes and why particle size was kept constant for a range of temperatures
9(a) As above, and suggest repeating the experiment	**9(b)** Carry out the above procedure systematically	**9(c)** Use the data from repeated experiments to draw graphs of results and to show that particle size affects the rate of reaction; comment on the accuracy of the experiment
10(a) Suggest that the rate of reaction depends on the surface area of the particles	**10(b)** As above, and calculate surface area of particles; check apparatus	**10(c)** Use the data from repeated experiments to draw graphs of results and to show that the rate of reaction depends on surface area; comment on the accuracy of the experiment

The pupils' book

C15.1 Why study soil?

Some books about environmental chemistry emphasize pollution, others concentrate on chemical changes in the natural environment. In this course it is not possible to go into these matters in any depth, but it is important to relate the impact of industry, farming and other activities on the environment to the scale of natural processes. This was hinted at in Worksheet C13E.

C15.2 How is soil formed?

The power of frost to shatter rocks can be emphasized by means of the demonstration suggested under Activities.

C15.3 What is in soil?

This section shows that ion exchange is not just a process used to soften water. Ion exchange is an example of a reversible process.

C15.4 Why does soil pH matter?

There is a diagram of the pH scale in the Biology pupils' book (Chapter **B**5). The practical work in connection with this section involves either a study of the effect of pH on solubility or the design of a kit to measure soil pH.

C15.5 How can the pH of soil be controlled?

This section provides an opportunity to revise the chemistry of limestone as described in Chapter **C**4. It also shows that the formulae and equations for the reactions of calcium carbonate and calcium oxide with acids can explain their neutralizing power, as described on garden and agricultural products.

Activities

Teacher demonstration: Freezing water

REQUIREMENTS

The teacher will need:
Either:
Small screw-cap glass bottle, such as a
  medicine bottle
Plastic ice-cream tub

Access to:
Freshly boiled, cooled water
Refrigerator with deep freeze compartment

Or:
Cast iron bursting bottle (available from
  suppliers of apparatus)
Plastic ice-cream tub with lid
Ice
Crushed rock salt
Freshly boiled and cooled water

Procedure

Either:
Carefully fill a screw-cap bottle to the rim with water which has been boiled and then allowed to cool. Screw on the lid, making sure that no air remains in the bottle. Stand the bottle in a plastic container and put it in the deep freeze section of a refrigerator. Leave overnight.

Or:
In advance cool the iron bursting bottle in ice. At the start of the demonstration fill the bottle completely with boiled, cooled water and screw the plug in tightly with a spanner. Submerge the bottle in an ice-salt freezing mixture. Cover with the lid. After about fifteen minutes a sharp crack will be heard – the bottle will split open.

Worksheet C15A1 Breaking down the rocks

REQUIREMENTS

Each group of pupils will need:
4 plastic cups (these should be strong, or the
  base is likely to bulge as freezing occurs)
4 saucers
Masses, 1 kg, 2 kg, 3 kg and 4 kg
Piece of sandstone, say 3–5cm across
Container to hold sandstone during soaking
Plastic bag
Burner, heatproof mat and tongs

2 pieces of granite, one of which can be
  comfortably held in tongs
Beaker containing water
Eye protection

Access to:
Freezer

The procedure is detailed on the worksheet. The three experiments might well be carried out in larger groups than pairs, and the results shared.

Answers to worksheet questions

1 Water is the main agent in the weathering of rocks. When it freezes it causes mechanical breaking; it dissolves the rock in chemical breaking; and the hydrostatic pressure it exerts within living roots causes one type of biological weathering.

2 Rocks are heated by the Sun during the day and then cool again during the night.

3 Desert conditions of hot days and cold nights would have the greatest effect. It might be thought that the role of water would be limited in this situation. In fact, it seems that even in the desert water is important and the damage is done by tiny amounts of water absorbed during the day and becoming frozen at night.

Planning lesson: Investigating reaction rates

If pupils are asked to make their own plans for the experiments to investigate rates of reaction, the teacher may wish to demonstrate the reaction first and then show the pupils a range of the apparatus which they might choose to use. For this purpose the teacher will need one example of each type of apparatus listed below for Worksheets **C**15A, **C**15B and **C**15C. The pupils' plans are prompted by box 1 on page 260. They can set out their requirements on Worksheet **C**0.

Worksheet C15A Particle size and the rate of reaction of a rock with an acid

REQUIREMENTS

The teacher (or each group of pupils) will need:
Copy of Worksheet **C**15A
Conical flask, 100 ml
Measuring cylinder, 100 ml
Stopclock, or watch
Top pan balance, reading to 0.01 g, preferably
  with a tare button
Eye protection

Access to:
Large marble chips, 20 g (see note 1)
Small marble chips, 20 g (see note 1)
Scrap paper
Dilute hydrochloric acid, 2 mol/L
Cotton wool
Graph paper, 1 piece per pupil

Note:
1 The marble chips should be washed beforehand in dilute hydrochloric acid and then in water to remove surface powder. They should then be allowed to dry in air.

This experiment can be organized as a demonstration carried out by a group of pupils while the rest of the class records the results and plots the graph. If the balance does not have a tare button, then one member of the demonstration group can use a calculator to work out the values for the loss in mass as the balance readings are read out. One group can do the experiment with large chips, then a second group can take over for the small chips. (If two balances are available, both groups can do their experiments at the same time.)

Alternatively this experiment can be set up as part of a circus with Worksheets **C**15B and **C**15C.

Worksheet C15B Concentration and the rate of reaction of a rock with an acid

REQUIREMENTS

Each group of pupils will need:
Copy of Worksheet **C**15B
Conical flask, 100 ml, with a wide neck
Bung to fit flask, with delivery tubes as shown on
  the worksheet

Trough
Measuring cylinder, 50 ml
Stopclock or watch
Eye protection

Access to:

Large marble chips, about 1 cm × 1.5 cm × 1.5 cm, 1 per group (see note 1 for Worksheet **C**15A)

2 mol/L hydrochloric acid, 100 ml per group, with 50 ml measuring cylinder

Graph paper, 1 piece per pupil

One large marble chip can be reused in each part of the experiment on the assumption that its surface area does not change significantly. If single large chips are not available use several chips of equivalent bulk. Alternatively, use four chips of approximately the same surface area, one in each experiment.

Questions 5–8 on side 2 of the worksheet ask pupils to calculate values for the rate of reaction and plot a second graph. This should be omitted if it will confuse rather than help the pupils.

Worksheet C15C Temperature and the rate of reaction of a rock with an acid

REQUIREMENTS

Each group of pupils will need:

Copy of Worksheet **C**15C

Test-tube in a rack

Stirring thermometer, 0–100°C

Burner, tripod, gauze and mat

Beaker, 100 ml

Stopclock or watch

Eye protection

Access to:

Balance, reading to 0.01 g

Small marble chips, about 3 mm across (see note 1 for Worksheet **C**15A)

4 mol/L hydrochloric acid – IRRITANT – 30 ml per group, with 10 ml measuring cylinder

Graph paper, 1 sheet per pupil

This experiment gives good results if the marble chips are carefully matched for size.

Questions 7–9 on side 2 of the worksheet should only be set to those who will not be confused by them.

Box 2 Problem: Measuring the pH of soil

Here the requirements will depend on the pupils' plans. The information for this exercise is given in box 2 in section **C**15.4 of the pupils' book. Two possible procedures are as follows:

Method A

1 Take 5 g of dry soil or compost.

2 Grind in a pestle and mortar.

3 Transfer to a boiling-tube and add 40 ml of water. (If tap water is to be used, its pH must be checked in case it is not 7.)

4 Shake.

5 Add a small amount of solid barium sulphate. (This helps the soil to settle quickly and prevents suspended soil particles from hiding the indicator's true colour.)

6 Add 3 drops of Universal Indicator solution and shake.

7 Read off the pH from a colour chart.

Method B

1 Take a 2-ml plastic syringe, remove the plunger, and seal the jet with a cap (or small bung which has been partially drilled).

2 Use a cork borer to cut a disc of filter paper and then push the disc down to cover the bottom of the barrel of the syringe.

3 Fill the syringe to the 0.5-ml mark with dry soil or compost.

4 Add water to the 2-ml mark, followed by 2 drops of Universal Indicator solution. (If tap water is to be used, its pH must be checked in case it is not 7.)

5 Insert the plunger just inside the barrel of the syringe, and shake the soil and Indicator together for 30 seconds.

6 Remove the cap or bung, and press in the plunger to force the solution through the filter paper into a test-tube.

7 Read off the pH from a colour chart.

Pupils can be asked to bring in soil samples from a range of localities. The pH of compost in pots for house plants can also be tested.

An important part of this problem for the pupils is the preparation of a clear set of instructions for the assembly and use of the kit.

Worksheet C15D Investigating the effect of pH on the solubility of soil minerals

REQUIREMENTS

Each group of pupils will need:
Copy of Worksheet **C**15D
Beaker, 100 ml
Glass rod
Measuring cylinder, 10 ml
Eye protection
1 mol/L aqueous ammonia in a dropper bottle
1 mol/L nitric acid – IRRITANT – in a dropper bottle

Access to:
The following aqueous solutions (approximately 0.5 mol/L) in reagent bottles:
  sodium sulphate (7 g/100 ml of the anhydrous salt, or 16 g/100 ml of the hydrated salt)
  potassium chloride (4 g/100 ml)
  calcium chloride – IRRITANT – (11 g/ 100 ml of the hydrated salt)
  ammonium nitrate – OXIDIZING – (4 g/100 ml)
  ammonium sulphate (6.5 g/100 ml)
  disodium hydrogenphosphate (18 g/100 ml of the hydrated salt)
  iron(III) nitrate – IRRITANT – (20 g/100 ml of the hydrated salt)
  magnesium nitrate (13 g/100 ml of the hydrated salt)
  manganese(II) chloride (10 g/L of the hydrated salt)
Small pieces of Universal Indicator paper

This experiment provides an opportunity for students to extend their knowledge of precipitation reactions.

It may be necessary for the pupils to measure the pH of the distilled water used to make the solutions first so that they can see whether the dissolved salts have made any difference. The pH of distilled water is often below 7, and this might lead to misleading interpretations if not noted.

Further information

Science at Work (old edition)
Two booklets include experiments to investigate soil. *Forensic science* describes an investigation to compare soil samples by measuring their pH. The suggested procedure suffers from the disadvantage that the indicator is added after the clay and humus have been filtered off. *Plant science* includes a series of experiments to analyse soil based on a commercial soil testing kit.

University of York Science Education Group
The unit in Chemistry in Action called *Gardeners' question time* is a practical exercise in which pupils are asked to apply their knowledge of chemistry to advise a market gardener to decide how to treat an acidic soil.

Video
"Soil" (ITV Science and Technology series) is useful for linking Chapters **C**15 and **C**16.

Chapter C16 Fertilizers

The syllabus section

Context

The use of fertilizers and agrochemicals has revolutionized farming in recent years. This section is a study of chemical aspects of this revolution. The work of Haber and Bosch can illustrate the contrasting roles of the scientist and the engineer. The section can include a discussion of the social and environmental issues involved in the use of fertilizers.

Knowledge and understanding

	Tier			

Syllabus statements	PoS	SoA
Know that materials can be converted into new, useful products through a range of types of chemical reactions, including ionic reactions, salt formation, oxidation and reduction.	3(iii)1	3.4(b)
Know that fertilizers are inorganic salts which supply plants with the elements they need, including nitrogen, phosphorous and potassium.	3(iii)1	3.4(b)
Know, through a range of reactions, that reactions with oxygen form oxides.	3(iii)1	3.6(c)
Appreciate the role of the chemical industry in manufacturing fertilizers and appreciate the need for catalysts, high temperature and pressure in the process.	3(iii)2 3(iii)11	3.7(f) 3.7(g)
Appreciate the difference between ammonia and ammonium salts.	**3(ii)2**	**3.7(e)**
Know the meaning of the term "nitrogen fixation" and appreciate that the chemical basis of the nitrogen problem is the inertness of nitrogen gas.	3(iii)1	3.7(g)
Understand equations which describe the chemical changes involved in the manufacture of ammonia and nitric acid.	3(iii)3,9	3.7(g) 3.8(f)
Be able to evaluate the fertilizer industry in terms of raw materials, energy considerations, waste disposal and profit margins.	3(iii)8,9	3.9(d)
Appreciate the environmental consequences of the use of fertilizers (e.g. leaching of nitrates).	3(iii)8	3.9(d)

Opportunities for co-ordination

References to the impact of fertilizers on the environment are in **B**7 and to aspects of the nitrogen cycle in **B**15. **B**17 deals with the advantages and disadvantages of pesticides from the biological point of view. The chemistry of agrochemicals is not accessible at this level.

The substantial energy cost in the manufacture of fertilizers links to **P**12.

There are links to the study of World War 1 in History. New methods of making ammonia and nitric acid were needed for the manufacture of explosives at the beginning of the war.

Routes and times

Basic	Central	Further
Replace sections **C**16.1 and **C**16.2 with appropriate videos. *1 hour*	**C**16.1 **Why do we need fertilizers?** Omit Q10 and 11. **C**16.2 **How has chemistry helped to solve the nitrogen problem?** (up to Q13) *³/₄ hour*	Q10 and 11 are suitable for homework.
Omit Worksheet **C**16C.	**Worksheet C16C Chemical equilibrium** *Optional*	Worksheet **C**16C should be done. *1 hour*
Replace this section by appropriate videos. *1 hour*	**C**16.2 **How has chemistry helped to solve the nitrogen problem?** (pages 272–275) **C**16.3 **The Haber process today** Omit Q21 and 23–25. *³/₄ hour*	Q21–25 are suitable for homework.
Omit Worksheet **C**16A.	**Worksheet C16A The catalyst crisis** (teacher demonstration) *³/₄ hour*	Worksheet **C**16A should be done as a class practical with the option of developing it into an Sc1 assessment. *1¹/₄ hours*
Omit box 1 and Q26 and 28. Replace with class practicals on the properties and preparation of ammonia. *1 hour*	**C**16.4 **From ammonia to ammonium salts** Include teacher demonstration of the properties of ammonia; omit Q28. *³/₄ hour*	All questions are suitable for homework.
Replace section **C**16.5 with SATIS Unit 505 "Making fertilizers" (omit page 6). *1 hour*	**C**16.5 **How are fertilizers manufactured?** Omit Q30–32 and 35–37. *¹/₂ hour*	All questions are suitable for homework.
Omit symbol equations in Q1 and 2. *³/₄ hour*	**Worksheet C16B Making a fertilizer** Omit Q3–6. *³/₄ hour*	Do Q3 in class; Q4 and 5 are suitable for homework.
Omit section **C**16.6 and spend longer on Q39.	**C**16.6 **What happens to fertilizers in the soil?** (homework) **C**16.7 **Are fertilizers a good thing?** *1 hour*	
Total: 5¹/₂ hours	*Total: 5¹/₄ hours*	*Total: 6³/₄ hours*

The pupils' book

C16.1 Why do we need fertilizers?

Plant breeding coupled with the use of fertilizers and agrochemicals has dramatically increased crop yields in recent years. Figure 16.2 attempts to show diagrammatically the contributions made by the various changes in farming practice.

As well as science and technology, the other big influences on agriculture are economics and politics. For the last forty years the main aim of agricultural policy has been to increase output. This is changing now that we have over-production in Europe with the notorious grain mountains, as well as increasing public concern about the effects of fertilizers and farm chemicals on the environment.

C16.2 How has chemistry helped to solve the nitrogen problem?

Chemistry and Biology textbooks often give a different emphasis to the treatment of the nitrogen problem and nitrogen fixation. In Chemistry nitrogen fixation is any method, natural or industrial, for producing nitrogen compounds from nitrogen gas in a form suitable for plants. The nitrogen problem is seen to arise from the chemical inertness of nitrogen.

In Biology the focus is on nitrogen fixation by bacteria. The nitrogen problem is seen to arise from the existence of other, denitrifying bacteria which result in losses of nitrogen from compounds in the soil to the atmosphere.

In this course we have tried to co-ordinate these two view-points, in this chapter and in Chapter **B**l5.

C16.3 The Haber process today

Pupils are not required to remember the details of the Haber process, but they should be able to show that they can understand an account of the process and interpret data about it. The effects of pressure and temperature on the yield are presented graphically and without reference to equilibrium ideas.

C16.4 From ammonia to ammonium salts

The study of gases has had an important place in chemistry ever since Jan van Helmont (1577-1644) coined the word "gas" from the Greek for "chaos" and Stephen Hales (1677-1761) developed techniques for collecting and handling gases. The chemistry of ammonia provides a good opportunity for teachers who enjoy demonstrations to show pupils a variety of interesting reactions. Some suggestions are included under Activities.

The reaction of ammonia with water is described in box 1 on page 205 in Chapter **C**11. The box in this section explains the difference between an ammonia molecule and an ammonium ion.

Factual recall of the process for the manufacture of nitric acid is not required, but pupils should be able to answer questions about this, and other similar processes, given appropriate information.

Worksheet **C**16A is a problem solving exercise based on events which faced German chemists at the start of World War 1. The Royal Navy cut off supplies of Chilean nitrates to Germany. So chemists had to find a replacement for the traditional process of making nitric acid by distilling a mixture of sodium nitrate and concentrated sulphuric acid. They had the difficulty of developing and scaling up the recently discovered, and little-used, catalytic conversion of ammonia to nitric acid.

Copper can be used as the catalyst, but the yield is low. The German chemists used iron–bismuth catalysts which were replaced by platinum after the war. Successful large-scale production of concentrated nitric acid from ammonia began in the spring of 1915, and may have added as much as twelve months to the fighting capability of the German High Command.

Haber's involvement in the preparations for the use of chlorine gas at this time is the basis of questions and discussion in the SATIS unit listed under Further information.

C16.5 How are fertilizers manufactured?

The ions taken in by plants from the soil are described in Chapter **B**15. This section describes the production of fertilizers to supply nitrate, phosphate and potassium ions.

The text points out the two uses of the word "compound" in this context.

Worksheet **C**16B provides an opportunity for pupils to carry out an industrial process on a small scale and then cost their product.

C16.6 What happens to fertilizers in the soil?

This section is based on ideas introduced by sections **C**15.3, **C**15.4 and Worksheet **C**15D.

C16.7 Are fertilizers a good thing?

The use of fertilizers and farm chemicals has become controversial; there are regular articles in newspapers and magazines which can be used to supplement the information in this section.

Activities

Teacher demonstration: The properties of ammonia

Possible demonstrations include the fountain experiment, the catalytic oxidation of ammonia and the reaction of ammonia with hydrogen chloride.

The fountain experiment

REQUIREMENTS

The teacher will need:
Apparatus for filling a round-bottomed flask with dry ammonia gas – TOXIC (see below)
Apparatus for the fountain experiment (see overleaf)
Spare dry flask to allow a repeat performance
Concentrated ammonia solution – CORROSIVE
Potassium hydroxide pellets – CORROSIVE

Mineral wool
Red litmus solution in dropper bottle
Red litmus paper
Eye protection for the teacher and the pupils

Access to:
Fume cupboard

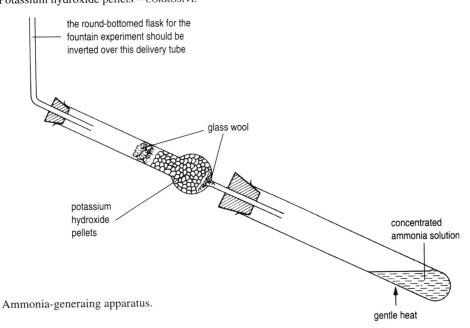

the round-bottomed flask for the fountain experiment should be inverted over this delivery tube

glass wool

potassium hydroxide pellets

concentrated ammonia solution

gentle heat

Ammonia-generaing apparatus.

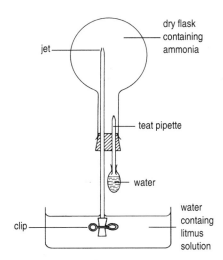

Fountain experiment.

Procedure

With many pupils it will be sufficient just to concentrate on this demonstration which illustrates several important properties of ammonia. One good demonstration will allow pupils time to work out for themselves how the fountain is created and what it shows about the properties of ammonia.

Fill the flask in a fume cupboard by upward delivery. Take some time over this because it is important to displace all the air. Moist red litmus paper held at the mouth of the flask will show when the flask is full.

Filling the flask with ammonia is part of the experiment – it is an opportunity to show that ammonia is a colourless gas which is less dense than air.

Assemble the apparatus as shown on the left. First do the experiment just with water in the trough to show that the presence of litmus is not necessary for the fountain effect. Repeat with litmus in the water for a more colourful demonstration and to show that ammonia solution is alkaline.

Start the fountain by squeezing the bulb of the teat pipette to inject a little water into the flask. The advantage of the apparatus shown is that it is simple, so that it is easier to visualize what is happening than with alternative arrangements with two flasks and more tubes.

The catalytic oxidation of ammonia

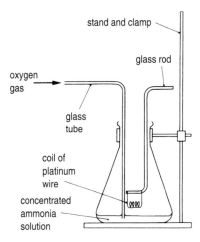

Catalytic oxidation of ammonia.

In addition to the apparatus for the fountain experiment, the teacher will need:
Apparatus shown on the left
Source of oxygen – OXYDIZING (see note 1)

Connecting tubing
Burner and mat
Safety screens
Eye protection for the teacher and the pupils
Fume cupboard

Note:
1 If no oxygen cylinder is available a gas generator is needed, together with 6% (20 volume) hydrogen peroxide solution and manganese(IV) oxide – HARMFUL. If a cylinder is used, a beaker should be used rather than a flask.

This demonstration provides a lead into Worksheet **C16A**. It uses the same apparatus.

Adjust the oxygen supply to deliver a steady stream of gas. This will produce a mixture of ammonia and oxygen above the liquid surface. Lower the coil of platinum wire into the flask. The catalyst should start to glow. If nothing happens, heat the wire to red heat in a Bunsen flame and then lower it into the flask. Once the reaction starts, the wire should continue to glow for a long time.

The reaction produces nitrogen dioxide which reacts with water vapour and ammonia to form ammonium salts so white fumes appear in the flask.

If the oxygen flow is too rapid there may be minor explosions; these do no damage, but it is important to use a safety screen for the demonstration and to insist that the class wear eye protection.

The reaction of ammonia with hydrogen chloride

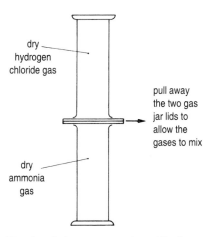

Reaction between ammonia and hydrogen chloride.

In addition, the teacher will need:
Gas generator, with tap funnel, and right-angle delivery tube

Crushed rock salt
Concentrated sulphuric acid – CORROSIVE
2 gas jars with cover-glasses

Fill one gas jar with ammonia by upward delivery. Fill a second jar with hydrogen chloride by downward delivery. Place the jar of hydrogen chloride upside down over the jar of ammonia as shown, then pull out the two cover-glasses.

Thick white clouds of ammonium chloride appear. The formation of a solid from two gases can be explained in terms of the theory in box 1 in section **C16.4**. Once the white powder has settled, point out the small volume of solid compared with the original volume of the gases. Pupils can be asked to use their knowledge of states of matter and structure to explain the difference.

Worksheet C16A The catalyst crisis

REQUIREMENTS

The teacher will need (see note 1):
Flask, 100 ml or 250 ml
Cork or bung with delivery tubes, as on the
 worksheet
Water pump
Eye protection for teacher and pupils

Access to:
Fume cupboard
Concentrated ammonia solution, 0.880 g/ml
 – CORROSIVE
Water tap and sink

Each working group will need:
Copy of Worksheet C16A
Bent glass rod to support the metal wires (as on
 the worksheet)
Eye protection

Access to:
Selection of metal wires, e.g. nickel, iron/steel,
 constantan, brass, nichrome, copper (preferably
 a range of samples of copper with different
 thicknesses)
Emery cloth to clean the surface of the wires

Note:
1 The worksheet is based on the assumption that pupils will plan their own investigations but that the
testing will be done under the immediate supervision of the teacher.

The situation presented by this problem was real in Germany during World War I. The
German chemical industry was cut off from supplies of Chilean nitrate by the British
blockade. Attempts to beat the blockade failed when the German navy was defeated in the
battle of the Falklands in 1914. Research chemists had little more than six months to
develop the ammonia oxidation process using a catalyst other than platinum, which was not
readily available.

This experiment must be done in a fume cupboard. It may be more convenient to
organize it as a class demonstration, with different groups preparing the various wires, and
then helping the teacher to demonstrate their effect (if any) to the rest of the class.

Pupils should have some success with copper wire, and they can then go on to
investigate whether the thickness of the wire or the way in which the wire is coiled has any
effect on the efficiency of the process.

Discussion of this experiment can be related to the information in section **C16.2** about
the way in which Bosch and his team found a suitable catalyst for the Haber process.

Worksheet C16B Making a fertilizer

REQUIREMENTS

Each group of pupils will need:
Copy of Worksheet C16B
Beaker, 100 ml
Beaker, 250 ml
Glass rod
Measuring cylinders, 10 ml and 50 ml
Filter funnel
Evaporating basin
Petri dish (see note 1)
Burner, tripod, gauze and mat
Eye protection

Access to:
Calcium phosphate, 6 g per group
Sulphuric acid, 2 mol/L – CORROSIVE – allow 40
 ml per group
Dilute ammonia solution, 2 mol/L, allow 40 ml
 per group
Distilled water
Balance
Filter paper
Labels
Chemical and apparatus catalogues with prices

Note:
1 The ammonium phosphate can be left to crystallize in the evaporating basin. However, the basins
may be required by other classes, in which case Petri dishes can be used as crystallizing dishes.

In step d, the ammonia should be added slowly, stirring and checking the pH all the while: 5 ml of ammonia may take the pH beyond 5.

This experiment is based on Experiment B in *Chemicals for Agriculture* which is number 5 in the *Experimenting with industry* series (see Further information).

For some groups it will be enough to make a sample of fertilizer. However, some pupils will enjoy the challenge of costing their product as described on sides 2 and 3 of the worksheet. Side 3 is based on an actual sheet for a production process in the chemical industry.

A: Materials

The materials used include the chemicals and filter paper. Prices can be looked up in catalogues. Capital costs may be ignored, but it should be pointed out that they are very important and a matter of great concern to industry.

B: Labour

Labour costs can be based on earnings from part-time work such as a paper round or a Saturday job. Companies often add a percentage to the labour rate (between 10 and 15 per cent) to cover administration.

C: Overheads such as fuel costs

The worksheet suggests that the fuel costs can be estimated given a value of the flow rate of the burner (typically of the order of 0.15 m^3/h).

The SATIS unit *Making fertilizers* gives details of a procedure for testing fertilizers using cress seedlings.

Worksheet C16C Chemical equilibrium

REQUIREMENTS

Each pupil will need:
Eye protection

Each group of pupils will need:
3 beakers, 100 ml
2 teat pipettes
White tile or sheet of white paper
Litmus solution (in dropper bottle)
Test-tube in test-tube rack

Access to:
Hydrochloric acid, 2 mol/L, allow 20 ml per group
Sodium hydroxide solution, 2 mol/L
 – CORROSIVE – allow 20 ml per group
Potassium chromate (VI) solution, 0.1 mol/L
 – IRRITANT – allow 10 ml per group

Optional (see below):
Hydrochloric acid, 0.1 mol/L, 20 ml per group
Sodium hydroxide, 0.1 mol/L, 20 ml per group
3 watchglasses

For the teacher (optional):
Eye protection
Fume cupboard
Apparatus and chemicals for generating chlorine
  (see note 1)
Iodine
Spatula
U-tube with bung and connecting tubing
Plastic gloves

Safety notes:
The pupils should be warned that sodium hydroxide is corrosive and that potassium chromate(VI) is poisonous and irritant.

The teacher should take great care with the demonstration experiment and should practise it or obtain technical assistance if unsure of the safety aspects. Iodine is corrosive and dangerous to skin and eyes, and chlorine is corrosive and toxic. The fume cupboard should be as closed as possible during the "pouring" of the chlorine. The chlorine should be "poured" away in the direction of the fan.

Note:

1 Use the apparatus shown to generate the chlorine (TOXIC) by adding concentrated (5 mol/L) hydrochloric acid (CORROSIVE) to fresh sodium chlorate(I) solution (CORROSIVE) , and dry it with silica gel.

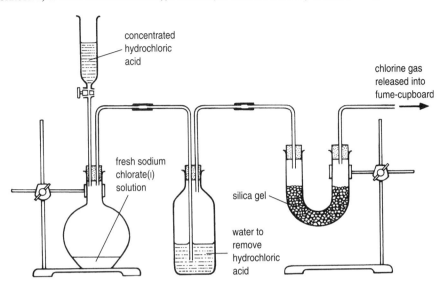

Apparatus for generating chlorine.

The idea of equilibrium is approached by first considering reactions which are reversible. Pupils then find the balance points of an indicator and of the reaction between potassium dichromate(VI) and potassium chromate(VI). In order to find the balance point more easily, it may be useful to provide some more – dilute acid or alkali to prevent "overshooting the mark". However, dilute acid must not be used in such quantity as to dilute the reaction mixture significantly.

It should be made clear that in such reactions, even when the reaction is apparently completely to one side, there are still traces of reactants as well as products. It can easily be shown that the "balanced colour" is an equal mixture of the colours of the indicator in acid and alkaline solution by placing a watchglass of litmus in acid solution over a watchglass of litmus in alkaline solution and comparing the colour with that of litmus in distilled water.

The importance that altering the concentration of reactants or products has on the reaction is discussed with reference to the synthesis of ammonia. In this case, an increase in pressure also increases the concentration of the reactants relative to the products so that the reaction moves to the right of the equation. However, do not make the mistake of extrapolating from this and assuming that an increase in pressure *always* increases the yield: this is not so – the reaction goes in the direction of a decrease in volume when the pressure is increased. It is sufficient at this stage for pupils to realize that an understanding of equilibrium is industrially important, although faster groups may study equilibrium in more detail.

The effect of altering concentrations may be demonstrated in a fume cupboard. The equilibrium between chlorine, iodine monochloride and iodine trichloride easily shows this. The position of the equilibrium

$$Cl_2 \quad + \quad ICl \quad \rightleftharpoons \quad ICl_3$$

green gas   brown liquid   yellow solid

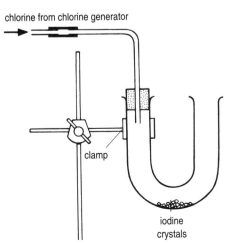

Apparatus for demonstrating the equilibrium between Cl_2, ICl and ICl_3.

may be altered by changing the concentration of chlorine gas passing over the iodine monochloride. Pass chlorine through a U-tube containing a few crystals of iodine. This forms the iodine monochloride, which will be seen as a brown liquid. The pupils' attention should then be drawn to these two reactants. Continue to pass chlorine through the tube, when yellow iodine trichloride will be formed. The excess chlorine pushes the reaction to the right of the equation. Then disconnect the U-tube and tip it up slowly until it is almost on its side. The brown iodine monochloride re-forms as the concentration of chlorine falls. The experiment could be repeated to show that the reaction is readily reversible.

Answers to worksheet questions

1 Add water.

2 A large amount will be required.

3 The reaction would be shifted to the left of the equation, and more hydrogen and nitrogen would be formed.

4 The reaction would be shifted to the right of the equation.

Further information

Experimenting with industry
Booklet 5 of this series (published by the Association for Science Education) is called *Chemicals for agriculture*. The experiments include investigations into the caking of fertilizers, the production of ammonium phosphate and the manufacture of protein by fermentation.

Science and Technology in Society
Unit 505 "Making fertilizers" could usefully be used for revision and homework. The first suggested experiment presents pupils with the problem of devising a procedure for making ammonium sulphate. The second experiment shows how to test fertilizers using cress seedlings.

Unit 207 "The story of Fritz Haber" raises the issue of the responsibility of scientists and the potential of science for good and bad. The unit includes an account of Haber's work in the development of chemical warfare.

Unit 810 "High pressure chemistry" includes reading and questions about the work of Carl Bosch and his ingenious design of a high pressure reactor for the Haber process.

University of York Science Education Group
The unit *Growing food* in Salters' Chemistry includes a series of sections which are relevant to this chapter.

Videos
"Chemical technology" (BBC Science Topics series), "Energy for sale – the story of ammonia" (BBC Great Experiments series) and "Soil" (ITV Science and Technology series) are useful here.

Topic C6

The Periodic Table, atoms and bonding

Chapter C17 The Periodic Table

The syllabus section

Context

The history of the discovery of the Periodic Table shows that it can take a long time for new ideas to be accepted in science. The story illustrates how the insight of Mendeléev led to the solution of a series of chemical problems.

Knowledge and understanding

	Tier	
B	C	F

Syllabus statements	PoS	SoA
Know that the soluble oxides of metals are alkaline while the soluble oxides of non-metals are generally acidic.	3(i)1	3.6(a)
Be able to compare the physical and chemical properties of elements and know what is meant by a periodic pattern.	3(i)1,2	3.7(b)
Know the major characteristics of metals and non-metals through a study of selected elements (Group II elements, hydrogen, noble gases and their compounds).	3(i)1,2	3.8(a)
Be able to recognize patterns in the properties of metals (Group II elements) and non-metals (halogens) and relate this information to their electronic structure and position in the Periodic Table.	3(i)2	3.9(a)

Opportunities for co-ordination

Carbon dioxide in plant growth links to **B**3 and acid rain to **B**17.

Routes and times

Basic	Central	Further

Basic

Replace sections **C**17.1 and **C**17.2 with an appropriate video.

³/₄ hour

Central

> **C**17.1 **How was the Periodic Table discovered?**
> Omit Q3–6.
>
> **C**17.2 **Patterns and problems**
> Do this in conjunction with Worksheet **C**17B
> "The Periodic Table"; omit Q7–9 from section
> **C**17.2.
>
> *1 hour*

Further

Omit Worksheet **C**17B.

¹/₂ hour

Use Worksheet **C**17B "The Periodic Table" and Worksheet **C**17A to show the positions of groups, periods, metals and non-metals.

³/₄ hour

> **Worksheet C17A A shortened form of the**
> **Periodic Table** (class + homework)
> Use in conjunction with Q3–5 of section **C**17.1
> and Q7–9 of section **C**17.2.
>
> *¹/₂ hour*

Q6 is suitable for homework.

Spend more time on this section. Omit Q11–15, 19 and 23. Put emphasis on acidic and basic oxides. Replace demonstrations with class practical work where it is safe to do so.

2¹/₂ hours

> **C**17.3 **Groups and periods**
> Include a variety of teacher demonstrations; omit
> Q11, 12, 14, 15 and 19.
>
> *2¹/₄ hours*

All questions are suitable for homework.

2 hours

Total: 4 hours   *Total: 3³/₄ hours*   *Total: 3 hours*

The pupils' book

This topic differs in character from the other five. Most of the course is designed to illustrate the importance of chemistry by placing it in its applied, social and historical contexts. This topic is intended to draw together many of the theoretical ideas which have arisen in other chapters and to show that it is possible to make sense of them in terms of atomic structure. Clearly this is of importance for those who are likely to continue to study sciences at a more advanced level.

There is no specified practical work for the pupils in this topic but teachers may wish to replace some of the demonstrations with with pupil experiments; appropriate safety precautions must, however, be taken if this is done. The two chapters review the chemistry that has arisen in the rest of the course; they have been written on the assumption that ideas about atomic structure have already been covered in the Physics Chapters **P**3 and **P**19. This means that they can be used for revision at the end of the course. However, some teachers will want to introduce ideas about atomic structure and bonding earlier, perhaps during the work on Chapter **C**5. There is no reason why they should not do so, but this will have to be carefully co-ordinated with the treatment in Physics. In both the Physics and the Chemistry books, the approach is to describe the model of atomic structure and then show what it can explain. On this basis, the picture of a nuclear atom made up of protons, neutrons and electrons can be described first in either Physics or Chemistry.

C17.1 How was the Periodic Table discovered?

The notion of periodicity is difficult, and pupils will need help with the idea. The historical background helps to emphasize the nature of the problem, which is to find some pattern in the properties of all the elements. The idea that there is a connection between chemical properties and atomic mass at first seemed ridiculous to many chemists, but was justified when explained in terms of atomic structure as described in Chapter **C**18.

Worksheet **C**17A is designed to make clear the repeating patterns of properties in the main groups of the Periodic Table.

Worksheet **C**17B is intended to help pupils with their study of this section.

C17.2 Patterns and problems

Pupils can appreciate the striking nature of the predictions based on Mendeléev's table. Some may be interested to know more about the discovery of the family of noble gases; there is a suitable account in the chapter on the Periodic Table in *A short history of chemistry* by Isaac Asimov. (See under Further information.)

C17.3 Groups and periods

Questions 11–21 are designed as revision exercises, reviewing many of the topics in the course.

It may help pupils if they see demonstrations of the properties of magnesium, calcium and their compounds. This might concentrate on the information tabulated in figure 17.11, in which the word "metal" implies "solid" (see under Activities).

The aspects of halogen chemistry featured in figure 17.13 might also be demonstrated (see under Activities).

Activities

Teacher demonstration: The properties of magnesium and calcium

REQUIREMENTS

The teacher will need:
Tongs
Burner and mat
6 boiling-tubes in rack
Eye protection
Safety screen

Access to:
Magnesium ribbon – FLAMMABLE
Calcium turnings – FLAMMABLE
Samples of the oxide, hydroxide, carbonate and
    sulphate of magnesium
Samples of the oxide – CORROSIVE, hydroxide,
    carbonate and chloride – IRRITANT – of calcium
Indicator paper
Distilled water
Soap solution in a dropper bottle

Safety note:
Use a safety screen and eye protection when heating a piece of calcium: it can jump dangerously when ignited.

The idea is to emphasize the similarities between the elements, not the gradation of reactivity down the group. The properties in the table in figure 17.11 can be demonstrated and discussed. If strontium or barium and their compounds are available this could be extended to making and testing predictions about their properties based on the Periodic Table. (Note that strontium and borium are flammable, and most barium compounds are harmful.)

Teacher demonstration: The properties of the halogens

REQUIREMENTS

The teacher will need:

Gas generator with tap funnel and right-angle
    delivery tube
2 gas jars with lids
6 boiling-tubes in rack
3 conical flasks, 100 ml, with bungs
Tongs
Burner and mat
Eye protection

Access to:

Bleaching powder, or sodium chlorate(I) solution
    (see note 1)
5 mol/L hydrochloric acid – IRRITANT
Bromine – CORROSIVE
Iodine – HARMFUL
Solid samples of the chloride, bromide and
    iodide of sodium
Silver nitrate solution (about 0.5 g of the solid
    – CORROSIVE – in 50 ml water) in a dropper
    bottle
Blue litmus paper
Distilled water
Fume cupboard

Note:

1 It is safer to make chlorine – TOXIC – by adding 5 mol/L hydrochloric acid – IRRITANT – to bleaching powder, or to a solution of sodium chlorate(I) – CORROSIVE. If potassium manganate(VII) and concentrated hydrochloric acid are used it is very important to check carefully that the correct acid is added. (The fumes of concentrated hydrochloric acid are very obvious.) It is highly dangerous if concentrated sulphuric acid is used by mistake, and so there must be no possibility of adding the wrong acid.

The purpose of this demonstration is to review the properties of the halogens and show their similarities as indicated in the table in figure 17.13, not the gradation of reactivity down the group.

Further information

Periodic Table
A colour version of the Periodic Table containing much useful information has been produced by The Association of the British Pharmaceutical Society, The Chemical Industries Association and The Royal Society of Chemistry (see Appendix).

Further reading
A short history of chemistry by Isaac Asimov (Heinemann Educational Books, 1972), *The elements*, an illustrated leaflet with poems by Roger McGough (Channel Four Television, 1991) and *The Periodic Table* by Primo Levi (Sphere, 1988) are all recommended.

Video
"The Periodic Table" (BBC Science Topics series) is useful here.

Chapter C18   Atoms and bonding

The syllabus section

Context

This theoretical section is included for those aiming for higher grades, to give an indication of the way in which chemists use theories of atomic structure to rationalize their knowledge. The section draws together ideas from many other sections in the course.

Knowledge and understanding

Syllabus statements	PoS	SoA
Be able to use the kinetic theory to explain how mixing and diffusion happen.	3(ii)1	3.7(c)
Understand and explain the difference between elements and compounds in terms of atoms, ions and molecules, and ionic and covalent bonds.	3(ii)2	3.7(e)
Know that the electrons in an atom are arranged in a series of shells around the nucleus.	3(ii)2	3.8(b)
Know the meaning of the terms atomic number and mass number.	3(ii)2	3.8(b)
Understand the meaning of the term isotope in terms of atomic structure.	3(ii)2	3.8(b)
Know that the elements are arranged in order of atomic number in the modern Periodic Table.	3(i)2	3.9(a)
Understand how the arrangement of elements in the Periodic Table can be explained in terms of atomic structure for the first 20 elements.	3(i)2	3.9(a)
Appreciate that the number of bonds formed by an atom in a molecule can be explained in terms of atomic structure.	3(ii)2	3.9(a)
Understand how atoms turn into ions, and ions into atoms, in cells and during electrolysis (with reference to simple examples).	3(iii)1	3.9(a)
Understand quantitative electrolysis and hence how the charges on ions can be determined by experiment.	3(iii)5	3.10(d)

Opportunities for co-ordination

Atomic structure is dealt with in **P**3 and **P**19. Isotopes and their uses are in **B**8, **B**9 and **P**3. The effects of ionizing radiations are dealt with in **P**3 and mineral salts are described in terms of ions in **B**15. Weak and strong forces between and within molecules are discussed in **P**2, **B**5 and **B**7.

Routes and times

Basic	Central	Further
Omit Chapter **C**18 at Basic level.		

C18.1 **Atomic structure**

Basic   **Central**   **Further**

Omit Chapter **C**18 at Basic level.

C18.1 **Atomic structure**

C18.2 **Atomic structure and the Periodic Table**
(pages 303–305)
Omit Q6.

1½ hours

All of section **C**18.2 is suitable.

C18.3 **Atoms into ions**
(up to Q22)
Omit "How can electrolysis be explained?".

1½ hours

All of section **C**18.3 should be done.

Worksheet C18B **How much copper is deposited?**
Include Faraday's laws of electrolysis.

1¾ hours

C18.4 **Bonding in molecules**
Omit Q32 and 33.

1¼ hours

Total: 4¼ hours   *Total: 6 hours*

The pupils' book

C18.1 Atomic structure

Probably the most convincing evidence for the model of electrons in shells is the way it can account for the Periodic Table and the similarities between the elements in a group. However figure 18.3 is included to show that there is other evidence to support the theory. Similar diagrams can be drawn for other elements given a table of ionization energies.

Answer to selected question

2	p	n	e
carbon	6	6	6
neon	10	10	10
protactinium	91	143	91
iodine	53	74	53
hydrogen ion	1	0	0
chloride ion	17	18	18

C18.2 Atomic structure and the Periodic Table

This section provides an opportunity to build on work which the pupils have done in Biology and Physics (see "Opportunities for co-ordination"). The explanation of the existence of isotopes should be related to examples from other parts of the course.

Answer to selected question

5 Average atomic mass $= 63.6$ u.

C18.3 Atoms into ions

It is important to stress that this section is a simplified introduction to the theory and that it only accounts for the formation of ions by a limited number of elements.

The word "stable" has been deliberately omitted because it is a thermodynamic idea which is too advanced for this course. Pupils likely to go further with their study of chemistry might be told that at advanced level they will study the reasons for the stability of compounds with noble gas electron arrangements in the ions. (See for example, Revised Nuffield Advanced Chemistry, Topic C6, section C6.5)

Explanations in terms of ions crop up frequently in Nuffield Co-ordinated Sciences. Most of the examples are reviewed in this section, and so the chapter can be used as a summarizing and revision topic towards the end of the course.

This section includes the final stage of the development of ideas about electrolysis. In Chapter C4 pupils look for patterns in the observations made when liquids and solutions are electrolysed. In Chapter C5 they are introduced to the idea that the changes during electrolysis can be explained in terms of ions. In this chapter they are shown how the changes at the electrodes can be described using ionic equations. Electrolysis is seen to reverse the process of electron transfer which takes place when an ionic compound is formed from its elements.

Figure 18.9 is designed to expose the thinking involved in working out what happens at the electrodes during electrolysis. Worksheet C18A can be cut up to make a flick book which gives a moving picture of ions turning into molecules at the anode. If pupils are able to make their own flick books to show other electrode processes it will demonstrate that they have an understanding of what is happening during electrolysis.

The section ends with an explanation of what happens at the electrodes during the discharge of a sodium–sulphur cell. The advantage of choosing this example is that it involves a reaction of a metal with a non-metal. So it has a close parallel with the reaction of sodium with chlorine, which has been used to explain how atoms turn into ions during reactions.

C18.4 Bonding in molecules

Here too the theory is limited in its application, but it does account for the numbers of covalent bonds formed in many of the molecules met in previous chapters. However, pupils should be warned that they will find that there is much more to the study of bonding than this chapter suggests, as they will discover if they continue with the subject at higher levels.

The misconception that covalent bonds are weak is remarkably common and persistent. As this course shows, it is essential that pupils should distinguish between the strong bonds **within** molecules as compared to the weak attractive forces **between** molecules. Covalent bonds are roughly one hundred times stronger than intermolecular forces.

There is no attempt to explain the nature of intermolecular forces. The existence of molecular liquids and solids is evidence for these forces.

Explanations in terms of molecules are common in Nuffield Co-ordinated Sciences. They are reviewed in this section which is designed for revision.

Activities

Worksheet C18A Ions into molecules at the anode

REQUIREMENTS

Each group of pupils will need:
Copy of Worksheet **C18A**
Scissors
Paper

Access to:
Stapler

Pupils make a "flick book" to show what happens to negative ions when they meet a positive anode. They can extend this work by making their own flick book to show what happens to positive ions at the cathode.

Worksheet C18B How much copper is deposited?

REQUIREMENTS

Each pupil will need:
Eye protection

Each group of pupils will need:
Power supply, 6V d.c.
Rheostat, 10 Ω
Ammeter, 0–1A
Stopclock or stopwatch
Beaker, 100 ml
Copper foil, 2 pieces each about 7 cm × 2 cm
Cardboard support for electrodes, as shown
Leads
2 crocodile clips
Scissors

Access to:
Distilled water
Propanone – FLAMMABLE
Steel wool
Paper tissues (for putting electrodes on while not being handled)
Copper (II) sulphate solution, 0.5 mol/L,
 – HARMFUL –100 ml per group
Balance, to weigh to 0.01 g

Safety note:
Copper(II) sulphate solution is harmful, and propanone is flammable. Pupils should take care not to raise dust when cleaning the electrodes.

Pupils are introduced to a simple quantitative method for measuring the amount of copper deposited during the electrolysis of copper(II) sulphate solution. They may devise experiments to find out the effect of current and time on the amount of copper deposited. Since there may not be time to carry out all these experiments, part i could be set for

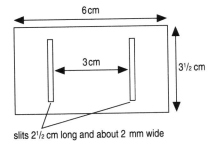

slits 2½ cm long and about 2 mm wide

Cardboard support for electrodes.

homework and the practical work carried out in class with different groups using different times or different currents. If this is done, however, the size of the strips must be standardized as well as the depth to which they are placed in the solution. The fact that the amount of copper deposited is proportional to time and to the current should be brought out. The quantitative questions should be photocopied separately from the top of side 2, so they do not give clues to the design experiment (part i).

Faster groups could discuss the quantity of electricity required to deposit one mole of substance in more detail, i.e. 96 500 coulombs are required to deposit one mole of a metal derived from a singly charged ion, 193 000 coulombs are required for a doubly charged ion, etc.

Answers to worksheet questions

1 Grease on hands could rub off onto the foils before electrolysis, or handling after electrolysis could rub off the new copper deposited; either of these would cause errors in quantitative calculations.

2 The mass of the cathode increases and the mass of the anode decreases.

3 The increase in the mass of the cathode equals the decrease in mass of the anode.

4 At the anode:
$Cu(s) \rightarrow Cu^{2+}(aq) + 2$ electrons.

At the cathode:
$Cu^{2+}(aq) + 2$ electrons $\rightarrow Cu(s)$.

5 0.429g.

6 The mass deposited is proportional to the time.

7 Current (A) = Charge (C) ÷ Time (s).

8 200 coulombs.

9 192 424 coulombs.

PHYSICS

Introduction to Physics

Topics and contexts

The content of the Physics course has been divided up into five topics:

Topic **P1** Matter
Topic **P2** Force and motion
Topic **P3** Energy
Topic **P4** Waves
Topic **P5** Electricity

Topic **P1** embraces material on weather (Topic **E1** in Earth and Space) and Topic **P2** covers Space (Topic **E3** in Earth and Space). The content of any one topic is never independent of work in the others. For example, an understanding of radioactivity in Topic **P1** cannot be achieved without some prior understanding of electric charge, dealt with in Topic **P5**. The transmission of energy using electricity, which is a part of Topic **P3**, also requires a prior understanding of electrical ideas.

Physics is not presented as a "linear" subject in which one topic leads inexorably to the next, but a web of interconnecting ideas. The ideas in one topic are developed around a common theme, but they are related to ideas developed in the other topics as well. Every point in this web of ideas is supported by strands which may come from many directions.

A web can be traversed by many different routes. One of the ideas underlying the Physics component of Nuffield Co-ordinated Sciences is that this sense of a self-supporting web of ideas is best appreciated by seeing that they connect together in many different ways. However, as pupils are told in the Introduction to the pupils' book, there is one route through the book's content that **cannot** be followed first time through – and that is the order of the chapters themselves! This encourages pupils to learn to read selectively, looking in the book for what they need, rather than reading it as one would a novel – from beginning to end. It also helps them to appreciate different ways in which ideas may be linked together.

Year 10			Year 11		
Chapter	Title	Time (hours)	Chapter	Title	Time (hours)
	Introduction		P6	Crashes and bangs	5
P1	Building bridges successfully	6	P7	Rising and falling	3½
P2	Cooking food quickly	6	E3	Space	2¾
E1	Weather	2¾	P18	Making use of electricity	5¼
P4	Motion	3¾	P3	Radioactivity	4½
P5	Controlling motion	5	P11	Energy where it is needed	2¾
P8	Machines and engines	4½	P12	Waste not, want not?	3¾
P9	Keeping yourself warm	3½	P19	Making pictures with electricity	3½
P10	Ideas in physics	2	P20	Control	4½
P16	Using electricity	3	P21	Communication	2½
P17	Energy and electricity	5			
P13	Fibre optics and noise	2¾			
P14	Making waves	3½			
P15	Making use of waves	5¼			
		53			38

A possible route through the Physics course.

One possible route through the Physics course is shown in the table above. Teachers will find other routes themselves. In devising new routes based on this material, two things have to be borne in mind:

• There is an overriding need to co-ordinate any approach with that of the other sciences – work in Biology and Chemistry will often depend on the prior development of ideas in Physics, and Physics will often need ideas from Biology and Chemistry. The charts shown in Chapter 2 of the General introduction show how the major themes of Nuffield Co-ordinated Sciences are cross-linked.

- At the end of the course, all pupils will benefit from revising Physics in the order in which it is presented in the book. In this way they will see new links between ideas and gain a better appreciation of the fabric of Physics.

Differentiation

The course materials – both the pupils' book and the worksheets – have been designed to be used by pupils of a wide range of ability and previous experience in science. No one pupil will find it appropriate to cover the entire content of the Physics book and the worksheets.

The commentary text in the pupils' book encourages pupils to make their own decisions about what is essential, seeking guidance from their teachers where this is needed.

Each chapter in the pupils' book can be divided up into three parts:

- core material which conveys the essential "message" of the chapter
- supporting material to provide more background and experience for pupils who need it
- extensions to take the work further – often in the form of exploratory investigations.

For example, in Chapter **P16** "Using electricity", the core material (developed in sections **P16.1**, **P16.2**, **P16.3**, **P16.5** and **P16.6**) is concerned with electric current. Pupils who are uncertain of their command of basic electric circuit ideas can gain additional experience in Worksheet **P16B**. Other pupils, who grasp these ideas readily, might find such work tiresome. For them there is a more detailed consideration of electric current as a flow of charge in section **P16.4**, and the more advanced Worksheet **P16C**.

Worksheets

Most, but not all, of the Physics worksheets are designed to accompany experimental work. Those designed to introduce pupils to practical skills or advance their understanding are generally presented as detailed guides to what should be done. Others, designed to accompany investigations, do no more than start pupils working in a profitable direction.

For some of the investigational worksheets, Help sheets have been produced. It is intended that these should only be a guide to pupils who ask for them.

Finally there is another type of worksheet designed to encourage pupils to take a broader view of Physics in its social context, or its relationship to other sciences and technology. Many of these worksheets have been based on Science and Technology in Society (SATIS) units. Teachers may want to make more use of SATIS (perhaps by replacing some of these worksheets with SATIS-derived worksheets or others of their own). In this way the social context of Physics will remain relevant as "live" issues change.

NOTES

Topic **P**1   **Matter**

This topic is about the particulate nature of matter. Chapter **P**1 shows how we can understand the strength and stiffness of solids in terms of the forces which act between the particles of matter. Chapter **P**2 is concerned with the kinetic theory of matter. It looks at the differences between solids, liquids and gases, and relates changes of state to changes in the kinetic energies of the particles. Chapter **P**3 is about radioactivity, and thus about the nature of the particles (atoms) which make up matter.

These three chapters cannot be taught in sequence. Chapter **P**1 is intended to be the opening chapter in the course. It builds on the example of Hooke's Law, taken to exemplify processes in science in the Introduction to the pupils' book. Chapter **P**2 must come early in the course because the ideas about moving particles, which are the essence of the kinetic theory, are essential to work in Biology and Chemistry. Chapter **P**3, on the other hand, requires some knowledge of electricity which will only have been gained by pupils who have completed work on Chapters **P**16, **P**17 and **P**18. This inevitably means that work on Chapter **P**3 must be postponed until the fifth year (the second year of the course).

The Introduction to Topic **P**1 revises the work of the third and previous years, which is essential to this topic. It can be used as a preparatory homework exercise prior to the first lesson. The questions are of the same standard as the original work – not harder questions on earlier themes. Ideas about energy are used in Chapter **P**2. A revision of what pupils should already know about energy is included in the Introduction to Topic **P**3 "Energy".

The introduction also explains to pupils the use of the word "particle" in this topic and its relationship to the words "atom", "molecule" and "ion", which are used in Chemistry. This may require some more discussion in class.

Chapter P1 Building bridges successfully
The strength of solids

Context

This section is centred around an investigation into the way bridges are constructed. The investigation leads on to a study of forces in equilibrium, the behaviour of springs, and ideas about stiffness. Pupils should also investigate the vector nature of forces in relation to the forces maintaining the equilibrium of suspension bridges.

Knowledge and understanding

	Tier			
Syllabus statements	**B**	**C**	**F**	**PoS**

Syllabus statements	PoS	SoA
Understand that the strength of solids derives from the forces between their constituent atoms and molecules.	3(ii)2	3.4(a)
Understand that unbalanced forces change motion and know that it is the size and direction of the resultant force that will affect the movement of an object.	4(iii)1	4.5(d)
Appreciate that a stable structure needs to be able to provide forces that counter-balance the external forces to which it is subject (including its own weight).	4(iii)5	—
Appreciate the spring-like nature of these forces by comparing the behaviour of materials under tension and compression with the behaviour of springs.	4(iii)5	—
Appreciate that the design of a structure must take account of the use to which it is put and the materials from which it is made.	3(i)7	3.10(a)
Appreciate the interplay of use and material by making a short study of a wide variety of bridge designs.	4(iii)5	3.10(a)

Opportunities for co-ordination

The study of materials is taken up in **C5**. **C6** looks at brittle materials. The reasons why metals are strong is dealt with in **C7**.

Plants and animals rely on the stiffness of tubular structures. This, and the elastic properties of muscles, are referred to in **B**10.

Routes and times

Basic	Central	Further

Spend more time on revision, including Brownian motion.

3/4 hour

Matter: Introduction (pages 10–11)
General review: questions optional or for homework.
1/4 hour

All this section should be done for homework.

P1.1 Structures

P1.2 Balanced forces
Include demonstration of weight hanging from a string.
3/4 hour

Demonstrate stretching of springs. Omit section on proportionality. Pupils build paper tubes and boxes as on page 22.
2 1/2 hours

P1.3 Changing shape
Include demonstration of spring, cantilever and foam-block model; omit Q7. Set Q5 and 6 for homework.
Worksheet P1B Cantilevers
Sc1 investigation.
1 3/4 hours

Restrict to comparing the strengths of differently shaped paper beams.
1 hour

Worksheet P1A Building a model bridge
Set the planning for homework.
3/4 hour

Worksheet **P1C** "Looking at bridges" may be used as an alternative to Worksheet **P1A**.
Optional

Worksheet P1D Moments
Worksheet P1E Balanced moments
1 1/4 hours

Brief revision only (class + homework).
1/2 hour

Worksheet P1F Centre of mass
Worksheet P1G Balancing tricks
1 1/4 hours

Spend less time on these activities.
3/4 hour

Sections **P1.4** "Suspension bridges" and **P1.5** "More about components and metals under force" are optional extension work for faster groups.

Total: 7 1/2 hours   *Total: 6 hours*   *Total: 3 3/4 hours*

Monitoring the progress of Sc1

Investigating cantilevers

Students should investigate what affects the deflection of a cantilever. This investigation may be carried out instead of Worksheet **P**1B Cantilevers.

Sample criteria are given below for an assessment between levels 4 and 6.

Strand (i) Ask questions, predict and hypothesize, e.g.	Strand (ii) Observe, measure and manipulate variables, e.g.	Strand (iii) Interpret their results and evaluate scientific evidence, e.g.
4(a) Suggest that the deflection may depend on the load	4(b) Control length, and measure the deflection of the same cantilever for two different loads	4(c) Conclude that a large load causes a bigger deflection than a small load
5(a) Suggest that a large load would produce a larger deflection because it exerts a larger force	5(b) Control length, and measure the deflection of the same cantilever for two different loads producing measurable deflections	5(c) Conclude that a large load causes a bigger deflection than a small load, but qualifying the conclusion
6(a) Suggest that the larger the load, the larger the deflection because the larger load exerts a larger force	6(b) For a range of lengths, measure the deflection of the same cantilever for a range of different loads producing measurable deflections	6(c) Conclude that a large load causes a bigger deflection than a small load because the larger load exerts a larger force

The pupils' book

P1.1 Structures

A slide presentation on bridges makes an effective introduction (see under Further information for suggestions). The exercise in building a model bridge to a given specification follows a brief introduction to structures. This is a popular activity and gives point to issues raised later in this topic. Not much over a period should be allowed for the model-building work with most pupils.

P1.2 Balanced forces

The idea that forces must balance if something is in equilibrium is introduced here at an intuitive level – something that will be returned to in Chapter **P**5. It is hard to justify experimentally, as many things like spring balances may well have been calibrated on the assumption that the spring pulls up with a force equal to the weight of any load on it acting downwards. In describing the counterbalancing force, the word "reaction" has been avoided deliberately. Considerable confusion is often caused by the different meanings which are attached to the word "reaction".

Answer to selected question
4 This question may seem trivial to many pupils – and if so is best left as such. To an interested group it can prove a good arguing point about assumptions made. In fact the balancing out of the forces is a special case of Newton's Second Law, since a net force will produce a change in motion – this has to be left until the work of Chapter **P**5.

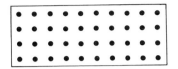

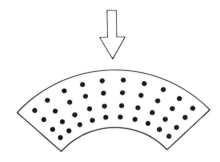

P1.3 Changing shape

This section poses the problem of how structures provide the counterbalancing force. By comparing the behaviour of solids with springs it is clear that structures must distort (if ever so slightly) in order to provide that force. The section picks up the results of the investigation into springs discussed in the pupils' book Introduction. Pupils who reach this point quickly (say within two periods including the bridge building) can go on to Worksheet **P1B**. Two periods should be allowed for this investigation to give time for thorough work with minimum help.

A large sponge, with black dots on it to represent atoms as in the diagram, is useful to show what happens to the spacing between atoms when a bar is bent.

The investigation into the behaviour of springs is used as an opportunity to think about proportionality. This is an important concept in Physics as it leads to easily expressed relationships between quantities. Three features of proportionality are emphasized. The first is the link between the straight-line graph and the algebraic representation. The second is the constant of proportionality and its dependence on the units of measurement. The third feature, developed in question 7, is the realization that there may be limits to proportionality in practical cases.

Answers to selected questions
7a 2 cm **b** 9 N
c i $36 = 3 \times 12$, so the extension might be expected to be 3×4 cm = 12 cm
c ii But such a force might well take the spring past its elastic limit.
d i 8 cm; **d ii** 2 cm.

8 Aircraft are an obvious example to give, where weight is important. Similar considerations can apply to boats. Keeping down mass (different from weight) is important in cars, rowing "eights", poles for pole-vaulters, etc.

P1.4 Suspension bridges

Much of this section is for pupils who have coped quickly and easily with the first three sections. Such pupils will have time in which to look at vectors and possibly do some of section **P1.5**. Worksheet **P1C** can be cut down to a homework exercise. For others, a longer time can be spent profitably on Worksheet **P1C**.

The distinction between physical quantities which have only size and those which have direction as well as size is an important one. In this course, not much more is expected than an appreciation that the distinction exists. The vector nature of velocity comes into Chapter **P4**, where it is contrasted with speed.

Answers to selected questions
11c The keel provides that force, as do crew members leaning over the sides. The closer the boat sails into the wind, the more the component of the wind's force on the sail is directed sideways onto the boat.

12 At right angles to the direction of the force.

P1.5 More about components and metals under force

Definitely extension work for the more able. The ideas are not difficult, but pupils will need to have covered the earlier work quickly if they are to do this section.

Answer to selected question
13c At the maximum force the cable will "run" and snap, as it can do this at a lower force than the maximum.

Activities

Worksheet P1A Building a model bridge

REQUIREMENTS

Access to:
Assorted paper and card
Scissors
Tape, adhesive
Blocks to act as piers
Metre rules
Assorted masses to act as test loads
Balance to check mass of bridge

The procedure to be followed is detailed in the worksheet.

Warning
Bench tops, the laboratory floor and pupils' feet should be protected from possible damage due to falling test loads. Ideally bridges should be constructed on benches and not across gaps between benches. If bridges are constructed across gaps, something (such as a carton containing foam offcuts) should be placed under them to catch any falling test loads: even an empty box suitably placed makes it difficult to put hands or feet under the suspended loads.

Worksheet P1B Cantilevers

REQUIREMENTS

Each group of pupils will need:
Two metre rules
G-clamp
Slotted masses, 100 g set
Graph paper

The procedure to be followed is given in the worksheet. Pupils have to devise their own way of carrying out this investigation.

Worksheet P1C Looking at bridges

This directs a pupil survey of bridges and their functions.

Worksheet P1D Moments

REQUIREMENTS

Each group of pupils will need:
Metal bar, e.g. clamp-stand rod
Large mass (at least 1 kg) which can be suspended from the bar

The experiment is described on the worksheet.
  Pupils will have investigated the turning effects of forces and may even have developed a law of moments during Key stage 3. If this is the case, this experiment may be done as a quick demonstration, which will give more time elsewhere.
  The experiment should give the pupils a real "feel" for the turning effect a force can exert. At a low level, an intuitive feeling for the moment of a force is enough to answer the questions on the worksheet; however, calculating the value of the moment will be necessary to carry out the investigation on Worksheet **P1E**.

Warning
A cardboard box underneath the mass helps to keep hands and feet away from the "drop zone" and gives some protection to benches and floors.

Answers to worksheet questions
1 The lever arms on the taps serve two purposes – they are easier to grip than conventional taps, and a smaller force is needed to turn them since the force is exerted at a greater distance from the pivot.

2 The revolving door is best pushed at its outside edge, where least effort is needed. (This could be tried with an ordinary classroom door too.)

3 For the same force you can have a larger moment by applying the force a longer distance away from the pivot.

4 90 N m; 27 N m; 96 N m; 8 N m.

Worksheet P1E Balanced moments

REQUIREMENTS

Each group of pupils will need:
Metre rule
Pivot (e.g. a pin through the centre of the rule pushed into a cork held by a
  boss on a clamp stand, or a seesaw-type pivot)
Masses to load the rule

This is a standard experiment to find the law of moments.
  The amount of guidance needed about the way the measurements are taken and how the loads are varied will depend on the ability of the class. Pupils should find that when the beam is balanced the anticlockwise moments equal the clockwise moments.

Answers to worksheet questions
1 Clockwise is the way that a clock turns, i.e. down on Joe's side, and anticlockwise is the opposite. Sally has to sit further from the pivot to have the same moment as Joe because her weight is less.

2 Assuming that the wheel is the pivot, the force of the man lifting upwards provides the clockwise moment and the force of the Earth pulling the barrow and its contents down provides the anticlockwise moment.

3 The concrete block counterbalances the crane when a load is lifted by the hoist. The block will move further from the centre for a bigger load.

4 1 m; 75 N; 1170 N; 0.6 m.

Worksheet P1F Centre of mass

REQUIREMENTS

Each group of pupils will need:
Irregularly shaped piece of stiff card
Large pin
Cork
Stand with boss and clamp
Ruler
Piece of thread and a load to make a plumb line

The instructions for this experiment are given on the worksheet. The idea of a centre of mass is quite difficult but the pupils are able to see that there is a balance point for a two-dimensional card.

Answers to worksheet questions

1 The centre of mass rises when it is initially below the pivot and falls when it is above the pivot.

2 The first cone is stable: its centre of mass rises when it is tipped a small amount. The second cone is unstable: its centre of mass falls when it is tipped a small amount. The third cone is an intermediate case. When tipped a very small amount the centre of mass rises, so the cone is stable for small disturbances. For larger displacements, the centre of mass falls and the cone is unstable. Technically, the cone is *metastable* (nearly stable), but pupils do not need to know this term. The centre of mass of the last cone neither rises nor falls when the cone is displaced: the cone will stay where it is put. Technically, this is *neutral equilibrium*.

Worksheet P1G Balancing tricks

REQUIREMENTS

Each group of pupils will need:
2 empty cans, both the same height but with different bases
Mass to fit in the cans, about 1 kg
Plank, wooden
Pencil
Drawing pin
Plasticine

This worksheet extends the idea of balancing and develops the idea that the stability of an object depends on it having a low centre of mass and a large base area. This experiment could be done as a demonstration; this would allow for discussion of many examples of stable and unstable situations, some of which are raised in the questions on the worksheet.

The balancing challenge is to balance a pencil horizontally on the point of a drawing pin (without pushing the pin into the pencil). This can be achieved by creating an object whose centre of mass is below the level of the pivot. Hang long "sausages" of Plasticine from either end of the pencil. The pencil will then balance on a pin held under its middle.

Answers to worksheet questions

1 A large base and a low centre of mass.

2 The full wine glass has a much higher centre of mass than an empty one.

3 A racing car has a large wheelbase and so a large base area. It also has a very low centre of mass.

4 A highchair is potentially unstable because putting the toddler into the chair significantly raises its centre of mass. To counteract this, the chair is given as wide a base as is practicable. Some highchairs also have a fairly heavy base (perhaps incorporating a table for later use) to lower the centre of mass. Another safety feature is the provision of a harness which prevents the child from standing up and raising the centre of mass still further. The harness also reduces the amount of "tipping" the child is able to attempt.

Demonstration experiments

Section P1.2: Balanced forces

REQUIREMENTS
Some arrangement whereby a large mass can be suspended by a string.

Section P1.3: Hooke's Law

REQUIREMENTS

It may be useful during the discussion to have a spring set up on a stand so that Hooke's Law can be demonstrated quickly. A cantilever made from a ruler can be compared with the spring.

Section P1.4: Force as a vector quantity

REQUIREMENTS

A 2 kg mass supported by strings at an angle. (See figure **P1.21a** in the pupils' book.) The exact arrangement is not important, but it should be possible to use force meters to measure the tension in the strings. (The "traditional" arrangement of pulleys and strings is best avoided – it makes for too many difficulties in interpretation.)

Further information

Science and Technology in Society

Worksheets **P**1A and **P**1C draw heavily on SATIS unit 501 "Bridges". While not really an alternative approach to this work (the two approaches are very similar) some teachers may care to refer to the original publication and perhaps develop the material more closely along its lines. Less emphasis will then be placed on the basic physics of balancing forces and vectors as these are **assumed** by the unit rather than **taught** by it.

Supplementary material

A set of slides or pictures, or the SATIS 14–16 Audio Visual unit 6 "Bridges", illustrating the wide variety of bridges will be useful.

Video

"Bridging the gap" (BBC Science in Action series) is useful here.

Chapter **P2**   **Cooking food quickly**
Molecules in motion

The syllabus section

Context

The kinetic theory, and the assumption that there are forces between atoms and molecules, together present a theory which enables many of the properties of liquids and gases to be understood, as well as the operation of things like pressure cookers, aerosol sprays, refrigerators and diesel engines.

Knowledge and understanding

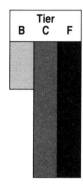

Syllabus statements	PoS	SoA
Understand the physical differences between solids, liquids and gases, and be able to explain evaporation and boiling in terms of the kinetic theory.	3(ii)2	3.6(b)
Understand and be able to use the quantitative relationships between the volume, pressure and temperature of a gas.	3(ii)1	3.7(d)
Be able to use the Kelvin scale of temperature.	—	—

Opportunities for co-ordination

The most important link on atoms and molecules is to **C**1 and **C**2. Mists and foams are discussed in **C**9 and evaporation and cooling in **B**12. **E**1 deals with the role of evaporation in the context of weather.

Routes and times

Basic	Central	Further
Worksheet **P2A1** "Pressure", is suitable at Basic level. *1 hour*	This is an appropriate place to revise the relation "pressure = force/area". *¹/₄ hour*	Omit this section.
	Worksheet P2A2 Pressure in liquids *³/₄ hour*	Worksheet **P2A2** is optional for faster groups.
Spend more time on section **P2.1**; omit Q6 and 8. Worksheet **P2A** "Marbles in a tray" should be included. *2 hours*	**P2.1 Solids, liquids and gases** Include demonstrations of figures 2.4 and 2.8, and omit Q4. Q1 is suitable for homework. *1¹/₂ hours*	Include Q4; spend less time on this section. *1 hour*
Omit this section.	**P2.2 Pressure and volume** Use demonstration apparatus where possible. *1 hour*	
Worksheet **P2B** "Aerosol spray cans" may be included.	**P2.3 Making use of evaporation** Demonstration of evaporative cooling is optional; omit Q12 and 13 and refrigerators. *¹/₂ hour*	The section about refrigerators is suitable for homework.
Omit this section.	**P2.4 Pressure and temperature** Include demonstration of heated tin and pressure-temperature experiment; omit Q15b and 16; additional gas-law problems should be added. *2 hours*	Q15b and 16 of section **P2.4** are suitable. Spend less time on this section. *1³/₄ hours*
Include Worksheet **P2D** and spend more time on this section. *1¹/₂ hours*	**Worksheet P2D Recording the weather** (optional) **E1.1 Air, hot and cold** **E1.2 Water in the air** Q4 and 6 are optional/homework. *1¹/₄ hours*	Omit Worksheet **P2D** and spend less time on sections **E1.1** and **E1.2**. *1 hour*
Spend more time on this section. *2 hours*	**E1.3 Which way does the wind blow?** Q2 may be done by teacher demonstration; omit Q7. **E1.4 Masses of air** Omit Q2 and 3. **Worksheet P2E Understanding weather maps** *1¹/₂ hours*	All questions are suitable. Replace Worksheet **P2E** by Worksheet **P2F** "Which way did the wind blow?". *³/₄ hour*
Total: 7³/₄ hours	*Total: 8³/₄ hours*	*Total: 6³/₄ hours*

The pupils' book

The kinetic theory is intimately bound up with the concept of energy. We interpret the changes in temperature which are associated with energy transfers with changes in the kinetic energy of atoms and molecules. Heating, as a mode of energy transfer, is considered in Chapters **P**9 and **P**10. A case could be made for establishing the connection between temperature change and energy transfer before looking in detail at the kinetic theory. In this course we have chosen not to do that. First, many of the details of the kinetic theory are useful in establishing a complete picture of matter as made up of particles (atoms and molecules) a picture needed at an early stage in Chemistry. Secondly, the connection between energy transfer and temperature change is more easily grasped in terms of the kinetic theory than in terms of the more abstract notion of energy on its own. So the relationship between energy transfer and rise in temperature is assumed in this chapter and its justification awaits the work of Chapter **P**10.

It is assumed that pupils will have gained some ideas about energy and its involvement in change in earlier work. They will also already have gained some insight into the association of "getting warm" with energy transfer. These ideas are used in this chapter when talking about the increasing kinetic energy of the molecules in a liquid and a gas as the temperature rises. Detailed enquiry into energy transfers starts with the work of Chapter **P**8. This will come after the present chapter. However, two important features of the way the concept of energy is developed in this course are also relevant to this chapter.

First of all, the concept of **forms of energy** as exemplified by such phrases as "electrical energy", "mechanical energy", "thermal energy", has been dropped. Secondly the word "heat" is **not** used as a noun, but as a verb. Heating is a process – a way of transferring energy. Both of these matters are discussed at greater length in Chapter 2 of the General introduction to this *Guide*. To be consistent with later work it will be necessary when talking about the ideas in this chapter to avoid using such terms as "heat energy" (which is meaningless in the context of this course), and to avoid talk of energy changing from one **form** to another.

P2.1 Solids, liquids and gases

Introductory work on the kinetic theory is assumed to have taken place in Key stage 3. In particular, pupils should have seen some evidence why matter is considered to be built from atoms and molecules and why we consider these atoms and molecules to be in a continual state of motion. Our work starts with a common piece of domestic equipment – the pressure cooker – and considers, in the light of the kinetic theory, how it works. This will lead to some revision of earlier ideas, but their inclusion at this point seems justifiable. The 2-D model is worth exploring in some detail. It is in fact much more fruitful than the more impressive 3-D model. Even so, more able pupils may not wish to spend very long on the associated worksheet (**P**2A).

We return to the pressure cooker, considering now the change in state from liquid to gas and the effect of pressure on boiling point. This involves some quite difficult ideas. In certain circumstances the change from liquid to gas can be described as *evaporation* (a surface phenomenon); in other circumstances, it is described as *boiling* (a bulk phenomenon). Evaporation can take place at all temperatures, its rate increasing with temperature. Boiling takes place at a fixed temperature which is determined by the external pressure. (Solids also evaporate, changing state from solid to gas. This does not concern us here.)

In both evaporation and boiling, energy has to be transferred to the molecules of a liquid as work is done against the intermolecular attractive forces. This process is referred to in the text as *vaporization*. To vaporize a liquid (whether by evaporation or boiling) energy has to be supplied. This is usually drawn from the surroundings. Normally liquids boil at temperatures well above normal room temperature, so the energy required is supplied by another hot object such as an electric heater, or a flame. In a refrigerator the liquid can be made to boil at a temperature below normal room temperature. In this case the necessary energy is drawn from the inside of the refrigerator.

Answers to selected questions

4a The kinetic theory explains gas pressure in terms of the collisions of the gas molecules with the walls of the container.

b The same number of particles will collide with the walls at a greater rate than before.

5a The rate of evaporation will increase because at any one time there will be a greater number of molecules with sufficient energy to break free from the attraction of the other molecules.

b The net rate of evaporation will increase because there will be fewer molecules returning to the liquid from the vapour state.

6a The number of people in the supermarket remains roughly constant because as many enter it as leave at any one time.

b See Biology pupils' book, Chapter **B**3.

7 130 kN/m^2; 170 kN/m^2; 200 kN/m^2.

P2.2 Pressure and volume

The pressure cooker directs attention to two features of liquids and gases which can now be followed up. The first, followed up in this section, is that the pressure rises in a pressure cooker as more molecules crowd into the space above the liquid. This suggests a relationship between pressure and number of particles, and leads on to Boyle's Law, where the increased crowding of molecules is achieved by a reduction in the volume they occupy. The relationship between pressure and particle impact is a necessary preliminary to this work and the demonstration illustrated in the pupils' book is a good one to show.

An experimental justification of Boyle's Law can be undertaken as a demonstration. Equipment to do this which is commonly found in many school laboratories is illustrated in figure 2.17b of the pupils' book. Question 10 gives some results for analysis which are typical of those obtained with such equipment. There is no necessity to use this particular equipment to illustrate Boyle's Law. Alternative equipment may do the job just as well. (However, you are advised against using the traditional equipment which involves an open reservoir of mercury. Apart from the safety aspect, pupils do not find it easy to understand what is happening.)

Answer to selected question

10 Testing for Boyle's Law is not easy because of the reciprocal relationship between *P* and *V*. Pupils can easily be told to plot *P* against 1/*V* and will do so. This does not necessarily imply they understand the relationship between the two quantities. This question tries to take them step by step through the testing process. If the experiment has been done as a demonstration, then experimentally obtained values should replace those of figure 2.18. If a value for **V** has been obtained at a pressure of 10 units, then only the value of *V* in part a will need altering.

The matter of units is a difficult one here. Volume is often marked out in "arbitrary units" on the equipment illustrated in figure 2.17b. To make the "arithmetic" straightforward and yet give values close to those recorded by such equipment, the volume is given in cm^3. This is very nearly equal to the length of the gas column.

For similar reasons, the pressure is given in kN/m^2.

The graph plotting suggested in question 10f may be beyond some pupils at this stage. It can be omitted from the question without affecting an analysis of the results. Straightforward graph plotting, such as that involved in the stretching of a spring (Chapter **P**1) is assumed to be something all pupils will have done by this stage. A further development of graph-plotting skills is provided by Worksheet **P**4C in Chapter **P**4.

P2.3 Making use of evaporation

The second aspect of the behaviour of matter arising from the pressure cooker has much more direct application in the everyday world – the change of state from liquid to gas. Two particular applications are considered – the aerosol spray (which is the subject of Worksheet **P2B**) and the refrigerator. The relationship between evaporation and temperature is important both for its applications and the way the kinetic theory is able to deal with it.

The energy transfers involved in vaporization are discussed further in this section.

Answers to selected questions

11a Since evaporated water molecules are no longer returning to the pond, not only is the net evaporation more rapid but also energy is being removed from the pond water more rapidly. Hence the pond's temperature falls more quickly and the pond freezes over.
b The evaporating water molecules remove energy from the liquid water, which consequently cools.

12a The temperature will fall.
b This will also fall.
c Its temperature will rise.
d The temperature of the pipes will rise.
e The temperature of the room also rises.

P2.4 Pressure and temperature

This section, which relates the pressure in a gas to its temperature and introduces the idea of an absolute zero of temperature, is targeted at tiers C and F. The experiment described in Worksheet **P2C** is discussed below and the comments on the necessity to have an experiment not plagued by leaks apply equally to such an experiment performed as a demonstration. Since it is difficult to have several sets of reliable equipment, it may be preferred to do this experiment relating pressure to temperature as a demonstration. The final section in the pupils' book makes a useful general point about the processes of extrapolation and interpolation.

Answers to selected questions

14i The gas molecules make more collisions per second with the walls of the container.
ii Each collision is harder as the particles are moving more swiftly.

15a From work done in compressing the gas.
b Less opportunity for the extra energy to be transferred to the surroundings. (In fact such compressions can take place under a wide range of conditions, extending from those that take place so slowly that all the energy is transferred to the surroundings and the temperature of the gas does, not rise at all – *isothermal* compressions – to those in which there is no transfer of energy to the surroundings – *adiabatic* compressions.)

16a The temperature of the gas rises.
b Due to the rise in temperature the oil reacts explosively with the air.
c This reaction transfers energy to the gas, raising its temperature and pressure. This excess pressure drives the piston downwards.

18 This question leads into the absolute zero of temperature. The value obtained will depend on the readings used and the line drawn through them. In an ideal situation, pupils should use results obtained experimentally in class – either from their own experiments or from a demonstration.

19a 373 K **b** 310 K **c** 90 K.

Activities

Worksheet P2A1 **Pressure**

REQUIREMENTS

Each pupil will need:
Large sheet of squared paper

Access to:
Bathroom scales
Calculator

The idea that exerting a force over a small area is more effective than exerting the same force over a large area is intuitive for many people and the pupils may need little more of an introduction to the idea of pressure than a brief discussion. For less able pupils you might wish to introduce the idea by looking at the impressions made in Plasticine by a variety of loads on blocks of different area.

The instructions for the experiment are on the worksheet. Less able pupils will need help with the calculation of area in square metres.

Answers to worksheet questions
1a 1.5 N/cm^2.
b 200 N/cm^2.
c Tessa exerts a greater pressure on the floor than Mark.

2 $15\,000 \text{ Pa}$; $2\,000\,000 \text{ Pa}$.

3 Skiers exert less pressure on the snow than people wearing ordinary boots because the same force is spread over a large area. They therefore sink into the snow less.

4 The main reason is to reduce the amount of friction. But a secondary effect is that the large pressure that results from a person's weight exerted over the small area of the skate's blade causes local melting of the ice, which reduces friction further.

5 An elephant's foot is about $0.3 \text{ m} \times 0.3 \text{ m}$, giving a total foot area (for its four feet) of 0.36 m^2. The pressure is therefore about $140\,000 \text{ Pa}$.

Worksheet P2A2 **Pressure in liquids**

REQUIREMENTS

The teacher will need:
Can or flask with several holes around its circumference, all at the same height
2 identical cans with holes near the bottom
Tray to catch water

Each group of pupils will need:
Two syringes of different cross sections, without needles
Plastic tubing (ideally pressure tubing), to connect the syringes

Access to:
Water

The procedure for the demonstration is detailed on the worksheet. The demonstration shows that the pressure of a liquid increases with depth and that the pressure is the same in all directions. (This, of course, assumes that the speed of the "fountain" depends on the pressure.)

In the experiment with the syringes, the pupils should be able to feel the way pressure is transmitted through the water to make the plunger at the opposite end move. The reading material at the end of this worksheet includes questions to extend the pupils' understanding of hydraulic systems.

Answers to worksheet questions

1 The pressure is the same in all directions.

2 The pressure is greater at greater depth.

3 It is easier to press on plungers of smaller area.

4 There are spaces between the molecules in the air but not between the molecules in the water, so you can compress the air but not the water.

5 The air at X would be compressed rather than fluid spreading out to all four brake cylinders.

6 Fluid would escape at Y instead of spreading out to all four brake cylinders.

7 To allow the driver to exert a larger force on each brake cylinder than his foot can on the master cylinder.

8a When X is pushed down, A shuts and B opens, pushing fluid into Y.
b If there were no valve at B, Y would go down when X was next pulled up.
c The valve at C allows Y to go down when required.

9a 100 N/m^2.
b 400 N could be raised on Y if there were no friction.

Worksheet P2A Marbles in a tray

REQUIREMENTS

Each group of pupils will need:
Tray with cork-lined base and ruler or piece of wood to reduce "volume"
25 marbles (about 15 mm diameter), one a different colour from the rest
Marble (about 25 mm diameter)

This 2-D kinetic theory model is one of the best for gaining an insight into the kinetic model of matter. The questions have largely been drawn from Revised Nuffield Physics. The worksheet will need some introduction – particularly in explaining why the tray has to be shaken continually, while the walls of any container **seem** to be stationary.

Worksheet P2B Aerosol spray cans

REQUIREMENTS

No particular equipment is needed, but it will be advantageous to have some or all of the following:
- An exhibition of a range of aerosol products.
- Any references to the use and mis-use of aerosols, for pupils' research.

This piece of work is designed to give pupils the opportunity to explore the application of a physical principle to a now common form of packaging. The range of products now packaged as aerosols and the criteria which govern the use of a material as a propellant are considered. There is widespread concern about the increasing use of aerosols and pupils are encouraged to see that the application is not without its disadvantages as well as its advantages.

Warning
Aerosols, misused, can be dangerous. Do not ask pupils to bring aerosols to school for the exhibition, except completely empty ones.

Worksheet P2C Measurements on air being heated

REQUIREMENTS

Each group of pupils will need:
Pressure gauge, 200 kPa
Round-bottomed flask, 250 cm^3 (**not** 500 cm^3)
Bung with hole through it
Glass tube, short length to fit in bung
Rubber tubing
Container (aluminium), large enough to hold the flask fully immersed in the water
Bunsen burner and heatproof mat
Tripod
Thermometer
Stand, boss and clamp
Stirrer
Eye protection
(Ice is an optional but valuable extra)

Notes:
The flask must be firmly clamped to hold it under water. The water level must reach the top of the neck of the flask, which may have to be tilted to achieve this. It may be best to have this set up for the pupils beforehand.

A supply of hot water from a tap or electric kettle is useful, and will speed up the experiment.

It is likely that only a minority of pupils will do this as a class experiment. However, the experiment itself is not difficult to perform, **given the right equipment**. If the amount of equipment causes overcrowding and makes supervision difficult, do this as a demonstration. It is essential that the flask used is airtight and that connections to the pressure gauge are as short as possible, commensurate with safety. The only way to test the equipment is to do the experiment and examine the results. Experiments which give invalid results due to air leakage or an insufficient proportion of the air being raised to the temperature of the surrounding water are worse than useless. They will undermine any teaching of the relationship between temperature and pressure either now or in the future. It would be much better not to do the experiment at all and rely if necessary on the sample readings in the pupils' book. However, given good equipment (and pupils should receive the flask already connected to the pressure gauge), there is everything to be said for able pupils arriving at the concept of an absolute zero of temperature on the basis of measurements they themselves have made.

This experiment may also be carried out (as a demonstration) using sensors and a data-logger or computer.

Worksheets **P2D** to **P2F** relate to Topic **E1** "Weather". Further information on this topic may be found on pages 521–23 of this *Guide*.

Worksheet P2D Recording the weather

REQUIREMENTS

Access to:
A range of measuring instruments, perhaps including: barometer, thermometer, hygrometer, rain gauge, anemometer, maximum and minimum thermometer, compass, sunshine recorder.

Safety note:
Pupils must be warned not to look directly at the Sun through the glass ball if a sunshine recorder is used.

This activity is an exercise in gathering information about the weather. It shows ways in which observations about the weather can be made. The data collected includes information that can be deduced from direct observation and some that can only be provided by measuring instruments.

The length of time for which pupils monitor the weather will depend on their motivation and the available time. A group of pupils should be encouraged to monitor the weather over an extended period and report back to the class. All pupils should record some aspects of the weather over a period of at least a week.

Pupils will need to be told which variables to record and how to record them. A full record of all the quantities below will need a table with more than a dozen columns. Such records are difficult for pupils to make and maintain. A possible alternative is to use a computer spreadsheet or database to record the results. If this procedure is to be adopted, pupils will need to invent keys to represent the precipitation and cloud symbols (perhaps by lettering them in order).

Cloud cover
A good way to tackle this estimation is to hold your arms out horizontally at right angles to each other, to delineate a quarter of the horizon. Look at the sky extending from this part of the horizon to directly overhead. This is a quarter, i.e. two eighths, of the sky. Split that area into an upper and lower part, each one eighth of the sky, and estimate the cover. Turn to face the next quarter, and so on. The sky is "covered" unless it shows clear blue.

Cloud type and height
Two recordings can be made: looking west ("where the weather usually comes from") and looking east ("where it's going to"). The official symbols are representations of the different types. If you can see both high and low clouds, record both.

Precipitation
It is important to write "none" if that is the case.

Visibility
Even on the coast and in the hills, mist and fog are relatively rare in Great Britain. If they are able to observe fog, pupils can enter the name of the furthest thing they can see through the fog and their observing point, and find out the distance later. If the air seems particularly clear, that should be noted too.

Wind speed
The wind force chart on side 3 of the worksheet can be used if the anemometer is either unavailable or inaccurate.

Wind direction
Pupils should be reminded that the wind direction is the direction from which the wind comes, not the direction in which it blows. It is difficult to measure wind direction accurately without a wind vane such as the one made in Activity **G**3 in Year 8. Pupils will need to know the compass directions. Later on, pupils may be told that we need the directions of both the upper and the lower winds in order to make local forecasts. The direction of the upper winds can only be found from observation of the high ("streaky") clouds, and these are not always present or visible. Turbulence around hills, buildings, trees and so on causes local variation in the wind at ground level, so that it can even blow in the opposite direction to the main current.

Air temperature
The worksheet warns pupils that the thermometer must be kept out of direct sunlight (which would give an artificially high reading). It should also be kept out of rain because evaporation of moisture on the bulb would lower the temperature. The distinctive white

boxes with louvered sides (called "Stevenson screens") provide an ideal environment for thermometers; schools may have one of these.

Air pressure

If pupils have not made the balloon barometer in Activity **G3** "Making weather instruments" in Year 8, they will need access to a factory-made one (probably aneroid type).

Water vapour

A wet-and-dry-bulb hygrometer is the traditional method of measuring relative humidity (the amount of water in the air), but the use of this instrument is complicated. Inexpensive direct-reading hygrometers, based on the change in length of a stretched hair, are easier to use.

Changes

These are important. Pupils should describe any changes since the last set of readings was taken.

24-hour readings of rainfall, maximum and minimum temperatures, and sunshine are important for two reasons: first because they give an idea of what has been happening during the night, and second because they build up into a body of data which may one day be usable for long-term forecasting.

Worksheet P2E Understanding weather maps

This activity enables pupils to make links between weather forecasting and weather maps, and contrasts the weather experienced at two different times of the year.

Answers to worksheet questions

1 This will depend on the location.

2a Anticlockwise.
b The winds are from the west because the air rotates anticlockwise around a low.
c The winds are moderately strong.

3a Because the warm front is crossing the west of Britain.
b Clouds associated with the frontal system will have insulated the land in the west during the night, keeping it warmer.
c Heavy showers may occur at the cold front. Then, after it crosses, the clouds can be expected to clear away rapidly to give blue skies in which small cumulus clouds gradually form.

4a Major differences are to do with the presence of a high near Britain rather than a low: this results in clear skies, with cold nights but bright days.
b A notable similarity is the large frontal system around the low in the northern Atlantic.

Worksheet P2F Which way did the wind blow?

REQUIREMENTS

Access to:
World atlas

Pupils use a knowledge of prevailing wind directions, together with information about wind directions in sedimentary rocks, to consider Britain's previous position relative to the Equator.

Answers to worksheet questions

1 Prevailing winds are from the south-west at present.

2 There is a gentle slope on the windward side (south-west) and a steeper slope on the leeward side (north-east).

3 The cross-beds slope down from the east to the west, showing that the wind was from the east.

4 The wind direction when the ancient sand dunes were laid down was different from the wind direction today. This may be because the wind systems were different then, or because Britain was in a different position relative to the same wind systems.

5 Prevailing north-easterlies occur between the Equator and 30° N. This could have been Britain's position in the past. The sketch should show a rough outline of the UK anywhere between the Equator and 30° N, rotated towards the east from its current position by about 45°.

6 Britain might have been at the bottom or the border of a tropical sea, with a corresponding climate.

Demonstration experiments

Section P2.1: Solids to liquids and liquids to gases

REQUIREMENTS
Kinetic theory 3-D model with driving motor
Power supply for the motor
Stand, boss and clamp, if required for the model

Demonstrate the effects of changing the speed of the driving motor or the weight of the piston. The procedure for using the model varies from one design to another.

Rise in boiling-point of water with increased pressure

REQUIREMENTS
Measuring cylinder, 500 cm^3
Pressure gauge, 200 kPa
Bunsen burner and heatproof mat
Round-bottomed flask, 250 cm^3
Bung with hole through it
Glass tube to fit bung
Rubber tubing
2 stands, bosses and clamps
Safety screens
Eye protection for teacher and pupils

The apparatus is set up as shown in figure 2.8 of the pupils' book. The pressure on the water boiling in the flask is increased by the depth of immersion of the tube in the cylinder of water.

Section P2.2: Model to show bombardment making pressure

REQUIREMENTS
Balance, 1 kg
Lead shot, or steel balls
Tray, large

The top of the balance is arranged as shown in figure 2.12 in the pupils' book. The balance is placed on a large tray, or inside a transparent container (plastic aquaria are a useful size).

The balls are poured in a steady stream from a height of 25 to 50 cm onto the inverted scale pan. As the balls hit the pan and bounce off they exert small impulsive forces – like those due to gas molecules hitting a wall. The comparatively great mass of the pan, etc. smoothes out these forces into a steady reading on the balance.

Warning
Avoid contact with or inhalation of the dust from lead shot.

Boyle's Law

REQUIREMENTS
Boyle's Law apparatus with pump to provide pressure

Apply pressure to the fluid in the reservoir. Read the pressure gauge and the corresponding length of the air column and record them.

Change in temperature when a gas is compressed

REQUIREMENTS
Gas syringe
Thermocouple and indicating meter
Cap or bung to seal the gas syringe

The thermocouple should be inserted through the cap or bung into the gas syringe to measure the temperature of the gas. When the gas is compressed, the temperature rises; when it expands, the temperature falls.

Section P2.3: Cooling by evaporation

Licking the back of the hand or putting a drop of alcohol – FLAMMABLE – on the back of the hand quickly demonstrates the cooling effect of evaporation.

Further information

Computer simulations
"Moving molecules" (Netherhall Education Software, available from CUP and AVP) and "Gas laws" (AVP) are useful for demonstration purposes here.

Chapter **P3** **Radioactivity**
The structure of atoms

The syllabus section

Context

Work on radioactivity is introduced by considering in what way these radiations can be dangerous to living things. The benefits that can be conferred by radioactivity are developed in a survey of the uses of radio-isotopes, which in turn requires an understanding of the properties of ionising radiations. The concept of half-life is explored in the context of using naturally-occurring radiations as a clock. The process of radiocarbon dating is discussed briefly.

Knowledge and understanding

	Tier	
B	C	F

Syllabus statements	PoS	SoA
Appreciate that radiations from radioactive materials are capable of breaking up other atoms and molecules.	3(ii)5	3.8(b)
Appreciate how radioactivity may be detected and measured.	3(ii)5	—
Understand why radioactivity can be dangerous to living things and be able to put these hazards into perspective.	3(ii)5	3.8(c)
Appreciate the uses to which radioactivity has been put.	3(ii)5	3.8(c)
Be able to relate radioactivity to the structure of an atom.	3(ii)3	3.8(b)
Appreciate how radioactivity changes with time and understand the concept of half-life.	3(ii)4	3.9(b)
Appreciate the idea of randomness in the decay process and relate this to half-life.	3(ii)4	3.9(b)

Opportunities for co-ordination

Ions are discussed in **C4**, **C5** and **C18**. The carbon content of living organisms links to **B3** and **B9**, and radioactive material as tracers to **B8**. **E2** discusses how the concept of radioactive half-life is used to measure geological time.

Routes and times

Basic	Central	Further
Chapter **P3** is omitted at Basic level, although some pupils may benefit from a simplified discussion of sections **P3.4** and **P3.5**.		Section **P3.1** "Radiation from atoms" is also suitable.

Central

> **Worksheet P3A What people say about radioactivity** (class + homework)
>
> **P3.2 Ionizing radiation**
> Demonstrations of spark counter, ionization chamber and Geiger counter; set Q3–5 for homework.
>
> *1¼ hours*

> **P3.3 What is background radiation?**
> Include demonstration of background count.
>
> **P3.4 Why are ionizing radiations dangerous to people?** (class + homework)
>
> *½ hour*

> **P3.5 Are all ionizing radiations the same?**
> Omit "Making use of ionizing radiations", and demonstrate absorption and deflection.
>
> *1¼ hours*

This is an alternative position for section **P3.7**.

> **Worksheet P3B Using radioactivity**
> Include "Making use of ionizing radiations" from the pupils' book.
>
> *1 hour*

> **P3.7 The structure of the atom**
> *½ hour*

Total: 4½ hours

Further

Spend less time on this section.
1 hour

Spend less time on this section.
¾ hour

> **P3.6 How long do substances stay radioactive?**
> Select material; demonstrate protactinium decay.
>
> **Worksheet P3C Using radioactivity to measure time**
> Refer to section **E2.6**.
>
> *1 hour*

> **P3.8 Random events and radioactive decay**
> The "dice decay" investigation, together with experimental data, might form the basis of an Sc1 investigation.
>
> *1¼ hours*

Total: 6¼ hours

The pupils' book

P3.1 Radiation from atoms

This chapter on radioactivity does not start, as other chapters have done, with an obvious application. Instead it takes up the commonly held view that "radioactivity" is to be associated with a "dangerous radiation". While radioactive substances do indeed emit potentially dangerous radiations, there are many popular misconceptions about its powers. Worksheet **P3A** lists some of the things popularly attributed to radioactivity. Pupils are asked to comment on their truth or falsity. At the end of the chapter they are encouraged to review their earlier responses to these statements.

The introduction sets out to show how radiations from radioactive substances can transfer energy to the surroundings. Radiation's ability to break up molecules is given as much attention as the production of charged particles. However, the latter effect leads to the industrial and research term "ionizing radiation" which it seems useful to employ in this context once the capacity of the radiations to ionize has been established.

P3.2 Ionizing radiation

Radiations from a number of radioactive materials are shown to have an ionizing capability, and the spark detector and Geiger tube are introduced. Although a relatively expensive piece of equipment, the spark detector gives a visual and aural impression of the energy associated with ionizing radiations.

The workings of a Geiger tube can be understood as an extension of the spark counter. The experiment shown in figure 3.8 of the pupils' book can be done to form a link between the two detectors, if the appropriate equipment is available. (See the notes on Activities which follow.)

The cloud chamber has been omitted from the work of this chapter. Many may regret this as it is the one class experiment that can be undertaken in radioactivity. However, this mode of particle detection has little relevance to modern work on radioactivity (although of course bubble chambers are a development). Many find diffusion cloud chambers difficult to set up and time-consuming and there is no guarantee of success. They also need a supply of dry ice. Having said all that, there is no reason why they should not be included in the work by a school which has always used them successfully.

Answer to selected question

5 The main advantage of these generators is that their power sources will keep them in operation for many years without attention. Such generators can be used on spacecraft and have been left to power experiments on the Moon's surface.

P3.3 What is background radiation?

No attempt is made at this stage to differentiate between different sorts of radiation. However, the Geiger tube observations lead easily to the observation of "background radiation".

A discussion on background radiation is essential to understanding the work of the next section which returns to the effect ionizing radiations can have on people.

The random nature of radioactive emissions might also emerge from Geiger tube observations. This is a difficult idea and has been omitted from this chapter for all but the fastest pupils. If, however, it is intended that a class will work through section **P3.8** "Random events and radioactive decay", now would be the time to introduce the idea of randomness of emission.

P3.4 Why are ionizing radiations dangerous to people?

This section introduces pupils to the units of measurement associated with the ionizing ability of radiations. From a "general knowledge" point of view these units are of as much importance as those of source activity, and it is important that pupils should be able to distinguish between the two. The term "radiation dose" refers to the ionizing capability of an ionizing radiation at a particular place. A high source activity does not necessarily imply a high "radiation dose". The radiation dose depends on the nature of the radiation, distance from the source, and the intervening material, as well as source activity.

No attempt is made to distinguish between ionizing abilities of the radiations in air and in tissue (what used to be referred to in terms of "rads" and "rems"). The correct unit of measurement for a radiation dose received by tissue is now the sievert, and this is used in the pupils' book. It might be useful in discussion to mention the older units of rad and rem as these are still in occasional use, but will soon disappear altogether.

Answers to selected questions

6c Workers exposed to known radiation hazards can be monitored carefully and the level of radiation to which they are exposed is carefully controlled. It is the lack of monitoring or control that necessitates setting low "safety levels" for the population-at-large. It is not (as might sometimes appear!) that risks are being taken with workers exposed to radiation.

7a Any answer to this question may appear to be contentious, but (bearing in mind the word "likely") the answer to this question is "No". There is a body of opinion that **any** level of radiation is harmful, but this involves an extrapolation of current data downwards into a region where the possible effects of radiation are overlaid by other hazards which might have similar effects. "Balance of risks" is not limited to the use and existence of radioactivity. For example, road transport has to balance convenience and necessity against the existence of road accidents. A useful discussion could arise from this question.

P3.5 Are all ionizing radiations the same?

The effect of magnetic fields on radiations leads into a discussion of the nature of the radiations and their differences. This discussion suggests that there is a "family" of ionizing radiations – alpha, beta and gamma. The approach to this is by comparing the behaviour of the radiations from americium, strontium and cobalt, which are respectively alpha, beta and gamma emitters.

This is the approach first introduced by the Nuffield Physics Project and later adopted by other projects such as the Schools Council Integrated Science Project. It is, in many teachers' opinion, much easier to understand than that which uses only radium as a radioactive source. In this alternative approach the ionizing radiation from radium is shown to be of three distinct kinds. It has the advantage of needing only one radioactive source but can lead to teaching difficulties.

The differences between the radiations lead to a more detailed enquiry into the uses of radioactivity. Worksheet **P3B** is based on the SATIS unit 204 "Using radioactivity". Work on the questions in this extensive worksheet will occupy the remainder of the unit. Some of the questions in it use the idea of half-life which pupils will meet in the next section.

Answer to selected question

8a The trails left by radiation from strontium (beta, and therefore negative) would be deflected in the opposite direction to the trails left by by radiation from americium (alpha, and therefore positive).
b The path of the particles from strontium would be more curved, as their mass (actually their mass-to-charge ratio) is much smaller than that of the particles from americium.

P3.6 How long do substances stay radioactive?

Radioactive decay as a "clock" forms the basis upon which ideas of half-life are developed. The unit in which source activity is measured is introduced here. This is the becquerel which has now replaced the older unit of the curie. As a unit the becquerel has the tendency to make even very small activities look uncomfortably large. It will be worth spending a little time getting this into perspective. Ordinary laboratory sources with an activity of 5 microcuries in the older unit, have, in the newer unit, an activity of about 200 000 becquerels.

The possibility of radiocarbon dating, is used as a good reason for wanting to know the rate at which sources lose their activity. The way in which radioactivity changes with time is investigated by measuring the decay of protactinium – an experiment first introduced by Nuffield Physics. The experiment described in the pupils' book uses a counter (scaler) to collect numbers of decays registered by a Geiger tube. A graph of these results then shows how the radioactivity declines with time, and the concept of half-life can be established.

There are now other and quicker ways of displaying the decay curve. The results can be accumulated by a computer via an appropriate interface and the graph displayed on a video screen. Alternatively, interfacing units such as the VELA enable the decay data to be collected and displayed as a graph on a CRO. Used with care, these newer methods can add greatly to understanding. Graphs obtained in this way are often closer to the expected form than those accumulated "by hand". On the other hand the complexity of the equipment can obscure the nature of the experiment too easily and the rapid production of results reduces "thinking time". Pupils who find the analysis of the results produced by direct counting difficult will benefit most from these "direct display" methods. More able pupils probably benefit most from seeing **both** approaches, if time permits. Alternatively, a combination of the techniques, in which pupils plot computer-collected results, is useful.

Answer to selected question
15a 256 decays per second **b** 128 decays per second.

P3.7 The structure of the atom

This section deals briefly with the nuclear model of the atom and its relationship to radioactive decay. No attempt is made to justify this model. Pupils are told it **can** be justified but that doing so is beyond the work of this course.

The model is used to show the nature of ionization as a change in the number of electrons associated with an atom. This idea is taken up again in Chapter **P**19 "Making pictures with electricity".

P3.8 Random events and radioactive decay

The chapter ends with a structured analysis of the relationship between randomness of the decay process and half-life. It is intended as an extension to the work of the chapter for more able pupils.

Answers to selected questions
17a 250 pulses per minute; **b** 250/12 = 21 pulses in five seconds;
c The number of pulses recorded each minute ranges from 230 to 265 – an average range of ±7% of the average value. The number of pulses recorded in five seconds ranges from 10 to 25 – an average range of ± 36% of the predicted value.

18a 100/5 (= 20 claims) would be expected.
b No, the numbers are becoming too small for certainty. **c** 1 or 2.

19a 20; **b** 100; **c** 100/6 = 17, to the nearest whole number; **d** 83.

21 The theoretical answer is "4.2 throws".

22a, **b** and **c** The answer should be the same as that to question 21.
e Again, the same answer.

Activities

Worksheet P3A What people say about radioactivity

This considers several statements about radioactivity, some true and some false.

Worksheet P3B Using radioactivity

This describes industrial, medical and domestic uses of radioactivity.

Worksheet P3C Using radioactivity to measure time

Geologists select isotopes with half-lives appropriate to the age of the rocks that they are analysing. Several kilograms of a suitable rock are collected from a field locality and then crushed to powder. For some isotopes the whole sample is used and for others certain minerals are physically separated from the rest; for example, uranium-bearing zircon crystals are easily extracted because they are very dense. The isotopes are dissolved out and "painted" onto a wire filament. This is made to glow hot inside a mass spectrometer. Streams of charged ions of the various isotopes follow different paths in the magnetic field of the mass spectrometer. Detectors measure the proportions of the isotopes collected at the ends of the different paths, and the information is analysed by computer.

Answers to worksheet questions

1 All once-living material contains radiocarbon: in this case, the wooden box, the woollen jumper, the cotton sheet and the bone. The iron sword is inorganic, and the nylon shirt is a petroleum product. (Oil does originate from plant matter, it is true, but it is far too old to give a radiocarbon value.)

2a A gram of a sample 5700 years old (i.e. one half-life old) would give about 7 or 8 counts per minute, i.e. half the value of the living sample.
b One would expect about 4 counts per minute per gram of the bone because it is about two half-lives old, with only a quarter of its original radiocarbon left.
c The flint arrowhead is inorganic and cannot be dated this way (there are other ways). The geologist assumes that the arrowhead was a likely cause of the death of the mammoth and is therefore contemporary with it.

3 With radiocarbon dating we are making the assumption that living things take up the same amount of radiocarbon from the atmosphere (in the gas carbon dioxide) throughout time. This is not really true, because the amount of atmospheric radiocarbon varies, especially if it is polluted by bomb tests. Radiocarbon dates have therefore been correlated against other dating techniques, e.g. dendrochronology (tree-ring counting), to account for the variation. Our bodies contain more radiocarbon than would be expected, and would give artificially young dates unless the pollution factor were allowed for by future scientists.

4 A safe level would be one similar to the background rate, i.e. about a twentieth of the current level. A period of four half-lives, or 48 years, would see a reduction to a sixteenth of the present level, and five half-lives (60 years) would reduce the level to a thirty-second. A safe time would therefore be around 50–60 years.

5 A time of 13 500 million years represents three half-lives, so one eighth (0.125) of the original number of uranium-238 atoms would be left. (This value can also be derived from graph 1.)

6a (Just under) 6000 million years. (The graph is needed to answer this.)
b The oldest rocks on Earth were formed about 4000 million years ago.

7 Too little of the sample will have decayed after so short a time. An examination of the graph reinforces this point.

8 Graph 2 gives a half-life of 700 million years. After three half-lives (2100 million years), only one eighth of the sample remains.

9a The original uranium-235 contents of the lower and upper lava flows would be $60 + 40 = 100$ atoms and $130 + 70 = 200$ atoms respectively.
b Given that $^{60}/_{100} = 0.6$ of the uranium-235 still exists in the lower flow, its age must be (just over) 500 million years. The upper flow has $^{130}/_{200} = 0.65$ of its uranium-235, so its age is about 430 million years.

c The limestone is sandwiched between the two lava flows, so one deduces that its age must be between 430 and 500 million years.

d Like all sedimentary rocks, the limestone will contain mineral grains which have been carried into the sea by rivers, and these grains may contain uranium-235. However, they originate from the erosion of some other, pre-existing rock, and the date they give will be of that previous rock and not the sediment they have been incorporated into.

10 Like all good scientists, those who date samples radiometrically like to get several results to reduce errors. In addition, certain isotopes reveal additional information about a rock. Some will produce several dates, for example corresponding to the several times a metamorphic rock has been reheated.

Demonstration experiments

Warning

In those experiments in which radioactive sources are used, it is essential to follow the guidelines laid down in DES Administrative Memorandum 1/92 "The use of ionizing radiations in Education Establishments in England and Wales" and the accompanying "Notes of guidance". All the sources listed here have the approval of the Department of Education and Science for use in schools provided that the regulations for use, storage and disposal are followed.

Section P3.1: Ions in a flame

REQUIREMENTS

2 metal plates with insulating handles
EHT power supply (or Van de Graaff generator)
Compact light source

Power supply for light source
Candle
White screen or wall

Procedure

The arrangement of the equipment is shown in figure 3.1 of the pupils' book.

Place the lighted candle so that its flame is a little below the plates. Place the light source 1 m or more away so that the shadow of the plates and the flame falls on a screen which should be at least a further metre from the plates.

When a high voltage is applied between the plates, the shadow of the flame and the gases above it divides into two parts, one towards the positive plate, the other towards the negative plate.

Sections P3.1 and P3.2: Spark counter

REQUIREMENTS

Spark counter
EHT power supply

Radioactive source, americium-241
Radioactive source holder

Procedure

Connect the spark detector to the EHT power supply without incorporating the 50 MΩ safety resistor. The terminal connected to the top plate of the spark counter should also be connected to earth.

Turn up the voltage **slowly** until it is just below the point of starting a spark. Usually a p.d. of at least 4500 V is necessary.

Hold the source just in front of the grid. Sparks will be seen and heard.

Section P3.2: Using a Geiger tube

REQUIREMENTS

Scaler counter
G-M tube, thin window type with holder
Radioactive sources of americium-241, strontium-90, cobalt-60 (see Notes)
Radioactive source holder

Notes:
Note that A.M. 1/92 requires that only one source may be out of its storage box at any one time.
A combined G-M tube/counter, such as the AEA "Radcount", may also be used.

Procedure
Connect the G-M tube to the scaler counter and apply the proper voltage from the scaler's built-in supply. This voltage can be most easily set by placing a strontium source close to the front of the tube and then raising the voltage until the scaler just starts to record pulses from the G-M tube. The correct operating voltage for the G-M tube is then about 50 V higher than this threshold voltage.

Experiments on the range of the radiations in air and the stopping power of various absorbers can then be demonstrated.

Section P3.5: Magnetic deflection of beta radiation

REQUIREMENTS

Scaler counter
G-M tube, thin window type with holder
Radioactive source, strontium-90
2 magnets, magnadur (slab)
Iron yoke

Stand, boss and clamp
Lead block (or any other material substantial
  enough to absorb the radiation from the
  strontium source)
Cork

Procedure
Connect the G-M tube to the scaler counter and hold it in a retort stand so that it is arranged as shown in figure 3.15 of the pupils' book.

Place the strontium source on the other side of the block. Fix it in a cork, pointing upwards as shown in figure 3.15.

The block shields the G-M tube from direct radiation from the source. Only a low count rate will be observed.

Arrange a horseshoe magnet of two slab magnets on an iron yoke. Bring up the magnet above the lead block. Place it so that its held is horizontal, across the path of the beta radiation. If the magnet is the right way round, radiation will reach the G-M tube and the count rate will increase. If the magnet is now reversed, the count rate should fall to its previous low value.

Section P3.6: Radioactive decay of protactinium

REQUIREMENTS

Scaler counter
G-M tube, thin window type with holder
Stopclock
Small polypropylene or high density
  polyethylene bottle (30 to 50 cm³ capacity)

Uranyl nitrate (or uranium oxide dissolved in
  nitric acid)
Hydrochloric acid, concentrated
Iso-butyl methyl ketone, or amyl acetate
Tray
Absorbent paper

Notes:
A combined G-M tube/counter, such as the AEA "Radcount", may also be used.

A.M. 1/92 advises that low density polythene bottles are not suitable; polypropylene or high density polyethylene bottles are suitable but should be replaced every five years. Bottles made from polytetrafluoroethylene would have an even longer useful life. If the cap of the bottle has a cork lining, screw a small piece of thin polythene under the cap for protection. Do not use polystyrene bottles.

The plastic bottle should be nearly full, containing equal volumes of organic reagent and acidified uranyl nitrate solution.

To make up a total volume of 40 ml of liquids proceed as follows:

Dissolve 2 g uranyl nitrate in 6 ml water in a beaker and add 14 ml of concentrated hydrochloric acid. Pour into the plastic bottle. Now add 20 ml of iso-butyl methyl ketone or amyl acetate. Screw the cap on the bottle tightly.

Other volumes can be made up by appropriate adjustment of the quantities above.

Procedure

Place the bottle in a tray lined with absorbent paper.

Support the G-M tube with a clamp on the tube holder and tilt it so that it points steeply downwards, slanting towards the neck of the bottle.

Beta radiation comes out to the G-M tube through the thin wall of the plastic bottle.

Shake the bottle vigorously for about 15 s and place it in position. As soon as the two layers of liquid have separated, start the scaler counter and let it count for 10 s. Take counts at 10 s intervals without stopping, or take 10 s counts every half-minute. Record each count.

Also record the "time of day" – that is, the total time from the start of counting to the start (or to the mid-time) of each count. That tells us the "age" of the source.

There is no need to continue counting longer than 5 minutes, when the activity will have dropped to less than 10% of its initial value, apart from background.

Allow for background radiation. Wait for 10 minutes after the start of counting and set the scaler to count for, say, 5 minutes, with the bottle still in position. That count will provide an average value of the background, some of which comes from the lower liquid.

Subtract the background **(reduced to a 10 s rate)** from each of the earlier counts. Discuss the obvious decay and try to find a rough value for the half-life. A graph can be plotted from the results as suggested in question 13 of the pupils' book. But how far the experiment is further analysed will depend on the ability of the class.

Section P3.8: A game with dice

REQUIREMENTS

Each group of pupils will need:
120 wooden cubes with one marked face (120 dice)

Further information

Films and videos

A number of films and videos are available which deal with the uses of radioactivity. One of these should be shown in connection with the uses of radioactivity discussed in section **P3.5**. (It is important at this stage not to show material connected with **nuclear power**. This is a separate issue dealt with in Chapter **P12**.)

Computer program

"Radiation game" (AEA Educational Services), in which pupils identify the isotopes present in different materials by carrying out tests, is recommended.

Topic P2   Force and motion

Introduction

It is not anticipated that the four chapters in this topic will be taught in sequence, although they are linked together by a common theme. Chapters **P4** and **P5** introduce the basic concepts associated with motion and relate the action of a force to them. Chapter **P4** gives considerable emphasis to the acquisition of skills in plotting and interpreting graphs, but otherwise the content of the chapters is qualitative rather than quantitative. They have been written on the assumption that they will be read and used early in Year 10.

Chapters **P6** and **P7** are more demanding, and it is anticipated that they will not be covered until early in Year 11. Chapter **P6** investigates the changes in motion that occur when bodies interact, and looks for laws relating these changes in motion. A simplified approach to the conservation of momentum is introduced for all pupils, called the "Law of Recoil". This can be used to solve several everyday problems. More able pupils are given the opportunity to extend this simple law to the more general pattern of momentum conservation.

Chapter **P7** extends the idea of simple "contact" forces to "action at a distance" and the concept of fields of force. It explores the force of gravity and contrasts the concepts of mass and weight.

As explained in the Introduction to this topic in the pupils' book, the work in these chapters tries to do much more than establish ideas about force and motion. Chapter **P4** is used as an opportunity to give practice in very important scientific skills – those of plotting and interpreting graphs. Chapter **P5** uses historical arguments about how bodies move to give pupils an opportunity to test out alternative theories in an investigative manner.

Chapter **P6** shows how ideas of force and motion are important in a wide range of practical situations, from the prevention of road accidents to the launching of space rockets. Chapter **P7** considers the universal nature of gravitation and uses this idea to direct attention to "predictability" in Physics.

Throughout these chapters, experimental work on motion has assumed the use of electronic stopclocks controlled by arrangements of lamps and photodetectors, as these seem easier to understand than the commonly used ticker-timers. However, the work of these chapters will in no way be hindered by the use of ticker-timers for time and distance measurements, if a school or teacher prefers, for reasons of expense and expertise, to use them instead.

Warning
Many of the experiments in this topic use dynamics trolleys on trolley runways. In all these experiments it is essential to have some form of end stop to prevent the trolleys from running off the ends of runways, to avoid injury to pupils and damage to the trolleys. It is also important to take due care in moving trolley runways about the laboratory and, if stored "on end", that they cannot fall and injure anyone.

Chapter **P4**   **Motion**
Speed, velocity and acceleration

The syllabus section

Context

Work on speed and acceleration is given some point by applying the ideas to the published performance characteristics of cars. Pupils are encouraged to discuss aspects of safety in relation to high speeds and high accelerations. Electronic timing techniques are introduced.

Knowledge and understanding

Syllabus statements	PoS	SoA
Understand the meaning of the terms speed, velocity and acceleration.	—	—
Be able to construct and interpret graphs showing relationships between distance, time, speed and acceleration.	—	4.6(e)
Be able to calculate mean speed from measurements of distance travelled and time taken.	4(iii)1	4.6(e)

Tier: B   C   F

Opportunities for co-ordination

Ideas about averaging and techniques such as graph-plotting link to Mathematics.

Routes and times

Basic	Central	Further
	Basic	**Central**	**Further**

The factors affecting the period of a pendulum could form an Sc1 assessment. *1½ hours*	**P4.1 Measuring time** *Optional*	
Omit Q13 from section **P4.2**. Worksheet **P4B** side 1 is also suitable. Spend more time on calculations. *1¾ hours*	**P4.2 Speed and velocity** Omit Q14 and 15 and "Velocity is a vector quantity". **Worksheet P4B Measuring time intervals** (sides 2 and 3 only) *1¼ hours*	All of section **P4.2** is suitable. *1 hour*
Worksheet **P4C** "Plotting a distance–time graph" is also suitable. Omit Q18 from section **P4.3**. *1½ hours*	**P4.3 Distance–time graphs** Include real-time graph plotting demonstration. *1 hour*	
Omit Q21c, d and e from section **P4.4** but spend more time on this section. *2 hours*	**Worksheet P4E Measuring acceleration** Omit the extension. **P4.4 Acceleration** Omit calculation of distance travelled from the speed–time graph and Q21e and 22c. *1½ hours*	All of section **P4.4** is suitable.
Total: 6¾ hours	*Total: 3¾ hours*	*Total: 3½ hours*

The pupils' book

P4.1 Measuring time

This chapter is about motion and measurement. Measuring the speed of a body in a laboratory presents obvious problems in measuring small time intervals accurately. The chapter thus starts with a brief history of timing devices. This could be expanded in class.

Pupils are challenged to produce a timing device of their own invention and help is given with this in Worksheet **P4A**.

The pendulum is introduced into the discussion and measurements of its period lead to a discussion of errors in measurement. More able pupils might care to discuss whether it is possible to "discover" that a pendulum always takes the same time to complete one oscillation. Against what yard-stick is this measurement made? To some extent adopting a particular "time-scale" is arbitrary. Decisions about atomic clocks being "more accurate" than pendulum clocks are based partly on fundamental laws of physics and partly on the ability of a particular timing device to keep time **with another similar timing device**. Two or three atomic clocks will keep time with each other to far greater precision than any other clock.

Investigations into the time-keeping properties of a pendulum do no more than show that a pendulum "keeps time" with a stopclock. The real importance of the pendulum is that changes in amplitude of (small) swings seem to have no effect on the time taken for each swing – this was Galileo's important discovery.

Along with the discussion of errors in measurement, the process of "averaging" is introduced, as well as the ideas of the "mode" and "mean" of a set of readings. Co-ordination with work in Mathematics will be useful here.

Finally, electronic timing devices are introduced and practice in using them is given in Worksheet **P4B**. It may be much easier for pupils to use and understand an electronic clock controlled by a light beam than to use and understand a ticker-timer. Because simple digital clocks controlled by a light beam are now available at a price which would enable schools to purchase class sets, it was decided to write worksheets using them. Some schools may, for reasons of expense and present equipment, wish to retain the use of the ticker-timer for measuring speeds and accelerations, perhaps confining the use of electronic stopclocks to a demonstration experiment. If this is done, it will be useful for pupils to have gained some experience in the use of ticker-timers in an earlier year, so that their understanding of speed and acceleration is not hampered by learning at the same time to interpret a record from a ticker-timer.

The use of ticker-timers rather than electronic stopclocks will necessitate the re-writing of Worksheets **P4B** and **P4E**. It is hoped, however, that all pupils will at least see a light-beam operated clock in use as well as a demonstration of the use of a microprocessor-based device such as a VELA, or similar device, or a microcomputer with an interface. The use of such devices is given more attention in Chapter **P20** "Control".

Answers to selected questions
1b 9.2 s; **c** 4 pupils.

2a The one obtained by pupil F.

4a 9.1 s;
b This result is lower than the mode. **c i** 9.1 s; **c ii** 9.2 s.
d This suggests that readings where a mistake seems to have been made should be discarded.

5c 5.3 s (Note the need to correct the answer to one decimal place.)

6a 25/10= 2.5 s **b** 25 × 4= 100 s **c** Her pulse rate was 60 beats per minute.

P4.2 Speed and velocity

The concepts of speed and velocity are introduced in this section. The latter part of the section, which highlights the difference between speed and velocity, depends to some extent on the previous introduction of the idea of vector quantities in Chapter **P1**.

An attempt has been made to maintain the distinction between speed and velocity which is defined in this chapter. Strictly speaking the term "velocity" should not be used unless an associated direction is stated or implied. Thus generally one can only say the **speed** of light is 300 000 km/s since this speed is independent of any direction. On the other hand it would probably be correct to say that the **velocity** of light from the Sun to the Earth is 300 000 km/s, since here a direction is implied!

Answers to selected questions
8a 6 km/h;
b 0.3 m/s (The data do not really justify an answer to better than one significant figure.)

9 4 km.

10 2 hours 40 minutes.

11 Average speeds for each ten-minute period are:
15.0 km/h, 12.0 km/h, 10.8 km/h, 9.0 km/h, 13.2 km/h.
i 12.0 km/h; **ii** 12.0 km/h.

12 A with 5, B with 6, C with 1, D with 4, E with 3, and F with 2.

13 500 s (about 8 minutes). The distance from the Sun to Earth is 150 000 000 km.

14a 3 m/s; **b** 1 m/s.

15b 3 cm/s due E at A, 3 cm/s due S at B, 3 cm/s due W at C, and 3 cm/s due N at D.

P4.3 Distance-time graphs

Distance-time graphs are introduced and the speed of an object is shown to be given by the slope of the graph line. This is extended to distance-time graphs which are not straight lines. Worksheet **P4C** gives detailed instructions on plotting such a graph and finding instantaneous speeds from it. Such detailed instructions may not be needed by all pupils.

Again it will be useful to co-ordinate this work on gradients of graph lines with work in the Mathematics department.

Answers to selected questions

16 See question 11.

17b A: 6 km/h, B: 0 km/h, C: −4.5 km/h.

18a The speed of car P is decreasing, while that of car R is increasing.
b Draw lines at a tangent to the curves at the point corresponding to $t = 2$ s and find the slopes of these tangents.
c Car P: 17 m/s, car R: 11 m/s. (Estimated from a graph.)

P4.4 Acceleration

Several points about the way acceleration has been treated may need explanation. First of all, it seems to be the experience of many teachers that establishing the **concept** of acceleration (as change in speed, or velocity) is very much easier than establishing what **constant** acceleration means.

Since Newton's Second Law of Motion is not developed formally in this course, there is no need to stress the idea of **constant** acceleration.

Secondly, problems arise over the fact that the word acceleration can have two meanings. It can mean "change in speed" which is its everyday use. It can also mean "change in velocity" which is its correct scientific usage. In the latter case, the vector nature of acceleration is also emphasized.

That an object can "accelerate" when **only** its direction of motion changes is usually introduced via a study of circular motion. It arises because of previous work on the relationship between force and change in motion. A force is found to be necessary to change the direction of motion even if the speed is not changed. However, Newton's Second Law, established for straight-line motion, relates force directly to rate of change of speed (along the straight line). This law is found to be directly applicable to, say, circular motion if the concept of acceleration is extended to "rate of change of velocity" rather than just rate of change of speed.

These ideas are beyond the scope of the present course, but will be important to pupils who study Physics at a later stage.

In establishing an understanding of any concept we believe it is important to relate it to any ideas the pupil may already have. In the everyday sense, "acceleration" means "change in speed". So for this reason, work on acceleration is confined to straight-line motion and the definition of acceleration is limited to such motion. It is left to later work to extend this definition to include change in direction.

Acceleration in this limited sense can be related to the slope of speed-time graphs. Such graphs are referred to as speed-time graphs since no particular direction is specified. Strictly speaking it could be said to be impossible to plot **velocity-**time graphs, since in general a velocity (which requires three co-ordinates in space as well as a size) cannot be represented on a single graph. But no simple rule can be given. If motion is specified as being in a straight line, some meaning can be given to a **velocity-**time graph. The direction of motion is implied as being either backwards or forwards along the straight line.

Deriving acceleration from a **speed-**(or velocity-) time graph has no meaning unless it is specified that the motion is in a straight line. On the other hand, the area under a **speed-**time graph gives the distance travelled whether or not a constant direction is maintained.

Many of these considerations are beyond all but the very fastest pupils. So this chapter keeps to the policy adopted in Revised Nuffield Physics of referring to all such graphs as speed-time graphs, but specifying that motion is in a straight line where it is necessary to do so.

Worksheet **P**4D applies the concept of acceleration to the performance of cars. This exercise may be more useful for pupils who have difficulty in grasping the concept of acceleration.

Worksheet **P**4E gives experience in measuring accelerations. The extended investigation that forms part of the worksheet (mentioned earlier) could form an alternative to Worksheet **P**4D for some pupils.

Answers to selected questions

20a 9 m/s; **b** It actually has this speed 3 s from the start.

21a i 0 to 1.5 minutes; **ii** 4 to 5 minutes; **iii** 1.5 to 4 minutes;
b i 20 m/s; **ii** 30 m/s; **iii** 30 m/s;
c 30/1.5 = 20 m/s every minute or 0.3 m/s every second. Both answers are perfectly respectable statements of acceleration, even though the first may be unusual.
d −30/1 = −30 m/s every minute or −0.5 m/s every second.
e To work out the distance, all times must be in the same units.
Area under the graph = ½ × 30 m/s × 90 s + 30 m/s × 210 s + ½ × 30 m/s × 60 s
= 8550 m (or 8.55 km).

22a 0.33 m/s every second; **b** −0.67 m/s every second; **c** 2700 m.

Activities

Worksheet P4A Inventing a timing device

REQUIREMENTS

No specific equipment is recommended for this investigation.

This is an investigation intended to be undertaken in the pupils' own time. If time permits it could be undertaken in class. Alternatively it could form part of a science-club activity.

Worksheet P4B Measuring time intervals

Experiment 1: Using a stopwatch

REQUIREMENTS

Each group of pupils will need:
Box with a set of blocks to fit in it
Stopwatch

This is quite a useful exercise for thinking about errors of measurement and averaging. The exercise is related to "time and motion" studies in industry.

Experiment 2: Using an electric stopclock

REQUIREMENTS

Each group of pupils will need:
Stopclock, electrically controlled
2 connecting wires
Track, grooved, with a 20 cm length of aluminium foil along each edge
Metal ball (ball bearing), about 12 mm diameter to run down track

A detailed procedure is given in the worksheet.

Experiment 3: Using an electronic timer

REQUIREMENTS

Each group of pupils will need:
Electronic timer
Lamp and photodetector, and supports for them
Dynamics trolley
Card: 20 cm × 8 cm

The aim of the experiment is to time the passage of a trolley through a light beam and work out its speed. A detailed procedure is given in the worksheet.

Warning
See the note about trolley runways in the Introduction to this topic.

Worksheet P4C Plotting a distance-time graph

Worksheet P4D Car performances

REQUIREMENTS
No equipment required.

Worksheet P4E Measuring acceleration

REQUIREMENTS

Each group of pupils will need:
Dynamics trolley
Card: 20 cm by 8 cm
Runway for trolleys
End stop
Electronic timer

Lamp and photodetector, and supports for them
Stopwatch
Blocks to tilt runway
Sticky tape, or some other means of marking
   lines on the runway

A detailed procedure is given in the worksheet.

Warning
See the note about trolley runways in the Introduction to this topic.

Using a microprocessor

REQUIREMENTS
Timing device (microprocessor-based), or microcomputer and interface
Lamp and photodetector, and supports for them, together with other equipment as needed

The use of microprocessors in a wide range of applications is investigated in Chapter **P20**. The use of a microprocessor-based timing device at this point will eventually assist that work. The procedure adopted will depend on the equipment used. The work can be based around either microprocessor-based timing devices such as VELA, or a microcomputer with an appropriate interface. Interfaces for the BBC microcomputer are available from all the major equipment suppliers. Setting-up details are usually available with instruction manuals packed with all such equipment.

Demonstration experiments

Timing a pendulum

REQUIREMENTS
Class set of stopwatches
Pendulum large enough for all to see

It is useful to have a pendulum set up for the work of section **P4.1**. Pupils time the swing and compare results. Many pupils benefit from first timing one swing and comparing results, then timing ten swings and repeating the exercise.

A motion sensor

REQUIREMENTS
Motion sensor (see Note)
Computer to interface with sensor

Note:

A suitable motion sensor is available from Educational Electronics, Woburn Lodge, Waterloo Road, Linslade, Leighton Buzzard, Bedfordshire LU7 7NZ. The motion sensor provides an excellent means of introducing and analysing distance-time graphs. Pupils predict, explain and produce distance-time graphs and their associated motions.

Further information

Manuals are provided with microprocessor interfaces. These usually give detailed procedures for carrying out experiments using the equipment.

Chapter **P5**   **Controlling motion**
The effect of unbalanced forces

The syllabus section

Context

It is intended that this entire section should evolve from a pupil-centred investigation into the cause of motion. Does it require a force, or is it something which continues indefinitely in the absence of a force? This investigation can be extended to relationships between force and change in motion.

Knowledge and understanding

	Tier				
B	**C**	**F**			
Syllabus statements				**PoS**	**SoA**
Know that to determine the effect of one or more forces on an object both the size and direction of the forces must be known.				4(iii)1	4.4(c)
Understand that unbalanced forces change motion, knowing that it is the size and direction of the resultant force that will affect the movement of an object.				4(iii)1	4.5(d)
Appreciate the effects of friction on the motion of objects.				4(iii)2	—
Be able to use and apply the quantitative relationship between applied force, mass and acceleration.				4(iii)1	4.8(c)
Understand the concept of centre of mass and appreciate its effect on the stability of vehicles.				4(iii)6	—

Opportunities for co-ordination

Friction in joints and the streamlining of fish are discussed in **B**10. Blood groups link to **B**7 and **B**8.

Routes and times

Basic	Central	Further
Guiding questions should be added to Worksheet **P5A** to make it accessible at Basic level. *1½ hours*	**P5.1 What makes things move?** Omit Q2. **Worksheet P5A What keeps things moving?** *1 hour*	All parts are suitable.
Spend more time on this section. *2 hours*	**P5.2 What stops things moving?** Omit Q5 and 6. **Worksheet P5B Investigating friction** Sc1 investigation. *1 ³/₄ hours*	All parts are suitable; spend less time on this section. *1½ hours*
Concentrate on balanced forces in section **P5.3**.	**P5.3 Aristotle, Galileo and Newton** Omit Q12. **Worksheet P5C Investigating frictionless motion** *³/₄ hour*	All parts are suitable.
Omit Worksheet **P5D**. Concentrate on unbalanced forces. *1 hour*	**P5.4 What if the forces are unbalanced?** The section on mass and inertia is optional; omit Q16–18. **Worksheet P5D Unbalanced forces** This leads to quantification of $F = ma$. *1½ hours*	All parts are suitable. Worksheet **P5E** "Inertia" may also be done if time is available.
Total: 5¼ hours	*Total: 5 hours*	*Total: 4³/₄ hours*

Monitoring the progress of Sc1

Investigating frictional forces

Students should investigate what affects the frictional force when a block is dragged over a surface. This investigation may be carried out instead of Worksheet P5B "Investigating friction".

Sample criteria are given below for an assessment between levels 4 and 7.

Strand (i) Ask questions, predict and hypothesize, e.g.	Strand (ii) Observe, measure and manipulate variables, e.g.	Strand (iii) Interpret their results and evaluate scientific evidence, e.g.
4(a) Suggest that the friction may depend on the load	4(b) Control nature and area of the surface and measure the frictional force for two different loads	4(c) Conclude that a big load causes a bigger frictional force than a small load
5(a) Suggest that a larger load would produce a larger frictional force, because there would be a larger force on the surface	5(b) Control nature and area of the surface and measure the frictional force for two different loads producing measurably different frictional forces	5(c) Conclude that a big load causes a bigger frictional force than a small load, but qualifying the conclusion
6(a) Suggest that the larger the load, the larger the frictional force because there will be a larger force on the surface	6(b) For different areas of contact, measure the frictional force for a range of different loads producing measurably different frictional forces	6(c) Conclude that a large load causes a bigger frictional force because the large load exerts a larger force
7(a) Suggest, with reasons that the surface material, surface area and load all affect the frictional force, and that one of the most important of these is the load	7(b) For a range of different areas of contact, measure the frictional force for a range of different loads producing measurably different frictional forces	7(c) Conclude that a large load causes a bigger frictional force because the large load exerts a larger force for the surfaces tested and within the range of loads tested

The pupils' book

P5.1 What makes things move?

This question leads to two opposing theories of motion. Scientists seeking explanations of events are compared with detectives trying to solve a crime. In many ways the procedures are similar. In both cases, there are to start with usually too few observations on which to form a judgement. Both scientist and detective look for more facts, usually guided by an expected solution. However, both try to keep as open a mind as possible during the investigation.

This leads to an investigation by pupils, into the effect of forces on objects. Little help is offered to them so they will need as much time as possible to suggest their own experiments that will help them distinguish between the rival theories.

When faced with the two theories, the reaction of many pupils may be "Well, it's friction, isn't it?" They may need to be encouraged to see that such a statement is meaningless as it stands. Discussion may reveal that what they are really trying to say is "Yes, we know a force is needed to keep things moving, but all that force is doing is overcoming friction". Pupils could be asked, "What would happen without friction?" They may suppose that things will then "just keep moving".

Pupils may need to be led to see that they are just "making up stories" about the world without attempting to justify them. They could be asked why such an explanation as they have advanced should be "better" than saying simply (as the first theory says) "A force is needed to keep things moving".

This may stimulate some lines of investigation. Pupils might, for example, measure the force needed to keep a particular object moving. They might ask, "Is that force always the same?" "What if the object is on wheels, or slides on a shiny table, or a rough table?" "What if the object is made to move at a higher constant speed?" Soon it is seen that Theory 1 asks more questions than it answers. If a force is needed to keep a body moving, why is it not always the same force? What patterns of behaviour describe the difference in the forces needed? Why, under some circumstances, is almost no force needed to maintain motion?

However, the alternative theory – that no force is needed to maintain motion – should by now seem equally implausible! But what if it were true? How could one explain the forces which are obviously at work in the "real" world when motion is maintained? Could the earlier observations be explained by assuming that some opposing force is simply being balanced by the push or pull that keeps the object moving? Could the opposing force (which we shall call "friction") be explained in terms of the way objects are built up from atoms and molecules? Can frictional forces be reduced? Or even removed? Are there any examples of motion where there is no friction?

Answers to questions such as these should make it clear that although "friction" is a necessary (contrived) force to overcome the difficulties involved in applying Theory 2 to the "real" world, it nevertheless leads to a much more self-consistent explanation of events.

Instead of tackling such an investigation, some pupils may benefit more from a class discussion which makes friction an obvious force to be taken into account when dealing with motion. They could then try the alternative investigation outlined in Worksheet P5B.

It is useful to establish pupils' current understanding of force and motion before starting this chapter. If they record their opinions at the beginning, they can review and modify them at the end.

P5.2 What stops things moving?

This section continues the discussion started in section P5.1. It considers some of the sources of friction and relates friction to the motion of a bicycle. An excellent video on force and motion has been produced by PLON, a Dutch Physics curriculum research group. (See Further information for details.) In this video, the relationship between force and motion is developed by observing children bicycling around the (flat) Netherlands landscape. If available, this would be an excellent time to show the first part, which deals with motion at constant velocity.

P5.3 Aristotle, Galileo and Newton

This section looks at the historical background to the two theories, and Galileo's inclined plane experiments are discussed. The argument which accompanies these experiments is covered in the pupils' book.

This leads on to Newton's work on force and motion, although only his First Law is being considered in detail here.

The acceptance of Newton's First Law of Motion is further encouraged by some examples of nearly friction-free motion. Worksheet P5C describes experiments with home-made pucks that float on a cushion of air and with an air-track. While the latter will clearly have to be demonstrated, it should be possible to produce sufficient "air pucks" for pupils to try their own experiments. Alternative or additional demonstrations are also possible, such as air pucks on a glass-surfaced table or pucks on an air-table.

This section continues by considering the bodies which move at a constant velocity in the everyday world – such as a table pushed at a steady speed across the room. If motion at constant velocity requires no force, it follows that the forces on such a moving table must be balanced. This reasoning leads, in fact, to the only way that the force of friction can be measured. When a body subject to friction moves at a steady speed, the size of the frictional force is equal to the size of the force doing the pushing or pulling, if we assume Newton's First Law of Motion to be true.

The section concludes by noticing that forces are required to change direction as well as to change speed. This point is taken up again in question 17c.

Answer to selected question

12a The forces are those of air resistance (friction) and gravity. Whether or not the forces are balanced will depend on whether the parachutist is falling at a constant speed or not.
b Once the parachute has opened, air resistance will balance the pull of the Earth and the parachutist will fall at a steady speed. (The effect of air resistance on parachutists is explored more fully in Chapter **P7**.)
c Forces of air and water resistance are balanced by the forward push of the engines if the hovercraft is travelling at a steady speed.
d At a steady speed, friction in the wheel bearings and between wheels and floor is balanced by the push of the man. (In this question the man and trolley have to be considered separately. The forces acting on the man involve Newton's Third Law – the force of the grocery trolley pushing back on the man. Newton's Third Law is not developed in this chapter, but the idea of action and reaction occurs in Chapter **P6**. More able pupils may care to discuss the point.)
e Again the sledge and the explorers need to be considered separately.
f The answer to this question rather depends on whether the piece of debris comes under the influence of unbalanced gravitational forces or not.
g An answer very similar to that for the hovercraft.

P5.4 What if the forces are unbalanced?

The chapter concludes with a qualitative investigation into the effect of unbalanced forces. The effect of the size of the force and the mass of the body on the acceleration it produces is considered. This should lead to a practical investigation into the link between these three quantities and a precise statement of Newton's Second Law.

All pupils may benefit from seeing the remainder of the PLON video "Force and motion" described above, if this is available.

Different bodies respond differently in the way their motion changes in response to the application of the same force. This is seen to be related to how "big" or "heavy" they are. This property is described as the **inertia** of a body – a property of its mass. No attempt is made to make this concept more than intuitive at this point. A more detailed consideration of the meaning of "mass" is given in Chapter **P7** "Rising and falling".

Worksheet **P5E** gives some experiments that highlight the inertial properties of bodies.

Answer to selected question

17a A full answer to this question is quite complex and obviously not expected here. The main point is that a passenger jumping from a moving bus is moving with the speed of the bus as he or she touches the ground. A (large) force is needed to bring the passenger to rest, and this is provided by friction between the passenger's feet and the ground. The complicated part is that it is the whole body that has to be brought to rest, but the stopping force is not applied through the person's centre of mass. The consequence of this is that the rotational effects will cause the passenger to fall over.
b If a car is brought suddenly to rest, a force is needed to do the same, harmlessly, to the passengers. A seat belt can do this. Collision between passenger and (say) windscreen may not! This is developed at greater length in Chapter **P6**.
c The change in direction of the car must be matched by a change in the direction of motion of the passengers. A force is needed to make this change, pushing the passengers round in the direction in which the car moves. Without this force, passengers will continue to move in a straight line – which they do until there is sufficient sideways force pushing

them round with the car. So passengers in a car **feel** as though they are being thrown outwards.

(Such a discussion is important when dealing with circular motion. It could form a useful background for pupils who intend to continue their studies in Physics beyond GCSE.)

Activities

Worksheet P5A What keeps things moving?

REQUIREMENTS

Each group of pupils will need:
Dynamics trolley
Runway for trolley
End stop
3 blocks of wood, different sizes, the largest about the size of a dynamics trolley
Slotted masses, 1 kg set
Force meter, 0–10 N
Electronic timer
Lamp, photodetector and supports
Card: 20 cm by 8 cm

Notes:
This is an open-ended investigation. Hints on how to get pupils under way have already been suggested in the notes on section **P5.1**.

Warning
See the note about trolley runways in the Introduction to this topic.

Worksheet P5B Investigating friction

REQUIREMENTS

Each group of pupils will need:
Wooden block, approximately 15 cm × 8 cm × 2 cm (but the precise size is not important), with hook to attach thread
Thread
Force meter, 0-10 N
Slotted masses, 1 kg set

A detailed procedure is given in the worksheet.

Worksheet P5C Investigating frictionless motion

Experiment 1: A model hovercraft

REQUIREMENTS

Each group of pupils will need:
Balloon
Hardboard disc, about 10 cm in diameter, with hole in centre to take a piece of dowel
Dowel, 25 mm length, 10 mm diameter, with 3 mm hole drilled down its centre

The way these air pucks are made up is detailed in the worksheet.

Experiment 2: An air track

REQUIREMENTS

Air track with accompanying accessories

The only thing demonstrated here is the apparent constancy of motion of the air track vehicles along the track. If pupils are allowed to try the experiment for themselves, they should be told that great care should be taken in launching the vehicles. This should be done using elastic bands at one end of the track as a catapult. There must also be similar elastic bands at the other end. Great damage can be done to vehicles by allowing them to "crash" into the far end of an air track.

Worksheet P5D Unbalanced forces

REQUIREMENTS

Each group of pupils will need:
3 dynamics trolleys
Dowels to help stack trolleys
Runway for trolleys
Stopclock
Electronic timer
Lamp, photodetector and supports
Force meter, 0-10 N, or dynamics elastics to tow trolleys along the runway.

Details of the procedure are left to the pupils.

Warning
See the note about trolley runways in the Introduction to this topic.

Worksheet P5E Inertia

REQUIREMENTS

For Experiment 1:
Card, about 10 cm square
Beaker or glass tumbler
Coin
Small piece of dowelling

For Experiment 2:
Glass or polystyrene beads, or a tray of glass marbles from the 2D kinetic model
2 hardboard discs
Masses, 1 kg and 100 g

For Experiment 3:
2 identical cans
Sand, to fill one can
String to suspend cans

For Experiment 4:
2 identical masses, each about 1 kg, held together by sticky tape
Thread
Thin cotton
Scissors
Stand, boss and clamp
G-clamp

For Experiment 5:
Inertial balance kit
G-clamp

These experiments can be set up as an experiment circus. Illustrations of the arrangement of each set of equipment are shown on the worksheet. The two cans in Experiment 3 can be suspended either from the ceiling or from a 1 m long lath resting on two stools.

Warning
For Experiment 4 the bench top will need to be protected in case the masses fall on it. Pupils should also be warned to take care that the masses do not fall on them.

Demonstration experiment

Section P5.3: Galileo's inclined plane experiment

This experiment can be shown using a pair of "planes" constructed from plastic curtain track.

REQUIREMENTS
Flexible curtain rail, 2 m long, screwed to 2 wooden laths (see Notes)
1 steel ball (or large marble), about 25 mm diameter
2 stands, bosses and clamps
2 G-clamps

Notes:
The rail should be of the symmetrical type with a lip along both edges. A good method of supporting a 2 m rail is to glue or screw a 0.5 m length of wooden lath (1.25 cm × 1.25 cm) to the underside of the rail near each end. Hold each end firmly with a stand clamp, 0.25 to 0.5 m above the bench. (It is not possible to hold the rail steady enough by hand.) If screws are used it is important to make sure the heads do not touch the ball.

Release the ball at the top of one end of the rail so that it rolls down the hill and up the other side. Tilt the rails to various slopes.

Further information

"Force and motion" – a video
Pupils will greatly benefit from seeing this video produced by PLON, the Dutch Physics curriculum research group. Copies can be purchased from the Audio-Visual Unit of York University. (See Appendix for address.)

"Sporting chance" – a video
Human-powered vehicles and racing bicycles are the focus of a discussion about air resistance and friction (BBC Science in Action series).

Chapter **P6** **Crashes and bangs**
Kinetic energy and momentum

The syllabus section

Context

The concepts of kinetic energy and momentum are developed in the context of an exploration into factors affecting road safety. Braking distances and the performance of seat belts are related to energy transfer. Understanding simple recoil phenomena both of an everyday nature and in jet and rocket propulsion leads to a development of the concept of momentum.

Knowledge and understanding

Syllabus statements	PoS	SoA
Understand the meaning of the terms kinetic energy and momentum.	4(iii)3	4.5(b)
Be able to use kinetic energy to solve simple, qualitative problems involving force and motion.	4(ii)4	—
Be able to use momentum in simple, qualitative problems involving recoil.	4(ii)3	—
Appreciate the way the concepts of kinetic energy and momentum can be applied to road safety.	4(iii)3	—
Be able to find both the kinetic energy and the momentum of an object from a knowledge of its mass and velocity.	4(ii)4	4.9(c)
Understand the use of the ideas of momentum and its conservation in relation to motion in systems such as collisions, rockets and jet propulsion.	4(iii)3	4.10(c)

Opportunities for co-ordination

B11 deals with the effects of alcohol.

Routes and times

	Basic	Central	Further
		P6.1 Motorway madness **P6.2 Stopping safely** Q6 and 7 are optional. *1 hour*	Spend less time on this section. *3/4 hour*
	Omit Q9–13 and quantitative work on kinetic energy. Do sides 1 and 2 of Worksheet **P6A**.	**P6.4 Force and change in motion** (up to page 102) Omit Q10–13. **Worksheet P6A Kinetic energy** (sides 2 and 3 only) *1½ hours*	All parts are suitable.
	Cover this in a qualitative manner.	**P6.4 Force and change in motion** ("Car safety belts" and "Braking distances") Omit Q15–17, 19 and 20. *3/4 hour*	All parts are suitable.
	Demonstrate Worksheet **P6B**, emphasizing the qualitative aspect of the "recoil law".	**P6.5 Recoil** Omit pages 106, 107 and 109–112, and Q23–25, 29 and 35. Include rocket demonstration. *1 3/4 hours*	All parts are suitable but some selection of material may be needed. The air-rifle experiment could be demonstrated.
			P6.6 Can we make more use of the idea of momentum? (class + homework) **Worksheet P6C Collisions** *1 1/2 hours*
	Pupils should discuss aspects of road safety in class. *3/4 hour*	**P6.3 A road safety investigation** *Extension activity/homework*	
	Total: 5 3/4 hours	*Total: 5 hours*	*Total: 6 1/4 hours*

The pupils' book

P6.1 Motorway madness

This brief introduction sets some problems about road safety which lead ultimately to ideas about kinetic energy and momentum.

P6.2 Stopping safely

An analysis of data provided by Department of Transport publications suggests a relationship between speed of travel and braking distance. This is extended by questions 5 to 7 to further considerations of road safety. At the time of writing, increasing pressure is being mounted on car manufacturers to advertise the "safe driving" aspects of their cars rather than "aggressive performance" aspects. This pressure may be relevant to answers to question 7.

Answers to selected questions
1a 30 feet. (Units of the foot and miles per hour have been used here as these are the only ones used in Department of Transport publications at the time of writing. Additional data in metres and km/h are given later.)

3a When the speed doubles, the braking distance increases by four times.
b Yes, braking distance again increases by four times when the speed doubles.
c An increase of speed from 40 km/h to 60 km/h is a 1.5 times increase. From the pattern above this should mean a $(1.5)2$ increase in braking distance: $8\,\text{m} \times (1.5)2 = 18\,\text{m}$ – just as the table shows.

P6.3 A road safety investigation

The material of this section could form the basis of a discussion for all pupils. But pupils who do not intend to work through section **P6.6** can undertake an extended group project. Each one of a group of five or six pupils can take one or two aspects of road safety. The group can then compile a report. These reports can be presented orally at the end of the work of the chapter. Aspects of kinetic energy and momentum will be important to many of the items. The effects of alcohol are a part of Chapter **B**11 "Detecting changes". Reaction times are also considered in the same chapter.

P6.4 Force and change in motion

The relationship between work and changes in kinetic energy is an alternative to Newton's Second Law as a method of solving problems involving force and motion. This section is based on an experimental investigation into kinetic energy (Worksheet **P6A**). It is difficult to establish the relationship between kinetic energy and the mass and speed of a moving body experimentally. Ideally, such an experiment should be able to measure the energy acquired by a body of known mass and speed. However, the most workable experiments transfer known amounts of energy to a body and then relate this to the body's mass and acquired speed. Such experiments are difficult even for able pupils to interpret without some prior ideas about the relationships expected. Experiments 4 and 5 on Worksheet **P6A** thus assume a relationship between kinetic energy, mass and speed and then test this experimentally.

Quantitative work with kinetic energy is the one area where a knowledge of Newton's Second Law is helpful. More able pupils who have done Worksheet **P5D** in Chapter **P5** may be given the Help sheet "Finding an expression for kinetic energy". This sheet assumes the relationship $F = ma$. This section ends by applying kinetic energy ideas to car safety belts and braking distances.

Answers to selected questions

9 The lorry has 5 times the energy.

10 The faster car will have 9 times the energy of the slower one.

11 The car has $^1/_3$ the mass of the lorry, but twice the speed.
So the energy of the car is $(^1/_3) \times (2)^2 = 1^1/_3$ times that of the lorry.

13a 12.5 J; **b** 50 J; **c** 250 J; **d** 125 J; **e** 200 000 J.

15 The actual energy is 3250 J.

20b Speed will have to be reduced to 20 km/h.

P6.5 Recoil

Most of the everyday applications of the conservation of momentum are concerned only with recoil – that is, the change in motion when two objects, initially at rest, push against each other to move apart. This particular aspect of momentum conservation is the one most easily tested. Experiment 2 in Worksheet **P6B** uses two sets of photodetectors and lamps. Clearly most schools will not be able to supply many such sets. For those which cannot, here are some alternatives:

1 Large groups of pupils can work round two or three sets, with individual pupils demonstrating the experiment to others.

2 One set of equipment can be set up and the experiment performed as a class demonstration.

3 An alternative arrangement, with trolleys colliding with end stops, can be used. While this latter arrangement is cheap to set up, it is more difficult for pupils to understand. Less able pupils, particularly, will benefit from seeing a direct measurement of speed using a timer controlled by light beams.

Similar experiments can be demonstrated using a linear air track. The law of recoil has been deliberately introduced in terms of mass and speed. The importance of "velocity" in considering momentum is developed in the next subsection "Introducing momentum".

The results are then applied to jets and rockets using a number of demonstration experiments. The carbon dioxide and water "rockets" are popular demonstrations, and both can lead to a number of searching questions. Some of these are given in questions 26–8.

The section ends with a more detailed look at the performance of rockets and jets. This will clearly be enhanced by the availability of appropriate visual material in class. The necessary launch speed of satellites is taken up again in Chapter **P7** "Rising and falling".

Answers to selected questions

22a The "mass × speed" of each vehicle is 600 g m/s.

23 The speed of the boat is 1 m/s.

29 The satellite moves about 20 times faster. (2000 km/h is 556 m/s. The satellite speed is 11 000 m/s.)

P6.6 Can we make more use of the idea of momentum?

This final section extends the use of momentum to collisions generally. Worksheet **P6C** describes investigations that can be undertaken. Again these are "expensive" in electronic timing terms. The alternatives suggested for Experiment 2 of Worksheet **P6B** can also be adopted here. Similar experiments using a ticker-timer are harder to carry out as considerable "friction-compensation" is involved in overcoming the drag of the tape.

The chapter ends by giving brief consideration to the law of conservation of momentum and the concept of interaction.

Answers to selected questions

37 A completed table of results is shown below.

Before collision

Mass of first vehicle in kg	Speed of first vehicle in ms^{-1}	Mass of second vehicle in kg	Speed of second vehicle in ms^{-1}	Total momentum before collision in kg m s^{-1}
0.4	0.29	0.4	0	**0.116**
0.4	0.25	0.2	0	**0.100**
0.4	0.23	0.8	0	**0.092**
0.8	0.17	0.4	0	**0.136**
1.2	0.24	0.4	0	**0.288**

After collision

Mass of first vehicle in kg	Speed of first vehicle in ms^{-1}	Mass of second vehicle in kg	Speed of second vehicle in ms^{-1}	Total momentum after collision in kg m s^{-1}
0.4	0.15	0.4	0.15	**0.120**
0.4	0.16	0.2	0.16	**0.096**
0.4	0.077	0.8	0.077	**0.092**
0.8	0.11	0.4	0.11	**0.132**
1.2	0.18	0.4	0.18	**0.288**

Differences between the total momentum before the collision and the total momentum after collision are a maximum of 4% of the total momentum. The speeds were measured by timing the passage of a 5 cm length of card through a light beam. Since the clocks read the time to 0.01 s and the cards could not be cut to better accuracy than 1 mm in 50 mm, an error of 4% is within the expected error of the experiment. Thus the results confirm the conservation of momentum for these collisions, to within experimental error.

Many pupils focus on the differences, rather than the similarities, between the readings, so this question needs to be discussed with the pupils once they have completed the calculations.

38a 2 m/s; **b** 8 m/s.

Activities

Worksheet P6A Kinetic energy

Warning
Pupils will need to be warned that falling masses can cause injuries. Some form of protection both for them and for the laboratory should be provided. A cardboard box with some newspapers in it will do. This has the advantage of making it more difficult to put feet and hands in the path of falling masses.

See the note about trolley runways in the Introduction to this topic.

Experiments 1, 2 and 3

REQUIREMENTS

Each group of pupils will need:

2 dynamics trolleys
Runway for trolleys
End stop
Single pulley on clamp

String
Slotted masses, 100 g set
Elastic catapult

A detailed procedure is given in the worksheet.

Experiment 4: Changing the mass

Experiment 5: Changing the speed

REQUIREMENTS

Each group of pupils will need:
2 dynamics trolleys
Runway for trolleys
End stop
Elastic catapult
Electronic timer
Lamp, photodetector and supports
Card: 20 cm by 8 cm

A detailed procedure is given in the worksheet.

Worksheet P6B Recoil

Warning
See the note about trolley runways in the Introduction to this topic.

Experiment 1

REQUIREMENTS

Each group of pupils will need:
Dynamics trolley, very smooth-running
Runway for trolley
End stop
Balloon
Pressure tubing, 50 mm long to fit firmly into neck of balloon
Sticky tape
Slotted masses, 100 g to place on trolley

A detailed procedure is given in the worksheet. A smooth-running "Dinky"-type toy, to which Plasticine may be added, is an alternative that sometimes works better.

Experiment 2

REQUIREMENTS

Each group of pupils will need:
4 dynamics trolleys, smooth-running (at least one must have a spring-loaded plunger)
Piece of wood (about 20–30 cm long and 50 mm by 25 mm in cross-section)
2 lamps, photodetectors, and stands for them
2 electronic timers
2 cards, both 20 cm by 8 cm

A detailed procedure is given in the worksheet. An alternative to spring-loaded plungers uses slab magnets attached to the front of each of two trolleys. This is detailed in the worksheet.

Worksheet P6C Collisions

REQUIREMENTS

Each group of pupils will need:
4 dynamics trolleys
Runway for trolleys
Block to support runway
End stop
2 electronic timers
2 lamps, photodetectors, and stands for them
2 cards, both 20 cm by 8 cm
2 corks, one fixed to each of two trolleys
Needle, fixed in one of the corks
Spring

A detailed procedure is given in the worksheet.

Warning
See the note about trolley runways in the Introduction to this topic.

Demonstration experiments

Sections P6.4, P6.5, and P6.6: Linear air track

Experimental work in both kinetic energy and momentum is enhanced by being demonstrated on a linear air track. Detailed procedures for experiments will be found in the manuals supplied with the accessories for the tracks.

Section P6.5: Carbon dioxide rocket

REQUIREMENTS

Expanded polystyrene block
Wire (minimum diameter 0.5 mm) run along length of laboratory
Carbon dioxide capsule, with mount that will slide along the wire (see figure 6.22 of the pupils' book)

The seal at the end of the carbon dioxide capsule is broken, with a round nail given a sharp blow by a hammer. On release it travels at high speed along the wire. A block of polystyrene or similar material should be mounted at the end of the wire to absorb the kinetic energy of the "rocket".

Section P6.5: Water rocket

REQUIREMENTS

Water rockets can be obtained from toy shops, but can easily be constructed from an old plastic washing-up liquid "squeezy" bottle.

Procedure

The "rocket" is half filled with water and the pressure of the remaining air raised using a pump. In the "home-made" version the end of the "squeezy" bottle is plugged with a bung carrying a small length of rubber tube. This in turn carries a car-tyre valve which is attached to a foot pump. The "rocket" is mounted vertically and the pressure raised by the pump. "Lift-off" occurs when the pressure in the container exceeds that which the bung will withstand. The experiment should be carried out outdoors!

Warning

Even a plastic bottle can inflict injury if moving fast enough. Make sure pupils are aware of the risks of rockets suddenly taking off – and coming back down!

Further information

Supplementary material

Any visual material (slides, posters, etc.) could help the work at the end of this chapter dealing with jet and rocket propulsion.

Chapter P7   Rising and falling
The force of gravity

The syllabus section

Context

Studying the effects of gravity introduces skills in stroboscopic photography and the interpretation of stroboscopic photographs. Safety in parachuting is explored. The possibility of Earth satellites leads briefly to communications satellites – a topic that looks forward to **P21**.

Knowledge and understanding

Syllabus statements	PoS	SoA
Appreciate that gravity is a force even though there is no direct contact between the interacting objects.	4(v)2	—
Understand the relationship between potential and kinetic energy for a falling object.	4(iii)2	—
Appreciate the distinction between mass and weight.	—	—
Understand the part air resistance plays in the way objects fall when close to the Earth's surface.	4(iii)2	—
Be able to use and apply the the quantitative relationships between mass, weight and potential energy.	4(ii)4	4.9(c)
Be able to relate the theory of gravitational force to projectiles, low orbit and geosynchronous satellites.	4(v)2	4.9(e)

Opportunities for co-ordination

E3 discusses the role of gravitation in space flight.

Routes and times

Basic	Central	Further
	P7.1 What goes up must come down? For Single Award, omit "Force fields". *½ hour*	
Worksheet **P7A** should be simplified to produce bar graphs from ticker-tape.	**P7.2 Finding out more about gravity** Some selection of material is necessary; omit Q4–6. **Worksheet P7A Free fall** This could be used as an Sc1 assessment. *1 ³/₄ hours*	
	P7.3 Air resistance **P7.4 Mass and weight** Discuss relationship between kinetic and potential energy for a falling mass. *1 ¼ hours*	Include section **P7.5** "Why what goes up does not always come down". *1 ½ hours*
Worksheet P7B Making a model of the Solar System **Worksheet P7G Measuring the distance to the stars** Revise. *1¼ hours*		
Omit this section but revise explanation of the seasons and day and night. *1¼ hours*	**E3.1 Gravity all around** **E3.2 Tides big and small** Omit Q2. **Worksheet P7C "... how heaven goes"** (optional/homework) *1 hour*	All parts are suitable but spend less time on this section. *³/₄ hour*
Omit this section but spend some time on revision of galaxies, the Solar System, the Universe. *1 hour*	**E3.3 Exploring Space** **Worksheet P7F Space!** (homework) *³/₄ hour*	Worksheet **P7D** "Planets" is also suitable.
Omit this section.	**E3.4 Space geology** **Worksheet P7E Ganymede** (class + homework) **E3.5 Air for life** *1 hour*	
		E3.6 Stars, old and young **E3.7 How did it all begin?** *³/₄ hour*
	Worksheet P7H In the beginning ... *Optional/homework*	
Total: 7 hours	*Total: 6 ¼ hours*	*Total: 7 hours*

The pupils' book It is assumed that Chapters **P4** to **P6** have been studied before undertaking this chapter.

P7.1 What goes up must come down?

The first part of this section gives some attention to the fact that Physics is very much concerned with general laws – with **predictability**. But it is asked whether the commonly held view that "What goes up must come down" is universally true. Pupils' current ideas about the way objects fall can be focused by demonstrating dropping a large and a small lump of Plasticine together. Pupils should predict the outcome of the experiment. If the outcome is contrary to their predictions, they can be assured that they are not the first in history to have made that mistake! While the effect of gravity may seem common enough on the surface of the Earth, the force itself is altogether strange. It is not a "contact" force, although our direct experience of it makes it seem so. We are aware of gravity through the counterbalancing force of the Earth pushing up on us to keep us at rest on its surface. Gravity is seen in action when a body falls freely towards the Earth's surface – but if the "body" is **you** the force is not then directly experienced as there is no counterbalancing force acting.

Indeed, in such circumstances a person is said to be "weightless"! Astronauts in orbit round the Earth are falling freely in this way – there is no counterbalancing force acting on them. More able pupils may enjoy discussing this point later on in the chapter where mass and weight are considered.

At this point, however, such discussion would probably not be fruitful. The points above are made to explain why gravity is introduced as a force which "causes things to fall" rather than something which leads to the experience of weight. The force is seen to act because an object, released above the Earth's surface, falls with increasing speed. Earlier work in Chapter **P5** has shown that a change in the speed or velocity of a body means there must be an unbalanced force acting on it.

The final part may be too difficult for some pupils and could be omitted by them. The idea of a "field of force" is developed and extended to electric and magnetic effects. Magnetic fields are introduced again in Chapter **P**18.

P7.2 Finding out more about gravity

This section is entirely concerned with making distance-time and speed-time records of falling bodies.

Familiarity with the way a camera works is assumed to come from Year 9 work on "Light". (See the Introduction to Topic **P4**.) The technique of multiflash photography is described in the pupils' book, and a photograph is displayed. It is hoped, however, that this will be demonstrated to the class and an analysis made of a photograph produced by them.

Detailed instructions are given in question 6 for plotting a speed-time graph from the data in a photograph. Such a graph, which should be a straight line, can be a little disappointing unless great care is taken in measuring the small distances involved in the photograph given in the text. Much better graphs can be obtained from a negative or transparency taken in class and projected onto a wall.

Worksheet **P**7A gives instructions for obtaining a similar distance-time record using a ticker-timer. This is the only occasion on which experiments described for this course use a ticker-timer. However, its comparison with a multiflash photograph (the timer makes a dot for the position of the falling object every 1/50th of a second) makes its use easy to understand. Results are easy to analyse and usually produce "convincing" graphs! Friction on the tape seems to have a negligible effect on the progress of the mass, and a range of masses from 0.5 kg up to 2 kg can be used, as described below.

P7.3 Air resistance

This section deals with the fact that "real" falling objects do not always move as the results of the experiments done in section **P7.2** suggest! A multiflash photograph of a model parachutist in descent shows that in fact the parachutist falls at a steady speed. Using ideas from Chapter **P5**, this suggests that the forces on the parachutist are balanced.

Pupils who have already studied Chapter **P8** and worked through section **P8.5** "Why do cars have a top speed?" will already be familiar with the idea that air resistance is a force that depends on the speed of the object moving through the air. This idea is also important here.

Also of importance is the fact that air resistance depends on the shape of the object. A piece of paper spread out experiences more air resistance than the same paper crumpled up into a ball, falling at the same speed. A short investigation into this shows why parachutes are effective in reducing the speed of fall.

P7.4 Mass and weight

Mass (or "inertia") was introduced in Chapter **P5** as the property of a body that influences the acceleration it acquires under a particular force. This property is contrasted here with weight, which is related to the everyday word "heaviness".

It is a matter of experience that these two properties seem to be related – big masses have a large weight and small masses have a low weight. The two properties of matter are also compared with a third – how much matter a body contains. This latter property (which is developed in terms of the number of meals different masses of potatoes will serve) is analogous to atom-counting and the mole concept in chemistry.

An investigation into whether heavy objects fall faster than light ones establishes the proportionality between mass and weight.

Answers to selected questions
11a 100 N; **b** 300 N; **c** 1000 N; **d** 1500 N.

12a 16 N; **b** 48 N; **c** 160 N; **d** 240 N.

P7.5 Why what goes up does not always come down!

This (optional) section looks at how objects can go into Earth orbit if they move fast enough. The approach is one first suggested by Isaac Newton and treats orbiting masses as a special case of free fall. The section assumes that the time and speed of fall are unaffected by the horizontal motion. Projectile motion is not studied in this course, but more able pupils may care to note the assumption being made here (and even suggest what tests might be done to verify its truth). The final paragraphs on communications satellites link with the work of Chapter **P21** "Communication".

Activities

Worksheet P7A Free fall

REQUIREMENTS

Each group of pupils will need:
Ticker-timer and power supply
Tape for ticker-timer
Sticky tape, if self-adhesive paper tape is not used
Several masses in range 0. 5 kg – 2 kg.
Clamp

A detailed procedure is given in the worksheet. The range of masses should not extend beyond those given. Friction on the paper tape will markedly affect the fall of masses less than 0.5 kg;

the weight of masses larger than 2 kg can too easily break the tape when they are released.

Less-able pupils benefit from making graphs directly from the ticker-tape: lengths of tape from between adjacent or alternate dots can be stuck onto graph paper, then lines of best fit can be drawn through the tops of the tapes and the steepnesses compared.

Worksheets **P7B** to **P7I** relate to Topic E3 "Space". Further information on this topic may be found on pages 529–35 of this *Guide*.

Worksheet P7B Making a model of the Solar System

REQUIREMENTS

Each group of pupils will need:
Tennis ball
Knitting needle
Ballpoint pen casing
Clamp and stand
Marble or Plasticine
Metre rule
Lamp or torch

Access to:
String
Scissors
Blu-Tack and sticky tape

This worksheet gives pupils a sense of the scale of Space. A darkened room is needed for the Earth/Moon experiment and, if the Sun is to be included, access to a large playing field will also be required. The Solar System model produces a useful wall display for the classroom or corridor.

The relative sizes of the Sun and the planets are not given in the worksheet. Their approximate diameters relative to the Earth are listed below.

Sun	109.6	Jupiter	11.2
Mercury	0.4	Saturn	9.45
Venus	0.95	Uranus	4.0
Earth	1.0	Neptune	3.9
Mars	0.5	Pluto	0.2

Answers to worksheet questions

1 This a problem currently taxing NASA scientists: if they see a cliff coming up, then the vehicle actually fell over it 15 minutes ago because of the transmission delay from Mars to Earth! A "stop" signal from Earth to Mars would take a further 15 minutes, making a total response time of 30 minutes. The proposed solutions include intelligent and/or indestructible machines.

2a From the figures in the question, about 450 000 km.
The mean distance is actually 384 400 km.
b From the figures in the question, about 150 000 000 km.
The mean distance is actually 149 600 000 km.

3 The Sun is far too close in this model!

4 If we say that a tennis ball's diameter in centimetres is approximately 6.38, this is equal to the radius of the Earth in megametres (1 megametre = 1 Mm = 1 000 000 m). So a scale model of Mercury, radius 2.42 Mm, would be 2.42 cm in diameter and the Sun, radius 696 Mm, would be 6.96 m in diameter.

5 The completed table is shown below.

Planet	Distance from Sun (in A.U.)	Distance on model (scale 25 cm = 1 A.U.)
Mercury	0.4	10 cm
Venus	0.7	17.5 cm
Earth	1.0	25 cm
Mars	1.5	37.5 cm
Jupiter	5.2	130 cm or 1.3 m
Saturn	9.5	237.5 cm or 2.375 m
Uranus	19.2	480 cm or 4.80 m
Neptune	30.0	750 cm or 7.50 m
Pluto	39.5	990 cm or 9.9 m

6 The gap is occupied by asteroids; these may be the remains of one or more planets destroyed in the early stages of the Solar System's formation, or may be where one or more planets were prevented from forming by adverse gravitational effects.

7 Proxima Centauri, the next-nearest star, is 4.5 light years away. Since one light year is 9 500 000 000 000 km, the scale distance would be 71 km.

Worksheet P7C "... how heaven goes"

Pupils start by role-playing an argument between Galileo (supporting a central Sun) and one of his opponents (supporting Aristotle's physics and a central Earth). This can help the pupils to empathize with the strong commonsense arguments for Ptolemy's scheme.

Next, pupils sketch a simple heliocentric model of our Solar System to help them understand its place within our galaxy, the Milky Way, which is one galaxy among many in a changing Universe. They should be able to differentiate between baseless speculations and informed hypotheses about the possibility of other similar systems. (The mnemonic "Many Valiant Explorers Make Journeys, Seeking Undiscovered New Planets" may help them to remember the planets' order – note both Mercury and Mars start with "M". The "undiscovered new planets" were found later – Uranus (1781), Neptune (1846) and Pluto (1930).)

Work on the phases of the Moon can be used to illustrate the way the phases of Venus disproved the Ptolemaic world-picture – yet did **not** prove the Copernican one. This exemplifies the development of one scientific theory and also shows the role of models in generating predictions.

Observing the largest four of Jupiter's twelve moons can enable pupils to develop their abilities to plan an investigation, select appropriate measuring instruments, identify relevant variables, record data in tables, produce an evaluative report and use an experiment to elucidate a theory or model. It can also illustrate the point that observation is an art, in which training is necessary.

The social, spiritual and moral dimensions of science are illustrated by some of Galileo's own writings about science and religion. Paragraphs A to D are from Seeger, R.J. *Galileo Galilei, his life and works* Pergamon, 1966, pages 270–275. The first quotation in question 11 is from SISCON-in-Schools *Space, cosmology and fiction*, page 4, and the second from Seeger (op.cit.).

Galileo's hypothesis that the tides are caused by the Earth's motion can be used to show how incorrect theories are often protected by subsidiary hypotheses, rather than discarded. Extension work could be done on theories of the origin of the Earth and the Universe. His efforts to prove the Copernican system furnish examples of the uses of evidence and the tentative nature of "proof".

An account, by the teacher, of the background to the "Galileo affair" provides an opportunity to show how social, spiritual and moral issues **affect**, and **are affected by**, the scientific enterprise.

Background information for teachers

Copernicus was not forced to his conclusions by scientific data alone. The astronomical tables he had would just as well have supported Ptolemy's view. Copernicus's preference for a Sun-centred system was in part mystical. He saw it as more fitting for the light of the Sun to be central. His scheme was not simpler than Ptolemy's. Copernicus was still wedded to the circular dogma – ellipses came later with Kepler's work. The attractiveness of Copernicus's scheme was that it was comprehensive, unlike the piecemeal one of Ptolemy. Contrary to one popular view, the displacement of humans from the central position was not seen as a threat to their uniqueness or to religious views of their importance to God. Copernicus said: "As to the place of the Earth; although it is not at the centre of the world, nevertheless the distance [to that centre] is as nothing, in particular when compared to that of the fixed stars."

It is a temptation to follow popular folklore and to present the "Galileo affair" as a conflict between science and religion. Such a view is simplistic, as is the "heroes and villains" style of writing history. But popular accounts of Galileo are often couched in terms of "goodies" and "baddies", even though faults are evident on all sides. The SISCON-in-Schools account of Galileo is inadequate in this respect. If Brecht's play on Galileo is used it needs to be treated with caution – it is a drama, with characteristic dramatic licence, not a historical sourcebook. It can be useful in raising moral issues about freedom of thought and the social responsibility of the scientist, but it gives no details of the trial itself. The SATIS 16–19 unit, "The retrial of Galileo", is imaginative but not without historical inadequacies. For instance, Cardinal Bellarmine is portrayed as a biblical literalist while Bruno's Copernican leanings are introduced, even though they played such a minor part in his indictment. No hint is given of the stormier side of Galileo's character or of the difficulties he often created for himself.

Points which need to be kept in mind are:

- Greek astronomy was already beginning to crumble.
- Galileo's initial enemies were the Aristotelian university teachers whose professional reputations were threatened.
- A League was formed to oppose Galileo, and one strategy was to try to make a religious issue of the dispute so as to discredit Galileo in the eyes of his employers and to stir up trouble with the Catholic Church.
- Galileo was publicly honoured in Rome by Pope Paul V and the Jesuit Roman College.
- Through the bitterness of his priority disputes (for example over sunspots), Galileo made many unnecessary enemies among the Jesuits, who had formerly been friendly.
- Galileo remained a loyal Catholic, saying of himself, "No saint could have shown more reverence for the Church or greater zeal."
- He wrote things about science and the Bible which were later in accord with the orthodox view of the Catholic Church.
- Despite his promises to prove that Copernicus was right, he never did so.
- A key issue in the affair was the sensitive one of who had the right to interpret the Bible for, in the wake of the Counter-Reformation and the Council of Trent (1545–63), this was vested in the Church Fathers; but Galileo was presuming to interpret the scriptures himself.
- Pope Urban VIII, in office at the time of Galileo's trial, was beset with problems of his own, although for much of the time he was Galileo's friend and ally. The kind of personality clash between the two is illustrated by Koestler's comment that Urban VIII's "famous statement that he "knew better than all the Cardinals put together" was only equalled by Galileo's that he alone had discovered everything new in the sky".

- Another key factor in the trial was the difference between two documents. One document was a report given to Galileo by Cardinal Bellarmine (dead by the time of the trial) of a meeting they had in 1616. The report said that Galileo had been told the Copernican scheme "cannot be defended or held". The second document was a Vatican record (unsigned) produced at the trial in 1633 which also claimed to be a report of that 1616 meeting. Its wording was much stronger, saying that Galileo had promised not "to hold, teach, or defend it in any way whatsoever, verbally or in writing". Scientific tests indicate that the Vatican report was not a later forgery, so the mystery remains.
- Galileo was threatened with torture if he did not recant his views; but both he and the authorities knew that this could not be carried out – it was illegal with a man of seventy – but it was very frightening.
- Galileo was not confined to dungeons, but was placed under house arrest in comfortable apartments.
- He called those who did not share his views "mental pygmies", "dumb idiots", and "hardly deserving to be called human beings".
- Galileo perjured himself, saying he had written the book to disprove the Copernican system. This could be seen to be ludicrous by anyone who read the book. Galileo tried to get himself out of this difficulty by claiming to have forgotten what he had written.
- Pope Urban VIII asked for his "unanswerable" argument – that God could use whatever means he liked to make tides and was not bound to use the motion of the Earth – to be included in Galileo's book. Galileo left it to the last page and put the argument into the mouth of a simpleton who had been wrong on every other point. The Pope said that Galileo "did not fear to make game of me".
- The authorities attempted an out-of-court settlement so it would "be possible to deal leniently with the culprit" and the Pope said they would "consult together so that he may suffer as little distress as possible".
- Galileo was forced to retract his ideas (there is no evidence for the legend that he muttered "nevertheless it moves" under his breath at the trial).
- He was sentenced to house-arrest and to recite penitential psalms; but he got permission for a nun to do it for him. The nun was his own daughter, one of three children he had by his mistress, whom he left on moving to Florence.
- The decline of Italian science was noticeable within a few years of the trial.

Worksheet P7D Planets

REQUIREMENTS

Each pupil will need:
Calculator

This worksheet enables pupils to calculate the orbital characteristics, volumes and densities of the planets. Pupils will need to be able to find squares and cubes of values with their calculators.

Answers to worksheet questions
1 Jupiter: (radius of orbit)^3 = 125; radius of orbit = 5 Earth orbits.
Saturn: (time of orbit)^2 = 900; (radius of orbit)^3 = 857.
Neptune: (time of orbit)^2 = 27 000; time of orbit = 164.
Pluto: (time of orbit)^2 = 62 500; (radius of orbit)^3 = 62 500; radius of orbit = 39.7.

2 Mercury has the smallest orbital radius and is therefore closest to the Sun and "ought" to be the hottest. However, the greenhouse effect on Venus makes its surface temperature even higher.

3 Pluto has the largest average radius of orbit and should therefore be the furthest from the Sun and hence the coldest. Again, however, there are complications: Pluto's fairly eccentric elliptical orbit sometimes carries it inside Neptune's orbit (where it is at the moment) and slightly closer to the Sun.

4 In theory, any planet with an orbital radius similar to the Earth's should be a candidate, i.e. Mars and Venus. However, both of these are unsuitable owing to atmospheric problems (see also section E3.5 "Air for life").

5

Planet	Volume relative to Earth	Density relative to Earth	Density relative to water
Earth	1.00	1.00	5.5
Mercury	0.05	0.98	5.39
Venus	0.88	0.92	5.06
Mars	0.15	0.73	4.02
Jupiter	1405	0.23	1.27
Saturn	857	0.11	0.61
Uranus	51	0.29	1.60
Neptune	43	0.40	2.2
Pluto	0.006	0.34	1.87

7 Saturn's density is considerably lower than that of water, indicating a gaseous composition (mainly hydrogen and helium, in fact). It is sometimes said that Saturn could be floated in a bathtub (if one large enough could be constructed on a planet big enough!).

8 Mercury is a small planet with a relatively low mass and weak gravitational field. So the escape velocity for gas molecules is low and the atmosphere has "escaped". In addition, Mercury is close to the Sun so its gas molecules are hot and fast moving, increasing their chance of escape anyway.

Worksheet P7E Ganymede

This worksheet introduces pupils to basic interpretation of planetary surfaces using standard geological techniques.

Answers to worksheet questions

1 Obviously, the longer a surface is exposed to bombardment by meteorites, the more craters it will acquire. In particular, surfaces which date from the early history of the Solar System are heavily cratered because there was a greater quantity of loose debris floating through Space at that time. If an ice surface is heated it will melt flat and later refreeze, obliterating the craters in the process. This has happened on Europa (another moon of Jupiter), which is thought to have been resurfaced relatively recently.

   If a lava flows out onto the surface of a planet or moon, it will bury any earlier features such as craters (e.g. the Mare of the Moon); if a fault (linear fissure between moving blocks of crust) forms, it will cut across any preceding features; and so on.

2 The most recent craters are, not surprisingly, those with fresh ejecta blankets surrounding them. In region A we see a crater with ejecta partly covering up an older crater and a linear crack-like feature.

3 The oldest areas are the blocks of crust between the cracks. We deduce this because they have the most craters.

4 Generally speaking, the north–south cracks are the oldest, followed by the NW–SE crack on the right of the diagram and then the ENE–WSW cracks, which come last. Other logical solutions may be suggested.

5 The cratered smooth areas are the oldest, the cracks (in the order described above) come next, and the craters with ejecta blankets are the youngest.

6 Although larger craters are usually surrounded by larger ejecta blankets, a careful inspection of the diagram shows that this is not always true. The important factors affecting ejecta fields are the gravitational pull of the planet or moon (in this case, this is the same for all the craters), the composition of the planetary surface (possibly variable in this case), the angle of impact (variable) and the kinetic energy of the impacting meteorite (dependent on its mass and speed).

Worksheet P7F Space!

REQUIREMENTS

Each pupil will need:
Calculator

The purpose of this worksheet is to familiarize pupils with the vastness of Space. They will need to be able to use the equation

　　speed = distance/time,

to handle large numbers (although standard-form notation is generally avoided) and to convert units, e.g. seconds to minutes to hours to days, etc.

Answers to worksheet questions

1 5429 hours (226.2 days).

2 The engine needs oxygen for combustion, the wheels would not be in contact with anything, and the passengers would need an air supply.

3 1.267 s.

4　Mercury:　307 s (5.1 minutes)
　　　Jupiter:　　2100 s (35 minutes)
　　　Pluto:　　　19 167 s (5.32 hours).

5 We have assumed that the planets are exactly on the same side of the Solar System as the Earth. If they are somewhere on the other side of the Solar System (quite likely), then the distances are greater.

6 $300\,000 \times 60 \times 60 \times 24 \times 365.25 = 9.467 \times 10^{12}$ km, i.e. about 9.5 million million kilometres.

7 237.5 million hours (27 100 years).

8 1990 + 520 = 2510 AD.

9 The radio signals have travelled 70 light years into Space by 1992. They have 86 light years in all to cover before reaching Beta Carinae so we would expect the first signals to arrive there in the year 1992 + 86 = 2008 AD.

10 One sees more stars along the plane of the galaxy, i.e. where the Milky Way (the next spiral arm to ours) runs. The constellation of Cygnus (the Swan) lies along this plane and many stars can be seen in it using binoculars. One would expect to see the most stars by looking towards the centre of our galaxy (in the direction of the constellation Sagittarius), but the view is obscured by clouds of dark dust. Infra-red and radio telescopes can "see" through this dust.

11 The Milky Way.

12 Over 100 000 light years.

13 Galaxies emit all kinds of electromagnetic radiation but particularly radio, infra-red and visible light. Certain galaxies emit streams of electrons which interact with surrounding gases to emit powerful radio noise. Some galaxies may have massive black holes at their centres causing these spectacular phenomena.

Worksheet P7G Measuring the distance to the stars

REQUIREMENTS

Each group of pupils will need:
Strip of wood, just over 1 m long
Metre rule
2 drinking straws
2 map pins
Plastic protractor

Access to:
Object to be sighted

Astronomers use a triangulation technique, known as the parallax method, to find the distances of the closer stars. Beyond this distance, the angular variation is too small to measure and other techniques are used instead. Likely stars can be selected on the basis of their proper motion, i.e. their gradual drift through the galaxy: close stars move more, and binary (pairs of) stars exhibit other tell-tale orbital motions.

In this experiment, a 1 m baseline is used. Astronomers use the diameter of the Earth's orbit (300 million km) as a baseline by taking measurements of the stars at six-month (half-orbit) intervals. The changing angle of a star is measured against the background of more distant, and therefore apparently fixed, stars. Pupils can simulate the effect by holding a pencil about 10 cm from their nose and viewing it through each eye in turn. The pencil will appear to move against the more distant background. Quickly switching from one eye to the other emphasizes the effect.

Pupils should start with an object about 2 m away so that they obtain significant angles. They can graduate to more distant objects later and, in doing so, learn of the difficulties involved in measuring small angles. The distance of the object is established using a scale diagram. The scale of this diagram will have to be reduced from the suggested 10 cm = 1 metre for longer rangefinding. It may also be necessary to stick several sheets of A4 paper together end to end or to use a length of tractor-feed computer printing paper.

Answers to worksheet questions
1a $4.3 \times 365.25 \times 24 \times 60 \times 60 \times 300\,000 = 41$ million million km.
b The triangulation sketch will be a very very thin triangle. Angle ADB can be calculated by trigonometry:
$$\sin (\text{or} \tan)\ \text{ADB} = \frac{300\,000\,000}{41\,000\,000\,000\,000}$$

So ADB $\approx 4 \times 10^{-4\circ}$

Obviously angle ADB is very small. A star giving an angle of 1 second of arc is 3.26 light years away, a distance called 1 parsec (short for "parallax second").

2a $300\,000\,000/(300\,000 \times 60) = 16.67$ light minutes;
$16.67/(365.25 \times 24 \times 60) = 0.000\,032$ light years.
b The triangulation diagram would be the same as that in question 1.

Worksheet P7H In the beginning ...

After considering the scientific view of the formation of the Universe (section **E3.7** "How did it all begin?"), it is interesting to analyse accounts of the creation from different religions. They are valuable reading in themselves but this worksheet also forms a useful exercise in looking for patterns of similarity and difference between pieces of information.

Answers to worksheet questions
The questions are open-ended and the following answers are only intended as a rough guide.

1 Important points, often common to more than one account, are:
- Nothingness before the creation.
- Separation of light and dark.
- Separation of the sky (and Heaven) from the land beneath.
- Separation of the sea from the land.
- A creator, although some accounts speak of gods being formed later.
- Some accounts include the first appearance of people, sometimes by creation or sometimes as offspring of gods/goddesses.
- Most accounts do not include a clear timescale, with the exception of Genesis and the Koran.
- Genesis mentions the creation of animals, whereas the other accounts do not.

Doubtless the reader can think of more. Pupils can build up a grid of items and the various accounts and check which are common to most or all of them (see question 3).

2 Scientific accounts of the creation of the Universe are largely concerned with what happened and the mechanism by which things happened. Theological and philosophical writings are concerned with matters that lie behind these mechanisms or which proceed from these mechanisms. A *theistic* philosophy considers the purpose of the God who made the Universe; an *atheistic* philosophy considers how meaning may arise in a Universe which has no creator. Pupils should be encouraged to realize that scientists, like the rest of humankind, can take either perspective.

The creation writings contain components relating to the nature of these issues.

3 Some points to consider are:
- The existence of a creator.
- Timescale.
- The separate formation of the Earth.
- The creation of living creatures and the order of their creation.
- The role of man and woman.
- The quality of the creation.
- Reference to specific individuals and their roles in the creation process.
- The completeness of creation.

Demonstration experiments

Section P7.2: Multiflash photography

The experiment described here uses a rotating strobe disc in front of a camera. The experiment described in the pupils' book uses a strobe lamp. The latter makes multiflash photography easier to understand but harder to do in the laboratory, as the level of illumination is much lower than that in the method described below. Strobe lamps are also expensive and schools may not wish to buy such equipment for this one experiment.

However, if the school has such a lamp it is well worth at least **demonstrating** a ball falling when lit by it, as pupils can see what the camera will "see".

REQUIREMENTS

Steel ball, diameter about 25 mm	Support rod for camera
Camera with shutter that can be kept open ("B" setting)	Metre rule
	Slotted base for metre rule (or stand and clamp)
Stroboscope, motor driven	Black cloth or paper for background
2 stands and bosses	Lamp (see Note)

Note:
The lamp should be a floodlamp or photoflood, or, best of all, a small slide projector pointed horizontally with its beam reflected down by a mirror at 45°.

Procedure
Set up the motor-driven stroboscope in front of the camera. Illuminate the ball strongly

from vertically above. Place a black background behind the path of the ball. The essence of success here is strong contrast between the bright ball and its surroundings, so the rest of the room should be three-quarters blacked out.

Include a vertical measuring stick in the picture, so that the photograph may be used later for an estimate of g. The measuring stick should have alternate centimetres marked black and white – a plain metre rule is not so good.

Set the camera to "B" and start the motor-driven stroboscope rotating.

Give a countdown. One pupil releases the ball. Another operates the camera and opens the shutter just before the ball is dropped. The shutter is closed when the ball reaches the floor.

Record the strobe frequency (motor-driven strobes driving a 5-slot disc usually give 30 pictures per second).

Section P7.4 The guinea and feather experiment

This experiment can either be demonstrated, or evacuated tubes can be prepared for groups of pupils to do their own experiments.

REQUIREMENTS

All pupils will need access to:
Vacuum pump
Pressure tubing, 1 metre long
Connecting tube (glass or brass)

Each group of pupils will also need:

Tube (see Note)	Small coin
Short piece of rubber tube carrying	Scrap of plastic foam
Hoffmann clip	Eye protection

Note:

The tubes are 60 cm long, and 5 cm in diameter. One end is closed with a plain rubber bung, the other end with a bung carrying a tube to take a short rubber tube with a clip (see page 125 of the pupils' book). Pressure tubing from the vacuum pump carries a short connecting tube to fit the short rubber tube while the pumping is done.

Warning

A cracked or dropped tube may shatter implosively when evacuated. For this reason, if in any doubt do this as a demonstration only.

Procedure

Put a small coin and a scrap of plastic foam in the tube. Close the tube with the rubber stopper. Pupils should first see what happens to coin and plastic when the tube is quickly turned upside down a few times.

The tube is now evacuated and sealed. The observations are then repeated. Finally the air is re-admitted and more observations are made.

Further information

Galileo Galilei and his views
The following publications provide further useful background material for Worksheet **P7C** "... how heaven goes":

Brecht, B. *Life of Galileo* Methuen, 1980.
Drake, S. *Discoveries and opinions of Galileo* Doubleday Anchor, 1957.
Drake, S. *Galileo* Oxford University Press, 1980.
Koestler, A. *The Sleepwalkers* Penguin, 1959.
Langford, J. *Galileo, Science and the Church* (revised), University of Michigan, 1971.
Poole, M.W. "The Galileo Affair" *School Science Review*, September 1990.
Poole, M.W. *Science and Belief* Lion Publishing, 1990. (A resource book dealing with other issues of science and religion.)
Santillana, G. de *The Crime of Galileo* Heinemann, 1958.
Seeger, R.J. *Galileo Galilei, his life and his works* Pergamon, 1966.

Topic P3   Energy

Introduction

A uniform treatment of energy has been adopted throughout Nuffield Co-ordinated Sciences and the terminology used in the National Curriculum follows this treatment. A summary of the main features is as follows:

- When things happen, energy is usually transferred.
- If energy is involved in a change, it will be transferred and re-arranged, but the total amount will stay the same.
- We become aware of energy only when it is transferred, and there are two important processes of energy transfer: work and heat.
  Heat is the name of a process whereby internal energy is transferred from a hotter to a cooler body.
  Work is the name of a process whereby energy is transferred when a force moves its point of application.
- Many changes involve energy being transferred to the surroundings. But the temperature rise which results is often so small that the energy appears to have vanished.

The concept of energy has two distinct aspects in science. On the one hand it is a **book-keeping** procedure. This is the aspect of energy relevant to the principle of energy conservation. On the other hand energy is something whose transfer is essential in bringing about **useful change**. In this aspect, energy becomes "degraded" or "unavailable" once it has been transferred to the surroundings. Many changes involving the transfer of energy to the surroundings produce a temperature rise so small that it is hardly noticed and the energy may appear to have vanished. It is this latter aspect of energy which is more apparent in everyday experience. The two aspects should be given equal emphasis.

More background to the treatment of energy will be found in Chapter 2 of the General introduction to this *Guide*.

The Energy topic in Physics is divided into three sub-topics:

Transferring energy	Chapters **P8** and **P9**
Internal energy	Chapter **P10**
Energy resources	Chapters **P11** and **P12**

This topic cannot be taught as one uninterrupted sequence. The work on transferring energy will have to come early in the course as the concepts developed here are needed in Chemistry and Biology at an early stage. Study of internal energy (which includes study of the conservation of energy) can come later in Year 10. Study of energy resources looks at, among other things, the importance of electricity as a means of transporting energy, and at nuclear power. It will thus have to come late on in the course. It might form a good end-point to the work in Physics.

Chapter P8   Machines and engines
An investigation into power and efficiency

The syllabus section

Context

The major concepts of energy, power and efficiency of energy transfer are developed in terms of a sequence of applications. The design of a domestic lift for disabled people is used to develop ideas about power and efficiency. These concepts are then applied to a wide range of machines and engines, including heat engines.

Knowledge and understanding

Syllabus statements	PoS	SoA
Understand, by investigating a variety of personal and practical situations, that when things happen an energy transfer is involved.	4(ii)1	4.4(b)
Understand that there is an energy transfer involved in making things happen and be able to identify the energy transfers involved in a variety of devices.	4(ii)1	4.5(b)
Understand that in the context of a range of energy transfers the total energy output is always the same as energy input.	4(ii)6	4.6(b)
Know that pressure can be calculated using the formula $$\frac{\text{applied force}}{\text{area}} = \text{pressure},$$ and use the concept of pressure to explain some simple everyday applications of hydraulics (e.g. car braking systems).	4(iii)	4.6(d)
Appreciate that machines can never be 100% efficient and evaluate means of reducing energy wastage in systems such as pulleys, electric motors and heaters.	4(ii)3	4.7(c)
Be able to calculate power and work done in a variety of situations.	4(iii)1	4.7(d)
Understand the law of moments and the use of levers as simple machines.	4(iii)6	4.7(e)
Understand that although energy is always conserved, in many processes it is inevitably spread out into the surroundings and so it becomes harder to arrange for further useful energy transfers.	4(ii)6	4.10(b)

The Tier column to the left of the table is labelled **Tier** with sub-columns **B**, **C**, **F**.

Opportunities for co-ordination

The use of fuels as an energy resource is taken up in detail in **C**13. The idea that the human body can in some ways be treated as an engine is developed more fully in **B**9. The idea of energy cost is considered in **C**16.

Routes and times

Basic	Central	Further
Spend more time revising previous work on energy. *1¼ hours*	**Energy: Introduction** (pages 130–131) *¼ hour*	
Omit section **P8.1**. Concentrate on energy transfers. Omit power calculations. *1½ hours*	**P8.1 Power** **Worksheet P8A Power** *1¼ hours*	Mainly revision for faster groups. *¾ hour*
Spend more time on section **P8.2**. Demonstrate a car jack or hoist to calculate energy input and output. *1 hour*	**P8.2 Machines** Include demonstrations of a selection of various machines. *¾ hour*	Section **P8.4** "The efficiency of engines" is suitable for homework.
Omit this section.	**P8.3 Energy cost** *¾ hour*	
Pupils should be guided to investigating force and/or energy.	**Worksheet P8B Using a ramp** This is suitable for an Sc1 investigation. *1½ hours*	Faster groups should investigate efficiency in Worksheet **P8A**. Section **P8.5** "Why do cars have a top speed?" is suitable for homework.
Total: 5¼ hours	*Total: 4½ hours*	*Total: 4 hours*

The pupils' book

P8.1 Power

This is the first chapter which deals with energy, so some time may have to be spent revising earlier ideas. Some questions which cover work assumed to have been done in an earlier year are given in the Introduction to Topic **P3**.

This leads, to the concept of power. The main difficulty here may be with the idea of "rate". For this reason, power is introduced as a way of expressing **how quickly** energy can be transferred. This is then related to the more precise word "rate" which pupils may already have met in Biology.

The concept of power is related to the design of a stair-lift in the pupils' book.

Since "force" and "power" are frequently used interchangeably in everyday speech, it seems worthwhile spending a little time explaining the similarities and differences between the two.

This introduction to power is consolidated by a circus of experiments (Worksheet **P8A**) in which pupils measure their own power in different circumstances. An interesting extension to this (easily tested with the arm ergometer) is a comparison between the maximum rate at which someone can transfer energy, and the rate that could be kept up for several minutes (or even an hour or so). Most measurements show that the human body's "continuous power" rating is about 50 per cent of its maximum power rating. There is usually no lack of fit and healthy youngsters prepared to demonstrate this fact!

Answers to selected questions
2a 3000 J; **b** 250 W.

3a 150 J; **b** 25 W.

P8.2 Machines

P8.3 Energy cost

These two sections introduce the idea that all jobs have a minimum energy cost which cannot be avoided. Machines and engines make it much easier to do many jobs, but often at an increase in the energy cost. The extent to which this cost is increased is measured by the efficiency of the machine or engine.

This leads to an open-ended investigation into the use of the ramp as a simple machine, introduced by Worksheet **P8B**. In contrast to the previous circus of experiments, the pupils are this time left largely to use their own initiative in performing the experiment, so most of two periods will be required for it.

Answers to selected questions
4a 80%; **b** 312.5 W.

5a 50 m; **b** 20 000 J; **c** 500 W.

P8.4 The efficiency of engines

This section looks at the possibilities of improving the efficiency of machines and engines. It ends with a brief look at "heat" engines and shows that some energy wastage is unavoidable. More able pupils may be interested to explore in rather more detail why this energy wastage **is** unavoidable.

Answers to selected questions
9a 1000 J; **b** 1250 J; **c** 80%.

10a 1000 J; **b** 1000 J; **c** 200 N.

P8.5 Why do cars have a top speed?

This extended problem uses partly real data and partly computed data. The frictional force data at various speeds has been computed by setting the top speed of a small car with a 37 kW engine at a speed of just over 80 miles/h and assuming the relationship $F = kv^2$ suggested in the text. k has the value of 0.74 N s^2/m^2.

Power output of a car engine can of course be varied at any road speed by using the engine throttle ("accelerator pedal"). The data in this question refers to an engine's maximum power output at particular speeds. It is this maximum power output that will help determine the maximum acceleration of a car. The maximum power output is the power obtained with the throttle fully open.

The second table in the question shows the way the maximum power output of the engine varies with its speed. All engines behave like this and have a highest maximum power. The difference between the maximum power available at each speed and its variation with speed is a difficult one to grasp (two **different** maxima are involved). This is explained in the text but may well require more verbal explanation.

The data for maximum engine power at various speeds is of course "test-bed" data. The question shows that this particular car is in fact incapable of a level road speed of 38.5 m/s! Test-bed data is given in terms of the number of revolutions the crankshaft of the engine makes every second. This has been converted to equivalent top-gear road speed in order that the data can be compared with the friction-power data.

Despite the assumptions made in the question, the fact that the moped turns out to need an engine of 50 cm^3 capacity is remarkable (or very lucky!).

Answers to selected questions

12a

Speed in m/s	5	10	15	20	25	30	35	40
Power in kW	0.1	0.74	2.51	5.92	11.6	20.0	31.7	47.4

c 37 kW.

d It will be travelling at a steady speed.

e 37 m/s; about 84 miles/h.

13a 37 m/s, same as in question 12.

14 The friction power, assuming the same relationship between friction and speed as for the car, is 1.82 kW (calculated). This means the highest power of the engine should be 1.82 kW. This would give an engine capacity of 49 cm^3.

Activities

Worksheet P8A Power

The experiments described in this worksheet are best set up as a circus. Experiment 5 takes longer to do and work out than the other experiments. It will be necessary to organize the work so that a queue of pupils does not develop at this point in the circus.

REQUIREMENTS

For Experiment 1:
3 sandbags, 10 N each
Stopclock (or watch)
Metre rule
Scales, to weigh bags

For Experiment 2:
"Step" about 30 cm high
Stopclock (or watch)
Metre rule
Personal weighing machine, calibrated in newtons

For Experiment 3:
Stopclock (or watch) Metre rule
Personal weighing machine, calibrated in newtons

Access to:
Flight of stairs

For Experiment 4:
Arm ergometer (joulemeter)
2 sand bags, 10 N each
Force meter, 0–50 N
Stopclock (or watch)

For Experiment 5:
Cycle ergometer (joulemeter)
Stopclock (or watch)

Detailed procedures are given in the worksheet.

Warning

While these experiments on pupil power are perfectly safe for any normally healthy pupil to carry out, it is important to watch out for pupils who have health problems which might be adversely affected by vigorous physical activity or for otherwise healthy pupils who suddenly appear distressed. Colleagues in the PE department should be able to advise teachers. This is preferable to relying on the pupils themselves to provide such information, even though they are given the same warning in the worksheets. It might also be worth advising pupils that these experiments are designed to find **normal** power capacities – they are not competitions designed to identify the most powerful person.

Worksheet P8B Using a ramp

REQUIREMENTS

Access to:
Ramp (see Note)
Metre rule
Pulley on a clamp
Blocks (to give a variable incline)
Tray on which loads can be placed, with hook to attach string
Slotted masses, 2×100 g sets and 2×1 kg sets
String
Force meter, 0–10 N
Dynamics trolley

Note:
A trolley runway would make a suitable ramp. Ramps must be as rigid as possible when supported at each end and will need to be about 2 m long and at least 10 cm wide.

Less-able pupils can investigate the force required and the energy cost by using ramps of different steepness; more-able pupils should be encouraged to investigate efficiency.

There should be enough equipment not to dictate the method of making measurements. The force needed to pull a load up the ramp can be measured directly with a force meter, but adding masses to a string passing over a pulley is a much more accurate method. In this way the force needed to just move the load on the ramp can be determined.

Investigations can be undertaken using or not using a tray to carry the load, varying the size of the load, varying the slope of the ramp, and perhaps varying the surfaces that slide over each other. Some may want to try the trolley – if possible all suggestions should be met with appropriate equipment.

Warning
Pupils need to be warned that falling masses can cause injuries. Some form of protection both for them and for the laboratory should be provided. A cardboard box with some newspapers in it will do. This has the advantage of making it more difficult to put feet and hands in the path of falling masses.

Demonstration experiments

Section P8.2

A car jack will be useful for demonstration purposes. A variety of machines will form useful focal points for discussion. These should be in as realistic a form as possible.

Further information

"Energy transfer" – a video
This deals with the idea of energy transfer in language that matches the treatment of energy in this course (ITV Science in Focus series).

Chapter P9 Keeping yourself warm
Heating: a way of transferring energy

The syllabus section

Context

The transfer of energy by heating is explored in the context of an extended investigation into home heating. Ways in which energy can be transferred from the home are investigated and pupils are encouraged to consider ways this transfer could be reduced.

Knowledge and understanding

Syllabus statements	PoS	SoA
Appreciate that, unlike work, heating as a mode of energy transfer is not measured directly, but in terms of the rise in temperature it can produce.	4(ii)1	4.5(b)
Be able to explain thermal transfer of energy through conduction, convection and radiation, using the ideas of motion of particles and the transmission of energy as waves.	4(ii)2	4.7(b)
Be able to relate the ways in which energy can be transferred by heating to an investigation into "energy efficiency" in home heating.	4(ii)3	4.7(c)
Be able to use the quantitative relationship between change in internal energy and temperature change to calculate temperature rises (specific heating capacity).	4(ii)1	4.8(b)
Understand that, although energy is always conserved, in many processes it is inevitably spread out into the surroundings and so it becomes harder to arrange for further useful energy transfers.	4(ii)6	4.10(b)

Tier: B C F

Opportunities for co-ordination

C13 makes use of the equation $E = mcT$ in order to measure the energy which can be transferred from a measured mass of fuel, and deals with comparisons of fuel costs. Energy and recycling (in terms of glass) are discussed in **C**6.

The transfer of energy that is involved when the temperature of a living organism is higher than its environment is dealt with in **B**9, **B**12 and **B**14. **E**1 deals with the roles of conduction, convection and radiation in the causes of various weather phenomena.

Routes and times

Basic	Central	Further
Worksheet **P9A** is a suitable Sc1 assessment at Basic level. *1³/₄ hours*	**P9.1 What should I wear today?** **Worksheet P9A Investigating warm materials** This could be used as an Sc1 assessment if Worksheet P9C is demonstrated. *³/₄ hour*	Optional /revision for faster groups; no class time given.
Part 2 of the home heating investigation only. Concentrate on survey of energy saving systems.	**P9.2 Keeping your home warm** (class + homework) *1 hour*	
Omit this section.	**P9.3 Measuring energy transfers** Q6 and 8 are optional. **Worksheet P9C Heating water** This could be used as an Sc1 assessment if Worksheet P9A is demonstrated. *1³/₄ hours*	Omit Q6–9 from section **P9.3**. Worksheet **P9D** "How efficient is your electric kettle?" could be set as homework.
Total: 2³/₄ hours	*Total: 3¹/₂ hours*	*Total: 2³/₄ hours*

The pupils' book

This unit of work has been written on the assumption that pupils can carry out, simultaneously with the work in class, an investigation into heating their homes. If this can be done, then probably all work out of school will be devoted to this project. Some pupils will probably need more "class time" support for this project than others. Such pupils could omit Worksheet **P9D** and even Worksheet **P9C**.

Under some circumstances, the "home heating" project may not be feasible. It might be possible to apply the project, to a school building or a boarding house – particularly if the project is carried out on a "group" basis with several pupils co-operating. Where circumstances do not permit the project to be undertaken at all, alternative material connected with the use of energy resources for home heating is suggested below. (See under Further information.) The computer program "CEDRIC", published by British Gas, enables some interesting quantitative work to be undertaken by pupils with access to a computer.

P9.1 What should I wear today?

The work on heating is introduced by an investigation into materials which can be used to keep people warm. Investigations of this sort need not take up a great deal of time in order to be useful. This particular investigation is the same as the one called "Survival" used by the Assessment of Performance Unit in testing investigational skills at age 13 +. Pupils who took part in the tests were only given half an hour in which to carry out the investigation. Older pupils should be able, with advantage, to spend rather more time on it, but even so should derive useful experience within the space of a double period.

Although Worksheet **P9A** is written as though for an individual experiment, the work could be organized in a number of different ways. Small groups could co-operate in a single investigation, or a class could be split into groups, with each group undertaking an agreed task. If the latter strategy is adopted, there will need to be time for the class to pool their findings.

The assessment of the investigation "Survival" is given detailed discussion on pages 5–13 of the Assessment of Performance Unit's *Science report for teachers 3: "Science at age 13"*.

Monitoring the progress of Sc1

Investigating the cooling of coffee

Students should investigate what affects how fast a cup of coffee cools. This investigation may be carried out instead of Worksheet **P9A** "Investigating warm materials".

Sample criteria are given below for an assessment between levels 4 and 10.

Strand (i) Ask questions, predict and hypothesize, e.g.	Strand (ii) Observe, measure and manipulate variables, e.g.	Strand (iii) Interpret their results and evaluate scientific evidence, e.g.
4(a) Suggest that volume matters and suggest how the rate might depend on the volume	**4(b)** Control initial temperature and time how long it takes two different volumes of coffee to cool to the same final temperature	**4(c)** Conclude that a big cup of coffee cools more slowly than a small cup of coffee
5(a) Suggest that a large cup of coffee cools more slowly than a small cup of coffee because there is more coffee there	**5(b)** Time how long it takes two different volumes of coffee to cool over a meaningful range of temperature	**5(c)** Conclude that a big cup of coffee cools more slowly than a small cup of coffee, but qualifying the conclusion
6(a) Suggest that the larger the volume, the slower the cooling because there is more coffee there	**6(b)** Time how long it takes a range of different volumes of coffee to cool over a meaningful range of temperature	**6(c)** Conclude that increasing the volume reduces the rate of cooling because the larger volume has more energy
7(a) Suggest, with reasons, that size of container, volume of liquid and initial temperature all affect the rate of cooling, and that the most important of these is volume	**7(b)** Time how long it takes different volumes of coffee to cool starting from a range of initial temperatures	**7(c)** Conclude that the volume of coffee has a bigger effect on the rate of cooling than the initial temperature over a range of volumes and temperatures between 60 and 80°C
8(a) Suggest, with reasons, that the time to cool between the same two temperatures is doubled if the volume of coffee is doubled and suggest a relevant investigation	**8(b)** As above, measuring temperatures to 0.5 °C and volume to 0.5 ml	**8(c)** Explain why the volume was kept constant for a range of temperatures and why the temperature interval was kept constant for a range of volumes
9(a) Suggest that the time to cool between the same two temperatures is doubled if the volume of coffee is doubled and suggest a relevant investigation; also suggests repeating the experiment	**9(b)** Carry out the above procedure systematically	**9(c)** Use the data from repeated experiments to draw graphs of results and to show that the rate of cooling decreases with volume; comment on the accuracy of the experiment
10(a) Suggest that the time to cool between the same two temperatures depends on the ratio of surface area to volume	**10(b)** As above, and calculates surface area; checks thermometer	**10(c)** Use the data from repeated experiments to draw graphs of results and to show that the rate of cooling depends on the ratio of surface area to volume; comments on the accuracy of the experiment

P9.2 Keeping your home warm

This section is concerned with setting up the "home heating" investigation. The first task is to collect data on the use of energy for heating the home. The important point being made here is that very little energy indeed has to be used to raise the temperature of a cold home to a comfortable level. Energy is mainly used to replace that being lost from the home to the "outside world".

It will take a week to collect enough data to show the use being made of electricity, gas, oil or coal. The second part of the investigation involves looking at the ways in which energy loss is being limited in any particular home or building. This work can proceed simultaneously with the collection of energy usage data. At the end of a week it should be possible to bring the two parts of the investigation together and suggest how it may be possible to reduce losses in a given home or building.

Some may feel it is worthwhile spreading this investigation over a longer period. In this case, all the laboratory and class work of the chapter can be completed in the suggested time, but the project can be allowed to extend over a longer period.

Less able pupils can carry out an investigation in which they survey the "insulation" features of their homes and those of friends and relatives. They should recognize common good and bad features, and make recommendations for improvements.

The class work associated with this section is concerned with a survey of the ways in which energy can be transferred from a room. The emphasis is on conduction and convection as the physical means of energy transfer. Useful material to support this work can be obtained from many manufacturers and also from government agencies concerned with "energy saving". Some examples are given in the Further information section.

The process of "free" and "forced" convection should be discussed: the pupils' book provides a context.

P9.3 Measuring energy transfers

The remainder of the chapter is devoted to measuring energy transferred by heating. This will be a sufficient length of time as this mode of measuring energy transfer is taken up again in Chemistry in Topic **C4**.

The transfer of energy from a hot object to a colder one is referred to as "heating". The text emphasizes that energy transferred in this way can bring about the same changes that can come about when work is involved. Both heating and working can raise the temperature of an object. When work is involved we measure the energy transferred from the forces and distances involved. There is no direct way of measuring the energy transferred by heating. We can measure the effect of the energy transfer – namely the rise in temperature it produces. All we can do at this point is see how the rise in temperature of an object might be related to the energy transferred to it.

A computer data-logger may be used to monitor the temperatures of a 1 kg block of aluminium, and 1 kg and ½ kg masses of water, all heated by identical heaters. Pupils explain the different temperature rises.

The concept of specific heating capacity (s.h.c.) is introduced, but cannot be measured until we have some means of relating temperature rise to the transfer of a known quantity of energy. This comes in Chapter **P10**. Figures for specific heating capacities are taken "on trust" and likened to the price labels that are put on vegetables. Worksheet **P9C** provides outline details of an experiment to test the relationship between energy transferred, mass and temperature rise. A Help sheet has also been prepared for those pupils who need it.

Finally, Worksheet **P9D** is intended as an extension to the work for the fastest pupils to try.

Answers to selected questions
7 £1.65; 84p; 64p; £1.55

10 Water.

11 Copper.

12a 1800 J; **b** 31 200 J.

13 3350 J.

14 204 000 J.

Activities

Worksheet P9A Investigating warm materials

REQUIREMENTS

Each group of pupils will need:
Stopclock (or watch)
Thermometer
Cans to hold warm water
Lagging materials, at least 4 different types, e.g.
  cotton, wool, plastic, nylon/wool mixture
Scissors

Sticky tape
Rubber bands
Pins

Access to:
Hair-dryer or fan, to blow cold air

This is an open-ended investigation and pupils devise their own experiments – which should nevertheless be checked for suitability and safety by the teacher.

Worksheet P9B Reading gas and electricity meters
Worksheet P9C Heating water

REQUIREMENTS

Each group of pupils will need:
Polystyrene beaker
Thermometer
Measuring cylinder, 250 cm³
Immersion heater, 12 V
Power supply, 12 V a.c.

Stopclock (or watch)
Joulemeter, electric (if available)

Access to:
Top-pan balance

The normal procedure is to use a clock to time how long an immersion heater has been switched on and to use this time as a measure of the energy transferred. Some pupils – and particularly those who find it more difficult to understand the experiment – benefit by having a joulemeter connected to the immersion heater. The joulemeter gives a direct reading of the energy transferred to the water.

Joulemeters of the pattern used for A-level work are expensive and would only be used here for demonstration purposes. However, simpler (and cheaper) joulemeters are now available. It may well be worth using them in this experiment.

Warning
Some low-voltage immersion heaters of the sealed sort have been known to explode. Do not use any in which the seal is cracked or deficient in any other way and do not allow the seals to be immersed in water.

Worksheet P9D How efficient is your electric kettle?

REQUIREMENTS

Each group of pupils will need:

Electric kettle

Measuring cylinder, 1000 cm³

Thermometer

Stopclock or watch

This is an optional experiment which can be set for homework. Pupils may have to estimate the temperature of tap water.

Warning

Although boiling a kettle is an everyday task, ten such kettles full of boiling water in a crowded laboratory could spell disaster. If in doubt demonstrate.

Further information

Children's Learning in Science Project

"Aspects of secondary students' understanding of heat: summary report"

   This report draws upon the results of the Assessment of Performance Unit (APU) testing scheme to show the difficulties many children have with the meaning of "heat" and "temperature". The report is particularly useful in highlighting the different ways in which children will use and come across the word "heat" in everyday conversation. It is for this reason that the policy has been adopted in Nuffield Co-ordinated Sciences of not using "heat" as a noun.

British Gas

"Domestic gas meters – how to read them"

"Transference of heat"

A short video that surveys ways in which energy can be transferred by heating. (Note that "heat" is used here as a noun for a "form of energy".)

There is a wide range of additional material available to support this work. The following list gives only a few suggestions.

- Advertising material on home insulation and double glazing – many manufacturers will provide material on request.
- *Energy package* – available free of charge from the Energy Efficiency Office.
- "CEDRIC 2" – a computer program available from British Gas, to run on BBC or RML machines. This program enables pupils to put in their own data and find out the consequences for energy usage in home heating.
- "Energy" – a video which concentates on methods of identifying and reducing energy losses from buildings by heating (ITV Science and Technology series).

Chapter **P10** Ideas in physics
Energy and change in temperature

The syllabus section

Context

The transfer of energy by heating is explored in the context of an extended investigation into home heating. Ways in which energy can be transferred from the home are investigated and pupils are encouraged to consider ways this transfer could be reduced.

Knowledge and understanding

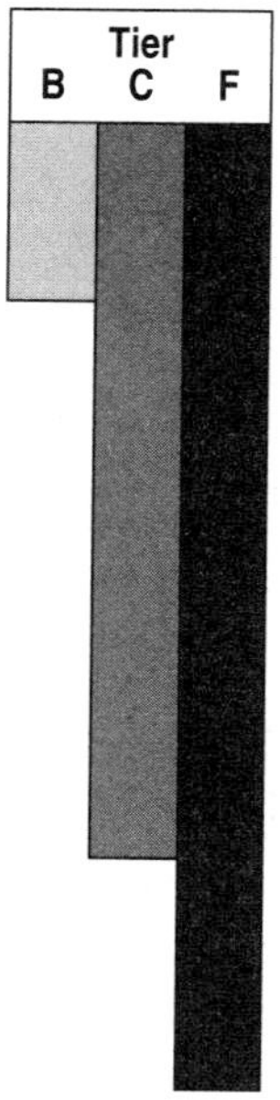

Syllabus statements	PoS	SoA
Appreciate that, unlike work, heating as a mode of energy transfer is not measured directly, but in terms of the rise in temperature it can produce.	4(ii)1	4.5(b)
Be able to explain thermal transfer of energy through conduction, convection and radiation, using the ideas of motion of particles and the transmission of energy as waves.	4(ii)2	4.7(b)
Be able to relate the ways in which energy can be transferred by heating to an investigation into "energy efficiency" in home heating.	4(ii)3	4.7(c)
Be able to use the quantitative relationship between change in internal energy and temperature change to calculate temperature rises (specific heating capacity).	4(ii)1	4.8(b)
Understand that, although energy is always conserved, in many processes it is inevitably spread out into the surroundings and so it becomes harder to arrange for further useful energy transfers.	4(ii)6	4.10(b)

Opportunities for co-ordination

C13 makes use of the equation $E = mcT$ in order to measure the energy which can be transferred from a measured mass of fuel, and deals with comparisons of fuel costs. Energy and recycling (in terms of glass) are discussed in **C**6.

The transfer of energy that is involved when the temperature of a living organism is higher than its environment is dealt with in **B**9, **B**12 and **B**14. **E**1 deals with the roles of conduction, convection and radiation in the causes of various weather phenomena.

Routes and times

	Basic	Central	Further

Central

> **P10.1 Scientific theories**
> ¼ hour

Further

This is suitable for reading homework.

> **P10.3 A kinetic theory of heating**
> **P10.4 Energy and temperature**
> ¾ hour

Replace section **P10.3** by section **P10.2** "The 'caloric' theory versus the 'kinetic' theory".

Basic

Simple energy transfer sequences should be revised.

> **P10.6 The conservation of energy**
> Demonstrate the experiments on page 170.
> 1 hour

> **P10.5 Comparing energy transfers**
> AND/OR
> **Worksheet P10A Measuring a rise in internal energy**
> **Worksheet P10B Estimating the specific heating capacity of lead**
> 1 hour

> **Worksheet P10C Energy conservation**
> ¾ hour

> **P10.7 Changes: from liquid to gas and solid to liquid**
> Optional

Total: 2 hours   Total: 2 hours   Total: 3½ hours

The pupils' book

The questions in this chapter ask for qualitative answers only.

This chapter, like Chapter **P5**, is concerned with scientific theories. In Chapter **P5**, pupils were presented with two different explanations of the cause of motion, and they set up experiments of their own to find out which explanation seemed the better. The theory eventually adopted (that in the absence of a force a body's motion cannot be changed) will probably have been new to most pupils and at first sight is by no means an obvious theory to apply to the world around them.

This chapter deals with explanations for changes in temperature. Unlike the work on forces, the theory eventually seen to be the better of the two (the kinetic theory) will already be familiar to pupils. A link between temperature change and the kinetic energy of particles is established in Chapter **P2** and pupils may already have met the idea of linking temperature with particle movement in an earlier year.

In the span of time that pupils can spend on Physics as a part of their general education, there is inevitably much that they have to take on trust. However, it seems important that pupils should at least realize that the models and theories presented to them are all based on careful thought and experimentation, and often represent the best (at present) of several conflicting alternatives.

The kinetic theory of matter, by its importance, justifies more than a simple description. So in this chapter it is set against the (historically older) caloric theory. After seeing a series of demonstration experiments in which the temperature of a body changes, pupils are asked to "explain" each set of observations in terms of both theories. At the end of their discussions they should see that the kinetic theory is better at giving an explanation of all the observations than the caloric theory.

Objections can be raised to setting the kinetic theory against the caloric theory in this way. Historically there was no such competition. The caloric theory was first of all replaced by establishing a link between energy transfer and temperature rise, in experiments such as the one in which Rumford drilled out cannons with blunt borers. The caloric theory was unable to explain these observations, but the then newly emerging concept of energy transfer could.

The kinetic theory of matter was established **after** the concepts of energy transfer and energy conservation had been understood. A model for matter based on moving particles gives a further explanation of what happens to the energy that is transferred when the temperature of an object changes.

However, the present approach does not try to suggest that the choice between the caloric theory and the kinetic theory is an historical one. It is felt that pupils may find it easier to grasp the picture of moving particles presented by the kinetic theory than the more abstract concept of "internal energy". So the account moves **from** this particle model **to** a more general interpretation of energy changes within a body, rather than the other way round.

P10.1 Scientific theories

The opening section looks at the important place theories (or "scientific explanations") have in science. More often than not these ideas of how or why things happen determine the direction of a scientist's research. As in Chapter **P5**, no attempt is made to distinguish between "theory" and "hypothesis". It is felt that such a distinction (if one really exists) would be beyond the understanding of pupils at this level.

P10.2 The "caloric" theory versus the "kinetic" theory

At this point in the chapter pupils can proceed by one of two routes. Many pupils will get interest and pleasure from trying to apply two different theories to the same set of experiments. But others may simply find this confusing. For the latter, the alternative section **P10.3** looks simply at the way the kinetic theory can be used to explain changes in temperature without bothering about the caloric theory.

The caloric theory and the kinetic theory are both introduced as simple explanations of what happens when things get hot. The pupils are then presented with four different experiments. For each one they are asked to say what **each** of the two theories will predict. They are then asked to observe what happens and to say which of the two theories seems the best at explaining this particular observation.

Both theories would predict a rise in temperature in Experiment 1 and in Experiment 2. As a rise in temperature is in fact found, there is nothing to distinguish between the two theories. In Experiments 3 and 4, however, only the kinetic theory predicts a change in temperature. So the kinetic theory is more successful than the caloric theory in predicting what will happen in each of these experiments.

The section concludes with a brief account of the historical evolution of the kinetic theory. The theory is seen to result from the atomic theory of John Dalton and others, combined with the relationship between energy and temperature which came from the work of such scientists as James Joule.

P10.3 A kinetic theory of heating

This is an alternative to section **P10.2**. It shows how the kinetic theory is able to explain the link between temperature rise and energy transfer. It limits itself to Experiments 3 and 4 in the last section and gives no consideration to the caloric theory as an alternative explanation.

P10.4 Energy and temperature

This short section links the kinetic theory to a more general relationship between energy transfer and change in temperature. It describes something of the contribution of the work of Joule and Mayer to the development of these ideas.

P10.5 Comparing energy transfers

Again, two alternative routes are suggested. This section shows how the relationship between energy and temperature change can be used to measure the specific heating capacity of a material. The way that specific heating capacities could be determined was left as an open question at the end of Chapter **P9**. More able pupils may be able to see that experiments such as these are necessary at some point in the determination of specific heating capacities. But once one specific heating capacity (say that of water) has been established in this way, it can be used as a standard in rather more convenient methods of establishing the specific heating capacity of other substances.

P10.6 The conservation of energy

The idea that energy is conserved (that is, not lost or gained in any interchange) will probably have been a part of the earliest teaching in energy. This is not, however, our everyday experience. Words such as "energy crisis" imply that we are continually using something that cannot be replaced. In pupils' early work on energy they may have learned that in fact energy becomes less useful when used and that this is why we seem to be "running out" of energy.

The relationship between temperature change and energy is a fundamental part of the concept of energy conservation. But the fact that energy is never lost does not solve the problem of the "energy crisis" if in many cases the energy cannot be re-used.

The time spent on this section will depend on the extent to which pupils may find it helpful to repeat energy transfer experiments performed in earlier years, and the time already spent on the work of earlier sections. More able pupils may enjoy the challenge set by Worksheet **P10C** in which they are asked to transfer as much of 10 J of energy to the kinetic energy of a trolley as they can.

P10.7 Changes: from liquid to gas and solid to liquid

The final section extends the idea of energy transfer to the particles of matter to consider what happens when a liquid changes to a gas, or a solid to a liquid. The idea of "internal energy" – that is, the energy associated with the particles of matter – is extended to include potential as well as kinetic energy. In this way we can understand how it is that heating can lead to a change of state without any change in temperature.

The chapter ends by looking briefly at the role of mathematics in physics. It is suggested that its use is in making predictions from theories and that being able to understand mathematics is not essential to understanding theories. Some hint is offered to the pupils of the way our ideas about energy have now been further extended by Einstein's work.

Activities

Worksheet P10A Measuring a rise in internal energy

REQUIREMENTS

Each group of pupils will need:
Mechanical heating apparatus and accessories
Electric heating accessories for the above, if available

Note:

There are a number of alternative versions of this equipment on the market. The actual equipment varies too much from one manufacturer to another to be able to give a detailed list.

The aim of the experiment is to transfer a measured amount of energy to the cylinder and measure the temperature rise which results. There may be a lag between the time when the pupil stops turning the handle and when the temperature stops rising. It is important to read the maximum temperature reached. The results can be used to give an approximate specific heating capacity for the metal of which the cylinder is made.

Accurate results will not be obtained, but the experiment is important as a matter of principle and a very useful vehicle for discussion of the sources of experimental error.

The experiment can be extended to electrical heating. A comparison between the energy transferred by the two methods to produce the same temperature rise in the metal cylinder amounts to a direct "check" on the calibrations on the voltmeter. Pupils may encounter just such an experiment if they continue their study of Physics beyond this course.

Warning

Pupils need to be warned that falling masses can cause injuries. Some form of protection for both them and the laboratory should be provided. A cardboard box with some newspapers in it will do. This has the advantage of making it more difficult to put feet and hands in the path of falling masses.

Worksheet P10B Estimating the specific heating capacity of lead

REQUIREMENTS

Each group of pupils will need:
Tube, cardboard or similar, 50 cm long, about 5 cm diameter with bungs or corks for both ends
Lead shot, 0.5 kg
Polystyrene beaker
Metre rule
Balance, 0–1 kg
Thermometer with 0.1°C gradations

Procedure

A detailed procedure is given in the worksheet. There is of course no need to know the mass of the lead shot in order to work out its specific heating capacity from this experiment. But pupils may find it easier to weigh the shot and use its value, first to find the energy transferred to the lead itself in falling, and then to work out the specific heating capacity.

Warning

Do not inhale dust from the lead shot. Wash hands after the experiment.

Worksheet P10C Energy conservation

REQUIREMENTS

Each group of pupils will need:

Dynamics trolley
Runway for trolley
End stop
Mass, 1 kg
Metre rule

String
Electronic timer
Lamp and photodetector, and supports for them
Card: 20 cm by 8 cm

Pupils use the energy from a falling mass to accelerate a trolley. The procedure is given on the worksheet.

Warning

Pupils need to be warned that falling masses can cause injuries. Some form of protection for both them and the laboratory should be provided.

Demonstration and pupil experiments

Section P10.2

Experiments illustrated in figure 10.7 of the pupils' book:

REQUIREMENTS

For Experiment 1:
Beaker, glass, 400 cm³
Thermometer
Bunsen burner
Tripod
Gauze
Heatproof mat

For Experiment 2:
2 beakers, 400 cm³, one containing hot
    water, the other cold water
Thermometer

For Experiment 3:
The same equipment as for Worksheet **P**10A.

For Experiment 4:
The same equipment as for Worksheet **P**10B.

Section P10.6

REQUIREMENTS

Optional (see figure 10.18 in the pupils' book)

This work involves the pupils in a wide variety of energy transfer demonstrations, set out as a circus. A range of experiments is illustrated in figure 10.18 of the pupils' book. Pupils may have come across these experiments in their work in Year 9, but many will find it helpful to discuss them again in terms of energy conservation and whether the energy is finally re-usable.

Further information

Children's Learning in Science Project
"Secondary students' ideas about particles" and "Secondary students" understanding of heat". Both these booklets provide helpful information on two ideas that many pupils find difficult. They are based on an analysis of the answers to questions obtained from tests administered by the Assessment of Performance Unit.

Chapter P11   Energy where it is needed
Energy transmission

The syllabus section

Context

This section is concerned with the problem of getting energy to the place where it is needed. The importance of efficient transmission of energy by an electric current is recognised and the performance of transmission lines and transformers occupies most of this section. Nevertheless, the advantages of other means of energy transmission are also considered.

Knowledge and understanding

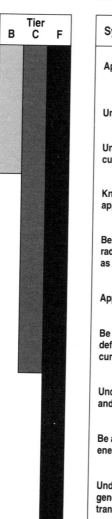

	Tier	
B	C	F

Syllabus statements	PoS	SoA
Appreciate the need for the transmission of energy.	4(i)1 4(ii)1	4.4(b)
Understand that energy can be transferred from fuels to electricity by dynamos.	4(i)5	4.5(b)
Understand, qualitatively, the effect of changing the voltage and resistance on the current flowing in a circuit.	4(i)6	4.6(a)
Know that an electric current itself has a magnetic field and that this can be applied to the design of electromagnets used in motors, relays and loudspeakers.	4(i)4	4.7(a)
Be able to explain thermal transfer of energy through conduction, convection and radiation, using the concepts of motion of particles and the transmission of energy as waves.	4(ii)2	4.7(b)
Appreciate the problems involved in the electrical transmission of energy.	4(ii)3	4.7(c)
Be able to explain that an electric current is a flow of electric charge and use the definition of the volt as a joule per coulomb to explain the energy transfer when a current flows.	4(i)7	4.8(a)
Understand the limitations and implications of worldwide patterns of distribution and use of energy resources.	4(ii)8	—
Be able to evaluate the economic, environmental and social benefits of different energy sources, and their transmission.	4(ii)9	4.9(b)
Understand the principles of electromagnetic induction by investigating the generation and transmission of electricity and devices such as dynamos and transformers.	4(i)5	4.10(a)

Routes and times

Basic	Central	Further
Spend more time on this section. *1½ hours*	**P11.1 Energy on the move** **P11.2 Generators** Include dynamo demonstration. *1¼ hours*	Omit section **P11.2** (covered in Chapter **P18**). Section **P11.3** "Using energy resources in the best way" is also suitable.
Omit section **P11.4**; some pupils will benefit from seeing power line demonstrations, however. *½ hour*	**P11.4 Transmitting electricity** Include power line demonstration. *1¼ hours*	
		P11.5 Transformers Include induction demonstrations. **Worksheet P11A Transformers** This is suitable for an Sc1 assessment. *1½ hours*
	P11.6 Other methods of energy transmission *¼ hour*	This section should be read for homework.
Total: 2¼ hours	*Total: 2¾ hours*	*Total: 4 hours*

The pupils' book

The work of this chapter centres around sections **P11.4** and **P11.5** in the pupils' book. Both of these sections involve laboratory work, much of which will consist of demonstration experiments.
Demonstration experiments play a large part in this work for two reasons:

- equipment based on transformers may be in too short a supply for individual experiments
- power line experiments using transformers involve dangerously high voltages. (The "a.c. power line" demonstration must be set up and supervised by a competent person and must comply with the "Electricity at Work" guidance note GS23 from the Health and Safety Executive, and IEC 1010–1.)

A further benefit conferred by demonstration experiments is the extent to which the class can discuss together the observations made when energy is transmitted along a "power line". Even so, some laboratories may have sufficient equipment to set up several transmission lines. In this case pupils can work in small groups, using the questions in the book as a basis for their own investigations.
It is likely that this central section of the work will take 3 or 4 periods. The time taken will depend on the extent to which pupils pursue the extensions to the work in sections **P11.4** and **P11.5**. One period, with the addition of possible homework, should be left to the last section and Worksheet **P11B**. The introductory section can be covered in a single period by more able pupils, but will need longer if section **P11.2** is to be included.

P11.1 Energy on the move

This introductory section looks at the need to move energy resources to the places where they are needed. The phrase "energy transmission" has been chosen to describe this; "energy transfer", introduced in Chapter **P8**, means something rather different. The delivery of coal and oil to houses by lorry and tanker are both methods of getting energy to places where it is needed. Natural gas is distributed through a network of underground pipes which make up an important method of transmitting energy for heating. However, nowadays the prime method of distributing energy to homes, industry, offices and public buildings is by electricity transmission lines.

To understand how electricity can be used as a means of energy distribution from primary sources such as fossil fuels, pupils will need to understand something about generators and dynamos. They may already have acquired a sufficient understanding from their work with Chapter **P**18. Those who have not are given a simple treatment of the ideas in section **P**11.2.

P11.2 Generators

This approach to the transfer of energy using electricity builds on some previous work pupils will have done in making an electric motor. Electric motors depend on an interaction between an electric current and a magnetic field to produce motion. This result is looked at as an "equation", with electric current and magnetic field on one side and motion on the other. Rearranging the equation suggests that motion (of a wire) in a magnetic field might produce an electric current.

It is ideas such as these that set Michael Faraday on his search for induced currents. Today we have the advantage of much more sensitive measuring instruments than he had, so the possibility of induced currents is easily tested by experiment. An experimental investigation is proposed in question 4 of the pupils' book. This could be undertaken by pupils in the laboratory. Then a mounted bicycle dynamo can be demonstrated. It may be helpful at this point to look at the sort of current this dynamo produces – one that surges backwards and forwards. This can be contrasted with the current from a dry battery, which flows in one direction only.

While the experiments emphasize the production of induced currents, the currents themselves are seen as a means of transferring energy. Generators and dynamos are described in the pupils' book as devices which can transfer energy from fuels to elsewhere, using the flow of electric charge (or simply "electricity" for short) in order to do this. This is a more accurate and more easily understood approach than to say that dynamos transfer energy to electric charge, and that this energy is then used elsewhere. This latter statement seems to imply that electricity can somehow store up energy for future use – and this is not the case.

P11.3 Using energy resources in the best way

This section is for pupils who have already spent some time investigating induced currents during work on Chapter **P**18. It explores two possible schemes for distributing energy on an imaginary island of Pylos, which has a single coal mine.

In investigating the efficiency of both schemes, pupils will need to recognize that energy wastage is more than losing energy to the surroundings by, say, burning coal and passing electric currents through wires, although both of these will be important. Paying people to deliver coal "costs" energy; so does building large power stations, or even small generators.

On the other hand, all members of a community need to be supported by food, energy, buildings and services. It might be preferable for the community to have a "labour-intensive" system for getting energy where it is needed if the alternative is that labour goes unused.

Arguments such as these, which may well appeal to more able pupils, show that decisions over alternatives in any field where technology can be applied are not easily made. The arguments are complex and it is difficult to know whether every factor has been considered.

Whatever conclusions are reached, work in Chapter **P**12 will show that the arguments over the best system of energy distribution are far from over.

P11.4 Transmitting electricity

(There is a short discussion about the use of the word "electricity" in the Introduction to Topic **P**5.)

This section is centred around an experiment with a model "power line". The power line is made of "resistance" wire, so that the effects of a real power line can be simulated in the short distances possible in a laboratory.

In the experiment, a 12 V lamp connected directly to a 12 V power pack (representing the power station) is found to be fully lit. Another lamp connected to the far end of the power line is lit only dimly. Measurements with a voltmeter show that in the transfer of the energy from the power pack to the distant lamp, much of it is "lost".

The power line is now rebuilt using transformers. This experiment must be demonstrated, even if the first one is not, as dangerously high voltages are involved. No attempt is made to explain the action of the transformers – they are "black boxes" which connect the power line to the power pack at one end and to the lamp at the other. At once it is seen that the two lamps (one connected to the power pack and the other at the far end of the power line) are equally bright. Voltmeter measurements show there has been little energy loss along the power line. But the voltage across the input and output ends of the power line is found to be 240 V, rather than 12 V. This leads on to the next section, which investigates how transformers work.

P11.5 Transformers

This section includes a simple introduction to induced currents, which can be omitted by pupils who have already covered this in Chapter **P**18. It is assumed that the experiments described in the pupils' book will either be demonstrated, or set out as a circus of experiments. If the latter course is adopted, the questions in the pupils' book will serve as a pointer to the pupils' own investigations.

These experiments lead directly to the transformer and the energy transfers that take place when it is in use. Finally the section ends with an investigation into the way the input and output voltages of a transformer are related to the numbers of turns on the coils.

For some pupils this may be a sufficient treatment of power lines. They will have learned that power lines transmit energy more efficiently if they work at a high voltage rather than a low one. They will have seen that transformers are capable of changing a.c. voltages and that despite the fact that transformers themselves waste some energy, their use can lead to considerable savings in transferring energy electrically.

Other pupils will want to know why there should be a difference in the energy wasted when low and high voltages are used. This section concludes with a more detailed investigation into the voltages and currents along power lines. It shows that transferring power electrically at a high voltage means a lower current in the transmission lines than if the same power is transmitted at a low voltage.

Energy loss comes from heating of the surroundings by the transmission lines through which the current is passing. The smaller the current, the lower the rate at which energy is transferred to the surroundings. So it is more efficient to transfer power at a high voltage than at a low voltage.

The section concludes with a brief reference to the National Grid and then asks some numerical questions about transmitting power electrically.

P11.6 Other methods of energy transmission

The introduction to this chapter showed that electricity is not the only method by which energy can be distributed. This final section looks at two more methods. Belt drives are still important where it is necessary to transmit energy over small distances. Hydraulic transmission of energy was once very important indeed. Over long distances it has largely been replaced by electricity. On a smaller scale, however, it still has a number of advantages.

In the future it may be necessary to replace one major energy resource not previously mentioned in this chapter, namely oil. Because it is a highly concentrated energy resource, it is extensively used for transport. Apart from modern rocket engines, no replacement for fuels extracted from oil has yet been found for use in air travel. Worksheet **P**11B reproduces two articles on possible modes of energy distribution in the future and asks pupils to think about some of their implications.

Activities

Worksheet P11A Transformers

Experiment 1 (demonstration)

REQUIREMENTS

Demountable transformer with 1 coil of 3600 turns
Lamp, 2.5 V MES
Lamp holder, MES

Wire, 4 m, flexible, insulated (one of the wires from twin lamp flex is better than solid core insulated wire)

Procedure

Place the 3600-turn coil on one leg of the laminated U-core of the demountable transformer. Connect it to the 240 V a.c. mains supply.

Connect the long flexible lead to the lamp holder with the lamp.

Switch on the 240 V a.c. supply and wind the long wire **turn by turn** round the other leg of the U-core. As more and more turns are wound on, the lamp begins to glow and then gets brighter and brighter. At least 25 turns will be necessary for this.

Provided a spare lamp is available, try placing the I-yoke across the top of the U-core.

Warning

The connections between the mains and the transformer must be made using a mains lead which has two layers of insulation over the conductors, and a proper plug and socket. Present standards prohibit the use of any mains lead with 4 mm plugs attached, or exposed wires.

Experiment 2

(This experiment may be a demonstration or group work, depending on the available equipment.)

REQUIREMENTS

Demountable transformer with 300, 600 and 1200 turn coils
or
2 C-cores with 60+60 turn and 120+120 turn coils

2 voltmeters, 10 V a.c. (ideally these should be demonstration instruments if this experiment is demonstrated to the whole class)
Low voltage power supply, 2 V a.c.
Connecting leads

Procedure

The circuit is set up as shown in Worksheet **P**11A. For use as a step-up transformer, a 2 V a.c. input is convenient. Outputs can range from 2 V to 8 V.

Faster groups can also see what happens if the output is used to light a lamp and the input and output currents are measured as well as the voltages.

Warning

If equipment is provided for pupils to carry out their own experiments it is important that no combination of transformer coils and input supply voltage can produce an output voltage in excess of 25 V. (See Health and Safety Executive Guidance Note 23 *Electrical safety in schools*: 18.) If 60 + 60 and 120 + 120 turn coils are used in conjunction with the low voltage (2 V a.c.) power supplies, as suggested, the maximum output voltage is 8 V.

Problem

REQUIREMENTS

Each group of pupils will need:
2 C-cores
Wire, pvc insulated solid core, 3 m
Lamp, 6 V MES

Lamp holder, MES
Power supply, 2 V a.c.

Pupils are set the challenge of lighting the 6 V lamp fully with the equipment provided.

Worksheet P11B Using hydrogen

This considers the future of hydrogen as a fuel.

Other demonstrations and pupil experiments

Section P11.2: To show that moving a conductor in a magnetic field produces an electric current

REQUIREMENTS

Each group of pupils will need:
Model motor (as constructed in Chapter **P**18)
Galvanometer
Connecting leads

Note:
Centre-zero galvanometers are ideal for this experiment, but many school meters allow for the measurement of small currents in both directions. Choice of a suitable instrument is best determined by trial and error beforehand.

The bicycle dynamo (demonstration)

REQUIREMENTS

Bicycle dynamo assembly
Meter, demonstration (or galvanometer), with
  2.5–0–2.5 mA scale or similar
Oscilloscope

Lamp, 6 V MES
Holder, MES
Connecting leads

Use the low-speed gearing on the dynamo assembly to demonstrate the output of the dynamo. The a.c. character can also be shown using the oscilloscope.

Driving the dynamo at a higher speed can light a lamp attached across its output, thus demonstrating the energy transfer from the operator to the lamp.

This experiment will have to be demonstrated when using a centre-zero galvanometer. Over-vigorous handle turning will permanently damage the meter movement.

Section P11.4: 12 V model power line

REQUIREMENTS

Each group of pupils will need:
Pair of power line terminal rods
2 bare Eureka wires, each 1.25 m long,
  0.40 mm diameter
2 stands and bosses

2 lamps, 12 V, 24 W
2 lamp holders, SBC
Power supply, 12 V a.c.
Connecting leads

The equipment is set up as shown in figure 11.16 in the pupils' book. Whether the experiment is done by the pupils or as a demonstration, it will save time and avoid confusion if the "pylons" and the transmission line are set up beforehand.

For each set, two dowels form the power line terminal rods. They are held horizontally in bosses at a height of about 30 to 50 cm above the bench and 1 m or more apart. Two lengths of high resistance (Eureka) wire are stretched between the terminals to form the power line.

The observations to be made are suggested in the pupils' book.

High-voltage model power line (demonstration)

REQUIREMENTS

One set of equipment from the 12 V model   2 pairs of C-cores with clips
  power line experiment, plus: 2 coils, 120 turns, to fit C-cores
Insulated sleeving to cover the Eureka wires   2 coils, 2400 turns, to fit C-cores

Tranformers are now added to one power line, for use as a demonstration. The circuit diagram is shown in figure 11.17 in the pupils' book. It is important to get the transformers the right way round (with the smaller coils connected to the power supply and the distant lamp respectively and the 2400 turn coils connected to the power line).

  The observations to be made are suggested in the pupils' book.

Warning

The Eureka wires **must** be covered with insulating sleeving: the method using high voltages between two bare wires **must not** be used. The ASE publication *Topics in safety* details several safer ways of demonstrating this. Alternatively, the experiment can be carried out using a 2 V a.c. supply which can be stepped up to 20 V and then down again; this reduces the risk of high voltages.

Section P11.5: Experiments demonstrating electromagnetic induction

REQUIREMENTS

For Experiment 1 (figure 11.19) each group of pupils will need:
Coil, 120 turns (as for use with C-cores)
Magnet, bar
Galvanometer, 3.5–0–3.5 mA
Connecting leads

For Experiment 2 (figure 11.20) each group of pupils will need:
C-core
Coil, 120 turns (as for use with C-cores)
Switch
Cell, 1.5 V, in holder
Connecting leads

For Experiment 3 (figure 11.21) each group of pupils will need:
2 C-cores
2 coils, 120 turns (as for use with C-cores)
Switch
Galvanometer, 3.5–0–3.5 mA
Cell, 1.5 V, in holder
Connecting leads

For Experiment 4 (figure 11.19) each group of pupils will need:
2 C-cores
2 coils, 120 turns (as for use with C-cores)
Power supply, 2 V a.c.
Lamp, 2.5 V MES
Lamp holder, MES
Connecting leads

Circuits for all the experiments are illustrated in the pupils' book (figures 11.19–22).

  The meters used must be sufficiently sensitive to give deflections which pupils can easily see.

Further information

Supplementary material
Useful supporting material on the supply and distribution of electricity is available from the Understanding Electricity Educational Service (see Appendix).

Chapter P12 Waste not, want not?
Energy resources

The syllabus section

Context

This section is devoted to a study of the world's energy resources. In addition to the use of fossil fuels, the use of nuclear power, both by fission and through the future potential of fusion, is discussed. Pupils are given the opportunity to discuss the social issues involved. Renewable energy resources are considered, and the benefits of increasing the efficiency of energy transference are discussed.

Knowledge and understanding

	Tier	
B	C	F

Syllabus statements	PoS	SoA
Appreciate the importance of energy in our day-to-day lives.	4(ii)1	4.4(b)
Appreciate the need for greater economy and efficiency in using energy.	4(ii)3	4.5(c)
Understand the difference between renewable and non-renewable energy resources, and the ways in which these can be used to generate electricity, including nuclear fission and fusion.	4(ii)7	4.5(c)
Understand that most energy resources ultimately derive their energy from the Sun.	4(ii)7,8	4.6(c)
Be able to evaluate the economic, environmental and social benefits and problems of different energy sources, including nuclear fission.	4(ii)8,9	4.9(b)

Opportunities for co-ordination

The human body, as an engine which needs fuel, is treated in detail in **B**9. Photosynthesis, as the means by which plants trap energy from the Sun, is covered in detail in **B**3. **E**3 links nuclear fusion to the energy in the Sun.

The refining of crude oil to produce fuels is the subject of **C**2. Energy from fossil fuels is dealt with in detail in **C**13. There are also links with **C**3.

Routes and times

Basic	Central	Further

| | **P12.1 Human resources**
P12.2 Energy from fuels
(pages 196–197 optional/homework)
³/₄ hour | All of section **P12.2** is suitable. |

| Omit Q8 and 9 from section **P12.3**.
A demonstration of the ionizing effects and the absorption of radioactivity could be included here. | **P12.3 Nuclear energy**
Worksheet P12A Nuclear power (optional)
1½ hours | Section **P12.3** should be done for reading homework and Worksheet **P12A** done in class.
1 hour |

| Omit Q15 from section **P12.4**, and Worksheet **P12C**. Supplement with suitable video material. | **P12.4 Alternative energy resources**
Omit Q11.
Worksheet P12C Geothermal energy
(homework)
P12.5 "Waste not, want not"
1½ hours | Sections **P12.4** and **P12.5** are suitable for homework.
³/₄ hour |

| Pupils at Basic level will benefit from a discussion of renewable and non-renewable energy resources.
1½ hours | **Worksheet P12B Ashton Island**
Optional | |

| *Total: 5¼ hours* | *Total: 3¾ hours* | *Total: 2½ hours* |

The pupils' book

The theme of the chapter is the world's continuing need for energy resources at a time when fossil fuels are becoming increasingly scarce. All pupils cover essentially the same material. However, section **P12.2** is optional and intended for pupils who may have the time and interest to study a recent experiment in transferring more energy from the Sun via plants.

The pupils' attention is focussed on two issues. The first is the nuclear fuel alternative to fossil fuels. The second is the availability of sources of energy which are alternatives to both nuclear and fossil fuels. These two issues have been made the subject of two class activities. They are based on two SATIS units: unit 109 "Nuclear power" and unit 107 "Ashton Island – a problem in renewable energy".

These two activities will occupy the majority of the time available for the chapter. Most of the other work can be seen as providing supporting material to these activities.

This chapter may be set as holiday work. Pupils carry out the worksheet activities after working through the pupils' book.

P12.1 Human resources

This introductory section shows how much energy a human being requires in a day, and how much of this can be transferred as useful work. From these figures it is shown that a day's human labour amounts, in energy terms, to just about 1 kWh – the "unit" in which electricity boards sell energy to the consumer.

The cost of this much energy from an area electricity board was about 7p in 1991. This shows clearly how the scale of human energy compares with that available from fossil fuels. It also demonstrates how the country's prosperity depends on the availability of cheap and plentiful energy resources.

P12.2 Energy from fuels

This is a short optional section for more able pupils. The section compares the time taken to produce fuels based on plant materials with the time taken to use them. It then considers an alternative to the traditional fuels of wood, peat, coal, oil or gas, which nevertheless still captures the Sun's energy through photosynthesis.

P12.3 Nuclear energy

It is necessary for pupils to have studied Chapter **P3** "Radioactivity" before tackling this chapter. The section starts with a review of the most important ideas arising from that chapter.

The section continues with a brief description of the way energy is released from the nucleus of a uranium atom in a nuclear reactor. It then gives a brief pen-portrait of the man who built the world's first nuclear reactor, Enrico Fermi.

The section concludes with an account of nuclear fusion and lists the advantages nuclear reactors based on fusion would have compared with those based on fission. If time permits, the material can be supported by showing one of a number of films that are available. Recommended sources are listed under Further information.

The entire section provides background for a pupil-based discussion group on the use of nuclear power. Worksheet **P12A** provides pupils with the essential material needed for the discussion groups. The worksheet is based on SATIS unit 109 "Nuclear power". The general briefing sheet in that unit has not been reproduced as the material contained in it is part of the present chapter. Teaching notes to accompany this worksheet are given separately below.

P12.4 Alternative energy resources

This section looks at the possibility of finding energy resources which are neither fossil nor nuclear fuels. Such energy resources are generally referred to as "alternative energy sources".

The material in this section can be supported by a range of display material, posters, and so on, some sources of which are listed under Further information. Again, if time permits, films are available which illustrate the potential for "alternative energy".

This material should be seen also as background for the second worksheet, Worksheet **P12B**. This worksheet sets pupils the problem of providing energy for a small community on an isolated island which has no fuel reserves and no nuclear power. The worksheet is based on SATIS unit 107 "Ashton Island – a problem in renewable energy". The details about alternative energy resources have been omitted as these are covered in the pupils' book. Detailed teaching notes are given in the notes on worksheets below.

P12.5 "Waste not, want not"

The chapter concludes with some consideration of the effect of greater efficiency in the use of energy on our available resources. The very small amount of energy usefully transferred from fuels is emphasized and examples are given of recent experiments in increasing this efficiency.

Activities

Worksheet P12A Nuclear power

The aim of this worksheet is to initiate an informed discussion between a group of pupils. To do this, each member of the discussion group becomes an "expert" in some field related to nuclear power. The group then discusses various aspects of nuclear power under the leadership of one member who takes the chair.

The class should be formed into groups of five. Each group should have a group leader, whose task it is to chair the discussions. The group leader will have to be chosen for his or her potential in this respect.

The group leader should be given the Chairperson's briefing sheet. Give the Experts' briefing sheets (1 to 4) to the other members of the group – a different sheet to each person. They should have time to study their briefings before the discussion – this could conveniently be set as a homework assignment.

The running of the discussion is in the hands of the group leader. Avoid intervening, if possible! A time limit will have to be placed on the discussions. The session could conclude with a "report back" to the whole class by each group leader giving the group's views on the "General points for discussion" listed in the Chairperson's briefing.

Worksheet P12B Ashton Island

Pupils tackle the questions on Ashton Island after they have made a brief study of alternative energy sources. They will probably do this best if they work in small groups.

At some time teachers may wish to contrast the problem of providing energy for a limited period of time to a few people (as in "Ashton Island") with the problems involved in using the same resources to replace our day-to-day use of fossil and nuclear fuels. At the time of writing, none of the alternative energy resources discussed in the chapter are viable in economic terms when contrasted with the cost of traditional energy resources. However they may become more attractive as the cost of traditional resources starts to rise, due to depletion of reserves.

Worksheet P12C Geothermal energy

REQUIREMENTS

Each pupil will need:
Calculator

Access to:
Atlas or map of the UK
Geological map of the UK

The worksheet considers the way in which temperature increases with depth in the ground and how this may be used as a source of energy.

Answers to worksheet questions
1a The geothermal gradient. **b** °C/km.

2 Water can get through permeable rocks but not through impermeable rocks. Permeable rocks, through which water can be pumped, are needed to extract the energy. Impermeable rocks are necessary around the permeable rocks so that the water is not lost.

3 All are near sites of volcanic activity.

4a Cornwall/Devon; Cumbria/Durham; County Down. **b** Granite. **c** Radioactive decay in the granite.

5 If the temperature is 120 °C at 7 km depth and 10 °C at the surface, a temperature of 40 °C would be expected at about $7 \text{ km} \times {}^{3}/_{11} = 1.9 \text{ km}$.

6 Rocks 6 km deep are at 250 °C. If the surface temperature is 10 °C, the temperature increases by 240 °C in 6 km, which is a gradient of 40 °C/km.

7 To allow the water to percolate.

8a 100 °C. **b** By keeping the water under pressure.

9 1 km³ of granite has a volume of 10^9 m^3, and a mass of $10^9 \times 2700 \text{ kg}$. The energy lost if it is cooled through 1 °C = $2700 \times 10^9 \times 820 = 2.2 \times 10^{15} \text{ J}$.

10 $2.2 \times 10^{15}/(30 \times 10^9) = 73\,000$ tonnes.

Further information

The basic processes of nuclear power
Several suitable videos are available from AEA Technology.

"The nuclear reactor simulation"
This is a computer simulation of an advanced gas-cooled reactor developed by the Education Service of the UKAEA and published by Longman.

The cases for and against nuclear power
Material dealing with the case in favour of the use of nuclear power is available from AEA Technology.

The case against nuclear power is laid out in a number of publications available from Friends of the Earth.

Other aspects of energy
"Alternative energy"
This video deals with geothermal and wind power, and looks at alternative lifestyle approaches (ITV Science and Technology series).

"Try and catch the wind"
In these group activities, in Pack 2 of *Problem solving with industry* (Centre for Science Education, Sheffield Hallan University, 1991), pupils consider whether wind-generated electricity is more acceptable than coal-generated electricity.

"Time for energy"
This film dealing with alternative energy is available from the Shell Film Library.

"Energy in profile"
A film available from the Shell Film Library.

"A quest for gas"
A film available from British Gas.
British Gas also produce a booklet on the history of gas called *Then and now*.

Topic P4   Waves

This topic is about the use that we can make of a wave model to describe a number of energy transfer processes. Particular attention is given to light, but this is extended to include the whole electromagnetic spectrum.

Sound and earthquakes are also included as other examples of energy transfer which can be described by wave ideas.

A wave, as a to-and-fro motion which can be passed "hand-to-hand" through a wave-carrying medium, is something which can only be seen on a medium such as water. To say that light and sound are waves, or that earthquakes travel as waves through the Earth is an exercise of the imagination which is both part of the beauty and power of physics and yet at the same time makes it seem "difficult". So in this course the properties of waves on springs and on the surface of water are studied. The behaviour of light and sound is seen in some simple respects to be like the behaviour of the waves observed on springs and water.

This leads to the possibility of light being some sort of wave motion. Further properties of light are explored on the basis of "let's see how far this idea will take us". These further explorations linking waves with light turn out to be very profitable, illustrating the usefulness of using the wave model to describe the behaviour of light. In a similar way, wave motion turns out to be a useful way of describing the behaviour of sound and earthquakes. In these two cases the model is given greater realism as we are able to explain what it is that "waves about" – a question that is very difficult to answer in the case of light and other electromagnetic waves.

Chapter P13 Fibre optics and noise
A revision of light and sound

The syllabus section

Context

The properties of optical fibres as explored are a means of surveying the basic properties of light (likely to have been covered before the two-year examination course). The advantages of optical fibres in communication and the importance of communication systems form a link between this section and **P21**. A study of the effects of noise similarly serves as a vehicle for exploring some of the basic properties of sound.

Knowledge and understanding

	Tier	
B	C	F

Syllabus statements	PoS	SoA
Understand reflection and explain that when light strikes an object some of it is reflected.	4(iv)8	4.5(e)
Appreciate how noise levels can be measured and appreciate the desirability of reducing noise levels, yet recognize the problems involved in doing this.	4(iv)5	4.6(f)
Be able to use the wave model of light to explain refraction in terms of the change of speed and direction of waves.	4(iv)8,9	4.7(f)
Appreciate how the properties of reflection and refraction can be applied to understand the transmission of light down an optical fibre.	4(iv)8	4.7(f)
Be able to use the wave nature of electromagnetic radiation to explain the processes of interference, diffraction and polarization.	4(iv)8,9	4.10(d)

Opportunities for co-ordination

B11 deals with sight and hearing.

Optical fibres make use of materials with a very high degree of transparency to light. Such materials may be made of materials like ordinary glass, or from plastic. Glasses are dealt with in **C**6; polymers are the subject of **C**8.

Routes and times

Basic	Central	Further
Spend more time on revision, including experiments on reflection and refraction. *1½ hours*	**Waves: Introduction** (pages 210–213) Revision of earlier work on sound and light. *¾ hour*	Spend less time on this section. *¼ hour*
Omit section **P13.1** and Worksheet **P13A**, but demonstrate the principle of reflection as applied to optical fibres. *¾ hour*	**P13.1 Fibre optics** Omit Q1. **Worksheet P13A Optical fibres** *1 hour*	
	Worksheet P13B Optical fibres, telecommunications and technology *¾ hour*	
Spend more time on this section. Worksheet **P13C** should be done in class. *1 hour*	**P13.2 Noise** Brief revision. **Worksheet P13C Noise** Select material. *¼ hour*	
Total: 4 hours	*Total: 2¾ hours*	*Total: 2¼ hours*

The pupils' book

Revising work on light

A revision of ideas about light, met in an earlier year, will probably be necessary. The section in the pupils' book entitled "What you should already know about light and sound" reviews the image-forming properties of a lens as well as basic ideas about reflection and refraction. Only the properties of reflection and refraction are essential to the work of this chapter. However, work on lenses and optical instruments is also a part of elementary work on light and is included here for the sake of completeness and inherent importance.

Some questions covering these basic ideas have been included in the pupils' book and could be used as the basis for deciding how much revision needs to be done.

P13.1 Fibre optics

The chapter opens by considering the way light has been used for signalling for hundreds of years. It is recognized that there are both advantages and problems in this method of communication. The main problems in using light for communication are hinted at by the questions "How far?" and "How fast?" Speed of communication is not simply a matter of the time taken for a signal to pass over a particular distance – it is also a matter of the length of the message being sent. For example, transmitting a document by Morse code would take rather more time than it does to read it. Digital communication systems have greatly reduced the time it takes to transmit messages; such systems have not increased the speed at which the signals cover space (this has been achieved at the speed of light for many years now). How messages can be compressed is dealt with in Chapter **P2l**.

Light has great advantages when it comes to "message compression". This is what is really meant when it is said that optical fibres can convey information faster than electrical cables. There is very little gain in actual signal speed.

The use of optical fibres has done much to increase the distances light signals can be sent. Worksheet **P13A** gives pupils a series of experiments that illustrate the way an optical fibre works. It introduces the concept of a critical angle and thus adds to the previous work pupils will have done on refraction.

The section concludes with a brief survey of the advantages of using optical fibres in telecommunications systems. Worksheet **P13B** widens the scope of the enquiry by not only asking questions about the use of optical fibres, but also considering more generally the impact of technology on people's lives. This worksheet is based on one of the same title published for the SATIS project by the Association for Science Education. The worksheet could be covered instead at the end of Chapter **P21** "Communication". Pupils who have had to spend some time on the revision of light will probably not benefit from doing Worksheet **P21C** in that chapter, and Worksheet **P13B** would be a good alternative.

Answer to selected question

1 This is an "estimates" question for which all but the most able pupils will require some help. The supplementary questions are:

i What is likely to be the average distance between beacons?

ii How long would it take one group of people to sight a lighted beacon and then get their own sufficiently well alight to attract others?

iii How far is it from the south coast of Britain to Newcastle?

The following answers are only personal estimates – others may differ markedly!

i An average distance between beacons might be about 25 km.

ii One might reckon on a time of 20 minutes at least between one beacon being lit and the next being sufficiently alight to pass the "message" on.

iii The distance between Newcastle and the south coast is more certain – it is almost 500 km in a straight line.

An estimate of the time the message would take is:
500/25 beacons × 20 minutes per beacon = 400 minutes.
This is a time of about 7 hours.

P13.2 Noise

Some revision of earlier ideas can take place first of all. Revision questions are given in the Introduction to Topic **P4**. Whereas the behaviour of light can easily be treated without any reference to its possible nature, it is common to treat sound as "waves in air" from the first. Thus early work on pitch will probably already have linked this with the idea of wave frequency. Speed of travel may also have been investigated. The companion features of light will probably have received no attention. On the other hand it is much more difficult to demonstrate the reflection and refraction of sound than of light. Since it is important to see later that sound shares many properties with light, and that both can be described as waves, it may be a good idea at this point to demonstrate that sound can at least be reflected.

Finally pupils can undertake all or part of the investigation into "Noise" described in Worksheet **P13C**. This worksheet is based on one of the same title published in the SATIS series. The final enquiry, "How noisy is your school?", is something that can be undertaken over a longer period than this chapter will take. It introduces another form of data collection – asking questions of others – and encourages a critical attitude to data collected in this way.

Activities

Worksheet P13A Optical fibres

REQUIREMENTS

Each group of pupils will need:
Transparent plastic block, semicircular
Transparent plastic strip, approximately 3 cm × 30 cm × 0.5 cm (see Notes)
Glass rod, 20 to 30 cm long with smooth-cut ends (neither scratched nor flame polished)
Optical fibre, 0.5–1 m long (see Notes)
Light source (reading or microscope lamp with non-clear lamp bulb)
Ray optics kit: lamp, holder and stand, housing shield, metal plate with slit in it
Power supply, 12 V
Paper, white
Paper, black
Card, white (such as a postcard)
Protractor
Stands, bosses and clamps to hold glass rod, optical fibre and screen

Notes:
The dimensions of the plastic strip are not critical provided it is long compared with its width, and sufficiently thick for a light ray to be seen in it.

RS Components Ltd (PO Box 99, Corby, Northants NN17 9RS) supply a suitable fibre optic cable under stock number 368-047. Maplin Electronics (Maplin Professional Supplies PO Box 777, Rayleigh, Essex SS6 8LU) also supply a suitable cable in 0.5 m lengths.

Experiment a

The ray of light is directed through the curved surface of the block along a radius. In this way the ray will be undeviated as it passes into the block. One way to achieve this is to mark the middle of the flat edge and then direct the ray at the mark. The angle of incidence of the ray falling on the back, flat surface is increased and it is noted that at first a refracted ray passes out into the air on the other side of the block. At the same time **some** of the light is internally reflected. As the angle of refraction approaches 90° the proportion of light reflected internally increases. At a particular angle of incidence, the critical angle, the angle of refraction is 90°. For angles of incidence greater than this, all the light is reflected internally in the block and the light ray emerges again from the curved face.

Experiment b

A light ray is directed into the short side of a clear plastic strip. By adjusting the angle of entry, a light ray can be made to travel down the strip by total internal reflection.

Experiment c

A piece of white card is flooded with light from the lamp. This acts as the source of light for the glass rod. Light can be seen emerging from the end of the glass rod at all angles. The black paper acts as a background against which the end of the rod can be viewed.

Experiment d

Experiment c is repeated using a length of optical fibre. The end of the fibre can be directly illuminated by the lamp. A small patch of light will be seen to emerge from the far end. This can be seen by directing the end of the fibre at a sheet of white paper. Bending the fibre is seen to have no effect on its ability to pass light along its length.

Further details of this and other experiments with optical fibres will be found in the ASE/SCSST publication *Optical fibres in school physics*. (See Further information.)

Worksheet P13B Optical fibres, telecommunications and technology

This discusses some applications of optical fibres.

Worksheet P13C Noise

An enquiry into noise and some of its effects on the environment.

Further information

Experimenting with Industry
"Optical fibres in school physics". This booklet, number 2 in the Experimenting with Industry series published by the Association for Science Education for the Standing Conference on Schools' Science and Technology, is primarily intended for work with sixth forms but provides interesting background information on optical fibres.

Videos
"The physics of optical communications" (BT Educational Service) covers refraction, internal reflection and fibre optics. "Picking up the vibes" (BBC Search Out Science Series) is aimed at Key stage 3 pupils but provides an effective review of sound, echoes and methods of reducing noise.

TOPIC P4 WAVES

The syllabus section

Context

In making a practical exploration of wave behaviour, this section paves the way for interpreting the behaviour of light and sound as a wave motion.

Knowledge and understanding

Tier		
B	C	F

Syllabus statements	PoS	SoA
Understand that a wave is a means of transferring energy in the direction in which the wave travels, without transferring matter.	4(iv)11	4.5(b)
Be able to distinguish between transverse and longitudinal waves and appreciate the circumstances in which either or both might occur.	4(iv)2	4.5(f)
Appreciate that, through their behaviour, both light and sound are examples of wave motions.	4(iv)2	4.5(f)
Know the meaning of the terms wavelength, frequency and wave speed.	4(iv)1	4.6(f)
Understand some of the properties of waves that distinguish this form of energy transfer from energy transfer accompanying the transfer of matter.	4(iv)8	—
Be able to use the equation "wave speed = wavelength × frequency" in simple applications.	4(iv)11	4.8(d)

Opportunities for co-ordination

Blood circulation and the human "pulse" are discussed in **B**8. **E**2 links the behaviour of waves to the study of earthquakes, and **E**3 links the use of electromagnetic waves to receive and interpret information about the rest of the Universe from space probes.

Routes and times

Basic	Central	Further
Spend more time on this section. *1½ hours*	**P14.1 Waves on the sea shore** (homework) **P14.2 Waves on a spring** **Worksheet P14A Waves on a spring** *1¼ hours*	Spend less time on this section. *¾ hour*
Concentrate on the meaning of frequency, wave speed and wavelength. Omit calculations.	**P14.3 Measurement of waves** *¾ hour*	
Omit most of section **P14.4** and Worksheet **P14B**. The reflection of water waves should be demonstrated. *¾ hour*	**P14.4 Waves on the surface of water** **Worksheet P14B Experiments with a ripple tank** *1½ hours*	Q13 of section **P14.4** is also suitable. The interference of water waves should be demonstrated.
Total: 3 hours	*Total: 3½ hours*	*Total: 3 hours*

The pupils' book

The study of wave motion is one of the easiest and most practically-based pieces of work found in elementary physics courses. Even so, its appeal to boys and girls is not uniform. Many enjoy the practical work involved, but others find it dull as it does not seem related to any obvious manifestations in their everyday world. By moving work on waves to a point when the use of wave models can be considered it is hoped that this chapter can be given a more universal appeal. It may help to refer back to Chapter **P**13 and ask "What is light?" and "What is sound?", and then to say that an answer to these questions, which we shall find in Chapter **P**15, requires us first to know something about waves.

P14.1 Waves on the sea shore

The introduction relates wave motion to an experience common to many pupils – sea waves. In discussing sea waves it seems worth making the point that their rolling motion makes them untypical. Sea waves have an association with water rushing up the beach – and thus the waves are seen to carry the water forward but it is just the opposite idea that is important: waves transfer energy **without** transporting matter.

Questions 1 and 2 encourage pupils to think generally about the nature of wave motion.

P14.2 Waves on a spring

It is worth spending a little while looking at waves on a rope or spring. Such wave motion enables the relationship between the "wave" and the movement of the material carrying it to be studied. If pupils can do their own experiments, they will inevitably set up standing waves. The effect can be simply explained without pursuing it in detail – its complexity makes clear the need to experiment with pulses rather than with continuous waves.

The pupils' book relates waves on a spring to the possibility of waves in solids, liquids and gases, and calls on some work from Chapters **P**1 and **P**2. It then describes the meaning to be associated with "wave pulse" and likens the word "pulse" to the use of the same word in Biology. It needs to be said, however, that a human pulse is caused by the heart **moving** blood round the body; wave pulses represent a transfer of energy, **not** material.

Not much more than a double period should be spent on sections **P**14.1 and **P**14.2.

P14.3 **Measurements of waves**

A single period can be devoted to the basic wave nomenclature and establishing the relationship between speed, wavelength and frequency. This latter could be omitted by some, to give more time on the first two sections, or on the last one.

Answers to selected questions
5a 400 cm/s; **b** 40 cm.

6 4 Hz.

7 1.5 km.

P14.4 **Waves on the surface of water**

This section is concerned with waves in a ripple tank. It should not be necessary to spend more than a double period on the work. Those familiar with the ripple tank will note that the continuous wave generator need not be used at all. Much more useful experimenting can be done with the finger or a small water "dropper" to make circular waves, or a rod to produce straight waves. Only the investigation into what happens when waves change speed may benefit from the use of a continuous wave generator. Question 14 refers to such a generator and pupils may be helped in answering it by seeing one in action.

Questions 8–10 and 13–14 should be done at the same time as the ripple tank experiments. No formal record of the ripple tank work is expected – the answers to the questions will provide a suitable record.

Diffraction of waves is introduced – it is an easy effect to see and is as unique to wave motion as wave interference (which is omitted). At this level pupils often confuse the words "refraction" and "diffraction". To avoid this, the word "refraction" is omitted when discussing the change of direction of waves. Diffraction, together with questions 11 and 12, enables some contrast to be made between wave and particle behaviour, without formally setting these up as alternative models of energy transfer.

The behaviour of waves with change of speed can be investigated with roller-generated pulses, but teachers may well feel this is better demonstrated with a continuous wave generator. If so, it is important to avoid spurious diffraction and standing wave effects. This is a case where the only worthwhile demonstration is a good one! This piece of work and the associated questions may be omitted by less able pupils.

Answers to selected questions
9b The reflected part of the wave should "fit into" the circle of the incident wave.

13 Dimensions have been given to encourage careful drawing. It is commonplace to find pupils making "changes" in wavelength in drawings of diffracted waves after they have passed through an aperture.

14 The plate edge is situated between ripple 6 and ripple 7; the plate is to the left of the drawing.

15 The expected phrases or words are, successively, "move up and down", "shallow", "up and down motion", "shallow side of the edge", "deep", "frequency".

16 The ratio of the wavelengths is 3 to 2; the answer is therefore 14 cm/s.

Activities

Worksheet P14A Waves on a spring

REQUIREMENTS

Each group of pupils will need:
"Slinky" spring
Sticky tape (to mark coils)

The procedure to be followed is detailed in the worksheet.

Worksheet P14B Experiments with a ripple tank

REQUIREMENTS

Each group of pupils will need:
Ripple tank kit
Power supply for ripple tank
Sheet of white paper
Ruler, 0.5 m
Protractor

The procedure to be followed is detailed in the worksheet. Failure to use a lamp with the correct filament is a common reason for poor ripple visibility. Any lamp will not do. Special lamps with the correct filament are provided for ripple tank work.

Refraction is difficult to demonstrate convincingly. The depth of water in the "shallow" area, over the glass plate, should be as small as possible.

Demonstration experiments

Sections P14.1 and P14.2: Watching water waves

It may be helpful to have a rectangular tank half filled with water and a wave "paddle" to show waves travelling over the surface of water. Optionally, the experiments in Worksheet P14A can be demonstrated.

Section P14.4: Refraction of ripples

A ripple tank, set up for demonstration with a continuous wave generator, may be useful to show the change of direction of waves as they pass into a shallower region.

Chapter P15 Making use of waves
Light, sound and earthquakes

The syllabus section

Context

This section begins by exploring the properties of colour, how we see colours: the making of colour photographs, and the production of colour pictures on a television screen. Energy transfer from waves leads to infra-red heating, microwave cookers and the reception of radio and television programmes. Sound as a wave is also explored.

Knowledge and understanding

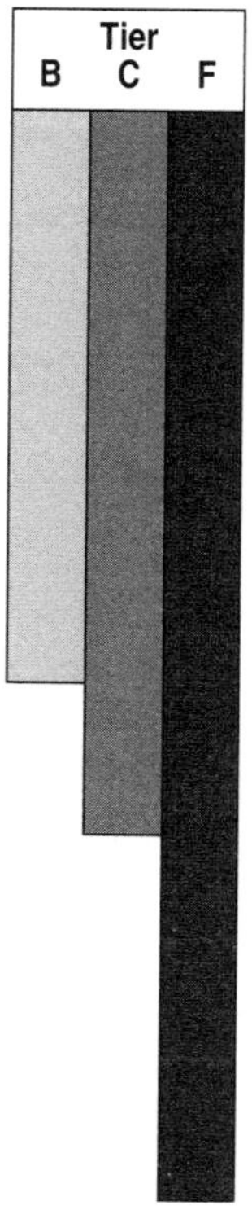

Syllabus statements	PoS	SoA
Know that light travels faster than sound.	—	4.4(d)
Be able to relate wavelength to colour and have some appreciation of the nature of colour vision, including primary and secondary colours.	—	—
Be able to explain that differences in loudness and pitch are a result of changes in the amplitude and frequency of the sound wave which is produced.	4(iv)1,3	4.6(f)
Appreciate the variety of possible uses of sound, for example in cleaning, pre-natal scanning and musical instruments.	4(iv)3,7	—
Be able to explain resonance in terms of forcing frequency equal to a natural frequency. Understand how this may or may not be desirable in certain circumstances.	4(iv)6	4.8(e)
Know the domestic, communication and medical uses, potential dangers, and properties of different areas of the electromagnetic spectrum and relate this information to position in the spectrum.	4(iv)10	4.9(d)
Be able to explain, in the context of the wave nature of electromagnetic radiation, the processes of interference, diffraction and polarization.	4(iv)8,9	4.10(d)

Opportunities for co-ordination

The work on colour is complemented by **C**11. Flame tests are introduced in **C**7. Colour as an indicator to test for acidity and alkalinity forms a part of **C**12 and **C**15. X-ray crystallography is studied in **C**5.

The selective absorption of colours is a fundamental part of photosynthesis and links to **B**3.

The work on earthquakes links with **E**2.

Routes and times

	Basic	Central	Further

Basic: Replace Worksheets **P**15A and **P**15B with Worksheet **P**15C "Colour vision". Worksheet **P**15D "Secondary colours" should be demonstrated.

Central:

> **P15.1 Colour**
>
> **Worksheet P15A Colour**
>
> **Worksheet P15B Examining colour filters**
>
> Demonstrate colour mixing using a projector.
>
> *1½ hours*

Basic: Omit section **P**15.2 but relate wavelength to colour. The speed of light should be demonstrated.

Central:

> **P15.2 More about light**
> Concentrate on wave model of refraction, and omit Q6 and 7; speed of light could be demonstrated.
>
> *½ hour*

Further: All questions are suitable. Diffraction, refraction and polarization should be demonstrated.

1¼ hours

Further:

> **P15.3 The electromagnetic spectrum**
>
> **Worksheet P15E The electromagnetic spectrum**
> (class + homework)
>
> *½ hour*

Basic: Omit all this section.

Central:

> **P15.4 Transferring energy using waves**
>
> **Worksheet P15L Resonance**
> (teacher demonstration)
>
> *1¼ hours*

Basic: Worksheet **P**15H "Making sounds" is also suitable. Spend time relating loudness to amplitude and pitch to frequency.

2¼ hours

Central:

> **P15.5 Other waves around us** (up to Q18)
> Demonstrate reflection and refraction of sound.
>
> **Worksheet P15J Ultrasonics** (homework)
>
> **Worksheet P15K How does sound travel?**
> (optional)
>
> *1¼ hours*

Basic: Selection of material is necessary.

Central:

> **P15.5 Other waves around us** ("Earthquakes")
>
> **Worksheet P15F Earthquakes**
>
> **Worksheet P15G Find that earthquake!**
>
> Select material from these as necessary and refer to section **E**2.3.
>
> *¾ hour*

Total: 5 hours   *Total: 5¼ hours*   *Total: 6½ hours*

The pupils' book

P15.1 Colour

The chapter begins with an investigation into colour. For less able pupils investigations into colour can occupy half the total time available (three or four periods). All pupils should have the opportunity of setting up their own spectrum and doing some colour mixing. However, many of the suggested experiments are more spectacular if carried out in a well-darkened room, using slide projectors carrying colour filters. If this is done, it is well worth spending some time adjusting the intensity of the light from each projector to be nearly the same. The intensity of the "blue" light will be lowest and it may be necessary to cut down the light from the other projectors by adding extra filters or running the lamps on a Variac. Trouble is, however, amply repaid.

Answers to selected questions
1 This requires a prism to analyse the light that has passed through the filter.

2, 3 and 4. The answers to these questions can all be derived from practical work with colour.

5 This can be demonstrated by overlapping, say, blue and red filters – nothing is transmitted. Many books on photography provide more details of the process of producing colour photographs but the details are very complicated.

P15.2 More about light

There will not be time to spend much more than a single period justifying the fact that we understand light to be a wave motion. No attempt is made to present incontrovertible evidence for this – rather the standpoint adopted is, "Many people understand light to be a wave. Is its behaviour, as we know it, consistent with this idea?"

A discussion of the speed of light is a more advanced option. The experiment measuring the speed of light down an optical fibre uses sophisticated equipment and is, of course, optional. This would seem to be a case where a description on its own can provide some useful experimental data, as the experiment is quite easy, in principle, to understand. However, if it can be set up, so much the better. Details are given under Demonstration experiments.

Answers to selected questions
6 Red light will have the longest wavelength.

7 Red light is spread out most by a diffraction grating. This is "opposite" to the prism, where blue light is deflected the most.

8 Light must travel slower in glass.

9 Light takes 500 s to travel from the Sun to Earth – about 8 minutes.

10 3.8×10^{13} km.

P15.3 The electromagnetic spectrum

This section deals with the electromagnetic spectrum and centres around Worksheet **P15E**. The worksheet not only asks pupils to prepare their own chart of the electromagnetic spectrum, but also introduces them to the logarithmic scale – seen simply as a device for coping with numbers which occupy a large range. It may be useful to have some additional information on the electromagnetic spectrum available, as pupils may need this in preparing their own chart.

Answer to selected question
11a 1 000 000 nm to the mm; b 500 nm.

P15.4 Transferring energy using waves

This section is an alternative to extended work on colour. It is based around a class experiment designed to show the transfer of energy from a wave to an oscillator. Experimentally it is shown that substantial energy transfer only takes place when the wave frequency matches the natural frequency of the oscillator. This is, of course, part of the whole phenomenon of resonance. However, no terms of this sort are introduced here. The fact of energy transfer is accepted empirically and then applied to such diverse applications as radio reception and microwave cookers.

It is tempting to go further with this work and link it back to colour. However, this involves energy level transitions in which electrons and atoms move from one natural state of vibration to another. Over-simplification could do more harm than good. Even with the microwave cooker there should be no attempt to add unnecessary detail. The "vibration" involved is actually a rotation and it will not be obvious to pupils that this takes place at some preferred frequency.

Despite these difficulties, the fact of resonant energy transfer seems worth including as giving a further important (and commonly observed) aspect of energy transfer.

Questions 15–17 need, for their answers, a knowledge of the relationship between voltage, current and power. This is dealt with in Chapter **P**17, so it might be a good idea to return to these questions later – perhaps as a form of revision.

Answers to selected questions
12 and **14** These questions should be answered after the demonstration experiment has been seen.

15c 33°C **d** 23°C.
e 260–270 s.
f This reinforces the comparison between extrapolation and interpolation made in Chapter **P**2.
g 48 300 J. **h** 65 000 J.
i No, **f** is bigger – not all the microwave energy is being absorbed by the water.
j 230 V × 5.9 A = 1357 W – yes, it is in good agreement.
l i 48 per cent; ii 36 per cent.
m The experiment could, for example, be repeated for a larger volume of water; different containers could also be used.

16a 155 400 J; **b** 200 000 J; **c** 78 per cent;
d These figures suggest that it is more efficient to heat water in an electric kettle.

17a 3×10^8 m/s; **b** 0.12 m (or 12 cm).

P15.5 **Other waves around us**

It is not easy to demonstrate the diffraction of sound waves and the variation of their speed in media other than air. It is difficult to separate diffraction effects from other factors leading to the spreading out of sound – such as reflections. On the other hand, it is obvious that sound is associated with a vibrating source and it is easy to see how a "sound" wave could travel through air. If pupils have studied sound in Year 9, they may already be familiar with the idea that sound is a "push-pull" wave motion in air.

Worksheet **P**15F encourages pupils to look at something of the nature and consequences of earthquakes, treated as a wave. Earthquakes and volcanoes feature in many geography courses, where the emphasis tends to be on geographical distribution and with theories of plate tectonics. This worksheet is complementary to that and puts more emphasis on the wave-like nature of earthquakes.

Answer to selected question
19a 11.3 m; 0.034 m.
b Room dimensions are usually smaller than 11 m. The "bass response" of room and loudspeaker decreases as the size of the room decreases, once room dimensions are less than the wavelength of the sound.

Activities

Worksheet P15A **Colour**

REQUIREMENTS
(The following equipment is part of the Nuffield Physics Ray Optics Kit.)

Each group of pupils will need:
Ray optics kit: lamp, holder and stand, lamp shield, 2 metal plates, each with a single slit in it, plano-cylindrical lens, +7D
Power supply, 12 V
2 prisms, each 60°
Screen

Note:

Examine the filaments of the lamps and replace any whose filaments are not straight and vertical. It will not be possible to produce a pure spectrum of this size from a crooked filament.

The procedure to be followed is detailed in the worksheet.

Worksheet P15B Examining colour filters

REQUIREMENTS

Each group of pupils will need:
Ray optics kit: lamp, holder and stand, lamp shield, metal plate with single slit in it, plano-cylindrical
  lens, +7D
Power supply, 12 V
Prism, 60°
Screen
Colour filters, primary blue, green and red, with holder
Coloured objects, various, in the primary colours and some in other colours for more able pupils

The procedure to be followed is detailed in the worksheet.

Worksheet P15C Colour vision

REQUIREMENTS

Each group of pupils will need:
Ray optics kit: lamp, holder and stand, lamp shield, 2 metal plates, each with a single slit in it, plano-
  cylindrical lens, +7D
Power supply, 12 V
2 prisms, each 60°
Screen
Bunsen burner and heatproof mat
Stand, boss and clamp
Sodium chloride (common salt)
Wire, steel, about 0.5 mm diameter
2 mirrors, small, plane
Colour filters, yellow, cyan and magenta
Eye protection

The procedure to be followed is detailed in the worksheet. With care and a well-darkened laboratory, surprisingly effective colour mixing can be done on a small scale. However, this is made more impressive if the effect of colour mixing can be demonstrated as well.

Worksheet P15D Secondary colours

REQUIREMENTS

Each group of pupils will need:
White light source (such as a slide projector)
Colour filters, yellow, cyan and magenta
Coloured objects or brightly coloured paper to make up a picture

The procedure to be followed is detailed in the worksheet. Most of these experiments are best demonstrated to the whole class.

Worksheet P15E The electromagnetic spectrum

Pupils produce a chart of the electomagnetic spectrum.

Worksheet P15F Earthquakes

This introduces the different types of earthquake waves and how they are recorded.

Worksheet P15G Find that earthquake!

REQUIREMENTS

Each pupil will need:
Pencil
Calculator
Pair of compasses

Answers to worksheet questions
1 1.6 s for P waves and 2.4 s for S waves.

2 0.8 s.

3 12.5 km.

4 Station	Lag-time	Distance
A	24 s	300 km
B	48 s	600 km
C	28 s	350 km

6 The epicentre is the point where all three circles intersect. Town D (Rome) is about 700 km from the epicentre.

Worksheet P15H Making sounds

REQUIREMENTS

The whole class will need access to:
Tuning forks
Rubber bungs (a striking surface for the forks)
30 cm rulers
Signal generator
Loudspeaker

This is a circus of experiments to look at how sounds are produced. For many groups, most of these activities will already have been covered at Key stage 3. The experiments introduce four basic concepts:
* Sounds are made by vibrating objects.
* Higher sounds (higher pitch) are produced by objects producing more vibrations per second than lower sounds.
* Louder sounds are produced by larger vibrations than quiet sounds.
* The smaller the sound-producing system, the higher the pitch tends to be.

Pupils should be encouraged to feel the vibrations of the tuning fork as well as see them. They should think about why the sound is louder if the stem of the fork is put on the bench. (They may notice that it dies away faster too.)

Answers to worksheet questions

1 By banging the tuning fork, flicking the ruler and connecting the loudspeaker to the signal generator.

2 It is vibrating.

3 Louder sounds correspond to larger vibrations.

4 The tuning fork will only produce sound of a single note. The pitch of the vibrating ruler can be changed by changing its length. The pitch of the loudspeaker can be changed by changing the frequency of the signal generator.

5 There are arguments for saying that any sound of a single pitch can be regarded as musical.

6 The movements were repeated oscillations.

7 Pupils should recognize that **all** things that make sounds involve some movement, even if that movement is difficult to detect.

Worksheet P15I More about sounds

REQUIREMENTS

The whole class will need access to:
Signal generator
Loudspeaker
Connecting wires
Oscilloscope
Microphone
Selection of musical instruments, e.g. a descant recorder and small electronic keyboard plus any
   brought in by pupils (who may wish to demonstrate them themselves)
"Help sheet" on musical instruments

This activity aims to make the connections between pitch and frequency, and loudness and amplitude, and the traces seen on the oscilloscope screen. The CRO patterns should also help to explain the difference in the quality of notes played on different instruments.

Answers to worksheet questions

1 As the frequency increases, so does the pitch.

2 Expect the highest audible note to be above 20 kHz for young ears, and considerably below that for older ears.

3 The patterns indicate the quality of the note.

4 For the same note, the frequency (i.e. the number of waves on the screen) is the same.

5 For most instruments, the source of vibration is obvious. In the case of the recorder and the flute, the vibrating parts are eddies of air passing either side of an edge.

6a Pattern (c), because it is a smooth (sine) wave.
b Pattern (e), because it is the largest-amplitude wave.
c Pattern (b), because there are the most waves in the screen width.

Worksheet P15J Ultrasonics

This worksheet gives examples of the applications of ultrasonics. Medical ultrasonics typically uses frequencies of around 3.5 MHz with waves that travel at around 1500 m/s through body tissue.

Answers to worksheet questions

1 Bats locate insects by sending out bursts of ultrasonic waves and listening to the echoes.

2 X-rays, but they have long-term harmful side-effects, and feeling through the abdomen, but that is only possible late in pregnancy; other methods are invasive. The advantages of ultrasonics are that it is non-invasive and provides high resolution – in the order of the wavelength (around 0.5 mm).

Worksheet P15K How does sound travel?

REQUIREMENTS

The whole class will need:
Bell jar containing suspended bell and battery (see note 1)
Vacuum pump
Safety screen and eye protection for the teacher and pupils (see note 2)

Each group of pupils will need:
Several "Slinky" springs
Sticky tape

Notes:
1 The battery for the bell should be strapped to the bell and the whole assembly hung inside the bell jar from elastic bands; this helps prevent sound from being carried to the jar by taut or stiff connections.
2 A safety screen **must** be used with the evacuated bell jar.

Pupils will discover both longitudinal waves and transverse waves in the course of their investigations. Transverse waves were investigated in more detail in Worksheet P14A.

Answers to worksheet questions
1 With a good pump the sound is very much reduced when the air is removed, and attention can be drawn to the fact that the bell is still visible, i.e. light can still travel through the space. (Lest we be too complacent about the "obvious" view that the experiment shows that sound cannot travel through a vacuum, we should be aware that even with the best vacuum pumps, sufficient air will remain for the sound to be adequately transferred! The reason that the sound gets much quieter is because the bell is less able to transfer its own energy to the air remaining in the bell jar.)

2 Energy (and information).

3 Shows the position of part of the spring.

4a If the air travelled to her ear, the area around the loudspeaker would be a vacuum.
b The air between the loudspeaker and her ear vibrates backwards and forwards and the wave travels through the air.

Worksheet P15L Resonance

REQUIREMENTS

Each group of pupils will need:
Dynamics trolley
Runway for trolley
2 clamp stands or G-clamps
4 springs, expendable
Thick rubber tubing, 1 m

The procedure is given on the worksheet. Explain that resonance occurs when the forcing frequency is equal to a natural frequency of vibration. The idea of forced oscillations is introduced and can lead to a discussion of resonance in other situations. Other demonstrations of mechanical resonance could be done if the equipment is available.

Answers to worksheet questions

1 The glass breaks because the amplitude of vibration it is forced to make exceeds the distortion that will break it. The driving frequency has to be equal to the glass's own frequency of oscillation.

2 You have to push them at a frequency equal to the natural frequency of the swing.

3 The car would bounce along the road, possibly completely losing contact with the ground. The effects would be even more startling if the frequency with which the car encountered the bumps corresponded to the resonant frequency of the suspension system.

4 The length of the tube of air controls the note in most wind instruments. The frequency of vibration is equal to the resonant frequency of the tube of air.

5 Higher frequency notes can be played by: plucking or bowing the thinner strings; tightening the string; shortening the string by moving the left hand's fingers towards the bridge; or producing harmonics, for instance by gently touching the string half or one third of the way along before plucking or bowing.

Demonstration experiments

Section P15.1: Colour mixing

REQUIREMENTS
3 light sources
Colour filters, primary and secondary, for light sources
Screen
Well-darkened laboratory

The three light sources need to project coloured light onto the screen. Ray lamps at the end of cardboard tubes may be used, or three slide projectors if available.

It is necessary to "balance" the intensities of the colours produced by the sources. This can be done by putting more than one filter in, or alternatively by controlling the voltage to each lamp through a Variac or rheostat, if this can be done without damage to the projector.

Section P15.2: Speed of light in an optical fibre

This is an optional experiment which some schools may care to include in the work of this chapter. The equipment used forms a part of the Revised Nuffield A-level Physics course and a complete set is sold by at least one of the leading equipment manufacturers. Once set up, the experiment works easily and well, and its results are easy to interpret. Nevertheless, the necessary equipment is expensive and schools may not wish to buy it simply to perform this experiment.

REQUIREMENTS
Oscilloscope, double beam
Speed of light apparatus
Metre rule
Leads

The detailed procedure for this experiment will be found in the booklet "Optical fibres in school physics". (See the Further information section.) Equipment manufacturers producing a kit of parts also give detailed instructions.

Section P15.4: Forced oscillations in a spring-tethered trolley

REQUIREMENTS
Dynamics trolley
Runway for trolley
2 stands
Springs, disposable
Spring, long and heavy, or length of rubber tubing

Note:
A heavy spring is much the best. The mass of the rubber tubing will have to be increased by filling it with sand if this is to be used instead.

The set up is illustrated in figure 15.22 in the pupils' book. This experiment needs setting up beforehand and the number of springs attaching the trolley to the retort stands should be adjusted so that the trolley responds to a wave arriving at 1 or 2 hertz. Attach three springs "in series" to each end of the trolley to give adequate amplitude. To obtain the right frequency it will be necessary to have two or three such sets of springs "in parallel" on each side of the trolley. With a little practice it is possible to demonstrate quite clearly the way in which the trolley will only take up energy at one particular frequency of wave oscillation. The system is quite "sharply tuned" – careful adjustment of the forcing frequency can lead to large amplitude oscillations of the trolley.

Section P15.5: Reflection and refraction of sound

REQUIREMENTS
Hard surface (such as a wall)
2 tubes, cardboard (internal diameter not less than 7 cm)
Clock, watch, or metronome with a loud "tick" (see Note)
Balloon filled with carbon dioxide

Note:
A loudspeaker driven by a signal-generator may be used as the source of the sound, with a microphone and oscilloscope to detect it.

The cardboard tubes are used to direct the sound at the hard surface and then to pick up the reflection as shown overleaf.

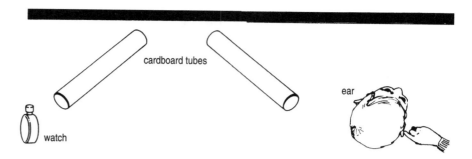

Detecting sound reflections.

A balloon filled with carbon dioxide gas can act as a "sound lens". The arrangement of the equipment is shown below. Careful adjustment of distances is necessary if the demonstration is to be effective. Trial and error will be needed as the precise distances depend on the curvature of the balloon. Try 2 m between clock and ear to start with. Interposing the balloon will make the "tick" seem louder.

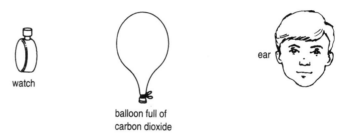

Using a balloon as a "sound lens".

Further information

"Optical fibres in school physics"
This booklet is number 2 in the Experimenting with Industry series published by the Association for Science Education for the Standing Conference on Schools' Science and Technology. Pages 17–20 give the details of an experiment designed to measure the speed of light in an optical fibre.

Topic P5   Electricity

Introduction

The importance of electricity in our lives has led to this being the longest topic in the Physics course. It is also the hardest. Only the effects of "using electricity" can be directly experienced. Matter, force, motion, even waves are things we can either sense or see. Even the transfer of energy (as when we get tired after "working") can be more directly experienced than electricity. It is this intangibility that makes the understanding of electricity especially difficult.

In starting this topic, it is assumed that pupils will all have had some experience of wiring up a simple circuit – to light a lamp, say. They may well have used an ammeter to measure an electric current. However, it is also assumed that many pupils will not have understood many of the things they have already seen. Consequently the first sections of Chapter **P**16 provide an opportunity for going over what may be for many pupils "old ground". The amount of time spent on this will depend on the pupils' understanding and ability. Certainly there will be no point in sacrificing understanding in order to take in the more advanced ideas in the rest of Chapters **P**16 and **P**17. Alternative routes have been provided in both chapters so that emphasis can be given to simple qualitative ideas if this seems more appropriate for some pupils.

Chapter **P**16 "Using electricity" is concerned with electric current. It seeks to establish the idea that much of what we call "electricity" is to do with electric **charge** moving round closed loops of wires and components – things we refer to as **circuits**. Chapter **P**17 "Energy and electricity" takes the story further. The flow of an electric current is associated with the transfer of energy – from the electricity supply to elsewhere. This chapter looks at the meaning of "voltage" and its relationship with electric power. Chapter **P**18 "Making use of electricity" shows how an electric current can produce a magnetic force which can be used to drive motors. Reversing this effect, the chapter goes on to show how dynamos enable the electrical transfer of energy from fuels to other uses.

Chapter **P**19 "Making pictures with electricity" looks more closely at the nature of electric charge. Chapter **P**20 "Control" is concerned with the way electricity can be used not only to help us do things by transferring energy where it is needed, but also to control this transfer of energy. This leads, via a discussion of simple switches, to some elementary electronics. Finally, Chapter **P**21 "Communication" is concerned with the way in which electricity is used in telephone and radio communication systems.

Note on use of the word "electricity"

The frequent use of the word "electricity" rather than the more specific phrases "electric charge", "electric current", or even "energy" needs some explanation.

The word "electricity" is in common use. If pupils are to make any sense of the ideas we associate with the study and use of electricity then it is important that they link these with their everyday language and their preconceived ideas. In everyday usage, the word "electricity" may take on several different meanings:

1 It may refer generally to a group of related phenomena, as when we speak of the study of light, or dynamics.

2 It may refer to the energy source that provides the electric current, as in the words "electricity supply".

3 It may refer to the energy we can transfer via an electric current, as when we refer to "using electricity".

4 It may be a loose way of referring to electric charge, as when we say "we depend more and more on electricity to transfer energy from fuels to where we need it."

In the pupils' book, all of these usages will be found where they seem to help clarify the ideas being developed by linking them to everyday experience and usage. However, in view of the fact that the word "electricity" is a loose translation of either "energy associated with electric charge" or "electric charge" itself, phrases such as "electricity generators" or "making electricity" have been avoided where possible, since neither charge, nor energy, can be **made**.

Chapter **P**16   **Using electricity**
Electric power and electric currents

The syllabus section

Context

An understanding of electric current is developed by linking this to the "power" ratings of domestic electrical appliances. Ideas about electric charge are developed. The section concludes by returning to domestic aspects of the safe use of electricity.

Knowledge and understanding

Syllabus statements	PoS	SoA
Appreciate the need for a complete circuit when making use of electricity, and recognize that electricity is a means of transferring energy and that the current can be read by an ammeter.	4(i)8	4.4(a)
Be able to use these ideas safely in circuits containing a number of components (cells, buzzers, bulbs and relays) which are controlled by switches.	4(i)2,8	4.4(a)
Be able to recognize and use the agreed symbols for bulbs, cells, switches, relays and buzzers.	4(i)8	4.5(a)
Know the function of components such as bulbs, cells, switches, relays and buzzers in the context of solving simple problems.	4(i)8	4.5(a)
Know that an electric current is a flow of electric charge, that electric charge is measured in coulombs and that a flow rate of one coulomb per second is called one ampere.	4(i)7	4.9(a)

Opportunities for co-ordination

C14, looks in detail at the way energy is transferred inside an electric cell. Electrical energy in atoms and groups of atoms links to **C**18.

Routes and times

Basic	Central	Further
Omit Q4. Spend more time revising basic electricity. *2 hours*	**P16.1 Using electricity** **P16.2 Simple circuits** **Worksheet P16A Simple circuits** Omit Experiment 3. *1¼ hours*	All of Worksheet **P16A** is suitable. Brief revision only. *¾ hour*
Simple revision of electric circuits and revision of the use of ammeters. *¾ hour*	**P16.3 Electric currents** Omit reference to charge and current. **Worksheet P16C Electric currents** (optional; side 1 only) *½ hour*	Section **P16.3** is suitable for revision homework.
		P16.4 Electric charge Include demonstration of the experiment in figure 16.12. **P16.5 Electric current again** **Worksheet P16C Electric currents** *1 ¾ hours*
Worksheet **P16B** "Using electricity in the home" is also suitable. *1½ hours*	**P16.6 Transferring energy using electricity** Omit Q18. **P16.7 Using electricity safely** Omit Q20. *1¼ hours*	All parts of this section are suitable, but spend less time. *¾ hour*
Total: 4¼ hours	*Total: 3 hours*	*Total: 3¼ hours*

The pupils' book

P16.1 Using electricity

The chapter starts by looking at the everyday use of electricity and asking some questions about it. Why is electricity often said to be dangerous? What do the labels found on all electrical appliances mean?

Attention is directed to the "power rating" given on such labels and some questions link this to earlier work on power in Chapter **P8**. The acceptance of power values of electrical appliances as being "what the label reads" is central to the development of electrical ideas in this chapter and in Chapter **P17**. It serves to relate electrical phenomena to other, more readily understood, phenomena involving energy transfer. It also helps the understanding of the meanings of both "amperes" and "volts". No circular argument is involved here, for while it may well be true that manufacturers have calculated these powers from "volts × amperes", they could in principle be measured directly.

Answer to selected question
4a Electric cookers do not, of course, always work at full power. Even if all the rings and the oven were switched on, the average power used would be much less than the maximum power (11 000 W in this case), due to the operation of temperature control devices.
b The input power is the power actually drawn from the supply; the output power relates to the (maximum) output to the speakers.
c This question revises the link between power and energy. Karen is quite right to suppose that a refrigerator will use much less energy – the refrigeration unit only works intermittently in response to thermostatic controls.

P16.2 Simple circuits

This short section revises ideas about simple circuits which pupils should already have met. However, two worksheets are provided (Worksheets **P16A** and **P16B**) which can provide more extensive practical experience for those who need it.

P16.3 Electric currents

This section introduces the main question posed by this chapter: "What happens in an electric circuit?". Two "mains" devices of different powers are connected to the mains supply via ammeters, and the readings of the ammeters are compared. These are seen to be related in the same way as the "power ratings". The higher power device is transferring energy more quickly. This suggests a simple explanation of energy being transferred from the supply by something that is flowing round the circuit – something we call the electric charge. Ammeters read this flow of charge in units called amperes. For some pupils this may be sufficient explanation. They could go on to section **P16.5** to look more closely at the meaning to be attached to the phrase "electric current". Others will benefit by a closer look, first, at electric charge.

Answer to selected question

8 The circuits may well be demonstrated. Pictures are included here to give pupils practice in drawing circuits and in reading ammeters. Many pupils find this difficult and the question could be supplemented by further examples of (low-voltage) circuits laid out in the laboratory.

P16.4 Electric charge

This section introduces pupils to electrostatic charging, which has obvious direct links with ions and electrons. Both of these are important concepts in later work in Physics and Chemistry. Charging by friction is a process of charge separation. This point is illustrated in figure 16.10a in the pupils' book but is not elaborated.

By using a Van de Graaff generator to produce the charge separation, it can be shown that these charges, when moving, will deflect an ammeter just like the charges from a battery. They are the same in all respects.

If a coulombmeter is available it is well worth using it to measure the charge on a charged polythene rod. The tiny amount of charge on the rod can be contrasted with the amount of charge flowing in a low-voltage circuit containing, say, a 12 V, 5 W lamp.

Answer to selected question

10 It would be necessary to transfer some charge from the black terminal of the battery to, say, an insulated conductor and then see if it repelled a charged polythene rod. This can be demonstrated using an EHT power supply.

P16.5 Electric current again

This section emphasizes that current is rate of flow of charge, not speed of charge. An analogy is drawn between electric currents and the flow of water in rivers and streams.

The section goes on to look at the readings of ammeters in series and branching circuits and investigates whether these readings are consistent with measurements of electric currents. This latter section could be omitted by pupils who have spent some time on the more elementary parts of the chapter. Worksheet **P16C** provides some experiments the pupils can do to test these ideas.

Answers to selected questions

12 2 A.

13 7200 C.

14 50 s.

15 A_1: 9 A; A_2: 5 A; A_3: 3 A.

16a A_2 and A_3 will both read 2 A.
b The lamp will dim; the readings on both A_1 and A_3 will both be 1 A.

P16.6 Transferring energy using electricity

This short section compares the transfer of energy using electric currents with the transfer of energy that can come about by pumping water round a closed circuit. In both cases energy transfer takes place as soon as the pump or battery is switched into the circuit. Energy is transferred **via** the water or the charges; it is not first **given** to the water or charges which **then** carry the energy round the circuit. This point is re-emphasized in Chapter **P**17. It is particularly important in understanding how alternating currents can be used to transfer energy. In an electric circuit work is done by the electric field set up by the battery pushing the charges through whatever circuit component is transferring the energy.

The section concludes by looking at how energy can be transferred to the surroundings by a wire, heated by an electric current. It shows how the temperature of a wire is related to the rate at which this transfer of energy has to take place. This leads to a discussion of one of the dangers associated with the use of electricity – the danger of fire. Fuses are discussed briefly.

Answer to selected question
18 This question compares the gain and loss of energy by a hot wire with the equilibrium of an evaporating liquid. The analogy with shoppers in a supermarket is again relevant. If the rate at which people enter a supermarket increases, the number of shoppers in the supermarket will increase until, once again, they are leaving at the rate at which they are entering.

P16.7 Using electricity safely

The issue of safety (which started this chapter) is continued in this final section by looking at the value of "earthing".

Activities

Worksheet P16A Simple circuits

REQUIREMENTS

For Experiments 1 and 2 each group of pupils will need:
2 lamps, 1.25 V, 0.25 A MES
2 lamp holders, MES
Cell, 1.5 V, in holder
Ammeter, 1 A d.c.
Connecting wires

Notes:
There is no particular reason why these component values should be adhered to. All that is needed is to match bulbs to batteries and holders, and to supply an ammeter of appropriate full-scale deflection. The main point is that "circuit boards" should not be used, except as cell holders. These would produce more constraints on how the circuit can be wired up than is required in these experiments.

For Experiments 3 and 4 each group of pupils will need:
3 cells, 1.5 V, in holders
2 lamps, 3.5 V, 0.3 A MES
2 lamp holders, MES
Switch
Ammeter, 1 A d.c.
Connecting wires
Resistor, 15 Ω, 10 W wire wound (see Notes)
Resistor, 4.7 Ω, 7 W, labelled "X" (see Notes)
Resistor, 10 Ω 7 W, labelled "Y" (see Notes)
Rheostat, 15 Ω

Notes:
Any resistors of a rated power suitable for the circuit will do, provided they are 15 Ω or less.

Again the circuits are meant to be wired up with connecting wires, rather than on a circuit board. "Clip component holders" developed for Nuffield A-level Physics are a convenient means of providing small components like resistors with sockets.

All four of these experiments could be set up as "stations" for a circus of experiments. As far as possible, pupils should work individually at setting up the circuits.

Worksheet P16B Using electricity in the home

REQUIREMENTS

Each group of pupils will need:
Torch, electric, working
Torch, electric, not working
Plug, 13 A mains
Wire, 3-core mains
Fuses, a selection, some of which have "blown"

Cell, 1.5 V, in holder
Lamp, 1.25 V, 0.25 A MES
Lamp holder, MES
Screwdriver
Wire strippers

Note:
A Worcester circuit board, with fittings, could be used as an alternative to the cell and lamp arrangement for testing fuses.

Warning
The 13A mains plug must be modified in some way so that a wired-up plug cannot be pushed into a socket, leaving bare wire exposed at the other end!
Plugs can be modified in several ways:

* by drilling the exposed "earth" pin and correctly fitting a heavy split pin;
* by bending the exposed "earth" pin at right angles about half way along its length;
* using "off-standard" plugs which cannot fit into standard sockets.

Pupils should be warned not to "try out" the newly wired plug for themselves. It is recommended that the power to the bench sockets is turned off during this work.

Worksheet P16C Electric currents

REQUIREMENTS

For Experiments 1 and 2 each group of pupils will need:
3 cells, 1.5 V, in holders
Rheostat, 15 Ω
2 lamps, 1.25 V, 0.25 A MES
2 lamp holders, MES
3 ammeters, 1 A d.c.
Connecting wires

For Experiment 3 (optional) each group of pupils will need:
Power supply, 12 V d.c. (or rechargeable cells)
Resistor, 15Ω 10 W wire wound
2 rheostats, 15 Ω
2 lamps, 12 V, 5 V SBC
2 lamp holders, SBC
6 ammeters, 1 A d.c.
Connecting wires

These circuits use so many ammeters that it will only be possible for one or two to be set up at a time.

A suitable circuit for Experiment 3 is given below. Adjust the rheostats so that the readings on A_2 and A_3 are different from each other, and from the reading on A_1. The total of A_1, A_2 and A_3 must not exceed 1 A (the maximum reading on A_6).

There is, of course, no need to stick to these values – an alternative circuit will do, but for the purposes of this exercise all the ammeters should be alike and should have the same full-scale deflection.

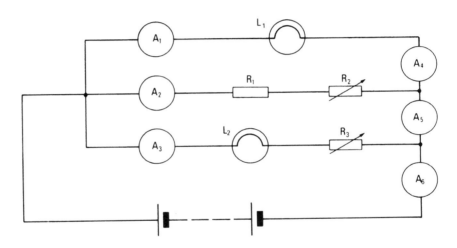

Circuit for Experiment 3.

Demonstration experiments

Section P16.1: Electric data plates

REQUIREMENTS
One or more appliances on which the data plate can be seen and read (an electric iron is illustrated in the pupils' book).

Section P16.3: Comparing electric currents (optional)

REQUIREMENTS
Mains electric fire, 1000 W
Mains lamp, 100 W
2 ammeters, 5 A a.c.
2 mains connecting blocks

It is best to keep to the same full-scale deflection for each ammeter in order to emphasize the difference in currents.

Safety note:

All connections used for this experiment **must** be inaccessible, for example within a junction box. Exposed 240 V connections must **not** be used. If 4 mm sockets are used, they must be of the shrouded type.

Section P16.4: Electric charge

REQUIREMENTS

For Experiment A:
2 electrostatics rods, polythene
Duster
Electrostatics rod, acetate
Stirrups to hang up rods
2 stands, bosses and clamps
Thread, nylon

For Experiment B:
Van de Graaff generator
Ping-pong ball coated with Aquadag and suspended on a nylon thread
2 circular brass plates, 125 mm diameter, on insulating handles
3 stands, bosses and clamps
Sensitive ammeter (see Note)
EHT power pack (optional)
Connecting wires

Note:

An ammeter or galvanometer reading currents of a few microamperes is required. Any such meter can be used. A light-beam galvanometer or electronic equivalent can be used.

The equipment is set up as in figure 16.12 in the pupils' book. The plates should be placed about 10 cm apart. When the Van de Graaff generator is started, the conducting ball should move back and forth between the plates, and the ammeter should record a current flowing. It is important to place the ammeter so that one terminal is connected to the "earth" terminal of the Van de Graaff generator. In this way the potential difference between the wire of the galvanometer coil and its surroundings is made as small as possible. Van de Graaff generators produce very high potential differences – higher than the galvanometer coil insulation is designed to withstand.

Changing the plate separation changes the rate at which the conducting ball shuttles between the plates – and consequently the current recorded by the galvanometer changes.

Optionally, the Van de Graaff machine can be replaced by an EHT power pack (giving 5000 V). The experiment can be repeated with the same result. This shows that charges from both sources are the same in nature.

Charging a coulombmeter

REQUIREMENTS
Acetate strip
Duster
Coulombmeter
Capacitor, 0.01 µF
Cell, 1.5 V

Charge the coulombmeter with the rubbed acetate rod. Charge the capacitor by connecting it to the cell, then connect it to the coulombmeter.

This experiment shows the similar nature of the charge from both the cell and the rod.

Section P16.6: Water circuit

REQUIREMENTS
Water circuit board
4 cells, 1.5 V, in holders
Electric motor, 6 V
Connecting wires

If available, this can be demonstrated here. It is an expensive piece of equipment to buy for just this one demonstration.

The behaviour of the water circuit can be compared with a similar circuit consisting of a battery and a motor.

Further information

"Electricity in the home" – a video
This is very relevant here. It deals with power, current, fuses, earthing and the heating effect of an electric current. (ITV Physics in Action series.)

Chapter **P17**   **Energy and electricity**
Voltage and electrical resistance

The syllabus section

Context

The energy associated with an electric current is introduced by surveying the wide range of applications in which this energy is used. The relationship between resistance, voltage and current concludes with a study of the design of a hair-drier and the factors affecting its performance.

Knowledge and understanding

	Tier		Syllabus statements	PoS	SoA
B	C	F			
			Understand that the "voltage" of an electrical supply is a measure of the energy it can transfer from an electrical supply to elsewhere.	4(i)7	4.6(a)
			Understand the meaning of the term electrical resistance and know that the resistance of a component (in ohms)=voltage across component/current through component.	4(i)7	4.6(a)
			Appreciate some of the factors affecting the resistance of wires, and fixed and variable resistors.	4(i)8	4.6(a)
			Know that a capacitor can store electric charge and thus energy.	4(i)8	4.8(a)
			Know that a potential difference of one volt is equivalent to an energy difference of one joule per coulomb of charge.	4(i)6	4.8(a)
			Be able to use the relationship "power = voltage × current".	4(i)5	4.8(a) 4.9(a)
			Be able to apply the idea of voltage numerically to circuits containing more than one component, and apply correctly the term potential difference.	4(i)6	4.9(a)
			Be able to use measurements of voltage and current to derive measurements of electrical resistance, charge, energy transferred and electrical power.	4(i)7	4.9(a)
			Appreciate the experimental evidence leading to Ohm's Law. Understand, and be able to use, the relationship between potential difference, resistance and current.	4(i)6	4.9(a)

Routes and times

Basic	Central	Further
Omit pages 264 and 265, and "Measuring voltage". *1½ hours*	**P17.1 Putting electricity to use** **P17.2 Energy in electric circuits** Pages 264 and 265 are optional; omit "Measuring voltage". **Worksheet P17A Voltage** Omit Experiment 3. *1¾ hours*	All of section **P17.2** and Worksheet **P17A** are suitable.
Replace section **P17.3** and Worksheet **P17B** with a simple introduction to $P = VI$.	**P17.3 Voltmeters, ammeters and power** (up to Q10) **Worksheet P17B Power in electric circuits** Set Q12 and 13 for homework. *1 hour*	All of section **P17.3** is suitable. Replace Worksheet **P17B** by Worksheet **P17C** "The efficiency of an electric motor" (this is a suitable Sc1 assessment for Further level). *1½ hours*
Replace section **P17.4** by Worksheet **P17F** "Electrical resistance". *2½ hours*	**P17.4 Electrical resistance** **Worksheet P17D Controlling the size of an electric current** **Worksheet P17E The resistance of a lamp** This is a suitable Sc1 activity. *2¼ hours*	Section **P17.5** "Changing electrical resistance" is suitable for homework. Omit Worksheet **P17E**. Worksheet **P17G** "Ohm's Law" is optional. *1 hour*
	P17.6 The design of a hair-drier *Optional*	Section **P17.6** should be set for homework.
Total: 5 hours	Total: 5 hours	Total: 4¼ hours

Monitoring the progress of Sc1

Investigating the efficiency of an electric motor

Students should investigate what affects the efficiency of an electric motor. This investigation may be carried out instead of Worksheet **P**17C "The efficiency of an electric motor".

Sample criteria are given below for an assessment between levels 7 and 10.

Strand (i) Ask questions, predict and hypothesize, e.g.	Strand (ii) Observe, measure and manipulate variables, e.g.	Strand (iii) Interpret their results and evaluate scientific evidence, e.g.
7(a) Suggest, with reasons, that load, power supply voltage and the make of motor all affect the efficiency of the motor, and that all these are important	**7(b)** Measure energy in and work done for a range of loads and a range of voltages	**7(c)** Conclude that the size of the load has a bigger effect on efficiency than the power supply voltage over voltages between 3 and 6 V and loads from 10 to 100 g
8(a) Suggest, with reasons, that the efficiency is doubled if the load is doubled, and suggest a relevant investigation	**8(b)** As above, reading meters to one scale division and length, time and load to within five per cent	**8(c)** Explain why the voltage was kept constant for a range of loads and why the load was kept constant for a range of voltages
9(a) Suggest, with reasons, that the efficiency is doubled if the load is doubled and suggest a relevant investigation; also suggest repeating the experiment	**9(b)** Carry out the above procedure systematically	**9(c)** Use the data from repeated experiments to draw graphs of results and to show how the efficiency changes with load; comment on the accuracy of the experiment
10(a) Suggest, with reasons, that the efficiency is dependent on the load because the work done on the load depends on the force times the distance through which the load is moved	**10(b)** As above, and check measuring instruments	**10(c)** Use the data from repeated experiments to draw graphs of results and to show how the efficiency changes with load; conclude that the efficiency is low when the load is low because the force is small even though the distance moved is large and that the efficiency is low when the load is high because the distance moved is small even though the force is large; comment on the accuracy of the experiment

Investigating the relationship between current and voltage

Students should investigate how the current through a conductor depends on the applied voltage. This investigation may be carried out after Worksheet P17G "Ohm's Law".

Sample criteria are given below for an assessment between levels 7 and 10.

Strand (i) Ask questions, predict and hypothesize, e.g.	Strand (ii) Observe, measure and manipulate variables, e.g.	Strand (iii) Interpret their results and evaluate scientific evidence, e.g.
7(a) Suggest, with reasons, that voltage, length of conductor and type of cell affect the current, and that an important variable is voltage	7(b) Measure the current in a range of conductors over a range of voltages	7(c) Conclude that both voltage and length of conductor affect the current with voltages up to 6 V and conductors up to 2 m long
8(a) Suggest, with reasons, that if voltage is doubled then the current will be doubled, and suggest a relevant investigation	8(b) As above, measuring current and voltage to one scale division	8(c) Explain why voltage was kept constant for a range of conductors and why the type of conductor was kept constant for a range of voltages
9(a) As above, and suggest repeating the experiment	9(b) Carry out the above procedure systematically	9(c) Use the data from repeated experiments to draw graphs of results and to show that current increases with voltage; comment on the accuracy of the experiment
10(a) Suggest, with reasons, that current is directly proportional to voltage	10(b) As above, and check apparatus	10(c) As above, and use results to show that current is directly proportional to voltage; comment on the accuracy of the experiment; explore the shapes of the graphs

The pupils' book

This chapter is concerned with energy transfer and electrical resistance. Understanding the process of energy transfer and its measurement in volts is one of the hardest parts of work in electricity at an elementary level. Yet it has to be understood if electric circuits are to be used sensibly and correctly. This introductory note is concerned with the background to the approach to energy transfer adopted in the pupils' book.

In the notes on Chapter P16 it was stated briefly that every attempt had been made to **avoid** the suggestion that energy was transferred in electrical circuits by a process in which the cell, battery, or power supply delivers this energy to electrical charges, which **then** transfer the energy elsewhere. This is not the mechanism of energy transfer and to suggest that it is can lead to many difficulties. For example, it can be shown that electrons move very slowly indeed round circuits even when there is a large current flowing. If the supply delivers energy to the electrons which then transfer it elsewhere, pupils can legitimately ask why, for example, lights come on as soon as a switch is closed. It is also not at all clear how these moving charges can carry energy.

In fact the transfer of energy in an electrical circuit involves work, in the same way as many other energy transfers. Forces within the conducting wires act on the charges in them and move those charges. Energy is transferred and can in principle be measured (as force on charges × distance moved in the direction of the force). The force comes from an electric field set up by the cell, battery, or power supply in the connecting wires and components in the circuit. The force acts on the charge in the wires and components. If there is a complete circuit, this force can move the charges and energy is transferred.

With this picture in mind it becomes clear how energy can be transferred in a circuit carrying alternating or direct current (a.c. or d.c.). Charges do not have to travel **from the supply** to transfer energy. It is sufficient that there is an electrical force capable of moving the charges in the connecting wires and components. Whether this force continually changes direction (as in a.c.) or is in one direction only (as in d.c.) is immaterial to its ability to transfer energy.

The charges act in some ways like the piston in a steam engine, or the oil in a hydraulic system. They are the mechanism which enables forces to do work.

This description of energy transfer in electrical circuits seemed inappropriate to an elementary course as it depends on some understanding of electric fields. Furthermore, these electric forces cannot be directly measured. Even in more advanced work their size is deduced from measurements of potential difference. So in fact we say nothing about the mechanism of energy transfer in electric circuits in the pupils' book and content ourselves with describing a cell's or power supply's "energy capability".

Unfortunately, just knowing something's energy capability does not give us all the information we need when assessing its usefulness for a particular job. As pupils will have seen in the problem of the stair-lift in Chapter **P8**, having a motor which will transfer the necessary energy is not sufficient to lift a person up the stairs. It has to be able to provide the necessary force as well.

Electric batteries, like many other sources of energy, vary in their "strength" as well as their total energy capability. That is, they vary in the electric force they can apply to charges in circuits. The "voltage" of a battery is a way of describing this "strength". This can be seen by comparing two circuits, like those shown below. The first circuit contains a 60 W mains lamp connected to the 240 V mains supply. The second circuit contains a 12 V, 3 W lamp connected to a 12 volt battery in an otherwise identical circuit. Identical currents flow in the two circuits. In four seconds, one coulomb of charge will have flowed round both circuits. In terms of electric forces, the force in both circuits will have moved charges the same distance. But in one case 240 J have been transferred and in the other 12 J have been transferred. So the electric force set up by the mains supply is 20 times bigger than that set up by the 12 V supply. Hence a description of the "energy capability" of a supply in terms of the energy it can transfer per coulomb of charge flowing in the circuit gives a measure of the strength of the supply as well as a means of calculating the energy it can transfer.

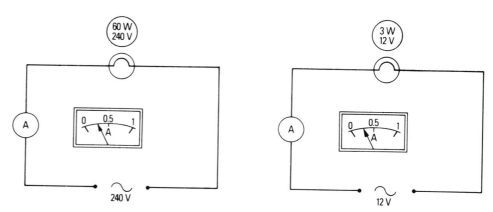

P17.1 Putting electricity to use

The first section "sets the scene" for the chapter as a whole by surveying a wide range of energy transfers in which electricity is involved. Question 1 is a "comprehension" question which tests understanding of the passage just read.

P17.2 Energy in electric circuits

The first part of this section compares the behaviour of two circuits which carry identical currents. The first contains a 60 W mains lamp connected to the 240 V mains supply. The second contains a 12 V, 3 W lamp connected to a 12 V supply. The energy transferred in the lamps by the time one coulomb of charge has passed through each lamp is calculated on the assumption that the marked powers of the lamps are correct. This leads to numbers identical with those describing the voltages of the supplies from which the lamps are run.

This introduction to the meaning of voltage may be sufficient for some pupils. They can now turn to the section headed "Measuring voltage" on page 267 and do Worksheet **P**17A.

There is no circularity of argument in this method of using marked power ratings to arrive at voltage. As has been said in the notes on Chapter **P**16, these powers could in principle be measured directly by transferring energy from the lamp to a known mass of water. More able pupils are given the opportunity in question 8 to devise such an experiment for themselves.

For pupils who will benefit from a closer study of voltage, question 2 gives an opportunity to apply the same arguments to a different pair of light bulbs and question 3 gives some practice in relating energy to voltage and charge.

The next subsection extends the idea of voltage to circuits containing more than one energy-transferring component. The behaviour of lamps in series is compared with that of lamps in parallel. The ideas emerging from this comparison are applied to an investigation of ring main circuits in question 6.

The way the energy transferred from the supply is divided up between components is generalized further in the subsection entitled "Potential difference". This introduces the term "potential difference" because it is particularly appropriate when considering energy transfers in circuits with many components. However, for the rest of the chapter the more colloquial term "voltage" is preferred. While such a policy has the benefit of linking a concept to commonly used terms, it does tend to lead to pupils also talking about "ampage" for current – something that may need to be actively discouraged!

The section concludes with a brief introduction to the use of voltmeters. No attempt is made to explain their working. Worksheet **P**17A provides a number of experiments in which voltmeters are used and are seen to give the readings that would be expected of such an instrument.

Answers to selected questions
2a 0.05 C/s **b** 20 s **c** 2.4 J/s, 0.7 J/s **d** 2.4 J/s × 20 s = 48 J, 0.7 J/s × 20 s = 14 J.

3a 60 s **b** 180 J **c** 15 C.

4 The current increases by 3 times (for 3 lamps) and by 4 times (for 4 lamps).

5a 0.25 A **b** 1.0 A **c** 10 C, 40 C **d** 9600 J.

7a 3 J **b** 4 C **c** 12 J **d** 12 J/10 s = 1.2 W.

9 A_1 and A_2: 0.5 A; V: 1 V.

P17.3 Voltmeters, ammeters and power

This section reverses the arguments that led to the introduction of voltage, and shows how values for power may be derived from the potential difference across a component and the current passing through it.

This work serves to enhance an understanding of the meaning of voltage, so most of the work derives "power" from values of voltage and current by going back to first principles rather than by relying on the equation:

power = voltage × current.

Answers to selected questions
10b 6 J **c** 2 C **d** 12 J.

11a 2 J/C **b** 0.5 C/s **c** 1 J/s **d** 1 W **e** 3 J/C × 0.8 C/s = 2.4 J/s;
f It will be brighter. **g** 2.4 W **h** Power = current × voltage.

12c Maximum power = 240 × 13 = 3120 W **d i** 36 000 W **ii** 132 MW.

13b 6 V × 0.8 A = 4.8 W.

P17.4 Electrical resistance

This section emphasizes the fact that batteries provide a force which drives a current round a circuit. The factor in a circuit which determines the size of the current is called the electrical resistance of the circuit,

Some of the factors which determine the size of the electrical resistance of pieces of wire are explored using Worksheet **P**17D. After this exploration has been completed, the electrical resistance of a component is defined as being the voltage across the component divided by the current through it. No reference is made at this stage to any relationship between current and voltage. In this way electrical resistance is understood to be a property of any component which passes an electric current. (Those particular components for which the current through them is proportional to the size of the voltage across them have a resistance independent of the current passing through them.)

Answers to selected questions
14a 1 A **b** 6 A **c** 3 A.

15 60 Ω.

P17.5 Changing electrical resistance

Sufficient work may already have been done on resistance for some pupils. They can now go on to the final section of the chapter – concerned with the design of an electric hair-drier.

The section starts by measuring the electrical resistance of a 60 W mains lamp, using a voltage of only 3 V. The expected output power of the lamp is calculated and found to be over 1000 W. This leads to an exploration of the way the resistance of a light bulb varies with the current passing through it. Data for a 60 W mains lamp is provided in the pupils' book, but pupils themselves are invited to carry out a similar investigation using a 24 W, 12 V lamp.

The results of these investigations show that the resistance of the lamp increases as the current through it increases. This might be due to the wire in the light bulb getting hotter (the obvious explanation). But it might also be that the current through a lamp is not proportional to the voltage across it, even if the temperature remains constant. This latter point is explored experimentally, using Worksheet **P**17G. The graph plotting necessary in this experiment to show that current is in fact proportional to voltage leads to a further comment about experimental error and the need to draw best straight lines.

The investigation leads to a statement of Ohm's Law, true if the temperature of the wire does not change. That it is the change in the temperature of the wire that leads to the variation in the resistance of a light bulb is confirmed by removing the glass envelope from a 24 W, 12 V lamp and showing that if the filament is kept at a constant temperature (by immersing it in water) then the resistance is the same no matter what current passes through it.

Answer to selected question
19a 3 A **bi** 1 A **ii** 120 A
c Probably not, in the case of the 240 V supply, as the resistor's temperature would increase.

P17.6 The design of a hair-drier

The section concludes by applying ideas of current, voltage, resistance and power to a design problem – that of designing a hair-drier. The problem is that of getting the energy transferred to the wire away fast enough, so that neither the air nor the wire gets too hot.

Answer to selected question
20a 1600 W/240 V = 6.7 A, 350 W/240 V = 1.46 A
b 36 Ω, 164 Ω.

Activities

Worksheet P17A Voltage

REQUIREMENTS

Each group of pupils will need:
2 cells, 1.5 V, in holders
2 lamps, 1.25 V, 0.25 A MES
2 lamp holders, MES
Voltmeter, 5 V d.c.
Connecting wires

The procedure to be followed is detailed in the worksheet. Circuit boards could be used for these introductory experiments.

Worksheet P17B Power in electric circuits

REQUIREMENTS

Each group of pupils will need:
2 cells, 1.5 V, in holders
Lamp, 2.5 V, 0.2 A MES
Lamp holder, MES
Electric motor, 6 V d.c.
Voltmeter, 5 V d.c.
Ammeter, 1 A d.c.
Connecting wires

The procedure to be followed is detailed in the worksheet. It is not essential to stick to any of the values listed. A larger motor and a more powerful lamp could be used with adjustments to the power supply and meters as necessary. All that is necessary is to give pupils the opportunity to measure electric power in two different circumstances.

Worksheet P17C The efficiency of an electric motor

REQUIREMENTS

Each group of pupils will need:
Electric motor, 6 V d.c.
Power supply, 6 V d.c.
or
4 cells, 1.5 V, in holders
Ammeter, 5 A d.c. (see Note)
Voltmeter, 10 V d.c. (see Note)
Rheostat, 15 Ω
Switch

Slotted masses, 100 g set
Stopclock
Metre ruler
String
Connecting wires
G-clamp, or similar, to anchor the motor to the bench so it can lift a load

Note:

A sensitive joulemeter may be used as an alternative to the ammeter and voltmeter.

The aim of this investigation is to explore the efficiency of a small electric motor. To do this, pupils will have to measure the input power (multiplying voltage by current) and work out the output power by timing how long it takes the motor to raise a known load a measured distance. More than one factor may affect the efficiency. It will vary with the input power and with the load lifted.

Worksheet **P**17C gives pupils a bare minimum of help. Those who need it can ask for a Help sheet which will give them some assistance with the investigation.

Worksheet P17D **The size of an electric current**

This worksheet is suitable for setting up as a circus of experiments

REQUIREMENTS

*For Experiment **a** each group of pupils will need:*
5 cells, 1.5 V, in holders
Resistor, 10 Ω, 7 W wire wound
Ammeter, 1 A d.c.
Connecting wires

*For Experiment **b** each group of pupils will need:*
3 cells, 1.5 V, in holders
Wire, resistance, fixed to a board (see Note)
Resistor, 4.7 Ω
Ammeter, 1 A d.c.
Connecting wires

Note:

Eureka resistance wire of diameter 0.28 mm (32 s.w.g.) has a resistance of about 10 Ω per metre. 0.5 m of such a wire would have resistance of about 5 Ω and the current recorded by the ammeter would vary from about 1 A to about 0.5 A.

*For Experiment **c** each group of pupils will need:*
3 cells, 1.5 V, in holders
2 wires, resistance, each 0.5 m long, one 0.28 mm in diameter and
　one 0.56 mm in diameter (see Notes)
Wire, copper, 0.5 m long and 0.56 mm in diameter (see Notes)
Ammeter, 1 A d.c.
Resistor, 4.7 Ω
Connecting wires

Notes:

One wire is the same as that used for Experiment **b** (0.28 mm in diameter, 32 s.w.g.). The other wire needs to be about twice the thickness (0.56 mm in diameter, 24 s.w.g.). Copper wire 0.56 mm in diameter (24 s.w.g.) has a resistance of less than 0.1 Ω per metre. This should have an almost negligible effect on the meter reading, end to end. This is the point that needs to be made.

The procedure to be followed is detailed in the worksheet. Different equipment can be used, depending on the resources available. The outcome of the experiments is largely qualitative. If component values are changed, a check should be made to see that ammeters cannot be damaged by overloading.

Worksheet P17E The resistance of a lamp

REQUIREMENTS

Each group of pupils will need:
Power supply, 12 V d.c. variable
Ammeter, 1 A d.c.
Voltmeter, 15 V d.c.
Lamp, 12 V, 24 W SBC
Lamp holder, SBC
Switch
Rheostat, 15 Ω
Connecting wires

Note:
It may be necessary to supply a 0–50 V voltmeter, or a dual-range instrument giving 0–10 V and 0–50 V or similar.

This is another investigative practical for those who cope easily with the work. Again the pupils have to design their own circuit and then take appropriate readings. They may have difficulty in adjusting the current and voltage if they do not have a power pack with continuous voltage control. Ideally they should also be left to work this out for themselves given sufficient time and careful use of the equipment.

Unusually perhaps (and as in the pupils' book) the graph plotted is resistance (defined as *V/I* for any particular pair of values) against current. This is consistent with the approach adopted to resistance in the pupils' book.

There is no reason to stick to the values given. It may be more convenient to supply a lamp of different power or voltage. Results which are in essence the same will be produced, but suitable changes will have to be made to the other pieces of equipment.

Worksheet P17F Electrical resistance

REQUIREMENTS

Each group of pupils will need:
2 cells, 1.5 V, in holders
Ammeter, 1 A d.c.
Voltmeter, 5 V d.c.
Wire, resistance, 0.28 mm in diameter (32 s.w.g.), Eureka, wound into a coil (see Notes)
Wire, resistance, 0.28 mm in diameter (32 s.w.g.), Eureka, mounted on board (see Notes)
Connecting wires

Notes:
The coil can be wound on any suitable small tube, but it should be fastened down onto the tube so that the turns of bare wire do not touch each other. Such a resistor will have a resistance of about 5 Ω. It can be fixed in a clip component holder (already referred to in the notes on Worksheet **P**16A). The board can be made up using four lengths of 0.28 mm Eureka wire: 60 cm, 45 cm, 30 cm, and 15 cm long.

The procedure to be followed is given on the worksheet.

Worksheet P17G Ohm's Law

REQUIREMENTS

Each group of pupils will need:
3 cells, 1.5 V, in holders
Rheostat, 15 Ω
Wire, resistance, 0.28 mm in diameter,
Eureka, 0.5 m long (see Note)
Ammeter, 1 A d.c.
Voltmeter, 5 V d.c.
Connecting wires

Note:
It is best to leave the wire loose so that its temperature does not change significantly during the experiment.

The procedure to be followed is detailed in the worksheet. This experiment is open to the traditional objection that the use of a voltmeter to establish Ohm's Law involves a circular argument. However, the voltmeter has been introduced empirically. While pupils cannot help but see that it is in some way related to an ammeter, the calibrations can in principle be checked by an energy transfer experiment which itself would involve no appeal to Ohm's Law.

Demonstration experiments

Section P17.2: Energy in electric circuits

REQUIREMENTS
Lamp, 60 W mains, in holder
Lamp, 12 V, 3 W, line filament, in holder
Power supply, 12 V a.c.
2 ammeters, 1 A a.c.
Mains connecting block
Connecting wires

The comparison of a 60 W mains lamp with a 12 V, 3 W lamp can be demonstrated. A suitable 3 W lamp is available from equipment suppliers as a line filament lamp. It is best to run both lamps from an a.c. supply so that the two ammeters are identical in appearance. The fact that a.c. is used rather than d.c. does not invalidate the argument, and the concept of voltage should be well established before pupils come to recognize the difference between a.c. and d.c. supplies.

Great care should be taken when wiring ammeters into circuits connected to the mains supply. All connections should be shrouded with insulating material; rubber tubing is very useful for this. No adjustment to connections should be made once the supply has been turned on.

Lamps in parallel and in series can also be demonstrated using 60 W mains lamps. Again, the same precautions need to be taken when wiring up circuits.

Warning
All connections used for this experiment **must** be inaccessible, for example within a junction box. Exposed 240 V connections must **not** be used. If 4 mm sockets are used, they must be of the shrouded type.

Section P17.5: Variation of the resistance of a mains lamp with current

REQUIREMENTS
Lamp, 60 W mains
Ammeter, 1 A a.c.
Voltmeter, 300 V a.c.
Variac, to vary input voltage
Connecting wires

In addition to the demonstration experiments, any of the circuits shown in the pupils' book could with advantage be set up in the laboratory. This helps in enabling pupils to relate symbolic drawings of circuits to the "real thing".

Warning
All connections used for this experiment **must** be inaccessible, for example within a junction box. Exposed 240 V connections must **not** be used. If 4 mm sockets are used, they must be of the shrouded type.

Further information

Computer software and interface
The current – voltage module of "Measurement toolkit" (available from Deltronics, 91 Hed-y-Parc, Cefneithin, Llanelli, Dywed) provides a quick method of plotting V–I graphs on a computer screen.

Chapter **P**18   **Making use of electricity**
Electromagnetism

The syllabus section

Context

An introductory study of the advantages of electrically-powered vehicles introduces the electric motor and the force which can act on a current-carrying wire in a magnetic field. A further investigation into electric motors leads to the option of an investigation into electromagnets and relays. Dynamos are introduced as "electric motors in reverse". This in turn leads to electromagnetic induction, alternating currents and power station generators.

Knowledge and understanding

Syllabus statements	PoS	SoA
Know that forces can act on an electric current when it flows through a magnetic field.	4(i)4	4.7(a)
Know that the force on an electric current in a magnetic field is at right angles to the directions of the current and the field.	4(i)4	4.7(a)
Be able to apply these ideas in understanding how an electric motor works.	4(i)4	4.7(a)
Understand that an electric current itself has a magnetic field and that this can be applied to the design of electromagnets, relays and loudspeakers.	4(i)4	4.7(a)
Understand that an electric current can be induced to flow in a wire moving relative to a magnetic field.	4(i)5	4.10(a)
Be able to apply this idea to understand the working of dynamos and alternators.	4(i)5	4.10(a)

Routes and times

Basic	Central	Further
Although Chapter **P18** is not required at Basic level, pupils may benefit from investigating electromagnets and motors.	**P18.1 Electric motors** Worksheet P18A **Electric vehicles** (optional) $1/4$ hour	Read for homework.
Revise magnetism. $3/4$ hour	**P18.2 Forces from electric currents** Worksheet P18B **Electric currents and forces** P18.3 **Magnets** (reading homework) 1 hour	
Omit section **P18.4**. $3/4$ hour	**P18.4 Magnetism and electric currents** Include demonstrations of figures 18.12 and 18.13. Worksheet P18C **Building an electric motor** $1^3/4$ hours	Spend less time on this section. $1^1/4$ hours
Omit this section but discuss electromagnets and their uses, and relays (page 287 only). $1^1/4$ hours	**P18.5 Electromagnets** Demonstrate figure 18.23. Worksheet P18D **Magnetism and electricity** Worksheet P18E **Electromagnets** This is optional but could be used as an Sc1 assessment. $1^3/4$ hours	
		P18.6 Making electric currents from magnetism (class + homework) Worksheet P18F **Induced currents** $3/4$ hour
		P18.7 Dynamos and alternators Demonstrate d.c. and a.c. dynamos and bicycle dynamo. $3/4$ hour
Omit.	Worksheet P18G **Magnetism in rocks** Refer back to section **E2.2**. $1/2$ hour	
Total: 3 hours	*Total: 5 $1/4$ hours*	*Total: 6 hours*

The pupils' book

Much of this work has been drawn from the Revised Nuffield Physics course. Originally intended for Year 9, experience suggests that pupils' understanding of this work more nearly matches their obvious enjoyment if the work is postponed to a later year.

Transformers have been included in Chapter **P**11 where they arise naturally in the discussion of problems related to the transmission of electric currents over large distances. This is a part of the topic on Energy, but both Chapters **P**11 and **P**12 are postponed until late in the course.

P18.1 Electric motors

This unit of work starts with the electric motor as a common mode of utilizing electricity. The advantages and disadvantages of electric motors can be investigated using Worksheet **P18A** "Electric Vehicles". This worksheet is designed to occupy a **maximum** time of 2 periods, but can be restricted to a shorter time by appropriate choice of questions. Teaching notes to accompany the worksheet are given under Activities.

Examples of commercial motors quoted in the following work invariably run from a.c. There might seem to be a problem in reconciling this with the treatment of motors adopted here. However, many domestic motors use brushes and commutators, just like d.c. motors. They run in this way because the a.c. passes through both the armature and the field coils of the electromagnet. Thus the a.c. nature of the supply is irrelevant to their operation – the current through the armature reverses fifty times per second, but so does the field direction. To explain their operation, it is best to regard them as d.c. motors. This point is not mentioned in the pupils' book, but a bright pupil may need an answer when he or she realizes that the domestic counterparts are running on a.c.

P18.2 Forces from electric currents

This section is based on Worksheet **P18B** which explores how forces can be produced by an electric current. This in turn introduces the magnetic field, extending the field concept already introduced in Chapter **P7**. While demonstrating the principle behind the working of an electric motor, there remain many design problems, such as getting the current into and out of the rotating coil and arranging that the forces on the coil produce continuous rotation.

Before dealing with these problems pupils are given the opportunity to revise ideas about the magnetic fields of permanent magnets which they will have met in an earlier year.

P18.3 Magnets

This section is a short revision of work on magnets that will have been covered in earlier years. Some pupils may wish to repeat some of the experiments.

P18.4 Magnetism and electric currents

This section is the heart of the chapter. It starts by returning to the results obtained from Worksheet **P18B**. The relationships between the direction of the force, the direction of the magnetic field and the direction of the current when the force is a maximum are summarized. The specific relationships summarized by Fleming's Left Hand Rule are not required in order to understand the working of the motor. It is sufficient to know that the force is at right-angles to the plane containing the field and the current, and that if either (but not both) of these directions is reversed, the direction of the force is reversed. However, many pupils feel more comfortable with an explicit knowledge of Fleming's Left Hand Rule and enjoy using it. They should not be denied this comfort if it helps them to understand what is going on!

The section continues by applying these ideas to the design of a simple electric motor, and the commutator is introduced.

Worksheet **P18C** gives details for the construction of a simple electric motor using components from the Westminster Electromagnetic Kit.

P18.5 Electromagnets

Little attention is given in this chapter to the magnetic field surrounding a current. The behaviour of an electric motor is treated in terms of the interaction between an electric current and a magnetic field, not as the interaction between two magnetic fields, as is often the case. The latter interpretation is too sophisticated for present needs and is appropriate only to abler pupils.

There is thus no need to make a detailed exploration of the patterns of the magnetic field surrounding a current-carrying wire. However, the magnetic field within a motor is commonly produced using an electromagnet. This provides an opportunity for an open-ended investigation into the factors affecting the strength of such a magnet (Worksheet **P**18E). The time spent on such an investigation will depend on the ability of the pupils and how much of the rest of the chapter is to be done by them. If the introduction to electromagnetic induction is left until the beginning of Chapter **P**11, then there should be time during this chapter for a thorough investigation into electromagnets. If, however, the pupils are to complete all of this chapter in the time available, the investigation may have to be brief.

This section concludes with a brief account of Oersted's work and uses it to make an important point about scientific discovery. The point made by Bernal in the extract quoted is that many people may well have observed what Oersted did, but only he was able to recognize its significance. The passage is in language which may be "difficult" for the pupils, but their understanding is encouraged by a "comprehension" question (question 10).

Worksheet **P**18D gives details of experiments pupils can do to repeat Oersted's observations and to see the pattern of a magnetic field around a straight wire.

P18.6 Making electric currents from magnetism

This work on induced currents is introduced by seeing what happens to the electric motor working "in reverse" – in other words, wires from the coil are connected to a sensitive meter and the coil is spun manually. This could be done as a class experiment, since both motors and galvanometers will be available. Worksheet **P**18F follows and its general conclusions are argued out with the help of the subsection headed "Induced currents".

The distinction between d.c. and a.c. can be made at this stage. In fact three types of current output are discussed in the pupils' book: d.c. from a cell is a current flowing in one direction which in the short term is of unvarying size if the circuit is not changed. The output from the model motor, however, is a current of varying size, but always in the same direction. If the commutator is replaced with slip rings, the output continually varies in both size and direction. This is best demonstrated at low speed using a centre-zero galvanometer.

P18.7 Dynamos and alternators

The link between commercial dynamos and alternators on the one hand and electromagnetic induction on the other is made via the cycle dynamo. This will probably be done by demonstration and class participation. (Traces from the cycle dynamo on a CRO seem to be more confusing than helpful and are best avoided.) The cycle dynamo introduces two useful points:

1 the rotation of a magnet rather than a coil, and
2 the fact that a.c. is just as good as d.c. when it comes to things like lighting and heating.

This is a good moment to review, with abler pupils, the nature of the process of energy transfer in electrical circuits as discussed in the notes on Chapter P17. If the process is seen to involve a force acting on the charges, then it becomes clear that alternating voltages are just as effective as direct voltages in transferring energy.

The importance of dynamos and alternators lies in the way they can be used in the process of transferring the vast amount of energy needed by an industrial society to the place where it is needed. A calculation is included in the pupils' book that shows how small a contribution the energy stored in a car battery can make even to our everyday domestic needs. This calculation may only be of relevance to the more able pupils, but it is a useful application of ideas developed in Chapters **P**16 and **P**17. Even so this would be a good opportunity to stress the dependence of an industrial society on very large energy resources, and so form a link between this chapter and the work of Chapters **P**11 and **P**12.

The chapter concludes by looking briefly at power station generators. This topic is returned to in Chapter **P**11.

Answer to selected question
16 14 300 A.

Activities

Worksheet P18A Electric vehicles

Though this worksheet does not involve experiments, the following notes may be helpful.

Questions 1 to 5 revise work from Chapters **P**8 (energy) and **P**6 (kinetic energy).

Question 7 reminds pupils that there is an energy loss in power stations which has to be taken into account when comparing the efficiencies of electrically driven vehicles and petrol driven vehicles. The data suggests that there is little to choose between the two methods of propulsion when it comes to overall energy losses.

Question 9 highlights one of the major difficulties electric vehicles have to contend with. Even though batteries used for vehicles can be recharged at much higher rates than normal battery recharging requires, they can never be "re-energized" as quickly as a petrol driven vehicle.

One section of the worksheet deals with pollution. As with efficiency, electric vehicles seem to score heavily over petrol vehicles at first glance. But again the problems are really transferred elsewhere. Power stations can cause considerable pollution. However, it might be said that pollution can be much more easily controlled in a few large power stations than in a large number of separate vehicles.

Worksheet P18B Electric currents and forces

REQUIREMENTS

Each group of pupils will need:
Power supply, low-voltage, Westminster type
Support block (see Notes)
Wire, copper, pvc covered, 0.6 mm in diameter, 0.75 m long
Wire, copper, bare, 0.45 mm in diameter, 0.25 m long
Wire, copper, bare, 0.28 mm in diameter, 0.25 m long
Iron yoke
2 slab magnets, Magnadur
Wire strippers

Notes:
All of the experiments included in Worksheets **P**18B to **P**18F make use of items from the Westminster Electromagnetic Kit.

The diagram on Worksheet **P**18B gives an idea of the support block required. Dimensions are not critical. Some varieties of power pack have their terminals in such a position that a support block may not be needed.

The procedure to be followed is detailed in the worksheet.

Worksheet P18C Building an electric motor

REQUIREMENTS

Each group of pupils will need:
Wire, copper, pvc covered
Iron yoke
2 slab magnets, Magnadur
Motor kit: base, 2 split pins, knitting needle, 4 rivets, armature, valve rubber

Sticky tape
Power supply, low-voltage, Westminster type
Wire strippers

Pupils are provided with construction details, but few motors work first time. The following instructions may help:

The brushes must press on the loops of the commutator firmly. Therefore:

1 Bend the brushes over until they cross as shown on the worksheet.
2 Slip the commutator end of the armature under the brushes where they cross, and insert the other end of the axle into the split pin, B.
3 Lift the armature, forcing the brushes to bend apart and push that end of the axle into split pin A.

This provides good contact because the brushes are "spring loaded".

Pupils should be given time to persevere with making their motors work – they get great satisfaction from it. Those fortunate enough to get theirs working quickly can go on to investigate its performance. Such pupils will need the following apparatus.

REQUIREMENTS

Each group of pupils will need:
Ammeter, 5 A
Voltmeter, 5 V
Plasticine, to make loads
String
Metre ruler

Access to:
Balance, 100 g

The procedure they might adopt is described in Worksheet **P**17C.

Worksheet P18D Magnetism and electricity

REQUIREMENTS

Each group of pupils will need:
Power supply, low-voltage, Westminster type
Wire, copper, pvc covered, 1 m long, bared at the ends
Card and supporting blocks
Plotting compass
Iron filings

The procedure to be followed is detailed in the worksheet.

Worksheet P18E Electromagnets

REQUIREMENTS

Each group of pupils will need:
Power supply, low-voltage, Westminster type
Rheostat, 15 Ω
Ammeter, 5 A d.c.
Wire, copper, pvc insulated, 2 m long
Steel rod pieces, 50 mm long or longer (see Note)

Access to:
Force meters, small masses, string, pieces of iron, small iron nails

Note:
Pieces of steel knitting needle can be used.
Pupils may want to bundle several together to form a core.

Pupils are expected to invent their own method of measuring the magnetic force of the electromagnet. They could do this by using a force meter to pull off another piece of iron, or by hanging masses on a piece of metal attracted to the electromagnet.

Worksheet P18F Induced currents

REQUIREMENTS

Each group of pupils will need:
2 magnets, Ticonal
Wire, copper, pvc covered
Galvanometer (see Note)
Iron yoke
2 slab magnets, Magnadur
2 iron C-cores, and a clip to hold them together
Cell, 1.5 V *or* low voltage power supply

Notes:
The major reason for disappointing results in these experiments is lack of a sufficiently sensitive meter. A suitable meter must be capable of responding to currents of a few microamperes. Centre-zero instruments or meters capable of reading a small negative current are not essential, but highly desirable. Transformer coils of 240 turns may be used to provide larger induced e.m.f.s if sensitive ammeters are not available.

The procedure to be followed is detailed in the worksheet.

Worksheet P18G Magnetism in rocks

REQUIREMENTS

Each group of pupils will need:
Plotting compass or small bar magnet
Lighter "flints"
Bunsen burner and heatproof mat
Tongs

Access to:
Samples of various rocks, including iron, magnetite, basalt and limestone
Microvoltmeter or light-beam galvanometer
Coil with about 20000 turns on it

The magnetism of strongly magnetic rocks can be detected with a magnet or compass. But weakly magnetic rocks often have magnetic fields that are small compared with the Earth's magnetic field. For these, other techniques have to be used. In this worksheet, pupils test weak samples for magnetic effects by seeing if they induce currents when moved near a coil connected to a sensitive voltmeter.

Answers to worksheet questions
1 Stroke the magnetite with a bar magnet or put it into a solenoid carrying an electric current.

2 Because the magnetic field of the rock sample is different in different directions.

3 Limestone has no magnetic effect because it contains no magnetic elements.

4 Limestone is a sedimentary rock and has not acquired a magnetic field by being cooled in the Earth's magnetic field.

5 Magnetic lighter flints are made of pyrophoric alloys, e.g. 65% "Misch metal" (a mixture of cerium and other rare earths) and 35% iron.

Demonstration experiments

The majority of the time spent on this chapter will involve pupils in their own experimental work. However, the following items will be useful for demonstration purposes.

REQUIREMENTS
Model motor already made up
Galvanometer, demonstration
Motor, fractional horse-power
Electric drill that can be taken apart
Bicycle dynamo
Bicycle dynamo that can be taken apart

Chapter **P**19   **Making pictures with electricity**
Electrons

The syllabus section

Context

The internal working of a television set requires an explanation which is satisfied by an exploration of electron beam tubes. This in turn introduces the cathode-ray oscilloscope and its use in, for example, medical applications, amongst others. The effect of magnetic fields on an electron beam shows how a picture can be built up on the face of a television tube.

This section can be presented in two ways. For pupils aiming at higher grades, all the work can be presented as a problem-solving activity. Not only are electron beams seen as a solution to the problem of how a television set works, but the behaviour of a diode valve can be presented in problem-solving terms as well. For others it will be enough to present the diode as a demonstration of the behaviour of an electron beam, which in turn can be used to show how a television set makes its picture.

Knowledge and understanding

Syllabus statements	PoS	SoA
Appreciate how the production of electrons from a heated wire has led to the cathode-ray oscilloscope and the possibility of television.	4(i)13	—
Appreciate that cathode-ray tubes can produce X-rays.	4(i)13	
Understand that both current and static electricity involve unbalanced charges and consider how static electricity may be safely used or discharged in everyday situations.	4(i)3	—
Appreciate that the behaviour of the thermionic diode can be interpreted in terms of negatively-charged particles given off from a heated tungsten wire.	4(i)13	—
Appreciate that the electron, as a basic component of the atom, could be the particle carrying an electric current in a thermionic diode and also the particle responsible for carrying charge round an electric circuit.	4(i)13	—

Opportunities for co-ordination

Ions as charged atoms link with **C**17 and **C**18.

Routes and times

Basic	Central	Further

Spend more time on this section. *1 hour*	**P19.1 Television** **P19.2 Electric currents in a vacuum?** Q2 is optional. **Worksheet P19A The diode** (side 1 only) *³/₄ hour*	
Do only "An electron gun" from section **P19.3**. Simple electrostatics, in terms of unbalanced charges, could be revised here.	**P19.3 The electron** *³/₄ hour*	Omit Q3 from section **P19.3**. Side 2 of Worksheet **P19A** is also suitable.
	P19.4 The cathode-ray oscilloscope **Worksheet P19B The cathode-ray oscilloscope** Demonstrate this if time is short. *1 hour*	
Omit Worksheet **P19C**. *¹/₂ hour*	**Worksheet P19C Rectification and smoothing** **P19.5 Making television pictures** *1 hour*	
Total: 3¹/₄ hours	*Total: 3¹/₂ hours*	*Total: 3¹/₂ hours*

The pupils' book

P19.1 Television

The introduction places the electron within a context which will be familiar to all pupils. Although brief, it is essential to the work and is returned to at the end of the chapter.

P19.2 Electric currents in a vacuum?

The approach to the diode depends very much on the ability of the class. The differentiation between various approaches is detailed above, under Context. No matter what approach is adopted, it is unlikely to take more than a single period. It is anticipated that pupils will see the experiment demonstrated and afterwards read an account of the experiment in their pupils' book. The arguments which relate the observations to an assumed cause are not easy. It is hoped that, by reproducing the observations in this way, pupils will have more opportunity to reflect on their meaning. The description of the results of such an experiment given in the pupils' book is not intended to be a substitute for the pupils seeing the experiment for themselves.

P19.3 The electron

The electron is first introduced into the Physics course in Chapter **P3**, where it forms part of the description of the structure of the nuclear atom. No attempt is made there to justify the description, but it is suggested that ionization could be described in terms of the loss or gain of electrons by an atom. This section shows that the behaviour of the diode valve can be understood in terms of a stream of negatively-charged particles emitted from the hot cathode. The picture of the atom as a positively-charged nucleus surrounded by a cloud of negatively charged electrons is recalled and it is suggested that the negatively-charged particles in a diode are in fact identical with the electrons surrounding an atom.

If this is so, then some electrons are easily detached from atoms in the formation of ions, as has already been suggested. The existence of these readily detachable electrons can account for the charges that can move freely through metal wires forming an electric current, and for the charging of insulating materials by friction. This short section ends by showing how an "electron gun" is made which provides the electron beam in both cathode-ray and television tubes.

P19.4 The cathode-ray oscilloscope

A period or maybe more should be allowed for pupils to familiarize themselves with the cathode-ray oscilloscope (CRO). The extensive Worksheet **P**19B has been provided in recognition of the fact that some of the more able pupils will in fact find their way round a CRO in a matter of minutes, and will have completed the first three investigations in not much more than fifteen minutes. For them, Investigation 4 provides adequate investigative work. Some schools may not have sufficient class CROs to make this a practical proposition as a class experiment (8 CROs will be required for a class of 32 pupils). Even so, the work should not be omitted. Using a demonstration CRO, pupils can still gain a helpful insight into its use. The Worksheet **P**19B should still be used as a basis for this (class) investigation.

P19.5 Making television pictures

The chapter closes by showing how an electron beam can be used to make pictures. Particular attention is given to the way the beam can be deflected using magnetic fields. This will give useful revision of the link between electric currents and magnetic fields established in Chapter **P**18. There is also a link with the use of a magnetic field to deflect beta particles in Chapter **P**3.

A picture is produced on a television screen by changing the brightness of the spot as the electron beam sweeps over it. This beam modulation can be simulated on some cathode-ray oscilloscopes. In such oscilloscopes there is a socket usually labelled "Z modulation" – implying a variation in beam strength perpendicular to the plane of the screen. The application of a suitable alternating voltage to this socket will produce a dotted line on the screen instead of the usual continuous line.

Colour television involves a more complex modulation procedure using a colour mask which produces a screen made up of spots of three primary colours which blend to produce the full colour pictures seen. This can be linked with the earlier work on colour covered in Chapter **P**15.

Activities

Worksheet P19A The diode

This worksheet is for use during a demonstration experiment.

REQUIREMENTS

Diode, hot filament type with stand   Ammeter, demonstration, 2 mA d.c.
Power supply for filament, 6.3 V   Connecting wires
Power supply, high tension (HT)

Notes:
The Teltron demonstration diode on which this description is based has a coil of wire (filament) at one side of the bulb, which is heated by passing a current through it. The other electrode in the glass bulb is a circular disc of metal, about 2 cm in diameter. In the description that follows, this disc of metal is called the "plate", while the coil of wire is called the "filament".

The maximum current from this tube is no more than 1 or 2 mA.

Procedure

Set the diode in the stand and apply 6.3 volts to the filament.

Connect the plate ("anode") in the tube through the demonstration milliammeter to the positive terminal of the power supply. Earth the other terminal of the supply and connect it to one of the filament terminals. The supply should be able to keep the plate at up to a few hundred volts either positive or negative relative to the filament.

Show the action of the tube, first with the filament cold, then with the filament hot.

Whatever the p.d. across the tube, no current flows as long as the filament is not glowing. When the filament is hot, a current flows if the plate is positive. No current flows if the plate is negative.

Warning

Pupils must **not** be allowed access to HT power supplies and only competent staff should use them. Although the voltage is much lower than that of EHT power supplies, the maximum current of the high tension power supply is much larger. Shrouded 4 mm plugs should be used to make connections. (See also Health and Safety Executive Guidance Note 23 *Electrical safety in schools 18*.)

Worksheet P19B The cathode-ray oscilloscope

REQUIREMENTS

Each group of pupils will need:
Oscilloscope designed for class use
3 cells, 1.5 V, in holders
Power supply, low voltage a.c.
Microphone
Connecting wires

Access to:
Tuning forks and other musical instruments for
  pupils doing Investigation 4

Note:
If this work is based on a class demonstration, a larger demonstration CRO should be used. Otherwise, the ancillary equipment will be the same.

The class CRO should be set up so that a bright, focussed spot is formed in the centre of the screen when it is switched on. It should then be switched off before class use. The rest of the details will be found in the worksheet.

Worksheet P19C Rectification and smoothing

REQUIREMENTS

Each group of pupils will need:
Motor
Battery pack or d.c. power supply
Power supply, 2 V a.c.
Diode, e.g. 1N5401
Capacitor, 4700 μF electrolytic, 6 V or greater
Connecting wires

Access to:
Oscilloscope

The procedure is detailed in the worksheet. Pupils find that the moment exerted by the motor is constant if the motor is connected to a d.c. supply, but that an a.c. supply causes the motor to vibrate backwards and forwards. A rectifier converts this a.c. to pulsed d.c., so that the motor produces a series of pulses all in the same direction. This pulsed d.c. may be converted to smooth d.c. with a capacitor that stores charge during times of plenty and gives it out in times of shortage.

Answer to worksheet question

1 In the same direction all the time.

Demonstration experiments

Electric and magnetic deflection of electron beams

The precise details of the equipment for the electric and magnetic deflection of an electron beam will depend on the equipment available. The details of equipment given here are for the Teltron fine beam tube. The requirements may differ slightly if other tubes are used (such as the Leybold fine beam tube, or the Teltron *e/m* tube).

Ideally when demonstrating both these experiments and those with the diode, the equipment should be wired up in front of the pupils. Ready-wired experiments that work "at the touch of a switch" are second best and can simply seem a confusing mass of wires to even the brightest pupils.

REQUIREMENTS

Fine beam tube, with stand   2 slab magnets, Magnadur
Helmholtz coils for the tube   Magnet, bar
Power supply, high tension (HT)   Ammeter, 1 A a.c.
2 rheostats, 15 Ω   Ammeter, 1 A d.c.
Power supply, 12 V d.c. smoothed, or 12 V battery

Notes:

The a.c. and d.c. ammeters are only used when setting up the apparatus. A 5 kΩ, 10 W resistor may be used as a safeguard for the tube anode circuit if the power supply does not have current limited output.

A 200 or 300 V d.c. voltmeter will be needed if one is not included in the power supply.

Procedure

Notes on setting up this and similar tubes are provided by their manufacturers. They should be read and their instructions should be followed carefully.

Set up the tube and connect **both** deflecting plates to the anode.

Switch on the heater of the electron gun which fires a horizontal beam. Adjust the current to 0.3 A. Wait until the cathode has become hot.

Raise the gun voltage (anode voltage) until the beam hits the end of the tube. Use 80 to 120 V for the demonstration.

1 Bring a bar magnet near the tube while the pupils watch.

2 Bring a magnet with face-poles (such as a Magnadur slab magnet) near the tube, taking care not to make sharp contact with the glass.

3 Without installing the coils in the tube base, turn on a current of about 0.2 A in one of them and bring this near to the tube.

The demonstration shows that the beam is bent most where the magnetic field is strongest, and that the deflection is at right-angles to the motion of the electron stream.

The beam may also be bent by a charged polythene electrostatics strip; this shows that the beam has charge.

Warning

Pupils must **not** be allowed access to HT power supplies and only competent staff should use them.

Chapter **P20** **Control**
An introduction to electronics

The syllabus section

Context

Electronics is introduced as "electricity in control". Untimed central heating control and a car ignition circuit are examples of relatively simple control (or "switching") units. More complex is the switching circuitry required to control an automatic gas cooker or to make a burglar alarm. Microprocessors are introduced as even more complex switching units which are used not only in computers but also in appliances such as washing machines.

Knowledge and understanding

Syllabus statements	PoS	SoA
Understand how a relay can be used to operate devices which need larger currents than detectors can pass.	4(i)8	4.5(a)
Know that a knowledge of changes in resistance can be used to produce detectors which can respond to changes in the environment.	4(i)8	4.5(a)
Appreciate how electronics can be used to solve simple problems in everyday life.	4(i)11	4.5(a)
Understand the use of diodes as "one-way valves" and transistors as "electronic switches".	4(i)8	—
Be able to use simple combinations of AND, OR and NOT gates to solve simple problems.	4(i)8	—
Understand how a bistable unit works and some simple uses that can be made of it.	4(i)9,10	—
Know the effects of feedback in control systems and be able to discuss the implications of information and control technology in everyday life.	4(i)11	—
Appreciate how knowledge of analogue and digital systems can be used to solve simple problems in everyday life.	4(i)12	—

Opportunities for co-ordination

Control sensors in living organisms are dealt with in **B**11 and **B**12.

Routes and times

	Basic	Central	Further
		P20.1 Switches *Reading homework*	
	Worksheet **P20A** "Switches" is also suitable for Basic level. *1 hour*	**Worksheet P20A1 Controlling current** (Experiment 1 only) **P20.2 Control circuits** Set box on page 306 for homework. **Worksheet P20A1 Controlling current** (Experiments 2–4) *1½ hours*	
	Most of this section should be omitted but pupils should realize how logic gates can be used to solve problems. *1 hour*	**P20.3 Another type of control unit** **Worksheet P20B NAND control units** AND, NOT and OR gates should also be discussed. **Worksheet P20C A bistable unit** **P20.4 Solving problems** *2 hours*	Spend less time on this section. *1½ hours*
	Omit this section.	**P20.5 Microelectronics** **Worksheet P20D Using input and output interfaces** (demonstration) *1 hour*	
	Total: 3½ hours	*Total: 4½ hours*	*Total: 4 hours*

The pupils' book

There are many arguments both for and against the inclusion of electronics in a Physics course at this level. Its inclusion in a broadly-based science course in which the constraints of time mean that other more commonly included topics have been discarded might seem to require more justification than usual. Here are some of the arguments for paying some attention to electronics.

1 Electronics is a technology that both draws heavily on scientific ideas and has in turn stimulated scientific research. One way of defining technology is to say that it is the process by which people cope with their environment. It is therefore a problem-solving process which draws on the knowledge and resources available to us, working within the constraints placed on it by scientific knowledge, society and the resources of our planet. Electronics is just such a technology. It is a technology which uses ideas about electricity, and it is in the context of electronics that people mostly deal with electricity. Throughout this course, pupils' attention has been directed towards the use that is made of scientific ideas. Including work from electronics is consistent with the inclusion of technological applications found in other areas of physics.

2 Because electronics is so often developed in isolation its relationship to basic electrical ideas of current and voltage is not always clear. This chapter concentrates on linking the technology to the basic physics.

3 Electronics is an excellent medium for problem solving, using equipment. It can thus contribute to the overall problem-solving aims of the course.

The approach adopted in this chapter owes a great deal to the work of the Independent Schools Microelectronics Centre and in particular the book *Electronics* by Foxcroft, Lewis and Summers.

P20.1 **Switches**

The first section looks at the way a switch can be thought of as a simple form of circuit control. Simple switches are introduced, as are switches that can be indirectly controlled such as the reed switch (a form of relay).

From make-and-break switching, attention is turned to the way in which a variable resistor can exercise similar control. A variable resistor, whose maximum resistance is so high that the current flowing through it is unable to drive a motor, can be used to turn a motor on and off just as a switch can. In this way the pupil is led to see that light-dependent resistors and thermistors can be used as switches, operated by light and by a change in temperature respectively.

Answer to selected question

2 A magnet could be inserted in the edge of the door. This magnet could be used to close a reed switch, inserted in the door frame, when the door closes.

P20.2 **Control circuits**

The difficulty in using light-dependent resistors and thermistors to control other devices directly is that the maximum current they can pass is usually low. This section shows how other devices, referred to as "control units", can be used as intermediaries, interfacing the device to be controlled (say a central-heating pump) with the controller (a temperature-dependent switch, say). The simplest control unit for pupils to understand is the relay, already described in Chapter **P**18.

Having shown how the relay can operate as a control unit, pupils are asked to accept that the same job can be done by other electronic devices. No attempt is made to explain how such devices (gates) work – they are simply shown to do the same job as the relay. This "black box" approach to electronics has already proved successful. It is not necessary to know how a device operates in order to make use of it; pupils merely have to understand what it will do.

Answers to selected questions

A suitable circuit for the "hot milk" detector is shown below.

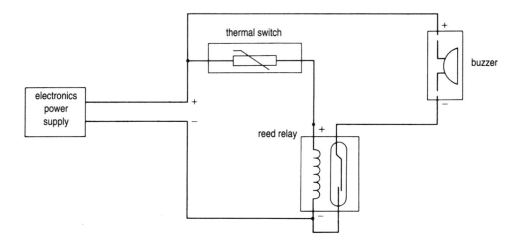

The circuit diagram below shows one possible solution to the rain-detection problem.

The "rain detector" consists of two sets of metal strips. Water, with a little salt added, will form a conducting bridge between the metal strips.

The diagram below shows one possible solution to the problem of turning on the fan.

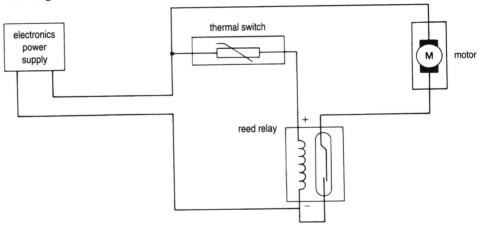

P20.3 Another type of control unit

This section shows that control units can be more complex than the sort just described. The NAND unit introduced here is a control unit that responds to particular settings of two inputs. The reason for the name of this control unit may be of interest to some pupils, but it is not intended to use the NAND unit as an introduction to a study of logic gates – as a family of such control units is called. However, pupils with the interest and the time may like to know about similar multi-input control gates – OR gates, AND gates, NOR gates and NOT gates. These, together with the bistable unit introduced next, are the "building blocks" of computers.

NAND gates are available in the form of "plug-in" units which enable circuits to be constructed easily. This aspect of easy circuit building is dealt with in the introduction to the Activities section below.

Once the operation of the NAND unit is understood, pupils are set the challenge of producing a burglar alarm. This leads to the introduction of the bistable unit – constructed from a pair of NAND units.

Answers to selected questions

4 The diagram below shows a suitable arrangement that could function as a cooker warning light.

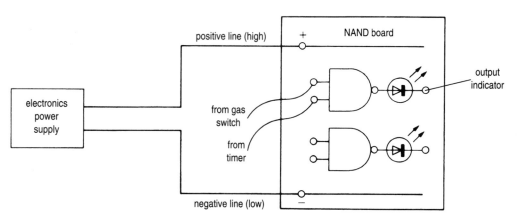

input A	input B	output Q
0	0	0
0	1	0
1	0	0
1	1	1

The diagram on the left shows the table of inputs and outputs expected from the two NAND gates shown in figure 20.21 of the Physics pupils' book. Such a combination of NAND units forms an AND gate.

P20.4 Solving problems

Provided pupils still have sufficient time, this section encourages them to formulate and solve a problem using the electronics control units they have now met.

P20.5 Microelectronics

This last section asks the pupils to make another step in their imagination and realize that microprocessors, which form the heart of personal computers and many domestic appliances, such as washing machines and sewing machines, are no more than very sophisticated control units.

Such microprocessors operate according to a plan called a *program*. In automatic machines the microprocessors are pre-programmed before installation. Such programs cannot be altered by the users of the machine. Microcomputers allow the user to program the microprocessor so that it can exercise control of external devices, via an *output interface*. They can also be made to respond to external inputs from light-, sound- or temperature-sensitive devices. This requires an *input interface*.

Pupils may be given the opportunity to program a computer to operate a set of lights as traffic lights. Special software is available which allows this programming to be done in "everyday English".

The chapter concludes by inviting pupils to develop ways of using computer-controlled systems to help handicapped people.

Activities

It is intended that most of the pupils' time during which this chapter is studied should be spent on practical work. The pupils' book itself is meant to do no more than assist this practical work and provide more problems to solve.

The equipment for practical work in electronics uses units that are mounted on boards which readily fit together to provide working circuits. Such circuits ought to be easy to wire up following simple instructions. It is hoped that the instant success that this gives will provide the confidence required to tackle problems using devices which may have been unfamiliar to pupils only minutes before.

There are already a number of units on the market designed to do the jobs suggested in this chapter and many schools may possess such units; the ones needed are listed under Requirements below. Schools requiring complete sets will be able to buy them as a set specifically put together for this course or they can use units developed for other courses, such as those used by ISMEC (the Independent Schools Microelectronics Centre).

Worksheet P20A Switches

This worksheet may be omitted or used as a reading homework in preparation for Worksheet **P20A1**.

REQUIREMENTS

Each group of pupils will need:
Power supply for electronics kit
Electronics kit: switch SPST, light-dependent
  resistor, thermistor, reed switch, light-emitting
  diode, reed relay, buzzer, motor, 2 NAND units
Connecting wires

Access to:
Hot water and freeze spray or ice, for use with
  the thermistor

Note:

If the NAND units do not have light-emitting diodes connected to the outputs of the NAND gates, an additional light-emitting diode module will be required. Ideally there should be one such set of modules to each pair of pupils in a class.

The wiring up of the modules and the experiments to be carried out are described in the worksheet.

Worksheet P20A1 Controlling current

REQUIREMENTS

Each group of pupils will need:
2 batteries or power supplies (see Note)
Electronics kit as for Worksheet **P20A**
Power transistor, e.g. TIP41A
Connecting wires, long
2 beakers, 250 ml
Resistor, 10 kΩ

2 loudspeakers, preferably 64 Ω
Capacitor, 100 µF electrolytic, 6 V or more

Access to:
Ice and hot water, for use with the thermistor

Note:
Batteries are preferable, to avoid the possibility of pupils touching mains switches with wet hands (after putting the thermistor into hot or cold water, for example).

Pupils first control a buzzer with electronic and electromechanical switches. They then try to control a motor with the same switches and find that the electronic ones (the LDR and the thermistor) will not pass enough current to power the motor.

The reed relay is then used so that the small current through the LDR or thermistor can control the large current through the motor. At first, two power supplies are used so that the controlling current and the controlled current are entirely separate. Then a single power supply supplies both currents.

The transistor is then introduced as an electronic relay, working in a similar way to the reed relay.

Experiment 4, which is optional, allows pupils to investigate the need for an audio amplifier. First two loudspeakers are connected directly together. This makes an intercom which **does** work, but which is best demonstrated with very long wires so that the loud sound of talking into one loudspeaker does not mask the tiny sound issuing from the other.

The rudimentary transistor amplifier that follows provides sufficient increase in performance to demonstrate the value of amplifiers, but extra stages are necessary for a proper intercom.

Worksheet P20B NAND control units

REQUIREMENTS
As for Worksheet **P20A**.

Worksheet P20C A bistable unit

REQUIREMENTS
As for Worksheet **P20A**.

Worksheet P20D Using input and output interfaces

REQUIREMENTS
Microcomputer, e.g. BBC and monitor (see Note)
Computer interface, output
Computer interface, input
Electronics kit
Cassette recorder or disc drive
Computer software to control interfaces

Note:
Other makes of microcomputer can, of course, be used if suitable interfacing units are available.

Full details of how to set up the interfaces and install the software are included with the kit of interfaces and software from the manufacturers.

Further information

Electronics
G. E. Foxcroft, J. L. Lewis and M. K. Summers (Longman Group, 1986). This book is essential background reading for the approach adopted in this chapter. It will also show how work in electronics may be continued outside this immediate science syllabus.

Chapter **P21**   **Communication**
Transferring information electrically

The syllabus section

Context

Ideas about electricity, magnetism and wave motion are used to explore the way in which communications systems have developed over the years. Starting with the electric telegraph, microphones, loudspeakers and the telephone system are explored. Radio transmission is investigated and its advantages discussed. The advantages of digital coding of signals over analogue transmission leads to fibre optics, satellites for the transmission of information and compact disc players.

Knowledge and understanding

Tier B C F	

Syllabus statements	PoS	SoA
Appreciate how, historically, the use of light greatly increased the speed of communication but that this required the use of a code.	4(iv)10	—
Appreciate how the use of electrical signals has improved long-distance, high-speed communication even further.	4(iv)10	—
Understand the difference between analogue signals and digital signals and recognize that the latter require an extension of the idea of a code for transmitting information and appreciate some of the benefits of digital coding for transmitting information.	**4(i)12**	**4.5(a)**
Understand the operation of the microphone and earphone and relate their operation to basic physical principles.	4(iv)4	4.7(a)
Understand something of the operation of the telephone system and of radio.	4(iv)10	—

Opportunities for co-ordination

Transmission of information within an organism is discussed in **B**13 and the comparison made with worldwide communication systems.

Routes and times

Basic	Central	Further

Omit section **P21.2** but discuss the difference between digital and analogue signals.

Central

> **P21.1 Introduction**
>
> **P21.2 Communication using electricity**
>
> **Worksheet P21A Sending messages using electricity**
> Side 2 is optional.
>
> This is a suitable place to demonstrate and explain the loudspeaker and microphone.
>
> *1½ hours*

Further

Spend less time on this section.

1¼ hours

> **P21.3 Radio** (class + homework)
>
> **Worksheet P21B A simple radio receiver**
>
> *¾ hour*

This is an alternative position for **Worksheet P13B** "Optical fibres, telecommunications and technology".

> **P21.4 Digital communication**
>
> **Worksheet P21C Sampling an analogue signal**
>
> *1 hour*

Total: 2½ hours　　　*Total: 2½ hours*　　　*Total: 3 hours*

The pupils' book

P21.1 Introduction

The aim of this introductory section is to show that increasing the speed of communication has often involved the use of some sort of code. Semaphore uses a complex coding system, but Morse code, introduced in the next section, is simpler, using only long and short sounds. Later in the chapter pupils will be introduced to digital coding which, with its **highs** and **lows**, can be seen to be closely linked to Morse. Just as Morse code represents each letter and number by an agreed sequence of short and long sounds ("dots and dashes") so the ASCII code, commonly used in computers, represents each letter and number by an agreed sequence of high and low voltages. (ASCII stands for American Standard Code for Information Interchange.)

P21.2 Communication using electricity

The invention of the electric telegraph came only a year or two after Oersted's discovery of the magnetic effect of an electric current. It demonstrates how a discovery in physics was used to satisfy an immediate need. The need for a reliable method of fast, long-distance communication arose in this country with the development of the railway system.

Worksheet **P21A** introduces pupils to the way in which messages can be coded in Morse, and at the same time shows that this coding method needs considerable skill to operate it. This worksheet paves the way for digital coding and helps illustrate the need for some automatic way of coding and decoding messages.

A more direct way of sending messages electrically is to use a microphone and an earpiece. The operation of this system depends on the same physical principles as the electric telegraph, but the message is not coded and decoded. It is an analogue system in which variations of electric current follow the variations of air pressure on a microphone produced by a sound wave.

This leads to a short discussion of the telephone system. Some of the problems encountered in the present-day telephone system have already been discussed in Chapter **P13**.

P21.3 Radio

The discovery of radio waves and their use by Marconi to send information from place to place is seen as overcoming one major disadvantage of the telephone system – it dispenses with the need to connect sending and receiving equipment with wires.

Instructions are given in Worksheet **P21B** for the construction of a simple radio receiver. The process of radio transmission by modulating a carrier wave is described briefly. It is recommended that this section is covered only if time permits. There are several methods of wiring up the simple radio. One method which involves no soldering is described in the notes on Activities that follow.

The section ends by considering some of the many uses to which radio communication is now put.

Answer to selected question
10 i 267 s (almost 4$\frac{1}{2}$ minutes);
ii 4270 s (about 1 hour 10 minutes).

P21.4 Digital communication

Digital coding of signals has two major advantages. First, it enables messages in both words and pictures to be sent with great accuracy. The signal is not subject to the same degree of interference that analogue signals are. Secondly, it enables a large amount of information to be sent in a very short time (as well as allowing it to be stored in a very compact form).

Two forms of digital coding are introduced in this section. The first is in many ways like Morse code. Each letter and number is given a code in the form of a decimal number: A = 65, B = 66, C = 67 and so on. This decimal number is then turned into a binary number. (So A = 100 000 1; B = 100 0010 and so on.) Turned into electrical voltages, A = high, low, low, low, low, low, high; B = high, low, low, low, low, high, low.

The second form of digital coding is able to transmit electrical signals which are analogues of variations in sound and light. This form of coding is harder to understand and may be omitted for less able pupils. In this form of coding the analogue electrical signal is transmitted as a sequence of numbers which represent the variation in voltage of the signal with time. The numbers are transmitted in digital form and the original signal is reconstituted by the receiver as a time-varying voltage. This is much the same as the way in which someone might pass on information about a graph in the form of a table of numbers to be plotted.

Worksheet **P21C** is a pencil-and-paper exercise along these lines. It shows pupils with what frequency these numbers would have to be sampled for a fairly faithful copy of the original graph to be reproduced.

The chapter concludes by looking at the use being made of digital communication techniques. Digital coding of analogue signals requires that numbers have to be transmitted at a very high rate if a faithful copy of the original signal is to be made by the receiver. To transmit pictures in this way involves very high rates of number transmission – something that can only really be achieved using light itself travelling down optical fibres.

Because optical fibres allow very high rates of information transmission, they are also being used increasingly for telephone communication. As this idea concludes the work of the chapter, this would be a good point at which to do Worksheet **P13B** if it has not been done earlier.

Activities

Worksheet P21A Sending messages using electricity

Experiment 1: Using the Morse code

REQUIREMENTS

Each group of pupils will need:
Power supply for electronics kit
Electronics kit: Switch SPST, buzzer
or
Morse key
Ticker-timer to act as "buzzer"
Power supply for ticker-timer
Connecting wires

The procedure to be followed is detailed in the worksheet. If the design task allowing two people to send and receive a message is undertaken, additional switches etc. will be required.

Experiment 2: Using a microphone and loudspeaker

REQUIREMENTS

Each group of pupils will need:
2 loudspeakers, small, moving coil
Amplifier (see Note)
Connecting wires

Note:
Amplifier kits based on the LM386 integrated circuit are available from Maplin Electronics (Maplin Professional Supplies, PO Box 777, Rayleigh, Essex SS6 8LU).

The procedure is detailed in the worksheet.

Worksheet P21B A simple radio receiver

REQUIREMENTS

Each group of pupils will need:
Battery, to power radio
Radio kit: ZN414 radio integrated circuit, resistor, 100 kΩ, resistor, 500Ω, capacitor, 0.1 uF, capacitor, 0.01 uF, capacitor, 330 pF (see Notes)
Earpiece, crystal
Coil, copper wire, 0.35 mm in diameter, 2.5 m long

Ferrite rod, 1 cm in diameter, 8 cm long
Cardboard, thin
Sticky tape
75 turn coil made with fine insulated wire with connections already attached to 75th turn and centre turn.

Notes:
It may be possible to use one of a number of kits to build a simple radio (for example, Unilab Ltd, Blackburn BB1 3BI supply two versions of a suitable kit). Each may use components different from those on this list. The list of components given matches the circuit on the worksheet, and can be used by teachers who wish to put together their own kit of parts.

The detailed procedure for connecting together the components for a simple radio will depend on the source of the components and the ability of the pupils. Schools may devise their own system working with basic components. Some pupils will benefit by being allowed to solder this circuit together, while for others it might be better to have an easier method of connection using either a connection board, or modules with 2 or 4 mm sockets.

If, alternatively, a kit of parts is purchased, the instructions enclosed with the kit should be carefully followed.

Worksheet P21C Sampling an analogue signal

Demonstration experiment

Section P21.3: Slow radio

REQUIREMENTS

Oscilloscope, demonstration type
Slow a.c. generator
Signal generator
Diode, any general purpose
Resistor, 1 kΩ
Resistor, 330 Ω, variable
Capacitor, 8 μF

A circuit diagram is shown below. Turning the handle of the "slow a.c." generator will "modulate" the 1 kHz signal from the signal generator. The modulation is displayed on the oscilloscope.

A diode and capacitor can be inserted, as shown in the circuit diagram, to show how the "carrier wave" can be removed, leaving only the modulating voltage.

The slow a.c. generator may be driven by a small electric motor rather than turned by hand.

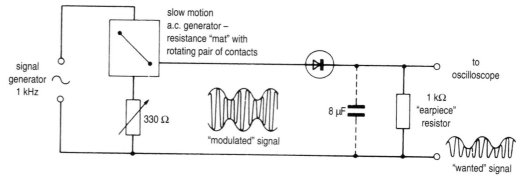

"Slow radio": this amplitude modulated signal goes to a diode and a resistor to represent the earpiece used in the "real" radio. The modulated signal across this "earpiece" resistor is shown in the middle of the diagram. Its average value rises and falls at the frequency of rotation of the slow motion a.c. generator. If a capacitor is placed across the resistor, the rapid 1 kHz fluctuations are filtered out, leaving only the slow "wanted" signal, which does not pass as easily through the capacitor.

Further information

Communication
This resource pack of slides and workcards is available from the BP Education Service, or the Science Museum, Exhibition Road, London SW7.

About Information Technology
(CRAC Publications, Hobsons Ltd for British Telecom and Rank Xerox.)

Science Museum publications
Telecommunications – a technology for change
Guglielmo Marconi by Keith Geddes. Useful background booklet for pupils.
There is also a permanent exhibition on communications technology in the Science Museum, Exhibition Road, London SW7.

EARTH AND SPACE

Introduction to Earth and Space

Topic and contexts

Earth and Space deals with three cross-curricular themes from the National Curriculum: weather, geology and Space. The themes fall loosely into two strands of the National Curriculum – Sc3(iv) "The Earth and its atmosphere" and Sc4(v) "The Earth's place in the Universe", but there are links with other strands.

These three topics are integrated principally into the Chemistry and Physics components of the rest of the course and provide valuable applications and extensions of these subject areas.

Chapter **P2** "Cooking food quickly" considers liquids and gases and the factors affecting their behaviour, and it is suggested that most of Topic **E1** "Weather" is studied with this Physics chapter.

Topic **E2** "Geology" integrates with both the Chemistry and the Physics courses. Activities on the different types of rocks revise the study of minerals (from Key stage 3) before pupils study the exploitation of the Earth's resources by the chemical industry in Chemistry Chapter **C4** "Chemicals and rocks". There are further links between Topic **E2** and Chapters **C15** "Soil", **P3** "Radioactivity", **P12** "Waste not, want not?", **P15** "Making use of waves" and **B23** "Changing with time".

Topic **E3** "Space" extends Chapter **P7** "Rising and falling". It considers Space travel and the information this has provided for scientists, as well as geological processes on other planets and theories of the beginning of the Universe.

Differentiation

Many of the concepts in Topics E2 and E3 are at attainment levels 8, 9 and 10 in the National Curriculum. According to the abilities of individual pupils, some of the sections could be used as extensions to areas of study for those who work more rapidly through the course; some will need to be omitted. There are no separate Routes and times for Earth and Space: the information is incorporated into the charts in the related Chemistry and Physics chapters, which give advice about which activities are suitable for which pupils.

Topic **E**1

Weather

Context

This section develops an understanding of the behaviours of gases and water vapour in the context of weather. Local atmos520pheric circulation leads to cloud formation and land and sea breezes. Global atmospheric circulation leads to the weather associated with fronts between air masses.

Knowledge and understanding

	Tier	
B	C	F

Syllabus statements	PoS	SoA
Know how measurements of temperature, rainfall, windspeed and direction describe the weather.	3(iv)1	3.4(d)
Understand the physical processes involved in the transport of water in the atmosphere and in rivers and oceans.	3(iv)3	3.5(d)
Understand how different airstreams give different weather related to their recent path over land and sea.	—	3.6(g)
Understand the principles which govern the behaviours of gases and water vapour in the atmosphere and how energy transfer processes drive some weather phenomena.	3(iv)1	3.7(h)
Be able to use qualitatively the ideas of conduction, convection and radiation, the behaviour of gases and water under changing pressure, and the relationship between pressure, winds and weather patterns to explain changes in the atmosphere that cause various weather phenomena.	3(iv)2	3.9(e)

Opportunities for co-ordination

C10 links with discussion of the water cycle. **P2** deals with evaporation and the relationships between the volume, pressure and temperature of gases. **P9** and **P10** discuss the physics of conduction, convection and radiation.

The pupils' book

Section E1.1 Air, hot and cold

This section is concerned with how temperature and pressure changes affect the movement of air. The variation of temperature and pressure with height and temperature changes connected with expansion and compression of gases are considered.

Answers to questions

1   $0.5\,°C \times 1085/100 = 5.4\,°C$

2   The atmospheric pressure decreases.

3   The mass remains the same; the density decreases.

4   When the gas is compressed, the temperature rises and the molecules move more rapidly; some of this energy is transferred by thermal conduction to the pump.

5   The person doing the pumping provides the energy that raises the temperature of the gas. The energy eventually spreads out into the surrounding air. (When the piston in the pump is stationary, molecules which hit it bounce back at the same speed as they arrive, rather like a ball hitting a stationary wall. But if the piston is moving towards the molecules, they bounce back at a higher speed, like a ball bouncing off a racket that is moving towards the ball. The speed of the piston is slow compared with the speed of the molecules, but the molecules have so many collisions with the piston that the net effect is significant.)

Section E1.2 Water in the air

This section considers evaporation and condensation of water and leads into cloud formation.

Answers to questions

1   Sources of water vapour in the atmosphere include: evaporation from seas, lakes, rivers etc.; respiration of animals and plants; combustion of fuels (e.g. in power stations); steam ejected as waste from industry (e.g. from cooling towers of power stations).

2   On a hot day, molecules move faster as they receive energy from the Sun; this means that they are more likely to be moving fast enough to leave the washing. On a windy day, the wind removes the molecules as they evaporate, so they are not likely to return.

3   A gas cools as it expands.

4   There are three main types of clouds:
   cumulus – a heap or pile
   stratus – a layer
   cirrus – a tuft or filament
This classification has been expanded to give ten cloud types: cumulus, cumulonimbus, stratus, stratocumulus, altocumulus, cirrostratus, altostratus, nimbostratus, cirrus and cirrocumulus.

5   The prevailing wind direction in Britain is from the south-west. Rain clouds generally move in from a westerly or south-westerly direction.
Rain-bearing clouds are cumulonimbus (from the Latin word *nimbus*, rain).
On sunny days, cumulus clouds often form as the ground gets warmer and patches of warm air carry moisture evaporated from the ground. As the air rises, it expands and cools; the moisture condenses and a cloud forms. Cirrus clouds may also form on sunny days at a high altitude (6000 m). These clouds are composed of ice crystals. They are slow to evaporate and change only slowly with time. The condensation trails of aircraft are a form of artificial cirrus.

6   Thunderstorms occur when static electricity builds up within a cloud. If there is a very large charge difference between the cloud and the ground or between two clouds, a spark sometimes "jumps the gap". This is lightning. Intense heating along the discharge path causes rapid expansion and this explosive expansion of air is heard as thunder.

The condition usually arises after a hot day, when rising currents of warm air (called "thermals") develop. As the air rises it cools as it expands, and the water vapour condenses to form cumulus clouds. Energy is released as the water forms, and a thunderstorm occurs as electrostatic charge develops.

Section E1.3 Prevailing winds

This section deals with the movement of large air masses and their effect on global weather patterns.

Answers to questions

1 Pupils should produce a diagram which shows that the Sun's light lands directly on ground near the Equator, but more obliquely nearer the Poles.

2 The Earth's circumference is about 40 000 km. A point on the Equator travels 40 000 km in 24 hours, a speed of 1670 km per hour.

3 Because air is arriving in this region from more or less opposite directions either side, and therefore moves upwards and not in any other clear direction.

4 Jet streams can help or hinder an aeroplane's progress according to their directions. An aircraft flying from New York to London will usually benefit from the strong tail winds of the polar front jet stream. Flying in the opposite direction, the pilot expects head winds. The pilot changes altitude or path to avoid the strongest winds.

5 During the day, the land warms up more rapidly than the sea does. As air from the land rises, cooler air from over the sea moves in as a sea breeze.

6 Pupils should notice that places which are well inland have much wider ranges of temperature than those which are near the sea.

Section E1.4 Masses of air!

This section describes how the movement and interaction of air masses produce the variable weather patterns of Britain.

Answers to questions

1 The total time for the depression to pass was from 18:00 one day to 17:30 the next – 23.5 hours.

2 As the warm front passed there was a rise in temperature, low clouds formed and there was some light rain or drizzle. The cold front was marked by the onset of heavy rain and a strong gusty wind; there was an accompanying drop in temperature.

3 When an occlusion passes, the warm-front conditions are directly followed by the cold-front conditions, with no warm sector in between.

4 This question involves collecting weather maps from newspapers. It could be of interest to collect maps from a variety of newspapers and to compare the different ways of presenting the information.

5 Anticlockwise around a low, clockwise around a high.

Activities

Experimental work related to this topic is contained in the following Physics activities:

Worksheet **P2C** "Measurements on air being heated"
Worksheet **P2D** "Recording the weather"
Worksheet **P2E** "Understanding weather maps"
Demonstration for section **P2.2** : Compressing air
Further information on these activities may be found at the appropriate place in the Physics section of this *Guide*.

Topic E2 | Geology

Context

This section considers the distribution of mineral resources and the theory of plate tectonics. Seismic evidence for a layered structure of the Earth is presented. Weathering and erosion introduce the formation of sedimentary rocks, which leads on to the rest of the rock cycle. Pupils study evidence for the time scales of these processes and the need for uniformity in making geological theories.

Knowledge and understanding

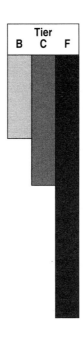

Tier B C F		

Syllabus statements	PoS	SoA
Know that weathering, slope processes and erosion lead to the formation of sediments.	3(iv)5	3.4(e)
Understand the scientific processes involved in the formation of igneous, sedimentary and metamorphic rocks including the timescales over which these processes operate.	3(iv)4,6	3.6(h)
Understand the theories for the formation of mountain ranges and the Atlantic ridge.	3(iv)4 3(iv)10	3.8(h)
Understand the use of radioactivity in the estimation of geological age.	3(ii)4,6	3.9(b)
Be able to describe and explain the seismic evidence for a layered structure of the Earth by comparing densities between the different layers.	3(iv)7	3.9(f)
Understand the geological evidence for the theory of plate tectonics and the contribution this process makes to the recycling of rocks.	3(iv)8,9	3.10(e)

Opportunities for co-ordination

The interpretation of the fossil record in the study of evolution is discussed in **B23**. **C4** and **C15** deal with the chemical processes of weathering and the formation of sediments and soils. **P3** links the concept of radioactive half-life to the measurement of geological time. The behaviour of waves in **P14** links to study of earthquakes.

The pupils' book

Section E2.1 Finding minerals

This section introduces the mineral resources of the UK and uses some of them as evidence that the climate when they were formed was different from the present climate. This leads into the idea of "continental drift".

Answers to questions

1 Mineral resources may be divided into the following categories:
- Precious metals and minerals (e.g. gold, silver, platinum, diamonds, rubies etc.).
- Major metals (copper, lead, zinc, aluminium, tin).
- Steel-industry metals (iron, chromium, cobalt, manganese, molybdenum, nickel, niobium, tungsten, vanadium).
- Speciality metals. This includes most other metals which do not fit into the categories above.
- Industrial minerals. These are generally minerals which may be used in the form in which they occur – as, of course are the minerals used for jewellery. They frequently have a metallic content but are not usually used for metal production: they include fertilizer minerals and minerals used in the production of ceramics, for example. Some examples are asbestos, graphite, magnesia, industrial diamonds, barite, potash, fluorspar, gypsum, salt, vermiculite, sulphur and phosphate rock.
- Energy minerals. This includes coal, oil, natural gas and uranium.

2 Whether minerals are classified as being plentiful or in short supply depends on the context of the question. The simplest answer is to classify abundant minerals as those which occur in large quantities, such as iron ore and bauxite. Rocks such as limestone, which are used for construction purposes, are in the same category. Other minerals, for which there is not a great demand, may not be abundant but on the other hand not be in short supply as there are ample mineral deposits providing society is willing to pay the price to extract them from the ground. Gold is an example of such a mineral.

3 A thousand years ago, there would be little geological difference – except in those regions where the coastline is being rapidly eroded, for example. The major differences would be those related to human habitation and activity.
  Although the end of the last glaciation is given as around ten thousand years ago, Britain was not an island until later – about 6000 B.C. – when the sea levels had risen sufficiently. There were humans who were hunters but at that time it was not warm enough for the spread of forests of the types of deciduous trees which are common today.
  Pupils should be reminded that their speculations (rather like scientific theories) are likely to be less accurate the more distant the time.

4 The answer to this question, about local mineral deposits, will depend on the area. Pupils might look for entries such as mines, quarries and brickworks in the "Yellow pages" if they are not already aware of local mineral resources.

5 Either the sea used to cover the mountains as they exist today, or the sediments have been uplifted since they were formed at the bottom of the sea.

Section E2.2 The moving Earth

This section considers the evidence for continental drift on a global scale.

Answers to questions

1 Africa and South America could once have been joined together.

2 Ridges are common to all the oceans. Trenches occur on the ocean side of island arcs and are numerous around the Pacific Ocean; they may extend down to 10 000 m. Some named trenches around the Pacific are the Mariana, Philippine, Japan, Kuril and, Aleutian trenches (all on the western margins) and the Central American and the Peru–Chile trenches on the eastern side.

3 In 1935, magnetic north was 11° west of true north, and in 1989 it was 5° west of true north. So the movement was 6° in 54 years, i.e. 1° in 9 years. So a movement through 180° should occur in 180×9 years = 1620 years.

4 Africa and South America were once joined as one land mass. They have been, and still are, moving steadily away from each other.

5 If the separation of 4000 km has been achieved at a steady rate of 4 cm per year, the continents were touching $4000 \times 1000 \times 100/4$ years ago, *i.e.* 100 million years ago.

Section E2.3 Earthquakes

Earthquakes regularly provide evidence of Earth movements generated by plate tectonics. They are responsible for mountain building where plates are moving together.

Answers to selected questions

1 Some other chains of mountains are the Rockies and the Appalachians of North America, the Alaska Range, and the mountain ranges of Iran and Iraq.

2 The location of copper mines in many places down the west coasts of North and South America illustrates how certain types of ore body have formed at or close to plate margins.

3 Seismometers will pick up all sorts of vibrations, including those from traffic. Hence they are usually located in a cellar deep enough to exclude such local vibrations.

4 The Earth's crust is solid, but the core is not (since S waves are not transmitted through it).

6 "Refraction" is the term used for waves changing speed and direction. Light waves will be the most familiar example.

Section E2.4 Recycled rocks!

The major rock types and the rock cycle are considered in this section.

Answers to selected questions

1 Gravestones that have lasted well are usually of igneous origin. The more ornamental rocks usually contain large crystals of contrasting colours (as in granite). Older gravestones are frequently made of a fairly local rock type, which may not be so resistant to weathering.

2 Bricks and concrete weather in the same way as rocks do. Pupils might also think of changes which occur to some plastics when exposed to sunlight.

3 Sediments become compacted and their particles cemented together, forming sedimentary rocks.

5 The highest geothermal gradients (50 °C/km) are in parts of the country where there are sub-surface masses of granite. South-west and northern England are two major regions where massive granite occurs. Other regions with a geothermal gradient of around 40 °C/km are the Wessex basin, the East Yorkshire and Lincolnshire basin, the Cheshire basin and the Northern Ireland basin. In all these areas there are sandstone aquifers up to 500 m in thickness at depths of 1–2 km. Wells driven into these aquifers have produced water at temperatures between 40 °C and 80 °C. Thermal springs occur at various spas, for example: Buxton (28 °C), Matlock (20 °C), Taffs Well (20 °C), Bristol (24 °C) and Bath (47 °C).

Geology in Britain

The photographs on this page illustrate some of the rock types found in different parts of Britain. No questions are asked but an exercise in matching them to locations on the geological map could be devised.

Section E2.5 How fast does it happen?

This section introduces the principle of uniformity and considers examples of how some changes occur.

Answers to questions

1 Pupils might consider the "obvious" changes through the life of a human or animal – that a child gets bigger as it gets older but at some stage will stop growing, for example. But the principle of uniformity extends to other areas as well. We expect objects to fall when we release them because other objects do: the law of gravity expresses that general observation. But such a law is no "proof" that things will **always** fall, nor a constraint on things rising: like other scientific laws, it is merely a description of our observations.

2 Assuming a constant rate of erosion of 0.1 mm per year, the limestone "should" have taken 200 years to be eroded 2 cm. St Paul's cathedral was actually built between 1675 and 1710.

3 The time for 30 cm of limestone to weather at a rate of 0.03 mm per year = 10 000 years. Erosion is faster in a city because of acid gases in the atmosphere which increase the acidity of the rain.

4 A cliff which has grown at the same rate as a coral reef would have taken 350 years to attain a height of 70 m.

5 100 years ago California would have been 500 mm (0.5 m) lower. In two million years, the uplift should be 10 000 m, which is about the height of Mount Everest.

Section E2.6 Geological time

Geological processes are on a scale that is difficult to observe directly. This section expands this idea and looks at different methods of finding the age of rocks. It has links with Chapter **B**23 "Changing with time", which considers the age of the Earth and the evolution of life.

Answers to questions

1 From their answers to previous questions, pupils might suggest that the Earth is some millions of years old.

2 11 140 years is two half-lives, so one-quarter of the original carbon-14 will be left. Over a period of 55 700 years (ten half-lives), the carbon-14 will have fallen to about one thousandth of the original level; this is too small an amount to measure.

3 One might have expected the rocks at the top to have solidified first. The rocks in the centre of the Pennines are Carboniferous limestone and millstone grit. These were uplifted and the deposits which were on top of them have been eroded as a result. Hence the Pennines are flanked by younger rocks to the east and west. For most of the time since the Pennines were uplifted, they have formed a land area so that no sediments have accumulated there.

4 Different fossil species will be found in the sands of differing ages. Fossils in the Thanet sands are mainly bivalves and gastropods. The older sandstones might contain different species of bivalves and gastropods, brachiopods, ammonites and echinoids, for example.

5 Pupils may have a variety of comments to make here. For instance, they might comment on the potential height of mountains if mountain building had occurred in the same regions throughout the Earth's history. A geological time chart is included for reference; this could be used in connection with questions on the pupils' local area to relate types of deposit to the age.

In general, in Britain, the oldest rocks are in the north-west and there is a general gradation to the youngest rocks, in the south-east.

Activities

Experimental work related to this topic is contained in the following Chemistry and Physics worksheets:

Worksheet **C4A1** "Igneous rocks"

Worksheet **C4A2** "Making sandstone"

Worksheet **C4A3** "Shifting sands"

Worksheet **C4A4** "Drifting apart"

Worksheet **C4A5** "The moving Earth"

Worksheet **C4A** "Making alum from shale"

Worksheet **C4B** "The story of the alum industry"

Worksheet **C4D** "Chemicals from salt"

Worksheet **C4E** "The limestone Inquiry"

Worksheet **C15A1** "Breaking down the rocks"

Worksheet **C15D** "Investigating the effect of pH on the solubility of soil minerals"

Worksheet **P2F** "Which way did the wind blow?"

Worksheet **P3C** "Using radioactivity to measure time"

Worksheet **P12A** "Nuclear power"

Worksheet **P12B** "Ashton Island"

Worksheet **P12C** "Geothermal energy"

Worksheet **P15F** "Earthquakes"

Worksheet **P15G** "Find that earthquake!"

Worksheet **P18G** "Magnetism in rocks"

Further information on these activities may be found at the appropriate places in the Chemistry and Physics sections of this *Guide*.

Topic E3

Space

The syllabus section

Context

Starting with the concept of universal gravitation, this section goes on to consider the role of gravitation in space flight and in tides. The use of the electromagnetic spectrum leads on to closer observation through space probes and the information they bring about geological activity elsewhere in the solar system. The unique nature of the Earth's atmosphere and its evolution are considered. The section ends with a study of the life cycle of stars and the "big bang" theory of the origin of our Universe.

Knowledge and understanding

Syllabus statements	PoS	SoA
Be able to explain day and night, day length and year length in terms of the movements of the Earth around the Sun.	4(v)1	4.4(e)
Be able to describe the motion of planets in the solar system.	4(v)1	4.5(g)
Know that the solar system forms part of a galaxy which is part of a larger system called the Universe.	4(v)1	4.6(g)
Know that gravity acts between all masses, that the magnitude of the force diminishes with distance and that gravity results in tidal activity with various effects.	4(v)2	4.7(g)
Understand the possibilities and limitations of space travel and the use of the data gained.	4(v)3	—
Be able to use data on the solar system or other stellar systems to speculate about the conditions elsewhere in the Universe.	4(v)6	4.8(f)
Understand the chemical and biological factors that maintain atmospheric conditions and consider how they may have been involved in the evolution of the atmosphere.	3(iv)3	3.8(g)
Know that other planets have been geologically active and that their present composition varies with their distance from the Sun.	4(v)4	—
Be able to relate the theory of gravitational force to the motion of satellites.	4(v)2	4.9(e)
Understand that the Sun is powered by nuclear fusion processes.	4(v)5	—
Be able to discuss the "big bang" theory of the origin of the Universe and some of the evidence for it.	4(v)6,7	4.10(e)

The image caption (tier legend): Tier B C F

Opportunities for co-ordination

B3, **B**7 and **B**9 deal with the role of photosynthesis and respiration in maintaining the atmosphere. **P**7 deals with gravity and discusses the physics and the uses of satellites. **P**12 links to the nuclear fusion energy in the Sun. In **P**14 there is material on the use of electromagnetic waves to receive and interpret data from the rest of the Universe.

The pupils' book

Section E3.1 Gravity all around

This section introduces pupils to the concept of gravity as a force and shows that it affects objects in Space as well as on the Earth. The Galileo and Mariner 10 probes exploited the gravity fields of the Sun and the inner planets to "catapult" them to new speeds and directions. No rocket would be powerful enough to do this.

All objects have mass and therefore exert gravitational pull on other objects. This effect is long range and operates across the Universe, but it does weaken with distance.

Satellites orbit the Earth because the gravitational pull keeps them in a (nearly) circular path. Without gravity they would continue along a straight line into Space (obeying Newton's first law). Thus, there is nothing "holding satellites up", only a downward force keeping them to their orbital path. This means that satellites are constantly falling towards the Earth, but their constant forward motion (given them by the launching rocket) ensures that their path of descent matches the curvature of the Earth's surface. They therefore never land (unless they lose speed owing to high atmospheric friction).

Satellites, including the space shuttle, are free-falling all the time and astronauts aboard them therefore feel weightless. They are not, however, in a so-called "zero-gravity environment". In fact, the gravitational field strength at their altitude is only 5 per cent less than on the ground. Pupils should expect gravity to affect a low-orbiting spaceship since the Moon, which is 200 times further away, is held in its orbit by the Earth's gravity.

Answers to questions

1 Typically, about 55 kg, 550 N.

2 Magnetic and electrostatic forces also act at a distance.

3 A simple example is an object swung round on a piece of string. The tension in the string is the (centripetal) force keeping the object in a circular path. If the string were cut, the object would continue in a straight line. Many fairground rides also involve circular motion, with pushes and pulls from rail tracks and connecting arms providing the forces. A car turning a bend is kept in a circular path by the force of the road pushing on the tyres.

4 A longer, more flattened, ellipse is said to be more eccentric. People who are said to be eccentric are unusual or odd, but it does not mean that they are mad!

5 Using the figures provided, one expects Halley's comet to reappear around the year 2060 or 2061. But its orbital period of 75 years is an approximate value and variation occurs. The comet returned slightly later in the mid eighteenth century than Halley had predicted. He did not live to see it then, and few people have ever witnessed it twice. This comet is mentioned in Chinese astronomical records that date back to 1057 B.C. It may have been orbiting the Sun for about 100 000 years.

Section E3.2 Tides big and small

This section introduces the idea that ocean tides are caused by the gravitational pull of the Moon. It suggests ways in which barrage schemes can store energy as a result of this work being done. Pupils are reminded that tidal effects are not confined to liquids: the atmosphere and the solid Earth are distorted too. Tidal working can make objects hot; an example is the volcanic moon Io.

Answers to questions

1 The next low tide will be about 6 hours 12 minutes later, i.e. 3.12 p.m. The next high tide will be 12 hours 25 minutes later, at 9.25 p.m.

2 The inertia of the water is responsible for this. As soon as the water is pulled, it accelerates. The bulge is produced when it has accelerated for some time.

3 The water initially behind the barrage transfers energy as it falls through the turbines.

The turbines drive generators and energy is transferred by the wires to the user. A barrage differs from a conventional hydroelectric dam in that the difference between the water levels on either side depends on the state of the tide on the seaward side, and this limits the optimum operating times.

4 Tidal barrages may seem to be an environmentalist's dream, providing clean power from a (seemingly) unlimited source without any fuel costs. The barrage may also double up as a crossing point for traffic across an estuary.

However, tidal barrages can increase pollution problems in estuaries and flood the margins used by bird life. Massive quarrying would scar areas of beauty, raise dust levels and congest roads with lorries carrying stone. Even a large barrage across the River Severn would only match the output of two to three conventional power stations, and it would not be able to provide power all the time (see the answer to question 3). A large barrage would take ten years or more to build, and its life span might perhaps be limited by silting up.

Section E3.3 Exploring Space

This section summarizes how Space is explored using ground-based instruments and spacecraft, manned and unmanned. Most information is derived from the gathering of electromagnetic radiation. The atmosphere screens out or spoils most of this radiation "picture", so instruments placed in orbit function more effectively. An even better option is to send spacecraft to nearer objects such as the planets. Automatic probes have landed on Mars and Venus, but the most versatile explorers are humans. Astronauts have explored the Moon and may one day visit Mars, although the current pace of manned Space flight is faltering, owing to US budgetary restrictions and the collapse of the USSR. On the other hand, there is a growing European and Japanese interest in space exploration.

Answers to questions
1 Pupils looking at the night sky are seeing visible light. The full electromagnetic spectrum, in order of decreasing wavelength, is: radio waves (including microwaves and radar), infra-red radiation, visible light, ultra-violet radiation, X-radiation, gamma radiation.

2 Approximately 2500 stars should be visible to an observer in the northern hemisphere at any one time, but this assumes a clear dark sky. In practice, massive "light pollution" from street lamps is banishing the night sky from our lives: in cities, only a hundred or so bright stars may be seen. Observatories have to be placed far from the urban sprawl and some have been moved as cities have spread towards them.

3 Rays parallel to the axis of the dish are focused to a point half-way between the dish surface and the centre of its curvature. This is where the receiver is placed.

4 Any type of mistake that goes undetected until after an experiment will do.

5 One or more powerful rockets will be needed. The crew (how many, and what skills should they have?) will need a large capsule to live in, with food and oxygen for two years, plus shielding in case of excessive solar radiation during the long voyage. A landing craft will be needed to descend to the Martian surface. Wheeled or tracked vehicles can be used to explore the surface. Space suits will be needed because the Martian atmosphere is very thin and not breathable. Sampling equipment and a laboratory will be essential: the pupils might like to think what geological, meteorological or biological experiments they could carry out. The astronauts will need to keep in touch with Earth using radio transmission of television images. (The delay time for the transmissions may be up to 20 minutes each way because of the great distance.) And so on.

Section E3.4 Space geology

This section extends geological ideas and knowledge beyond our own planet to other bodies in our Solar System. Thirty years of planetary exploration has replaced dim and fuzzy images from Earth-based telescopes with pin-sharp images.

The difference between comparative planetology (as Space geology is called) and Earth-based geology is that few landings have been made and samples collected (the Moon being a notable exception). So geologists have to make educated guesses about what they are looking at by comparing planetary features with similar ones seen on Earth. If this method fails, new physical mechanisms are proposed on the basis of theories and experiments to simulate likely planetary conditions in the laboratory. Ideas are superseded rather rapidly!

Answers to questions

1 Modern tankers (known as very large crude carriers, VLCC) can reach 500 000 tonnes fully laden. An iron–nickel meteorite has a density of (over) 10 tonnes per cubic metre. Based on this round figure, the Barringer meteorite which struck Arizona could have been up to 50 000 cubic metres, equivalent to a cube with sides of about 37 metres. Most of the meteorite vaporized on impact.

2 Typical shield volcanoes have slides sloping only 6°. Photographs of more viscous andesite–rhyolite volcanoes, e.g. Mount Fuji and Mount St Helens, will show that they have steeper sides.

3 Ammonia, NH_3, contains nitrogen and hydrogen. Methane (CH_4) contains carbon and hydrogen.

4 The field would be torroidal, *i.e.* doughnut-shaped. This is a "flatter" version of the dipole field surrounding a bar magnet. One face of the loop would be a north pole and the other face a south pole. Planetary fields are (mainly) dipolar and the connection with circulating charge carriers at the core is crudely simulated by the field caused by a current through a loop of wire.

5 The elements mentioned are hydrogen, helium, carbon, nitrogen, oxygen, sulphur, iron and nickel. Basalt is also mentioned, which contains magnesium, silicon and calcium, along with iron and oxygen. The same elements are found in the Sun, although in different proportions, suggesting that the Sun and planets formed from the same cloud of dust and gas.

Section E3.5 Air for life

This section reminds pupils that the Earth's atmosphere is essential for life and that, as far as we know, no other planet in our Solar System – or perhaps in the Universe – can support living organisms. Plants and animals exchange gases with the atmosphere through respiration and photosynthesis.

The Earth's atmosphere is thought to originate from the volcanic production of gases, with modification of those gases by evolving photosynthetic single- and multi-celled organisms. The result was rising levels of oxygen and the development of an ozone layer, which screens out harmful ultra-violet radiation.

Humans have recently modified the atmosphere through ozone depletion by CFCs and the build-up of carbon dioxide through combustion of fossil fuels.

Answers to questions

1 All three are highly adapted for flight and feed on insects. The house martin (bluish-black above and white underneath, with a white rump and a short forked tail) and the swallow (bluish-black above and white beneath, with a reddish throat and a long forked tail) belong to the same family. The swift is the "odd one out": it has a short forked tail, longer wings and is dark all over except for a whitish throat.

2 The main pollutants are carbon dioxide (a combustion product of all fossil fuels), sulphur dioxide (mainly from burning coal), nitrogen oxides (from car exhausts) and chlorofluorocarbons (from aerosols, a wide variety of manufacturing processes and the dismantling of domestic refrigerators).

3 In its simplest form: carbon (from fuel) + oxygen → carbon dioxide.

4 The best answer is an oxidation reaction in which iron(II) is changed to iron(III), *e.g.*

iron(II) oxide + oxygen → iron(III) oxide   (word equation)

$$4Fe_3O_4 + O_2 \rightarrow 6Fe_2O_3 \qquad \text{(chemical equation)}$$
$$Fe^{2+} \rightarrow Fe^{3+} + e^- \qquad \text{(simplified ionic equation)}$$

Note from the last equation that oxidation is the process of losing electrons.

5 Ultra-violet radiation is that part of the electromagnetic spectrum with wavelengths just shorter than visible light. Strong ultra-violet radiation kills micro-organisms and there is now well-established evidence that it inhibits the growth of crops. Reddening and peeling of the skin (i.e. sunburn) is caused by ultra-violet radiation killing and damaging skin cells. It can, in some cases, damage the genetic information in skin cells and cause them to become cancerous. In this respect it is no different from X-rays and gamma radiation, yet people are still prepared to lie in the sun and take the risk!

Section E3.6 Stars, old and young

This section introduces the idea that stars are other suns and that our own Sun is a relatively small and long-lived example.

Stars in the sky have different brightnesses and colours. Their colour relates to their surface temperature. Stars are "black body radiators" and as such glow from red through white to blue the hotter they are. Hot stars have fewer spectral lines because they contain only simple atoms. Cooler stars exhibit multiple-line spectra because they contain heavier atoms and molecules.

The meaning of brightness depends upon the distance of the star. Dim, closer, stars will still appear brighter than more distant luminous ones. Fortunately, several range-finding techniques exist. Closer stars can be measured using parallax, some distant stars (called Cepheid variables) have known luminosities, and many stars exist in binary pairs or groups whose mutual orbits are measurable (and thus their distances from us known) because they obey Newton's and Kepler's laws.

Hertzsprung and Russell independently established that hotter stars are also more luminous. It follows that they also use up their hydrogen fusion fuel faster and have lives in the order of only one to ten million years before they explode as supernovas. Small stars, such as our Sun, last around 10 000 million years.

Answers to questions

1 A heated piece of metal glows dull red, then bright red, orange, yellow, white and bluish-white as its temperature increases. The colours of stars are related to their temperature in the same way.

2 Pupils' diagrams should show dispersion occurring at the first face of the prism with red light refracted least and violet light most. The prism would also refract infra-red and ultra-violet radiations beyond either end of the spectrum.

3 The light source is sunlight reflected off the atmospheres of these planets. They produce no light of their own (except a little lightning on Venus). Gases in the atmospheres absorb some of the wavelengths, giving absorption lines. Astronomers collect the reflected light with telescopes and examine it using spectroscopes. In practice, Earth-bound spectroscopy of planetary atmospheres has proved difficult as some gases, *e.g.* nitrogen, do not give strong lines. Space-probe data has altered our perceptions many times.

4 A helium atom contains two neutrons and two protons in its nucleus and two electrons surrounding the nucleus; so, empirically, we need to start with four protons and four electrons, *i.e.* four hydrogen atoms. The actual fusion process involves joining deuterium with tritium (both isotopes of hydrogen) to produce helium plus a spare neutron left over.

5 The estimated age of the Earth is 4500 million years. If the life expectancy of our Sun is 10 000 million years then it is middle-aged and has about 5500 million years to go.

Section E3.7 How did it all begin?

In the late twentieth century, science is pushing back the frontiers of the unknown at a greater pace than ever before. In each human lifetime the sum of mankind's knowledge now expands tenfold. Nevertheless, the simplest questions will always exist to challenge us all. What is the nature of the Universe? Where did it come from? Where is it going? Why are we here?

In civilized Europe, the Aristotelian/Ptolemaic view of an Earth-centred Universe held for 1500 years before it was tentatively challenged by the Polish priest Copernicus. He merely sought a simpler explanation for the motions of the heavenly bodies, but he opened the floodgates of cosmological discovery. His successors, Galileo, Kepler, Newton, Einstein, Hawking and many others, have revealed an astonishing Universe of staggering dimensions and vast age.

The growing complexity of scientific knowledge is almost frightening, but it is to be hoped that young minds will delight in the challenges that cosmological science presents.

Answers to questions

1 This question provides the opportunity to encourage pupils to realize some of the limitations of science as well as some of its power. They might reflect that science gives us the ability to do many things, but is unable to direct us in what should be done and for what reason.

2 Pupils will probably suggest intelligence, abstract reasoning, tool making, power to control our environment, and complex social behaviour. Some of these factors are unique to humans and others are not. For example, chimpanzees make simple tools and have complex social relationships within groups. More clearly unique might be seen to be mankind's self-knowledge, moral and religious awareness and knowledge of eternity. People differ as to whether they attribute this merely to the 2 per cent of differences between our genetic make-up and that of the chimpanzees.

3 The pitch of the siren is higher, indicating a higher frequency and shorter wavelength. Light from a star moving towards us is similarly shifted and therefore appears bluer. The opposite effect is observed for a receding siren (lower pitch) or star (red shift). This is known as the **Doppler effect**.

4 One million million seconds, or 32 000 years.

5 Pupils may choose all sorts of things! The frontiers of science seem to be at its extremes of scale, from quantum physics to cosmology. Certainly, books on these subjects date most quickly. Even as this book is in preparation a new discovery about the "microwave background" has been made. Variations in its intensity have been mapped by an orbiting radio telescope after several decades of claims that it was totally uniform. It happens that recent discoveries support existing theories about the beginning of the Universe. But great breakthroughs in science often proceed from evidence which is in conflict with existing theories.

6 The "steady state" theory obeys the principle of uniformity in that it predicts an unchanging Universe. In the "big bang" theory, the uniformitarian statement "the present is the key to the past" does not hold true because the Universe has radically altered.

7 10^{-43} s $= 0.000\,000\,000\,000\,000\,000\,000\,000\,000\,000\,000\,000\,000\,000\,000\,1$ s
10^{-35} s $= 0.000\,000\,000\,000\,000\,000\,000\,000\,000\,000\,000\,000\,01$ s
10^{35} °C $= 100\,000\,000\,000\,000\,000\,000\,000\,000\,000\,000\,000\,000$ °C
10^{28} °C $= 10\,000\,000\,000\,000\,000\,000\,000\,000\,000\,000$ °C

8 Pupils may consider that all kinds of people, from artist to scientist and from musician to poet, have chosen to reflect on this.

9 Iron has a mass number of 56 and an atomic number of 26. So it has 26 protons, 26 electrons and $56 - 26 = 30$ neutrons. If each neutron were made from a proton and an electron, the whole atom would be equivalent to 56 protons and 56 electrons. (See also question 4 in section **E3.6**.)

Activities

Experimental work related to this topic is contained in the following Physics worksheets:

Worksheet **P7B** "Making a model of the Solar System"

Worksheet **P7C** "... how heaven goes"

Worksheet **P7D** "Planets"

Worksheet **P7E** "Ganymede"

Worksheet **P7F** "Space!"

Worksheet **P7G** "Measuring the distance to the stars"

Worksheet **P7H** "In the beginning ..."

Further information on these activities may be found at the appropriate place in the Physics section of this *Guide*.

Appendix 1   Apparatus lists

The following lists contain all the items required for Nuffield Co-ordinated Sciences. They are comprehensive in that they contain items needed both for basic and for optional experiments. Schools do not need all the equipment listed here to carry out the course successfully, but successful completion does demand that a very large majority of the experiments should be available.

The descriptions given below are not rigid specifications. Teachers should always make their own judgement about the appropriate equipment to use. Manufacturers, too, should not be constrained by these lists from offering alternative equipment. The question that should be asked of any equipment is "Does it do the right job?" rather than "Is it the right piece of apparatus?"

In the lists for Biology and Chemistry, a rough guide of quantity is given for those items where multiples are needed. A letter p means that the item is required for pupil experiment and that class sets will be needed: p3, for example, means that three are required per pupil group. Other numbers in this column refer to the **maximum** numbers that will be needed, and (a) indicates that pupils only need **access to** the item.

Biology apparatus list

New or unusual items

The following list collects items that may not already be present in schools and items that require more than the normal preparation.

Quantity	Item	Chapter
p	apparatus for constructing model biogas generator	**B**17
	bare ground, patch about 15 m² (a)	**B**23
p	blindfold	**B**10
p	block, wooden	**B**15
	books for identifying plants, lichens and protists (a)	**B**16
	cups, drinking (a)	**B**20
p3	cups, plastic	**B**13
p	dental mirror	**B**4
	electric fan (a)	**B**8
	grass, patch about 15 m² (a)	**B**23
p	key to freshwater organisms	**B**13, 14
p	keys to soil organisms, and other appropriate keys	**B**14, 15, 18
	large-scale Ordnance Survey map of the area (a)	**B**18
p3	markers, soil	**B**15
p	maze	**B**10
p	mesh, plastic, 1 cm mesh	**B**15
p	metal sheet, thin, with raised and depressed patterns of dots	**B**10
p	net curtain, pieces of	**B**15
p	nutritional information, especially concerning size of regular portions	**B**6
	parallelogram model of human ribcage (a)	**B**7
	paths, tarmac or concrete (a)	**B**16
	polythene hoods to cover potometers (a)	**B**8
p	samples of Braille and Moon alphabets	**B**10
	scale for measuring pupils' height (a)	**B**20

p	scale, e.g. Scalafix or strip of graph paper, attached to capillary tubing	**B**8
	scales, bathroom, measuring in kg (*a*)	**B**20
p3	spoons, dessert	**B**13
p200	straws, 100 green and 100 red, cut into about 10 cm lengths	**B**23
p	string, marked at 10 cm intervals	**B**16
p	string, nylon	**B**15
p	syringe model of human thorax	**B**7
p	tablets, dental disclosing	**B**4
p	teatowel	**B**12
p	tights, pieces of	**B**15
	toothbrush, brought from home by each pupil	**B**4
	toothpaste, 4 brands (*a*)	**B**4
p	variety of food labels giving nutritional information	**B**6
p	varnish, clear nail, or clear adhesive	**B**3
	walls, a variety, e.g. old brick, cement, shady, sunny, etc. (*a*)	**B**16
	wooden blocks to simulate organisms (*a*)	**B**7
p	yogurt pots with holes in the bottom	**B**17

General laboratory equipment

The following items are likely already to be present in schools.

Quantity	*Item*	*Chapter*
	aquarium containing a variety of organisms (*a*)	**B**13
	aquarium tank, transparent plastic	**B**3
p	balance, accurate, for measuring mass	
	beaker, tall, 500 cm³ minimum	**B**3
p2	beakers, 250 cm³	
p	beakers, 100 cm³ and 500 cm³	**B**12
p3	beakers, about 400 cm³, for beads	**B**22
p	bench lamp fitted with 60 W bulb	**B**3
	blacked-out laboratory (*a*)	**B**13
p	boiling-tube	**B**3, 14
p3	boiling-tubes with bungs (as alternative to large glass container)	**B**13
p2(2)	bosses, retort	
p	bowl for 1 m glass tube to stand in	**B**10
p	box or cupboard, light-proof	**B**7
p	box, light-proof, with inside blackened and a hole at one end	**B**10
p	bung, split rubber	**B**3
p4	bungs	**B**8
p2	bungs fitted with delivery tubes	**B**9
p	Bunsen burner	**B**3, 5, 14
	capillary analysis (J) tube with greased adjustment screw/rubber tubing	**B**3
p	capillary tubing, fine	**B**3
p	capillary tubing, fine, 30 cm lengths	**B**3
p	caps for specimen tubes, thin rubber	**B**7
p	chair or stool	**B**12
p	choice chamber	**B**16
p3	clamps, retort	
p2	clamps to support conical flasks	**B**3
p	clipboard	**B**16, 23
p	clock	**B**19
p	compass	**B**18
p2	conical flasks or boiling tubes	**B**3

	connector, T-piece, glass	**B**7
p	container for collecting water dripping from soil	**B**17
p	container, large glass, with tight-sealing lid and glass well	**B**13
p6	containers for organisms, e.g. beakers	**B**1, 14
p4	containers, plastic or glass, with loose covers	**B**15
p	cork-borer	**B**3, 13, 15
p	cork-borer or scalpel	**B**10
	dish for collecting ash from burning cigarette	**B**7
p	dish, collecting	**B**15
p	dish, dissecting	**B**10
p	dish, large	**B**16
p	dish, Petri or white porcelain	**B**3
p	dish, Petri with lid	**B**19
p	dish, Petri with lid, sterile, containing potato dextrose agar	**B**13
p	dishes	**B**1, 8, 10
p	dishes, Petri, one for each radiation dosage	**B**22
p	eye protection	
	filter pump	**B**7
p	filters, coloured	**B**3
p	flask, 250 cm^3, with side arm and bung with hole to take shoot	**B**8
2	flasks, conical, with rubber bungs fitted with 2 bent glass tubes	**B**7
p	forceps, blunt	
	fume cupboard (*a*)	**B**7
p	funnel	**B**3
	funnel, glass, short stem	**B**3
p	graticule, eyepiece	**B**19
p	hand lens	
p	incubator at 25° C (*a*)	**B**13
p	jar, large, or small tank	**B**16
p3	knives (as alternative to scalpels)	**B**13
p	lamp, bench	**B**3, 13
p	lamp, bench, covered except for small aperture for light	**B**14
p	lead shot	**B**10
p	light source	**B**7, 10
	light source, powerful	**B**3, 15
p	light sources, a variety	**B**3
p	load, for base of retort stand	**B**10
p	McCartney bottles (*a*)	**B**4
p	means of shielding apparatus from other light sources	**B**3
p	measuring cylinder	**B**12
p	measuring cylinder, 100 cm^3	**B**14
p	measuring cylinder, 250 cm^3	**B**17
p	measuring cylinder, very large (as alternative to 1 m glass tube)	**B**10
p	microscope with high-power (×40) and low-power objective lenses	
p	needle, mounted	**B**14, 23
p	needle, to fit 2 cm^3 syringe	**B**7
p	paintbrush, small thin	**B**1, 10
p	pestle and mortar	**B**3
p	pins	**B**13
p	pipette, dropping	
p	pipette, 10 cm^3 graduated, or syringe	**B**10
p7	pots, 7.0 cm	**B**10
p6	pots, flower	**B**15
p	pupils' book (*a*)	**B**3
p	quadrat, 0.25 m^2	**B**13

p	quadrat, 10 cm^2	B16
	receptacle for waste liquid (a)	B3
p	rod, glass, 20 cm long	B8
p	rulers	
p	sampling equipment appropriate to the habitat studied	B14
p	scalpel	B7, 8, 10
p	scissors	
p	scissors or razor blade	B3
p	scissors, dissecting	B10
p	seeker	B7, 8
p	sink or bowl	B4, 8
p	slide, microscope, with counting cell if possible	B23
p2	slides, microscope	
p11	specimen tubes, flat-bottomed, 7 cm × 2.5 cm, 3 of them stoppered	B7
p3	stand	B12
p(2)	stand, retort	
p	stand, tripod	B3
p	stopclock	
p	stopwatch	B7, 17
	syringe, 2 cm^3	B3, 7
p	syringe, 10 cm^3, and needle	B8
p2	syringe, plastic, 5 cm^3	B5
p	syringe, plastic, 20 cm^3	B3, 5
p	tape measure	B13, 22
p	tape, measuring, 30 m long	B18
p	test-tube holder	B5
p	test-tube rack	
p3	test-tubes	
p2	test-tubes, 10 cm^3	B9
p6(3)	test-tubes with rubber bungs	B3, 10
	thermometer	
p	thermometer, clinical	B13
p	thermometer, stirring	B14
p	tile, spotting	B4
p	tile, white	B8, 10, 13
p	tin can (as alternative to water bath)	B13
p	towel (a)	
p	tray, seed, with plastic or glass top	B22
p	trays, for leaf litter and collected organisms	B15
	trough, bowl or sink of water at room temperature	B3
p	tub, plastic, sealed	B13
p	tube, glass or clear plastic, 1 m × 2 cm, with rubber bung at lower end	B10
p2	tubes, glass, 20 mm diameter and 30 cm long	B8
p2	tubes, specimen	B9
2	tubes, hard glass, with bungs fitted with tubes shaped as cigarette holders	B7
p	tubing, capillary, about 15 cm long with a 90° bend	B8
p	tubing, PVC, short length	B8
p	tubing, rubber, short length	B3
p	Tullgren funnel apparatus	B15
p	watch with second hand	B23
p2	watch-glasses	B10
p	water bath, electrically heated, with variable temperature settings (a)	
p	wooden board or white tile	B3

Organisms

Quantity	Organisms, etc.	Chapter
p	blowfly larvae	**B**13
p	compost heap, undisturbed for several months	**B**15
p	cones from a conifer e.g. Scots pine, male and female of different ages	**B**2
p	crab, lobster, prawns, shrimps, cockles, whelks, mussels	**B**2
p	dandelion, inflorescence stalk	**B**10
p	dish, plastic Petri, prepared with nutrient agar and inoculated with *Micrococcus luteus*	**B**4
p20	duckweed plants	**B**15
p	*Elodea*, free from dirt and filamentous algae	**B**3, 7
p	eye, sheep's	**B**10
p	ferns	**B**2
p	flowers, insect- and wind-pollinated	**B**19
	freshwater organisms, in aquarium (*a*)	**B**13
p5	gammarids	**B**16, 17
p	garlic clove	**B**13
p	groundsel, or other plant with flowers and fruit	**B**23
p	heart	**B**8
p	herring roe, hard and soft	**B**23
p	leaf litter	**B**15
p	leaves of sun and shade plants, e.g. dandelion and dog's mercury	**B**13
	leaves, flat, e.g. alder, apple, ash, beech or oak (*a*)	**B**15
p	leaves, fresh green, e.g. busy lizzie, grass, nettle, spinach or bamboo	**B**3
	leaves, freshly picked, e.g. privet, ivy-leaved toadflax, lilac, busy lizzie	**B**3
p	leaves, holly, some of which are mined	**B**14
p	leaves, a selection, e.g. variegated, kept in the light, green kept in the dark and green kept in zero CO_2 for 48 hours	**B**3
p	leaves, variegated or red, e.g. copper beech, *Coleus*	**B**3
p	leaves – rue, rosemary, basil, potato	**B**13
p	maize, barley, broad bean and pea seedlings grown in Knop's solution	**B**2
p	mosses or liverworts, showing sporangia	**B**2
p	mould on bread, e.g. *Mucor*	**B**23
p	onion, raw	**B**10
p	peanuts, unroasted	**B**14
p	pig's trotter	**B**10
p	plants, potted, e.g. *Pelargonium*, kept in dark for 24 hours	**B**3
p	pluck (heart, lungs, trachea, larynx and diaphragm) of sheep or pig	**B**7
p	pond weeds	**B**17
p	potato, raw	**B**10
	protists, photosynthetic, e.g. *Spirogyra, Cladophora, Euglena, Chlamydomonas* (*a*)	**B**1, 2
p	protists, photosynthetic, multicellular, e.g. *Fucus* and *Laminaria*	**B**2
p	seeds – maize, barley, broad bean and pea, washed in 1% sodium hypochlorite solution and soaked overnight in distilled water	**B**2
p	seeds, cress	**B**16
p100	seeds, cress or grass	**B**13
p	seeds, irradiated at several different doses	**B**22
p50	seeds, *Nicotiana*, soaked overnight	**B**13
p42	seeds, pea	**B**10
p4+	seeds, pea or bean	**B**15

p	seeds, chlorophyll-deficient strains of tobacco, tomato or barley	**B**22
p	seeds, tomato – P1 and F1 of crosses involving single major genes for stem colour and leaf shape	**B**22
p2	shoot, transparent leafy, e.g. groundsel, celery, flowering spinach, kept in weak dye for 2 hours before lesson	**B**8
p	shoot, leafy, with stem just wide enough to fit PVC tubing	**B**8
p	skull of rabbit, sheep, dog or cat (at least one herbivore and one carnivore)	**B**4
p	slides, prepared microscope, of leaf sections	**B**3
p	specimens showing measurable variation for obvious characteristics, e.g. stick insects, woodlice, pea or bean pods, etc.	**B**22
	trees in or near school grounds (*a*)	**B**13, 16
p	water animals such as water snail or *Gammarus*	**B**7
p	water weed, rotting	**B**16
p10	woodlice	**B**16
	woodlice, a collection, preferably containing several species (*a*)	**B**1

Consumable items

Quantity	*Consumable item*	*Chapter*
	aluminium foil or black polythene	**B**3
	ash from burnt wood (*a*)	**B**17
p	bag for waste material	**B**8
p	blotting paper (as an alternative to filter paper)	**B**8
p	cement, polystyrene	**B**2
p	chalk (as alternative to marker pen)	**B**22
2	cigarettes	**B**7
p	clingfilm, as covering material for tubes	**B**7
	compost or manure (*a*)	**B**17
p	compost, damp	**B**22
p	compost, seed	**B**10
p	cork and pins, or aluminium foil, or black paper and paper clips	**B**3
p	cottonwool	**B**3, 7, 8
p2	coverslips	
p	gauze	**B**3
p	glass wool	**B**3
p	gloves, plastic	**B**10
p	glue	**B**7
p	glue, paper	**B**23
p	labels	**B**22
	matches	**B**7
p	paper, absorbent	**B**8, 19
p	paper, drawing	**B**2, 4
p	paper, filter	
p	paper, filter, 3 strips about 2 cm × 5 cm	**B**10
p	paper, graph	
p	paper, red litmus	**B**8
p	paper, pH	**B**17
p	paper, thin tissue, 2 cm²	**B**10
	paper towels	**B**3
p	paper, white	**B**2
p	paper, writing	**B**4
p	pen, marker (as alternative for chinagraph pencil)	
	pencil, chinagraph	

p	pencils, sharp	
	pens	**B**4
	Plasticine	**B**3
p8	rubber bands	**B**3, 6
p	sand or gravel	**B**16
p	silt or mud	**B**16
p	soil samples e.g. acidic, basic, neutral	**B**17
p	soil samples, e.g. vermiculite, sterile sand, sterile organic potting compost, garden soil rich in nitrates, garden soil in which beans have been grown, sterilized garden soil in which beans have been grown (*a*)	**B**15
p	soil, from different places under a tree	**B**13
p	soil, in which to bury mesh bags	**B**15
p	stones, large	**B**16
p	stones, small	**B**17
p	tape, adhesive	**B**4
p	wallpaper paste	**B**10
p	wood, strips	**B**7
p	writing materials	**B**9

Chemicals, etc.

Item	*Chapter*
agar jelly cubes, side 2 cm	**B**8
agar jelly cubes, with eosin incorporated, side 2 cm	**B**8
ammonia solution, 2M (*a*)	**B**8
ammonia solution, 9M (*a*)	**B**8
amylase, 1% solution	**B**5
amylase, 1% solution through which cigarette smoke has been bubbled (*a*)	**B**5
Benedict's solution	**B**5
broth, nutrient	**B**4
complete mineral nutrient solution	**B**15
complete solution lacking iron	**B**15
complete solution lacking magnesium	**B**15
complete solution lacking nitrogen	**B**15
culture solution (15% sucrose, 0.01 g boric acid, 0.01 g yeast)	**B**19
diazine (Janus B) green, 0.03%	**B**9
dilute hydrochloric acid	**B**5, 8
drying agent, e.g. calcium chloride	**B**16
egg white suspension	**B**5
ethanol	**B**3
ethanol, 10%	**B**15
ethanol, for sterilizing	**B**13
glucose solution,10%, boiled, cooled and with yeast added	**B**4
hydrogencarbonate indicator solution, previously equilibrated with atmospheric air	**B**3, 9, 13
iodine in potassium iodide solution	**B**3, 5
paraffin, liquid	**B**9
petroleum jelly (*a*)	**B**17
potassium hydroxide solution, concentrated	**B**3
potassium manganate(VII) solution	**B**8
potassium pyrogallate solution	**B**3
potato dextrose agar	**B**13
propanone (acetone)	**B**3

protease, 10% solution	**B**5
silver sand, well washed	**B**7
sodium chloride (*a*)	**B**5
sodium chloride solution, 10%	**B**10
sodium chloride, 0.9% solution (*a*)	**B**20
sodium hydrogencarbonate	**B**3
sodium hydroxide pellets wrapped in muslin bag	**B**3
starch, 1% solution	**B**5
sucrose solution, 2 mol/dm^3	**B**10
water	
water, distilled	
water, distilled and acidified to different pH values (*a*)	**B**17
water, iced	**B**13
water, pond, adjusted to pH 4, 5 and 6	**B**17
water, rain (*a*)	**B**17
water, river or spring (*a*)	**B**16
water, running (*a*)	**B**15
yeast suspension added to boiled, cooled 10% glucose solution	**B**4
yeast suspension, fresh, 10%	**B**4

Chemistry apparatus list

New or unusual items

The following list collects items that may not already be present in schools and items that require more than the normal preparation.

Quantity	Item	Chapter
	apparatus to demonstrate the conductivity of molten glass	C6
p	bag, plastic	C15
	bottle, small glass with screw-cap, e.g. medicine bottle	C15
	brushes, paint (*a*)	C9
2	cans of tomato soup	C4
	cigarette (*a*)	C10
p4	cup, strong plastic, with lid	C3, 14, 15
	dish, shallow, heat-resistant, at least 7 cm deep and 15 cm diameter	C4
p	fabric, cotton	C11
	file (*a*)	C7
p	frames, wire	C9
	hammer (*a*)	C7
	ice-cream tub, plastic with lid	C15
p	jugs, measuring (not measuring cylinders) (*a*)	C3
p	paper, absorbent (e.g. paper towels)	C11
p3	paperclips, plastic	C7
	pliers (*a*)	C7
2	plywood, approximately 1 cm × 2 cm × 5 cm	C4
p4	saucers	C15
p	sink or bowl	C11
	snips (*a*)	C7, 14
	spoons, plastic (*a*)	C3
	stains – motor oil, moist clay, powdered charcoal, lipstick, cooking fat, dust (*a*)	C10

p	stick, wooden, or other suitable agitator	C10
p	straws, drinking	C3
	string (a)	C7
p	washing line	C10

General laboratory equipment

The following items are likely already to be present in schools.

Quantity	Item	Chapter
p	ammeter, 0–1 A	C18
	ammeter, demonstration, 3 A	C4
	apparatus for fountain experiment, with spare flask for repeat	C15
	apparatus for the catalytic oxidation of ammonia	C15
	apparatus to fill a flask with dry ammonia	C15
	balance (a)	
	balance, to weigh 20 g (a)	C4
	balance, to weigh to 1 g (a)	C13
	balance, to weigh to 0.5 g (a)	C10
	balance, to weigh to 0.01 g (a)	C13, 15, 18
	balance, to weigh to 0.1 g (a)	C8
	balance, top-pan, to read to 0.01 g, preferably with a tare button (a)	C15
p	basin, evaporating	C4, 7, 16
p2	beaker, 10 ml	C8
p3	beaker, 100 ml	
p	beaker, 250 ml	
p	beaker, 400 ml	C11, 13, 14
p	beaker, 500 ml	C4, 5
p	beaker, plastic, 250 ml	C8
p	boat, weighing, or small pieces of paper	C14
p5	boiling tube	C3, 4, 11
p	boiling tube, with stopper	C9
	book of data or textbook giving formulae of alkanes (a)	C2
p	boss	
p	bottle, dropper	
p	bowl, or trough large enough for washing fabric samples	C10
p	bulb, in holder, 1.25 V/0.25 A	C14
p	bung, to fit wide-necked 100 ml conical flask, with delivery tubes	C15
p	bung, with delivery tubes	C16
p	Bunsen valve to fit delivery tube	C2
p	burette, 25 ml or 50 ml	C12
p	burner	
	burner, batswing, or flame spreader (a)	C6
	burner, gas fuel (a)	C13
	burner, spirit	C13
	bursting bottle, cast iron	C15
p	can, metal	C13
p	cardboard support for electrodes	C18
p	clamp	
p	clock, wall, or wristwatch	C10
p	cloth, emery	C16
p	container, waste, for hot residues (a)	C13
p	cottonwool	C8, 9, 15
p	coverslips	C9

p2	crocodile clips	C18
p	crucible	C6, 7, 13
	d.c. supply, 2–6 V	C14, 18
p	d.c. supply, 6–12 V	C4
	d.c. supply, 10–12 V	C4
p	d.c. supply, 20 V	C5
	d.c. supply, low voltage (a)	C4
p	delivery tube with bung to fit hard-glass test-tube	C2, 4
	desiccator (a)	C4
p	dialysis apparatus	C9
p	dish, Petri	C7, 16
2	electrodes, carbon	C4
2	electrodes, carbon (or preferably platinum)	C5, 9
	electrodes, copper, iron, magnesium, nickel, zinc and others (a)	C14
2	electrodes, hydrogen, platinized	C14
p2	electrodes, lead, 3 cm × 5 cm	C14
p	electrolysis cell	C4
p	eye protection	
	flask, Buchner	C12
p	flask, conical, 100 ml	
p	flask, conical, 100 ml, with wide neck	C15
p	flask, conical, 250 ml	C4, 12, 16
p	flask, graduated, 250 ml	C12
	flask, round bottomed, 500 ml or 1 litre	C4
	fume cupboard (a)	
	funnel, Buchner	C12
p	funnel, burette	C12
p	funnel, filter	
	gas-generator, with tap funnel, and right angle delivery tube	C16, 17
	gas jar and lid, or large beaker with aluminium foil cover	C7
p	gas jar, with cover glasses	C16, 17
p	gauze, copper, strips 10 cm × 3 cm (a)	C2
	gauze (for tripod)	
p	generator, Van de Graaff (or induction coil and low voltage d.c. supply)	C9
	gloves, protective	
p	glue	C5
	insulator, strip, or two tubes	C6
	ion exchange column	C10
p	jar or other container	C9
	kettle(s) with scale	C10
	knife, glass-cutting, or file (a)	C6
p	labels	C9
p	leads	C18
2	leads, long	C5
p	lens, hand	C4
p	light source, bright, or projector	C9
p	lolly sticks or spatulas	C10
p	masses, 1, 2, 3 and 4 kg	C15
p	mat, heatproof	
p	measuring cylinder	C3
p	measuring cylinder, 10 ml	
p	measuring cylinder, 25 ml	C8, 9, 12
p2	measuring cylinder, 50 ml	C11, 15, 16
p	measuring cylinder, 100 ml	

p	measuring cylinder, 200 ml (*a*)	C11
p	measuring cylinder, 500 ml (*a*)	C10
	microscope (*a*)	C4
p	microscope, with high and medium-power lenses	C9
	mineral wool (*a*)	C2, 13
	models, ball and spring	C2, 3, 13
p	muslin cloth	C8
	nail, iron, 5–10 cm long	C4
	newspaper (*a*)	C4
	oven (*a*)	C4
p	paper, blotting, or paper towels	C8, 11
	paper, blue litmus (*a*)	C8, 17
p	paper, chromatography, Whatman no. 1	C7
	paper, cobalt(II) chloride	C13
p	paper, filter	
	paper, filter, Buchner	C12
p	paper, gummed, or grease pencil	C9
	paper, indicator, universal, full range (*a*)	C3, 4, 17
	paper, red litmus	C15
	pen, marking (*a*)	C10
	pestle and mortar	C4
p	pipette, 10 ml or 25 ml, with filler	C9
p	pipette, 25 ml	C5
p2	pipette, dropping	
p	pipette, graduated, 25 ml, with safety filler	C12
	plate, smooth metal	C7
	porcelain, broken chips (*a*)	C2
p	power pack, 25 V d.c.	C9
p	pump, filter	
	refrigerator (*a*)	C4
	refrigerator, with deep freeze-compartment (*a*)	C15
	rheostat	C4, 18
p	rod, glass	
p	rod, glass, long enough for glass blowing	C6
p	rod, glass, to support metal wires	C16
	rod, soft glass (soda glass, 6–8 cm long, 7–12 mm diameter)	C6
p	scissors	
	screen, safety, for teacher and pupils	
p	seeker	C9
p	Sellotape	C5, 8
	sink (*a*)	C16
p9	slides, microscope	C4, 9
p	spatula	
p	splints	C4, 13
p	stand, burette	C12
p	stand, retort	
p	stapler	C1, 17
p	stopwatch or stopclock	C3, 15, 18
p	syringe, 10 ml, with end cut off	C4
p	syringe, plastic, 25 ml	C3
p	test-tube holder	C4, 9
p	test-tube rack	
p	test tube, hard glass, small hole blown near closed end	C4
p	test-tube, with bung	C10
2	test-tubes with side arms, and bungs	C13

p3	test-tubes with bungs, to collect gas	C2
p5	test-tubes, hard glass	C9
p4	test-tubes, stoppered	C14
p	thermometer, −5 to 110 °C	
p	thermometer, 0 to 100 °C	C9, 15
p2	thermometer, stirring, 0 to 100 °C	C3, 9
p	thread, strong fine, for tying Visking tubing	C14
p	tile, white	C12, 16
p	tile, white, or piece of white paper	C4, 5
p	tin lid, or sand tray	C8, 13
p	tin lid (for heating sulphur, sand, etc.)	C4
	tin lid, small, about 1.5 cm deep	C18
p	tissues, paper	
p	tongs	C9
	tower, drying, adapted as shown on page 284	C6, 7
p	triangle, pipe-clay	
p	tripod	C7, 9, 15
p	trough	C2
p	trough (or large margarine tub), or large crystallizing dish	C8
	trough or margarine tub (a)	C4
p	tube, glass, 3–5 mm internal diameter, length about 10 mm	C6
p	tube, sample, or test-tube with stopper	C7
	tubes, fine glass (a)	C16
	tubing, connecting	C6
p	tubing, glass, to make a dropping pipette and a right-angle bend	C13
	tubing, glass, including thistle funnel	C3
p	tubing, Visking, 15 cm, soaked in distilled water	
p	tweezers	C4, 5
	U-tube	C16
	U-tube, with bung and connecting tubing	C14
p	voltmeter, 0–5 V	C14
	voltmeter, high resistance	C12
p	wash-bottle	C8, 16
p3	watchglass	C7
p	watchglass, large, or dish	C4
p	watchglass, to cover 250 ml beaker	C14
	wires, connecting	
p2	wires, connecting, crocodile clip at both ends	
p4	wires, connecting, crocodile clip at one end, plug at the other end	C4

Chemicals

Item	Chapter
acetic (ethanoic) acid, glacial (a)	C8
acetic (ethanoic) anhydride (a)	C8, 12
alizarin (a)	C11
alloy samples (a)	C7
alum solution (a)	C11
ammonia solution (a)	
ammonium nitrate solution (a)	C15
ammonium sulphate solution (a)	C15
aqua regia (a)	C7
aspirin tablets, commercial (a)	C12
basalt (a)	C4

bath salts (*a*)	C10
Benedict's solution (*a*)	C3
bleaching powder	C17
boric acid (*a*)	C6
bromine	C17
bromine, aqueous (*a*)	C2
calcium, turnings (*a*)	C17
calcium carbonate (*a*)	C5, 17
calcium chloride	C17
calcium chloride solution (*a*)	C15
calcium hydroxide	C17
calcium oxide	C17
calcium phosphate (*a*)	C16
Calgon (*a*)	C10
candle wax (*a*)	C5
charcoal, powdered (*a*)	C7
citric acid solution (*a*)	C14
clay (*a*)	C4
cleaning agent for metals (*a*)	C7
copper (*a*)	C5
copper(II) sulphate, anhydrous	C13
copper(II) sulphate solution	C9, 14, 18
copper carbonate, powdered ("malachite") (*a*)	C4
copper chromate (*a*)	C5
copper foil (*a*)	C7
copper foil, pieces about 7 cm × 2 cm	C18
corrosion indicator (*a*)	C7
corrosion inhibitor, commercial (*a*)	C7
decorating filler, powdered (*a*)	C4
derusting agent (*a*)	C7
descalers, commercial, in original packs	C10
detergent, soapless, powder (*a*)	C10
detergent, washing-up (*a*)	C8
diaminohexane in water (*a*)	C8
disodium hydrogenphosphate solution (*a*)	C15
dithio-oxamide in ethanol (*a*)	C7
dolerite (*a*)	C4
ethanol	C13
fresh or UHT milk	C9
fructose (*a*)	C3
fructose solution (*a*)	C3
gelatine	C9
glucose (*a*)	C3, 5
glycerol (propane-1,2,3-triol) (*a*)	C9
granite (*a*)	C4
granite pieces, one easily held by tongs (*a*)	C15
graphite (*a*)	C5
grease paint (*a*)	C9
hexane or naphtha (*a*)	C4
hexanedioyl dichloride (adipyl chloride) in 1,1,1-trichloroethane (*a*)	C8
high-alumina shale (*a*)	C4
hydrochloric acid (*a*)	
hydrogen, cylinder	C14
hydrogen peroxide (*a*)	C11
ice (*a*)	C5, 15

indicator, screened methyl orange (*a*)	C12
indigo (*a*)	C11
iodine, crystals (*a*)	C5, 16, 17
iodine solution (*a*)	C3
iron (*a*)	C5
iron wool (*a*)	C2
iron(II) ammonium sulphate solution (*a*)	C14
iron(II) nitrate solution (*a*)	C15
iron(II) sulphate solution (*a*)	C4
lead (*a*)	C7
lead(II) bromide (*a*)	C4
lead(II) oxide (*a*)	C6
limewater	C13
liquid fuels – methylated spirits, paraffin, petrol (*a*)	C13
litmus solution, red (*a*)	C16
magnesium carbonate	C17
magnesium hydroxide	C17
magnesium nitrate solution (*a*)	C14, 15
magnesium oxide (*a*)	C5, 17
magnesium ribbon (*a*)	C7, 17
magnesium sulphate	C17
magnesium sulphate solution	C9
manganese chloride solution (*a*)	C15
marble chips, about 20 g (*a*)	C15
marble chips, small (*a*)	C15
metal wires, nickel, iron/steel, constantan, brass, nichrome, copper (different thicknesses) (*a*)	C16
methanal (*a*)	C8
milk of magnesia tablets (*a*)	C12
nitric acid (*a*)	
obsidian (*a*)	C4
oil (*a*)	C7
oxygen, cylinder	C14, 16
paint, various types	C7
paraffin, liquid (*a*)	C2
perfume (*a*)	C9
petroleum jelly (*a*)	C4
plaster of Paris (*a*)	C4
plastics, samples of	C8
polystyrene (*a*)	C5
polythene (*a*)	C5
potassium alum solution	C9
potassium chloride solution (*a*)	C15
potassium chromate (*a*)	C16
potassium dichromate, acidified (*a*)	C11
potassium hydroxide pellets (*a*)	C4, 9, 16
potassium hydroxide solution (*a*)	C4, 14
potassium manganate(VII), aqueous (*a*)	C2
potassium manganate(VII) crystals	C4, 5
potassium nitrate solution (*a*)	C14
preservative (*a*)	C9
Procion yellow dye (*a*)	C11
propanone (*a*)	C7, 18
rock salt, crushed	C15, 16
salicylic acid (*a*)	C12

salol (phenyl salicylate)	C4
sand (*a*)	C4, 5
sandstone, pieces of, in container for soaking (*a*)	C15
sandstones, samples of (*a*)	C4
silver nitrate	C17
soap powder (*a*)	C10
soap solution (*a*)	C10, 17
sodium bromide	C17
sodium carbonate, hydrated (*a*)	C11
sodium carbonate solution (*a*)	C3
sodium chloride (*a*)	C5, 11, 17
sodium chloride solution (*a*)	C4, 9
sodium dithionite (*a*)	C11
sodium hydrogencarbonate (*a*)	C12, 14
sodium hydroxide (*a*)	C11
sodium hydroxide solution (*a*)	
sodium iodide	C17
sodium sulphate solution (*a*)	C15
solids – very small pieces of wood, coke, coal, wax, paper, straw (*a*)	C13
solutions of metal ions – Ag^+, Cu^{2+}, Fe^{3+}, Ni^{2+} (*a*)	C7
starch (*a*)	C3
starch solution (*a*)	C3, 9
stearic acid (*a*)	C9
steel wool (*a*)	C18
sucrose (*a*)	C3, 9
sucrose solution, fresh (*a*)	C3
sulphur, lumps or crystals (*a*)	C5
sulphur dioxide, solution in water (*a*)	C11
sulphuric acid (*a*)	
titanium oxide	C9
urea (*a*)	C5
Vaseline (*a*)	C7
water, distilled (*a*)	
water, freshly boiled and cooled	C15
water, hot (*a*)	C10
water, tap (*a*)	C5, 16
zinc – metal, lumps, foil and powdered (*a*)	C4, 7, 14
zinc oxide (*a*)	C6
zinc sulphate solution (*a*)	C14

Physics apparatus list

Item	Chapter
air track and accessories	P5, 6
air track blower	P5, 6
ammeters – *see* meters	
aerosols, various	P2
amplifier	
(One which can produce a clearly audible output into a small loudspeaker when a similar loudspeaker is used as a microphone.)	P21
atlas, world	P2
ball bearings, 15 mm and 25 mm in diameter	
balloons	P5, 6
bathroom scales, calibrated in newtons	P2, 8
balances: 5-kg, domestic	
balances: 100-g	
ballpoint pen casing	P7
beads, glass or polystyrene	P5
beakers, glass, 400-cm³	
bell jar with suspended bell and battery	P15
bicycle dynamo assembly	P11, 18
bicycle dynamo which can be taken apart	P18
Blutack	P7
box with set of about 24 wooden cubes which fit into it – dimensions are not important	P4
Boyle's Law apparatus with pump	P2
bung with hole to fit 250 cm³ round-bottom flask	P2
Bunsen burners and heatproof mats	
C-cores with clips	P11, 18
CO_2 capsule with mount that can be suspended to propel itself along a wire stretched across a laboratory	P6
CO_2 cylinder	
camera with shutter that can be kept open	P7
candle	P3
cans, tin	P9
capacitors, 0.01 µF, 100 µF and 4700 µF electrolytic, 6 V or greater	P16, 19, 20
card	
cells, 1.5 V in holders	
(For most experiments, Worcester 1601 circuit boards are an acceptable alternative.)	
circular brass plates on insulating handles	P3
clip, Hoffmann	
coils for C-cores: 120 turns	P11, 18
coils for C-cores: 2400 turns	P11
colour filters, set of primary red, blue and green	P15
colour filters, set of secondary yellow, magenta and cyan	P15
coloured objects, various, in primary and other colours	P15
compact light source	P3
compasses, pairs (for drawing circles)	P15
computer, with disc drive or cassette recorder	P4, 20
computer interface, input	P20
computer interface, output	P20

computer software to control interfaces	**P**20
connecting leads	
container, aluminium	**P**10
corks	
coulombmeter	**P**16
curtain rail, flexible, 2 m long	**P**5
demountable transformer kit	**P**11, 18
dice	**P**3
diode, hot filament with stand	**P**19
diode, e.g. IN5401	**P**19
dowel, 10 mm diameter	
drawing pins	**P**1
drinking straws	**P**7
electric drill which can be taken apart	**P**18
electric heating accessories for mechanical heating apparatus (q.v.)	
electric kettle	**P**9
electric motor, 6-V	**P**17

electronics kit containing:

light-dependent resistor	reed relay
thermistor	buzzer
switch SPST	motor
reed switch	2 NAND gates
light-emitting diode	power transistor, e.g. TIP41A

(A power supply (q.v.) will be required)	**P**20
electrostatics rod, polythene	**P**16
electrostatics rod, acetate	**P**16
expanded polystyrene block	
fan or hair-drier to blow cold air	**P**9
fine beam tube and base	**P**19
force meters, 10-N	**P**5, 8
force meters, 50-N	**P**8
G-clamps, 50-mm	
G-clamps, 100-mm	
galvanometers – *see* meters	
gauzes	
Geiger–Müller tube, thin end-window type, with holder	**P**3
glass rod, 20 to 30 cm long, with smooth ends (neither cut nor flame polished)	**P**13
glass tubing	
glue, general purpose	
hammer	
hardboard disc with hole in centre to take a piece of dowel	**P**5
Helmholtz coils for fine-beam tube	**P**19
hydrochloric acid, concentrated	
inertial balance kit	**P**5
immersion heater, 12-V	**P**9, 10
ionization chamber, simple open type to detect α-particles	**P**3
iron filings	**P**18
iron yoke for Magnadur magnets	**P**11, 18
iso-butyl methyl ketone	**P**3
joulemeter, arm – to measure energy transferred by arm	**P**8
joulemeter, cycle – to measure energy transferred by legs	**P**8
joulemeter, electric – to measure energy delivered by 12 V a.c. supply. (Rewound domestic electricity meters or electronic	

equivalents are already present in many schools. A simpler
version that causes a light to flash for every 100 J transferred
is to be preferred for pupils' use.) **P**9, 10
kinetic theory model kit
    (An apparatus with an integral motor is easier to use than
    those driven via a belt from a separate motor.) **P**2
lagging materials, e.g. strips of cotton cloth, foam rubber,
cotton-wool, wool scarf, to lag tin cans **P**9
lamp, e.g. photoflood, for bright illumination **P**13
lamp, 2.5-V, 0.2-A, MES
lamp, 1.25-V, 0.25-A, MES
lamp, 12-V, 24-W, SBC
lamp, 12-V, 3-W (e.g. line filament type with holder) **P**17
lampholder, MES
lampholder, SBC
lath, about 25 mm × 50 mm × 1 m **P**1
lead block, about 1.5 cm × 5 cm × 5 cm **P**3
lead shot **P**10
light gate, any arrangement for timing interruption of light beam **P**4, 5, 6, 15
lighter "flints" **P**18
loudspeakers, small moving coil **P**15, 21
magnets, bar, Ticonal **P**18
magnets, Magnadur, slab **P**18
mains electric fire, 1000 W **P**16
mains electric lamp, 100 W, in holder **P**16
mains electric lamp, 60 W **P**17
mains connecting block
    (A means of connecting equipment safely to the mains supply,
    and of measuring currents and voltages, is required in some
    experiments.)
map of the UK **P**12
map of the UK, geological **P**12
marbles, 15 mm in diameter **P**2
marbles, 25 mm in diameter **P**2, 5
masses, 1-kg
masses, 100-g
measuring cylinders, 250-cm^3
measuring cylinders, 100-cm^3
mechanical heating apparatus with equipment for heating it electrically
meters, electric, for class use:
    ammeters,   1 A d.c.
                   5 A d.c.
    voltmeters,   5 V d.c.
                   10 V a.c.
                   5 V d.c.
    galvanometers, 3−0−3 mA, or similar
meters, electric, for demonstration use:
    ammeters,   1 A a.c.
                   5 A a.c.
    voltmeters,   5 V d.c.
                   10 V d.c.
                   15 V d.c.
    galvanometer, 3−0−3 mA, or similar **P**11 and
                                       16−20

(The ranges quoted above are a guide to the size of the readings likely to be obtained. The meters can have any ranges that are clear and easy to read, provided a measurably large deflection is obtained in use. 100 μA meters, diode protected, are electrically robust and are conveniently used with plug-in shunts and multipliers. For such meters, those with ranges of 0–3 and 0–10 need fewest shunts and multipliers and should be considered as suitable alternatives to the ranges specified above. It is important that pupils are easily able to interpret the meter scale in terms of the measuring range in use. Less able pupils may benefit from using direct-reading meters.

Low-cost digital meters are becoming more common and are useful in circuits in which the current and voltage are not changing quickly. When a reading is changing rapidly, as in electromagnetic induction experiments, a moving coil (analogue) meter is essential.

The same criteria apply to demonstration meters. Ease of use and clarity of reading are paramount considerations. Demonstration meters based on the same movements as corresponding class meters are convenient as they both use the same set of shunts and multipliers.)

metre rules	
microphone	**P**15, 19, 21
mirrors, plane	**P**13
motion sensor	**P**4
motor kits, electric, containing:	
base	
2 split pins	
spindle	
4 rivets	
armature	
valve rubber	**P**11, 18
motor, fractional horsepower	**P**18, 19
musical insruments, a selection	**P**15
nails	
needles	
optical fibre, 0.5–1 m length	**P**13
oscilloscopes, single beam	**P**19, 21
oscilloscopes, double beam	**P**15
paper, black	**P**13
paper, squared	**P**2
paper, white	
pressure tubing, short length to fit neck of balloon	**P**6
ping-pong ball coated with Aquadag and suspended on nylon	
thread	**P**16
pins	
Plasticine	
plotting compasses	**P**18
plug, 13-A, mains	**P**16
polystyrene beaker	**P**9, 10
polythene bottle, 30 to 50 cm^3 capacity	**P**3
power supply, 2 V a.c.	**P**19
power supplies, 12 V a.c./d.c.	

(Pupil experiments frequently need low voltage a.c. and d.c. supplies for electromagnetic experiments and 12 V a.c./d.c. supplies for lamps and heaters. It would be convenient to have these combined into a single, economical unit.)

power supplies, 0–12 V d.c., variable, smoothed

power supply, HT

power supply, EHT

power supply for electronics kit

    (Different kits will have different requirements. Many can be
supplied from dry cells. Some will need a regulated supply.)

pressure gauge, 200 kPa

    (This gauge should read absolute pressure. It should be either
stand-mounted or designed to be mounted directly into a
bung or tube.)   P2

prism, glass or plastic, 60   P15

protractors   P1, 13

pulley on clamp   P10

radioactive sources:

    americium-241, 5 µCi (0.18 MBq)   P3

    strontium-90, 5 µCi (0.18 MBq)   P3

    cobalt-60, 5 µCi (0.18 MBq)   P3

radioactive source holder   P3

radio kit, to allow easy assembly of radio (A DIY kit can be
made up from:

    ZN414 integrated circuit

    capacitors,   0.1 µF

                  0.01 µF

                  330 pF

    resistors,   100 kΩ

                  500 kΩ

    crystal earpiece

    ferrite rod, 10 cm × 1 cm diameter.)   P21

ray optics kit (cylindrical lenses are not required)   P13

resistors, 15 Ω, 10 W, with sockets   P17

resistors, 4 Ω, 7 W, labelled X   P17

resistor, 10 Ω, 7 W, labelled Y   P17

resistor, 10 kΩ   P20

ripple tank kit

    (Any simple arrangement to demonstrate simple wave
phenomena; a motorized vibrator is not required.)

rock samples, including iron, magnetite, basalt and limestone   P18

round-bottomed flask, 250-cm³   P2

rubber bands

rules, 30 cm and half-metre

runway for dynamics trolley   P4, 5, 6, 10

safety screen   P15

sand   P8

sandbags, 10 N and 20 N   P8

scaler counter, for GM tube   P3

scissors

screen, white

screwdriver, small

signal generator   P15

slotted masses, 100-g sets

slotted masses, 1-kg sets

slotted base

spark counter   P3

speed of light apparatus

    (A cheap DIY version is described in "Experimenting with
Industry" No. 2, published by ASE/SCSST.)   P15

spring, long, heavy	**P**14
springs, disposable	**P**15
spring, Slinky	**P**14, 15
stands, bosses and clamps	
steel rod pieces, 50 mm long or greater	
(Pieces of knitting needle can be used)	
step (strong box to stand on, about 30 cm high)	**P**8
stirrer	
stirrups to suspend electrostatics rods	**P**16
stopclock	
stopclock, electrically controlled (for use with light gates)	
string	
support block for electromagnetism experiments	**P**18
support rod for camera	**P**7
switch, on–off, with sockets	
syringe, gas	**P**2
syringes, plastic	**P**2
tape, adhesive	
tape for ticker timer	**P**7
tennis ball	**P**7
thermocouple and indicating meter	**P**2
thermometer	**P**2, 9, 10
thread	
ticker timer	
(Any reliable mechanism to mark tickertape for dynamics experiments.)	**P**7 (Optional: **P**4, 5, 6)
tongs	
torches, electric, one working and one not working	**P**16
track, grooved, with 20 cm aluminium foil fitted along each side of part of groove	**P**4
transparent block, plastic or glass, semi-circular	**P**13
transparent strip, plastic, approximately 0.5 cm × 3 cm × 30 cm	**P**13
tray, about 20 cm × 30 cm, with hook to attach string	**P**8
tray for 2-D kinetic theory model	**P**2
tripod	
trolley, dynamics	**P**4, 5, 6, 10, 15
(See note under "runway".)	
tubes, cardboard, about 50 cm × 5 cm diameter	**P**10, 13
tube for "guinea and feather" experiment	**P**7
tube, rubber	**P**15, 19
tubing, plastic	**P**2
tuning forks	
uranyl nitrate	**P**3
vacuum pump	**P**7, 15
Van de Graaff generator	**P**3, 16
voltmeters – *see* meters	
water circuit board	**P**16
water rocket	**P**6
weather-monitoring instruments	**P**2
(A selection, perhaps including barometer, thermometer, hygrometer, rain gauge, anemometer, maximum and minimum thermometer, compass, sunshine recorder.)	
wire, flexible, insulated, e.g. 16 × 0.5 mm	

pvc insulated, solid core, e.g. 0.6 mm diameter
tinned copper, 0.45 mm (26 s.w.g.)
bare Eureka, 0.56 mm (24 s.w.g.)
bare Eureka, 0.40 mm (28 s.w.g.)
bare Eureka, 0.28 mm (32 s.w.g.)
3-core mains
steel, about 0.5 mm diameter
wire strippers
wire resistance board with 4 different lengths of 0.28 mm bare
Eureka wire
Worcester circuit board
(Basic electricity kits which connect with conventional plugs
and sockets are an acceptable and sometimes preferable
alternative to circuit boards.)

Appendix 2 | Useful addresses

This list of addresses and telephone numbers covers the suggestions for sources of visual aids and further information that we have made in this *Guide*. It is not an exhaustive list. Some of the smaller organizations, especially the charities and campaigning societies, appreciate it if you enclose a stamped addressed envelope.

Association for Science Education (for Science and Technology in Society – SATIS – units)
College Lane, Hatfield, Hertfordshire AL10 9AA. (Tel. 0707 267411.)

Films, slides, videos and television programmes

Argus Film and Video Library (for ICI videos)
15 Beaconsfield Road, London NW10 2LE. (Tel. 081–451 1127.)

AVP (for computer programs and audio-visual resources)
School Hill Centre, Chepstow, Gwent NP6 5PH. (Tel. 0291 625439.)

BP Educational Service (for BP tape–slide sets)
PO Box 30, Alton, Hampshire GU34 4PX. (Tel. 0420 22638.)

BP Film Library (for BP films and videos)
15 Beaconsfield Road, London NW10 2LE. (Tel. 081–451 1129.)

BBC Education Information
BBC White City, 201 Wood Lane, London W12 7TS. (Tel. 081–746 1111.)

British Gas Education Service (for British Gas slides)
Room 707A, 326 High Holborn, London WC1V 7PT. (Tel. 071–242 0789.)

British Plastics Federation
6 Bath Place, Rivington Street, London EC2A 3JE. (Tel. 071–457 5000.)

Independent Television Publications (for ITV videos)
6 Paul Street, London EC2A 4JH. (Tel. 071–247 5206.)

National Coal Board Film Library
Hobart House, Grosvenor Place, London SW1X 7AE. (Tel. 071–235 2020.)

Nuclear Industry Education Programme (for AEA videos and other teaching aids)
Building 329, Harwell Laboratory, Didcot, Oxon OX11 0RA. (Tel. 0235 433359.)

Philip Harris Education (for Philip Harris slide sets, filmstrips and videos)
Lynn Lane, Shenstone, Lichfield, Staffordshire WS14 0EE. (Tel. 0543 480077.)

Phillips Petroleum Film Library
15 Beaconsfield Road, London NW10 2LE. (Tel. 081–451 1127.)

Scottish Central Film Library (for Unilever films)
74 Victoria Crescent Road, Dowanhill, Glasgow G12 9JN. (Tel. 041–334 9314.)

Thames Water
Customer Centre Manager, Customer Centre, Thames Water, Bath Road, PO Box 1850, Swindon SN1 4TW. (Tel. 071–837 3300/0345 200800.)

Viscom Ltd (for British Gas, British Steel, De Beers, Esso, RTZ Group and Shell films and videos)
Audio-Visual Library, Unit B11, Park Hall Road Trading Estate, London SE21 8EL. (Tel. 081–761 3035.)

University of York, Audio-Visual Unit, (for PLON video "Force and motion")
Heslington, York YO1 5DD. (Tel. 0904 433031.)

Booklets, leaflets, wallcharts and other sources of information

AEA Technology (formerly **UKAEA**)
Harwell Laboratories, Didcot, Oxfordshire OX11 0RA. (Tel. 0235 821111.)

Allied Breweries (UK) Ltd
107 Station Street, Burton-on-Trent, Staffordshire BE14 1BZ. (Tel. 0283 45320.)

Aluminium Extruders Association
Integrated Marketing Services, Whitegates House, Rudge Heath Road, Claverley, Wolverhampton WV5 7DJ. (Tel. 0746 710310.)

Anglian Water
North Street, Oundle, Peterborough PE8 4AS. (Tel. 0832 276000.)

The Association of the British Pharmaceutical Industry
12 Whitehall, London SW1A 2DY. (Tel. 071–930 3477.)

Bass Brewing Ltd
137 High Street, Burton-on-Trent, Staffordshire DE14 1JZ. (Tel. 0283 511000.)

BP Educational Service (for enquiries)
Britannic House, Finsbury Circus, London EC2M 7BA. (Tel. 071–496 4000.)

BP Educational Service (for ordering materials)
PO Box 30, Alton, Hampshire GU34 4PX. (Tel. 0420 22638.)

The Brewers' Society
Technical Secretary, 42 Portman Square, London W1H 0BB. (Tel. 071–486 4831.)

British Agrochemicals Association
4 Lincoln Court, Lincoln Road, Peterborough PE1 2RP. (Tel. 0733 349225.)

British Ceramics Manufacturers' Federation
Federation House, Station Road, Stoke-on-Trent ST4 2SA. (Tel. 0782 744631.)

British Gas Education Service
Room 707A, 326 High Holborn, London WC1V 7PT. (Tel. 071–242 0789.)

British Glass Manufacturers' Confederation
Northumberland Road, Sheffield S10 2UA. (Tel. 0742 686201.)

British Museum (Natural History)
Cromwell Road, London SW7 5BD. (Tel. 071–589 6323.)

British Steel Corporation
9 Albert Embankment, London SE1 7SN. (Tel. 071–735 7654.)

BT Education Department
BT Centre, 81 Newgate Street, London EC1A 7AJ. (Tel. 071–356 5000.)

Carnauld Metal Box Technology Plc
Downsview Road, Wantage, Oxfordshire OX12 9BP. (Tel. 0235 772929.)

Chemical Industries Association
Kings Buildings, Smith Square, London SW1P 3JJ. (Tel. 071–834 3399.)

Chloride Motive Power
PO Box 1, Salford Road, Bolton, Lancashire BL5 1DD. (Tel. 0204 64111.)

The Coeliac Society
PO Box 220, High Wycombe, Buckinghamshire HP11 2HY.

Copper Development Association
Orchard House, Mutton Lane, Potters Bar, Hertfordshire EN6 3AP.
(Tel. 0707 50711.)

Council for the National Parks
246 Lavender Hill, London SW11 1LJ. (Tel. 071–924 4077.)

Cystic Fibrosis Research Trust
Department PD 130, Alexandra House, 5 Blyth Road, Bromley, Kent BR1 3RS.
(Tel. 081–464 7211.)

Davis Gelatine
Upper Grove Street, Leamington Spa, Warwickshire CV32 5AN. (Tel. 0926 422795.)

De Beers Diamond Information Office
17 Charterhouse Street, London EC1N 6RA. (Tel. 071–404 4444.)

Duracell UK
Duracell House, Church Road, Lowfield Heath, Crawley, West Sussex RH11 0PQ.
(Tel. 0293 517527.)

Ecton Educational Centre (formerly **Mineral Industry Manpower and Careers Unit**)
Room B315, Dept of Mineral Resources Engineering, Royal School of Mines, Prince
Consort Road, London SW7 2BP. (Tel. 071–584 7397.)

The Electricity Association
30 Millbank, London SW1P 4RD. (Tel. 071–834 2333.)

Energy Efficiency Office
1 Palace Street, London SW1E 5HE. (Tel. 071–238 3474.)

Esso Petroleum Co. Ltd
Esso House, Victoria Street, London SW1E 5JW. (Tel. 071–834 6677.)

Ever Ready Ltd
Ever Ready House, 93 Burleigh Gardens, Southgate, London N14 5AQ. (Tel. 081–882 8661.)

The Farm and Food Society (s.a.e. when writing please)
4 Willifield Way, London NW11 7XT. (Tel. 081–455 0634.)

Fertilizer Manufacturers' Association Ltd
Greenhill House, Thorpewood, Peterborough PE3 6GF. (Tel. 0733 331303.)

Food and Farming Information Service
European Business Centre, 460 Fulham Road, London SW6 1BY. (Tel. 071–610 0402.)

Friends of the Earth Ltd
26-28 Underwood Street, London N1 7JQ. (Tel. 071–490 1555.)

The Green Party
10 Station Parade, Balham High Road, London SW12 9AZ. (Tel. 081–673 0045.)

Greenpeace Communications Ltd
5 Bakers Row, London EC1R 3DB. (Tel. 071–833 0600.)

Guinness Brewing GB
Park Royal Brewery, London NW10 7RR. (Tel. 081–965 7700.)

Health Education Authority
Hamilton House, Mapleton Place, London WC1H 9TX. (Tel. 071–383 3833.)

ICI Agricultural Division
PO Box 1, Billingham, Cleveland TS23 1LB. (Tel. 0642 553601.)

ICI Educational Publications
PO Box 50, Wetherby, West Yorkshire LS23 7EZ. (Tel. 0937 844443.)

ICI Education Liaison Officer
PO Box 6, Bessemer Road, Welwyn Garden City, Hertfordshire AL7 1HD.
(Tel. 07073 23400.)

ICI Mond Division
PO Box 13, The Heath, Runcorn, Cheshire WO7 4QF. (Tel. 0928 511111.)

ICI Petrochemicals and Plastics Division
PO Box 54, Wilton Works, Middlesbrough, Cleveland TS6 8JE.
(Tel. 0642 454144.)

Institute of Biology
20-22 Queensberry Place, London SW7 2DZ. (Tel. 071 581 8333.)

Institute of Materials
1 Carlton House Terrace, London SW1Y 5DB. (Tel. 071–245 9555.)

Institute of Physics
The Education Officer, 47 Belgrave Square, London SW1X 8QX.
(Tel. 071–235 6111.)

JET Joint Undertaking
Abingdon, Oxon OX14 3EA. (Tel. 0235 528822.)

Kodak Limited
Photo Information Services, PO Box 66, Hemel Hempstead, Hertfordshire HP1 1JU.
(Tel. 0442 61122.)

Lead Development Association
42-46 Weymouth Street, London W1A 2BG. (Tel. 071–499 8422.)

London Brick Company Ltd
Public Relations Officer, Stewartby, Bedford MK43 9LZ. (Tel. 0234 851851.)

National Centre for Alternative Technology
Llwyngwern Quarry, Machynlleth, Powys SY20 9AZ. (Tel. 0654 702400.)

National Coal Board
Hobart House, Grosvenor Place, London SW1X 7AE. (Tel. 071–235 2020.)

National Dairy Council
National Dairy Centre, 5–7 John Princes Street, London W1M 0AP.
(Tel. 071–499 7822.)

National Society for Clean Air
136 North Street, Brighton BN1 1RG. (Tel. 0273 26313.)

The National Stone Centre (for high–alumina shale)
Wirksworth, Derbyshire DE4 4FR. (Tel. 0629 824833.)

Oxfam (for "Poverty game")
Oxfam Youth Department, 274 Banbury Road, Oxford OX2 7DZ. (Tel. 0865 311311.)

Pilkington Glass Ltd
Group Public Relations Department, Prescot Road, St Helens, Merseyside WA10 3TT.
(Tel. 0744 28882.)

Royal National Institute for the Blind
For Braille texts: 224 Great Portland Street, London W1N 6AA.
(Tel. 071–388 1266.)
For Moon texts: Moon Branch, Holmesdale Road, Reigate, Surrey RH2 OBA.
(Tel. 0737 246333.)

The Royal Mint
Llantrisant, Pontyclun, Mid Glamorgan CF7 8YT. (Tel. 0443 222111.)

The Royal Society of Chemistry (Education Department)
Burlington House, Piccadilly, London W1V 0BN. (Tel. 071–437 8656.)

The Royal Society of Chemistry (Distribution Centre)
Blackhorse Road, Letchworth, Hertfordshire SG6 1HN. (Tel. 04626 72555.)

RTZ Corporation Ltd
PO Box 133, 6 St James's Square, London SW1Y 4LD. (Tel. 071–930 2399.)

S.C.A. Aylesford Ltd
West Mill Newsprint, Aylesford, Kent ME20 7DL. (Tel. 0622 883532.)

Science Museum
Exhibition Road, South Kensington, London SW7 2DD. (Tel. 071–589 3456.)

Sheffield Hallan University (for "Problem solving with industry")
Centre or Science Education, 36 Collegiate Crescent, Sheffield S10 2BP. (Tel. 0742 532209.)

Shell Education Service
Shell UK Ltd, Shell-Mex House, Strand, London WC2R 0DX.
(Tel. 071–257 3000.)

The Sugar Bureau
Duncan House, Dolphin Square, London SW1V 3PW. (Tel. 071–828 9465.)

TEAR Fund
100 Church Road, Teddington, Middlesex TW11 8QE. (Tel. 081–977 9144.)

Thames Water
Nugent House, Vastern Road, Reading, Berkshire RG1 8DB. (Tel. 0734 593704.)

The Tidy Britain Group
The Pier, Wigan WN3 4EX. (Tel. 0942 824620.)

Understanding Electricity Educational Service
30 Millbank, London SW1P 4RD. (Tel. 071–834 2333.)

Unilever Educational Publications
PO Box 68, Unilever House, London EC4P 4BQ. (Tel. 071–822 5252.)

The Warmer Campaign
83 Mount Ephraim, Tunbridge Wells, Kent TN4 8BS. (Tel. 0892 524626.)

The Wiggins Teape Group Ltd
PO Box 88, Gateway House, Basing View, Basingstoke, Hampshire RG21 2EE.
(Tel. 0256 842020.)

Worldaware (formerly **Centre for World Development Education**)
1 Catton Street, London WC1R 4AB. (Tel. 071–831 3844.)

The Zinc Development Association
42 Weymouth Street, London W1N 3LQ. (Tel. 071–499 6636.)

Sources of further addresses

Chemical Industry Education Centre
c/o The Chemistry Department, University of York, Heslington, York YO1 5DD.
(Tel. 0904 432523.)

Education in Chemistry
Published bimonthly by The Royal Society of Chemistry, Burlington House, London
W1V 0BN. (Tel. 071–437 8656.)

Education in Physics
Published bimonthly by the Institute of Physics, 47 Belgrave Square, London SW1X 8QX.
(Tel. 071–235 6111.)

Education in Science
Published five times a year by the Association for Science Education, College Lane,
Hatfield, Hertfordshire AL10 9AA. (Tel. 0707 267411.)

Goldmine
A catalogue of resources for teachers, available from the Association for Science
Education.

The School Science Review
Published quarterly by the Association for Science Education.

STEAM
Published by ICI Educational Publications, PO Box 50, Wetherby, West Yorkshire LS23 7EZ.
(Tel. 0937 844443.)

Chemistry: practical evaluation

Some of the Chemistry practical work was more widely tested.

A detailed evaluation of the whole programme of practical work was carried out by
Roger Norris of Wymondham College. In addition, useful comment and advice was
received from groups of PGCE students who tested selected experiments:

London Institute of Education, working under Brendan Schollum:
Mehboob Ahmed, David Colledge, Terry Gould, Nicky Greenbat, Jennifer Hiew, Jeff
Hoadley, Josephine Percival, Kerry Ridpath, Gurdip Sagoo, Alison Spurling, Dawn
Webster, Andrew Wooley, Nuei Yu

Sheffield City Polytechnic, working under Bill Harrison:
Ian Campbell, Shamima Ditta, K. J. Garner, Ron Green, Keith Young

St Mary's College, Twickenham, working under Tim Brosnan:
David Horsan, John Mollins, John O'Driscoll, Paul Sexton, Neil Young.

Index